A E I

ARABIA EGYPT INDIA

A E I

ARABIA EGYPT INDIA

A NARRATIVE OF TRAVEL

ISABEL BURTON

WITH FIFTEEN ILLUSTRATIONS
AND TWO MAPS.

GYAN

Published by

GYAN

Gyan Publishing House
5, Ansari Road
Daryaganj, New Delhi-110002
Phone: 011-47034999, 9811692060
E-mail: books@gyanbooks.com

Distribution Network
gyanbooks.com
India, USA, Canada, UK, Australia, France

ISBN : 978-81-212-9642-7 (PB)
First Published, 1879

2nd Impression 2023

Printed at: Gyan Press, Delhi.

A E I ARABIA EGYPT INDIA
Author: ISABEL BURTON

OUR ROUTE FROM LONDON TO INDIA.

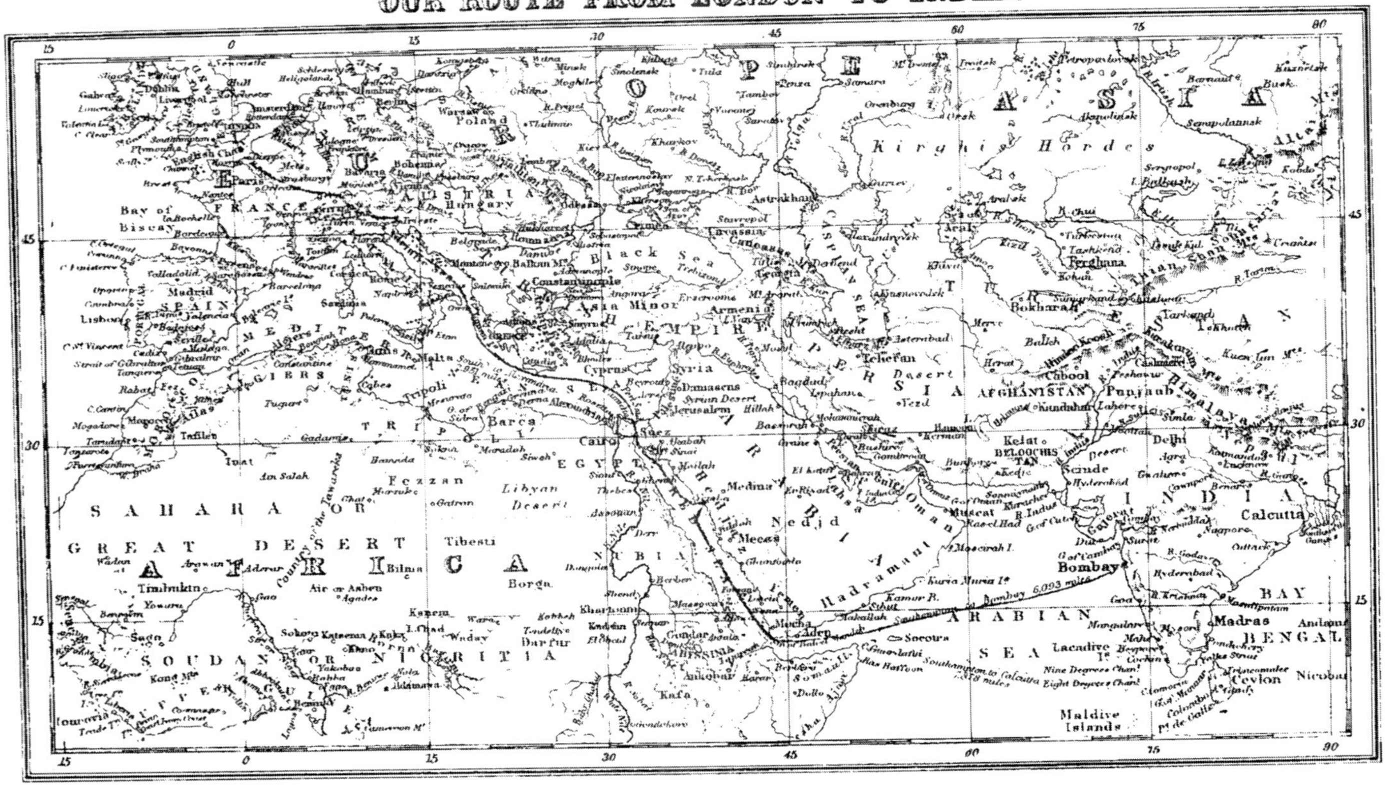

THE WELLS OF MOSES IN THE ARABIAN DESERT.

A E I

Arabia Egypt India

A NARRATIVE OF TRAVEL

BY

ISABEL BURTON

Author of "Inner Life of Syria"

WITH FIFTEEN ILLUSTRATIONS AND TWO MAPS.

LUX EX LITERIS

1879

TO

My Dear and Honoured Father,

HENRY RAYMOND ARUNDELL,

WHO HAS ALWAYS TAKEN THE PROFOUNDEST INTEREST IN OUR TRAVELS AND WRITINGS; WHO HAS HELPED US WITH HIS COUNSELS; AND WHO HAS EVER SHOWN THE TENDEREST SOLICITUDE FOR OUR WELFARE.

Isabel Burton

May God's choicest blessings crown his good works;
May he, like the holy patriarchs, have a long, happy, and peaceful life;
May we console and support his old age, and when he leaves us
May the mantle of his noble, simple, upright life fall upon us his children.

CONTENTS.

LIST OF ILLUSTRATIONS.

OUR ROUTE THROUGH INDIA.

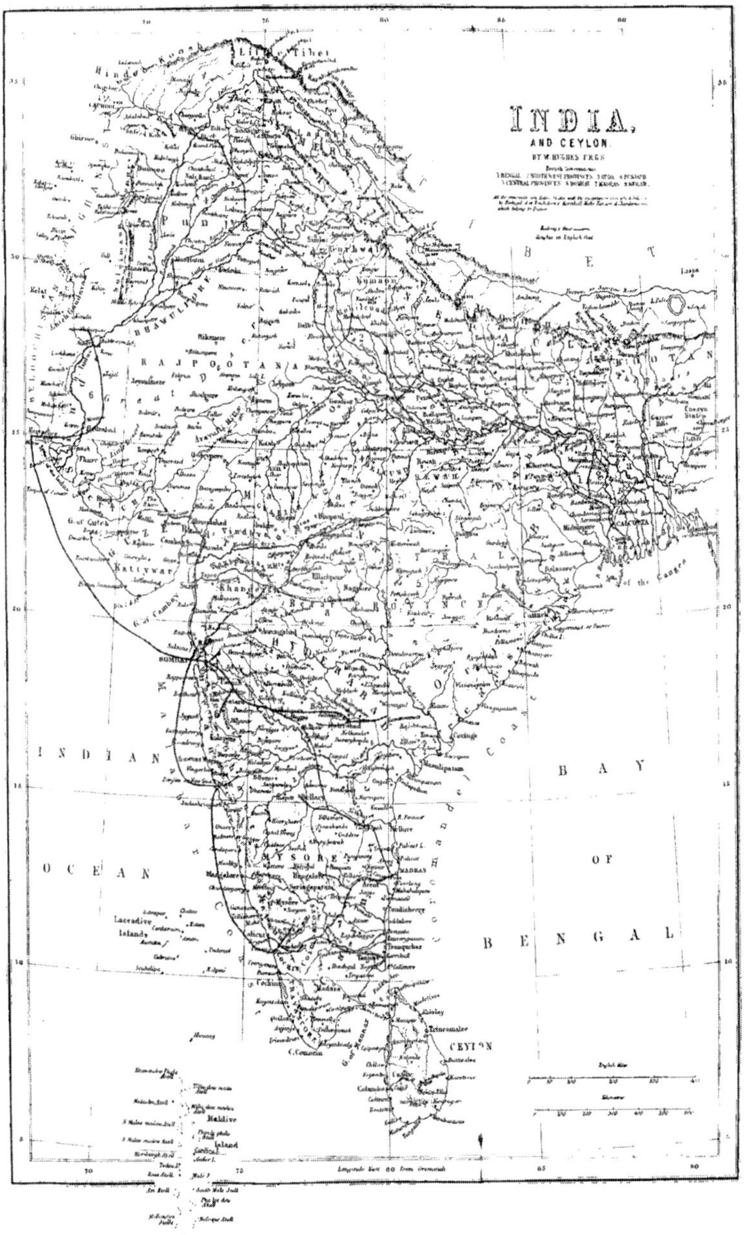

INTRODUCTION.

VERY PERSONAL.

THE kindness shown to my "Inner Life of Syria" makes me long to presume on another narrative; but I picture to myself the following conversation with my publisher:—

"No really, Mrs. Burton, I cannot undertake your book, because we all know everything about India; we have sucked it dry, and are sick of it."

"True, Mr. A.," I reply, "but you said the same of 'Syria, Palestine, and the Holy Land,' and yet I found enough of unwritten matter to give you MSS. which you had to cut down to two big vols. Perhaps, with my 'griffin' eyes, ears, and brain, I may have seen something from a different aspect to those who have preceded me for the last few hundred years. Do try me, dear Mr. A.! Give me another chance!"

Mr. A. relents, and accepts my MSS. Then the printers have to be conciliated. They always strike work when MSS. from Captain Burton or myself go in, we write so badly. Also I have to think of my readers, who are ever kind, generous, and just; and will not, I trust, be disgusted with a somewhat hackneyed title. For my part, I hope that between London and Goa we may chance to find something which is not generally known.

I always think of a *prima donna* at Trieste, with regard to the public. We import our operas from Milan two years before they appear in London. We have an excellent Opera house and three theatres, always full, and the Triestines are so severe and so critical that *artistes* become extremely nervous; they know if they can pass Trieste they may sing anywhere. One evening, a very plain, but first rate, *prima donna* appeared on the stage. She had not yet opened her mouth ; they all began to hiss and hoot. She advanced with great resolution to the footlights, and said : "*Cari Triestini*, I know I am frightful, but I did not come to be looked at, I came to sing. Hear me before you hiss." There was a dead silence. She opened her mouth, and before she had finished the first few bars, the applause was deafening and prolonged. She remained a favourite ever after.

Our English public is colder perhaps, but just, and generous, and sincere.

CHAPTER I.

FROM LONDON THROUGH FRANCE AND ITALY.

AFTER a delightful year in England, publishing my last book, in the gay season of 1875, and being *fêtéd* by all my friends and relations enough to spoil me for ever, my husband, finding he had still six months' leave, asked me what I should like to do. I consulted my heart, and it answered, "India." He had been nineteen years in the Bombay Army, and eight of them on active service through all those exciting years from '42 to '49, on the staff of Sir Charles Napier, whose fortunes as a soldier he may be said to have followed. Indeed, the old General's fate seems to have overshadowed him, and later on, Lord Stratford de Redcliffe had a like effect in the political line, of whose school, and whose fervent disciple in Eastern affairs, he was. Do not start. This book is *not* going to be "weighted with a grievance." This only serves to explain that I had never seen India, and that I proposed that he should take me there and show me all his old quarters. He liked the idea; so we got a map, cut India down the middle lengthways, from Cashmere to Cape Comorin, and planned out how much we could manage to see on the western side, leaving the eastern for another year; we were already too far advanced in the season for such an expedition.

The 4th December, 1875, was remarkable for being as black as midnight during the livelong day: thick snow lay upon the ground and covered every object; dense, murky fog filled the air; through which a dull red, lurid gleam just rendered the darkness visible—and horrible. In any sunny land we should have feared an earthquake, or the last judgment, but here

(London) we only remarked that there must be something extra "odd" about the elements, with a passing smile at the unhappy foreigner who had come over to see London. Our dear "village" gloomed like a snow Inferno fit for Dante and Gustave Doré, and the "Squares" appeared like spectre Christmas Trees. "It looks," said my husband, "as if London were in mourning for some great national crime;" but I answered, "Let us try to think our Vaterland wears mourning for our departure into exile."

Everyone that day seemed ill and miserable; I felt as if I could never rise to face the day. To be sure we had been having a farewell dinner, which festivity devoted to leave-takings had been unduly prolonged to five o'clock a.m., and we were obliged to force ourselves to get up at nine, and put our shoulders to the wheel for our sins. We lunched with my father and family by lamp-light at one in the day, and set out, a large family party, by the 4.45 train to Folkestone; arriving cold and hungry, but merry, we enjoyed a delightful supper at one of the best hotels in the world, albeit somewhat expensive, and that is The Pavilion,—the redeeming point of Folkestone, for poor is the station through which so much wealth passes. There we found Carlo Pellegrini, of Ape celebrity, full of fun, who joined our family party. He was staying there some months for painting.

The next day, Sunday, the snow was eight feet deep, and we went with difficulty to the small pretty church, where the priest gave us a short, but sensible, sermon, in consideration of our pinched fingers and toes. All that day neighbouring friends and relations flocked over to spend the day with us; and one act I shall never forget, and that was my cousin's wife, daily expecting her confinement, wading four miles in the snow not to miss wishing us God-speed, because no carriage could be got to undertake the journey. Heart and pluck like that are not to be found out of the British Isles. Meanwhile the train stuck in the snow; the down train from Folkestone to Dover, usually an affair of twenty minutes, occupied from six till one p.m.—seven hours. The night train could not come in at all. The boat did not go, and it was "blowing great guns."

That night—the 5th of December—I bade adieu to all my friends and relatives, and one parting in particular still wrings my heart. I little thought to meet no more Rodolph Arundell, the last of four dear beautiful brothers, who have all died young by untoward accidents. The wrench costs me a feverish attack every time I leave, which is once in every three or four years; nor do age and experience steel the heart nor wither the ever green memory. On Tuesday, the 7th, my husband and I found ourselves in a sleigh, which took us over the snow from hotel to boat. The weather seemed to stay its fury for our crossing the Channel, or else we are so used to rough it that it seemed only a healthy breeze and a heavy swell. The sun once tried to peep from his couch of clouds, and one passenger gleefully pointed out to another passenger a square inch or two of pale blue sky, which of course was duly smiled at by us tropicals. How hard it is to leave home! I even linger over it on paper; but now I am across Channel, and the deed is done, I will brace myself up and not be so tedious.

In our company for a week was that remarkably clever and brilliant writer, Andrew Wilson, the author of "The Abode of Snow." The old port of Boulogne stretched out its two long lean arms to our cockle-shell of a steamer. We enter somewhat differently to the manner of the old time. There was a new regulation, which is an extreme disadvantage to the town,—that of landing on the *gare* side, to the right. So that instead of remaining a few days in the town, as in the old time, it is easier to jump into the train and find oneself at Paris—*tant pis pour Boulogne!* The fact is that the Railway, perhaps the *most* despotic power of our modern day, willed it so. The Municipality, foreseeing that their City would, to the great detriment of the hotel-keepers, become a mere station, a place of passage, a "half-way house" between London and Paris, fought manfully against the change. The Railway simply said, "Either *here* or *nowhere*," and the Municipality was forced to yield.

Hôtel Christol is a grand place in Boulogne, but after The Pavilion it looked more than *mesquin*. Long, long ago, I passed two years of my school days in this town. My husband was then a young lieutenant on furlough from India. He was just beginning to spring into fame, after twelve years' service and his famous expedition with the Hajj to Mecca, and was staying with his family and writing a book. It was, therefore, interesting for us to stop a few days and visit all our old haunts, where we first met when we were young. The Church of St. Nicholas; Constantin, the fencing master, where "the Burton *une-deux*" is still taught, and which afterwards earned him. his *brevet de pointe*. The present Cathedral, in the Haute Ville, was building: now, a magnificent, but slightly crooked and very badly proportioned, pile. Dear old Abbé Haffreingue was its author. He died happy in 1871, after devoting half of his eighty-six years to its erection; and in gratitude to the English, who gave the greater part of the money, the statue of Our Lady, on the summit, has her face turned towards England.

Then the old ramparts where we first made acquaintance, and where he used to follow us when we were sent out to learn our lessons *al fresco*, and he used to chalk up, "May I speak to you?" and I used to chalk back, "No, mother will be angry"—and mother found it, and *was* angry. The Rue de l'Ecu, the Grande Rue, the Quai, the Pier, where we used to come on summer evenings and hear some Swiss strollers play on the guitar or fiddle, and sing little *jodelling* nothings, and thought it heavenly. How lovely everything is when one is young! And what a dear, picturesque old town it is, this capital of old Morinie,—the City of Julius Cæsar in ancient times, and of the Blessed Virgin in the present day, with its background of dull brown cliff, broken by the broad valley of the river Eln, Elna, Elnboga, now Liane! How many happy boating excursions we used to make upon that river when we were all young and living.

And then I hunted out my little brother's grave, and planted fresh rose trees. I visited Caroline, the Queen of the Poissardes, who used to be a friend of my childhood, a great ally of my brothers and sisters and self. She is still a beautiful and majestic creature in her costume. She reminded me of a promise I made her then, which I had long since forgotten, that if ever I went to Jerusalem I would bring her a rosary. I little dreamt then of marrying Richard Burton, who would be Consul of Damascus, and that I should ever go to Jerusalem; but things come about strangely, and I *did* go there fifteen years later; and now, to her great delight, I was able to fulfil my promise.

I often wonder that nobody writes the history of the Poissardes of Boulogne. They are a race apart, — a fine cross between Flemish and Spanish. They are the original stock, and the townspeople are a new and mongrel breed whom these despise and do not mix or intermarry with. The Poissardes have their own church on their hill-top, and their own town, laws, customs, manners, and habits, a separate register of births, deaths, and marriages, and they live under the rule of Caroline. The lower class are the shrimping girls,—and a rough lot too, but remarkable for their virtue. If they chaff the funny passing Britisher a little too much, a reference to Caroline brings them to order at once. On great feast-days and religious processions they form by far the prettiest part of it, with their lovely varied costumes, big white caps, embroidered white kerchiefs, and the huge gold ornaments that are heirlooms. Boulogne is materially changed since our time. It used to be a very fast place, full of amusing, but not *all* desirable, acquaintances, although there was a large sprinkling of happy exceptions. In fact, it was a City of Refuge, "The home of the stranger who's done something wrong," and the *good* people came either for economy or for the education of their families.

On the 10th we went up to Paris. The Ligne du Nord is the only comfortable line of railway in France,—the only one which has porters and civil officials ready to give you the value of your "tip." We sped past the Dunes, loved of rabbits, where father used to shoot, *faute de mieux*, and I used to carry the bag and lunch; along the winding shore of ancient Picardy, through the peat beds leading to Abbeville, and over the utterly uninteresting plains of La Belle France, *i.e.*, the northern section, till we rushed by the black silhouettes which denote the fortifications of the Capital. We compared them with the workmen's Cities outlying our own Babylon, and we felt grateful to that "streak of silver sea," our Channel. May they who propose to tunnel under it never see their folly carried out. Much better is it to allow a few old women to be sea-sick for a couple of hours, than to waste millions in constructing a thing at whose entrance we should always require a "Woolwich Infant." With our institutions, England placed in a continental position could not last a week. With our laws and customs, a foreign nation could not live a year. It is our birthright, a gift of God, that we are an island, and we want to sell it for the veriest mess of pottage,—a step which would be regretted but once and for ever as soon as it is irrevocable.

I found Paris terribly changed since the Franco-Prussian war. The weather was bad, for one thing, and that put one into an extra bad humour. Paris was full of Miss Blackford ("Fanny Lear") and her sale,—her black-draped drawing-room hung with Imperial likenesses, and her funny *meubles* engraved with her family motto "Prends tout."

The only amusement I found was going to hear Rossi in Hamlet and Macbeth. My husband and I had for some time past taken an interest in reading together and studying the various acting and difference of opinion as to the interpretation of Shakespeare's tragedies. The quarrels and excitement occasioned by Salvini's appearance in England, with his Italian reading of Hamlet, Macbeth, and Othello,* his magnificent voice and presence, and that of our own great tragedian Irving's appearance in these characters, with the latest, and perhaps truest, reading, gave the desired opportunity. It had become almost a party question amongst the dramatists, and we had entered warmly into it, visiting all these representations as often as we were at liberty; we were desirous of comparing these with Rossi, the only other great name at present in connection with Shakespeare in Europe, and so we went to "Les Italiens" every time he performed.

I found the scenery after London shabby to a degree, the dresses flashy and tinsel; there were no appliances for sensational effect. Rossi is a short man, with a bull throat, a chest suggestive more of fat than muscle, a big trunk upon incompetent legs, dark hands, a pale, unwholesome face, and light hair. He

* It may not be uninteresting to remark that Salvini read Shakespeare with our respected and talented predecessor, Charles Lever, at Trieste, who expounded the author's hidden meanings to him.

appeared to have colourless small eyes, and was obliged to shut them for passionate scenes. This on the stage; and as his pictures represent him as a fine, handsome, dark young man, I conclude it is the effect of the "make-up." In Hamlet he is too mad, and rants. He lacks the dignity, the finely-strung imagination and refinement and facial expression of Irving; nor has he the majesty and the glorious Tuscan Italian of Salvini, whose voice is like a Cathedral bell. And yet no Italian can help being artistic. Some of his actions are large, noble, and graceful, and he handles his sword like a man who lives with his weapon by his side. To say he cannot act would be absurd, but he can only rank as third. In Macbeth he was very good in the murder scene, from "Why have you left the chamber?" till "Wake Duncan with thy knocking." He has a pretty trick of looking at his blood-stained hands and hiding them, when he thought nobody was observing him; and again, when the Queen's death is announced, he looks sad for one instant only, and then, seizing what appears to me the true idea, that Macbeth would soon have poisoned her, to silence those somnambulisms and nightly tellings of his secret murders, gives himself a shake and casts his sadness off, as if he would have said, "Better so; what matters whether to-day or to-morrow?" Then, *en revanche*, he staggers like a drunken man to commit his murder, and in his conversation alone with his wife he treads upon his own cloak, and feigns to think it is the ghost of Banquo. Terrified by his guilty conscience, he flounders on his back like a turtle, his crown rolling away. Now, Shakespeare was an Englishman, and an Englishman rolling on his back from fright was never seen, nor could such an idea enter an English brain. Had he drawn his sword to cut the ghost down, it would have been more in tune with our ideas. His wife drags him off after the murder, pommelling him as a fish-wife would a drunken husband. The ghost scene, supper, and fright, were not merely a *fiasco*, but contemptible. In Hamlet, he danced upon his uncle's picture like a monkey. All that is neither English nor Shakespeare. I am a fanatic about Shakespeare, so I enter into these minor details *con amore*. The last story I heard in Paris concerning Rossi was a conversation between two *petits crévés*:—

A. As tu entendu Rossi?—

B. Qui est Rossi?—

A. Comment! tu ne sais pas? Mais ce monsieur qui fait une conference sur un crâne.

And now for a serious bit of moralizing, from gay to grave. The radical changes of the last five years in Paris deserve chronicling and deep study. The War and the Commune have made a New World. "*La nation la plus aimable la plus aimée et peut-être la moins aimante,*" has been translated—"The light and joyous character may lie below; but there is a terribly hard upper crust of sulkiness and economy run mad—rage for lucre, and lust *pour la revanche.*" There is only the *ancienne noblesse*, the Faubourg St. Germain, the souls loyal to their King and to their Faith, who remain pure. So far, the Parisians are like the Irish Kelt,—a blathering, bumptious, bull-and-blunder loving race. The former have been converted in half-a-century by politics and polemics into a moping and melancholy brood. It is no longer the fashion in France to speak without an introduction. Men will sit side by side at *table d'hôte* in dead silence for a month; they travel twenty-four hours in the railway without opening the mouth; and if a loud laugh be heard in public it is sure to come from some *triste Anglais*. Even the women, although they still fling the look of hate at a pretty toilette, seem to have abdicated the supremacy of the toilette. Once you never did, now you often see the absence of corsets upon figures that can't stand it. They are badly painted, and it is a sin to paint badly. They are *outrées* in their dress, and the neglect of these things is a bad sign in Paris. The middle and the lower classes, who used to be *à quatre epingles*, were *mal coiffées*, with their petticoats hanging below their dresses, as we were in the days of *les Anglaises pour rire*. We have learnt many things from our French friends, and amongst the *good* things, how to dress; but dress never made *our* women's beauty—it did that of the French.

The theatres are clearing 27,000,000 of francs (1875), when during the palmiest days of the Empire they never exceeded 17,000,000. Except at the new Opera, the scenery and decorations are those of our penny gaffs. "Les Italiens" bears the palm of dowdyism, and actors and actresses seem to have decayed with the decorations. The *cuisine,* except in special instances, has notably fallen off. The bottles are all "kick," the famous bread-and-butter has lost caste. The *café au lait* is all chicory,—maximum water, minimum beans. Mammonolatry is rampant, and the grand problem of manufacture and depôt, of store and shop, is how to charge the most for the worst article. Economy has now become a vice instead of a virtue, and 1,852,000 souls manage to pay 12,280,000 francs in taxes per annum.

It is impossible to pass a day in Paris without hearing and speaking politics. The French, I have said, are sulky, especially with the "Perfidious," because she had supplanted them in Egypt, where for so many years England had by a tacit convention supplied the material and France the personal. They question the wisdom of our last dodge. It is the first move in the coming Kriegspiel. I hate half-measures, and I would have bought the Canal wholly out and out, and put a fortress at each end and taken a mild nominal toll to show my right. I would protect Egypt and Syria, occupy the Dardanelles, and after that let the whole world wrangle as much as it pleased. What is the use of having a Navy superior to all the united Navies of the rest of the world, if we can't do this? The world will never be still till Constantinople returns to the old Byzantine kingdom; and we might put a Royalty there, say the Duke of Edinburgh, who, being married to the Czar's daughter, would unite the interests of Russia and England. Let the Turk live, but retire into private life; he is a good fellow there, and we can respect El Islam so long as he has nothing to butcher.

Let Austria become a mighty empire,—nineteen million Slavs, eight million Germans, five million Hungarians. Let Italy be satisfied with her Unity and Freedom, and Progress, and Prussia repose upon her Bismarck, and France keep quiet and look after her health. But as it is, the three Emperors may say to us, "Gentlemen, you have got what you want; we will follow suit—look on, and don't spoil sport." Taken *per se,* this Suez Canal measure is a patch of tinsel gold plastered upon the rags of foreign and continental policy which our Ins and Outs have kept up during the last decade, whilst under-authorities are apparently told off to declare periodically that England has lost none of her prestige abroad. Listen to the average politician of the multitude.* Were I a man I should fight once a day about the doings of my own party (I am a red-hot Conservative); but being a woman I can only use my tongue and drop hot caustic upon the unhappy offender who ventures too much upon hoping that, being only a woman, I do not see to the bottom of the well; and what irritates me more is that little as *he* knows, there is sound truth in what he says.

The fact is that England has repudiated the grand old rule of Aristocracy which carried her safely through the Titan wars of the early Buonaparte ages, whilst she has not accepted the strong repulsive arm of Democracy, which enabled the Federal to beat down the Confederate. She rejects equally the refined minority and the sturdy majority; she is neither hot nor cold; she sits between two stools, and we all know where that leads to.

This Suez move would have been a homogeneous part of a strong policy,—that is, a policy backed by two millions of soldiers, by a preponderating fleet of ironclads, and by a school of diplomatists which has not been broken in to "effacing" themselves. Of our politicians generally, the less said the soonest mended; but I have unbounded confidence in our Premier, in our Navy, and the good heart, rough common sense, firmness, and *esprit de corps* of our British public. The next shake—and it will be heavy and soon—will give us the Euphrates Valley Railway, despite the cleverness of an Ignatieff. The first disaster will bring on a revival of the Militia Law, and I should not be surprised if we live to see ourselves revolve round again to a general conscription, and the "do nothings" will eventually go to the wall. It is a pity to tie the hands of so long-sighted a Premier.

Revenge is still the dream of Paris, and the dream is not of the wise. The three Emperors love the three Empires, and hate one another; the Government and the Lieges are blinded by jealousy; each wishes to be the first in the race, and to see the

* Written in 1876.

other two distanced. All are mounted upon a war footing *au piéd de guerre;* which means that they intend fighting, and Germany especially must fight or she is lost; to her peace is more ruinous than war. France is cutting her up with the purse instead of the sword. The great Triad might alter the map of Europe. "The Sons of Hermann" would absorb Belgium and Holland; the Muscovite swallow Constantinople with its neighbouring appendages, and Austria *convey* ("the wise it call") the remainder of Turkey's Slavonic provinces. But they will do nothing of the kind. Germany has proved herself the natural guardian of the Eastern frontier of Europe.

A Franco-Russian alliance is now, in 1876, in everybody's mouth. France is for the moment safely republican, with a chance of M. Thiers, the Kingmaker, succeeding to the Presidency.* She casts the blame of the Communal excesses upon the Buonapartists, because she fears them; but she has clean forgotten Legitimists and Orleanists. As regards the Franco-Russian alliance, opinions follow two courses. The sensible and far-seeing, which (like councils of war) never fights, would unite with Russia and temporarily keep the peace. The majority of hot heads and Hotspurs would use it for another "*à Berlin*" to attack Prussia from the east as well as the west.

Yet if truth be told, France is far less ready for war than England. She can hardly raise 400,000 men to defend her own frontiers. We assisted at various reviews, and inspected many of the camps; we saw artillery, cavalry, and infantry equally unfit to face an educated enemy. Every order given by an officer was answered or questioned by a private,—"*Mais, ce n'est pas cela du tout, mon Capitaine.*" Guns, horses, and men were equally inefficient. True the chassepot is being changed for the fusil Gras, the sword bayonet is being supplanted by a neat triangular weapon unfit to cut cabbages and wood, and the six arms manufacturers of France are not wasting an hour. But after seeing the skirmishes and advances in line, one cannot help feeling certain that at this rate half a century will elapse before the Frenchman is ready to fight the Prussian. Meanwhile, every

* This was written in 1876.

head of man, woman, and child here pay half a franc (fivepence sterling) per diem, and the Municipality of Paris spends, I am told, an income inferior only to the six great Powers of Europe.

The part of the Regal-Republican, Imperial-Republican Capital showing least change is that Conservative Quarter which may be called "Anglo-American Paris." This "West End" is bounded north by the Boulevarts des Italiens, and the Madeleine; south by the Rue Rivoli and the River (a mere ditch, but not so dirty as Father Thames), east by the Rue Richelieu, the Palais Royal, and Véfour, west by the Embassy and the Chapel, with the Vendôme Column as a landmark. Here the northern and western barbarians have their King Plenipo, and their Consul, their Chaplain and Physician, their pet hotels, English (Meurice's), their club and library (Galignani's), their tavern (Byron's, famed for beer) their dentists, their pharmacies, and their shops labelled, "English (or American) spoken here,"—which generally means, "I'm a thief, you're a fool." We can tell a compatriot a mile off—the men by their billycock hats and tweed suits, their open mouths, hats well at back of head, and red guide-books; the women by their wondrous dress and hats,—for which there are especial shops,—their turned-up toes and noses, their manly strides, their taking men's arms,—one on each side,—and the glum faces of both sexes on the Sabbath, when the guide-book is exchanged for the Common Prayer Book and the Bible. In this region where the snuffle of the Yankee mixes with the *h*aspirations of the Cockney, the really Parisianized Englishman is never seen, and if compelled to pass through it he hurries with muffled face in trembling haste, like Mahomet rushing down the demon-haunted defiles of El Hidjr.

I was so glad to leave Paris at the end of a week, to move out of the raw white fog sunwards. This line from Paris to Modane is the worst in France; it bears the palm of badness. It is expensive, and yet parsimony haunts you. The night lamps are so scantily filled as to soon die out. At the *buffet* one pays a franc for a cup of hot milk. Discomfort is rampant. Every carriage must be filled before another is put on. Porters seem to be unknown. Lap-dogs are muzzled and put in a dirty cold dog-box, to howl out their miserable twenty-one hours thirty minutes. *Orders* never end; you are even ordered to remove the old labels from your travelling-boxes. At Modane when passing into the Custom pen I was gruffly addressed,—"*On ne passe pas!*" *Comment on ne passe pas?* "*On ne passe pas.*"

The only thing wanting, I afterwards ascertained, was a visiting card; but the opportunity of being safely insolent was too tempting to be passed over. Jacques Bonhomme can never wear a rag of uniform without becoming a "Jack in office." The Midi should reform its disreputable terminus; the Parisian station should be modelled on that of the Nord; Modane should be cleaned out and reorganized. The Company has little idea of what a delight it is to arrive at Modane, and to exchange the discomfort and petty official tyranny and rudeness of the *petits employés* of the France of the Republic, for the dear, good-natured Italians and civil, gentlemanly Austrians. What *would* have happened if these *braves* had reached Berlin? Europe would have been uninhabitable. France as a second-rate Power *or* as a Monarchy, would be charming; as a republic, she is detestable.

The journey was performed in twenty-three hours, and the Italian country passed through was Bardonnechia, Meana, Bussolino, Borgone, Sant' Antonio, Condove, Sant' Ambrogio, Avigliana, Rosta, Alpignano, and Collegno. Turin showed us the sun of the *Bel Paese* at nine in the morning, and we stared like mine-born children, brought to the top for the first time, at the charming mixture of sun and frost,—the gold dust of the beams raining upon the pure ermine of the snow. After the long, dull brown plains of central France, the aspect of a silver-topped Alp was a relief to eye and heart; and we greatly enjoyed glimpses at Monte Viso and the Grand Paradis,—all was, in fact, a change for the better, except the presence of unclean paper money.

The site of Turin is a shelf between the mountains and the river Po, and the kidney-stones of the streets drain off the heaviest rains in a few hours. She has a tramway, which Rome and Milan have not (1876). She has her intellectual conquests, and can boast of being in the foremost rank of modern Italian Cities. The Royal Academy of Sciences has enlisted the services of many great men. Amongst her bright particular stars are MM. Cristoforo Negri, President—founder of the Italian Royal Geographical Society, the most genial and least pugnacious of geographers; Professor Fabretti, the Etruscologist of the world; Professor Gastaldi, whom anthropologists love to honour; and last, because youngest, Guido Cora, originator, proprietor, and editor of the *Cosmo.*

After bath and toilette we breakfasted, and passed the day with these friends, and visited all our old haunts at Turin. The Museum here is almost unrivalled in Egyptology, and the prehistoric and Etruscan periods are of the highest importance. The sooner they are moved to the Palazzo Carignano the better. It is worth while to spend a week at the comfortable Hotel Feder, or the Europa, and see the churches and private galleries. There is a Roman *Ruina Recente;* a Jewish synagogue of Signor Antonchi, a modern imitation of the Tower of Babel, a Temple of Herod with double proportions, which has cost one million of francs, and which wants another five hundred thousand pounds;* and, finally, there is the drive to La Superga, with its glorious view of peak and plain. Here I had the honour of sending my "Inner Life of Syria" to the Principessa Margherita di Savoja (now Queen of Italy), and of receiving a gracious letter of thanks and approval.

On the 18th, provided with a mighty flask of *Vermout di Torino*—the best known—we proceeded to cross the fat flats of Northern Italy, which extend almost without a break as far as Istria and Trieste, passing through Chiavasso, Santhiá, Vercelli, Novara, and Magenta. After the hills of Montferrat and historic Chiavasso, the Paduan valley supports a host of villages, which are towns in miniature,—most unlike the Alpine hovels, plastered against hillsides as wasps' nests stuck to a ruined wall. We passed and admired the Campanile towers and lantern of the Vercelli Cathedral, and laughed at the six-storied, pepper-box dome of Novara and the truncated obelisk of Magenta.

The lime quarries supply abundance of granite, black and white

* It is noticed by the learned Mr. Ferguson, in his late work "The Temples of the Jews."

and red and white; so that even the humblest offices have their monolithic jambs. It is hard to explain the neglect of the vast turbaries of this rich region. *Mottes* of peat are sold at Venice, but no one has apparently started the exploitation, upon a large scale, of a material which would be most valuable for the iron trade. Can the long arm of the Coal League extend thus far? And we philosophized upon the beggar-plague, which now begins to rage. Mendicancy, when it is not caused by actual want—as is often the case—appears to me the logical result of making poverty an ecclesiastical virtue. So in Syria, well-to-do villagers will exchange the Lebanon in winter for Beyrout, and beg, because such was the custom of "our Lord and the Apostles." *Al fakro fakhri* (Poverty is my pride), quoth Mahomet, who thus engendered the Fakir and the Dervish. Climate and scanty wants have something to do with this pest, for we see it increasing as we go further south; and yet Piedmont and Lombardy are not soft and sunny regions, though hotter than England; and the rosy-faced women, with big straw hats, working in the fields, show that industry, and the *objects* of industry, are not yet wanting. We threaded the watermeadows, which bear rice, and the rich pastures that produce the cheese familiarly known as Parmesan.

The approach to the most civilized and joyous town in Italy, where animals are not illtreated, namely Milan, is that of an Imperial City. The *Gare*, if not watertight, is at least ornamental, and the tracery is laid down by art. The Hotel de la Ville and the Feder are both good, and we installed ourselves in the former, which opens upon the Corso Vittorio Emanuele, the popular walk where, on Sundays and holidays, the world admires its neighbour's wife; where the *Madamina* (Milanese grisette) shows the fine stalwart Lombard figure; where the English Ulster and the Pastrano cloak contrast with the black and scarlet cap of Turin; where the fan-like silver combs of the Brianzuola nurse compare with the Paddy-like tailcoat of the southern peasantry and with the huge green felt of the Tyrolese man. We both knew Milan well, so we revisited only the scenes most cared for, despite the cold of that nineteenth of December. For instance, who would pass through and miss a chance of gazing at that magnificent work of sculpture, the Duomo? What more beautiful than the white marble of the Borromei, standing out against the pure turquoise sky of Italy? We went to the very top, and spent hours there, quietly enjoying the perspective of floriated flying buttresses, known as "the garden;" of spires, pinnacles, statues, and lace-work of marble. The interior is more Spanish than Italian. It commands a beautiful view, but we only caught sight of the tips of the mountains of Lecco through the mist, capped with snow, and rosy in the sun.

The City here becomes quite a panorama, and we could see at a glance its complicated system of irrigation. Two outlets, from the Lago Maggiore and the Como water, meet within the walls, and forming a fan, radiate southwards over the gentle slope leading some fifty miles down to the banks of Father Po. Then, of course, we went to look at Leonardo da Vinci's "Last Supper" in the Dominican refectory of Nostra Signora delle Grazie, used in these heretical days as an artillery barrack. The old relic looked much more damaged than when I last saw it; to me a forecast of what Italy will become when she casts out Christ's Church. What a pity that there is no way of conserving this splendid wreck with more certainty. Now a stove has been built to dry the glorious fresco, whose colour began to fade even in the days of a contemporary (Lanuzzi).

We then went to the Brera, only to look again on Raffaelle's "Sposalizio" (or "Marriage of the Virgin"), with the rejected suitor breaking the rod,—his first style. Then to the tower called St. Gothardo of Azoni Visconti, where Gian Maria Visconti was murdered; and what a beautiful bit of Lombard architecture it is! Then to the hospital (Ospedale Maggiore), with its splendid *façade* of brick and mouldings wonderfully carved in terra cotta, and its cloistered court of the same material, showing that the genius of the Vicentine, Palladio, has not been ignored by the Milanese. Then to the Ambrogian Library, rich and rare in volume and manuscript Then to the little church, made of bones and skulls, which smells fearfully corpse-like. The Scala Theatre was not to be opened till the 26th. These things I visit every time I go to Milan: I love the little place. The streets are gay, the people are gay; the animals are happy, and not tortured. You see well-dressed men and pretty women, who seem to belong to a world, —not ours, perhaps, but still a world. We finished up our amusements by dining with our genial colleague, Mr. (Consul) Kelly, who made our short stay so pleasant.

The Capital of Lombardy is a place where you *can* dine, and the Rebecchino Trattoria has a national *cuisine*, and we had a delicious Milanese dinner, *ravioli* and all. This restaurant is evidently composed of a *cortile*, a court-yard roofed in by iron girders and glass. I wish we adopted this manner of enlarging space in England. The decoration is florid—in fact, that of Pompeii—and the white groundwork of the walls does not absorb the light. The *menu?* None! It is not Trattoria fashion, so we made it out in our memory. First, the cold *hors d'œuvres*; trout, mixed with Mayonnaise cream; and a plate of sausage, jelly and gelantine stuffed with truffles and pistachios. Instead of soup, the *Risotto a la Milanese*, which the Italian loves; the fish, boiled *branzino;* and for *grosse pièce*, fillet of beef with *ravioli*, the prince of Italian pastes. The gem of the feast was a *boudin à la Richelieu*, here called *Flambe di Selvaggiume*—our game pudding; *poulet à l'aise* (chicken made easy), followed by ice pudding, by Goronzola, a cheese of the Stilton and Roquefort type, made, like Parmesan, about Milan; and lastly by dessert, in which grapes figured most. The wines are the Lombard Gattinara (whose fame we cannot accept), and the Piedmontese Barolo, the only Italian brand that resembles claret, though still far from its rosy bouquet. *Vixi diem!*—I know that we have dined.

Milan is bravely raising a monument to Napoleon III., whilst the popular feeling of young Italy runs strong against the French. The main reasons appear to be the abstraction of Nice, and the domineering tone assumed by the late Empire. Moreover, "the *peoples*" (Kossuth still lives at Turin) do not readily pardon their benefactors. Witness the aversion of Spain and Portugal for England since the days of the Peninsular War. In the next campaign the general voice of the younger and more fiery sort, and of that solid power, the Left Centre, will compel the constitutional Government of Victor Emmanuel, despite all his prepossessions and prejudices, to side with Germany against France. This was written two years ago, but it is, methinks, still true.

A few words touching the Italian character, which is so little appreciated by the stranger. Of course, the sentimental and moral element, the produce of the middle lobe, as opposed to the frontal or intellectual, is well known to all the world. Foreigners love him for his high spirits, his love of nature, of art, of music, of romance, of the picturesque; combined with a simplicity and a genuineness of feeling, and an absence of shyness, which to the grave, pompous Northern appears almost childlike, and proportionately charming. Few know the basis of his character,—an absolute Scepticism, which throws into the shade that of France, and a hard and rugged Realism, a rock crowned with flowers. We must not waste paper, but simply compare Dante's Commedia Divina with any other Epic. An iron purpose runs through the great poem; not a page but what tends to the real and material unity of Italy. Many a passage and a prophecy might head the chapters in "Italy Revisited," and the national worship of the Florentines led directly to "Ettore Fieramosca," the celebrated novel by the Marchese d'Azelio, the first blow struck by those who would be free.

Milan looks forward to the *concurrence* which the St. Gothard tunnel will cause, and aspires to piercing the Splügen, which will connect the Lakes of Constance and Como. She has serious causes of complaint against the French Ligne du Midi. The minor *employés* are careless of her goods, and their masters, the directors—who were, unfortunately, left uncontrolled by convention—have placed an almost prohibitory tax of fourteen and a half cents per kilometre on each thousand kilogrammes. This arbitrary proceeding is done for the purpose of forcing trade *viâ* Genoa and Marseilles and Paris, where the fourteen and a half cents are reduced to three cents. The St. Gothard will not be finished for, say, four years. Meanwhile we look forward to the day which will deliver us from the horrors of the Paris and Modane Stations.

Amongst the two hundred and sixty thousand souls, Milan numbers about one hundred and sixty English, children included.

Many families are here for economy, some for education, especially young people (American and British), hoping to make a musical *carrière*. They have their consul and chaplain and missionary, who advertises himself as follows: "Italian Evangelization (!) in connection with the Methodist Episcopal Church . . . . Christian friends passing through Milan are cordially invited to encourage the work of Evangelization by their presence, and will be thankfully welcomed by the Missionary and his family if visited at their home." For myself, I confess I do not understand what it means. Roman Catholic processions are not allowed to go about the streets, but are confined within their own temple walls, and all the little churches are secularized so as to stamp out the national religion as much as possible.

At Milan we relapsed into the regular style of Italian society, so remarkable at once for the exquisite amenity of its old civilization,—as far as manners are concerned,—and for the stiffness and mediæval semi-barbarism of its surroundings. We send our letters of introduction, with a visiting card, by the *commissionaire*, asking when we can call. The reply is "*Va bene*" (all right)—pleasant, but vague. We take heart of grace, and enquire at the door if the Signor Conte be visible. The janitor replies, "His Excellency receives at eight o'clock p.m." We reply that eight o'clock p.m. will find us on the railway. The domestic, whose movements are leisurely, leaves us in the hall, and dawdles upstairs to report the remarkable case. He returns, and, by order of the *Padrone*, shows us into the saloon. It is the usual huge, bare, fireless room, with a few ludicrous photographs and French prints; with that stiff, green sofa against the wall, and that semi-circle of chairs, also stiff and green, which suggest those horrors the *conversazione*, the *tertulia*, the "little music,"—in fact, the Southern equivalent of an English "tea fight." The Signor Conte keeps us waiting twenty minutes, whilst he shaves and exchanges his dressing-gown for that suit of sables, which is the correct, the only correct, raiment of the Latin race. Nothing can be more polished than his manners; he receives us with a cordiality and a *bonhommie* which at once win our hearts. But we are introduced to him by a bosom friend. Our pursuits and tastes are the same. Why, then, can't he ask us up to his cosy study, and give us a cup of coffee and a cigarette? *Sarebbe proprio indecente* (it would be really too rude) is the reply, although both he and we would like it extremely. After the fifth or sixth visit we should, perhaps, be more fortunate; but how long it takes to arrive at cosiness! And so for want of time to crack this hard nut-shell, to get at the kernel, we are choked off. This style of *gêne* grows like beggary as we go south, and will reach its zenith in Iberia and Greece.

On the 20th, another pleasant stretch of eight hours' travelling, fast for Italy, which separates the Capitals of Lombardy and the Venetian. The train passes through Treviglio, Bergamo,—which is built like Sâo Paulo in Brazil,—Bresera, Desenanzo, Peschiera, with its extensive ramparts and battlements. We are now in the Mediterranean regions, where every feature of the landscape falls into picture as naturally as the *figurante* into *pose.* Very grand and gracious is the accompaniment of Alp, the Lecco, and the Splügen,—those masses of polished steel and frosted silver, washed with gold and vermilion by the setting sun, as they advance upon and retire from the chocolate plain, based upon boulders and water-rolled pebbles, and bearing the mulberry, the poplar, and the vine, married to the elm. Foot of hill and face of lowland are dotted and lined with white cities and towns, hamlets, villages, and villas, churches, chapels, convents, and cypress-shaded cemeteries. After romantic Bergamo and Brescia, —which manufactures the sword,—we come suddenly upon the Lago di Garda and its artistic surroundings; a lovely country, with snowy mountaius,—an old friend that I have sketched, and gladly see again, and now feel that I am in familiar lands. It looks the most peaceful of its kind; it enjoys absolute repose, as is shown by its washings of varied blue; it slumbers an enchanted sleep at the feet of its guardian, the tall snow-peaks to the east flushing fiery red in the last beams. Unfortunately it is three hours of rail from Milan, somewhat too distant for the *villegiatura;* and the consequences are an absence of country houses and the presence of pauper villages. Then we passed through Verona and Tavernelle, three hours' drive from Recoaro, in the Italian

Dolomites. Recoaro is an iron-water drinking and bathing snuggery, which we go to occasionally for a month's refreshment in the waning summer. Then Vicenza, Padua, and Mestre, and, finally, dear old Venice.

Venice is our "happy hunting ground" whenever tired of Trieste, for it is only six hours from us by boat, and nine by rail. The "Silent City" took us to her damp bosom at dusk. It seemed, after the "flesh pots" of London, for which I was still sighing, so silent, so dark, so sad; and the plash of the *Gondola*, so often longed for when worn out and weary with the dissipated season or the busy world, sounded less soothing to me than I thought it would. Was I changed, or it? I suppose neither, really, for it took its effect at last. The mind is too much wound up sometimes, the nerves too finely strung; but the rest always brings one back. Try, reader, enduring great fatigues and anxieties, on a stretch, for a year and a half, and then come to Venice, and lie at the bottom of a *Gondola*, rowed about by a couple of *Gondoliers*, with a cushion for your head, half awake and half asleep in Dreamland. If you are not too unhappy to rest *anywhere*, you will find that do you good. It is the perfection of luxury and repose,—the plash of the oar is a lullaby.

However, nothing depends more upon complexion than the ex-Queen of the Adriatic; to-day she is enveloped in white fog, and we steamed up the Murazzi in a Scotch mist. The network of lagoons meanders through streets of the foulest mud,—a perfect Maleboge (see Dante), a wet place of punishment, with the domes and towers rising ghostly through the mist. But see Venice on a fine Adriatic day, when the blue sea dances to the bluer air; when the light of a golden sun picks out each beauty of detail, and when the horizontal cast of the landscape is set off by the misty forms of the Rhætian and the Julian Alps, towering like a monstrous Chinese wall, as if to keep out the "northern barbarian." Venice is, in fact, although the world in general does not know it, pre-eminently a *sommerfrisch*, a hot-weather City. In the winter, with her cold canals and wet alleys, her deep rains and dense mists, her huge unwarmed palaces, and her bare, draughty hotels, she is no better than she should be. Yet throughout the year her climate is essentially sedative, like that of Nice, of Madeira, and of Görz (Gorizia), and most unlike the exciting, *jumpy* air of Trieste, of Istria, and of the east Adriatic shores in general. She is more composing than even Rome.

With such reflections we wend our noiseless way, awaking now and then a drowsy echo by a conventional grunt, as we plough round the corner of some narrower water-wynd. After a quarter of an hour we stand under the familiar Bridge of Sighs, and we emerge upon the splendour of the Riva dei Schiavoni, of the Slavs who founded Venice, and who supplied her with Mocenigos, Gradenigos, and all that ends in "igo." Here, upon a sandbank, rising barely above high tide, as you may see in the Piazza San Marco, when the pavement slabs are raised to repair the gas-pipes, dwelt the fishermen, around whom clustered in course of time the big crannoge (pile village), which became "a noble and fantastic City."

We went to the Hotel Danielli. One should always go to the best, because second-rate inns are not only devoid of comfort, but in the long run are dearer than the best. I have a *penchant* for the Europa, because I am old-fashioned: my husband likes Danielli. We paid only twelve Italian lire per diem, which can't be called dear, and all, save wine, included. Danielli (MM. Genovesi and Campi) also owns the chief restaurant at the Lido (the Littus, or shore), the great natural breakwater, seven miles long and one-and-a-half broad, which stands between the Adriatic and the lagoons. Here Byron used to ride and lunch when he lived and learned Orientalism with the "Doctors of Penitence," the Armenian brotherhood, now called after Abbot Mekhitar, the Consoler. The pious community makes the best liqueur in the world, called "Benedictine," and sells little books. To the Lido, in the hot season, crowds go to bathe, to drive, to pick up the "flowers of the sea," shells, and to gaze for hours on the lazy Adriatic, which looks in the moonlight like a vast sheet of quicksilver, albeit somewhat ragged about the edges. A small octavo, copiously illustrated, called "A Week in Venice," shows you how to "do" the Sea City in ten days, but it is hard work. Dine, when tired, at the restaurant Français (Quadri), on the north of the Piazza San Marco, and take your coffee and *petit verre* at the Café Florian, on the opposite side. To the west of the square is an excellent library (Munster's). There are several clubs, especially the Società Quirina, which takes the newspapers of Europe; and the theatres open on the 26th December.

The first impression of the stranger at Venice, especially after a trip through the minor canals, is that the smells are abominable. A naturalized Englishman has obtained from the Municipality a commission for bringing in the waters of the Brenta river by an aqueduct into the city, and the abundant supply will speedily dilute the drainage. At present, water is carried from the rain cisterns by *bigolante*, as these Friuli girls, with men's felt hats, are called—after the *bigolo*, or yoke, which, passing over the shoulders, connects the two copper pots. The latter contain some twenty litres, costing five soldi, whereas M. Ritterbrandt proposes to supply one hundred for six soldi. The Brenta is rapidly silting up the lagoons, and threatening to make Venice, like Ravenna, an inland city. Against this evil two measures have been proposed: the first is to dredge away the deposit, a long task, which will cost millions of francs; the second is to favour the mud growth on the land side, and to reserve the clearing and cleaning for the main approach to the port.

Perhaps the most urgent improvement called for, is a reform of the Custom-House. Merchants and Skippers complain aloud of its vexatious formalities and immense delays. It is even whispered that, as soon as possible, the P. and O. will refuse to renew the postal contract. Why not make the old place a free port, and let Trieste and Venice be King and Queen of the Adriatic? There should be room enough for both. In the Piazza San Marco I met an Englishman who appeared to grow more and more bilious as he increased the distance from his native shore. He saw me, as usual, in a state of happy contemplation at the picturesqueness around me; so he began,—

"Eh! what! staring as usual at the Stones of Venice? Stuff! You're always staring, and one can't get a word from you. What are you thinking of? Look at the Doges' palace. How it has been bespattered with flattery! Why, it is a building turned upside down. The light, airy part is below, the solid and weighty is above. The whole affair looks top-heavy. And the fine marbles of the upper half have been cut so as to look exactly like bricks. Then that pudgy cathedral, which seems to be a Mosque gone mad, and its huge campanile contains as many square feet of accommodation as the cathedral itself. It slopes, you see; so do the two columns of the Piazetta,—so does every tower in Venice. They all lean in a languid way, without energy, like the monsters of Bologna. Look about you, and you won't see in all the masonry a tight joint or a straight line. By this general crookedness I explain the moral obliquity of Austrian policy in the so-called palmy days of the turbulent and treacherous '*Serenissima Republica.*' The physical effect must have acted upon the *morale.* Now come to the Piazza dei Leoncini to see the Lionlets, to the north-west of the Cathedral, and stare at the classical patriarchal palace. I am glad that it looks upon Manin's tomb, though! and the St. Basso Church in another style of the classical. How they swear at that dwarf heap of Byzantine domes! Only one specimen of how incongruous is art in the 'Stones of Venice.' But it's all the same to the mob of sightseers and travellers. Like sheep, one takes the path, and the rest follow, too glad to save the trouble of thinking for themselves."

I saw he had the spleen, so I had the tact to turn the conversation upon himself, and gave him an opportunity to *sfogarsi*—in plain English, "to let off the steam."

There are few novelties in Venice. Some hideous iron bridges, veritable engineer's, as opposite to artist's, Art, which are found cheaper and more lasting than those of masonry. The flower girl, the minstrel boy, and the gondolier are still institutions. Picturesque figures still haunt the Rive, the red-capped and stockinged fisherman, the blue-capped peasant, and the mountaineers in the tightest of tights. But the old Venetian type of beauty—the Desdemona—is waxing rare, except in the two extremities of the City, north and south. Patrician dames of old used to bathe their locks in sea water and expose them to

AN ENGLISHMAN WITH THE "SPLEEN" AT VENICE.

the burning sun. They didn't know of henna, perhaps. Now they prefer the raven's wing, and to rival the pretty Jewesses of to-day.

Here also I sought out and found some interesting Shakesperian memories; the dress of the Patrician of Venice in the 16th century, "Il Costume Antico e Moderno di Guilio Ferrario," in the Biblioteca Marciana; see especially pages 700—925; 3 vols., coloured plates, published in Milan 1823, and to be found in our British Museum; and "Gli Abiti Antichi e Moderni," by Vicellio, published, Venice, 1598, and not found in England, I think gives all the costumes, and some of the manners and customs, of the days of Shakespeare and Othello. The original Desdemona was a fair specimen of the Venetian beauty of that day—blonde hair, dark brown eyes, thin, high, prominent nose, delicate small mouth, tall and graceful figure, narrow shouldered, with small hands and feet, and a generally thorough-bred appearance and carriage. Othello's family is not yet extinct; Signor Moro-Lin represents the two houses, and has two stout folios in MSS., showing Cristofalo Moro, 67th Doge of Venice, in 1462, after his return from Cyprus, wearing the Phrygian cap of office, and all guiltless of his gentle wife's blood. Consult also the "Storia dei Doge di Venezia," Grinaldi: Venezia, 1867.

I had with me a German maid, who had never seen Venice, never heard of lake villages, nor seen Rotterdam, nor Pernambuco: she was swimming in a gondola for the first time, and was at the highest pitch of excitement at finding that all was water, and that she had to step into a gondola at the door, instead of a carriage, or trudging on *terra firma*. She marvelled at the absence of cabs and dust, and exclaimed perpetually, "Nothing but water, water, everywhere!" which we old hands naturally finished off by—"And not a drop to drink," till I believe she fancied that was the only thing we English ever think of. I took heart of grace to show her all the chief beauties of the place,—the Duomo, with its *et ceteras;* the Piazza San Marco, the Piazetta, the Doges' Palace; the Frari, Canova's tomb, the Scalzi full of marbles, the Prigioni, the Bridge of Sighs, the Lido and Rialto, —not forgetting Rietti's and several other people's curiosity shops and glass works, more interesting to her, probably, than the buildings.

Then I had the good fortune to make acquaintance with the Montalba family. The mother and two of the daughters were here. These interesting girls are so well known as sculptors and painters of high degree that I can only say what a treat it was to make their acquaintance, and how charming I found them.

I was astonished to find the Italianissimo feeling so rampant in Upper Italy, and the people so excited upon the subject, when their Government have set them an example of calmness, common-sense, moderation and constitutional spirit of compromise, which go far to redeem the character of the Latin race, even in this the darkest day of its history. Because Dante made the Quarnero Gulf finish Italy, and because Petrarch established the Alps as the surroundings of his fair land, their new geographical politicians would absorb Trieste and Istria; and when Jove shall wax wroth, he will probably grant them their silly prayer.

On the 23rd we left by the midnight boat, and all who knew us came to see us off; the plash of the gondola and the distant "good nights" dying away upon the water seemed to keep time like a glee. At seven a.m. next day (Christmas Eve) I was at Trieste, my much-loved home for four years and a half, which I found all to a hair as I left it a year ago. Christmas night was, however, a little sad, for my husband was not well, and I could not go to the various festivities to which I was invited and leave him alone. So, having ordered nothing at home, and having given the servants "leave of absence" to their respective families, I was obliged on this our greatest feast to dine alone on bread and olives, which was all I could find.

The remaining days of 1875 were spent in Christmas visits, Christmas boxes, Christmas cards, Christmas dinners. Our kind friends were as glad to see us back as we were to see them, and gave us a perfect ovation during our eight days' stay. Baron Pascotini, one of the most eminent public men here, presented me with a diploma from the Societá Zoofila (Prevention of Cruelty to Animals), electing me a life member; and, curiously enough, I was also the bearer of one for him on the part of our Society in Jermyn Street, which he richly deserved. He is a fine old man, past eighty years of age, and as active as a youth; ever prominent in all cases of humanity and charity. He is decisive in his judgment, and his great position in Trieste enables him to carry out the dictates of his noble heart. I was also elected, by unanimous vote, President of another Society, a religious and charitable *réunion*, numbering some ten thousand members in Trieste and its environs, enabling me to do some good work for the Church, and for the poor of all denominations. I had also the pleasure of presenting my "Inner Life of Syria" to the Civic Library of the town. These affectionate marks of goodwill and approval on the part of the Town and society in which we had lived for three years were a great source of pleasure and gratification. During my leisure I received and paid all my *intime* visits and re-organized my house, unpacked from England, and repacked for India. On the last day of 1875 we were fully prepared for our Eastern tour, but with a feeling that we were starting two or three months too late, and would have to encounter some of the hot and fatal season to accomplish it; but, you know, "Consuls, as well as beggars, can't be choosers."

CHAPTER II.

TRIESTE, AND GENERAL POLITICS IN THAT QUARTER.

AND now for a few words about my beloved Trieste. There are two ways of getting here. Either embark in a small Lloyds at Venice at midnight, and find yourself at Trieste at five or six a.m., or go by train round the top of the Adriatic, nine and a half hours from Venice. Slow travelling, but, with its glorious contrast of Carnian Alps and rich riverine plains which belong to the lowlands of Northern Italy, one can bear it sometimes in fine weather. The gliding down the steep incline extending from Nabresina, in the Karso, to old "Tergeste" (Trieste), is truly glorious. Nothing can be more beautiful than coming into Trieste from the Karst or Karso, a wilderness of stone like Syria, forming the mass of the Carniola, and the broken surface of fawn-grey limestone, pitted with huge pot-holes, and seamed by a few goat paths. It is as grisly a scene as man's eye could see, until you emerge at Opçina, a Slav village, near which stands a rural inn and a single obelisk. This height shows Trieste and the Adriatic like a map at your feet. The view of azure sea, coasted by long projecting points, and deeply recessed bays of emerald green, hill range and valley and dale waxing faintly blue in the airy distance; a noble City, crowning heights spreading over the subject plain, sending forth skirmishers of villa and farmhouse, and sapping with her moles and piers the covered way of the waves, is a sight worth gazing upon.

About 1835, there were English merchants at Trieste. They lived in good style, and kept foxhounds, though I can't think how they could ever have had a chance with a fox, whose immediate refuge would be the impassable Karst. They throve upon imported sugar, but the vile beetroot stuff from Hungary, Moravia, and Bohemia, has supplanted the business. The Jews and Greeks who now monopolize commerce have long since "eaten them up," to use a Kafir phrase. The Jew makes money, and spends it: he does all the hospitality of the place. The Greek makes and hoards it, or else he is hospitable only to his own people.

We have a new port. Unfortunately the only breakwater is built to leeward, not to windward as it should be. Its huge moles and diminutive basins, gigantic expense, and utter disregard for local interests, smells, etc., duly prove the omnipotence of the Railway system in these our days. The combined effect of station and harbour will be to build a new town, and to reduce by half, the value of house property in the older city, where some tenements, like the Casa Carciotti, let for £3,000 per annum. The reason, say the Railway authorities, is, that by making Trieste a mere half-way house, they will benefit the many to the detriment of the few. But the Citizens who lose all, can hardly be expected to adopt that aspect of the matter, and already there are loud complaints that the new Port, though already costing some twenty millions of florins, and far from finished, is seriously disturbing trade.

The effect of Californian and Australian gold has been to build here, as elsewhere, a bit of the capital, contrasting strongly with the antiquated and pauper *Città Vecchia* (pronounced in Triestine, Vetchia). The thoroughfares are lined with slabs, like Florence and Pisa; not with kidney stones and bands, as in Upper Italy; and the fine material, easily quarried in the seaward face of the Karso escarpment, is profitably exported to Alexandria. But never was a maritime city less maritime. Not a yacht, not a private boat, appears off the quays,—everything is for traffic. The worship of the almighty florin in dirty paper is universal, but there is a doleful lack of labour-saving appurtenances. We have only just laid down a tramway. Porterage is done by the back of man and the one-bullock carts (*zaje*), as in Madeira, and long trucks (*carradori*), drawn by the well-bred carriage-horses in the morning, in most instances, who in the afternoon draw the carriages of the local aristocracy to St. Andrea, our Rotten Row, and at night take the same pleasure-seekers to the balls and *conversazione.* I often wonder when these horses sleep; Trieste is the only town I know that is never still day or night. The horses show a good deal of "blood." There is a Government stud at Lipizza, two hours from Trieste, where Arab stallions are crossed with Hungarian, Croat, and sometimes English mares, and all the produce that does not reach a certain standard of excellence is sold to the riding and driving public. The former are to be counted on the fingers of one hand. I have seen only one lady who can be called a horsewoman. The local *jeunesse dorée* are beginning to drive "fast trotters," but these things are in their babyhood. There are no rich, idle, horsey people. If I kept anything, it would be a couple of strong Croat ponies, to scramble over the Karso with my gun, and bring back, perhaps, a hare for dinner now and then; but even so small a stable as this would be attended with great difficulty, as with my English ideas of horseflesh, I could not trust a Triestine groom, and to attend to one's own one must live in the country, with a stable attached to the house.

The "victorias" and "coupés" of Paris here appear so civilized after the hideous and impure "growlers" of London, the worst-cabbed capital in the world (save our hansoms, which are most creditable); and they ply amongst a kind of drosky, the *carrettella* used by the peasantry, with its single pony harnessed to the near side of the pole. The driver wears a conical cap of black Astracan, with a coat of skin, the hairy side in, extending to his ankles; and his nether limbs are clad in Hessian boots. Parisian toilettes and the Italian costume of the lower orders—calico jacket and petticoat—jostle the Slav market women from the neighbouring villages. Some of the girls, especially those of Servola, are exceedingly beautiful,—the profile purest Greek, the outline a regular oval, and there is a general delicacy of form and hue that startles one. But the eye is washed-out, nay, colourless, and the blonde hair is like tow; it wants the golden ray. The dress is as remarkable as the face, a white triangular head-kerchief with embroidered ends hanging down the back, a boddice either of white flannel picked out with slashes of colour, or a black, glazed, and plaited stuff; a skirt of lively colour, edged below with a broad belt of even livelier green, blue, pink, or yellow; white stockings, and short stout shoes. The ornaments on high days and holidays, when the country girls come out to dance, are gold necklaces and crosses, a profusion of rings and ear pendants, sometimes of brilliants: often of the enamelled work for which Fiume is celebrated, turbaned Moors' heads, probably a survival of the Turkish wars. Opposed to the *contadina* is the *sartorella*, "the little tailoress," a local institution like the French *grisette* and the Milanese *madamina*. I always call Trieste "Il Paradiso delle Sartorelle e l'Inferno degli animali," because the former is a prominent figure in Trieste, and Fortune's favourite. She fills the streets and promenades, especially on festa days, dressed *à quatre épingles*, powdered and rouged and *coiffée* as for a ball, with or without veil (never a hat or bonnet). She is often pretty, mostly has a good figure, but she does not always look nice, and her manners, to use a mild word, are very *dégagées*.

There are 4,000 of these girls, who fill the lower-class balls and theatres. There is one in every house, off and on: for example, a family have a dress to make, or a petticoat. They send for their *sartorella*. She comes for eighty kreuzers or a florin a day, and her food, and she is supposed to sew for twelve hours, leaving at six, when she begins her evening. She is always well dressed outside, but often has not a rag, even a chemise, under it, unless she is in luck. Luck, I grieve to say, means that every boy, or youth, or man, beginning at twelve, and up to twenty-five to twenty-eight, is in love with a *sartorella*; and I may safely assert, without having a *mauvaise langue*, that she does not give her—shall we say heart?—gratis. She generally turns the servants' heads by relating that she is immediately going to be married to a real *Graf* (Count) as soon as he is independent of his parents. The children are brought up much too precociously, and allowed to enjoy the world before their studies are over. An old colonel told my husband that, in consequence of this premature dissipation and late hours, out of one hundred and eighty recruits for the army, often only eight are passed as sound.

By the *Inferno degli animali* I mean to say that no foreigners, however rich and charitable,—and they are immensely so,—would ever think of giving a florin to secure the comfort of a beast; and that the lower orders do not yet know that an animal can feel; so that what with ignorance, carelessness, and brutality, their lives are made truly wretched. I have tried to remedy this great want by kindness, good manners with the people, and making in England a collection of twelve hundred florins to give in prizes for every class of humanity, and to abate every sort of cruelty here practised. My English sentiment for animals was long looked upon as a harmless lunacy, which I was allowed to indulge in, as it hurt nobody; and it raised only a passing smile and shrug when some one saw me rushing in between a broken-down horse and infuriated driver using his knobbed stick, to save the beast. They would laugh and exclaim, "*Corpo di Bacco! Quella è ammalata Bisognerebbe mandarla all'ospedale!*" But truth almost always prevails. I have won a hearing, and at last all the authorities, and even the people, with few exceptions, are with me, and we are getting things very nicely into order.

But to return to our population. To the east of the town the Wallachian "Cici" charcoal dealers from Inner Istria, show the dress of the old Danubian homes. The Friulano with his velvet jacket and green corduroys, the most estimable race in the land, is often a roaster of chesnuts at the corners of the streets; whilst his wife, the best of *balie* (wet-nurses), bravely attired, often makes her *padrona*, or mistress, look, if civilized, at least commonplace. Trieste has a mixed population. North of Ponte Rosso is Germania, composed of the authorities, the *employés*, and a few wealthy merchants. They have a maniacal idea of *Germanizing* their little world, a mania which secures for them abundant trouble and ill will, for eight millions cannot denationalize thirty-two millions. There are twelve thousand Italians at Trieste who speak a corrupted Venetian; eleven thousand of these are more or less poor—one thousand perhaps are too rich. However, their civilization is all Roman, and they take a pride in it, whilst the *exaltés* and the Italianissimi hate their rulers like poison. In this they are joined by the mass of the wealthy and influential Israelites, who divide the commerce with the Greeks. The former subscribe handsomely to every Italian charity or movement; and periodically and anonymously memorialize the King of Italy. The lower class take a delight in throwing large squibs, here called by courtesy "torpedoes," amongst the unpatriotic petticoats who dare to throng the Austrian balls. The immediate suburbs, country, and villages are Slav, and even in the city some can barely speak Italian. This people detests all its fellow citizens with an instinctive odium of race, and with a dim consciousness that it has been ousted from its own. Thus the population may be said to be triple. Politics are lively, and the Italianissimi thrive because the constitutional Government, which has taken the place of the old patriarchal despotism, is weak, acting as if it feared them. Austria of to-day is feeble and gentlemanly, and as such is scarcely a match for the actual Italy. Let us lay out a little map of politics immediately around our small corner of the world.

Being a devoted Austrian, I have many anxieties concerning the political health of this admirable country. Austria, once so famed for the astute management, the "Politiké," which kept in order the most heterogeneous of households, between Bohemia and Dalmatia, and from Hungary to the Milanese, is suffering from a complication of complaints. The first is the economic: her deficit for 1877 is already laid at twenty-six millions of florins; she lives on paper, and she habitually outruns the constable. Secondly are the *modus vivendi* with Hungary, the Convention, the Bank, and half-a-dozen other troubles, which result from the "chilling dualism" of Count Beust (1867). The inevitable rivalry of a two-fold instead of a three-fold empire is now deepening to downright hostility. The Slavs complain that the crown of the Empire is being dragged through the mire by the "Magyarists;" and on December 9th the Vienna Chamber of Deputies heard for the first time a proposal to substitute Trialism for Dualism. Third, and last, is the Eastern Question, in which the poor invalid is distracted by three physicians proposing three several cures. Doctor Hungary wants only the integrity (!)

of Turkey: alliance with England, war with Russia. Dr. Germany, backed by the Archduke Albert, and aided by the army, looks to alliance with Russia and to the annexation of Bosnia and the Herzegovina when Turkey falls to pieces. Lastly, Dr. Progressist with the Club of the Left, advocates the cold water treatment, absolute passivity: no annexation, no occupation, no intervention. The triad division seems inveterate: even the Constitutionalist party must split into three—a Centrum, a Left, and a *Fortschritts-partei.* Hence Prince Gortschakoff, not without truth, characterized this mosaic without coherence as "no longer a State, but only a Government."

Austria, like England, is suffering from the manifold disorders and troubles that accompany a change of life. At home we have thrown over for ever the rule of aristocracy; and we have not yet resigned ourselves to what must inevitably come—Democracy pure and simple. Accordingly, we sit between two stools with the usual proverbial result. Austria, in 1848, sent to the Limbo of past things the respectable "paternal government," with its *carcere,* its *carcere duro,* and its *carcere durissimo;* and threatened to make sausage-meat of M. Ochsenhausen von Metternich. Constitutionalism, adopted by automatism, found the Austrians utterly unfit for freedom; and the last thirty years have only proved that constitutionalism may be more despotic than despotism. Austria has ever been the prey of minorities German and Magyar. Her *Beamter* class has adopted the worst form of Latin *Bureaucratie.* Her Press has one great object in life, that of "Germanizing" unwilling Slavs. Her fleet has lost Tegetthoff and Archduke Max. Her army, once the best drilled in Europe, and second to none in the *ingens magnitudo corporum,* has been reduced by short service to a host of beardless boys; and the marvels of the Uchatius gun will not prevent half the regiments being knocked up by a fortnight's work. But these are the inevitable evils of a transition system, and if Austria can only tide over her change of life she will still enjoy a long, hearty, and happy old age.

Hence Austro-Hungary is freely denounced as "disturbing the European Areopagus." Hence Paskievich declared in 1854 that the road to Stamboul leads through Vienna. Hence Fadajeff, the Panslavist, significantly points out that Europe contains forty millions of Slavs who are *not* under the White Czar. These ancient Scythians have hitherto shown very little wisdom. Instead of cultivating some general language,—for instance the old Slavonic, which would have represented Latin,—they are elaborating half-a-dozen different local dialogues; and, at the last Slav Congress, the Pan-Slav Deputies, greatly to the delight of the Pan-Germanists, were obliged to harangue one another in German. If "Trialism" be carried out in the teeth of Hungary, what and where can be the capital of the Jugo-Slavs—the Southern and Latin, as opposed to the Pravo-Slavs or orthodox? Where shall be the seat of its Houses? Prague is purely Czech, utterly distasteful to Slavonía, Croatia, and Dalmatia. Laibach in Krain is the only place comparatively central; but that means that all would combine to reject Laibach. Meanwhile the Slavs declare that they are treated as Helots, and that they will stand this treatment no longer.

Austria will hardly declare war against Russia even at the bidding of the Turko-Hungarian alliance,—even if menaced with her pet bugbear, the formation of a strong Slav kingdom, or kingdoms, on her south-eastern frontier. She is thoroughly awake to the danger threatened by her friends: that of falling into her four component parts, each obeying the law of gravitation,—Styria, Upper and Lower, absorbing herself in Germany, and Dalmatia and Istria merging into Italy. She has made all her preparations for occupying Bosnia, which the Turks are abandoning, and for which it is generally believed they will not fight. Count Andrassy, the rebel of '48, the Premier of '76-'78, will keep his own counsel and carry out his own plans. He has been unjustly charged with a vacillating and uncertain policy; as if a man who is being frantically pulled diametrically in four opposite directions were not obliged to stoop at times in order to conquer.

Italy has of late made strong representations at Vienna against the possible occupation of Bosnia by Austria. She knows that the step would for ever debar her from the possession of Dalmatia; and that the old Kingdom, the mother of Emperors, will never rest satisfied till her extensive seaboard is subtended by a proportionate interior. Italy would prefer to occupy Bosnia *in propriâ personâ;* but, that being hardly possible, she would leave it unoccupied, or, worst of all, occupied by the Turks. Italy is the deadliest enemy of Austria, and wears the dangerous aspect of a friend. Such is the present standpoint of the Empire,* and you see, she is still, as she has been for years, a "political necessity." We, her well wishers, can only say to her, in olden phrase, *Tu, felix Austria, nube,*—Yea, marry, and take unto thyself the broad and fertile lands lying behind the Dinaric Alps.

Meanwhile, Italy, the rival sister of France, the recipient of many favours from her, and, *par consequence,* her bitterest foe, bides her time, remains quiet as a church mouse, and, like the Scotchman's owl, thinks hard. She is at present the last, the only hope of Latinism. She has shown, since 1870, a prudence, a moderation, an amount of common sense, comparatively speaking, which have surprised the world. Ethnologists, who scoffed at "Pan-latinism," were over-hasty in determining that the game of the Latin race was "up;" and that the three progressive families of the future are the English (including the German and the Anglo-American), the Slav, and the Sons of the Flowery Land. The present standpoint of Italy is this. She has a treaty with Russia which makes her a spectator. She has returned an overwhelming majority of the progressists, who aim at converting her into a Republic; and Italy, classical and mediæval, has never attained her full development except under Republican rule. Meanwhile, her "citizens and patriots" look forward to recovering Nice, where in 1860, some 26,000 votes against 160 were polled in favour of annexation to France. She wants an Algeria, and would like to find it at Tunis, with Carthage for capital. And finally, she would fain round off her possessions by annexing from Austria the Trentine, the County of Gorizia,

* This was written at the end of 1876. It would be impossible to-day (1878) not to sympathise with and admire Austria and her brave army struggling single-handed and manfully in the great Bosnian and Herzergovinian difficulty, but when it is over her reward will be great. It is a large step in the right direction, but we who want a great Austrian Empire, wish she had had all the nineteen million Slavs, not a part.

the Peninsula of Istria, including the chief emporium, Trieste, and even the Kingdom of Dalmatia.

It was not a little amusing to note the expressions of simple amazement with which the general Press of England acknowledged the discovery that Italy "actually contemplates" this extension of territory. Would they be surprised to hear that such has been her object for the last six hundred years; that in her darkest hour she has never abandoned her claim; that during the last half-century she has urged it with all her might, and that at the present moment she is steadily labouring to the same end?. We, who derive experience from the pages of history, firmly believe that the prize would even now be in her hands were it not for Prussia, who calculates upon the gravitation of the Austro-German race, and who already speaks of Trieste as "our future seaport." But why, we ask, cannot Italy rest contented with Venice, which after a century of neglect, might by liberal measures again become one of the principal commercial centres of Europe?

Under Augustus the whole of Istria was annexed to the Xth Region of Italy; the south-eastern limits being the Flumen Arsæ, the modern Arsa, that great gash in the Eastern flank beyond which began Liburnia. Hence Dante sang (Inferno, IX., 113-115):—

> "Sì come a Pola presso del Quarnaro
> *Che Italia chiude e i suoi termini bagna,*
> Fanno i sepolcri tutto 'l loco varo."

Hence Petrarch (Sonnet CXIV.) declares of his Laura, whose praises he cannot waft all the world over:—

> "—— udralo il bel paese,
> Ch' Apennin parte, e 'l mar circonda e 'l Alpe."

And who can forget the glorious verse of Alfieri, the first to discern Italy in the "geographical expression" of the eighteenth century?

> "Giorno verrà, tornerà giorno in cui
> Redivivi omai gli Itali staranno,
> In campo armati," etc., etc., etc.

Italy bases her claim to the larger limit, upon geography,

ethnology, and sentiment, as well as upon history. Only the most modest of patriots contend that the Isonzo river, the present boundary of Austria, was a capricious creation of Napoleon I. The more ambitious spirits demand the whole southern watershed of the Julian Alps; nor are they wanting who, by "Alps" understanding the Dinaric chain, would thus include the whole Kingdom of Dalmatia inherited from the Romans.

Ethnologically again, Istria declares herself Italian, not Austrian. Her 290,000 souls (round numbers) consist of 166,000 Latins to 109,000 Slavs, the latter a mongrel breed that emigrated between A.D. 800 and 1657; and a small residue of foreigners, especially Austro-German officials. The Italians are, it is true, confined to the inner towns and to the cities of the seaboard; still, these scattered centres cannot forget that to their noble blood Istria has owed all her civilization, all her progress, and all her glories in arts and arms. Lastly, "sentiment," as a factor of unknown power in the great sum of what constitutes "politics," is undervalued only by the ignorant vulgus. The Istrians are more Italian than the Italians. Since the first constitution of 1848, they have little to complain of the Government in theory, much in practice. Austria, after the fashion of Prussia, unwisely attempts to "Germanize" her Italian subjects, who in Istria outnumber the Teutons by five to one. The true policy of Austria would be to Italianise the Italians, to Slavonise the Slavs, and to Magyarise the Hungarians; in other words, to elicit the good qualities of her four component races, instead of attempting to unrace them. And her first practical step should be to abolish all idea of "Germanizing." If she did not try for it, it might settle itself.

The chief danger of Italy, at present, is wishing to go too fast. She would run before she can walk steadily: she forgets the past: she ignores that her independence and unity were won for, and not by, her; that each defeat was to her a conquest. She had the greatest statesman in Europe, Cavour; who so disposed his game, opening it in 1854 with the Crimean War, and following it up with a seat for Piedmont amongst the Great Powers in the Congress of Paris, that it led by a mathematical certainty to Solferino in 1859, and to securing Rome for a capital in 1870.

But "Milor Camillo" is dead, and Prince Bismarck, who rules in his stead, bluntly says: "No one can doubt, even beyond the Alps, that an attack upon Trieste and Istria would meet the point of a sword which is not Austrian." Italy must put her house in order before she can aspire to extend her grounds. Her income is insufficient for her expenses; her gold is paper; her currency is forced, and her heavy taxes breed general discontent. She has a noble estate for agriculture, but her peasants prefer the stocking to the Stocks, the Funds, or the Bank. Her Civil Service is half paid, and compelled to pay itself. Her Custom House duties are a scandal to a civilized power, and her post office is a farce. Her army cannot compare, in fighting qualities, with that of Prussia, Austria, or even France. Her sailors are not tailors, but she cannot afford a first-rate armour-clad fleet; she was beaten at Lissa, and her seaboard would easily be blockaded by a great maritime power. Moveover she has that dual Government at Rome, and a terrible skeleton in the cupboard,—her treatment of the Pope.

The Liberal press and the "indignation meetings" of Italy have been alternately severe and sarcastic upon the *entente cordiale* between the Vatican and the Seraglio. But the Papal logic is clear and sound. It says:—"The reverence of Constantine for the Keys transferred the seat of civil empire to the Byzantium, whereas Anti-Christ Russia founded the pseudo-throne of Saint Peter in the far north. We fought against the Moslem when he was an aggressor. Innocent XI., not to mention the crusader-Popes, preached the liberation of Vienna. Pius I. worked up to the Battle of Lepanto. But things are now changed. You, Bulgarian and Bosnian Catholics, have religious liberty, and you will have political liberty when you deserve it! Meanwhile, obey the Sultan, who has nothing to do with Christianity, and shun Anti-Christ—the Czar." Good logic, I say, cold and clear-drawn; but powerless to purge away the sentiments, the prejudices, and the passions of mankind.

Italy drives the coach too fast. Patriotic Italians declare that England has no right to hold Malta. Cyprus was under Venice; *ergo*, they think it should be under Italy. The Trentine, the

Southern Tyrol, Istria, and Dalmatia are in the same condition. The Latin kingdom has achieved a great position in Japan. She sends her travellers to explore New Guinea. She aims at being the most favoured nation in Egypt, where she lately received a severe *schiaffo*. The Italian national expedition landed in the dominions of the Khedive without having had the decency to call upon him in Cairo. You know how the Egyptian noticed the affront. Finally, she talks of herself as one of the Powers, ready to occupy the insurgent districts which the Porte cannot reduce. Such is the actual standpoint of United Italy.

I will now sketch the state of Hungary, whose ambition threatens to make her aggressive, entitled, by the press of England, the "backbone of the Austrian monarchy;" and praised for the "superior political organisation" with which she has crushed her Slav rivals.

Since the days, now forgotten, when Prince Esterhazy first flashed, in London society, his diamond jacket upon the dazzled eyes of the "upper ten thousand," the name of Hungarian has been a passport to favour amongst us. We meet him in the shape of a Kinsky, an Erdödy, or a Hunyadi,—well-born, well-clad, and somewhat unlearned, except in the matter of modern languages. But he is a good rider, a keen sportsman, and a cool player for high stakes,—qualities in one point (only) much resembling Charity. He looks like a gentleman in a drawing-room and in the hunting field; he is quite at home at a fancy ball; he wears his frogged jacket, his tights and his tall boots, his silks, satins, and furs with an air; his manners are courteous, cordial, and pleasant; in money matters he has none of the closeness of the catankerous Prussian, none of the meanness of the Italian; and, lastly, he makes no secret of his sympathy with England, with the English, and with all their constitution-manias. What can you want more? You pronounce him a nice fellow, and all, women especially, re-echo your words: "he is *such* a gentleman!" and—he received the Prince of Wales so enthusiastically!

But there *is* another side (politically speaking) to this fair point of view. The Hungarian is a Tartar with a coat of veneer and varnish. Hungary is, as regards civilization, simply the most backward country in Europe. Buda-Pest is almost purely German, the work of the Teutons, who, at the capital, do all the work; you hardly ever hear in the streets a word of Magyar, and the Magyars have only managed to raise its prices and its death-rate to somewhat double those of London. The cities, like historic Gran on the Danube, have attempts at public buildings and streets; in the country towns and villages the thoroughfares are left to Nature; the houses and huts, the rookeries and doggeries are planted higgledy-piggledy, wherever the tenants please; and they are filthier than any shanty in Galway or Cork, in Carinthia or Krain. The Ugrian or Ogre prairies have no roads, or rather they are all road; and the driver takes you across country when and where he wills. The peasantry are "men on horseback,"—in this matter preserving the customs of their Hun and Tartar ancestors. They speak a tongue of Turkish affinity, all their sympathies are with their blood-kinsmen the Turks, and they have toiled to deserve the savage title of "white Turks," lately conferred upon them by Europe.

Fiume, the only seaport of Hungary, is a study of Hungarian nationality. The town is neatly built, well paved, and kept tolerably clean by Slav and Italian labour, the former doing the coarse, the latter the fine work. The port is, or rather is to be, bran-new. Because Austria chooses to provide a worse than useless and frightfully expensive—in fact, ruinous—harbour for Trieste, whose anchoring roads were some of the best in Europe, therefore (admire the consequence) Hungary demands a similar folly for her emporium, Fiume, whose anchoring roads are still better. After throwing a few millions of florins into the water, the works are committed to the charge of the usual half-dozen men and boys; moreover, as the port is supposed to improve, so its shipping and its business fall off in far quicker ratio. Commerce cannot thrive amongst these reckless, feckless people. There is no spirit of enterprise, no union to make force, no public spirit; the dead cities of the Zuyder Zee are bustling New England centres in comparison with Fiume; and the latter, which might have become the emporium of the whole Dalmatian coast, and a dangerous rival to Trieste, is allowing her golden opportunity to pass away never to return. For when Dalmatia shall have been vitalised by the addition of Bosnia and the Herzegovina, her glorions natural basins—harbours that can hold all the navies of the world—will leave Fiume mighty little to do, except what she does now, look pretty and sit in the sun.

All Englishmen who have lived long amongst Hungarians remark the similarity of the Magyar and the southern Irish Catholic. Both are imaginative and poetical, rather in talk than in books; neither race ever yet composed poetry of the highest class. Both delight in music; but, as the "Irish Melodies" are mostly old English, so the favourites of Hungary are gipsy songs. Both have the "gift of the gab" to any extent, while their eloquence is notably more flowery than fruity. Both are sharp and intelligent, affectionate and warmhearted; easily angered and appeased, delighted with wit and to be managed by a *bon-mot;* superficial, indolent, sensitive, punctilious, jealous, quarrelsome, passionate and full of fight. Both are ardent patriots, with an occasional notable exception of treachery; both are brilliant soldiers; the Hungarians, who formerly were only cavalry men, now form whole regiments of the Austrian Line. They are officered by the Germans, who will not learn the language, justly remarking, "If we speak Magyar, we shall be condemned for ever to Magyar corps, and when the inevitable split takes place, where shall we then be?" Both are bold and skilful riders; and, as the expatriated Irish Catholic was declared by Louis Le Grand—an excellent authority upon such matters—to be "one of the best gentlemen in Europe," so Europe says the same of the Hungarian *haute volée.*

As regards politics and finance, Buda-Pest is simply a modern and eastern copy of Dublin. The Hungarian magnate still lives like the Squireen and Buckeen of the late Mr. Charles Lever's "earliest style;" he keeps open house, he is plundered by all hands, and no Galway landowner of the last generation was less fitted by nature and nurture to manage his own affairs. Hence he is drowned in debt, and the Jew usurer is virtually the owner of all those broad acres which bear so little. An "Encumbered Estates Bill" would tell strange tales; but the sabre is readily drawn in Hungary, and the "chosen people," sensibly enough, content themselves with the meat of the oyster, leaving the shells to the owner.

This riotous, rollicking style of private life finds its way into public affairs; and as a model of "passionate politics," the Hungarian is simply perfect. He has made himself hateful to the sober-sided German and to the dull Slav; both are dead sick of his *outrecuidance;* the former would be delighted to get rid of the selfish and short-sighted irrepressibles, who are ever bullying and threatening secession about a custom tax, or a bank, or a question of union. They are scandalized by seeing the academical youth, the *jeunesse dorée* of Magyar universities, sympathising with Turkish atrocities, declaring Turkey to be the defender of European civilization, *fackelzug*ing the Turkish Consul, insulting the Russian, and sending a memorial sabre to a Sirdar Ekrem (Commander-in-Chief) whose line of march was marked by the fire-blackened walls of Giaour villages, and by the corpses of murdered Christians, men, women, and babes. Could the Austro-Germans only shake off the bugbear of Panslavism, they would cut the cable, allow the ne'er-do-well Hungarian craft to drift away waterlogged into hypostatic union with that big ironclad the Turk; they would absorb the whole of Bosnia, the Herzegovina, and Albania; they would cultivate the Slav nationality, and they would rely upon racial differences of dialect and religion to protect them against the real or imaginary designs of Russia. Prince Eugène of Savoy, in the last century, a man of wit, was of that opinion, and so are we.

Hungary, indeed, is a tinder-box like Montenegro, and much more dangerous, because her supply of combustible is on a larger scale. The last bit of puerile folly has been to press for an Austrian military occupation of Servia; and why? Because an Austrian monitor, being in a part of the river where "no thoroughfare" is put up, was fired upon with ball cartridge by a *schildwache* (sentinel) from the fort walls, and exploded, bungler that she was, one of her own shells. The Hungarians had been raving at the idea of "occupation" in Bulgaria, but the moment they saw an opportunity of breaking the Treaty of Paris, they proposed doing so at once. By-the-by, now that Prince Wrede, a *persona ingrata*, is removed from Belgrade, you will hear no more of Servian outrages against Austria. To the "Magyarists" we may trace most of the calumnies against the brave and unfortunate Servian soldiery,—lies of the darkest dye, so eagerly swallowed by the philo-Turk members of the English Press, and as freely vomited for public benefit. And here is the main danger of Hungary and her politics of passion. Russians and Turks might be safely put into the ring together, like "Down-Easters" in a darkened room, and be allowed to fight it out till one cried "Enough."

If these views of Hungary and the Hungarians be true,—and they are our views,—you will considerably discount the valuation set upon them by the Turcophile Press. They were once a barrier against Tartar savagery, a Finnish race, invited by the Byzantine Emperors to act as a buffer against Mohammedanism. The three orders of Magyars—Magnates, Moderates, and Miserables—hate Russia for the sensible and far-seeing part which she played in 1848–49; all excitement is apt to spread; even so in a street dog-fight, every cur thinks itself bound to assist, and to bite and wrangle something or other, no matter what. And where, we may ask, is the power that can muzzle these Eastern ban-dogs? who shall take away the shillelaghs of these Oriental Paddies?

A taste of Hungarian quality has been given by M. Vambéry in the columns of the *Daily Telegraph*. M. Vambéry was born in Hungary, of Israelitish German parents. Like the sons of Israel generally, he hates Russia, and he loves England, and probably he has good and weighty reasons both for his hate and for his love. He was daring enough to tell us, in his first book of travels, that after dining with the Turkish Minister at Teheran —and a very good dinner it was—he just disguised himself as a dervish, and travelled perfectly *incog.* for months and months under Russian eyes, partly through Russian territory. The Russians must have known every step taken by M. Vambéry. He saw only what he was allowed to do; and thus Mr. Schuyler, whose name has, we regret to say, been altered by the irreverent Turcophile to "Squealer," roundly declares that he never visited the places which he has so well described. You will therefore regard M. Vambéry's opinions upon the subject of Turkey with suspicion, and reserve all your respect for his invaluable publications upon the Turanian dialects, his *specialité.* Lieutenant Payer's book will disappoint you; its main merit is that of having been written by a Magyar.

Do not believe these Ugrians to be "the backbone of the Austrian Empire," whatever they may be to its element of weakness, the Monarchy. And if you are driven to own that the Hungarians "play the leading part in the events of Southern Europe," understand that the chief end and aim of Magyarist policy is to ruin the Slavs. I am a strong Austrian, with a great admiration for the Hungarians, who are to me, personally and individually, most attractive; but this does not blind me to the disadvantages they, *en masse,* bring to Austria. I believe the Slav to be the future race of Europe, even as I hold the Chinese to be the future race of the East. In writing politics and history which may live after one is long forgotten, one must speak the truth, and bury repulsions and attractions.

Were I Emperor of Austria, I should have the police organized on English principles. I should punish with death the first two or three cases of brutal crime. The people are excellent; it speaks highly for them that, with weak laws, and authorities that act as though they dreaded the independent Triestines, the worst crimes are only stabbing when drunk, and suicide; and the latter is entirely owing to the excitability of the climate and the utter throwing off of religion, whilst all moral disgrace or dread is removed by the applause conferred on the suicide, and sympathy with the surviving family,—which last is good and noble. I have seen thousands accompanying a *felo de se* to the grave, with verses and laurel leaves and a band of music, as if he had done something gallant and brave. Indeed one was considered very narrow-minded for not joining in his eulogy.

They say that forty years ago Trieste was a charming place to live in; but that with increase of trade, luxury and money flowed in, and faith flowed out. Let us say that the population is 130,000, with suburbs: 30,000 are practical Catholics, 20,000 are freethinkers, and 90,000 are utterly indifferent. In fact, the national religion is dying out; and when that is so in a Catholic land, there is nothing to replace it except materialism. After repeated outrages and torpedo-throwing, the Habeas Corpus would have been at once suspended in free England, and the French would have placed the City under martial law. The Empire-Kingdom does not, however, disfranchise the turbulent city by suppressing the local Diet till such time as the public expression of disloyal feeling shall have disappeared. A more manly policy would suit better. Trieste is also allowed to retain peculiar privileges. She is still a free port; her *octrois* are left to her for squandering and pillage, and are so heavy that till lately the adjoining villages consumed sugar which came *viâ* Holland all, round and through Europe. Trieste has three towns, as well as three races. The oldest is the Citta Vecchia, which dates before the days of Strabo. Filthy in the extreme, it is a focus of infection. Small-pox is rarely absent from it, and it swells the rate of mortality to the indecent figure of 40–50 per 1000 per annum; London being 22, and Madras 36. The climate is peculiar. It has three winds,—the Bora (Boreas), the Baltic current, the winter wind—cold, dry, highly electrical, very exciting, and so violent that sometimes the quays have been roped, and some of the walls have iron rails let in to prevent people from being blown into the sea. And there have been some terrible accidents in my time. An English engineer has been blown from the quay into the hold of a ship (thirty feet); I saw him in the hospital, a mere jelly, but nothing broken; he is well, and at work. A cab and horse have been upset, and also a train. The summer wind is the Sirocco, straight from Africa, wet, warm, and debilitating; whilst the *contraste* means the two blowing together, and against each other, with all the disadvantages of both.

Trieste, the chief Port of Austria, is a harbour greatly coveted equally by the Italian and the German. Mr. Freeman says that the chief glory of Trieste is its being on the way to Spalato. We thank him. He enters at some length into the origin of the City, and has well described the cathedral of San Giusto. But he should have read our little guide-book, "Three Days at Trieste," which carefully describes the ruins of the Roman temple, Jupiter Capitolinus, and the classical Arco di Riccardo (Richard of England), who never was here. The old gateway to the temple is not, however, in any sense a "double arch." He says nothing of the remnants of the Roman theatre and aqueduct in the old town; nothing of the Museums (Winckelmann and Civico Ferdinand Maximilian), and nothing of the old Keltic (?) castellieri, or proto-historic villages lying within cannon-shot of the city of Augustus.

Trieste, wealthy as she is, still wants all modern improvements. The reason is simply that the two rival parties act like the two bundles of hay in the fable; between them the ass starves. Thus, the water, being not only scarce, but dear, exceedingly ill-flavoured, and unwholesome, a fresh supply has been demanded for years. The *Italianissimi* proposed to bring it from the Risano stream to the south-west, thereby ruining one of the happiest valleys in Istria. The Tedeschi put forward the Rekka, or San Canziano rivulet to the north-east,—a mere ditch in summer, and mightily foul at all seasons. Let us hope that Mr. Ritterbandt, C.E., after satisfying Venice, may bring the Timavo, the classical Timavus, bodily into the City. The effect of better water at Vienna has been at once to reduce the mortality by one quarter. Similarly, Trieste trade is being ruined because Trieste wants a northern railway to Salzburg; the Laak line is advocated by one lot, the Predil by the other, and meanwhile transit and traffic must describe a long semicircle, *viâ* Venice or Vienna.

In two points Trieste can claim a pre-eminence. The first is her Exchange (the *Tergesteo*), which probably originates half the views about Herzegovina and Bosnia which fill the papers of Europe. The second is her new Municipal Palace. The ancient building had the true Venetian cachet, but was small and low, and so was improved off. The new is of the order which I have heard called "bastard nothing," and has not a straight line in the frontage. The joints converge like a Chinaman's eyes; it cost 270,000 florins, and the sharp natives name it Sipario—stage-curtain palace. The masons of Trieste are nevertheless admirable. They run up a five-story house of cut stone, with walls two feet

4

thick, with a surprising rapidity. These buildings are not pretty, they are like deal boxes; lack balconies, verandahs, are painfully wall-sided, and unconscious of light and shade, and they ignore all that adorable, straggling, no-shapedness and picturesqueness which makes one long to buy. But this is the architect's want of soul, not the mason's.

Trieste is a political and coy personage, hotly wooed by Italy and by Germany. The latter openly declares that she is part of the new Teutonic Empire, and that the eight millions or so of Austro-Germans ought to belong body and soul to the Fatherland. Meanwhile she is enjoyed by the Empire-Kingdom, greatly against the grain. A powerful rival is rising a few miles to the south, in the person of Croatian Fiume, which has long ago repented her of having cast her lot with Hungary. The Flanatic Bay of the ancients is magnificent, almost equalling the scenery of Naples. A French company is building a port, which will avoid much of the expense and some of the errors fatal to Trieste, and but for the inveterate backwardness of the people, the utter ignorance of what progress means, and the miserable local jealousies, Fiume, connected by a railway with Agram or Zagabria, might already have risen upon the decline of Trieste; but Fiume does not see her advantage, and we retain our supremacy.

Beyond the Sinus Flanaticus begins the kingdom of Dalmatia, with a line of natural harbours between Zara and the Bocche di Cattaro, which are perhaps the finest in the European world. Unhappily, at present these ports have nothing to export or import. After long and careful consideration of the question, based upon the impartial hearing of both sides discussed, we have come to the conclusion,—firstly, that the dualism of 1867 has not been successful; secondly, that Austria should have been a *Triregno;* thirdly, that H.I.M. Franz Josef might still be crowned King of Bohemia as well, and thus establish a nucleus about which the divided families of Slavs, especially the estimable Slovenes, the Wends who founded Venice, could and would group themselves. I am essentially Austrian by sympathy and ancient family ties, as I have said; but I do not like the Germans to chuckle when they tell me that the last great Slavonic Congress, which met in 1845, was compelled, after various failures, to make speeches in German; because the laughers ignore the fact that Panslavism is still rampant in Austria, and the clergy puff up the patriotic movement with all their might, and that schools and colleges are teaching the rising generation its rights as well as its wrongs. None but an inveterate theorist who holds that the Slav race is not to be the race of the future, would neglect the importance of a people constituting nearly half the total of Austro-Hungary—nineteen millions out of the thirty-four which remained after the cession of Venice in 1866.

The evil action of this unfair dualism is now causing profound discontent. Dalmatia is the narrowest kingdom in Europe, —300 miles long by 0 to 15 miles broad, the cypher representing the two spots where Turkey touches the sea. She is a face without a head; the latter would be Bosnia and the Herzegovina. She has a profusion of ports which have nothing to port, and a fine seafaring population ready for, and capable of, any amount of carrying trade, but condemned to be professors, custom-house officers, and fishers of sardines. Bosnia, with her unworked mines and forests, her unimproved flocks and herds, and her hundred other sources of neglected wealth, is the complement of, a political necessity to, Dalmatia. Some day she must become Dalmatian, and the sooner she connects herself with Austro-Hungary by a *plébiscite*, or some such civilised instrument, the better it will be for both. The only drawback to this movement in the far west of the Ottoman Empire is that it appears to be somewhat premature. Russia has her hands full in Eastern Asia, and Austria has for some time had a hole in her pocket. No one knows how sick the famous Sick Man really is since his last attack of Russomania, following his chronic Russophobia,*—an attack brought on by our own disgraceful (Liberal) abandonment of the Black Sea Treaties. None know, save those who have sat by his bedside, looked at his tongue, and have felt his pulse. He was breaking fast when he determined to risk a national bankruptcy. Finding the so-called "tax of blood" too heavy, he was already talking of a Christian recruitment, which

* N.B.—This was written January 1876.

would have been the beginning of the end; and the paroxysm induced by sending a few thousand troops to ravage and lay waste his discontented outlying estates, has reduced him to the last gasp. For the rebellion, although premature, is a reality,—it will not be put down by paper; it means to last till next spring, and when the fighting season comes it will call for the armed intervention of Europe.

The integrity of the Ottoman Empire has been, since the days of Chatham, a fortieth article of faith to English statesmen; although since the publication of Macfarlane's "Turkey and her Destiny," every traveller from Mostar to Bussorah, from Candia to Circassia, has shown up the miserable misrule which oppresses those fair and fruitful regions. The British Cabinet till now has not opened its eyes to ask "How long?" or has had originality enough or irreverence sufficient to pull down the old idol, and to propose a remedy for the present condition of things. The official mind was made up: there was no more to be said upon the subject. A Government that preferred peace and present prosperity to the discharge of an arduous and distasteful duty, laid down its law, determined to let sleeping dogs lie, till that little matter of the Turkish debt, the neatest thing done by the arch-enemy of the Ottoman, came like a thunderbolt and "roused the spirit of the British Lion."

Meanwhile the action of Austria has been sadly trammeled by the Dualism which she has brought upon herself. The German population of the Empire naturally dislikes being swamped by the new influx of Slavs, but it has not proved itself unpatriotic. The contrary is the case with the kingdom of Hungary,—the five millions of Magyars who, strengthened by the position and the character of Count Andrassy, have opposed themselves with all their might to the development of Dalmatia. This is a mistake, because sooner or later Dalmatia will develop herself without them. The reason that Austro-German officers joining Hungarian regiments avoid as much as possible studying the language is that they fear not being allowed to exchange, and they do not see their way in case of a separation between the Empire and the Kingdom.

The British philo-Turk, if any there be now, would characterise the absorption of Bosnia and Herzegovina,—I would even add Montenegro and Albania, with the frontiers of Greece,—as a spoliation of Turkey. Let him prove that it is not a just and right retaliation for the centuries of injury which she has inflicted, which she still inflicts, and which she will ever inflict, upon tht sacred causes of civilization and progress. If any casuist declare that the misrule of a government, as in the case of Oude, does not justify the annexation by powers professing faith in the development of man, in the religion of humanity; if he put forward that old saw that "the end does not justify the means;" let him be answered that Europe has duties which she owes to herself, that the first rule of conduct is her own safety, and that the second is the support of her co-religionists in Europe and Asia, throughout the Ottoman Empire. The Christian population equals, if not exceeds the Mahometan, and the evident hope with which it looks forward to emancipation from Islamism deserves the most careful consideration.

For the last ten years the relations of Great Britain with Turkey have been peculiar and unsatisfactory. The Ottoman voice has openly said: "The last Englishman who cared for us was Lord Palmerston. You will assist us if it be to your interest, no matter how we treat you, well or ill. You do not fight for an idea, like France. You will not fight for love of us, as in the days of Silistria and Eupatoria. We prefer an open enemy to a false friend. Go to! We have had enough of you." And they showed their especial contempt by their treatment of English subjects in Turkey; the debts owed to them by the Turk remain unpaid, and in Syria our fellow countrymen were the last to receive the compensation for the destruction of their property in the massacre of 1860.

Again, the present is, if any, the moment for us to act, or to encourage action in others. The stride of the young Colossus is temporarily, not lastingly, stayed. In future times* *quien sabe?* (but God avert it!), we may be so hampered by civil disturbances between Capital and Labour, so trammeled by intestine

* I fear that the Future now threatens to be the Present (1878).

troubles in Ireland, or so engaged in external war, that moral force only will not suffice to give our voice any weight in the European world. And the effect would be allowing Russia, a vigilant enemy of overpowering resolution, to annex Turkey in Europe without any attempt to preserve the last rag of balance of power by strengthening the hands of Austria.

Again, there are thousands of our fellow countrymen scattered over the surface of Turkey, and were England known to be incapacitated from using arms, yet having arms and money, it is to be feared that the first Russian gun fired from Constantinople would be the signal of a miserable butchery. But it will be said that the Sultan has begun the task of reform, his last rescript has been more favourable to the Rayyahs than anything ever issued by Turkey. I reply, it is easy to have dust thrown in our eyes provided we open them for the purpose. What have all the Hatts Shereef or Humayoun yet done for the Christian Turk? We must be made, after the image of David Urquhart, to believe in such pie-crust promises. Grant we that H.I.M. the Sultan is sincere, yet he cannot act himself, and there is no one to act for him; the Turkish official—and, for the matter of that, the unofficial—society is much like her army. The private is an excellent man, sober, honest, truthful, brave, and docile to a degree. Promote him, and he runs through the several grades of bad comparison, not *repenté*, but with an agility which surprises the slow northern mind. As a non-commissioned officer he is bad; higher he is worse; and command makes him worst. The same with the French peasant: give him a small *emploi*, a bit of gold lace, and he falls from an angel to a demon in a week, without stopping to look round.

Now back to *notre premier amour*, Trieste. I, as a woman, should naturally know but little of these things of myself, but associating with politicians and clever men all day, with open eyes and ears, an average amount of intelligence, and an occasional peep at a despatch, make one learn a good deal, and form strong opinions. I am neither philo-Turk nor Russ. I am John Bull to the backbone, with hereditary and personal Austrian sympathies, and a strong leaning to all that is of Arab blood.

This port was once a favourite with the British bird of passage, especially when embarking with the Austro-Hungarian Lloyd for Alexandria. But the Northerner did not approve of the line. He liked his beef and mutton in huge joints, not in slices and cutlets; he preferred his potatoes in their jackets to *pommes de terre à la maître d'hôtel;* in fact, he grumbled about everything, and at Suez he transferred himself on board the P. and O. like one that had found a home. The stranger has also been put to flight by the hotel managers. This city is one of the dearest in Europe. The shilling, the lira, and the franc have become the florin, but these gentlemen gild refined gold, and charge highly for the operation. There are three establishments which call themselves first-rate, and which Englishmen would consider decently comfortable. Unhappily, they belong to companies, not individuals, and they are farmed out to managers, who squeeze you as the tax-gatherer does the Rayyah. There are no tables of charges hung up in the rooms, so you pay according to length of purse, real or supposed. Thus, the late Lord Dalling had a bill of £45 for two days, during which he never dined in the house, and the present Prince Ypsilante was plundered at the same time of 950 florins. It is said that he sent for the manager, and, after settling his account, warmly complimented him upon being the greatest rascal he had ever had to do with. So the late Lord Hertford, when paying off his Parisian architect, politely regretted that he had ever had *le déplaisir de sa connaissance.*

All the world here is reading M. Charles Yriarte. That popular writer, the Ipsilon of the *Revue des deux Mondes,* who spent the winter of 1873–4 in Istria and Dalmatia, Montenegro and Herzegovina, published his trip in the illustrated journal, the *Tour du Monde;* and, the time being propitious, it was translated into Italian at Milan, with a variety of notes taking the Italianissimo view of the matter, and converting a delightful tale of travel into a rabid wrangle of politics. The Austrian Government has shown a want of knowledge of human nature, put the book *à l'index,* confiscating every copy found in the libraries; consequently we are all devouring it *en cachette.*

Now, having vivisected Trieste from a manly, business-like, and political point of view, I return to my own nature, that of a tender and indulgent woman, very much in love with her home. Trieste is *beautiful;* I know of no more fascinating panorama than that of the Carnian Alps from the *rive* (quays) of Trieste. In summer they are hid by the exhalations of the Aquilejan lowlands, but in winter, when they raise their giant heads, hoar with snow, and extend their lower garments of light azure over the plain, whose foreground is the deep blue Adriatic, dotted with its lateen sails, they give an inconceivable majesty to the north-western horizon. All round our bay the hills are covered with woodland and verdure, and are overtopped on one side by the bit of wild Karst, which looks like stony Syria. The town fills the valleys, and straggles up these wooded slopes; the sky is softly blue; on a balmy day, the birds and bees, the hum of the insects, the flowers, fresh air, and the pretty peasantry on gala days, combine to form a picture which makes one glad to live. The boisterous winds and bad climate have never hitherto, thank God, given me anything but the strongest health.

You can live exactly as you please here; you can be as retired or as gay as you like. If you have money there is every creature comfort; and if you do not find it here, you can have it in a day or two, for you are near Vienna, Paris, London, Berlin, Rome. If you have not money, you must be content with modest living. There is abundance of society of all kinds,—and it is so good-natured and amiable; it does not care whether you are rich or poor, whether you receive or do not receive; it only asks you to be nice, and opens its arms to you. I daresay my visiting list, private and consular, comprises 300 families; but we have our little *intime clique,* which is quite charming, and includes some sixty or seventy persons, the *crème* of Trieste. It is a great deal to say in a small town of 130,000 inhabitants, that I have found twenty-six women friends whom I should be glad to see again in any part of the world. They are mostly pretty, have charming figures, are beautifully dressed, have delightful manners, are well educated and accomplished; all speak three or four languages, are good musicians, and swim like fish, to say nothing of being good-hearted and most pleasant company.

One gets to know the male portion of society less well because they are all (except the Austrian authorities), in some profession, or mostly on the Bourse, so that they are rarely seen, except at a ball or party, and so we do not get very intimate. All are married or mere boys; there is a scarcity of what we should call "young men," so there are few weddings. And I would strongly recommend any friend who has a wife *tant soit peu légère,* to come and reside here. We have what Captain Burton is pleased to call "hen parties,"—*Kaffee gesellschaft,* which is really five o'clock tea, where we meet, dance (together), play, sing, recite stories, and have some refreshments; but a man, except the master of the house, is never seen. Then, *en revanche,* we have plenty of evening entertainments, for both sexes, when a rigid decorum is observed. No one dares indulge in the most innocent flirtation.

Captain Burton and I have drawn out a line for ourselves. We rise at three or four in summer, and five in winter. He reads, writes, and studies all day, out of Consular hours, with occasional trips for health; and I learning Italian, German, and singing. We take our daily exercise in the shape of an hour's swimming or fencing at the school, according to the weather. Then, what with writing, reading, looking after the poor, working for the Church, or for the Society for the Prevention of Cruelty to Animals (here an arduous and much-needed mission), the day is all too short. You can, in one word, occupy yourself as you like, and have the best of masters for everything. The prettiest thing of all is the swimming school. It is moored out at the entrance of the harbour. We reach it in a boat, and get hold of "Tonina," the old woman who provides us with a *camerino,* or little stall to undress in, and grins from ear to ear at our "chaff," and prospects her *bakshish.* Our costumes are short trousers, boddice, and belt, of blue serge, or black alpaca, trimmed with white, and we plunge into the great *Vasca,* or basin,—an acre of sea, bottomless, but enclosed on all sides with a loaded net to keep out the sharks. There are twelve soldiers to teach us; they begin with a pole and rope, like a fishing-rod and line, and to the end of the latter is a broad belt, which goes round the waist of a beginner whilst she learns the movements; and you hear the incessant "eins, zwei, drei" of the drill. Next they lead you round the edge of the *Vasca* with a rope, like a pet dog. Some swimmers cast away the rope after the third, fourth, fifth, or sixth time, and some, who will never swim, keep it for forty or fifty times; it is a mere matter of courage, as it is natural for every animal to swim. The adepts plunge in head first from a sort of trapeze, or from the roofs of the dressing rooms, making a somersault on the way. They do the prettiest tricks in the water,—young married women meeting in the middle, and shaking hands and holding long conversations; scores of young girls romping about, ducking each other under, climbing on each other's backs for sport in deep water; and children of three or four swimming about like whitebait in and out between us all. One old lady sits lazily on the water like a blubber-fish, knitting, occasionally moving her feet (we call her the buoy, and hold on to her when we are tired).

We have a curious local custom. On the 24th August you find the streets full of baggage, carts, and trucks, processions of boxes and furniture. The impression of a stranger is, that the town is being bombarded, or there is an earthquake, and we are taking flight with our "little all." No such thing; if you wish to change your house, you must give notice this 24th August, and you must change next 24th August, and on no other day, and that the hottest of the year, or you may option to lose a year's rent. There are two or three other curious local customs, already dying out in my time,—that of two friends or relations meeting in society, and perhaps after embracing affectionately, dropping each other a Court "curtsey." Visiting hours are from twelve to two; men are required to go in white cravats, kid gloves, and evening costume. This "Minstrel"-like mode is happily also fading out. Every lady has her reception day, fixed, say, every Monday or every Friday, from such to such an hour. When I first came, I was often invited *en intime* to tea with half-a-dozen friends, all related to each other, and to come "just as you are, my dear," and would find them *décolletée* with diamonds, whilst I, being English, had taken them *au pied de la lettre*, and gone "as I was." A friend once said to me, in confidence, "You know, my dear, we are so fond of our *toilettes* and diamonds, so it gives us pleasure to dress, even for one another; but don't you do it if it bores you." An invitation received in the morning to "drink a cup of cold water" at a friend's house in the evening, generally means a splendid ball, with Parisian supper and *toilettes*. All these *extremes* are, however, dying out, even during my stay here, or else I have grown used to them and do not perceive it. It is, taking it all in all, a most cordial and generous town, and nowhere have I been received with more kindness, affection, and consideration. I shall always return to it with pleasure, and even if it should be my lot to leave it officially, I shall never desert it. This I can say both as to its private and public life, for the latter is always progressing, always in movement, and always trying to improve itself. The people have a good heart, and are amenable to kindness, and to reason and good manners. It is a most talented, a most tolerant, and charitable town, with its purse ever open to distress of all kinds.

CHAPTER III.

TRIESTE TO PORT SAID—1st *JANUARY*, 1876.

A PARTING mid-day dinner with friends. At 3.15 the Government boat, containing the *Capitaine du Port* and sailors, in uniform, with the Chevalier d'Alber, his daughter, and son-in-law. Baron and Baroness Czœrnig came to take us to our ship,—an honour seldom accorded to any but high Austrian officials. At the ship we were joined by a large party of friends,—H.R.H. the Duke of Würtemberg, Commander-in-Chief at Trieste, who has again so much distinguished himself in the Bosnian campaign; Baron Pascotini, and several others, who came to wish us "God-speed." I cannot say how touched we were at those affectionate proofs of popularity, and the honour we received; doubly so, that after all those who were not about to sail were obliged to leave the ship, many lay to in their boats till five p.m., to see us steam out by the departing daylight of the old year. Never shall I forget so much kindness.

At five p.m. we backed out of the old port of Trieste, and turned the *Calypso's* head southwards. The flags bent lazily northward, as if a *scirocco* were coming, and we expected to meet the tyrant of these seas, who is apt to rage furiously between Albania and Corfu. In the darkening air we sped past the Muggia Bay, with its queer old Venetian port; past Capo d'Istria, where "the most Serene Republic" had her Istrian headquarters; past Isola town, no longer insulated; past picturesque Pirano, famed of yore for pirates; past the lighthouse of Salvore,—that long, grassy, wood-tipped point, whose name, "Salvo Ré," denotes that it once saved a king from drowning. After this the world, as the Arabs say, "grew dark before our eyes."

The *Calypso* (Austrian Lloyd's) is a good old tub, originally built in Glasgow for a cattle boat, is two thousand tons and two hundred horse-power. We were the only passengers, so Captain Bogojevich and his six officers and engineers and ourselves were soon established on the footing of a family party, and I never was so comfortable in any ship before or since. Soon I established my bed on the floor of my cabin, and slept for twelve hours, as I had had but little rest since leaving London, twenty-nine days ago.

The day after the start was a complete *bonanza* (calm). The seas slept as we sped by the beautiful islands of the Istrian archipelago, sighting to starboard the hills of Abruzzo Citeriore, and the *Massif* of Monte Gayano. At eight in the evening we saw the new lighthouse of Pelagosa,—a quaint, isolated bit of limestone in the sea, whose radius is twenty miles. We hug the Italian coast because the current runs southward, at the rate of 1·30 to 1·45 knots an hour, setting the reverse way up the shores of Illyria. It was Sunday and a Catholic ship, but there was no service as on the P. and O. These poor fellows boast of their irreligion all the time of meals, and are somewhat blasphemous. How foolish it sounds to me, and how they will cry out for one of those despised and maligned priests when they come to their last hour. Our days were passed between eating, drinking, sleeping, walking, reading, writing, and studying.

The third day showed us, at 9.30 a.m., the Brindisi harbour; this is the very filthiest town of all Italy: and about noon the bluff Cabo di Otranto, a name loved by romance. Two hours later we reached the Bocca del Golfo, where Adriatic storms are supposed to cease, whereas they as often begin and rage as far as Zante. We have to-day rougher weather, both wind and sea. I passed my day reading the Life of Moore and "The Veiled Prophet of Khorassán," called by Moore "Mokanna," but whose real name was Hasan Sabah, or Hasan es Sayyah. On our port bow was a lovely sight. The snow-clad mountains of Albania blushed pink in the sun of eventide, as they reclined upon their bed of billowy purple cloud; and we were told frightful tales of the Cimariot Highlanders, a race as savage as the Somal or the Kervosje (bloodmen) of the Bocche di Cattaro. The last smile of day lit upon Fanó, the *outlier* of Corfu, Mr. Gladstone's folly, which will cost us pretty dear now that we want Mediterranean stations for our ironclads.

The fourth morning's first beams fell upon the white cliffs and blue-shaded ravines of Zante; and beyond is the little bay of Arkadiá. The wind got stronger and the sea rougher. After another range of misty, storm-wrung highlands, we steered right across the mouth of the glorious Navarino bay, a fine harbour for refuge, backed by a country abounding in game, ducks, and wild geese. I passed the day in writing, and reading "Lallah Rookh." We had a bad night, and although we fondly hoped that all had been made "taut" and snug for the night's bad weather, things rolled from one side of the cabin to the other all night, enlivened by distant crockery smashes. I think, by the way she danced, the *Calypso* carried but little cargo that voyage; however, she behaved very well in a heavy sea.

The next day (fifth) the morning light showed us Mount Selinon of rugged Candia, and at noon we ran through the narrow channel between Crete and the Gavdo rock, which our captain calls Gozo; and by evening we were beyond land, and nothing remained to us, as Ovid says, but blue sea and azure air,—the latter waxing warmer and warmer every day. We already begin to feel Egypt. I sat on a chair all day, lashed to the deck, and read "The Light of the Harem." The waves were glorious, much higher than the ship.

The sixth was passed in the same manner. It is fatiguing when such a storm lasts long, to be so knocked about, and baths are impossible. One can only sit and read and write, make a hasty toilette at most, being obliged to hold on to something with one hand, or be knocked the while from one side of the cabin to the other; and dining on the balance, the food ever sliding into one's lap, is dreadfully tiring. To-day I read "The Adventures of Roderick Random," and "The Memoirs of a Lady of Quality," by Smollett, which I found coarse but interesting. I was told that this course of reading is supposed to be necessary to form one for novel writing, and so I took it on board to save time, in case I should ever wish to write a novel. I felt rather displeased when Smollett's Lady of Quality married her second husband, and quite *bouleversée* long before I arrived at, let us say, her fifteenth lover.

The seventh.—We put up several dozen letters, written on board, for friends in Europe, as we were to reach Port Said at 3.30. The run from Trieste is six days and six nights. Port Said shows itself upon the southern horizon in two dark lines, like long piles or logs of wood, lying upon the sea, one large and one small. It is the white town and the black town, apparently broken by an inlet of sea and based upon a strip of yellow sand, which stretches from the north to the west. We steamed in slowly, with the Pilot in charge, on a calm and balmy afternoon. The two big lighthouses at the entrance of the canal are striking. There are the old red Crimean huts, zebra'd white and red, and the two-storied bungalow of the Governor, Ibrahim Rushdi Bey, the fatal Hospital, and the Convent of Carmelite nuns. This is a sort of Egyptian Wapping.

A foul swamp, an arm of the Lake Menzaleh, separates the white town, where Christian pigs are hunted by Moslem dogs, from the black town; the latter is an African cross between a Fellah and a fishermen's village; it taints the air and adds to the deadly chill-breeding damps from September to December. The slightest of dams, extending from the general establishment to the opposite side, would suffice to gain much ground and abate the malaria plague. This place contains nine thousand souls, including about thirty English. It leans to Socialism. The Maltese *canaille* are fond of murdering and burying in the sand, so at night men carry a Derringer in their pocket. Regarding its morals, I am told, the less said the better. Here we saw an Austrian Lloyd from Constantinople, with the danger signal (the yellow flag) up; an English steamer, the *El Dorado*, and with ourselves and a "Bibby" as long as the sea serpent, made four steamers to enter the Canal. We went ashore into this sandy settlement and posted our letters, but no one, either at the post or at Austrian Lloyd's office, would take Austrian paper, of which I had a quantity. We wandered about with the Consul (Mr. and Mrs. Perceval), Mr. Buckley, of the F.O., Colonel Stoker and Salih Bey. Mr. and Mrs. Stephen Cave arrived on their Egyptian mission, and the distinguished Monsieur de Lesseps.

The houses look like painted wooden Swiss toys. The streets are broad; the shops are full of penny dolls and gingerbread nuts, crackers, shilling straw hats, and similar rubbish, and are surrounded by dogs and half-naked dark brown gutter boys.

The eighth day.—We visited the Arab town, and had a most pleasant dinner party with the Percevals in the evening.

Port Said is simply two towns lying on a waste of sand, with an unwholesome stagnant Lagune between. That near the sea is the European, and that behind the Lagune is the Egyptian. But for this Lagune, with its stagnant water, and smells of dirt, and dogs, it ought to be a healthy place, as it immediately faces the sea and inhales all its breezes. There is a circular garden in the centre of the European part, with faded flowers, and a kiosk in its centre for the band to play in the evening. There is a casino, or low-class *alcazar*, a few donkeys, but no horses or carriages; some small hotels, of which the "Louvre" is the best; and there is a great deal of low-class music, dancing, and gambling; add to these a French chapel and a Greek chapel. The most picturesque, characteristic, albeit dirty part, is the Arab town, with its tumbledown houses and bazar; the people in gaudy prints and dirty Abas (mantles) bespangled with gold.

Whilst strolling about this town, my German maid, who was in an Eastern place for the first time, came upon a man filling a goat-skin with water. She saw a pipe, and the skin distending with a sound. She had often heard me say how cruel the Easterns are to animals, and knowing my weakness on that point, she ran after me in a great state of excitement, and pulled my arm, saying, "Oh, *Euer Gnaden!* the black man is filling the poor sow with gas, do come back and stop him!"

There is no night travelling on the Canal, but at six a.m. in the morning we began to steam up the long ditch. The piercing of the Isthmus took ten years, and now we no longer say right and left, but Asia and Africa. For little more than five years the line has been open to trade, and it is a wonderful work. It has cost sixteen millions, and it is said half more will be required to finish it properly. England lent the Viceroy £10,600,000 for the works. Almost every steamer one meets upon the Canal is British. The heavy toll is roughly estimated at ten shillings a ton, and the maritime Canal has greatly increased the traffic between Great Britain and the East; it is the last link riveted in the great belt of trade, and the road for our ships is completely defensible. It forms an admirable moat against the Bedawi, and a grand line of defence on the Eastern frontier. It has produced, they say, a change of climate,—it breeds fogs and clouds, and draws a strong wind from the north. At blue, stagnant Suez there is a cool in draught in the worst season. Two winters ago Jebel Atakeh and the opposite range of Asiatic mountains were for forty-eight hours covered with snow, which astonished the oldest inhabitants. Violent showers fall in January over the northern third of the Red Sea, and the climate of Jeddah has been materially changed.

This interesting work is eighty-two to eighty-six *nautical* miles long,—the one hundred and sixty-nine kilometres are marked up on posts along the sides,—and it is cut through the sand of the wildest desert. All the large depressions form lakes; the least prepossessing is about Lake Menzaleh, whose dismal banks are flanked on the African side by a mirrory sheet of water, skimmed over by butterfly sails, supporting troops of birds, which are magnified by mirage to the size of men; we often mistook them for camels and Bedawin. At certain distances are stations, inhabited by Frenchmen, with posts and conveniences for making-fast steamers to let others pass; for, except in the lakes, there is hardly room for two to lie abreast; therefore the greatest speed allowed is five and three-quarter knots an hour.

At length, to the far east, we trace a gladdening glimpse of the Desert,—the wild, waterless wilderness of Sur, on the Asiatic side, with its tall waves and pyramids of sand catching the morning rays, with its shades of mauve, rose-pink, and lightest blue; with its plains and rain sinks, bearing brown dots, which are tamarisks; the manna trees. It has a charming simplicity which wins the heart. In the young day nothing can be softer or more tender than the colouring of the old Lion, one of the fiercest, by-the-bye, of his kind. The utter barrenness becomes a thing of absolute beauty. The sky was heavenly blue, the water a deep band of the clearest green, the air balmy and fresh. The golden sands stretch far, and on all sides end in horizon; an occasional troop of Bedawin, with their camels and goats, passed, and reminded me of my old life. I have not enjoyed myself so much with Nature for four years and a half. Noon will wash out its coat of many colours, and under the cold rays of the moon it will suggest a broken expanse of snow. We stand and gaze upon Life by the side of Death.

Much comforted at once more "smelling the desert air," we felt thankful for the slowness of the pace. In the event of hopelessly sticking fast, the Company has reserved to itself the right of blowing us up. We reached, after five hours, El Kantarah, the northernmost ferry for the Syrian caravans. There are two others south of Lake Timsah, and in the cutting of Shalúf, a station of importance, is the transit for the Hajj or Pilgrimage Kafilehs. The scene is that of all Eastern pictures,—the Nizam regular soldiers, and negroes, Bedawin draped in usual cloak and *kuffiyyeh*, and women in blue garments, not changed a hair since the days of Abraham, except that they now carry matchlocks instead of spears. The tawny camels squat upon the ground, and the black sheep and goats form separate huddled knots, vainly attempting to shade their heads. A seedy *dahabiyyeh* rolls past us; it is a craft belonging to a bygone age, and is hustled out of the way by the fussy, high-pressure *mouche*, which carries the daily mails to Ismailiyyah. This was the pleasantest two days imaginable,—like a river picnic; we read, wrote, and lounged on the bridge, glass in hand, with the captain and the surly Maltese pilot.

At 4.20, after forty miles, we entered the Crocodile Lake. The approach is a picturesque but dangerous curve crowned in Africa by a pretty little pavilion, striped red and white, and capped with quaint little *crenelles* built by the Khedive * as a breakfast-room for his royal guests of 1869. This blue sheet of water is about three miles across and six long, and it rages, when high winds blow from south and south-west, but lately the Egyptian gunboat, now at Port Said, was blown ashore, after losing two anchors. The channel, twenty-four feet deep, is well marked by buoys and iron posts painted red.

Ismailiyyah is a pretty mushroom town, with palaces, consulates, and gardens. It has a telegraph and a steam launch for Lake Timsah, and railway to Cairo, Suez, and Alexandria. The Vice-regal Palace is a monstrous pile of building, and the fine gardens form dense clumps of verdure. It contains two thousand souls, and hoists nine various national flags. The situation is charming, and dulness reigns supreme. M. Lesseps will, however, make it a second Alexandria. At present there are only fishing boats and a steam yacht returning from a Red Sea cruise. It is interesting to know that we have the land of Goshen, mentioned in Genesis, immediately to our north-west. A little steam launch, or *mouche*, as coquettish as a humming bird, buzzing with importance, came fussing alongside with a smart French-looking official with neat uniform and gold band, and exchanged our surly Maltese for a handsome grey old pilot who was rather reserved, but answered courteously if spoken to. "Ecco una bestia che non ha lingua affatto mi pare," said our captain. Presently he heard my husband and I exchange a word or two. His face changed, his eye brightened, and he hailed us in English, his native tongue, and we fraternised; his name was Young,—a nice old man.

We took on board 100,000 florins in gold, to pay the troops in El Hejaz, and the guard is a single soldier, whose quaint sitting at squat amused us. After forty minutes' delay we issue

* *N.B.*—The proper word is "Khediw,'—a Persian word, meaning "Prince." Why we should pepper the last syllables of our Oriental words with a barbarous acute accent I don't know, unless to please the French so please let us be independent and pronounce it "Khedív."

from Lake Timsah, and proceed on our way, and after the forty-sixth mile, at dusk we anchored in the deep narrow cutting of Serapeum, near No. 2 ferry, which communicates with a Bedawi village in Asia. The hues of evening were surpassingly tender and lovely, although some clouds in the west presaged a mist. Foxes abound, and one squatted upon the sand bank and stared at us. We dined at anchor. It was a glorious moonlight; the rays silvered the sand, and all was replete with a freshness and stillness which I cannot make any reader feel save those who know it.

We unmoored at dawn, and again ran up the deep channel. The desolation around, barren sand, contrasted with the splendour of the heavens, the glory of the East, the sun elongated into egg-shape by the mirage, and the filmy cloudlets' sublimed dew, mauve above and below burning with the fire of the opal. About seven, we came upon the Serapeum village. The Persepolitan ruins lie to the W.N.W., and the native craft appeared to be sailing inland. Some twelve miles from Timsah, we crept into the Great Bitter Lake,—a small sea some ten miles broad, whose tiny waves are like cream on a surface of sapphire. North and east lies low ground, with marshes and backwater; and southward and westward rise the sandy cliffs of Jebel Jeneffeh, and towering above all is the outline of Jebel Atakeh. It reminded us of Lake Tiberias. At 9.15 we hurried by the southern lighthouse, and hugged the African shore, which trends to meet the Asiatic. We could see the mail train puffing through the desert, and the butterfly boats sailing over the sand, in a sweet-water canal which we cannot see.

At 10.50 we passed into the last cutting—Shalúf. We are but twelve miles from Suez, and we recognised the old familiar features of the scene, Fort Ajrud, the British Hospital, the house of the Government-agent for troop ships, the minaretted town' and the English island-cemetery, gleaming white.

Soon ragged lads, boys like spiders, and girls in blue nightgowns, form a running line on the Asiatic side, and shout the well-known cry, "*Bakshish! ya Kawajah!*" It is the first time for four years and a half I have heard that sound which irritates like the buzz of a mosquito. The soldier throws them a bit of bread, but as we throw them nothing, the petitions change to curses,—"Na'al abukum, ya kilab!" ("Drat your fathers, O ye dogs!") We pass the ruins of old Arsinoë in Asia, creep down the last curve, called (no one knows why) the Quarantine. On the African side is a double dam, and the other shore is left to nature. We sniff the breezes of the sea as we round the new port, and at 2.30 make fast to the buoy. Suez is a most inaccessible place, and steamers anchor in the bay, an hour's steam from the town, and much more by sail; if you leave your steamer, and if there is a contrary wind you can never be sure of getting back to it. Inasmuch as we were to sail at six, prudence forbade our trying it: we only sent our letters off; I had written some twenty-five. The civil and obliging agent of Austrian Lloyds came off and took our post (Mr. Mahorcich is his name); our peace and quiet was all spoiled by gaining two quite tipsy Russian passengers, one a professional spy, and the other a merchant's son, who was addicted to drink, and who was put under his care for cure. The first limped, and therefore was called "The Leg;" the other was forthwith christened "Champagne Charley," and they hereafter led us a terrible life. We dined at five, and sailed at six.

January 1st, 1870, was a sad day for Suez. It was the opening of the Canal;* and, as if by magic, all that had passed through Suez, now passed through the Egyptian Bosphorus, ruining the former, so that after six years she wears the appearance of a Red Sea town lately bombarded, and not yet repaired. She suffers from the Canal as Trieste from her railway the Südbahn; but these accidents are transitory, position is essential and paramount. To the north-east are the ruins of Arsinoë; on the west lie the old reservoirs, and the Tel el Klismeh, preserving the old Greek name Clysma, from which the Arabs took their term, Sea of *Ḳulzum*. Suez is, however, safer at night than a few years ago, when the ready knife or pistol of Greek or Maltese

* Suez is now a big village with, say, three thousand native inhabitants, about seventy-five Europeans,—chiefly English,—employed in the telegraph, steamers, railways, and post-office. She sits solitary under the sky, in the sand, on the borders of the sea, far from all civilization or progress. She has had a past, and will have a future.

made it dangerous as the leading of a forlorn hope; and nothing has ever been heard of an American who, in 1869, set out for a solitary walk. The Suez Roads are lively, scores of steamers starting for the north and south,—these bound for India, China, Australia; those, for Europe. Two Turkish transports await their "food for powder," cargo for Abyssinia and Arabia; three thousand camels are being shipped for Massawwah, and *on dit* that thirty thousand troops have been collected in that unhappy land and its sterile shore. Here we also shipped a pious pilot, one Mohammed Salám, who said his prayers regularly, and carefully avoided touching my dog. Of course he was from Mecca, as every Frenchman is Parisian; but, unhappily for his reputation, the first night spent at Jeddah gave him a broken nose, the effect of a scrimmage in some low coffee-house. An Egyptian Fellah amused us very much by coolly asking the captain if he had provided a sentinel to stand over his oranges all night. The bumboat men are mostly Maltese, and scud up to us under their huge lateen sails. Their decks were a mosaic of fruit, vegetables, bottles and flasks, cigars and tobacco, work-boxes, needles and thread, in fact, every kind of *chow-chow* under the sun; and they seemed to be the chief consumers of their own merchandise.

Most interesting were the views on either side of this most memorable sea. Eastward, painted pink and plum-blue by the last floods of sunlight, rose the regular wall of the Asiatic mountains; an offset from the great line which begins far north of the Lebanon, and which extends southward to Aden,—a counterpart of the Moab range, which would have served Holman Hunt for a background to his famous "Scapegoat." Opposite them, in Africa, stood Jebel Atakeh, "The Mountain of Deliverance." It looks as if the hand could almost touch it, and yet it is several hours' ride from Suez; the heights are very bad climbing, the loose material crumbling in blocks under the foot. Atakeh is separated from its southern neighbour, Abu Daraj, "The Father of Steps,"—so called from its distinctly trap-like outline,—by the Wady Musa, down which the Great Deliverer is supposed to have led the chosen people.

My husband saw here, twenty-five years ago, many monas

teries and hermitages, which seemed to prove the holiness of the ground. He showed me where the Israelites are popularly supposed to have crossed the Red Sea. Christians have three places above Suez, and the Arabs two below. The Serbonian swamp and lagunes, south of the Mediterranean, he says, is the real place, as proved by Dr. Brugsch Bey, from Egyptian papyri. The "Red Sea" is nowhere mentioned in the Pentateuch. The only name is Yamm Suf, which means "sea of weeds," or papyrus; utterly inapplicable to the Suez Gulf, but well fitting the Mediterranean lagune. We were taught to believe that they started from near Cairo, not far from Memphis, and now we are told that the children of Israel started from Goshen, near Tanis, or the modern Sán, on the extreme east of the Delta; that upon the Serbonian swamp, where the Egyptians in pursuit were drowned, they doubled back to the south-west, and then turned north-east over the Tih; the latter is still translated "Valley of the Wandering," whereas it means a "wilderness where man can wander."

There was a beautiful moon a little past the full, with a fresh northerly breeze down the Red Sea, as we set out about nightfall; it allowed us to sleep under a fur, and propelled us at the rate of ten knots an hour. I had always thought that the Red Sea was like a broad river, and was surprised to find a big, rough sea, between Asia and Africa, with Arabia on one side, and on the other Egypt, Nubia, and Abyssinia; and that after we leave the Gulf of Suez, at Ras Abu Mohammed, we see no more land. To starboard, Africa rises wild and very grim; its sugar-loaves, caps, and slope hills are of dull murret colour, patched with yellow sand. This is the dangerous shore, and requires a number of lighthouses: the Zaaferanah, the Gharib, the Ashrafi, The Brothers (North and South), and the Dædalus, or Abd el Khisán,—a sort of lighthouse like an iron buoy, where a couple of guards reside, who are relieved twice a month. Yonder big block is the Shadwán, a large, waterless desert island, half submerged: on its northern reef, in 1869, the P. and O. lost a steamer, and we a friend.

On the morning of the eleventh my husband called me on

deck by dawn to see Mount Sinai, lone in the Tih desert, Bir Hatt, and Musa Tur, called after Tyre, founded by the Phœnicians, and Ras Mohammed, the last cape, or point, of Egypt. Then, far towering over the deep blue waves, with their caps of snowy foam, sit three old Monarchs of mountains, bearing, as the Arabs say, heaven on their brows, and based upon broad carpets of golden sand. The pilot, however, calls them Jebel Serbal, Horeb, and Jebel Musa, Mount Catharine (? Sinai). We are too far off to see the Hammam Musa and the little harbour of Tur, still occupied by Justinian's Jebelíyeh (mountaineers). They are at the southern point of the low dark bank subtending the sea. It is interesting to me, because in my husband's Arab days he landed at Tur, and bathed at Hammam Musa on his way to Mecca.

On the other side of Ras Mohammed is the Gulf of Akabah, the Stormy, whose Wady (valley) Arabah is said to have given Arabia and the Arabs their name; and I expect a year or two more will increase its fame; but of this I shall not speak. The Gulf of Suez is narrow, so that we seem close to these mountains of Egypt and Africa. It was rough, but the weather delicious; and having worked all day at a memorial for a newspaper in England, I went to pass the evening on the bridge. We ran by "The Brothers" at about eleven p.m. These are two most dangerous rocks, not easily seen at night, barely covered over by the water. The Red Sea is strewn with these hidden slabs, and scarcely a lighthouse; it makes one reflect seriously how many gallant ships must have foundered on dark nights, through the inexperience of a commander or the derangement of a compass; whilst so many millions are thrown away on useless buildings, a penny cannot be found for such an object! During the night we ran along the Highlands of the Hejaz, and passed El Wijh (Wedge), the frontier point, where Egypt and Arabia meet. Here pilgrim ships going northward must perform quarantine.*

* Shortly after we passed it, Wedge lost the quarantine establishment, which was transferred, most unwisely, to Tur. Readers will find the subject discussed in the "Land of Midian," my husband's *second* book.

The weather was rough, with a strong north wind, on the 12th, and there was not much to see till we passed Jebel Ridwah, a notable item of the mountains in the Moslems' Holy Land. At its base lies the turbulent and fanatical little town of Yambu, the port of Medina, and behind it are the winding valleys which eventually lead to the death-place of the Apostle of Allah. We asked our pious pilot about Saad, the sheikh of the Harb Bedawin, the Robber Chief of the Jebel el Fikrah. He replied that "the dog had long since gone to Jehannum;" that he "regretted that his son Hudayful, who is also a dog, and the son of a dog, still breathes the upper air."

13*th.*—To-day, at dawn, the Highlands of the Hejaz began gradually to define themselves on the south-east horizon, until the whole range of Jebel Kara was visible; first, blue brown, then dead chocolate brown, based upon a yellow flat, the Tehamah, or lowlands of the Moslem Holy Land, quite shadeless, not a speck of green; these outliers are backed by a hazy blue line, the Jebel el Surúriyyeh, of which the far-famed Taif forms a part. We then neared Jeddah, the port of Mecca, about which I have a good deal to say. I never could have imagined such an approach to any town. For twenty miles it is protected by nature's breakwaters—lines of low, flat reefs, huge slabs of madrepore and coralline that cut like a knife, barely covered, and not visible till you are close upon them; there is no mark or lighthouse, save two little white posts, which you might mistake for a couple of good-sized gulls; in and out of these you wind like a serpent; there is barely passage for one ship between them, and no pilot will attempt it, save in broad daylight; so a vigilant look-out is necessary as soon as we near Shaab el Kebir, or Great Shoal, to which ships give a wide berth. It is *sans* lighthouse, and grim to look upon in the southerly gales. About noon the *Calypso* slackened speed, and seemed to be running straight towards a long line of breakers; and all the crew were piped to the forecastle, ready for dropping anchor or working the jib sails. When at length we reached the Inner Reef, at about three p.m., we found the open roadstead full of ships, with hardly room to swing, and a strong north-west wind, so that we could not get a place; we ran right into the first at anchor, the *Standard*, a trading-ship of Shields, built of iron. Fortunately it was broad daylight. My husband and I were standing on the bridge, and he touched my arm, and said,

"By Jove! we are going right into that ship."

"Oh, no!" I answered, "with the captain and pilot on the bridge, and all the crew in the forecastle, it can only be a beautiful bit of steering; we shall just shave her."

The words were hardly out of my mouth when smash went our bulwarks like brown paper, and our yard-arms crumpled up like umbrellas. I had jokingly threatened them with the 13th the day before, and they had laughed at me.

"Il tredici!" shouted the second officer as he flew by us.

The crews of both behaved splendidly; the fenders were let down, and the cry on board our ship was,

"Il Capitano! Dov 'è il Capitano Inglese? non lo vedo." ("Where is the English captain? I don't see him.")

"No!" we answered, "ma noi lo sentiamo." ("No!" we answered, "you don't see, but *we* can hear him.")

He was all there, and "swearing quite like himself." There is nothing like an Englishman for a good decisive order, and who can blame him if he adds at such times a little powder to drive the shot home? We were about three hours disentangling ourselves, and I believe the damage was about £200, but absolutely no one to blame. The *Calypso* had been lengthened to three hundred feet, the wind was blowing hard, there were thirty ships in a place not big enough to swing round in, hemmed in on every side with reefs.

Jeddah bears a whimsical resemblance, and has a relative position, to Jaffa, not only in situation, but form and distance from their respective Holy Cities. Jeddah is the most lovely town I have ever seen, to gaze upon from a quarter-deck (perhaps I ought to say *bizarre* and fascinating), by sunlight, especially at the setting thereof, and ghostly in the moonlight. It looks as if it were an ancient model carved in old ivory, so white and fanciful are the houses, with here and there a minaret. The most remarkable buildings are the dark *façade* of the Sherif Abd el Muttalib's palace, and that of the late Sherif Mohammed bin Aun, whose son, Sherif Abdullah, now rules the Holy Land. It is doubly interesting to me, because my husband came here by land from Mecca, and on return embarked here for England in 1853. Mecca lies in a valley between those high mountains at the back, and a second higher and more distant range, a little to our right. As I write now from our quarter-deck, the reefs are all around us, the sun is declining on the water, which is of the brightest green, like a prairie, the whole shore is yellow sand, backed by ranges of mountains of various altitudes, bathed in rose and purple tints. The sky is heavenly, and the ivory town lies on the golden sand. There are four or five small slave settlements of huts, built of mud, some in conical shape, like bell tents, and others like claret-cases; and I see a troop of camels grazing in the distance. These *Arish*, or huts, of the Bedawin and camels are all scattered about the sandy shore. The former are dark clumps of dry wattle, brushwood, and matting.

On the 14th, Mr. Wylde, the Vice-Consul, son of our old friend Mr. Wylde of the Foreign Office, hearing we were on board, sent a boat and Kawwas to bring us off, and invited us to live at the Consulate so long as the ship remained, which we gladly accepted, as we were to anchor there eight days, to embark pilgrims. The only boat that carries one comfortably in a rough sea in and out of these dangerous shoals and reefs, is that used by the natives, a large flat-bottomed *Sambúk*, carrying a big lateen sail, and then with a good wind and enough depth of water, it is managed in an hour.

The houses are made of white coralline, with brown wood shutters, jalousies, and balconies of fanciful shape, mostly all crooked, but as finely carved as delicate lace. The Consulate is the best of all, close to the sea, with a staircase so steep that it is like ascending the Pyramids. There is a room at the top, a sort of Belvedere, with windows opening to all sides, which I used to call "The Eagle's Nest;" from here there was delicious air and view. The party consists of Captain Beyts (Consul) and Son, merchants, and Mr. Wylde, Vice-Consul; Mr. Oswald and

Mr. Russell, also in the business. On the ground-floor is the Consulate on one side and the "Firm" on the other; in the middle of the house (upstairs) is the residence of the five bachelors, whom I call the "wreckers," because they are always looking out for ships with a telescope. They keep a pack of bull terriers, donkeys, ponies, gazelles, rabbits, pigeons, and all sorts of animals; they combine, as far as possible, Eastern and European comfort, and have the usual establishment of Dragomans, Kawwases, and servants of all sizes, shapes, and colour.

Our first excursion was to Eve's tomb. This building is 479 feet long and 15 feet broad, the whole enclosed in low white walls. At her head is a little building with a palm over it, "El Surreh." The Navel is a square crenelled chapel, surmounted by a dome, whose entrance is flanked by false minarets, and inside which, by favour and bakshish, and removing our shoes, we were admitted. It contains the usual little whitewashed room, with lamps, inscriptions, and prints of Mecca and the Kaabah. A stone box is covered with a green cloth, which they lifted up and disclosed two long blocks of stone lying side by side, and a black slab carved with Arabesque patterns. It terminates very plainly at the end with a fanciful wall, and a low column with inscriptions over her feet. The whole inside of the enclosure is planted with a green bramble, called "Jiram." One or two famous and holy people are buried in the enclosure. This grave is the centre-piece of about five acres of land, also enclosed by low whitewashed walls, in which are many tombs, although it is not by any means full. There is a small broken well, whose rain water is to them as "Holy water;" and two large mounds where the cholera patients were buried. The cemetery commands a view of the distant mountains, lovely in the setting sun, behind which lies Mecca. The prison is hot, damp, and mosquitoey enough to bring any refractory persons to their senses, and is hallowed by the tomb of Sheikh Abd el Salám, the Bayrakdar or standard-bearer of Omer the Caliph; and the Grand Sherif's flag—green ground, bordered red—flies from here on Fridays. There are five mosques, six windmills, barracks to lodge one thousand men, and two large Bedawi villages. There

EVE'S TOMB AT JEDDAH.

The building is 479 feet long, and 15 feet broad. The low white wall encloses about five acres of ground. To the right hand in the interior of the desert lies Mecca.

are also the slaughter-place, the domed tomb of Shaykh Yúsuf, and the place where fish is taxed. The troops (Turkish) are five hundred regulars, kept generally eighteen months in arrears, and then receive paper, which they must sell at 50 per cent. to their officers.

Beyond Eve's tomb are cisterns, which supply the town with brackish water, and greatly increase the death-rate. An excellent supply of running water might be brought from "Baraymán," a place at the foot of the Kara hills, distant some two hours' ride, and various depressions in the Jeddah plain would yield an abundant supply; but this is opposed, for pecuniary reasons, by several, and one in particular, of whom his fellow citizens sang:

> "Ahwar el Yamín, aduww 'el Muslemín
> Ahwar el Shimál, aduww 'el Jemál."
>
> "Blind of the right, hates the Moslem;
> Blind of the left, hates men all."

There are some two hundred Nautch girls at Jeddah, but they are forbidden to dance before men. I have heard, however, that the law can be evaded on occasions. There are two different types of villages in the plain—the Bedawin and the settled men. The former are represented by the Banú Malik, who besides dealing in sheep, are professed sheep stealers. They are distinguished from the others by black cloth of camel skin, often taking the place of wattle; by the ferocity of their dogs, and by the insolence of their manners.

The latter sort, "settled men," put to death their own murderers, and they use their pistols like men. The huts, even those of the Shaykhs, are wattle, with compounds of the same material, and each settlement has its mosque and Santon's tomb of stone and lime. Here and there in the village is a solitary acacia, Zaazafán, or camomile, a tamarind, a nebk, a tamarisk, or a palm, which helps to cool the eye. They live well, eat meat, fish, dates, butter, grain, dukhn, millet, and rice, which is their staple food. They amuse themselves with rough swings and merry-go-rounds. The lower village shows few children, and sickly adults; those built on higher ground, where the sand is clean, produce a fine, strong, healthy race. We used frequently to ride out into the desert, by the Hajj way, and it was tantalizing to find oneself so near Mecca, and to have to turn round and come back. There was a rumour that two American and two English had gone up "for a lark" to Mecca, and had been killed. This was not *quite* true, but not exactly the moment to show blue eyes and broken Arabic upon holy ground; we therefore consoled ourselves by returning through the Mecca gate and through the bazars, half dark and half lit, to see the pilgrims and camels. They are larger and cleaner than Damascus bazars, but less rich and picturesque; still, the scene is much a repetition of that described by me at the Hajj of Damascus in the sixth chapter of my "Inner Life of Syria:" every Eastern Moslem under the sun is here represented; there are only ten Christians in the whole place, and I am the only European lady.

To have taken these rides, and have walked through the Mecca gate in 1853, when my husband went to Mecca, would have cost us our lives by sabre slashes and clubbing. The bazars literally swarm with the picturesque and variegated mob, hailing from all lands between Morocco and Java, Moscow and the Cape of Good Hope; every race imaginable, with their different costumes and languages. This is a grand time for the *bric-à-brac* hunter, especially porcelain with Arabic inscriptions. We must remember that this year, 1875-76, is a great pilgrimage,—*Hajj el Kabir,*—on account of the "Day of Arafat" falling on a Friday. The total number of devotees collected at the Hill of Arafat and the Valley of Muná for the Eed el Kabir (Courban Bairám), between the 6th and 9th of July, 1876, was 137,980.

Here are camels, donkeys, Takhtarawán (litters), and Bedawin in quantities, but scarcely a horse to be seen. I feel quite happy in the atmosphere, and the Arabic sounds so musical and so familiar. Here is the open-air mosque, the Hindi Eedgáh, where the prayers of the Ramazan are recited; here are the pits where lime is burnt, the fuel and charcoal which is brought in by the Bedawin, and a short street of wattled and matted booths, where meat and other provisions are sold, and where the pariah dogs are fiercer than in all other quarters.

We must look through the great bazar, however, to see all the splendour and misery of the East side by side. All the pilgrims bring back something to sell, especially the tall-capped, long-bearded Persians, who sell fine carpets, cutlery, precious stones, especially turquoises, gulf pearls, and *káliúns* (water-pipes) of great elegance.

Yemen sends her old hoards,—weapons studded with the gold coins of the Venetian republic; her guns from the opposite coast, her perfumed coffee, and her delicate filigree work and chiselled silver. The pale-faced and tarbushed Turk, dressed in furs even in the dog days, contemptuously offers his arms, jewellery, rugs, and perfumes to the greasy Greek,—Asiatic above and half European below. Short and thin dark men, whose white cottons proclaim them to be Indians, deal with substantial Arab merchants in silks and dry goods, spices, drugs, tea, rice, and building timber. The Nizam officer, cigarette in hand, draws into a dark corner the sooty-faced Zanzibar man, or the Kuzayriyyah, the Mulatto, one of the most persistent of *Jellábs* (slave-dealers), in order to settle the terms of some fair purchase, Abyssinian or Galla. The vulturine Takrurí, from western inner Africa, once so common, now so rare, since the Viceroy of Egypt has wisely closed the way to an army of starving mendicants, views with scant favour his rival, the Bengali beggar, carrying a *coco de mer;* and the regular dervishes, who generally go in pairs, are singing,—one to the tambourine, the other offering a brass pot for contributions.

Turkomans wearing huge mushroom-like caps of Astrakan wool, and Caucasians, Central Asians with wadded skull-caps, retailing to crabbed-faced and spectacled Scribes the goods which they collect in the way. Here and there a small, neat horse is urged through the crowd by an Egyptian Fellah, loudly crying the price, —say 1,200 piastres, or 12 Napoleons,—whilst the soldiers in uniform chaff him. That tall and sinewy Kurd, with the gold-threaded *kuff'iyyeh* veiling his dark face and shaven chin, and his uptwisted moustachio, is a sheep dealer, for he wrangles with the lamb sellers from the neighbouring villages. The tall and lanky Sawákin Moslem, with the sphynx-like curls hanging to his shoulders and over his brow, whilst the upper hair forms a mighty tuft, sells to the clerks of Mohammed Banáji the mother-of-pearl fished on the coast.

The savage Somali, who has attempted to humanise himself by shaving off his mop, brings little parcels of gums, incense, and myrrh, the produce of the wild hills, which he offers to the priestly elders yonder. Every few minutes we meet strings of camels of every class, from the high-bred to the diminutive, charity-made beast, laden with grain, and led by Bedawin (if possible, leaner still) in kerchiefs bound to the head with ropes, and in long blouses stained yellow with saffron or acacia bark. All are armed with the jambiyeh-dagger, either long and straight or short and curved, and carry the crooked stick of the wilderness and the dwarf spear with tapering head, which they will barter but not sell. Here the skeleton of a donkey, holed with many a raw, and laden with water-skins, is cruelly driven along by a peasant lad in blue rags. Here an animal of better breed is ridden by a huge Haji, whose peculiar Aba, or cloak, proclaims him to be an Abú Sham, or "Father of Syria." There the rough and surly Slav Turk from Europe, clad in the old garb of the Serb, swaggers, with his belt full of weapons, past the natty, sneering Hejazi, who mutters Ghashim (Johnny Raw). This son of the Holy City affects the tenderest colours. A white turban bound round an embroidered Surat cap, a Cashmere shawl, a caftan of fine pink cloth, a green worked waistcoat, silk mixed with cotton, a dagger with silver hilt, and the elaborate slippers of the country.

The pauper Javanese, with his pock-marked face, Chinese features, and crook-bladed crease (Malay dagger), glides past the Jedáwi, who is selling at auction the produce of his seas, the white soft coral bought by Indians *in memoriam;* and the black coral, much like bog oak, found in thirteen fathoms of water some ten miles down the coast; and—to bring the too long but most imperfect review to a close—four brawny Hayramis, the *hammáls* (porters) of these regions,—men even stouter and stronger than the far-famed Armenian porters of Constantinople, carry a lean corpse, whose two big toes are tied together, and trot through the seven negrolings whose oiled black skins and snowy sheets—not to speak of the yearning looks with which they watch us—tell the world that they are for sale.

The bazar presents, at this season of the year, a panorama of Eastern life, where costume becomes more *bizarre* by contrast, where the most various types blend for a brief moment, and where difference of language, of manners, and of customs, combine to form a veritable kaleidoscope. All is complicated; the very air ranges in temperature between the damp reek of the watered and shaded mainway, the dry heat of the tropical sun darting through the plank joints, and the pleasant coolth of the coffee-houses, where the tall, crooked water-pipes bubble. An endless variety of odours assail the nose; it is an atmosphere composed of every sort of drug and perfume of the Orient, of the pipe, the kitchen, and others less pleasant. Equally confused are the sounds,—the grunt of the camel, the howl of the trampled dog, the chaff of the boys, the prayer-cry of the Muezzin,—peculiar, by-the-bye, to Jeddah; the chaunt of the Fakir, the blare of the trumpets, and the roll of the drum; the titter of muffled anonyma at meeting the Frank's eye, the blessing, the curse, the shrill cry, the hoarse expostulation; briefly, a Babel of tongues and a *bourdonnement* of distant voices like the hum of insects on a drowsy summer noon. All come and go, rush and halt, pass and cross, eat and drink, smoke and chew, talk and doze, elbow and jostle, without disorder or difficulty, as though they were the born denizens of Capitals. Every one is armed to the teeth, but no one ever draws a weapon. Not a case of drunkenness to be seen, and about sunset the whole of this crowd will begin to melt away. The bazar, when they light up at dusk, is wonderfully picturesque. Then the wealthy pilgrims retire to their *wakalahs* (caravanserais), the middle class to their tents; and the majority to their carpets and rugs and coffers spread in the open street; the few hybrid and friendless Franks, the "mean whites" of the land, will find shelter in the Greek coffee-house, or in the two dens called by courtesy hotels. By eight p.m. the bazar will be as silent as the desert, save a few pariahs quarrelling over a bone.

I saw the Khan where my husband lived as one of these very pilgrims in 1853, and the minaret he sketched in his book,—and am pleased to see that all regard him with great favour; and the Governor, and all those who knew the whole story, called upon him and were very civil.

One cannot state the population of Jeddah. Some say 18,000, others 20,000, and some give 40,000, for the town and its dependencies, including the eleven villages in the plain. There are ten resident Christians,—Europeans, officials, or merchants; no ladies. Great Britain protects about 5,000 natives. The Greeks are very unpopular, on account of their cowardice during the Jeddah massacre; whilst in the Damascus massacre the *only* brave native Christian was a Greek.

There are three Consuls; the Frenchman is a sanitary officer, Dr. Buez, also a lover of *bric-à-brac*. He has now the French Consul of Bussorah on a visit, and these two gay Gauls combined to enliven our visit. The French Kawwas is very *chic*, with a bit of tricolour round his arm and a decoration. The Consul for the Netherlands and our own complete the Corps.

In 1858 there was a cruel, cowardly massacre of the few Europeans and Christians, including the English and French Consuls, which was revenged by the French with two bombardments and a fine of 2,241,016 francs. It arose from our suppression of the Slave Trade, and jealousy at finding that the Europeans, whose exports and imports are worth about £3,000,000, were absorbing the commerce; moreover these two feelings still exist. Our present Vice-Consul, Mr. Wylde, is a man well fitted to the post, which is anything but a pleasant one. His open-hearted, straightforward, and fearless ways of dealing with the natives succeed perfectly; he knows what the native disposition is, and how to treat it, whilst he is of a joyous temperament, and quite insensible as to any danger. Still, (as he laughingly remarked to me one day,) it would doubtless be much more comfortable if the morning and evening *shell* (instead of gun) were fired into the town; and, joking apart, every passing man-of-war ought to have orders to look in, *en passant*, just to call on the authorities, and to see what the delightful natives have been up to since the last ship passed. Some day the Wali Pasha of the Hejaz may be a fanatical hater of Europeans, the Kaimmakám of Jeddah may be a weak-minded, good-intentioned man who cannot keep things in order, or intestine troubles may draw away the troops; and these visits are more necessary in places where perpetual orders from home necessitate an interference with the Slave Trade, which the Arabs are ever ready to resist. There ought to be Cruizers perpetually visiting and reporting upon the condition of all the outlying little ports, where at present British subjects are unfairly left to take care of themselves.

One day we had a delightful sail in Captain Miller's Chinese boat, after that in one of the native craft (*Sambúk*), and lastly went to see the interior of some native houses; they are handsome, but inferior to Damascus, like the picturesque streets and bazars. In the evening we used to sit outside the Consulate, and have some sherry and a cigarette, and play with the dogs.

One evening my husband came in, and found me nursing what I supposed to be a dying negro. He was very angry, as I had sent for the French Doctor-Consul, who pronounced him to b only tipsy,—and those terrible boys teased him by putting snuff up his nose. They are awful boys, but such fun. When the food is bad, they call the cook in, and make him eat it.

"Babarchi, what's that, eh?"

"No! no! massa; me lose caste!!"

"Hold your tongue, you —— scoundrel! eat it directly."

One day it was seven big *smoked* onions. In this way the table is usually excellent. I wish we could do it in England, *still more* at Trieste. They all worship Mr. Wylde nevertheless. I think the dogs are worse than the boys. There are about ten bull-dogs, that worry everything they see, and send every pariah flying out of the bazars. I have heard since that the natives have poisoned all the dogs.

In the afternoons we used to ride out Mecca-wards; and I remember, on one or two occasions, the animal was thin and the girths too large, so the saddle came round with me, and I had a spill on the sand, which greatly delighted the boys, and did not hurt me. Sometimes we had a very jolly dinner-party at the Consulate, to which the captains of the steamers and the two Frenchmen came.

After eight exceedingly pleasant days, which we shall always remember, we received notice to embark. The great hospitality shown us, the unbounded kindness from our own countrymen, the courteousness of the *Turkish* authorities, and the civility of the fanatical Jeddáwis, will not be forgotten. We had furious southerly squalls; our ship was anchored at least six miles away; we started, therefore, in a *Sambúk*, the large flat boat with big sail, which can go close to the wind without upsetting. All our friends accompanied us, and thus we crossed the reef and reached our ship, and were truly sorry to give the last shake hands, and sail at 2·30. We found 800 pilgrims on board; we were packed like herrings. It was very rough, and I sat on a chair lashed to the deck. My last recollections of Jeddah were sailing straight for a long reef, over which dashed gigantic breakers, until we came so near that my heart sank, for we had our pious pilot on the bridge, who ran us into the *Standard* at Jeddah, and I prayed that we might have no more of his "beautiful fine steering." We veered off, it appeared to me, just in time. I think my face amused him as we got nearer and nearer. We escaped well, but others did not; another ship had also taken pilgrims—some three hundred—and went out about the same time that we did; she dashed on this reef, which is about twenty miles from Jeddah, that same afternoon; the ship foundered, and all hands were lost, save one or two who clung to spars, and were picked up. I do not suppose the truth of that story will ever be known. It was said that the captain and officers were English, and were drunk; that the fanaticism of the pilgrims was aroused; that they combined and lashed the Captain and the officers to the masts, and took charge of the ship themselves,—and that means that she managed herself,—and ran on to this long bank of rock, upon which breakers foam higher than the ship. The only survivor I ever heard of was a Portuguese doctor, or shopkeeper, or something like that, who of course tells the story his own way.

Although I am on board ship, I still want to talk about Jeddah, and that seriously; and firstly I will relate the promised history about the Americans and English who were said to be taken at Mecca. Mr. Arthur Brown, who had been employed on the

Bombay Gazette, after landing at Aden, proceeded, in company with the Turkish Consul for Western India, to Jeddah, and thence found his way to Mecca. At Arafat he was found unable to speak Turkish and Arabic, and, being asked his nationality, he replied Indian,—which was absurd, as he had light eyes and hair. When led before the authorities, he declared himself a Moslem. He was examined by the brother of the Grand Sherif Abdullah, and he avoided all difficult questions by pleading that he was a new Moslem. He was then released, and on January 15th he came to Jeddah, where I saw him. Captain Beyts, the British Consul, wisely sent him on board one of the steamers, and as he said he had been robbed of all his money, kindly gave him a passage gratis. He told us he had not been able to do anything at Mecca; watchful eyes followed him everywhere, and he was not even allowed to count the columns of the Beyt Allah, or Kaabah, and faithfully promised not to publish anything. However, he published copiously as soon as he returned to Bombay. He could tell us little of the second *pseudo* pilgrim, except that he was an American supercargo, who, after Islamizing some seven years ago in Ceylon, had become a regular loafer. He also being blond, was arrested at Arafat and put into chains; but, after a while, the authorities released him, and allowed him to go to El Medinah, at the expense and under the charge of his Indian friends. For such mean results as these men are not justified in risking their own lives, and in rousing popular murmurs against the European residents of Jeddah and other Red Sea ports.

CHAPTER IV.

HOW CHOLERA SPREADS.—THE JEDDAH MASSACRE OF 1858.

ONE must read "Une Mission au Hedjaz Arabie," par Dr. Buez (Paris : Masson, 1873, Académie de Médécine), which treats of the epidemics which this Hajj engenders,—the focus of infection for Egypt, the Mediterranean, and consequently for Europe. At any rate, one may note the nine conclusions.

1. Arabia, and especially El Hejaz, with its pure air, does not originate the morbid elements which express themselves in dysentery and typhus, cholera and plague. Small-pox, however, in certain places, is always to be dreaded.

2. Cholera is at present the special genesis of India.

3. Steamers, though, on the whole, beneficial to the general health of the pilgrims, produce new sanitary conditions, and aid greatly in propagating the choleraic element; thus becoming a permanent and, at times, a real danger to Europe. The same is the case with railroads, but to a much less extent.

4. All the great outbreaks in the Hejaz, notably that of 1865, when five hundred *per diem* died at Mecca during the Hajj, were imported, indirectly or directly, from India, and then spread over the civilized world.

5. The problem of preserving Egypt, Syria, the Levant, and Europe from cholera is to be resolved only through the strictest surveillance, by competent men, over pilgrims bound from India to the Hejaz; and to Egypt from the Red Sea ports—Jeddah, Rais, Rabegh, Yambu, Lîth, Gonfodah, Jisán, Hodaydah, Lohayah, Mocha, etc.

6. The question is complicated by the existence of choleraic

foci, which may be termed secondary and local—as opposed to primitive or original—where the epidemic has lingered, and possibly has incubated till again exasperated by occult conditions, —telluric, atmospheric, or hygienic. This fact demands increased measures of surveillance; they may not be thoroughly satisfactory, but because we cannot close all the doors, we need not leave all the largest open.

7. At the period of embarking from the Red Sea ports, where *bakshish* is the key to most consciences, the local Health Office and the member of the Sanitary Council annually sent from Stamboul after the International Conference of 1866 should be assisted by a special commission of European physicians, who could, moreover, modify and improve the different "Passenger Acts."

8. "Long Desert," a march of twenty-one days, is the best of *cordon sanitaires*, alone able to "purge" infected caravans.

9. *Ergo:* when the Hejaz is attacked by cholera the sea road should be peremptorily closed to all pilgrims, an operation whose difficulties have been greatly and needlessly exaggerated; nor should it be re-opened till after at least one pilgrimage season has passed away without accident.

To these wise conclusions I would add a truth. All quarantinary measures are unpopular with Moslems, who regard them as inventions of the Evil One, or, as our vulgar say, "flying in the face of Providence." Moreover, at Mecca it is every man's interest to conceal the outbreak, and there is always a danger of the earliest cases finding their way to Jeddah before the existence of cholera is suspected at the port. Indeed, clean bills have been given under such circumstances. Evidently, the only remedy for this evil is to make the special sanitary commission of European physicians meet annually at Mecca.

I took some trouble to investigate the causes which led to the horrible massacre of June 15th, 1858. This is far from being an old tale of times which will not return: it is an example of what may occur any day in the present excited state of the Moslem world. Moreover, the conditions under which it occurred are precisely those of the present moment, and an ugly symptom has just appeared:* the villain Moplah (Malabar Moslem), who murdered Mr. Conolly, has been allowed to escape from surveillance at Jeddah, to embark at Líth, and probably to return to India *viâ* Makalla in Hadramant. But as popular memory in England is short upon such subjects, it is necessary to give a *résumé* of the facts.

The innovation of appointing European Consuls to Jeddah, the "Gate of the Holy City," was resented by the Moslems, both on the grounds of religion and of private interests,—especially when protected foreign subjects began to absorb the greater parts of the commerce. Several *ballons d'essai* were launched. In 1848 an attempt was made to assassinate, near the Medinah Gate, M. Fulgence Fresnel, the famous Arabist, who was often consulted upon questions of casuistry by the D.D.'s of Mecca. The criminal was saved by a certain Abdullah Muhtasib, a Fellah of Lower Egypt, who began life as a baker, and who rose to be farmer of the *octroi* and Chief of the Police; thus being able to bribe and bully *à discretion*. In 1849, Mr. Consul Ogilvie was openly insulted in the Bazar, and obtained no redress. During my husband's first visit to Jeddah, Mr. Consul Cole had avoided all troubles by his firmness and conciliatory manners; but, after his departure, the so-called "War of the Sherífs" (1854) suggested a grand opportunity for despoiling the Christians. Abdullah Muhtasib again appeared as the villain of the play; he was, however, arrested, and exiled to Massawwah by the *Wali* of the Hejaz, Namik Pasha.

In 1856 Abdullah Muhtasib returned triumphant from his exile, and the Sepoy war of 1857 once more offered him a tempting opportunity. Actively assisted by his son, he brought into the plot the Kadi (Abd el Kadir Effendi), the Sayyid el Amúli, the Shaykh Bagafur, Abdullah Bakarum, and the wealthy merchant Yusuf Banáji. Presently, in June, 1858, during the height of the pilgrimage, it became known that Captain Pullen, H.M.S.S. *Cyclops*, intended to carry off the *Irania*, an English ship upon which Turkish colours had been hoisted. Abdullah Muhtasib and his friends met at the Custom House *café*, and

* This was written in 1876.

sat, *en permanence*, to direct the issue of their conspiracy. At two p.m., on June 15th, the ship was worked out, the boats of the *Cyclops* left, and the coast was clear.

Violent harangues in the Bazar roused the cry of "Death to the Infidel!" The plot burst like a barrel of gunpowder, and at six p.m. the massacre began. The Sayyid el Amúli took charge of Mr. Page, whom he beheaded with his own hand; the body was thrown into the streets to be hacked to pieces by the mob; the house was plundered, and the flagstaff was torn up. M. Sabatier, however, is in error when he reports that the English dragoman and kawwás were murdered: one died lately, and the other, a very old man, is still living.

Meanwhile, two bands of ruffians attacked the other objects of their hate. One rushed to the French Consulate, and broke in the doors when they were closed by the Kawwás. Madame Eveillard was first stabbed and then her husband was cut down, despite the heroic defence of the daughter, Mdle. Elise, who, after seizing one of the chief murderers by the beard, and severely biting his arm, was wounded by a yataghan in the face. She and the lady's-maid, saved by the tardy arrival of the *Kaim-makam* (commandant) and two Government Kawwáses, were taken from the blood-bespattered home to a Turkish house. Mr. Emerat, the Chancellor, after bravely fighting for fifteen minutes, was preserved in the same way; and, sabred in three places, was led by his faithful Algerian, Haji Mahommed, to the quarters of Hasan Bey, commanding the artillery. M. de Lesseps was, therefore, misinformed about Mdle. Eveillard saving herself by drawing the cushions of the divan over her body, and by simulating death whilst the murderers slashed at her legs. He says nothing of the *Kaim-makam*, and he attributes the honour of saving the two lives to a negro boy and the old Algerine soldier.* The flagstaff was torn down, the tricolour trampled upon, and the Consulate given over to plunder.

* See "Lettres Journal et Documents," vol. ii., p. 298-300. He rates the mob at five thousand, and writes dramatically. The cushions of a divan do not form an *espèce de tombeau*, where a woman can be *ensevelie vivante*. M. de Lesseps says that he had the details from the chief actors of the drama, but I prefer M. Sabatier's account.

The other band rushed to the house of Sabá Mascondi, the richest of the Greek merchants, and therefore the most obnoxious of all the Christians. My husband well remembers this amiable and inoffensive man. He had been repeatedly warned, but he refused to believe a massacre possible till he and his party, some twenty men, mostly from Lemnos, met one evening. At length, when it was reported that the Consulates were being pillaged, three of them went out to enquire. Meanwhile the armed mob rushed in, and instantly cut down eight, the rest jumping out of the windows, and flying over the terraces and down the streets, to reach the sea. Poor Sabá veiled his head, and also tried to escape. M. Sabatier heard two accounts of his death: one was that he was killed in the house of the English dragoman (an error); the other, that he was recognised in his rude disguise by the son of Abdullah Muhtasib, who blew out his brains with a pistol. This is a fact.

The French Consul-General also relates that the *Cyclops*, anchored only three miles off, perceiving a tumult in the town, armed her boats and sent them to find out the cause; that the crews were fired upon, and that they returned, without further action, to their ship. It is hard to believe this. A few shells thrown into Jeddah would have cleared every street in half-an-hour. No justification was wanted for resenting so gross an insult, and instant measures might have saved some unhappy lives. But in those days we were still under the glamour of that most unfortunate Crimean War, and modern England does not, as a rule, encourage her officers to incur any manner of responsibility.

The first act of retribution was on the early morning of July 25th, when the *Cyclops*, at the distance of twenty-five hundred yards, bombarded Jeddah for two hours. This was repeated till noon on the 26th, when the new Governor-General, Namik Pasha, arrived. The people, of course, evacuated the town; a few houses were injured; a minaret was knocked crooked, and some fifteen boats were destroyed.

Presently France, who, whatever may have been her sins, of omission and commission, has ever shown a noble jealousy of her national honour, determined not to be played with after this fashion; and she sent, not a "person of rank," but M. Sabatier, the fittest head and hand for the work. The inapt and treacherous politic of the Porte on this occasion, bears a fraternal resemblance to her manœuvres adopted after the massacre of Damascus (1860), with this difference: at Beyrout there was no Sabatier, but there was a certain trickster of the first order, Fuad Pasha, whose reckless ambition had caused the catastrophe. The Sultan appointed, as his commissioner, one Ismail Pasha, who hastened off to the Hejaz, and, in concert with the feeble and negligent Namik Pasha, put to death half-a-dozen poor devils, compiled a voluminous *Mazbatah* (*procès verbale*), and hurried back to Constantinople with thirty-nine "compromised" individuals. Heavy bribes had induced him to estimate the damage done to Christian property at twenty thousand francs. *Il était difficile de faire associer les consuls de France et d'Angleterre à meilleur marché*, is M. Sabatier's only comment upon this part of the proceeding.

As Ismail Pasha persisted, in conversation with his two fellow-commissioners, that his part of the work had been thoroughly done, and that he was expected at Stamboul, M. Sabatier and Captain Pullen, R.N., set out in the *Cyclops*, with the English and French flags flying together on the mainmast, and reached Jeddah on October 12th, 1859. Here they found Commodore Seymour with the *Pelorus* (twenty-one guns); the corvette *Assaye* (ten guns); and the *Chesapeake* (fifty-one guns) expected. Five days afterwards Namik Pasha arrived from Mecca; and, as the Turkish Commissioner had admitted that all the local authorities were accessories to the murder, M. Sabatier proceeded to examine all witnesses, Moslems as well as Christians. Even he, accustomed for long years to the abstruse chicanery of the East, must have been surprised to hear the Turkish authorities laying the blame upon Captain Pullen; as if a mere question of maritime and international law could have borne such fruits. Even he, so well inured to the contempt of European intelligence,—which is an article of faith with all Orientals,—must have been startled, as well as shocked, to see the abominable Abdullah Muhtasib sitting side by side with Hasan Bey, the wretched commandant of artillery, when the Consulate of France was still a mere shell, and the walls were bespattered with the blood of his fellow-countrymen.

It would be tedious to relate how bravely and how well M. Sabatier did his duty. Briefly, in January 1859, M. Tricoult, *Capitaine de Frégate*, appeared upon the stage, and a few hours brought the authorities to their senses. The miserable Ismail Pasha lost his head on "Raven's Isle," within sight of Jeddah; Abdullah Muhtasib and the Sayyid el Amúli on the Custom-house square (January 12th, 1859). The fine for the losses of the Christians amounted to 2,241,016 francs, of which 500,000 were paid to the Eveillard family, 100,000 to M. Emerat, and 100,000 to Saba Moscondi's relatives.

The Jeddah massacre was made the stalking-horse to bring down Slave Trading in the Red Sea, which had already been abolished theoretically (1855) under the effects of the Crimean War. In June, 1869, vizierial letters were addressed especially to the Hejaz, without any effect beyond causing a disturbance; they were essentially dead letters, worth only their weight of spoiled paper. This is not the place for so extensive a subject. I will only state that the traffic still flourishes at Jeddah; that the market, till lately, was under the eyes of the British Consulate; that on representation it was removed a few yards off; that the Turkish authorities, even if they wished, are unable to stop or even to hinder it; and that the only remedy is armed intervention, serious and continued,—in fact, a "Coffin Squadron," like that of the Persian Gulf, stationed in the Red Sea, with "Slave Approvers" all around the coast of Arabia. I need hardly say that we should demand the right of search, and that a Consul-General or a Slave Commissioner, with a sufficient Staff and salary, the use of a gunboat, and a roving commission, should be appointed to the Red Sea, independently of the Consul-General of Egypt, and in lieu of the trading Consul of Jeddah.

M. Sabatier on the occasion omitted only one step, probably because he judged that the hour to take it had not struck. He should have insisted upon Mecca being opened to the world, and upon all travellers being protected there as they are at Jerusalem and other "Holy Cities." It is high time that these obsolete obstructions to the march of civilization should everywhere be swept away; the world will endure them no longer. Mecca is not only a great centre of religion and commerce; it is also the prime source of political intrigues, the very nest where plans of conquest and schemes of revenge upon the Infidel are hatched; and, as I have before said, the focus whence cholera is dispersed over the West. Shall a misplaced sentiment of tolerating intolerance allow her to work in the dark against humanity? Allah forbid it!

The pilgrimage over, thirty or forty steamships lying in the reefs, and five or six hundred *Sambúks* propose to embark the eighty thousand who go by sea; agents and pilgrims both trying to cozen and rob each other. We heard the cracked voice of the old town-crier singing out, in Arabic,—"The steamer *Camel* will sail for Mecca, Medinah, Taif, and other *inland* places. Apply immediately for bills of lading."

The *Calypso* was one of the first to leave, having stowed away eight hundred pilgrims. In short, the old cattle-ship seemed to have returned to her original trade,—not that I mean to compare men and women with divine souls to cattle, but because they are stowed away like, and have the habits of, cattle. It is usual, after leaving Jeddah, to slip from spring to hot midsummer, but we kept a strong northerly breeze the whole way; and our pious pilot explained that this had been the case ever since the opening of the Canal. Our weather was bad the whole way to India, at the season it is supposed to be the best.

Now, if such great meteoric changes can be affected by a mere riband of water let into the sand, what will happen when we submerge a great part of the African Sáhara (whose eastern limits are unknown), and thereby create a sea, perhaps, bigger than the Mediterranean? We cannot calculate the possible amount of climatic modification which such a new offset of the Atlantic might induce; and some clever men think that the Sáhara Sea is likely to affect many parts of the Mediterranean basin, and even the whole southern seaboard of Europe, with changes which may be deleterious in the extreme. The sirocco from Africa is the summer wind *par excellence* of the "White Sea," as the Arabs call it, blowing through half the year, and that half the most dangerous.

On the 20th it blew very hard, the waves were higher than the ship. It was a grand sea for those who were not sick, but the poor pilgrims suffered horribly. I crawled about and tried to help them a little; one died, and was buried at sunset. They washed the body, and then put a bit of white stuff like mull muslin round the loins, and a bit of money—to show that he is not destitute when he arrives in the next world. Then they tied him up in a sheet, or at least a white clean bit of linen or stuff, and when his head and feet were tied, he looked just like a big white cracker. He was laid upon a shutter, with a 5 lb. bar of iron bound to his feet; and then, with a short Arabic prayer —*Allahhu akbar*—they took him to the side and heaved him over. This happened twenty-three times between 20th January and 2nd February. All were very jolly, and seemed to think it very good fun; of course, according to their way of thinking, he would be glad to die, and go straight to heaven.

But I must say it made me feel very serious. I kept saying to myself—"That poor Indian and I might both be lying dead to-day. There would be a little more ceremony for me, and (not, of course, including my husband) it would cast a gloom over the dinner-table for a couple of days. Once we left the ship's side, the sharks would eat us both, and perhaps like me a little the best, because I am fat and well-fed, and don't smell of cocoa-nut oil. And then we would both stand before the throne of God to be judged; he with his poverty, hardships, privations, sufferings, pilgrimage and harmless life; and I with all my faults, my happy life, my luxuries, and the little wee bit of good I have ever done or ever thought, to obtain mercy with,—only equal that our Saviour died for both." All are laughing because it is only a poor, ugly, old skeleton of a "nigger;" not one of them thinking, "Supposing that were *me!* My turn *will* come, and then the rest will think it jolly fun to see *me* thrown over the side."

We passed, on Friday 21st, Jebel Teer, and a group called Zubayr Islands.

One might write a chapter on the Hajis. It is an experience I am glad to have made once, having escaped without injury, but one which (God willing) I will never again attempt, unless some unforeseen necessity compels me to take a passage on a ship about to carry pilgrims. Imagine eight hundred Moslems, ranging, in point of colour, from every shade, from lemon or *café au lait* to black as polished as your stove; races from all parts of the world, covering every square inch of deck and every part of the hold fore and aft, half our quarter-deck and the holds having no cargo; packed like sardines, men, women and babies, unwashed, smelling of cocoa-nut oil; the tedium of the long days, the air stagnant and heavy, tainted with the reek of this oil; unwashed bodies, sea-sick, covered with sores, the dead and dying; cooking their messes, and—save to cook or fetch water, or kneeling up to prayer—never moving out of the small space or position which they assumed at the beginning of the voyage. Gaudy jackets and wraps were on the strong and richer ones; the poor were barely covered. They were skin and bone, and half naked, with a rag round the loins at most.

They die not of disease, but of privation, fatigue, hunger, thirst, and opium,—die of vermin and misery. They have each their cooking-pot, their opium, a handful of grain, perhaps, and a pot to drink out of. No one would believe the scene unless they saw the dirt and smelt the horrible effluvia that arises from them. They have two insatiable wants, and no ship ought to be permitted to carry pilgrims unless it can provide them—a copious supply of fresh good water to drink, and wood to cook with. A third thing is that pilgrims are allowed to embark in a dying state, or without a penny, relying that some charitable person will give them food; perhaps there *is* no charitable person, and then the poor wretches die. Either there should be a law preventing ships from embarking such paupers, or there should be a charitable provision of rice.

Being rather soft-hearted, I can't tell you what I suffered during those fifteen days. Many of them won't ask; but if they see a kind face they speak with the eyes, as an animal does. I daresay some will think it weak, but I can't stand that imploring expression of dumb, mute, patient pain which, brutelike, appeals for help without speaking. I cannot eat my dinner if I see a dog looking wistfully at it. I therefore spent the whole day, from light till dark, staggering about our rolling ship with sherbert and food and medicines, treating dysentery, fever, diarrhœa; and during my short snatches of sleep I dreamt of the horrors, showing the effect of fatigue and the motion of the ship. But nobody can know how disheartening it was, owing to religious fanaticism, and from want of their knowing their own Korán.

I will just take my journal as I jotted things down, because it will be more true. The Somalis were full of wonder, and listened to me with more faith about food and medicines because I could recite their Bismíllah, and their call to prayer. We have not only Somalis but Hindís, Arabs from Bokhara, Kokand, Kashgar; Turcomans, Persians, natives from Tashgand; Russian subjects, Bengalee, and every sect of Mohammedans,—but I can't classify them till the ship rolls less. At nine we passed the Harnísh Islands, and last night Jebel Zoogur; at one p.m. we saw Mocha, whence the good coffee comes. It is just like Jeddah, dice-like houses, lumpy maritime hills, and distant curtain of tall blue mountain, but it looks larger and rises in the middle, as if built on a hill. At four we passed the straits of Bab el Mandeb,—at school called Babelmandel. The straits are very narrow; a steamer was running dangerously near the rocks, and we thought she was aground, but she made no signals for help, so we passed on; the sea was very rough.

Sunday the 23rd we arrived at Aden very early. At once came on board the Somali lads, with their bawling voices and necklaces, their mop heads of mutton wool, now and then plastered down with lime. They sell the vulgarest wants,—water, firewood, fowls and eggs; and they are all numbered, in case of being "wanted." The Jew youth, with his blinking eyes, ram-like profile, his olive-green skin, and his corkscrew curls, demands with his harsh rude voice double price for third-rate wares; and so, for the benefit of purchasers, I will tell them the proper terms. The sale is chiefly *ostrich feathers*.

Boa of ostrich feathers	. . . .	10 rupees
Muff	. . . .	3 ,,
Tin box for feathers	. . . .	6 annas
Coral black necklace	. . . .	4 rupees
,, white rock	. . . . . .	8 annas
Single feathers, ostrich (best white)	. .	50 to 60 rupees per doz.
,, ,,	2nd white . .	40 to 48 ,, ,,
,, ,,	inferior . .	30 to 36 ,, ,,
,, ,,	best grey (female)	9 rupees
,, ,,	medium . .	6 ,,
,, ,,	black . . .	8 ,,
Skins—Zebras'	. . . . . .	10 to 15 rupees
,, Lions'	. . . . . .	10 ,,
,, Panthers'	. . . . . .	8 ,,
,, Monkeys'	. . . . . .	3 to 5 ,,
A silver Somali necklace	. . . . .	40 rupees
A knob stick	. . . . . .	8 annas
Spoons	. . . . .	4 ,,
Spear or dagger	. . . . .	3 rupees

All this mob of possible thieves is kept in order by the water-police—a disciplined body, whose uniform, white cottons and marigold turbans—makes them as conspicuous as yellowhammers. Their Subahdar, Mohammed el Hammàl, who accompanied Captain Burton, the explorer of Harar (Hurrur), died about a year ago; of his old party Long Guled, and the two women Shahrazad and Dinarzad, still live, the former in camp and the latter in Somali-land. Abdo, *alias* Akhir el Zamán, the "End of Time," died a natural death. Yusuf, the "monocular one," was murdered by the Isá tribe. Hasan Ahmed, the boy of the party, is now Havildar (sergeant) of the Water-Police. He tells us that the Egyptian troops who have occupied, happily for travellers, Berberah and Zayla, where they have imposed duties amounting to 12 per cent., entered Harar without fighting; and that the Amir Mohammed conveniently died as soon as he could—under suspicious circumstances. Rauf Pasha, the Governor, however, is now invested on all sides by the Gallas and the Somalis; the reinforcements cannot reach him, and he is in considerable danger. Hasan promises to procure for us, on our return, the coins of Harar.* They have on one side, *La illáha 'ill Allah*, and on the

* Just brought by my husband to England, in 1878.

reverse, Zaraba Amir Mohammed. Colonel Gordon Pasha, Governor-General of the Equator, has promised to send me specimens.

In 1840 what is called the Turkish wall of this our military station witnessed a peculiar attack, which, as far as I know, has never been described. A certain Fakih (D.D.) Sáíd, who had assumed the title of *El Mehdi el Muntazar* (The Expected Regenerator), resolved, before dethroning the Imam of Saná'a, to strengthen the sinews of war by plundering the infidels of Aden; and his first step was to promise all his fellows (some thousand men lent by Abdáli, the Sultan of Lahej) invulnerability against Kafir sword and gunshot wounds. One fine morning, the mob, utterly unarmed, and wearing white shrouds, rushed, in a rude column, shouting *Allah-hu Akbar!* towards the Turkish wall; the defenders waited to the last moment, but seeing that mischief was meant, they fired half-a-dozen rounds of grape, which had the effect of causing a *sauve qui peut.* The survivors, sorely disappointed, fell upon Fakih Sáíd with threats and reproaches, which that cunning madman silenced by saying, "True, I told you that the cannon of the *Mushrit* (polytheists) would have no effect upon true *Gházis* (fighters for the Truth). But your hearts were black, you dogs! as your faces are now. You went, not to purify the Faith, but to plunder the goods and to carry off the women of the Infidel." His dexterity saved him this time, but in December of the same year he was defeated, and killed by the Imám.

We landed for a few hours, and drove in canopied carriages, with poor lean nags, bullied by brutal Somali drivers. Amongst the hotels are de l'Europe, Prince of Wales, and Sorel. The first is the best; but the hospitality of the residents never allows friends to taste of their horrors. The unique Tanks, Reservoirs, and the Camp of Aden, are five miles distant; we shall go there on returning from India.

Aden is garrisoned by two regiments, three Artillery batteries, a company of Sappers and Miners, and a troop of irregular Cavalry. She fears no attack, and could be easily reinforced from Bombay in case of need.

My husband and I, and Nip, our little terrier, went ashore to spend the day with Mrs. Schneider, the wife of the Governor, or Station Commandant, who was absent, and her nice little daughter. Their house seemed peculiar to a "Griffin:" a long ground-floor verandah, supported by columns and all the rooms opening on to it, and covered with net-work and mats. Separate is the servants' house, and the guest-house, and the stables, —like a settlement. There is a Parsee shop belonging to the ship's agent (Cowajee Dinshaw), which contains everything, from a needle to an anchor. I asked for skates, for fun, as I thought it was the only thing they would not have, and I was right. Englishmen are always glad to see a Parsee. The old Iranians appear to be, and are, a perfectly different race from those around them. They maintain the high physique which distinguishes them in their essentially Aryan homes, and the only artistic mistake they make is that of shaving the beard.

Aden is a wild, desolate spot; the dark basalt mountains give it a sombre look. It would be dull work for any one to live here without resources. Poor Dr. Steinhaüser, our old friend, lived here, however, for twenty-five years, and died in Switzerland. Many will remember him. It is terribly hot in the summer season. I think it is to Aden that is attached the legend of the sailors who died and went to a certain fiery place, and appeared, and on being asked why they came, they replied that they had caught cold, and had leave to come to fetch their blankets. We embarked at 4.30, leaving two of our passengers ashore, who were too late, and we sailed at six. It was a delightful, balmy evening. We wrote some letters, and went to bed early, and next day I resumed writing my account of the Pilgrims.

Our northern pilgrims provided themselves with "Tilá Khokandi,"—gold pieces, each worth about 12 shillings (more exactly, 6 rupees 4 annas = 4 roubles 20 kopeks): they also take "Rosizio" (Russians; gold coins of 6 roubles 40 kopeks), and the precious metal is everywhere, except perhaps at Bombay, changed with profit. They object, on account of the mountain roads, to the shorter line *viâ* Káshghar—which, like Yarkhand, belongs, or rather belonged, to hard-fighting Atalik Ghâzi Yakub

Khan, now closed; they might have passed over the more civilised Russian line, *viâ* Orsk, Orenburg, Samara, the Railway, and the Don River, to the Azov Sea; but that would have cost them 65 instead of 40 Tilás (=Rupees 250). Their living for 158 days at a private house in Mecca, including the visitation of Medina and lodging at the Madrasch Akhuna Jan, was laid down at 15 Tilás (=Rupees 95), and the return journey will be the same as the outward-bound. Thus the whole of a pilgrim's expenditure from High Asia is 95, we will say 100 Tilás (= Rupees 750). He takes with him a few kerchiefs of the handsome silk made at Marghílán, and he carries back Medina dates, Zamzam water, and common stones of Mecca, which, in those far regions become *quasi*-sacred.

The middle class of pilgrims, numbering twenty-four, are Hindís from Western India, who call themselves Hindostanís, including a yellow and sour-faced little Sayyid from Sind. They occupy the starboard side of the quarter-deck, paying 13 to 23 Rupees, and some few of the poorer—chiefly Aghans and Pathans—are in the hold; they surround their women and children with a curtain, and if the weather be bad, they will pay for a cabin. They live comfortably on curry and rice, they smoke water-pipes which make the Turkomans look grave, they chew *pán-supárí* (betel); they pay as regularly as they can, and they dispose decently of their one corpse. One of them, Haji Ishak, who signs himself "timber-merchant, Puna," is returning from his second pilgrimage: in virtue of superior business qualities he takes command of the lower orders; he organises a begging committee to feed the sixteen starvelings, and he makes himself generally useful in settling disputes and in keeping people in their proper places. His pilgrimage has cost him between 2,500 and 3,000 Rupees, and he pays a passage for his family and friends at the rate of 17 Rupees a head between Jeddah and Bombay.

The third order, which at first numbered six hundred and odd, including twenty-three deaths, is composed of Bengalis,—the very meanest specimens ever seen, equally contemptible in body and mind. They are distributed upon the fore and middle decks, and both holds have been cleared to receive them; the fare varying, according to bargain, from Rupees fourteen to twenty. The women go about with unveiled faces, and both sexes wear the scantiest of *toilettes;* they seem to think only of muffling the head. Their food is a little rice and, perhaps, fish-like strips of sun-dried meat, which they have cut from the victims of Muná. All are half-starved; many are so old that they can hardly move, and not a few die with hoards of rupees in their waistbands, refusing to buy a meal or to engage a servant for a few annas. These *misérables* are indescribably filthy. Fresh from the pilgrimage, they rob one another. Squatted like apes and crowded like herrings (men like mummies and the women like the witches in *Macbeth*), they pass their time in chattering, in squabbling, and in calling for *páni* (water), which is served out morning and evening; and in the "Caccia del Mediterraneo" with occasional attempts at praying and cooking. They are so ignorantly fanatic that if an Infidel give them a plate of rice and curry, they will, even when starving, throw each mouthful out of the scupper-hole whilst pretending to swallow it; yet the sensible law of El Islam allows man to save life even by eating pig. If, at their request, you give them medicine, they will heave it overboard; and if they die after taking it, their caste-fellows will declare that you have poisoned them to lighten the ship. They freeze up the very fountains of Charity; you never can know that you are not bestowing alms to a comparatively rich man. They have no more sympathy than cattle; none will give a draught of water to the dying, and as for praying over the corpses before throwing them overboard—who will take the trouble?

The only thing for which we envy them is their excessive facility of departing this life. Their powers of vitality seem to be at the minimum; a few hours of cold wind kill off half-a-dozen like flies,—they eat rice, they beg a few lumps of sugar, they lie down, and they give up the ghost. All go directly to *Firdaus* (Paradise), where curry and mango-pickle, sherbet and *pán-supári* drop into their mouths,—where there is no collector, no Government peon, no Banyan usurer, no paying of rent. What a contrast is this quiet dropping to sleep with the horrors of the English death-bed, with the barbarous predilection for prolonging the agony, with the atrocious boast that the moribund was enabled to keep his senses to the last! When will education conquer these stubborn and detestable prejudices? When can we expect to see the Euthanasia, by ether or chloroform, sanctioned by public opinion and practice in cases of extreme pain, when a man is prepared, as far as in him lies, to face Death? When may we hope to see Death robbed of his sting by abolishing the trappings of woe, the expensive funeral, and all the other indications that we have weak faith in the glorious Future we preach of; still sanctioned by the respectable religious Public's opinion and practice? When shall we be advanced enough in Education and Civilization to check infectious vapours and spreading disease by Cremation?

The officers and crew never maltreat these wretches, who, child-like, want everything to be done for them. They simply neglect them,—and that is doing the worst. There would be much more "kicking about" on board an English steamer, but our rough seamen would be generous with water and fuel. The pilgrims, we are told, are allowed to cook, but we know that the canny commandant of the galley cannot afford to admit those who cannot pay.

Twenty-five years ago, a British pilgrim to Mecca (R. F. B.) described this state of things, which is simply disgraceful to Anglo-Indian rule. It partly justifies the charge brought against us by European unfriends, namely, that England does nothing for India beyond looking after her Commerce, her Armies, and her Coolies. The French of Algeria and the Dutchmen of Java put us to shame by the conscientiousness with which they regulate the transit of pilgrims; and, until we can learn for ourselves, we should take a leaf or two out of their books.

A new Passenger Act is, I believe, about to appear; let us hope that it will abate one part of the nuisance. At present we can never feel safe on board these crowded cattle-pens. An epidemic might break out any moment; in case of shipwreck all would be lost; and even if the screw were injured, or the main shaft were to break, hundreds on board would die of starvation.

Each ship should be compelled to carry a condensing apparatus and cooking-ranges, calculated to accommodate the pilgrims; while one passenger per two tons (registered) should be the maximum of freightage. Before departure, the devotees ought to be severally and carefully inspected by the Port Surgeons; at Aden the Health Office should take them in charge; and in case of infectious disease having appeared on the voyage, they should be quarantined at Perim or at the Kumarán Islands, off Lohayya. No one after a certain age should be allowed to embark, the Korán allows him to send a substitute; and the same is the case with the infirm and with invalids. Each person should prove that he carries at least 400 Rupees in ready money, and that he has left with his family sufficient to support it according to its station: such is the absolute order of the Hanafi school, to which all these Bengalis belong. On arriving at Jeddah, all should take out passports from Her Majesty's Consulate, paying a fee of one Rupee per head, and the same for visas after return: the French and the Dutch charge a dollar. Proclamations in Hindostani and Persian should be issued at the several Presidencies, and be published in the local papers every year before the annual preparations for the pilgrimage begin. I am certain that all sensible Hindí Moslems would be grateful for a measure relieving them from exorbitant charities, and from the reproach that Hindostan is the "basest of Kingdoms;" whilst we should only be doing our duty,—a little late, it is true, but better now than neglected till the evil shall have become inveterate. That everlasting incuriousness and *laissez-aller* of the Anglo-Indian are the only reasons why precautions were not taken twenty-five years ago.

24*th*.—The weather became very rough, and during the night a Bengali, it is said, fell overboard. His companion, who witnessed the accident, said nothing; and on being asked, replied, "I saw him fall overboard about three hours ago." Such are the ways of this, to me, peculiar people. The sea is too rough for reading and writing, and, to add to our discomfort, the two Russian passengers drink, fight at table, and call each other "liar and coward, snob and thief, spy and menial." I feel despondent, because thirty pilgrims are dying of starvation and dysentery, and they won't take our food or medicines, though the Korán enjoins them even to eat pig to save life; but they are too ignorant to know the laws of their own faith. We fear some disease may break out.

On 27th we passed Socotra, the last shelter in monsoon time. It is very unpleasant not to be able to stand or walk, read or write; and to stagger about, and be flung hither and thither. It is all very well to talk of a "soul sickening o'er the heaving wave," but I should like to have seen fastidious Byron in an Austrian Lloyd, stationed to windward, rough or smooth, of eight hundred reeking filthy pilgrims, and serving them, ill or well. We ought to organize a fleet of hospital ships, each with a good doctor, and a detachment of nurses and Mohammedan cooks; a large supply of firewood and fresh water and sherbet; plenty of eggs, fruit, rice, and chickens, sufficient accommodation and baths, and each a separate bed or rug. Then they might live, but packed like sardines in a rough sea, suffering from age, poverty, disease, and sores, after the hardships and privations of the Hajj; foot-sore, without money, food, or friends who care whether they live or die; so ignorant that they will perish sooner than touch our food; suffering from cold and heat, sea-sick; in a worse condition than a beast in a stall,—who can wonder that we had twenty-three sea funerals, or that the ceremony is performed within the hour of death, and as cheerfully as if it were of small account? It is a heaving mass of cocoa-nut oil, rags, filth, and putrid sores and misery. All this the head-wind blows back into our cabins, and it is a wonder we are not all ill. One feels like a drop of water in the ocean to do good amongst them, and they are so disheartening. As I write this a man is dying absolutely from hunger. I fetched him a large plate of rice, and carefully scraped away all the outside that he might not suspect us of having touched it. He took it, looked wistfully at it, and thanked me, and as soon as I turned away, threw it in the sea. I then gave him two apples, and he ate those because I could not touch the inside. They beg for medicine; some few drink it, others spit it out and think it is arrack. I say, "No, verily! Allah knows that it is not arrack." It was generally chlorodyne or peppermint. A Bengali is so weak that he cannot take a dose fit for a child. To one poor man I gave a dose of calomel, and enjoined him not to take cold. In the night I got up and went to look after him, and found him lying, naked and dying, in a through draught from a cutting wind, and his strong wife wrapped up (fast asleep beside him) in a good blanket. She had watched until he was too weak, and had taken it from him. Once they bid fair to die, their dearest leave them lying in the fierce blaze of the sun, or in the night wind and damp, and give them neither to eat nor to drink. "Khalás!" they say, "it is finished!" it is not worth while, it is wasted. It is the dying hours of such as these I try to comfort, but our Russian passenger brings me word that, when those who must inevitably die, expire, they say it is *I* who have poisoned them. If so, why does the whole ship run after me for help? Others have lots of money, and die of starvation, saying they can't afford to "eat Rupees," forgetting they cannot take it with them. "Come, O Bountiful One! and sit a little amongst us, and examine my wife, who has the itch, and give her something to cure it," said one to-day. But if I were to give her anything, she will presently die of weakness, and I shall be blamed for her death. I used sometimes to ask my maid to help me, and she made us laugh by looking disgusted and saying, "No, thank you; I have the nose of a Princess, and cannot do such work." Several come to me daily to wash clean, anoint, and tie up their feet, covered with sores and worms, already enough to breed a disease. I did it for one very old man, who, touchingly, offered me a Rupee. I told him, laughing, that I had plenty, but if he would give it to the starving ones it would greatly please me. All these smells blow back upon us night and day, and what a mercy of God that we catch no disease! We have not lost a man under sixty, one eighty, and one was said to be (however incredible) one hundred and twenty. I am sure he looked it. This last had one hundred and fifty Rupees, and two hundred in gold,—and died of starvation. Amongst the pilgrims, however, are fine, strong, hale men, who do well; the Arabs, the Somali, and northern races, who are Russian subjects, and look almost like Japanese. The Bengali and the Hindi are the most fragile and unfit.

To-day north-east winds set in with violence, and destroyed all our peace. Everyone was dreadfully sick. The ship rolled heavily. The pilgrims howled with fright; six died. They shouted "Allah-hu Akbar!" lustily all day and night. The waves were very high. The ship danced like a cricket-ball. The captain said, "If this is not the north-east monsoon it is his brother."

30th.—The weather much better, and it lasted till we reached Bombay. We saw five birds. Mosquitoes came into the cabin. We had a delightful evening, with balmy air, crescent moon, and stars under it; and with the balmy wind, a gentle, undulating sea. The Dalmatian sailors sang glees; I have heard many a worse opera-house chorus; yet they are quite untutored. To-day another pilgrim died, and was robbed, his body was rifled of his bit of money as he lay dying, and they fought like cats before his eyes for the money he had been too avaricious to eat with and keep himself alive.

I made a curious entry in my journal on the 31st:—"A delightful day, without events, and nobody died."

There were thousands of dolphins at about 4.45, performing their water leap-frog before our bows.

February 1st.—We have been a month at sea.

At last, betimes, on February 2nd, the thirty-third day after leaving Trieste, a haze of lumpy hills arose from the eastern water-horizon; and we knew it to be the mountain backing Panwell. Then the blue water waxed green, greenish and brown, likest to liquid mud; the gulls became tamer and more numerous, and jetsam and flotsam, mostly empty barrels, drifted past us. We gathered on the bridge to enjoy the run in, which, however distasteful to the jaundiced eye of Indian veteran, is picturesque in the extreme.

We sighted land very early. It was again rough weather, so we did not see the "milk-white seas" recorded in the "Periplus," nor yet the broad lateen sails of coloured cotton and lug-rigged boats always written about in old books. Two more pilgrims died, completing twenty-three deaths. As we were running in, the pilot ran alongside, and called up to the captain, "Have you any sickness on board?" Answer, "Yes." "Run up the yellow flag; I will keep alongside in a boat, and you make for Butcher's Island"—a horrible quarantine! I was standing on the bridge, and seeing the yellow flag hoisted, and hearing the orders, felt convinced there was a mistake. So I made a trumpet of my hands, and holloed down to the pilot, "Why have you run that flag up—we've got no disease?" "Oh yes you have; either Cholera, or Smallpox, or Yellow Jack." "We have nothing of the sort," I answered. "Then why did the captain answer 'Yes'?" he replied. "Because it's the only English word he knows," I cried. Then he asked me all particulars, and noted them, and said he would go off for the doctor, and we were to stand out at a respectful distance from Bombay. This took place running up the spacious bay, surrounded by mountains and hills,—a poor copy of Rio de Janeiro. The doctor arrived, and my husband explained, and we were allowed to land. Never shall I forget the thankfulness of those pilgrims! They carried off their sick; they swarmed like rats down the ropes, hardly waiting for the boats, and gave us a sort of cheer, as they attributed their release to our intervention. Indeed, if we had been together a few more days, some disease must have broken out. What would happen in case of a fire or shipwreck, goodness only knows. All rushed up out of the holds, whilst the large-limbed Turkomans, bent upon not losing a moment, transferred themselves from under the bridge to the two gangways. The Bombay pilgrims, dressed in their Sunday best, leek green and flowing scarlet coats, and gold-threaded turbans; the small girls, Fatima Bái and Khadija Bái, have new nose-bags, rings, and bangles, and will hardly condescend to look at us; and the last we saw of the Holy Mob was a stream as of black ants trickling down the ladders and the ropes.

CHAPTER V.

BOMBAY.

" Below her home the river rolled
With soft melodious sound,
Where golden-finned Chuprassies swam
In myriads circling round,
Above, on the tallest trees remote,
Green Ayahs perched alone,
And all night long the Mussak moaned
In melancholy tone.

And where the purple Nullahs threw
Their branches far and wide,—
And silvery Goreewallahs flew
In silence side by side,—
The little Bheesties' twittering cry
Rose on the fragrant air,
And oft the angry Jampan howled!
Deep in his hateful lair."

—*Edward Lear's Book of Nonsense, "The Cummerbund."*

I will say two or three words upon the land we are about to enter, for those foreign readers who are not so familiar with Indian history as we are obliged to be in England.

It would be too extensive to say much about the state of India and its rulers in the early days. I want merely to trace, in a few sentences, our connection with it.

The Mohammedans entered India about the year 1000, and under Mahmoud effected a permanent establishment. The famous Akbar became heir to the throne in 1555. His reign was the most admirable and magnificent India ever enjoyed, and it extended over fifty-one years. He died in 1605. His empire was divided into fifteen viceroyalties. He was succeeded by his son Jehangir, in whose reign Sir Thomas Roe, the first English Ambassador to the Great Moghul, arrived in India. Shah Jehan (his son) succeeded him, and was eventually supplanted by his son, Aurungzeb, who kept his father in confinement at Agra, till he died seven years after. Shah Jehan was a splendid monarch. The Peacock Throne, the new City of Delhi, the Jamma Masjid, and the Taj Mahal, that "dream in marble," are all monuments of his taste and splendour. Shah Jehan left a gigantic Moghul empire, and Hindustán under Aurungzeb enjoyed profound peace and prosperity for eighteen years; but in 1678 he had to be incessantly in the field, quelling rebellion, and fighting hosts of enemies. During his reign, the Moghul Empire attained its acme of prosperity, in extent, population, and riches; its annual revenue being thirty-two millions sterling.

Thomas Stevens, a student of New College, Oxford, was the first Englishman who visited the western coast of India, and landed at Goa in 1579. Then a Mr. Newberry and a Mr. Fitch travelled through Syria to India, carrying a letter from our Queen Elizabeth to Akbar. The first English expedition destined for India was rather of a buccaneering nature; a cruise against the Portuguese was sent out in 1591, under Captain Raymond, but it failed. In 1599 a little Company was formed in London, with a subscribed capital of £30,133 6*s*. 8*d*. Out of this nutshell came our mighty Eastern Empire. In 1600 the Company received a Royal Charter (conditionally) of privileges for fifteen years. In 1601 a little fleet of five small vessels, under Raymond's lieutenant, James Lancaster, set out, furnished with letters from Queen Elizabeth to various potentates. In 1612 the Emperor of Moghul (then Jehangir) granted them a Firman, to establish themselves in India, and a little factory speedily rose at Surat. This was the cradle of Bombay and British India. The factory at Surat grew speedily enough to maintain a President at £500 a year. He is described as living in great state from the earliest days. "A banner and a horse went before him, and a company of native servants, armed with swords and shields and bows and arrows, before and behind." Whenever the dignity of his "Lodge" was at stake, he "put on more side." "Before him were carried two large English Ensigns; Persian and Arab horses, with rich trappings, were led, the Captain of the peons on horseback, with forty or fifty attendants on foot; then the Council, in large coaches drawn by state oxen; then the factors, in more coaches, or upon horses with velvet saddles, richly embroidered, their head-stalls, reins, and croupers covered with solid wrought silver."

Ovington says that "the grand style of living of the English made all the great people of India exceedingly to value their friendship."

"About six in the morning the whole company came together to hear prayers read by the chaplain. They then dispersed, some to the morning meal, others to the 'groves and gardens' near the water side, and a few of the young writers to the teacher provided for their use by the Company. At ten business began, and went on till noon. Then dinner was served, all sitting down after the English manner, in a public place, according to their seniority in the service. The table, spread at the Company's expense, was adorned with drinking cups, dishes, and plates of pure silver, 'massy and substantial.' The dishes were filled with the choicest meat Surat or the country round could afford, prepared to please 'the curiosity of every palate,' by an English, a Portuguese, and an Indian cook. With equal freedom, generous Persian wine and arrack punch were served round the table. This was the everyday fare; but on Sundays and public festivals the table was 'still further embellished' by game, fruit, European wines, and English beer. In the afternoon, about four o'clock, business was resumed, and was carried on till dark. Then, after prayers, at eight, a public supper and some 'innocent easy recreation,' all retired to their rooms, no one being allowed, without liberty of the President, 'to lie abroad or leave the factory.'"

But with the restoration of the Stuarts at home, we find that orders had also to be issued here against drunkenness, profane swearing, and uncleanness. For his first crime the offender was admonished; for the second, fitly punished; for the third, sent to England by the next ship. Still in hard drinking they were beaten by the Dutch,—though, says Ovington, "brandy was by the wiser sort seldom taken unless it were a spoonful or so before dinner, or a drop at night before they go to bed." The "wiser sort" must, however, have been in a minority, for, according to Mr. Campbell, "the best known of the Surat tombs was that raised over a jovial Dutch commander, a great drinker, and said to be a relation of the Prince of Orange. At the top was a great cup of stone, and another at each corner. Opposite each cup was the figure of a sugarloaf. Dutch drinking parties used to frequent this tomb, brewing their punch in the large stone basins, "remembering," says Ovington, "their departed companion so much, that they sometimes forgot themselves." With the transfer, in 1687, of the head-quarters of the English Company to Bombay, the distinctive features of Surat life came to an end. But these merchants and factors were to serve as a model for our present Civil Service; and this Company at Surat was to be the conqueror of India; and so the story of this period must always have a charm for Anglo-Indians.

A Scotch surgeon, named Boughton, having in early days performed important professional services for Jehanghir and his family, a good understanding was established between the Imperial Government and the English at Surat. In this year (1612) Captain Hawkins was in the Gulf of Cambay, and Sir Henry Middleton at Surat, and Sir Thomas Roe's embassy was in 1615. In 1640 the site of Madras had been obtained, and a fortress was erected by order of Charles I.; that at Hooghli followed in 1656.

The English sadly wanted Bombay, and had made several fruitless attempts to obtain it from the Portuguese, who made no use of it. In 1661 our Charles II. married the Infanta of Portugal, Catherine of Braganza; and, as they considered it a useless place, they threw it in with her dowry, as well as Tangier in Africa,—which we certainly ought to have kept,—and thus Bombay became ours.

In 1668 Charles II. made it over to the East India Company, for a payment of an annual rent of £10 in gold, on condition they bound themselves not to part with it; and that all persons born there should be considered British subjects. The Company then left Surat and made Bombay their head-quarters. They afterwards purchased Calcutta, and made that their head-quarters on the north-eastern coast of India, and Madras on the south-eastern coast.

When the Portuguese made this concession, they saw no use to put Bombay to, and it puzzled them to imagine that it would be of any benefit to the English; but by giving the English what was so much desired, they secured their protection against the Dutch, so all parties were pleased. This is not to be wondered at, for it was a sickly salt marsh, occupied by a poverty-stricken, barbarous population. There was no corn, no cattle; indeed, a sheep or two was considered a grand present. The water was horrible, it was filled with malignant vermin and reptiles; and the air was foul and corrupt; wounds never healed; men lost the taste of the palate, and out of five hundred, perhaps one hundred Europeans lived to leave it. Cholera was their worst of some twenty prevalent diseases, and up to late times, say fifty years, it was a common English proverb that "two monsoons were the age of a man." It is not, therefore, astounding that it was accounted of so little value, when Sir Gervase Lucas, the Governor, sent out at that time, reported the total revenue of Bombay (1667) to be £6,490 17*s.* 4*d.*, paid by a population of ten thousand souls. The English, however, all will admit, are essentially made for successful colonization; and the sagacious Company immediately built a Fort and Castle, and garrisoned it to replace a small, ill-fortified house, with four little brass guns. They exempted the inhabitants from five years' taxes, ordered religious liberty, and freedom of foreign trade; they fostered national industry, built a harbour with docks, gave waste lands to settlers, provided them with looms, encouraged all sorts of manufactures, native or otherwise; so naturally the whole world flocked there. When the world saw that the English knew what to do with Bombay, everybody wanted it. After disposing of the Dutch, they had to contend with the Maharattas (that Imperial banditti which overran all India), the Malabar pirates, and the French. But the superior genius and valour of Clive won the day. He was born in 1725, died 1774. It was he who caused Bombay to become something better than a foreign settlement, holding a precarious existence in the midst of a host of enemies. His

GENERAL SIR CHARLES NAPIER, OF SIND, CALLED BY THE NATIVES "SHAYTÁN KÁ BHÁI."

successes turned the tide. From then till now the Natives have always called our troops the "Red Wall," as our Infantry are terrible in crossing bayonets. The moment a vacant place was made, it was filled up, and if a whole line were swept down another would instantly take its place, as long as the army lasted. Our men never know (as Napoleon said) when they are beaten. They never retire, never give way. An Englishman is phlegmatic, and slow to provoke, but once rouse him and he will never leave off. The more he fights the more he likes it, like a tiger that has tasted blood. Sir Charles Napier (my husband's old Chief) made it a rule never to retreat before an Indian army. In the campaign of Assaye, 1803, our troops suffered much from the Maharatta artillery, but their army always broke the moment the British regiments got within musket shot. In short, the conquest of India is due entirely to the incomparable fighting qualities of the British soldier. Foreigners fancy we have no soldiers. If we have fewer than they, ours make up for it by their bull-dog determination and courage, and "never knowing when they are beaten." The names of Commodore James (Bombay Marines, 1770), Major-Generals Stewart and Hartley; General Lake, Sir Arthur Wellesley (Wellington); General Sir Harry Smith, and a host of other gallant names, have an evergreen memory in India.

It was in Clive's time that Siráj ed Dauleh confined 170 English residents in a small, loathsome dungeon called the Black Hole, and most of them died of suffocation in one night. Clive, with only 900 English, took signal vengeance on Siráj and his 40,000 men, and afterwards totally defeated him at Plassey, with 1000 Englishmen against 50,000 men and 40 pieces of cannon. He converted an association of traders into the Rulers of a large and magnificent Empire.

Old Bombay was a town only a mile long, in which lived, confusedly, according to Fryer, English, Portuguese, and Topasses, or Indo-Portuguese, Gentoos, Moors, and Coolies, mostly fishermen. The houses were low, and thatched with cocoa leaves; oyster shells were used instead of glass for windows,—which is still the case in Portuguese India. Mr. Forbes a "writer" in

1770, says in his memoirs that "for want of means to buy a supper or candle (the salaries were low in those days), he used to sit on the flat roof of their office and read Shakespeare by moonlight."

The Bombay Navy, after the peace of 1805, extirpated Pirates in the Indian Ocean, Red Sea, and Persian Gulf, and made careful surveys of those Seas.

Clive's administration lasted from 1757 to 1760.

Vansittart and Spencer, 1760 to 1765.

The first Sepoy mutiny was in 1764.

Clive's second administration, from 1765 to 1767.

Verelst, Cartier, and Hastings, were successive Governors of Bengal, 1767-74.

The first Governor-General of British India was Warren Hastings, in 1774. Fox's India Bill and Pitt's India Bill passed in 1784. Lord Cornwallis succeeded as Governor-General in 1786, and Lord Teignmouth (Sir J. Shore), 1793. The Marquis of Wellesley (1798) retired in 1805.

Lord Cornwallis Governor-General (second time), and Sir George Barlow Governor of Madras 1805-7. Lord Minto in 1807. The Marquis of Hastings, 1813. The Maharatta war took place in 1817—1823. Lord Amherst went out in 1823 as Governor-General, and Lord William Bentinck 1828.

In 1833 the Overland Route was established. It was an enormous advantage, for though the East Indies still sent cargo round by the Cape to prevent Indian merchandize from being too cheap in the Levant, passengers and mails began to go, instead of by Jeddah, *viâ* Suez through Egypt in vans, and through the desert to Alexandria, where other steamers awaited them; whilst the monsoon mails were sent round by the Persian Gulf as late as 1840. Once it took five months to send, and five months to get an answer to a European letter; by the "Overland" people could write and receive an answer in five months, afterwards reduced to three months, now to *one*. Sir Bartle Frere was, I am told, the first Anglo-Indian civilian who performed this journey, in 1833. He traversed the Red Sea and Indian Ocean in an Arab Dhow, a plucky feat, and he was so damaged by the voyage that when he landed no one recognized him, and treated him as an impostor.

Lord Auckland became Governor-General in 1836. In 1839 we occupied Cabul, and the Afghan outbreak took place in 1841. In 1840 to 1842 was the first Chinese war; Lord Auckland retired and Lord Ellenborough went out. In 1842 General Pollock advanced on Cabul. We evacuated Afghanistan. The Sind troubles, under Sir Charles Napier, were going on in 1842. We annexed Sind in 1843, and fought the battles of Miani and Hydrabad.* There were troubles in Gwalior, and we fought the battles of Maharajpur and Panniar. In 1844 Lord Ellenborough was replaced by Lord Hardinge. In 1845 the Sikhs crossed the Sutlej. The battles of Mudki, Firozshahar, Aliwal (Sir Harry Smith's great battle), and Sobraon were fought, and in 1846 the Punjab was settled. Lord Dalhousie went out in 1848. There was a fresh outbreak in the Punjab, and the siege of Mooltan. In 1849 was fought the battle of Ramnagur; the storming of Mooltan took place, and the great battle of Chilianwallah (the fiercest of all the great Indian engagements); lastly the battle of Gujerat, and in 1849 the Punjab was annexed. In 1852 we had the second Burmese war, and in 1853 we annexed Nagpur. In 1856 we annexed Oudh. Lord Canning went out in 1856. In 1857 were the Persian war, the expedition to China, and the great Sepoy mutiny. In 1858 the confiscation of land in Oudh. In 1858 the East India Company transferred the government of India to the Queen. Lord Elgin went out as Viceroy in 1861; Lord Lawrence in 1863; Lord Mayo succeeded in 1869; he was murdered by a fanatic Afghan in 1872, and was replaced by Lord Northbrook; now as I write (1876) Lord Lytton is taking his place.

I suppose no one has any idea (and certainly no foreigner has) of the amount of diplomacy or the responsibility incurred by the Viceroy of India. The India House may well be quoted as "the focus of politics for nearly all Asia, and the storehouse of romance of all the East." It has to regulate our relations with all the neighbouring foreign powers *beyond* the limits of Hindustan, and with the four hundred and sixty dependent Princes and Chiefs within our own Indian Empire.

* My husband was on Sir Charles Napier's staff in Sind between 1842 and 1849.

Talking of early history, a house, now pulled down, at the foot of Malabar Hill, on the Back Bay side—Mr. Maclean in his admirable "Guide to Bombay" has told us—is pointed out as that which was inhabited by the subsequent Duke of Wellington, and that an old lady (probably Mrs. Hough, who died three years ago at Kolaba) used to relate that in 1803 she danced with Sir Arthur Wellesley at a *fête*. Mr. Maclean regrets that before her death she burnt memoirs she had kept extending over three-quarters of a century; they would have been invaluable material for a domestic history of Bombay at that time.

On arriving at Bombay, we were housed at Watson's Esplanade Hotel, a very large-sized building. We called at Parell; Government House two hundred years ago was a church and convent belonging to the Jesuits; they were expelled in 1720, and their property was given to the Carmelites; the lower storey forms the now desecrated Church. We went to see the Victoria Gardens, which are charming; and the Museum, a gorgeous pile of architecture in Renaissance style, but it contains, as yet, only specimens of cotton and trap-rock. I am new in India, and am therefore struck by the cows with humps; by brown men with patches of mud on their foreheads, a stamp showing their Brahmin caste; by men lying in closed sedan chairs (palanquins), so like our hospital litters that I said, "Dear me, the smallpox must be very bad, for I see some one being carried to the hospital every minute;" and by children, and big children too, with no garment save a string of silver bells. I was impressed by the picturesque streets, the coloured Temples, the irregular houses, and by the Parsee palaces garnished for weddings; but the populace struck me as being stupid and uninteresting—not like the Arabs. I became more interested as I knew more. The town was very fine; the weather was beautiful. The principal occupation appears to be driving to green, picturesque Malabar Hill, with its pretty bungalows, and afterwards to the American *café* to hear the band play.

Next morning was spent at Ali Abdullah's stables, where we saw some perfect colts. He is the son of an Anazeh Arab who married a Christian, and is settled here; he is Europeanized, and keeps stables of four or five hundred horses, imported from Persia, Syria, and from the breeding districts of Turkish Arabia, at the head of the Persian Gulf. He *makes* them perfect, and sells them. I saw about two hundred Kadishi, fourteen hands high; useful, not pretty, and worth £12 or £14 each in Syrian estimation; some blood colts, two or three faultless for £200; and two fine English stallions.

Then some friends took us in a steam launch to see the Caves of Elephanta.* We were a party of five. We had a first-rate view of Bombay harbour, of the shape of a round arch, which claims to rank high amongst the beauties of the world; and soon the bold and fretted line of the Western Gháts began to define itself on the horizon. This huge ridge of basalt extends some seventy miles from Bassein to Alibagh, with occasional breaks, especially where the creeks open into Bombay harbour.

After an hour or more steaming, we neared the southern point of Elephanta, or Gharapúri Island, and passed on to Hog Island, a little to the north-west, where we saw Mr. Edwin Clerk's hydraulic lift for steamers; it cost £170,000 and then proved an utter failure, having completely broken up a French steamer. It is placed at the mouth of the Panwell river, where the current sweeps strong, and is bad and dangerous; it is separated by six miles of water from the establishment required for repairing ships, but the engineer says that is not *his* affair. The object was to land troops here, and send them directly, *viâ* Kanjat and the great Kalyan junction, up the Bhor Ghát, thus saving them an immense round; but the lift is never used because they are not sure about its strength.

We then come to a pierlet of concrete blocks, a long, easy flight of basalt steps, which leads us up to the Caves. The elephant which gave the Portuguese name to the island, is a broken-up heap lying in a flower-bed of the Victoria Museum Gardens, where it was transferred in 1864. We continued the endless steps, and visited the well-known wonderful Hindú caves,

* Vehar Lake, in the island of Salsette, fifteen miles from Bombay, is a charming picnic place. It is a long day, and one can visit also the Keneri caves by a long scramble; but I did not go there.

covered with gigantic carvings of their Triad,—Shiva in his triune form; and also of other gods, carved or hewn out of the solid trap-rock. The entrance is clothed with luxuriant verdure. The cave is in the form of a cross, one hundred and thirty-three feet in length, divided into three parts by two rows of beautiful pillars. There are two chapels on each side, like an ancient basilica. The principal statue, nineteen feet high, represents Shiva as their Trinity, Bramha, Vishnu, and Shiva; Creator, Preserver, and Destroyer. Another is Ardhnarishvar; Shiva in his character half male, half female, leaning on a bull, his constant attendant. The next figure is Shiva and his wife Parbati, with one breast. From the god's head flows the Ganges, with three figures representing the Ganges, Jumna, and Saraswati, which unite the other two. These figures are from ten to fourteen feet high. We admired the great hall, with its cushioned pillars, carved out of the stone which supports the massive roof, and which recede in vistas on all sides. We noticed the sword blade of Arjúna: it is long, straight, and bevelled off to a point; the guard is a mere cross; the hero's hand fills the grip, and the pommel is a large, striped "mound," with the projection below. The steamer had great difficulty in getting back, as the sea was very rough, but we had plenty of grapes and sandwiches and champagne, so we did not mind being late for dinner. We returned by Magazon and ran straight down the harbour, stopping at the American *café* at the Apollo Bunder, for a glass of Vermouth, to give us an appetite.

6th.—Mr. F. F. Arbuthnot drove us with his own team out to Bandora, about twelve miles from Bombay, where he has a charming bungalow in a wild spot close to the sea, and where one can get a little quiet and fresh air. First we passed through the Esplanade, then through the Bhendi Bazaar (native)—the most striking part of Bombay—and afterwards through native villages, huts of dirty thatch under palms, with pigs, goats, mangy dogs and cats, kids, and children, all intermingled. The finest thing I have seen in India, the only thing that impressed me in the vegetation line after South American experience, lay on our way—the Máhim woods, a grand, wild, straggling forest of palms (cocoa palms, date palms, fan palms, dom palms, betel nut palms), acacia, banyan trees, and creeping all over with *poincietta bourgainvilla*, lilac and scarlet. Then we passed over a bridge across an inlet of the sea, which looks like two lakes separating Bombay Island and Salsette Island, to which we are going. Turning the hill which ascends to the house is a narrow curve and a deep well. Here a fatal accident occurred not many years ago. A picnic party were coming down the hill too quick in a coach, which caught the parapet and tilted; two ladies fell into the well, and were killed on the spot, and others were seriously hurt.

At the end of our drive we found a charming bungalow facing the sea. It was rural, solitary, and refreshing, something after the fashion of our Bludan in Syria; and attached to it was a stable with six horses. This became our weekly resort from Saturday to Monday, and very pleasant days we used to pass there. There is a delightful walk to a point which juts out into the sea. A pilgrimage is made by climbing up to the church of Nossa Senhora do Monte, a little old Portuguese country chapel and shrine, built two hundred and thirty years ago, in the best situation, on a height, with a Scala Santa for descent. The summit commands a delicious view of the two sheets of water separated by the bridge; it is surrounded by rising country and wooded hills, except on the side open to the sea, the fore scene having the Gháts for a background. Towards sunset arrived the Duke of Sutherland, Admiral (Rim), now Sir R. I. Macdonald; Admiral Lambert, and Mr. Albert Grey, one of H.R.H.'s suite, and we had a very jolly dinner and evening. It was the eve of a great feast, and young boys, dressed like tigers, came and performed some native dancing, with gestures of fighting and clawing one another, but exceedingly graceful. The meaning of the performance I shall presently notice.

7th.—We drove back in the cool of the morning all together in Mr. Arbuthnot's break. We were just in time for the *Tabút*, or Mūharram feast, this tenth of the month,—a Moslem miracle play, like our Passion Play at Ober Ammergau. It celebrates the martyrdom and death of Hassan and Hossein, sons of Ali and Fatima, son-in-law and daughter of Mohammed. Here the Moslems are so ignorant they make it a day of rejoicing and fighting, instead of grief. But then, of course, here, as in all other religions, are three classes :—

1. Who believe, and practise.
2. Who practise, and do not believe.
3. Who believe, and do not practise.

What astonished me was that no European seemed to care about the sight, whilst in any other land there would be crowded express trains and excursion steamers to catch a glimpse of it.

I went to the Imám Bárrá, where the Shiahs (Persians) assemble: my husband had seen it so often he did not go. The crowd was so great I had to get a policeman's help. They let in the Hindús and us, but not the Sunnis, who are their religious enemies. The whole place was a blaze of lamps, mirrors, a brazier of wood flaring up, and a large white tank of water (Hossein died fighting his way to the Great River). Men form themselves into a ring, moving from right to left with a curious step, beating their naked breasts with their hands. It makes a noise like the thud of a crowbar, but in musical time: the Arabs dance that way, but do not beat their breasts. The blows are given with such violence that they sometimes die of them, and often faint, and think themselves happy to suffer in the cause. They become more and more fanatical, working themselves up to frenzy, crying, "Hossein! Hossein Shah!" and with this wail the blows are dealt with noise and regularity like a huge sledge hammer, till it becomes a maddening shriek. They become raw as beef, and bleed, and are distorted. To see those hundreds of men, in the prime of life, brawny and muscular as they are, carried away by religious fanaticism, awes you; and you know what a terrible thing it is, and what a tremendous force it is, when roused, to twist the world in and out of shape with.

Then comes a procession of horses bearing little boys of six or eight, the children and nephews of Hossein, carried off prisoners; their white clothes and the horses' trappings stream with blood (painted wonderfully well). A group of mourners hang round each horse, crying real tears, and shrieking, "Hossein!" which thrills our nerves, and all the spectators sob. Then comes the bier with Hossein's corpse, and his son sitting upon it sorrowing and embracing him, and a beautiful white dove in the corner, whose wings are dabbled with blood. The effect upon the excited crowd is awful. Then follows a litter with the sister and widow of Hossein, throwing dust and straw upon their heads. One horse has a score of arrows stuck in its housings. We must here call to mind that Fatima was the daughter of the prophet Mohammed, was married to Ali, the prophet's favourite companion, and was mother of Hassan and Hossein. Fatima expected Ali to succeed her father, but Ayesha, the last and youngest wife of Mohammed, managed that her own father, Abubekr, should become the Caliph. Then came Omar, then Osman. When Osman died, Ali, who was still alive, became Caliph, and was assassinated A.D. 660, leaving his two sons Hassan and Hossein, blessed by their grandfather Mohammed as the foremost youths of Paradise. Hassan renounced his rights to save civil war, and was poisoned at Medina by his wife, at the instigation of Muáwiyah. Hossein went to Medina, invited to return by the subjects of the treacherous Yezíd, was caught in the snare, and slain in battle at Kerbala (Arabia).

I was then invited by Persian friends of H.H. Agha Khan, Chief of the Khojahs, to go to the Jumat Khana, the place of assembly of the Khojah caste,—an immense building, enclosing a large space of ground.

This was the tragedy represented there:—

First came Hossein, six feet high, with fair complexion, and black beard cut close. He walks with dignity, as becomes so great a personage. His green and gold turban is like a crown, and shows his relationship to the Prophet. He is draped in a black cloak. Then the wife and sister came, veiled; then four little children; then attendants. Hossein seats himself in a large armchair on one of three dais; his family on a similar one opposite; and a sick youth, the son of Hossein, lies on a mattress on a third. His son was ill when Hossein died, but lived to become the progenitor of all the Sherífs of the East.

Then the villain Shimr, inviting Hossein to return, was hooted; and a noble reply from Hossein was received with murmurs of applause. Then rises up Hossein's sister, imploring him not to go to destruction. The wife dâre not speak; she may feel the most, but in the East she dares not show it, even by a murmur. Hossein says that he is called to be the Imám of the Faithful. If slain, he will die for the people of the true Faith; if he lives, he will do Allah's will. The sister cries aloud, and casting dust on her head, flings herself on his neck. He embraces her tenderly, but will go and die for the sins of all. Sobs burst from all sides—and real sobs. Everything is so earnest, so simple, so distinct, and expressive. Then the little daughter comes forth and caresses him: the child really weeps. He takes it in his arms, soothes, and puts it back to its mother's lap. He then goes over to his son's sick bed and bids him a tender adieu. A splendid horse then comes in, and the sister brings him a white linen shroud, and puts it on him. When about to mount, the child rushes from her mother's arms and catches his cloak. He sinks on the ground, and wraps the child in his arms. As he rises the child pulls off the shroud, covers herself with it, and stretches herself on the earth. He takes it from her and mounts his horse. The child flings herself in front of the horse's hoofs, and the animal stands still. A servant picks the child up, but she breaks away, and clings to the horse's legs: her little hands clutch its hoofs.

The audience have been sobbing the whole time, but now there is a perfect spasm of grief. An Angel then comes, and offers to slay Hossein's enemies; but he refuses, and the Angel throws dust over his head. Then he draws his cimitar. The villain Shimr appears, and they ride off. The battle, the treachery, want of water, and the slaying, are left to the imagination; and we next see the procession of the Imám's captive children, sister, and widow, and his headless corpse upon a bier. The procession of last night follows again, shrieking, "Ya Ali! Ya Hossein!" with beating of breasts. The Tabúts are set up in every nook and corner, and are a fanciful representation of the tombs of Hassan and Hossein—gay, glittering grimcracks and tinsel. They are carried through the streets by men and boys as merry as grigs, dancing, and shouting, to fling them into the sea. The explanation is that the Shiahs mourn for Hossein with despair, but the Sunnis consider him not a martyr to be mourned for, and turn the occasion into ridicule; and these Tabút processions are conducted by the Sunnis as a caricature, which sometimes ends in a serious fight.

I believe few people know how contagious religious emotion of this kind is. I will recount an instance rather in self-ridicule. I went up to a Slav country church on a mountain with a Slav maid on a Sunday not long ago. We had a nice country service and Slav sermon. The congregation wept bitterly, and I cried too. All of a sudden I had a wish to laugh. I said to myself, "What a fool I am! here I am crying, and I don't know a word of Slav;" and it struck me as being so ridiculous that I could not recover my gravity. I turned round to my maid and said to her in Italian, "Netti, what are we crying for?" "Because the priest is going away, and is taking leave of his flock." There were we two women sobbing our hearts out because a priest whom we did not know was saying good-bye to his people and church whom we had never seen before, and should never see again.

In the evening we went to Kolaba Point, which is the other tip of the round, arch-shaped bay, and corresponds to Malabar Hill,—Malabar Hill to S.S.W., Kolaba Point S.W.; two and a half miles from the middle to either point.

8*th.*—In the afternoon took place a Regatta, where all the youth, beauty, and fashion of Bombay was gathered under a tent; and the races seemed very good; after which there was a Regatta-club-dinner in tents, and bands playing.

9*th.*—I went to see the Convent of Jesus and Mary, where live the Right Reverend L. Meurin, S.J., Bishop of Ascalon, i. p. i., Vicar Apostolic of Bombay, with Father Cook, and other Ecclesiastics. The nuns educate and attend to the poor, and are very simple. The smallpox is raging in Bombay at present. To-day we called upon Sir Charles and Lady Staveley, and lunched on board the *Undaunted*, with Admiral Macdonald, and then drove to

Breach Candy. Mr. Mannockjee Cursetjee and a Persian friend of my husband's came to breakfast. I then went down to our ship to get something left on board, and heard all the news; how the Italian officers had ridden on donkeys three hours to Lanaulí, and had come back very stiff, and unable to sit down. How "Champagne Charley," one of our Russian passengers, was in the hospital with delirium tremens, and bound down; and how the other, who was popularly called the "Leg," had written to the papers to say that he was not the man of the same name, who is a Russian spy. In the evening I had the pleasure of meeting the philanthropist Miss Mary Carpenter, who at so advanced an age undertook that solitary and laborious journey to Bombay, for good works.

11*th*.—We drove to see the Docks, where there are splendid projects for more than ever can be used. Millions thrown away in reclaiming sea, and heaps of land are lying waste. In 1858, twenty-two acres of sea ground were reclaimed, and it has so expanded that forty acres are given to Dock purposes; but one good result is that the exhalations from the mud have ceased, and cholera, which was seldom absent from the sailors, is now rare.

The next day we drove through the Palm woods, and by the sea to Amballa Hill, to breakfast with some friends. There was a forest of Cotton Mills below (like Wigan), which prevented our enjoying the magnificent view of Bombay, the sea and the distant mountains.

My husband inspected the Cotton Mills, but I was too hot and too lazy to care about the difference between Bombay and Manchester. It is, however, evident that India must become a manufacturing country, or it can no longer defend its teeming millions from famine. When this great work shall have been done, Great Britain, with one foot on Hindustan and the other on China, will command the cotton and wool manufactures of the world, and be the greatest producing power ever known.

Then we went to the Races at Byculla. There was a Nawwab (Nabob) in rainbow and gold, a rainbow carriage with a hammercloth, upon an open barouche. It was like a Catherine-wheel, green, red, and yellow; and black servants, in gorgeous costumes, to match, and two ditto in dirty white rags as a contrast. There was one of each sort before, and one of each sort behind. The Eastern "swells" were on the ground and in carriages, and the Europeans in the Club Stand. The racing distance was a mile and a half. One jockey, named Hankey, was the only rider, and whatever horse he rode won, even when others were more likely. There was an Arab horse, which, with a man on its back, must have beat everything, but the clumsy-made black riders sat like sacks, and ruined their chances. I saw that at once, and won nine bets one after another. Arabs will not run against "Walers," New South Wales horses; tall, long, lanky, weedy nags, with immense stride.

We dined with Sir Charles and Lady Staveley, at the Commander-in-Chief's quarters. I noticed that everybody went out by military rank, Mrs. Colonel G—— being the "big-wig" on this occasion. The native women beat the Syrians in colours, —everything as bright as a rainbow, but not "swearing." They are graceful and interesting, have fine eyes, but are not pretty. I see no cruelty in their disposition, nor temper, nor quarrelling.

On the 10th I went to see Mr. Mannockjee Cursetjee's (he is a Judge of the Small Cause Court) Alexandra Native Girls' English Institution; an English school for sixty-five girls, Parsees and Hindús. They also have fine eyes, and are graceful. They learn the elementary business of a national school,—music, needlework, and drawing. They sang and recited for me in English and Guzerattee. Amongst them was D. A. H. Wadia, daughter of Hormasjee Ardaseer Wadia, of Lowjee Castle, who illustrated so well that she could earn a living, but, as is usual in these cases, she is a rich girl, who will forget her talent in a too luxurious home. This family were great shipbuilders, and possess many testimonials from England for their cleverness and honourable dealings; amongst other things, the freehold of Parell was granted to them sixty years ago.

12*th.*—We breakfasted with a Persian Mirza, who knew my husband when he was here in '48. He had three sons and one daughter; the former breakfasted with us. We had a Persian feast, fruit, vegetables, every kind of sweets and rice, seasoned in various ways; rice with carraway seeds, pilao with saffron, savoury and aromatic; prawn-curry with plain rice, sweet rice with rose-water, and spices and sweet paste from Muskat. Afterwards I went to the Harím, and found a charming old mother, very much *kohl'd;* an interesting and ladylike married daughter with splendid eyes, who spoke English perfectly, without an accent, and she appeared very sensible, but extremely melancholy. There was a fat, furious, and untidy-looking old aunt; other women and negresses. I smoked a *narghileh* with them, and we chatted chiefly upon religion. The mother was very bigoted; they did their best to convert me to El Islám, and were generally pleased with my religious sentiments. They would not breakfast with us because of my husband's presence, —"*not*," they said, "that it was exactly a *law*, but their practice; and if God were pleased with them, what matter what men thought?" The Mirza sent me away in his carriage, and my husband remained with him. We then visited the new burial grounds at Suri, which are very pretty, and when they were opened, in 1867, the Sonápur cemetery, being too full, was closed.

14*th.*—I went to the wedding feast of the daughter of Venayek Ramchunder Luxumonjee, at Bhau Russell House, Girgaum Road. It was one of the handsomest entertainments I have ever seen. A long saloon was brilliantly lit: every sort of luxurious carpet: benches, chairs, and sofas, ranged top, bottom, and sides, were covered with gay colours; hundreds of Easterns were present in gorgeous dresses, one or two black coats, and I regret to say I was the only European lady. There was a Nautch, which consisted of three little girls, twisting their fingers and toes, singing "Jinny minny puddy-ah"—at least it sounded like that—and then "God Save the Queen." I should have stood up, only I did not recognise it till too late. The manners of the host were worthy of the most polished English gentleman, natural, courteous, and dignified; and he showed sincere pleasure at having Europeans at his house.

15*th.*—My husband and I made a party to be vaccinated. The smallpox was very bad, and daily four hundred people clustered round a cow at the hospital and were operated on. I had a very bad arm for a long while, but the others did not take. After our operation, Mr. Ormiston and his brother took us in a steam-launch to see his work, the revolving light at the Prongs, the handsomest thing I have ever seen. It is one hundred and sixty-nine feet high, it flashes every ten seconds, is seen eighteen miles off, and was finished in 1871 for £60,000: it saves hundreds of shipwrecks in the monsoon. It is eight stories high, each story containing a comfortable little room. The man who keeps it is named George Warden. I believe he has been there nine years, and a dull life he must have of it; I think it would be very kind if any good soul, having some amusing books to give away from time to time, were to send some to him.

We then went to the Steeplechase. There were four very good races; Cossack was a charming horse, and Kerosene a first-rate pony. There was a very large and good attendance.

17*th*.—We were invited to a Garden Party at Parell (Government House), a beautiful place, with grounds to match. There was a large attendance and much dressing,—something like a very mild Chiswick party. I amused myself with talking to the Bishop. At dusk I drove to Bhau Russell, to the same Hindú wedding before described, to the Harím of the gentlemanly, manly, well-mannered host, courteous without servility, and speaking excellent English,—Venayek Ramchunder Luxumonjee. He took me into the Harím. The little bride and bridegroom were aged nine and ten. There was a profusion of rose-water, bouquets, nuts wrapped in leaves, and cocoa-nuts. The children, covered with jewellery, sit in two chairs opposite each other, and an embroidered sheet is put between them; prayers are recited; she hangs a necklace of strung white blossoms round his neck, and he throws a necklace of black beads, something like a shabby watchchain, round hers. The marriage lasts for days. She goes to his home on a horse, behind her husband, their faces shaded by flowers, and, indeed, altogether covered with flowers, like two little Jack-in-the-greens, and there they are received; next day she is brought back to her parents, and stays with them until she is ready for practical marriage. But there are no more ceremonies, they are actually, though theoretically, married to-day: and there is no going back from it, nor possible change, if they do not like each other afterwards, any more than at our marriages. The houses on these occasions are lit up at night like a transformation scene in a pantomime, and it makes Bombay look very gay and pretty.

We dine out every evening. Everyone is so hospitable, and these long drives out to dinner and back are delicious on the balmy Indian nights; but when dinner is in town, we lose our only possible drive and breath of fresh air.

18th was the Byculla ball,—a very gay affair. They do everything well at the Byculla Club, except not admitting ladies inside, unless on such occasions.

19*th*.—We went again to the races. Five were very good. "Dutchman" was ridden by Hackney. There were many splendid horses, and some good "Walers." I again won every bet by betting on Hackney, and my friends taking the field. To-day I saw the Mango trick for the first time, and it is apt to astonish one at first, to have a tree planted and grow before one's sight without any apparent means to accomplish it. The Indian jugglers are clever, but the best I have seen is at Cairo. We are tired of the child being killed in the basket, and the mango tree is old to residents in India. In the evening we all went off to Bandora, Mr. Arbuthnot's country retreat.

On the 21st we left by a 1.30 G. I. P. R. train for Mátherán, passing the stations Byculla, Chinchoogly, Parel, Dadur, Sion, Coorla, Bhandoop, Tannah, and Derwa. The easy access of Mátherán is an immense advantage, but, as in many other cases, it causes her to be despised, whilst more difficult places become fashionable. At Parel we noticed the hills of the Island of Bombay, and we left the lovely Máhim woods to our left. As we proceeded we saw a few new things; for instance, the hay was hung in trees, to protect it from ants; the burial grounds were full of little flags or pennants, like those on a lance. We crossed Salsette, an island and a plain, surrounded by a river which separates it from the mainland. After Sion came

Coorla, with its cloth factory; and the salt Bombay Flats. Low cactus hedges line the way, till the country begins to get hilly. The outlines of the Gháts are seen in the distance. Woods, cactus, jungle, goats, sheep, cows, huts, and buffaloes, and signs of agriculture, are all intermingled. Near the hills of Vehar we smelt some delicious aromatic herb, almost like eau de Cologne. Tannah is a big village, an unhealthy-looking place, with two old crumbling forts in the river.* We saw some small bluish-black birds with long tails, and several black and white birds of blackbird size, and one like an ibis. Then we came close to the basaltic Gháts, where we saw curious natural formations, resembling churches, and domes, steeples, castles, and battlements, which are most striking. We passed a river and woods, and came to Kalyan Junction, the third halt. This poor village-port was, in A.D. 200, the far-famed Kalliénapolis, which shipped dry goods and precious woods to the outer west, and we are now on classic ground, near the northern extremity of the Shurpáraka, or winnow-shaped region, the Greek Limyrica, where some have placed the Ophir of Solomon.

We ran up the valley of the Ulas river, which separates the block of Mátherán from the main line of the Western Gháts. The Konkan lowland at this season is like the Arabian desert, it is tawny, not with sand, but with straw-like stubbles, and black patched with fire. Here we turn down towards Madras, joining the Calcutta railway and pass Budapoor. The land is semi-pastoral—hay, woods, beautiful mountains, thatched huts, jungle, and agriculture. After two hours of Deccan hot winds we finished the thirty-three miles between Bombay and Narel (pronounced Neral), and alighted at the little Maharatta village, on the river plain at the eastern base of Mátherán. Narel is the birthplace of the famous Náná Sáhib. At five we reached Narel, left the train, and started for Mátherán with a mob of lean Nasik ponies, and coolies; and a *tonjon* for my maid, who was carried between

* It is a Collectorate. There used to be five thousand velvet weavers here; they used also to cure large quantities of bacon. In the thirteenth century four friars went to dispute with the Moslem Kadi, and told him Mohammed was in Hell with his father the Devil, on which he executed them with such tortures that his own King banished him, and the Portuguese took signal revenge.

some twenty bearers, something after the fashion of the grapes of Eshcol on the antique brass platters. We have here seven miles of splendid mountain scenery; an ascent of two thousand seven hundred feet; ever turning, and each turn giving glorious panoramas of plains below. Carriages could not come here, unless they were carried upon the head, like the philanthropists' wheelbarrows by the African of Sierra Leone. Our road lay through zigzagged corniched and shady woods, the mountain wall rising on one side, and the precipice yawning on the other. Our ponies stumbled and shied at dogs. I was badly dressed for the occasion; my small hired saddle cut me, it was loose; it had a too long stirrup, and though we were only two hours and a quarter ascending, and six hours out, I was tired. After climbing up four plateaux, marked by milestones, we arrived at J. C. Pinto's (Alexandra Hotel), Máthérán, and at 7.15 sat down to an excellent dinner,—better than at Watson's.

The day after our arrival we began at 6.45. a.m. I was charmed with the wooded lanes and wild flowers, the pure atmosphere, the lights and shadows playing on the big foliage, and the birds rustling and singing in it. The contour of Máthérán is like a badly-made letter H, with the crossbar running upwards; the breadth of the three limbs forms the plateau, which covers eight square miles; in fact we are standing on a table-land of about five thousand acres, covered with bungalows, in lovely woods, seamed with riding-paths, regular leafy screens, whose several ends lead to the famous Points, each showing a magnificent view, with the Konkan beneath; around, the rugged Ghâts, rocky coast, City and harbour, always the same scene more or less extensively, Panorama Point being far the best—the vantage ground which commands Bombay. It is the north-eastern head, and is prolonged southwards, after a break by the abrupt Chandni cone, which books call Chandora. We looked down magnificent ravines, amongst buttress-shaped mountains, light and shade sharply defined, burnt yellow grass, green trees, and black basalt. The ground we stand on, and the mountain tops, are laterite stone: it cuts soft, is bright red, like brick, afterwards it hardens, and is lasting and durable. The scenery is large and bold. The highest peak is two thousand seven hundred feet above sea level.

The fresh, vivid verdure of the woods, which are raised above the level of the fetid, jungly undergrowth, is a repose to the eye, wearied by the tawny lowlands. You enjoy bright green grove, black rock, and red-yellow laterite, and the luxuriance of fernery is a change from palm and bamboo, aloe and cactus. There is one patch of virgin forest, the Rambagh, below Alexandra Point. The chief items of the second growth are the jambul and the párjamb (wild olive): the most striking is the ghela, with its stiff thorns and yellow-white flowers, and its crab-like poison apple, a dwarf, contrasting with the gigantic anjun or iron wood, whose lilac and pink bloom look like patches of morning sky peeping through the foliage. Wild animals are not wholly killed off. Tigers and lions no longer haunt the hill, but you may see a hyena or a shrinking panther. You may shoot spur fowl and button quails, but it is not worth while; and in early morning you may hear the Wánúrú monkey barking like a wolf. Mátherán has two seasons, the heats before and after the rains: it is not habitable during the deluges that last from early June to mid September.

North-west lies Porcupine, and south-west Great Chauk Point; and the other minor views are Hart, Louisa, Echo, Landscape, Battle, Monkey, Little Chauk, and Alexander, each of which has its particular history. Ghárbát is best for inland view, and for seeing Amrai or Rambagh and its magnificent grove of trees, with gigantic creepers in festoons.

The fantastic Gháts rise up out of the plain before us. We are looking upon Lion Ridge, which has a natural cap of basalt, like a funnel. This is the spur at the south end of Prabal. We enjoy a lovely view of Bombay, and the sea with bright sun shining upon it. Near Karanja is Negotna Creek or river. Prabal Ridge, commonly spelt Parbul, is like a wall; its name means "strong hill." On clear days at Bombay it is distinctly visible against the north-eastern sky, and the bold fretted outline of the Mátherán Organ Mountains show every shape that naked basalt can assume. That part opposite Louisa Point is the block called Prabal. My husband says these are formed by submarine volcanoes, which have been gradually upheaved. It has the appearance of a funnel and a tooth. In the Bháo Malang, which is like a church, Moslems have a praying place.

Porcupine Point is a tongue or buttress of a valley running out over a fearful gorge, where we heard in the depths beneath, first what we thought was a wolf, but which was the howling monkey. I crept on hands and knees to the edge, and looked over. Malet House was built by a Member of Council, the first house erected in this beautiful exhilarating air. We ascended the turret for the grand view, and commanded the green wooded hill for a radius of five thousand acres from this table-land with precipitous sides: below is the plain, with those wonderful spurs and ridges. Though every point is much the same, Panorama Point decidedly gives us the best idea of the great Konkan river-valley-plain, ten miles broad, with its river and railway bounded on either side by mountains. Then we stood on the root of the tongue, which we call Cathedral Spur, and look down on the station, Narel, and another Maharatta village. One feature is the sharp little "Parrot's Beak," as the Brazilians call these spur-like rocks, and another the "Doctor's Nose." Northernmost towers the huge sloping and detached block known to landsmen as the "Cathedral," to seamen as the "Queen of the Maharatta's Throne," and to Moslems as "Bháo Malang," from the Santon whose tomb occupies the dizzy top. There is the "False Funnel," or shattered tower of trap, and "*The* Funnel," or Karnáli, a truncated cone of naked basalt, some hundred and eighty feet high, useful to ships clearing the south-west Prong: it reminds one of the "Old Man of Hoy." Were these points some twenty miles nearer the harbour head, Bombay would have been one of the most picturesque of bays, but unfortunately they can only be seen just before or just after the rains. All our excursions are through wooded, shady walks; our first was to Landscape or Echo Point. We passed the bazar full of seeds, grain, natives, and buffaloes.

The jungle people, of whom I shall say more by-and-bye,

are simple, cheerful, and laughing: even the baby giggled at us. Only one man looked surly. Bright women, with good figures, wear a cloth round their thighs, which fastens up to the waist, and is carelessly thrown about their shoulders. They gave us milk from goats, and we gave them some silver. They had only goats, fowls, and calves; when they halt, they build a little thatch place covered with a cloth, and the cradle hangs in the trees, so their resting-place is ready in a moment. They wear a single scalp-lock, and are half naked: the children are pretty, like pups. They set a trap composed of a little hurdle upheld by twigs, the bait under, and the hurdle covered with huge stones, poised so as to fall easily, and it catches jackals and small deer.

Besides the new Bazar, there is a Gymnasium, and Roman Catholic and Protestant churches. There is a Chauki, or pike, where tolls are paid; a superintendent's quarters, with a post and telegraph. There are some seventy bungalows, built of laterite, which cuts red, and waxes rusty. We went to see some tanks, four higher and one lower, for washing clothes. Ex-convict Chinese live here, and the place is surrounded by garden and wood, enclosing a holy place where they annually sacrifice a cock and a goat. The officers' Sanitarium is a horridly-smelling, melancholy, deserted, almshouse-looking row, painted black, with black mat-screens; it looks like a stationary hearse, and would make one sick, even if the air were not redolent of smallpox. The rooms looked evidently fresh from some horrid disease, and uncleaned. We shuddered, and spat, passed on, and left the tainted atmosphere.

Mátherán, unlike Tungá and Máhábáleshwar, was utterly ignored by the sacred annals of the Hindús, till the seventeenth century, when a fort was built upon Prabal Ridge by Sivaji, the founder of the Maharatta kingdom, a hero who, like many others, thoroughly deserved hanging. It was also a favourite haunt of another Maharatta scoundrel, Ragoji Bángria, who, between 1844—46, was the *cauchemar* of the Konkan and of the Násik districts. In those days some three hundred men of the Ghát Light Infantry were encamped upon the hill, and shortly after it was well explored by the Conservator of Forests, an old friend of my husband, Dr. Alexander, whose *sobriquet* was "Daddy Gibson." Mr. Hugh Poyntz Malet, of the Bombay Civil Service, who followed in 1850, built the "Byke," and got a grant of £50 for road-making. In 1855, Mátherán was visited by Lord Elphinstone, who built Elphinstone Lodge, and liked it better than Malabar Hill. Yet Mátherán is not fashionable; it is affected by the commercial classes, who can be absent only from Saturday to Monday, but not by the "Services." Lord Mark Kerr, however, has lately patronized it, so let us hope it may see better days. Mátherán, Máhábáleshwar, and the Neilgherries, may be likened to Margate, Brighton, and Biarritz.

Mátherán has a pleasant night and morning. We saw fly-catchers (green birds), wild fig; anjún, the tree with a plum-like leaf and pink and lilac blossoms coming out of bough and trunk, which makes you fancy, at a distance, you see blue air *through* the tree, till on coming close the delusion vanishes. Our hotel-bungalow was not at all uncomfortable: it contained a tolerable cook, large tubs for baths, and good beds. There are four hotels, the "Alexandra,"—good fare, but no view; the same at "Hope Hall;" "Chauk Hotel" has a beautiful prospect, comfortable house, and bad food; and the same at the "Clarendon." You must choose between the *physique* and *morale*. We chose the *physique* at home, and went out for the *morale*. There are five compounds for tents: and tent life is what I would choose if I went to reside. Thieves, of the caste called Paggi or Ramosi, are employed to guard the houses and keep off other thieves. One slept outside our bungalow. They call all down the lines at night, to ascertain if the others are awake. It is really a pity that this charming summer quarter is not much used. We rode out and dined with a pleasing, intelligent, and ladylike Mrs. Douglas, with whom it was our good fortune to meet; and she invited Dr. N. and his pretty wife to meet us.

23*rd*.—We were up at five, and started at seven for Narel, carrying with us some of the quartz crystals, called Hill diamonds, from the mountain called Ghárbat; walked down the steep descent, and then rode. The way was lined with wild fig, and cotton trees, haunted by many birds and squirrels. We saw the *bagla* or white demoiselle-crane, in abundance, sitting on and picking the ticks off the cows; and plenty of blue and green fly-catchers. We arrived, hot, and a little tired, at the station, and the train came in at ten o'clock. We mounted the break, and much enjoyed the ascent of the Highlands, arriving at 11.45 at Lanauli. The Lanauli section of the Bhore Ghát is one in forty-five to one in thirty-eight. The line is, here a cornice, there a succession of tunnels, and the effect of light is most curious. We ran up the valley of the river Chauk, and passed an overhanging rock inhabited by monkeys. The first station, Karjat Khandalla, is a very pretty, pleasant place, on a height, where the soldiers are sent for change of air. The nights are cool, and it is charming from October to December. There is a bungalow belonging to Mr. Byramji Jijibhoy perched on a spur of the Ghát, high above the incline, which is very fine. Here is a thick jungle, where one finds panthers and cheetahs. Then comes the reverse station, where the rail makes a detour like a capital V, and then Lanauli begins.

This famous Bhore Ghát is one of the most splendid engineering triumphs in the world. The incline is fifteen miles long, the level of its base is some two hundred feet above the sea, and its summit two thousand and twenty-seven feet.

At No. 5 viaduct the air changes sensibly, and gets cooler. They say that it is quite lovely during the rains, the whole length of country being on each side covered with rice. The line is continually tunnel and viaduct, bored mountains and bridged valleys. The scenery is wild, bold, grandiose: the mountains are all curiously shaped, as in Brazil, and are dotted with patches of hot, withered grass. There are on the way two Maharatta Forts, called Ráo Machi, one on each hill. There is a ravine between them, and one is surrounded by ravines like a gigantic moat, making this great block a sort of island. This was defended by a Thakur, or Maharatta chief, and was the scene of a great fight in 1846, when our second European Regiment took these Forts and unearthed the Chief. The conductor, who was on our break, had been a soldier fighting in it, and gave my husband, who was then in the Bombay army on Sir Charles Napier's staff in Sind, a most spirited account of it. We passed another overhanging rock, which they say is usually covered with monkeys, some nearly as big as a man, and the others a small species; and the two kinds do not associate or intermarry. We fell in with troops of Brinjari, whom I will presently describe.

On arriving at Lanauli, we went to the Hotel (comfortable for roughing it, with a good cook); this place consists of a series of small detached bungalows in a square enclosed space, surrounded by a Maharatta scattered village; with Protestant, Methodist, and Catholic Churches, a Post Office, and a row of bungalows for railway officials. These corrugated iron roofs are dreadfully hot; but if thatched freshly once a year they would be cool. They are terrible for clothes, as they sweat rusty drops all over the room, which leave lifelong stains on your linen and dresses. I came away with everything ruined. The railway officials are everywhere in India, and especially here, most civil. The air was delicious, like that of São Paulo or Damascus in spring.

We were up and off at dawn to the Karla caves, so called after the village. There was bronght to the door at dawn a jibbing, backing pony, with vicious eyes, for my husband; and for me, a mangy horse like a knifeboard, spavined, with weak legs, and very aged, but, nevertheless, showing signs of "blood." At the top of this poor beast was a saddle big enough for a girl of ten: I being eleven stone, felt ashamed to mount. The Caves front west, and are in a bay or recess of the ancient geological northern bank of the Indrauni river, four miles from the hotel, on a good road, quite French and Napoleonic, straight and tedious, with trees on each side. I noticed coming along the road that the men wear sandals, with a sort of mouse-tail to ornament them. We passed a beautiful tree with clumps of orange flowers, called Ashook.

At the end of four miles we left the road and crossed the river-valley, to the mountains. Here we descended, and began to climb a goat-like path, and came to what looked like a gash or ridge in the mountain's side, with a belt of trees; here we sat on the stones facing one of the most wonderful Buddhist temples in India, constructed about two thousand years ago. It was shaped just like our cathedrals, body and aisle, with a horse-shoe roof of teak wood, declared to be the original, which has defied the ravages of time. The nave is separated from the aisles by fifteen columns on each side, whose capitals are two couchant elephants, with a man and woman upon each; a dome on a round base, surmounted by a coloured ornament and an umbrella at the top takes the place of High Altar,—the ornament being, like the pedestal, for the Blessed Sacrament, and the umbrella for canopy or tabernacle. The space behind the High Altar is a continuation of the horse-shoe shape, and separated by four plain columns. All the light comes from an open space, where a large window should be, above the entrance, behind the organ and choir of a church; and it is artistically done, so as to shine only on the High Altar and dome, like those in the Spanish and the Portuguese churches. The Kenneri Caves have the same arrangement.

The Brahmins keep this temple, and it is honoured by them as that of Mahadeo. Horse-shoe shaped wooden rafters adorn the ceiling. This is Buddhist architecture, if it is not a "bull" to say so, when it is not *built*, but cut out of the solid rock, pillars, capitals, façade, and all. On either side of the entrance are carved three splendid elephants, larger than life, and the whole is covered with niches and figures of (Buddhist) men and women. Four (now three) enormous columns front it with a gigantic slab of stone across the entry, forming a screen against curious gazers from outside; and again, further on, stands a huge column, with three lions for its capital. A little temple outside is consecrated by the Brahmins to Devi. We were not allowed to go nearer to this goddess than past a triangular ornament covered with big bells; but they lit it for us and let us peep in, and it disclosed a woman's face and figure, so horribly ugly as to give one a nightmare: a large, round, red face, with squinting glass eyes, open mouth, hideous teeth, and a gash on her chin and forehead for caste marks. She is the Goddess of Destruction, and is purposely made frightful.

Then we visited the water-tank close by the northern recess of the Indrauni river, bored with little caves like a beehive, and full of carved inscriptions and figures. Most curious of all was the Monkery. Cells were scooped out all around, and opened into the large, round centre room, and besides the ground-floor cave, there were a first, second, and third story. The stairs were no more, so we climbed up on piles of stones and a broken bit of ladder, and were pulled up by the men who accompanied us. They say sometimes that the Jesuits always pick and choose the best situations. The Buddhist monks did the same thing. This place commands the whole country. In fact, the more I travel, see, and learn, the more I perceive that all the ancient religions show that but one has existed from the Creation, for every faith tells the same tale as ours, with different actors under different names, but all the facts are the same. The cave was cut in basalt, hard green stone, and we saw quartzes, crystals, and agates. We "bakshished" our men, and a grey-haired grandmother, because she was so very old. On our return we saw many pretty plants and trees, flowers and birds, and wild absinthe perfumed the mountain. The flower, however, which pleases me the most in India is a luxuriant creeper, like a violet or purple honeysuckle, and I think its name is *Clipea hernandifolia*, or *Menispermacea*, and it is very plentiful at Bombay.

It was hot returning. The poor horse constantly faltered, giving a wrench to one's back, and bringing one's heart in one's mouth when it almost sat down behind. We passed troops of Brinjari, whose procession lasted for about two miles. This wild tribe intermarries only amongst themselves, and has its own laws. It is a very strong race ; men, women, and children are good-looking. They grow their own corn, have their own bullocks, spin their own sacks, and, with huge dogs for guard, walk leisurely along, about two miles an hour, to sell their grain. The women's dress is picturesque; their legs are covered with heavy leglets of brass, half-way to the knee. They wear a short coloured petticoat and peculiarly-shaped red and gilded bodice. Their arms are loaded to the very top with ivory, glass, and metal bracelets; an *izar*, or mantle, covers head and shoulders, and from their foreheads, heads, ears, and noses, hang knobs, and balls, and jangling things of every kind, like a war horse, of gold, jewels, brass, silver, bone, or glass. They looked defiantly if one laughed or spoke, and they carried their babies in a basket on their heads. We reached the hotel at eleven a.m., having started at six, making an excursion of five hours, losing no time. The horse arrived without falling.

We visited the Maharatta villages. These Hindús are a fine, manly race. Their habitations are thatched huts, divided by screens of sticks and boughs into rooms, one of which would be big enough to keep a small animal in. They contain nothing. They seemed surly, and even the dogs wanted to bite: they were like Scotch rough-hided terriers, turnspit shaped. I got some one to ask them if they disliked my staring at them, and then they became civil, gave me a stool, and swept a clear place for me; the man that was spoken to was civil, the woman less so. They were pounding maize in the ground for meal. I gave them a Rupee, which they seldom see, and then they *all* wanted me to visit them.

After breakfast and bath we went to the Station. The Master had just shot and wounded an otter and put it in a tub of water. Soon our train came up, and we were about two and a half hours getting to Poonah through the Indrauni river-valley, with mountains in the distance.

Poonah was the scene of all the Peshwa intrigues against the English and the great battles with the Maharattas. Their dynasty lasted only seventy years, but Bajee Ráo might have been Peshwa all his days if he had not quarrelled with the English. This was in Mr. Mount-Stuart Elphinstone's time, with whom at that time was Grant Duff, the historian. General Sir Arthur Wellesley (Wellington), General Sir Harry Smith, Lieutenant-Colonel Burr, Captains Ford and Staunton, General Pritzler, Sir Thomas Munro, and Colonel Prother, are names of that period that will ever be remembered in Poonah.

The stations we passed were Kurkulla, Tulligaum, Chinchwud, Kirkee, a large European military station, and very pretty, with its green trees, creepers, and flowers, pagodas, and cypresses. Finally we reached Poonah at 6.30, and went to "Napier's," a very nice-looking hotel, and far the best, kept, as usual, by an obliging Parsee. There is something nice about an intelligent Parsee; they are a progressive race; they like and imitate the English, and they are loyal. It is a curious fact that at the Parsee riot in 1874 everything was hacked to pieces except Her Majesty's picture, and by common consent that was respected, and stood intact amidst the general wreck. In 1825 a journey to Poonah, one hundred and nineteen miles, before railroads, occupied twenty-four hours, and cost six pounds. The first bit of rail was open in 1853, twenty-five years ago. However, in Gujerat there was no communication at all for four months in the year, and eight months only by riding.

25th.—We drove all about Poonah, and went to see the Palace of the Peshwas, in the Indian bazar. It is now used as a library below, and native law courts above; the chief ornaments are curious carved wooden columns, with elaborate capitals. Then we went to Parbati, the Maharatta Chief's palace and stronghold, from which the last Peshwa, Bajee Ráo, as he "sat on the rocky brow," saw his troops defeated by the English in the plain. He fled on horseback down the other side, and was hunted about the country for months, until he gave himself up to Sir John Malcolm. He was pensioned with eighty thousand a year instead of being hanged, and retired to Bithoor, on the Ganges, where he rewarded British clemency by adopting a child, born in the village of Narel, at the foot of Mátherán, who lived to be the infamous Náná Sáhib, the same that afterwards tortured and killed so many of our people. The English have such mistaken notions of clemency: they always scotch their snake, but are too generous, or hold it too much in contempt, to kill it, and let it run about to sting *ad libitum.* You mount by long, easy, sloping steps, which are seen in Bologna and some parts of Italy, but unknown in England. From the top is a noble view of the whole country, of the European town, the military lines, the native town, the green oasis, the jungly-looking tract beyond, the river, canal, and lake immediately below us, and mountains in the distance. Most of the private houses here are of the Italian or Brazilian kind, and covered with brilliant creepers.

There are three pagodas in this building, dedicated to Vishnu, Shiva, and Wittoba, but one small temple particularly, to Kalee or Bhowanee, wife of Shiva and patroness of the Thugs. Being sunset, the wild yet mournful, *bizarre* sound of tom-tom, and kettle, and cymbal, and reed (making a caricature of bagpipes), suddenly struck up. I could have shut my eyes and fancied myself in camp again in the desert, wild sword-dances being performed by the Arabs. Then we descended and got into a boat; I steered and they rowed. It was dark, and there was a good deal of "chaff" about our reaching safely. We dined with Mr. and Mrs. Peterson, Captain Yates, and Dr. Machonochie. Kharekwasla Tanks, or the Lakes, were laid out by Mr. Joyner, C.E. (a wonderfully clever work), and he made a water-party that we might see them; and then Lady Agnes Danyell took us to the brass bazar, where one picks up most curious things of all shapes and kinds. My husband and I were to meet at Mr. Peterson's to dinner, but the coachman of the carriage which Lord Mark Kerr lent me, did not know the way. There are "new lines" and "old lines," miles apart from each other, and we went to the wrong one. I was three-quarters of an hour sitting in a dark lane, for when they found they had made a mistake, instead of trying to rectify it, the black servants sat down in the road and made no attempt to move. Finally Dr. Sexton passed, and seeing an Englishwoman in a very uncomfortable position, helped her out of it; and I arrived for dinner, very much ashamed, an hour too late, during which Lord Mark, who was also going out, was minus his carriage, a double mortification.

27th.—We went to the Convent of Jesus and Mary, erected in 1863, by subscription, costing eighty thousand rupees; it had a home for destitute women added in 1872. The institution is especially established for the orphans of British soldiers, who receive a sound education, and are taught singing besides. There is also a day school for ladies, and a free school for the lower class. It is called St. Joseph's School-Convent-Lines, Poonah. The staff-surgeon attends the establishment, medicines are provided by the Government, and there is an infirmary for the sick. The children have four meals a day, and everything is beautifully clean, the children's persons, dress, lodgings, and bedding. The Reverend Mother, a superior woman, who seems to be widely known and beloved (Mother Catharine, called Madame St. Catharine), took me over the whole building, and initiated me into all its affairs. There were nine Sisters, a very nice chapel, and a magnificently organized convent and orphanage, all begun without a sou. There are one hundred and twenty soldiers' orphans, one hundred day scholars, one hundred natives, in the free or charity school; in fact, four hundred annually pass through: they have married ninety-eight of their pupils well, and I saw one happy bride, two days married, in her white wedding-dress. The greatest trial to the nuns is to get the soldiers' orphans not to be ashamed of honest work. They cannot understand that white people must work as well as black, and that should they go home their position will not be so good as in India. The Reverend Mother asked me to address a few words to the school, which I did with much pleasure; I tried to explain their folly to them, and the stake they would find it in after life. It was just the same with the children in Syria; after they have received some education, the first impression always is that they are too good to work, and that their parents, who cannot read, must wait upon them.

We made all ready for departure for the Nizam's territory that evening, and before starting dined with Lord Mark Kerr, Lady Agnes Danyell, Major Kerr, Major Hume, Mr. Danyell, and others; and went off to the station, where we met Mr. and Mrs. Norman, who travelled a little way with us.

CHAPTER VI.

THE JOURNEY TO HYDERABAD IN THE DECCAN.

THE train left at nine o'clock. In the night we passed Soonee, Ooroolee, Kheirgaum, Patus, Dhond, Deeksal, Bheegwan, Poomulwaree, Schwoor, Keim, Barsee Road, Marheh, Unger, Mohol, Packney, Sholapoor, Hoodgee. The first station I was conscious of passing, having slept like a top, was Kurrubgaum, at 5.59 a.m., on the morning of the 28th. I give the names of the stations because it shows a reader on the map, or reminds one who knows India, what country we passed through. We then passed Doodneh, Goodoor, Goolburga, and then Shahabad. There we changed the G. I. P., or Great Indian Peninsula, for the Nizam's State Railway, and passed an hour at this station; and very pretty it is, full of plants, flowers, and gardens, cultivated with taste and care. After Shahabad the stations were Wadi Junction, Chitapore, Seram, Hepore, Tandur, Dharur, Illampallee, Pattapore, Singampallee, and Hyderabad at 5.33. The train was slow, but safe and comfortable, with all possible comforts and accommodation, washing places, couches, and comfortable cushions. The greater part of the journey was over a broad plain or prairie: it is too undulating and cultivated to be called a desert. At 7.30 in the morning we passed through a green palm grove, where is a village that looks like an old castle, with walls in ruins. The country seemed a very gradual ascent, and full of flocks. One striking object was a curious grey old temple, a solitary cupola, with walls and battlements on a rising ground. There were domed mosques everywhere amongst the trees. I was struck by the villages and towns being so like Syria, only the plain was greener.

Shahabad, a large station, was very pretty.: it was our last before entering the Nizam's territory and railway. The change impressed me in favour of the Nizam's Government: ours looked poor and taxed; that of the Nizam comfortable and prosperous. I regret to say that this is the case throughout the part of India which we visited. Mr. Hyndman has lately startled the India House by his shocking details concerning the semi-starvation of India. In English society people say, "Nonsense! India poor! why, it was never richer." But this certainly will be altered and remedied as soon as it is made known. I am John Bull enough to believe that England never sins with her eyes open.

This part of independent India is full of Moslem villages, fortified towers, pretty stations, and neat buildings. I saw an old bit of rail hung up to serve as a gong. The conductor told us that the heat in a month or two will be unbearable, but that it is a charming line in the cold season. We passed a splendid avenue of tamarind trees at ten o'clock. This would be a capital hunting country, but a fox would have no chance. We seemed to pass various features in each different few hours; for instance, the tamarind country at ten o'clock; then we changed for yellow broom, tall trees lining the railway, not furze or bush as in England; then came jungle, which reminded me of a very poor Brazilian wood. At 1.45 we were amongst yellow magnolias and red silk-cotton trees, showing well against dark myrtle green, and many a new bird, tree, and plant, also cattle and fields. At 4.45 all this changed to a strange formation, an outcrop of huge granite boulders, which look as if arranged by art, but it is wild Nature. It is like an ancient town with battlements and castles, and this extends all over the country an hour's rail before reaching Hyderabad, and covers a radius of thirty miles round that City, like natural defences.

Hyderabad lies 1800 feet above sea level. By far the largest and most important Native State in India is that ruled over by our faithful ally, the Nizam. It is the Moghul Subah (Viceroyalty) of the Deccan. It was founded by Asaf Jah, a son of one of Aurangzeb's officers, who after a long life of political intrigue at Delhi, established his independent power as Subedar of the Deccan in 1724, with Hyderabad, on a tributary of the river Krishna, as his Capital. The present army numbers about 30,000 men, chiefly Cavalry, of whom 600 are Arabs. The area is almost 95,337 square miles, and the population is about 11,000,000. Major and Mrs. Nevill, our kind hosts, met us cordially at the station. He is the English officer who commands the Nizam's troops, and though he ranks as Major, is really Commander-in-Chief, having no one over him excepting Sir Salar Jung.

Whilst we were at Hyderabad, we jotted down the following notes together, upon railway travelling in India. It may not be uninteresting to some, and others may skip it, and go on with my story.

The British public, whose ideas about India are even less formed than about all other Colonies, is gradually learning that Aryavarrtá—the Land of Men as opposed to that tenanted by us "missing links"—is a big word. Formerly when you sailed Bombaywards, you received a multitude of introductory letters to, and commissions for, Calcutta and Delhi, Madras and Bangalore. During the Crimean war "Indian officers" were appointed to the Turkish Contingent and the Bashi Buzuks *because*, knowing India, they must know Turkey. I need hardly say that a career of commanding Hindús and Hindís (Moslems) was rather a disadvantageous education for commanding Ottomans. So also when Sir William F. Williams, of Kars, stood up in the House of Commons to speak upon a Chinese question, and declared that a long service in Asia Minor entitled him to form an independent opinion concerning the "Flowery Land," Mr. Bernal Osborne groaned out, *magno cum risu audentium*—"Oh, the Fall of Kars!" Whereupon "Kars" fell, never to rise again.

We now know, even at home, that India is not a country, but a continent. It contains as many races as the whole of Europe: here we have the Jángali or wild men; the Dravidians or old Turanian immigration; the pure Aryans from Persia, as the Nágar Brahman; the vast variety of mixed breeds between Dravidian and Aryan, such as the Telinga Brahman; and, besides these four great families, a number of intrusive peoples, Christians from Chaldea and Portugal; Jews, white and black; Rohillas ("hill-peoples") from the Afghan Mountains; Sidis (Wásawáhili) from Zanzibar; and Arabs, pure or mixed, the latter showing its type in the Mapillahs (Moplahs) of Malabar. After all, in Europe there are only three; the great Slav race, occupying the Eastern half of the Continent; the Scandinavo-Teuton; and the Græco-Latin races. Europe also speaks three great forms of language; here we have the three, Semitic, Hamitic, and Japhetic or Turanian, with some thirty modifications of the Prakrit, which in the hands of the literati, became, like the modern Greek spoken at Athens, the Sanskrit or finished speech. It was the same with the *Latina Rustica,* not the language of Virgil and Cicero, but the quaint country tongues which branched off into the neo-Latin family.

Again, the climate of India has a far wider range than that of Europe, even if we throw into the latter Iceland and Spitzbergen. The west regions of the mighty Himalayas, the "Homes of Snow," represent the Polar regions; and we run through the Temperates into the Tropical, or rather the Equinoctial, about Ceylon. And what a richness and diversity of productions in the animal, the vegetable, and the mineral worlds, compared with the poor produce of the temperate regions! What untold wealth still hidden in the soil, and awaiting the skill and energy of the nineteenth century! What a grand field for exploration and discovery! Dr. de Marchesetti, a young Italian botanist from Trieste, assures us that the fungi, one of the most interesting families of plants, have hardly been studied at all. And how much remains for us to learn; for instance, no sword-cutter in Europe can tell you anything about the steel which makes the far-famed Khorásáni blades, miscalled "Damascus;" and the diamantiferous regions between the valleys of the Ganges and the Krishna, are in great part unexplored ground.

But at this rate I shall never reach the G. I. P. R. We begin by observing that the *affiche* at the hotel, "Madras time is thirty minutes in advance of Bombay time," may be intelligible, but is not generally understood. All assured us that 2.30 p.m. at Madras meant three o'clock here; whereas practical experience showed us that it represents two p.m. at Bombay. It may also be wise to assume Madras time as the mean between that of Bombay and Calcutta; but railways are powerful, and confusion results. Poonah time is nearly that of Frere Town and Sassoon Town: but at Hyderabad (Deccan), when an hour is named, you must ask if it be railway time or Hyderabad time, a difference of nineteen minutes.

We had heard the G. I. P. Railway highly spoken of as the most finished in India, and therefore we scrutinised it somewhat carefully and critically. The Bombay station must be only provisional: no country-town of any importance in Europe would content itself with such a hovel; and the peel of plantains and oranges scattered about the table of the first-class waiting-rooms, suggested that the station-master requires an increase of staff, and the stations generally the eye of the travelling director. With a few exceptions near the Presidency, they have no sheds to keep off the burning sun from the standing train: yet a tiled roof like that of Karjat, or a corrugated metal *hangar*, as at Khandalla, would not be a ruinous expense. As it is, the want gives the whole line an unfinished aspect, to be compared only with the Suez Canal. At the minor stations the basins are rarely clean; the tea is a decoction of tannin; the native buffet-waiters are often "grasp-alls," and the Goanese waiters are not so civil as they might be. *En revanche* the station gardens are neat and pretty, a pleasure for the eye to dwell upon. The European station-masters and guards are exceptionally obliging, and render a journey as happy and pleasant as they can; they seem to belong to a higher class than those at home; "tipping" is unknown, and perhaps the habit of dealing in rupees instead of shillings has raised them in the social scale. But the driving between Poonah and Shahabad is, without exception, the worst I have ever experienced; you start with a jerk which, at night, almost flings you off your improvised bed. There is, it need hardly be said, as much difference in driving an engine as in tooling a four-in-hand; and in the former care and attention at the start are particularly required. Again, it is almost impossible to write in the train, a sure sign that something is wrong, probably in the coupling chains. Beyond Raichor, I am assured, all runs smoothly.

The waggon-carriages must also be provisional. They have double roofs, but no flying roofs with a draught of air all round as in Brazil. Sleeping-cars are not wanted, we are told, because the seats draw out; this, however, is not the case with all, and lying upon the sofa is like resting on a knife-board. At this season we require little defence against the hot winds of the Deccan, but apparently no efficient cooling system has as yet been invented. The ventilators do little in the way of ventilation. The wet *tatties* to windward dry after a few minutes. The *pankah* merely agitates the furnace-blast. The water-wheel below the floor is apt to get out of order. Finally, the water-basins and the other offices attached to the waggons, are highly convenient, but too often the tubes strike work.

Coming to the Nizam's State Railway, between the G. I. P. station Shahabad *viâ* Wadi junction, we find Madras time in advance, not thirty but fifteen minutes. Here the evils of the main trunk line are exaggerated. The stations are palaces, yet totally lacking shelter from the sun. The names are not yet written upon them; and there is abundant want of finish. Briefly, the whole affair shows an enormous expenditure, much of it, apparently, spent in the wrong direction.

As far as Poonah the trip is interesting enough, especially if you visit Mátherán and the Karla caves. After escaping from Bombay and Salsette Islands, which are in rapid process of being buckled to, of becoming one ground, you skirt the picturesque peaks and tables of the modern sanitarium; Chandora, the sharp little spur to the left of flat-topped Bháo Mallang, *alias* the Queen of Maharatta's throne; the haystacks of Mátherán and Prabál, the latter infamous for shutting out the sea-breeze; the "False Funnel," very like the "old man of Hoy" in romantic Orcades; and the "True Funnel," or Karnali, useful as a landmark to sailors clearing the South-Western Prong. Were these bold and fretted outlines of the Western Gháts placed a few miles nearer its head, Mumbadevi Bay would rank high amongst the conventional bay beauties of the world,—Spezzia and Dublin, Naples and the Cove of Cork, Fiume and New York, Rio de Janeiro and Bahia (de Todos os Santos), Bantry Bay, Port Jackson, and Sydney. But then the atmosphere would also require alteration: at this season dust and 'smokes" hardly ever allow a clear horizon.

Let me also note another change, which may now be ripening in the womb of time. Bombay wants an Alpine Club. She has Peaks and Passes enough, yet who has ever ascended and investigated them? Badminton is good, so are rackets, so is cricket, so is polo, but none equal the climb in mountain air. Possibly some future Home Government, liberal but not *Liberal*, may relax the extreme strain of official labour, and allow its leisureless servants some spare time for literature, Alpine work, and Shikár. The latter is fast waxing obsolete; who now takes the place of Colonel Shakespear (the "old Shikári"), Colonel Campbell (the "old Forest Ranger"), Colonel Rice (the *Chasseur du Tigre*), and Colonel Marston, who has polished off half the game in Sind?

The ascent of the Bhore Ghát is picturesque when seen for the first time; a second view makes the "Indian Semmering" appear somewhat monotonous. However, the G. I. P. Railway Company has done its best by attaching passenger-breaks to the rear of the train; and the conductor, an old soldier, is thoroughly well up in all the details, and obliging as he is locally learned. Of Karla I will say nothing, except that the ascent to the caves is in a shameful state, when a few hundred rupees would make a decent road; and that a *Pattewála* or two should be stationed there to keep off the self-constituted *ciceroni*, the peasants of Vehar, the little village below, who are a bore. Better to charge a shilling for entrance, if money be scarce.

There is little to detain the traveller at Kharki (Kirkee) except to sketch that caricature, the Ganesh-Khind (cleft of Ganesha), and note that the guns and gunnery are admirably exposed to a *coup de main*. At Poonah one visits the stock sights: the Parbati hill, or Acropolis; the historic Sangam, and the native town with its Budhwara, the Peshwa palace, and the house of Nana Pharnavis, "the Indian Machiavel." The new lines beat hollow the proverbially "magnificent distances" of Washington. They give you a mild idea of infinity in space. Look at "Lothian Road," broad enough for Xerxes to march his host, with a dwarfed bit of building at either end, and a scatter of bungalows on both sides, the whole like a skeleton of Rio de Janeiro or Bahia.

On the other hand, the Kharekwasla Tank and the noble dam, built by Mr. Joyner, C.E., are well worth visiting, both on account of the intrinsic excellence of the work, and the great consequences to which such works must lead. It not only supplies the "Monsoon Capital" of the Bombay Presidency, but it will diffuse life and plenty over some ninety linear miles of now waste ground. Travelling from Poonah to Hyderabad, you remark that the land at this season is mostly fit only for the traditional dragon and wild ass; it is, like Sind, a cross between an oven and a dust-bin. Yet where the smallest rill flows, all is life and verdure; the emerald-green topes, and the leek-green paddy fields, are a repose to the sight, a "coolness to the eye," as the Arabs say; and you hasten to plunge that hot and weary organ into the damp lush vegetation of orchard, and field, and kitchen-gardens. The first step will be to supply water, as Mr. Joyner is doing; the second, to regulate its use. Here the golden fluid is wasted in a way which would scandalize the Arab, the Egyptian, the Sindi, and the "Heathen Chinee."

And this leads us to notice another popular error which has gained possession of the British brain. Certain statistics, which may be correct, have taught it that India is an overcrowded land, and that its population per square mile, exceeding that of England, approaches that of Belgium. This, as with all statistics, is both true and untrue. Parts of Bengal, for instance, teem with human life; and as native wars are no more, and famines are to be turned, regardless of expense, into plenty, or rather profusion, the peasantry will end, in Caffre phrase, with "eating one another up." For note that the true cause of Indian famines is concealed from England. There is plenty of provision. There is an abundance of transport. But the people are so penniless that when grain rises one penny a pound, they must live on wild roots or starve.

The statement that India is overcrowded is utterly misleading as regards the whole of India. Throughout the peninsula the lands are of three kinds, not including the jungles and forests, which cannot be touched without danger of diminishing the rain supply. There are the fertile, as Gujerat; the wholly desert, mostly sandy and stony tracks; and the half-desert, which grows luxuriant crops only during the rains. And the latter are so extensive that with irrigation they would support at least treble the actual number of inhabitants.

India, then, has more than one string to her bow: she will dispose of her increasing millions in three ways. Firstly, she will keep them at home and feed them by irrigation which costs much, gives slow profits, but ends by being the best of investments. Secondly, she will export them to our other colonies, where labour is so much wanted, and where, as free hands, they will take the place of our old friend, the "a'mighty nigger." Sind, I need hardly tell you, calls aloud for them, and can offer the richest of soils. Thirdly, she will retrench her useless expenditure; abolish a host of local Governors who should be Secretaries; of Commanders-in-Chief who should be Major-Generals; and of Members of Council whose chief work is to spoil foolscap. Lastly, she will become a manufacturing country. She has coal and iron; she breeds millions of human beings, hireable at sixpence a day; her men can mine, and her women and children can work at *la petite industrie.* Despite the "mildew" with which mildewed Manchester, *pace* Mr. E. Ashworth, is attempting to inoculate India; despite the timidity of statesmen, and despite the jealousy of the manufacturing mob, which wishes to buy dirt-cheap from India, and to make her pay 100 per cent. for working her own produce, we have a conviction, as we have before said, that Indian manufactures will succeed; and that Great Britain, with one foot on Hindostan and another in China, whose three hundred millions work at threepence a day, will command the wool and cotton markets of the world, and will become the greatest producing power that the globe ever bore.

Let me end this long sermon with a short comparison of a railway station village and a Hindú hamlet, dating long before the days of the iron road. Our types shall be Lanauli, whose name does not even appear in Murray's Handbook for India (1859), and Walwán, the old settlement on the great traffic road to Poonah, distant about a musket-shot from its younger brother.

Lanauli is a place of some importance, being the locomotive station at the head of the Bhore Ghát, whilst the site upon the edge of the Sahyadri Range, renders it tolerably healthy for the Europeans. Consequently, where a few huts formerly rose, the place now contains some two hundred pale faces. I saw with immense satisfaction fifty-three men of the new Railway Volunteer Corps, which numbers a total of one hundred and fourteen, being drilled by a red-coated sergeant, under the eye of Captain Buckley. This is truly a patriotic movement, and one which may prove far more important than we expect in these days, when the native powers have armies far exceeding our own in numbers. There is hardly an "Indian officer" who does not expect another "Sepoy Mutiny" within ten years, and yet we do little to prepare for it. Were I Viceroy every station should have its cannon-armed and casemated place of refuge.

The long walls of the ill-laid-out, inconvenient station, stretch from east to west. They contain the usual conveniences of one at home; and the only novelties are the parts allotted to native travellers, the facilities for ablution, and the refreshment of fruits and sugar-cane for the herd, which is penned up in its two-storied waggons, like a flock of sheep, and which seems to use only one word of its own language—*Pâni* (water).

The station divides the settlement into two. The southern half is the native town and bazar, also the Roman Catholic Church. Europe lies to the north, beginning with the neat, stiff bungalows, whose gardens suggest those of Clapham Junction, tenanted by the humbler *employés*. My only objection to them is the corrugated metal roof, which is hot in hot weather, cold in cold, damp in damp, dry in dry, and generally unwholesome, unless covered with thatch. Then, detached to the west, come the scattered necessaries of an Anglo-Indian station, all surrounded by "compounds," whose low walls enclose nothing worth enclosing. The items are the English Church, of course Gothic; the Methodist Chapel prefers the east end, and thus the various sects separate to three of the four cardinal points; the little Post Office; the Hospital and the "pukka" stone-built house of the Hindu Contractor; the Dharmsala, or Native Travellers' Bungalow, and the "Lanauli Hotel," two detached bungalows kept by Mr. (Parsee) Ardashir Merwanjee. The servants are rather a rough lot; the doors do not shut, and the locks are torn off, which somehow or other prevents one feeling quite at home in one's inn: but the owner is civil, and the charges are not exorbitant. Lastly, in aristocratic seclusion, far to the north, removed from the daily and nightly roar, whistle, and sniff of the engine, and sheltered by magnificent "topes," especially mangoes, whose fruit is not worthy of its outer show, lie the whitewashed bungalows of the Chief Officers. Lanauli has its season, as if it were in Dover or Scarborough, for here the Balaghat region enjoys the benefit of the sea breeze.

Walwán, lying upon a highway, is hardly a fair specimen of the average native villages. To see these in perfection you should visit the out-of-the-way parts of Gujerat or Kutch. As in the mining settlements of Brazil, Walwán (mentioned by Murray) consists mainly of one long line of tenements along the road, doubtless so placed for the convenience of selling and buying. The suburbs are *Jhompris* (hovels) of torn matting and ragged leaf-thatch, while here and there a big well, with wheel or log, spreads an emerald patch over the golden stubbles. The "High Street" shows wattle-and-dab houses, and the usual shady verandahs of the "native town," porches supported on posts, with or without carved corbels; while the neat bazar, under the charge of crummy Banyans, occupies the post of honour in the centre. Flags, grain-baskets, and straw-stacks raised above ground, are attached to the houses and the courts. The east end is the religious part of the hamlet, the residence of the Brahmin and of the Ramosi, who has planted a few stems of tobacco along his wall. Here lies the great tank, stone revetted during its palmy days; the masonry, however, in most places has now given way to mud. Here the women of the village gossip and draw water, and here the juvenile population gathers to chaff and jeer the passing stranger. The sheet of water is girt by the tallest trees, chiefly figs, the mandrukh, and the gullar, whose fruit is relished by monkeys; and under the spreading canopy rises the whitewashed Tulsi altar, and another of cut basalt, with two steps, four horns like the classical forms of Greece and Rome, and the vermilioned tablet which bears the alt-relief of the god.

You will rarely pass through Walwán and its congeners, between six a.m. and noontide, without seeing a string of Brinjaris carrying down grain to the coast or salt into the interior on their padded oxen, which straggle about at the rate of two miles an hour. Each caravan is under a Naik, and evidently these people are of many castes; some wear the Janeo (thread of the twice-born), others do not; the former refuse to touch meat, which is not forbidden to the latter. Much has been written about the women and the three breeds of dogs, but I shrewdly suspect that much more remains to be written. Generally the Brinjaris have been identified, as also have been the "Nats" or "Naths," with the Gipsies, to whom they bear a superficial resemblance. This is a mere mistake; the Romani are an Indine people, from the great Valley of the Indus. My husband settled this question as early as 1849.

Finally, the characteristic odour of Lanauli is coal; that of Walwán a mixture of spices, strong smelling flowers, at times roast Hindú, and always "gobar," which the Americans of the Far West call "buffalo chips." There we have the symbol of European restlessness, the voice of the steam-engine; here morning opens with the chattering of human beings, the cries of the crows, and the chirping of birds, while sunset ushers in a dead silence as of the grave.

A FIGHTING ELEPHANT.

CHAPTER VII.

HYDERABAD IN THE DECCAN.

OUR first visit, *en route* to Major Nevill's bungalow, was to the beautiful public garden called the Nizam's, where the military band was playing. Our charming quarters were rooms in Major Nevill's "compound," divided into sleeping and bath-room, and tents thrown out from either entrance, the front opening to the garden. Two servants, one man and one woman, were placed at our disposal; in short, nothing was wanting to perfect hospitality. We had to dress quickly, as that evening there was a dinner-party given to the 16th Lancers, and a ball at Sir Richard and Lady Meade's. Government House has a splendid frontage, like the Madeleine (a couple of stone lions at the entrance), a grand staircase, and hall. It was an exceedingly gay ball, and the Governor and Lady Meade are charming: he a straightforward, honest, manly English gentleman, and she a soft, pretty, lady-like, merry wife.

29*th.*—Next morning we were up early, and out on elephants, to see the town. These beasts look very imposing when they are in large numbers, with gaudy trappings; but the first mounting and the curious motion are decidedly new sensations. We went all through the City unarmed and without guards, and met with nothing but greetings and blessings. I mention this because everyone knows what a bad name Hyderabad has, or had. The horses are good country-bred, and show blood: they are frightened of elephants, and "shy" to avoid them. You see everywhere wild-looking men in gaudy dresses, and unveiled women. The very great "swells" have troops of men before and behind with drawn swords; everything is on the old feudal system. You will meet with many a brown Noble, riding with troops of retainers in white burnous, carrying the arms and wearing the uniform of their Chiefs. The houses are flat, like those at Damascus. The town is clean; in spite of open drains I only smelt a bad smell three times in ten days: I wish I could say the same of my beloved Trieste. The streets are broad, and spanned by high arches, whose bold simplicity is very striking. The Nizam's palace, at least a mile long, is carved with delicate tracery; and many a mosque, like lace work, rises here and there, but the *cachet* of all in Hyderabad, is size, boldness, and simplicity.

After going over the town, we proceeded to the palace of His Excellency Mookhtar ool Moolk, Sir Salar Jung, G.C.S.I., called till lately the "wily minister" in our papers. He is a noble, chivalrous, single-hearted Arab gentleman, of the very best stamp. His palace contains about seven courts, with fountains, and various suites of large halls opening on to them: it is perfectly magnificent. But, unfortunately, instead of being furnished with Oriental luxury, which is so graceful, so rich, and characteristic, it was full of European stuffs, glass, porcelain, and bad pictures, which they value as we do *their* things. One room, however, was unique, the ceiling and walls being thickly studded with china (cups, saucers, plates, etc.), and would have been an envy to fanciers and collectors in London. After a luxurious breakfast of European and Eastern dishes, and wine for us, but water for himself and party, our host showed us his weapons, swords, and daggers, and many arms I had never seen before, all with beautiful blades, inlaid sheaths, and covered with gorgeous jewels. I forgot to mention that the party consisted, besides Sir Salar Jung and ourselves, of his two sons; the youngest, whose *sobriquet* was the "Fox," took my fancy exceedingly; he was about ten, very serious looking, as sharp as a needle, and full of courage and spirit. The others were all ministers, the cousin, the brother-in-law, the Persian Secretary, and the Private Secretary of our host. We then went to the stables, a place like the Burlington Arcade, open at both ends, and loose boxes where the shops would be, each opening into the passage running down the centre. There are about one hundred horses, and every horse has its own groom, nearly all thoroughbred Arabs and Persians; "blue" and "red" being the favourite colours, which means the same as our grey and light bay. On returning we were each presented with four bottles of ottar of roses, and Sir Salar bade us adieu near the carriage which took us away.

In the evening was a dinner party at the Residency, given by Sir Richard and Lady Meade to Sir Salar Jung and ministers, to which we were also invited.

March 1*st,* Ash Wednesday.—I was not allowed to go to Mass (there is a little Catholic Chapel), because of the cholera. There are about thirty cases a day, and I should have to pass through the most dangerous part to get to church. Sir Salar Jung lent me a beautiful grey Arab, large, powerful, and showy. He had never before had a side-saddle on, but did not seem to mind it after a bit. Mrs. Nevill, the eldest daughter of our talented and lamented predecessor, Charles Lever, the celebrated novelist, who is a perfect horsewoman, accompanied me. She had broken in four thoroughbreds for her husband and herself during the short time she had been there. We enjoyed our ride very much.

In the evening there was another dinner-party at Major Nevill's.

2*nd.*—We breakfasted with Sir Salar Jung and the officers of the 44th, who arrived on troops of elephants with scarlet trappings.

We drove to the tomb of General Raymond, a French General who once commanded the Nizam's forces: he is now called Shah Rahman, and is made a saint of. There is a saint or fakir's tomb, by name Ujala-Shah-Ká Dargah, called by the English "Johnny Shaw's" grave, situated amongst, and near a group of, lovely little temples that you would like to put under a glass case on the drawing-room table.

The day finished by a dinner-party and a "little music" at Lady Meade's in the evening.

3rd.—We started very early to visit the Tank Mir Alam, a lake dammed up by a "band." It is one big horseshoe, divided into twenty-two segments. The water is forty-five feet deep, and full of fish: the banks are covered with huge boulders: the sloping borders are groves of young palms; under the surface was once a garden, and the fish-hawk watches his prey from the top of the half sunk Masjid or the Hindú Temple. Under some trees ashore is a natural spring, whose water is kept for the Nizam; and not far is a beautiful height crowned by a castle and mosque, belonging to Mir Mahbub, who was a dervish or fakir.

After some early hours in a boat, we drove to the palace of the Wikar Shums ool Umárá, K.C.S.I., one of the three great dignitaries of the Nizam's country. We were received by a guard of soldiers and a band of music; and the secretaries ushered us up into a splendid palace, perhaps the finest we have seen; but here also, alas! we found gaudy European furniture, cheap glass and china, and pictures worth a couple of francs. Everything else was *splendid.* The Chief is a thin, small, well-bred old gentleman, in a yellow silk robe, and a necklace of large emeralds. He was attended by a fat, jolly son, in a green velvet dressing-gown; and one tall, thin, sallow-faced youth, who looked like a bird with the "pip," which I was told was meant for dignity, he having married the late Nizam's daughter. We were taken to a room to wash our hands, where I actually found powder for the face, and puff, as carefully provided as in Paris. We had a capital breakfast: the cooking was delicious. The hall was full of retainers and servants, who pressed me to eat as they served the dishes; and "Take mutton cutlet: 'im very good," was whispered close to my ear with an excellent English accent.

We then visited the jewellery, a perfect Catharine-wheel of diamonds, Geneva musical boxes, with birds jumping out to sing, mechanical toys of monkeys pulling out each other's teeth, and Punch rolling a barrel. Then came, far more interesting, the weapons,—shields, inlaid with gold; and a coat of mail belonging to our host's great-grandfather, every link and every ring containing an engraved verse of the Koran.

This was sacred armour, and a warrior was supposed to be invincible in it. Then there was a beautiful lance, well balanced, whose point was shaped like a flame. There was every sort of gun, sword, and dagger, with jewelled inlaid hilts, and often dangling pearls and emeralds attached to them. Quite at the top of the palace is a very large room, with windows to the four quarters, and here the eye commands the country for forty miles round. At last we saw something very unique and *bizarre*—an ostrich race. The man mounts, sits back, puts his legs under the wings, and locks his feet under the breast. The birds go at an awful pace, and kick like a horse.

Towards the cool of the evening there was a garden-party at Lady Meade's, with lawn-tennis, badminton, and refreshments. I was shocked to see European ladies sitting in rows, and Lady Meade walking down the rows to present her husband, the Governor, Sir R. Meade, to those ladies, or those ladies to him, I should say; and they all kept their seats, whilst the host and hostess stood before them, and only acknowledged this gracious courtesy by a very stiff motion of the head. I suppose it was meant for a dignified bow, and I said to myself, "Are these Indian manners? and if so, what a hard time Excellencies must have of it." The only one whose natural instincts gave her the habits of society was a little French governess, who immediately sprang to her feet, and with a graceful bow, and a few pretty words, acknowledged the compliment paid by the personages representing Her Majesty.

I wish some of these Indian military ladies could know what an effect their manners produce upon one for coarseness and arrogance when they come to Europe. Of course those who are in high military position in India, and are in society in England, will know what I mean, and will have experienced the same amusement or disgust. I could tell some good stories on the subject, but it would not be good-natured.

There was a dinner-party given that evening by Major Nevill to his native officers, Sayyid Ahmad and Ahmad Abdullah being the two nicest; they are Arab descendants of Anazeh (Bedawin), and Sayyids (Prophet's race).

There are two parties in India on a certain question, the treatment of the Native. One is all for keeping him down and treating him harshly; the other condemns this, and wants to make him on an equality. Neither party actually mix freely with the native, and the native says, "The English are just, but they are not kind,"—and that's about the truth. I have no right to offer an opinion,—I was only a few months in India,—but I have experience in other lands, where the natives are brown and black, and I think neither are right (I speak, of course, not of us individually, but as a nation). I think we have vulgar manners and weak policy; in other words, we want more polish and more firmness. It would be a good thing if we could send those officers and *employés* who are destined to serve in countries we want to maintain, to learn the politeness of foreign courts first.

I have frequently remarked the courtesy, delicacy, and civility of a high-class native, to Brown, Jones, and Robinson of ours. I have seen them apply to that native for everything they want; use all his benefits, his carriages, horses, anything; accept all his gifts and pretty attentions, take them as a matter of course, because Brown, Jones, and Robinson happen to be white, and the native black, and then on the first possible occasion ignore him, snub him, or refuse him harshly any little request. Further, I have heard of the highest-born natives being obliged to stop their carriages, and get out, and stand aside on the road whilst Mrs. Brown, Jones, and Robinson swept by in their carriages, not even deigning a bow of recognition for the extreme civility. And yet we wonder we are not loved. I should like to know who would make way for Mrs. Brown, Jones, and Robinson in "Dear old England;" and whether they would not be too happy to get an invitation to any of the balls given to meet one of those black Highnesses by the "Upper Ten" in London?

Do not let me confuse the idea. I am all for firmness; and what *has* to be done, should be done with a hand that never relaxes; but we should be kind and courteous too; and I am certain that if we *were*, we should never want *force*. It is the gulf that hinders all good, and breeds all evil feeling; and such English people as I have generally described, do everything to widen it.

With regard to the reports about Hyderabad, I can only say that we sleep in open tents, and have never missed anything. We have no arms, no guards, only because they are not necessary. I cannot say how much the Court felt not receiving a visit from the Prince of Wales. They said, "The very fact of his being our guest would make him sacred; but in *his* case his life would be dearer to us than our own." We were all sorry: it was quite one of the most interesting things to see in India, and H.R.H. could not have failed to have been pleased.

Our next pleasure was an Assault of Arms. There were about two hundred performers, and three hundred to look at them. There was no keeping the ground; they broke Major Nevill's flower-pots and trees. There were some very good gymnastics, sword exercises, single stick with small shields that were soft and about the size of a plate. Their actions were wild and graceful, with something of the tiger in their defiant gestures. An old man performed wonderful *tours de force* for his age, and there was emulation even amongst the children; every youth, wild to win his spurs, sprang into the arena to perform, thereby hindering one another, but without the slightest ill-temper. We thanked them all before leaving.

They also showed us some cock-fighting, and indeed all sorts of fighting. They fight every kind of animal, goats, birds, even quails and larks, which are very plucky, and *want* to fight, but they pull them off when they ill-use one another too much. I did not care to see this, and went away.

There was a dinner party of European ladies in the evening.

Next day we drove to the country palace of the Amir el Kebir. There are three great men in Hyderabad who jointly manage the Nizam's affairs: Sir Salar Jung is Regent and Prime Minister, the Amir el Kebir is co-Regent and Minister of Justice, the Wikar ool Umárá is his brother, and they are all relations of the Nizam. The palace was a succession of beautiful buildings in gardens, full of storks, pigeons, and other birds. They made the pigeons giddy by shaking them, and then they turned head-over-heels for ever so long; but that did not please me much, as I should not like it to be done to me, and I always consider animals in the same way. It is not from a morbid or sickly disposition, but an acute sense of justice and fair play, and a horror of cruel tyranny or oppression to what is weak and miserable. I do not mind seeing men fight, nor yet beasts, *if they do it of their own accord;* but I object to their being "*set on*" at one another, and *forced* to fight *whether they like it or not;* and the contempt instead of pity for the weaker side I cannot understand. Besides birds there were flowers, and all the gardens and terraces were covered with that beautiful purple Indian honeysuckle which I have before mentioned. In the palace was the usual defect, a profusion of singing clocks, mechanical pictures, toys, and model wax-fruit under glass cases from Europe. We rode each on a separate elephant, and went once more through the town, and visited the Masjid (Mosque) el Mekkah, the main street, and the wonderful arches, and kindly words and blessings greeted us on every side. We then went back to breakfast with the Amir; and a charming breakfast it was, with delicious mangoes. Our host wore a lovely cashmere robe like a dressing-gown, and gorgeous jewels.

Our last recollections of Hyderabad are brilliant, for Sir Salar Jung gave a magnificent evening *fête*, which I have never seen equalled. One of the large courts of the palace is a quadrangle, the centre of which is occupied by a huge basin or tank of water as big as a small lake, and full of fountains. The *salámliks* all open out into it with flights of marble stairs. The starlight was above us, but a blaze of wax lights and chandeliers lit up every hall, and coloured lamps and flowers spangled the whole centre. The company consisted of the Nizam's court and ministers, and about thirty-six picked Europeans. First there was a Nautch, which was stupid, as the girls really did nothing but eat sweetmeats, and occasionally run forward and twirl round for an instant, twisting their hands and feet, with a self-conscious, half bold, half *mauvaise honte* look, and only one was barely good-looking. Perhaps that is the Nautch to dance before ladies; but in Syria they are much better, without being "shocking." A beautiful dinner of about fifty-six covers was then served in the principal *salámlik* by retainers in wild, picturesque costumes. The band played, we walked about and conversed, were presented with ottar of roses, and went home. We regretted much to have been obliged to miss the following tempting invitation: "Reseldar Mohun Sing, and the native officers of H.H. the Nizam's 3rd Lancers, present their compliments to Captain and Mrs. Burton, and request the honour of their company at their Lines at Assuf Nagur on Wednesday, 8th March, at eight o'clock p.m., to witness their Holee Tamasha."

Next day we went to Secunderabad. It is a prosperous European station, with three regiments; some splendid old bungalows to be had for a mere song, as it has the bad reputation of being unhealthy. We saw the Indian bazar. There is a good parade and riding ground, with a sort of club or establishment, a few good shops, a burial ground, churches, and good roads, but it is not in the least interesting, and I would much rather live at Hyderabad.

We then went on elephants to Golconda, a most interesting place, about which there is much to say; but as no European has ever been permitted to enter it, and even Sir Salar Jung or the Nizam himself had never done so, we could not ask or hope for such a favour. This great event was to come off in a few months, when the Nizam would have attained the age permitted to visit Golconda.

I can only describe that which we were allowed to see. We viewed the town from outside, and saw a hill covered with buildings. The throne-hall, with arched windows, they say is a mere shell. The King's Palace and defences occupy the mound, which is in the midst of the town. The town is on the flat ground, is surrounded by walls, battlements, curtained bastions, and towers thrown out, and reminds one of old Damascus and Jerusalem; and in it dwells many an old feudal Chief. Past those walls no European nor Christian has ever been allowed. The Tombs of the Kings are very ancient, and are outside the town; to those we were admitted, and they reminded me of the Tower Tombs of Palmyra. Picture to yourself enormous domes, set on a square broad base, the upper section beautifully carved, or covered with Persian tiles, or tiles from Sind, which bear Arabic and Hindustani inscriptions. The lower part or entrance of one is arched, and supported by slender needle-like monolithic columns. Abdullah's and his mother's are the two best. Thanah Shah, the last King, was taken prisoner, so he is punished by having his tomb left in an unfinished state. There is a beautiful garden of palm trees, and a labyrinth of arches; we wandered about this romantic spot, of which we hear in the nursery tales as "all the *mines* and *riches* of Golconda,"—by a crescent moon, on a balmy night, the fireflies spangling the domed Tombs and the Palm Gardens. About a mile away we saw a mosque, built on a height, and on a corresponding height (at a distance) a palace, but both were more or less ruins.

As I found myself at such a pleasant hour surrounded by the romances of which I had so much read and heard, I could not forget that I was in the birthplace of the far-famed Koh-i-noor, whose history I gave to the *Morning Post*, September 28th, 1875. I would fain here reproduce my actual letter, the better to record the adventures of that stone to my readers.

SIR,—I brought out a book this season called "Inner Life of Syria." That book has met with a success which could not fail to gratify the most ambitious author, but especially a beginner like me. The reviewers have accorded me terms of praise far beyond my deserts. But they have had a duty to perform to their public, and though they have done it conscientiously, they have also, to their great honour, doubtless on account of my sex, handled my foibles (?) most tenderly and courteously. For this I thank them. The gem of my book, to which the rest is but a framework (to my thinking), is a Dream which fills the whole of Chapter XXVII.—some fifty pages. This is the raw which the press has been obliged, however delicately, to touch up. Some say I write like two persons, or with a double nature. Some say one thing, and some another, but all, thank God, give me credit for honesty, and they are right. It would surprise them to know how many persons who have read my book have come to me and said (privately, of course), "I am so thankful to find that some one else has dreams besides me; I often have them, but I should not dare to own it for fear of being thought foolish." Now I knew that it would be thought foolish, but I could not resist giving the public a specimen of those things to which I, amongst many, am subject. There is some excitement in not being believed when one is speaking the truth, and I am forced to cry with Galileo, "Eppur si muove." I have read my Dream over carefully, and I have now picked out what I conceive to be the silliest-sounding thing in it—the passage about the Koh-i-noor. I will reduce that to practical common sense, and I think that I could perform the same office, in course of time, for every line of my Dream. I must remark that when I dreamt and wrote in 1871 I was not aware that the Koh-i-noor had any history or antecedents, but as I dreamt so I wrote. Since my dream has been set before the public, one friend sent me "Rambles and Recollections of an Indian Official," by Lieutenant-Colonel Sleeman (1835), and another friend, who held a high post in Hyderabad, has given me a quantity of interesting information from various old Indian sources, relative to this wonderful ill-fated stone, now the property of our Crown.

Do you not see what a vein of Dreamland runs through our two inspired books, canonical and uncanonical—the Bible and Shakespeare? In the Bible everybody "dreams a dream," and these have become visions and revelations. Shakespeare meant the same thing when he said—

> "And therefore as a stranger give it welcome.
> There are more things in heaven and earth, Horatio,
> Than are dreamt of in your philosophy."

Do you believe that any one man, in one life, could have known so much of human passion if he had not been inspired by dreams? And do you believe that, because we have become a practical £ *s. d.* kind of people, there are no more dreams going about amongst the highly-wrought, nervous, sensitive exceptions, who live a higher kind of life? I do believe it; nay, I *know* it.

I will now give you the history of the Koh-i-noor, as I believe my dream was given me to do. I know how the English nation glory in the possession of the thing, simply because it is worth a million—how reluctantly they would part with it. I know they like a veil to be drawn over their hidden sores, and abhor the knife and cautery; therefore if I would contribute my mite to saving our country a disaster, I must do so at the risk of popularity. But if, after reading it, Englishmen agree with me, let me tell them that there are two ways of getting rid of it. To break it up, sell it, and give the proceeds to the poor would be the Eastern way of dispelling the ill luck. My way would be to sell it to Russia for less than its worth (£800,000), pass our ill luck on to our bugbear, and use the money to send our future King out to India as an Emperor should go. But it is not for me to suggest, but only to give its history.

The Koh-i-noor, or "Mountain of Light," is the largest and most celebrated diamond in the world, and is famous throughout the East as the "Accursed Stone" that brings misfortune and, eventually, destruction upon the dynasty of every successive possessor. In the East there is a belief as to good or evil fortune attending particular precious stones. It was the same in England in the reign of Elizabeth and the first James, and Shakespeare alludes to this belief in one of his minor poems, but the modern Englishman rejects the absurdity, despite the fact that evil fortune has actually always followed the owner of this particular gem, showing how curiously actual fact co-operates with superstitious theory.

The Koh-i-noor was first discovered in the mines of Golconda about A.D. 1650, and has cursed the world for two hundred and twenty-five years. The famous Mir Jumla was then farmer of the diamond mines, and the King's chief minister, a Persian who had been brought young to India, and who rose by rapid gradations to power, was famous for the sagacity of his plans and the ruthless cruelty with which he carried them out. The poor people under compulsory labour had to give their services for a bare subsistence to all the farmers of the mines, and under Mir Jumla their condition was desperate; this tempted them occasionally to elude the vigilance of their taskmaster and secrete a stone if they could. The cruelties that followed the smallest suspicion of such a fault rendered the mines a perpetual scene of horror, especially under Mir Jumla, and it is supposed that some frightful act of fiendish brutality occurred at the finding of the Koh-i-noor, which was cursed by the innocent victim—a curse which ever since, according to the natives of India, has remained attached to it and to its possessors.

Certain it is that before the King of Golconda had long been in possession of it he quarrelled with Mir Jumla, who in return treacherously invited the Mogul Emperor of Delhi, Aurungzeb, to invade his master's territory, promising to join him with the whole of the forces under his command. This he did, and the King of Golconda had to sue for peace, which was granted by Aurungzeb only on his giving him one of his daughters in marriage; making over to him a large portion of his treasures, including the Koh-i-noor, as well as a considerable slice of his territories; and consenting to hold the rest as a fief of the Great Mogul Empire. Some time after, the King of Golconda thought he saw a favourable opportunity to recover his territories, rose against his oppressor, and lost all the rest of his kingdom, nay, all that he possessed. Mir Jumla died a miserable death of disease in exile.

Aurungzeb, the second royal possessor of the Koh-i-noor, was at the time of getting it in the zenith of his power; but immediately trouble after trouble rained upon him, and accumulated till he died in 1707. After his death a war began amongst his progeny. The first who succeeded him, the third royal possessor of the Koh-i-noor, was Shah Alum, who died in 1712, five years after his succession. The next King of Delhi, the fourth possessor of the Koh-i-noor, was Jehander Shah, who was deposed and strangled at the end of one year (1713). Ferok Shah, the next in succession and fifth possessor of the Koh-i-noor, met the same fate in 1719, in the course of which year two other occupants of the throne (sixth and seventh possessors of the Koh-i-noor) passed in the same way thence to the grave.

So, in twelve years from the death of Aurungzeb, five princes of his line who had ascended the throne and possessed the Koh-i-noor, and six others who had been competitors for it, had come to grief. Moreover, the degraded state of the royal authority during this period had introduced an incurable anarchy, and a disposition in all the governors of provinces to shake off their dependency on the head of the Empire. The next King of Delhi, and eighth possessor of the Koh-i-noor, was the Emperor Mahmoud Shah, under whose reign the once great empire of Aurungzeb almost fell to pieces. He succeeded, in 1719, twelve years after the death of Aurungzeb, being the son of Akter, son of Shah Alum, the son and immediate successor of Aurungzeb,* and it was in 1739 that the final blow was given to his authority; his ill-fortune culminated in the capture of Delhi by the celebrated Nadir Shah, who in that year invaded India, and after defeating the army of Shah Mahmoud at Kurnaul, entered as conqueror into the capital. Then, in consequence of hostile acts of some of the people, he delivered over the whole city to massacre and pillage; and from the dawn of light till the day was far advanced, without regard for age or sex, all were put to the sword by his ferocious soldiery.

Fifty-eight days afterwards Nadir Shah commenced his march homewards, carrying with him treasure amounting to twenty millions sterling, jewels of enormous value, and the Koh-i-noor, which was considered by the Persian conqueror to be his greatest prize. Nadir Shah, ninth possessor of the Koh-i-noor, was no more fortunate with it than the previous owners had been, for shortly after his return to Persia, in the height of his glory, he was assassinated, leaving no heir to his kingdom; while Ahmed Abdallee, chief assassin, and once his trusted officer, went off, carrying with him most of Nadir Shah's treasure, and amongst

* Consequently great-grandson of Aurungzeb.

it the Koh-i-noor. He meant to found a kingdom for himself out of the territories now known as Afghanistan.

The dynasty which Abdallee, this tenth possessor of the Koh-i-noor, founded, having been crowned at Kandahar in the year 1747, met with the same fate that attended the dynasties of all the possessors of this celebrated stone. His son Timour, after a short and inglorious reign, left his throne to his eldest son Humayoon, twelfth possessor of the Koh-i-noor, who fell into the hands of his next brother, Zemaun Shah, by whom he was cruelly blinded, and rendered incapable of reigning. The same fate befell Zemaun Shah, the thirteenth possessor of the Koh-i-noor: he in turn fell into the hands of another brother, Mahmoud, who also put out his eyes and succeeded him; but who was in his turn soon conquered by another brother, Shah Shooja, our Afghan ally. This last did not long maintain his position, and, after various vicissitudes, fled to the Punjaub with his brother Zemaun Shah, carrying with them the Koh-i-noor, of which Shah Shooja was the fifteenth and last Mohammedan possessor. His fate is known to all who have heard or read the story of our fatal expedition to Cabul and its consequences, including Shah Shooja's end. Shah Shooja being now dependent on Runjeet Sing, the then sovereign of the Punjaub, for his very existence, soon found himself compelled to yield to the requirements of this powerful and most unscrupulous potentate, who insisted upon the Koh-i-noor being given up to him. The captive prince had no alternative, and yielded, when the great Sikh potentate became the sixteenth possessor of the Koh-i-noor.

At that time no native sovereign in India was so great as Runjeet, and no kingdom seemed more likely to last than the great Sikh monarchy he had founded, but by a curious coincidence the same ill fate that had always followed the possessor of the Koh-i-noor pursued it into this great family. Runjeet himself died, leaving the Koh-i-noor, which he valued at £1,000,000 sterling, to the priests of Jagannath (Juggernath); but it was preserved in the Lahore Treasury. Runjeet was succeeded in 1839 by his son Kurruck Sing, who was poisoned the following year. Before the funeral ceremonies were completed, his son was purposely killed by a falling archway. A competition for the throne (now vacant) ensued, between the widow of Kurruck Sing and a reputed son of Runjeet Sing, named Shere Sing, who, though born in wedlock, had been stigmatised by his father as illegitimate. Shere Sing, however, succeeded, but his triumph was of short duration. Near the close of 1843 he was assassinated, and this led to wide-spreading anarchy, culminating in the two successive wars with the British, that of

1846 and 1848-9, ending in the final annexation of the Punjaub by the British, and the acquisition by it of the celebrated diamond the Koh-i-noor.

The natives, with their belief as to the peculiar properties of the stone, prophesied what would happen. The East India Company carried off the booty, which should have been sold and converted into prize-money. They broke up almost directly after the "accursed" had entered their hands, when Lord Dalhousie, the Viceroy of India, presented it to Her Majesty (3rd July, 1850). It was considered by loyal natives the most sinister circumstance that could have befallen our royal family. Lord Dalhousie did not live very long, and died just as he might have expected to be raised to the highest honours of the State. The Duke of Wellington, who gave the first turn to the cutting, died three months after. We then lost Prince Albert, and I do not believe we any of us knew what we were losing until he was gone.

When my friend, the then Collector of Hyderabad, was sitting with the Nawab Mahmoud Khan, the former Minister of that State, and one of the Queen's most loyal subjects after the conquest of the province, he informed the Nawab of the stone's destination. The latter spat upon the ground, and with an expression of horror uttered the usual Mohammedan exclamation under the circumstances, "Tobah! Repentance in the name of God! Are they going to send that accursed thing to our Queen? May she refuse it!" All natives spit with an exclamation of horror whenever they hear it mentioned. It is impossible for me to go into the causes, nor perhaps ought I to say how, according to Eastern theory, the curse might be averted. Nevertheless, I have done so. May I ask if, barring £ *s. d.*, our position or *prestige* has progressed or declined since we became the possessor of the accursed stone? I ask all non-£ *s. d.* Englishmen whether they consider the Koh-i-noor a comfortable ornament for the English Crown, or a pleasant legacy for our most deservedly-popular and well-beloved Prince of Wales?

Will the Press absolve me from utter imbecility in my dream? Here is the most ridiculous item. Our ancestors were not so sceptical, and many a noble foundation and a splendid action has had its origin in beliefs, or, if you like it better, in superstitions, of a not very dissimilar kind.

I am, Sir, with regret at having so trespassed on your kindness, yours obediently,

Isabel Burton.

As might be expected, the *Western Press* said, with good-natured irony, "Mrs. Burton advises that the jewel should be sold to the Emperor of Russia, not considering that the Emperor of Russia *is England's declared friend.* Perhaps if the notion of the curse is really believed in, it would be better to keep the diamond until we go to war, and then present it to the potentate who is our enemy; in which case we should probably be spared the cost of maintaining an army in the field."

The *Daily Telegraph*, however, was "quite too awfully" ironical, and expended a whole "leader" of playful caustic on my "fad," saying, "Mrs. Burton would have Her Majesty sell the gem now at once to the Emperor of Russia, which is such a compliment to the Czar's strength of mind, that we are sure he will excuse the slight indifference to his personal fate which the proposal implies."

After the opening of the following Session I received dozens of letters out in India, saying, "What will you feel when you hear that Her Majesty actually opened Parliament with the Koh-i-noor in the centre of her Crown?" The end of that Session left us saddled with a war with Russia, and if it is closed up now, it will only have to break out later, and worse, till all the virus is out; but I see the world rolling on very slowly, but surely, towards the fulfilment of my dream. Her Majesty has since become an Empress. Princess Louise and the Marquis of Lorne are governing Canada. There are whispers of a Royalty going to Ireland. There is a matrimonial alliance with Russia; and a coming one with Germany, besides the Crown Princess. Victor Emmanuel was reconciled to the Church before he died; and Pope Pius IX.'s greatest sorrow was not to be carried to his bedside, personally to give him the last Sacraments. There are secret whispers of the Vatican being some day at Jerusalem. All the rest is equally rolling round to its destiny.

Shere Ali Khan is an ill-conditioned Prince,—prond, coarse, and violent. Yet there is something to be noted on the side of this little Highland chief. His hostility dates from those early days when, perhaps, we deserved scant friendship. During the Sepoy Mutiny he urged the invasion of the Punjaub upon his wise old father, Dost Mohammed Khan, whom a Russian paper reports on the throne, although he has been dead for years. The masterly inactivity which Lord Lawrence still dares to recommend, did not prevent that Viceroy acknowledging the claims of Afzal Khan, the brother who had deprecated the Punjaub invasion. Shere Ali had a pet grievance against Lord Mayo, and he was especially hurt by Lord Northcote refusing to pay his subsidy—"tribute," the wise would call it—with the desired regularity. His relations with the present Viceroy need hardly be noticed. The truth is that a policy of alternate do-nothing, bullying, and cajoling, have persuaded him firmly that he holds the road to India; that the keys of the treasure-house are in his hands. Hence he persistently refused to receive the Kàshgar mission; "their blood be upon their own heads if they come to Cabul!" Hence he admitted no English representative, and he hardly permitted the Wakeel, or resident Agent of Her Majesty's Government, to address him in Durbar. That he despises us, we cannot fail to see; nor less can we fail to feel that we have not forced him to respect us. We might have withdrawn that phantom of a Wakeel: we might also have withdrawn his subsidy or tribute, a lakh of rupees *per mensem*, till his manners improved; or, better still, we might have reserved it for his successor. But a high-principled Viceroy objected that such proceeding would be a "premium upon rebellion."

That unhappy mission has placed us between the horns of an ugly dilemma. If we do not fight, we offend public opinion at home and abroad, in England and in India. If we do fight, we play Russia's own game. Although never committed to paper, there was an implied agreement between the two great Europo-Asiatic Powers that our Asiatic army should not be employed in European wars. The policy of the moment thought fit to throw a new weight into the scale; and Russia's comment must have been something of this nature: "Oh! you will employ your Sepoys in Europe, will you? All right; meanwhile you shall have enough to do with them in India!" Whatever alarmists told the world, Russia has hitherto meddled mighty little with our Eastern Empire. Now, however, times have changed, and we may look out for squalls. Our Imperial "Bakht," our conquering star, our unbroken good luck, may yet be our shield and our defender. Not the less this Afghan war threatens to be the beginning of serious, nay, of fatal troubles, which may shake our Indian Empire to its very foundation. Behind it stand General Scindia and the Nawab of Hyderabad,—now the great Moslem power, the Delhi of the Peninsula. Behind all, terrible and menacing as the Spirit of the Storm which appeared to Da Gama, rises that frightful phantom, a starving population reduced to the lowest expression of life by the exorbitant expenditure of our rule.

I would willingly point a moral with the state of the Sepoy army, now reduced to a host of irregulars; with the cost of a march *à Cabul* against an enemy whose improved weapons have been supplied by ourselves as well as by Russia; with the Russian claim to wage aggressive and non-official war, even as we did in Turkey; with the effect which our intense sensitiveness to every step taken by Russia must exercise upon the Sultan and his Ministers; and lastly, with the possible results to England, which under the workings of a Free Trade, the reverse of free, threatens to become a Macclesfield on a very large scale. Is the prophecy of the Koh-i-noor to be fulfilled after all, and a ridiculed superstition to become a reality?

Next day we rose at four o'clock at Hyderabad: and took the train at seven o'clock to return to Bombay. I was very anxious to possess some photographs before leaving, but Major Nevill was unable to procure me any. Our kind host and hostess and Sir R. Meade, our Governor, saw us off, and gave us the last kindly greeting; and a good-hearted Parsee ran up and slipped some fruit and wine into our lunch basket. We had a comfortable carriage, and the railway officials were all most kind and civil. The heat was so great that they were walking up and down periodically to wake up the passengers, as they have been occasionally found dead. I think two or three cases happened about that time.

The following ancient account of Hyderabad, given to us by Sir Salar Jung, may not be uninteresting, being a *literal* translation by a native from an ancient Hindostani work in that City:—

"Up to the reign of three kings of the line of Khootoob Shahs, the Fort of Golconda, which was so large as to contain forty thousand cavaliers, was the seat of the Capital, but during the rule of Mohammed Khoolee II., son of Ibrahim Khootoob Shah, the Capital, being crowded by the people, and densely populated, created a foul air, from which most of the people were subjected to all sorts of illness; and besides the King, taking consideration of his rank and dignity, found that the place was unworthy of his residence, and thereby resolved to build another City, which, both in expansion and pleasantness, was to be the next to the Paradise of Rest. In this meditation he rode for hunting, and went in search of game. Whilst going here and there he happened to pass into a forest, which, being put up into a beautiful spot of ground, was in pleasantness and purity of climate, envied by the blue sky and the garden of heaven. There the King was pleased to build a City, and ordered the astrologers of great skill and discernment, to fix an auspicious moment to lay its foundation. This being accordingly done, the cleverest architects laid the design of the City, containing four extensive bazars and four elevated arches (Chár Kámán), and each of the bazars was equal in size to the other; also several other bazars, which are said to have been forty thousand in number, were made with streams flowing through, bordered with shadowy trees; and each bazar was confronted by a large edifice; and besides there were planned twelve thousand buildings, of the kind of baths, monasteries, schools, mosques, poor-houses, and inns. The residence of the King being settled to be in the northern part of the Capital, several grand and beautiful palaces were erected. The Capital was at first named Bhag Nugger, after the name of a woman, Bhag Mutty, to whom the King was attached, and upon her death it was changed into Hyderabad, which is bounded on the north by Meduck, on the south by the Coelconda Circars, on the east by the Bhonghur Circars, and on the west by the Mozuffer Nugger Circars, called also Mohamadabad Beder. The year of the commencement of the City can be found out from the word 'Ya Hafiz,' said by some poet, which comes to 1000;

and of its completion from the word 'Furkhonda Boonad,' which is 1006.

'As the King was very fond of propagating the Mussulman Creed, and at the same time mindful of the benefit of the Public in general, likewise ordered the erection of Mukka Musjid (or mosque), which was called by some poet Baitool Ateekh, from an Arabic word meaning Caba, which is also expressive of the year of its erection, 1023. Its height from the surface of the ground to the roof is calculated at about thirty-six yards, and the cost is estimated at eight lakhs of rupees. It is said that no other building like it was ever witnessed by anybody in all the Mussulman countries. Char Minas (four minarets), containing four arches, each facing the broad road of the four bazar lines, being firm and lofty, is situated in the centre of the city, each of the minarets containing rooms intended for students; and in the centre of the building lies a cistern with a fountain. Char Soo Ká Howz (water cistern), standing at the junction of the four roads, is beautifully situated in the centre of the four arches (Chár Kámán). The Daroosh Shiffa (general hospital), and several other works of public utility, as baths, etc., etc., were constructed and supplied at the expense of Government, with all their requisites."

CHAPTER VIII.

HYDERABAD.

I WILL now give you the two descriptions of our actual rides about the City upon elephants; and then my husband's observations upon the diamonds. These few remarks were written on the spot, and meant for publication, by my husband and myself. Those who like my story best can skip the official relation, but the accounts of the diamonds and undeveloped resources of India, I will recommend all to read who are interested in real information. That is why I insert such matter here, at the risk of certain passages being a repetition.

We have just returned from our first survey of the "Lion City," and as we saw much that was unexpected, and nothing that we were entitled, after reading certain popular and newspaper accounts, to expect, I am bold enough to believe that your readers will find interest in these few lines.

The country about Hyderabad in the Dekhan (Deccan) is very picturesque to all eyes; except those of the jaundiced Anglo-Indian, whose main, if not his only view in life, is "privilege leave." Nowhere more decided contrasts of sunburnt granite and syenite in bristling ridges, solitary boulders, loggan-stones, weathered into likenesses of man and beast; castellated rocks piled as by the hands of art; in ruddy fallows, in little green paddy-fields, in sky-blue distances, in golden stubbles almost pulverised by burning suns and deficient showers; in glorious "topes" of mangoes, tamarinds, and shady wild figs, and in scattered plantations of the cocoa; the fan palm, and the phœnix which bears toddy instead of dates. Almost every wave of ground swelling above the level of the rolling uplands, opens a vista of pleasant fore-plan backed by the great City, and wanting nothing but a few hours' downfall to lay the dust and to wash out the blue glaze from the distant picture. At this season, too, the nights, the early mornings, and the evenings are delicious; the air of the plateau, 1,800 feet above sea level, is that of Damascus and of Brazilian São Paulo; and though the "Whites," grumbling about the sun, are preparing for the annual flight to the hills, we find nothing oppressive in the mid-day, which is cooled by the brisk westerly breeze. The Deccan proper, I need hardly tell you, begins south-west of the Narbada (Nerbudda) River, and ends on the left bank of the Krishna, only a few miles to the south.

Early this morning "Sundargaj," one of H.E. Sir Salar Jung's tallest and bravest elephants, in all the bravery of bells and scarlet trappings, knelt down to receive us, and with that queer one-sided gait, which makes the cabriolet-haudah pitch like a little boat in a short chopping sea, began to lumber over the three miles separating us from town. Hyderabad can show a goodly procession of these intelligent monsters; and a body of nine hundred collected within a few hours surpasses the famous exhibition of Típú Sáhib. The *point de départ* was High Gate, the quarters of Major R. Nevill, commanding regular troops of H.H. the Nizam, fronted by his parade-ground, Fath Maydan; backed by the pretty gardens called after the Chádar Ghát, and showing eastward, beyond Nizam Yar Jang's "compound," the time-blackened walls of the stout old French cannon foundry; and eastward the "Black Rock," *alias* the Naubat-pahar (band-hill), a huge grey slide of newly-worked granite, crested by a little mosque with its tree and Hindú flag. The broad highway, "Chádar Ghát Road," not unworthy of Bombay Frere Town, is lined on either side by "compounds" of gorgeous shrubs; and by villas, which affect the classical (*e.g.*, Board of Public Works and "Mount Charles"), the Gothic (church and Nizam's gardens), and the homely thatched bungalow of no earthly order. It ends in the Afzal Ganj, the native bazar of the regular troops, parallel lines of shops and booths, mostly flat-roofed, sometimes tiled, one-storied, verandah'd, and clean with white-wash and red paint. This quarter leads to a substantial bridge of cut granite, the Náyá Pul or Ponte Nuovo, that spans the bed of the Músí stream, here some four hundred yards wide. At this season two-thirds of the ground are under cultivation, the garden of cucumber giving additional likeness to Syria; but the rains will convert the valley, with its Hindú *Smashán* (burning ground), into a roaring torrent, dark with *ragar*, the black cotton-soil, and ruddy with *chilka*, gritty ferruginous mould, apparently half composed of termite hills. The new bridge bears the date 1860. Up stream we see the arches of the old bridge, or "Oliphant's," whilst the windings of the bed conceal from us No. 3, called after Marrett or Kandú Lál. The river should be dammed between the two latter bridges, when a fine sheet of water would front the town.

Here we have our first view of the city, whose crumbling towers and ramparts, abutting upon the right bank of the River Valley, contrast queerly with the prim Gothic battlements of the North-Eastern or Palace Gate: its neighbour is the Delhi or Water Gate, where elephants are taken down to bathe. A little to the left, half hidden by the luxuriant orchards which make Hyderabad, like Poonah, look more countrified than cities are wont to do, rises the Barahdari or pavilion of the Prime Minister: when public entertainments are given, the building becomes a blaze of light. Further still, down the left bank, a flag, rising from a mass of white masonry, denotes the "Residency."

Before entering the castellated Palace Gate, we must remember that Hyderabad is not an ancient city. It owes its origin to Sultan Mohammed Kuli II., of the Kutub Shahi or Golconda dynasty, who, about A.D. 1520, built a country palace for one of his mistresses, the lady Bhágwati (not "Bhagamuttee"), a Hindú of no particular caste; and, after assigning to her a guard of a thousand horsemen, called the outpost Bhagnagar. The quaint Persian history tells us that, with the thought of founding a new capital, Mohammed Kuli Khan "rode out a-hunting, and while going here and there in search of game, he passed into a

12

forest which, occupying a beautiful spot, was envied for its pleasantness and purity of air by the blue sky and the garden of heaven; there he was pleased to build a city, and to order astrologers of skill and discernment to fix the auspicious moment for laying the first stone." The year when the city began is known by the words "Yá Háfiz" (A.H. 1000), and that of its completion by "Farkhundah-bunyad" (A.H. 1006), the modern title. It throve by the black death which in 1590 wasted the Diamond City of Tavernier, then capable of sending out forty thousand sabres. Finally it became the capital of the Nizam el-Mulk (Regulator of the State), the head of the Asuf Jahi house, shortly after the Emperor Aurungzeb, in 1687, captured Golconda, and led prisoner the last Kutub Shahi King, Abd el Husayn, popularly known as of Thana Shah; his unfinished sepulchre still tells the tale of his misfortunes. Why it was baptized Hyderabad—the abode of Haydar or of the lion—none can tell us, but we are reminded of its origin by the frequent tigers, terrible monsters in gamboge stripes, black beards, and red appendages, which here take the place of the king of beasts.

We now pass into the Shah Rah or main street, which, running north and south, nearly bisects the city. Our first pleasant surprise is the comparative absence of that characteristic which Coleridge attributed to Cologne. Hyderabad presently expects once more to rival Salt Lake City, when pure water, conducted by leats from the Mir Alam tank, south-west of the town, will flow in twin ribbons down the sides of the principal streets. There is no pavement except in patches of black basalt, which reminded us of the Salahíyyah Causeway at Damascus; and in places the original granite still outcrops in uninjured boulders. The main thoroughfares are well kept, sprinkled with water, and stamped with small hand-stamps, though a steam roller stares us in the face. There is a something of that marvellous animation and diversity distinguishing the great market of civilised and progressive Bombay, the "Bhendi Bazar," which politer men call the "Kalbadevi Road." We miss, however, the quaint mixture and jostle of

Europeans in military and naval, clerical and civilian garb; of dark Portuguese and sallow Eurasians; of Parsees, whose hats look like chimney-pots blown backwards by a gale of wind; of Banyans with beaked turbans, red and gold; of Máráthás, whose head-gear assumes the dimensions of flat small tea-tables; and of Moslems, clad in costumes almost as numerous as the individuals that wear them. Here the chief foreign items are dark, wiry Arabs from Hazramant or the Persian Gulf; sturdy Sulaymanis or Afghans, and large-limbed Zanzibar Sidis (Wásawáhíli), sometimes *pure sang*, oftener mixed with Asiatic blood. The Wahhabis conceal their tenets; the Shi'ahs are numerous, and the Bábis are unknown. The stranger at once observes that every respectable man is armed with gun or matchlock, pistol, sword or dagger, and that all the women show their faces, which means that they are mostly Hindús and never high-caste Moslemahs. As in all "native" Cities, the Fakirs, Dervishes, Sanyasis, Jogis and religious mendicants, Hindí and Hindú, are many and noisy, but beyond the exercise of their vocation they give us no trouble.

A marked feature in Hyderabad is the Tak or Kamán, the plain building that here takes the place of the triumphal gate. It is a pointed arch with horizontal coping and side windows, which, towering above the lower tenements, crosses the thoroughfares, relieves the monotony, and forms a resting-place for the eye. The royal Founder directed the four main bazars to be fronted by as many elevated arches, the Chahár Kamán, and, says the guide-book, "the forty thousand other market places (read streets and alleys) were made with streams flowing under borders of shadowy trees; and each was faced by a large edifice; besides which he planned four thousand buildings of the genus mosques and praying-places, baths, schools, poor-houses and inns." You may think the account exaggerated, but a ride round the official or walled city will occupy two hours of sharp canter; and the suburbs, as the graveyards show, must have extended to a distance measured by leagues.

The next object of note is the Makkeh Masjid, also built

about A.D. 1600, by Mohammed Kuli; the huge doors with their big studs of bronze, the two bulbous domes of the eastern or main entrance, the fine tank and the spacious prayer-hall, and the noble simplicity of the proportions deserve all praise. Unhappily the inner walls of the latter are whitewashed, after the fashion of mosques in general. The architect was, they say, a Persian, and the name we are told records the fact that this is a facsimile of the "Haram" at Mecca; if such is the case, either the latter has wholly changed its shape, or, more probably, the failure to catch the likeness is as remarkable as the many European imitations of Roman Saint Peter. The date of its completion (A.H. 1023) is known by the words "Bayt el Atik" (the old House, or Ka'aba). The cost was thirty-three lakhs, and the height above the ground is one hundred and eight feet. Hyderabad may well be proud of her *Jama'a* (cathedral).

"Sundargaj" then rolls for a few yards up the High Street, and shows us the Gulzar-hauz (garden cistern), formerly known as the Chaharsu-ka-hauz (bazar cistern); it is a pretty tank, holding a midway rank between the Place Lesseps at Port Said, and the modern improvements effected in the old "Bombay Green." It forms the centre of the Chahár Kamán (four arches) before alluded to. Beyond it, in the very heart of the city, denoting the intersection of the four main streets, rises the Chahur Moonar, also the work of Mohammed Kuli. The Gazetteers misinform us that this "Chaur Moonar" was "formerly used as a school of arts and sciences, but now turned into warehouses." At present it bristles with scaffolding, but when finished the four minarets will serve the Muezzin or prayer-caller; the upper rooms will be a mosque, and a cistern-*cum*-fountain on the shady ground floor will be a very satisfactory place for the *flâneur*. The four fronts are broken by long lines of windows, and the minarets are not very top-heavy, the main fault of Hyderabad church-architecture in general, whilst the strangulated dome too much resembles the onion. The block to the south-west, with the upper latticed windows, is mostly occupied by the palace of His Highness; and the sepoy-guard, with the quaint chimney-pot shakos, whose top-knot is split in two, dating from the days of the old Jack Sepoy and the French officers, removes us to the last century.

We now approach the southern or Madras Gate, which was once protected by the deserted lines of the old guard. These entrances, except only the Palace Gate, are in true Oriental style, large doors, with huge bronze knobs like the umbos of shields, and with crenelled summits instead of battlements. They are somewhat higher than the ramparts, but none are remarkable for beauty or dignity. Five of them break the northern wall. As a rule they have fanciful names like the eastern feature, Dudh-baoli, the "well of milk," so-called after a pit which supplies sweet water. The number is not excessive for a city said to measure fourteen miles in circumference, and to contain four hundred thousand souls.

The pleasant ride, which was protracted through the bye-ways as well as the highways of the city, ended with a charming breakfast at the palace of the Mukhtar-el-Mulk (Prime Minister), Sir Salar Jung, G.C.S.I., a name already known and highly respected. The morning showed us not only a glimpse of the "Lion City," but an *aperçu* of the general errors which afflict it. Forty years ago Hyderabad may have been a turbulent city, into which Europeans could not enter without insult or injury, and where lawlessness and recklessness of life were the laws of the land. But, although a couple of generations, and, let me add, the progressive measures of an enlightened Minister have completely changed the condition of things, still popular and even official opinion, whose watch is always an age or two behind the time, refuse to admit the change. "You come from a place where you may be murdered at any moment," was the address of a late Viceroy to an Englishman, who had taken service under His Highness the Nizam; and yet during the last thirty-five years, I am assured, not a single European has been murdered in the Moslem dominions, and the only one wounded suffered the consequences of his own fault. Nothing was done here by the enraged peasantry to the gentlemen sportsmen who engaged on a battue of the Prince's tame deer. Such is the impression left upon us by a first visit to the City, and a second did not alter it except for the better. "Of course you had a large escort," said a friend to me in Bombay, on hearing my tale. We had nothing beyond a *mahaut;* but prejudices engendered are not easily disposed of.

And now I have told you how clean we found the City which Murray has branded "one of the filthiest in India;" how we escaped the "insult and perhaps personal injury" threatened by Bevar, and how pleasantly we were received by "the most disorderly, turbulent, and ferocious set of ruffians within the limits of India." It is a favourite Anglo-Indian theory that "Native States," Moslem and "Gentoo," should be left, like plague-spots, by way of contrast, with the clean and orderly state of society under Christian England rule, and upon this model the theorist often trims his facts, not a little to the detriment of the facts. The Native States are sometimes happier and more flourishing than ours—at least, to be fair, this is a case in point.

After our happy but unconscious escape from the interior of the "Lion City," we gathered courage to attempt the three normal trips to the environs—Raymond's grave, the Tank, and the Tombs of the (Golconda) Kings. We will attack them severally, and we will religiously avoid repeating what the Guide-books say or think.

To reach General Raymond's "little landed estate" we pass the handsome Residency Park, whose trees, by-the-by, require abundant clearing, and traverses the northern markets, containing some thirteen thousand souls; the Gulbazar, where the steam-roller is at work, and the Russell ganj. You go nowhere in India without stumbling upon a Russell and a Smith, a Grey and a Brown, an Elliot and a Jones. Then it crosses the Marrett or lower bridge, bisects Champarpeth, where it is proposed to barrack the new Regulars, and takes the highway to Madras. The characteristics of the scene are booths, tombs, and a yellow-flowered weed; on the ground-wave to the right rise the white walls of the modern gaol, and to the left lies a little patoh of sepulchres, *Ujále Sháh ká dargáh,* which the British soldier of Secunderabad (Sikundarabad) converts to "Johnny Shaw's Tomb." At certain seasons crowds of both sexes here meet to pray and make merry at the last resting-place of the Pir or saintly man and his neighbours of the grove. The tombs are the prettiest toys in the world; the material is the wax-like Jaypur marble, famed for statuettes, and the shape is that of the Nizam's monuments in the Mecca Mosque. They look as if carved in ivory at some Giant's Dieppe, ready to be placed under a glass case; the fretted and open work is an admirable lacery in stone, and the sharp shadows of the dark green trees set off their snowy whiteness.

We must dismount to ascend the Raymond hillock, and skirt a walled orchard, in which cocoas grow luxuriantly. It is by no means usual to find them flourishing at this distance from the sea, two hundred direct geographical miles to the south-east, and over three hundred to the west. The Orient half of the hill is occupied by a Hindú *dewal;* the rest belongs to "Monsieur Raymond," as he was called by the English writers of his own stirring day. He appertained to the epoch following the heroic age of Dupleix, Bussy, and Lally Tollendal; when the idea of a French Empire in India had not wholly died out of the Gallic brain. He was to the Nizam what M. de Boigne was to Sindhia (Scindia), Commander-in-Chief of some fifteen thousand troops, *le corps François de Raymond,* officered by his compatriots, and devoted to himself. He was a red-hot Revolutionist, an ardent believer in the Age of Reason and the Rights of Man—especially French man—and not the less a Gaul to the backbone; he introduced the idea of Citizenship to the native mind till it culminated in *le citoyen Tippoo;* and, after his death in 1798, the heir-apparent of the Nizam used to swear "by the head of M. Raymond." These ancient warriors are still remembered with affection, the chief reason being their pliability in conforming to "country customs"—a good quality for serving, a very bad one for ruling in India. The descendants of Raymond's sepoys, Moslem as well as Hindú, who fought under the stout old Frenchman at a time when the Máráthá Pindarís (free lances) were making war support war, still burn incense, and hold religious meetings at the tomb; and the ignorant have sanctified the tenant under the title Sháh Ráhman. It reminded me of the Nikkal Sinis, who took General Nicholson as their patron, and of a celebrated *convert* at Jerusalem, to whom everybody was saintly, even *le Saint Goliath*.

There is little to be said of the monument—a truncated, built-up obelisk of stone, inscribed "J. R." on the four faces. Four slabs of black marble, apparently greased, are wholly ignorant of the epitaph, but have not yet been stolen, as the Indian fashion is, to serve for curry-grinders. It is adorned westward by a little open pavilion, which commands a suggestive view northward; beyond the foreground tombs of other French officers lies the sun-burnt and now barren plain, the shore of the sea of verdure, which appears to overwhelm Sikandarabad. We easily distinguish the forms of the ancient square fort, with its round bastions; the mud redoubts, old and new; the huge parade-ground, cut up by its intrusive cemetery; the rococo heads of half-a-dozen "temples," belonging to as many different "persuasions;" and the clock-towered St. James's Police Office and Court House—in these days the "Bobby," like the British flag, girdles the habitable globe. Sikandarabad was once equal to Lahore in dignity as the largest stations in English India; but now the glory is gone from it, as we see by the long, empty lines of officers' bungalows and the deserted *palazzi* standing out from the southern bazar. The fever and the engineer have prevailed against it, and "the spider spins her web in the halls of Afrasyáb." Fine houses will be cheap till the right species of Eucalyptus dries the soil and perfumes the air. In the far distance run long, jagged rock ridges, capped, as usual, by sparkling white walls; this is Trimalgadi (Trimulgherry), the head-quarters of the Artillery, where, unlike Karkhi (Kirkee), the guns are defended from a *coup de main*, as they always should be, by an entrenched camp. The granitic pile intercepts Boláram, head-quarters of the Hyderabad Contingent, where strawberries grow, and where Sikandarabad has gone out of town. Ichabod may now be written upon the old cantonment.

Less suggestive, but more picturesque, is the prospect which opens to the south. Here the world is greener, and the face of water cools the eye. We see the broad Madras highway winding over the "Band" (dyke) of Sárú Nagar, and damming up the precious element which, all about Hyderabad, is sadly wasted. The townlet with its curtains and towers, built to keep out the Pindárí, forms the centre of the Nizam's preserves, and spotted deer wander over the plain tame as sheep; pea-fowl, very good eating during the first year, and jungle cocks, which make the "griff" suspect that he has murdered a barn door, abound; here also, it is said, the wild dog, not the Pariah, runs wild, hunts in packs, and pulls down the largest game.

A favourite place of picnic is the Mir Álam (not Allum) tank —these lakelets, with their cool, damp air and verdant borders, are always pleasant to the visitor of a thirsty land, subject to hot, dry winds, and much neglected by Jupiter Pluvius. It derives its name from that notable Minister, the firm friend of the English, who died in 1808. This maternal grandfather of Sir Salar Jung, and the first *Diwán* of a family from Ispahan, some seventy-two years ago (A.H. 1221), when Mr. H. Russell was Resident (1805-6), enlarged the old pool of unknown origin. The work, directed by Captain R. Russell, cost twenty-three lakhs, which sum, however, included the Diwán's *Bára-dari* (pavilion). The well-made road, not a macadam, traverses the Begum Bazar, where the cemetery seems to have the advantage of the dwelling-house, and crosses Oliphant's or Old Bridge, which is fronted by the double-towered *Pul-ká-darwázáh*, opened in the north-western wall. It then runs through the suburbs amidst a scatter of mosques, pagodas, and tombs, Hindí and Hindú. On the right is the rocky river-bed, showing a chaplet of pools; to the left are paddy-fields watered by the tank, and a little farther, or due south, is another cemetery of the old French officers. It is kept in far better repair than that at Poonah; the Maltese Cross still stands, and Catholics are buried here even now.

After a devious drive of some four miles to the south-west, we alighted at the Walad Garden, the villa, and the neat

Ghát, or pier of cut-stone, belonging to the Mir Álam Tank. A few yards' walk over the crest of the new "Band," shows us its peculiar shape. The single large arc of ashlar and waterproof cement, the latter lately applied, is divided into thirty-two semi-circular segments, with strong buttresses supporting the several bases, as may be seen by the back view. The general effect is that of a huge bridge laid horizontally on the water. Small square sluices can be opened near the east and the west ends; and, at the latter, a range of fifteen rough monoliths denote the *chadar* (sheet) or waste weir. In unusual floods the surplus overflows the whole dam, now only two feet nine inches above the water level; and discharges into the lower or escape tank, which finally drains to the Músí Fiumara. Thus there is little risk of Hyderabad being visited like Sheffield, a fate often predicted for Poonah, where the Kharewasla reservoir, a miracle of economic architecture, admirably calculated and carried out by Mr. Joyner, C.E., has excited the absurdest alarms. The season is exceptionally dry, yet the depth now reaches forty-five feet, and there is water sufficient, not only for the rice fields, but also for the streets of Hyderabad.

The Mir Álam tank is fed by a canal from the river Usi, which falls, almost at a right angle, into the Músí below Golconda Fort, thus resembling the Mutamula farther north: all the great cities on this line, we may observe, occupy either the heads or the upper courses of streams that feed the Bay of Bengal. The new or northern tank is a parallelogram running roughly east and west, whilst the older part is triangle, attached to the south-western side, and disposed with the apex southwards. The site of the old "Band" is shown by a rock islet, containing the stone tomb of the patron saint (*Sayyid ká dargáh*), while a submerged mosque, a pagoda, and a gate denote the extension. Vast beds of water-plants, which it would be an useless expense to remove, support eels, the Marram-fish, said to be the best, and the Parram (a Silureis'), reaching 100 lbs., and shot instead of being netted. These again feed the alligators, and the solitary fish-hawk dives for the smaller fry. The total circumference is laid down at seven miles, or five less than the extreme circuit of the enlarged Husayn Sagar north of Hyderabad city. Nothing can be more justifiable than lavish expenditure upon this branch of the Public Works Department. The neglect of tanks and irrigation-canals has converted many tracts of the Nizam's dominions into fiery wildernesses; and their restoration under the present enlightened rule will tend to "avert," as the local historian says, "those fearful seasons of want which brought fear and death to every door."

We embarked upon the little steam-launch of ten tons, superintended by M. P. de Louney: there is also a paddle-wheeler of some fifty tons upon the Mir Álam, whilst the rival Hossein Ságar can boast of yachtlets and regattakins. Cruising around the shores we failed to remark with Mr. Briggs ("The Nizam," ii., 249) that "but for the Oriental character of the tombs by, and the native villages, the scene might be believed to lay in the south of Europe." Everything here is essentially Deccani (Dekhani),—the rocks, the vegetation, and the sky. To westward of the old tank towers the sepulchre of another reverend man, Mir Mahboob Sáhib; it is the normal article, a whitewashed dome tall and straight, based upon a parallelogram, and supported by a quadrangle of cut stone, connected, they say, by a tunnel with Golconda. On the level ground to the south-west, flooded during the rains, are the tents of the engineers, and a little to the east of them a fine "tope" denotes the source known from some "Begum" as the "Bíbí-ka-Chashmah" (Lady's Fount): its supplies are reserved for the Nizam's palace.

On return we drove southwards, and passed through the Dudhbaorí Gate to the *Kothi* (palace) or *Báràdari* (pavilion), the fine establishment of the Chhota Nawab Sahib, alias "Wikár el Umárá" (Honour of the Emirs), the younger brother of the "Shams el Umárá" (Sun of the Emirs), better known as the Amír el Kabír. The Gardens and Courts could easily lodge a small army, and a band directed by an English master awaited to play "God save the Queen." Our host, whose gold-fringed turban denotes his connection with Royalty, received us as though we had been old friends; and, after a succulent breakfast, showed his curiosities, especially his weapons. The most interesting were the defences carried by his grandfather, who wielded a ponderous *Gurz* (mace); the small Hyderabad turban of steel bands with bar nose-piece, and the heavy mail-coat with an *ayat* (verset) of the Koran worked in relief on every ring;—the latter does not, however, equal in finish that of the Tower collection. Our visit ended with enjoying the lovely view of the Lion City from the upper windows, and H. E. presented me with his history of the Kings of India, the "Taríkh Rashíd el Dín Khaní," a lithographed folio containing detailed notices of Hyderabad. His distinguished brother the "Bará Amír," or Co-Regent, though long an invalid, did not allow us to leave the city without carrying away the most agreeable reminiscences of his courtesy and hospitality: he is the type of the Indian *Grand Seigneur*, and his second nephew, the Bashír ed Daulah, was equally sympathetic. The establishment known as the Jehán-numá (not Jaenuma) Palace, the "world exhibiting," because built on high ground, is of goodly proportions. You pass through the barracks surrounded by a strong wall, and enter an *enceinte* facing north, and showing, through the trees, glimpses of the Royal Tombs. A succession of parterres, popularly called "hanging gardens," each with its fountain and flower-plot, is separated by as many tall and airy pavilions: the vegetation is gorgeous, and the only failures are the cypresses, which, like those of Poonah, suggest huge asparagus.

The most interesting of trips in the neighbourhood of Hyderabad remains to be described:

> "I'm going to fair Golconda,"

as the old song runs. It is the first and the most famous of the six independent Moslem kingdoms, which, in A.D. 1399, rose on the extinction of the Toghlak (Delhi) dynasty, and it survived till 1688, when Aurungzeb brought all India under one sceptre. The lump of rock crowned by an empty wall and conspicuous from almost every part of Hyderabad, adds greatly to

> "The poetry of the distant view."

Strangers, however, go *to*, not *into*, Golconda. It is a state prison, in which, after the ugly affair of March 5th, 1815, the sons of the Nizam were confined; and as such, it is entrusted to a high official, the Kiladar Mohammed Khan, who is responsible for its not being entered. Visitors are admitted only when "Huzúr" (H.H. the Nizam) makes a royal progress to the venerable ruin. After the return of Sir Salar from England it was said there would be a grand "Tamasha." If so the boy-king would call upon his Prime Minister for the first time, and promenade through Golconda in state, a little matter which would cost him a lakh or two of rupees.

Early on March 5th, after elephants had been sent forward, we drove westward through the northern suburb, and found fault with Major Malleson.* He describes "Char Mahal" as "a walled enclosure about five hundred yards square in the north-west angle of the town, on the banks of the River Moussi;" for which read, "in the northern suburb, separated from the city by the Musi bed." But even Níebuhr, the great historian, was a poor topographer; and we have read "The French in India" with pleasure and profit. Passing the Goshah Mahall, Púran Mal's Tank, and the proposed cotton manufactory, we came to the Hindú quarter, shown by frequent Pagodas with gilt finials and strong coped walls defending shady gardens. These people (Máráthás, Telingas, and Canarese) number in the capital 1 to 1·5 Moslems, and throughout the country 9 to 1. To the left is the stony spine of Afzalganj, crowned with a white *Dewal*, and sheltering Sir Salar Jung's village and pleasure-gardens in what our host, Major Nevill, calls "The Happy Valley." Amid the rich cool verdure, I noticed a few vines of which a very fine old specimen lines a porch attached to the "Wikár el Umárá's" Palace: Dionysius, however, does not flourish in his own realms. The same is the case throughout Brazil, because in both countries the ripening summer is also the rainy season.

We then took the fine new road connecting the modern with the ancient capital: its predecessor, running southwards along

* "The French in India." London: Longmans, 1868.

the Músí Fiumara, is the highway of Poonah, when Capital of the Peshwa, the Moslem's bitterest enemy. The four white *gumbaz*, or domes, denoting the tombs of the Kings, which are visible from most parts of Hyderabad, form the main body of a line here scattered, there grouped, which begins immediately beyond the faubourgs, and which runs up the left side of the River-Valley. On the right towers a huge syenitic boulder carved by the Hindús into the semblance of a "Gumat," the pyramid-tower covering the Holy of Holies; and south of the Músí there is also a pagoda pierced in the ruins of an incipient Cave-temple. As we approach the short ruins and the long homes of the Kutb-Shahi house, the several features begin to define themselves. The tall *Aywán* crowning the Bala Hisar (upper or inner Fort), which rises some two hundred and fifty feet above the plain level,—a mere shell of building, once a throne hall,—shows one window to east and west, and five arches, here a favourite number, in the northern and southern faces. It stands sharply out from the rock, and seen against the sunrise or sunset, it wears an Italian look, like many a *Sala* in Genoa or fair Verona. The buildings around and below it form a kind of "Hof," or Palace; and the northern spur of the rocky hill carries down a curtain to the north-east. There is a similar line to the south-west, and thus the eastern part of the subject town is cut off from the western. The lower or outer works of the City, about three miles round, are the usual curtain and bastion: the former is capped by crenelles with large stones placed upon the sky-line ready for hurling; and the latter, long sections of ovals, number eighty-four. Each "burj" carries from one to three guns, the smaller cast and the larger built up; some of these are regular "Mons Megs." Major Nevill has just saved from the smelting surface, he tells me, a specimen twenty-nine feet long. The defences are strong towards the east, and raised high to prevent being commanded; and on the south they are doubled: they were, however, successfully attacked from the site of the sepulchres. There is an attempt at a glacis, a moat and a covered way, so that the fortified camp of Golconda is still, against native assailants at least, the barrier of

Hyderabad. A few white honses, reserved for the Nizam and his chief officers, rise above the grey ruins, which look as if lately bombarded by Aurungzeb. The main fault of the tracery is not having taken in the tank on the north-west.

About five miles from the Residency gate we passed a new house surrounded by neat gardens, and said to be famous for the "nautch." A few paces beyond it begin the Tombs of the Kings, which lie about five hundred yards north of the Petta-burj (bastion). The first noticed is the unfinished pile of the unfortunate Tháná Sháh: the dome is only half a cup, and the ground floor has been converted into a "buggy-house." "Sundargaj" and "Ikbal-tikkeh," the two elephants, bore us carefully over the rough ground girthing the northern *enceinte*, and affording an excellent view of the *tout ensemble*, while the cicerone, Mohammed Lal, of Hyderabad, supplies the necessary information. To the north-west, and separated by a bit of plain, is a separate group of sepulchres flanking the *Gumbaz* (dome) and *dargáh* (shrine) of a local saint, Shah Wali Sáhib: here also is a fine old caravanserai, still used by rare wanderers. The tombs straggle far and wide about the valley, and even climb the curtaining rock-ridges; the best, however, are those in and around the well-watered Government gardens. Here the mixture of oasis and desert is truly Arabian; Arabian also are the pigeon-holes and dove-cots of the walls, while the song of the water-wheel reminded my husband of Egypt. We remark the tanks of neatly cut stone, the masonry channel, and the aqueduct of flat arches, which may have supplied the Delhi Emperor during his investment of the City. We then pass on towards the Músí river, which has now shrunk to infantine size. Near the left bank rises the five-arched, double-halled mosque of Ibrahim (Bagh) Bádsháh, probably unfinished, as it lacks minarets; a fine ramp leads up to the vaulted and now uneven platform where worshippers were lodged; and a little village still occupies the plain. Close to the stream is the Mahállah (Palace) of the same king, approached by three distinct flights of steps; here the arches are also five. Viewed from the Sangam, or junction of the Usi and Músí, the

Bálá Hisar gains height and distinction; the Throne-Hall towers over the River-Valley, and the double lines of defence show to the best advantage.

We now dismount and inspect, not for the first time, the most interesting remains of Mohammedan splendour. I can hardly compare them, as some have done, with the "sea of ruins" at Fathpur Sikri; and still less with the tombs of the Mamlúk kings outside the Gate of Victory, Cairo, these triumphs of mediæval Egyptian architecture, so faultless in their relation to the surrounding scenery. They hardly equal the large, whitewashed piles of Bandeh-Nawáz and Shah Husayn at Gulbarga, the old capital of the Bahmani dynasty. The style of the Indian mosque has generally a something of grotesqueness, as if borrowed from the Hindú pagoda, many of which were converted to El Islam: most parts appear to be built for show, not for use; whilst a profusion of ornament, pastry-cook's work in stone and stucco, fritters away the length and breadth of the lines. The Mecca Mosque of Hyderabad, whose majestic simplicity places it far above all its neighbours, is a notable exception; but the architect was a Persian.

The prevailing style of the Golconda tomb is a dome standing upon an oblong or a square, both of grey granite: the shape of the cupola is various, from the orange, or rather the onion, strangulated at the base, which is invariably Arabesqued, to the segment of a circle, either straight with, or bulging beyond, the drum; the finials are of silver, not of gold, as in the modern city. The parallelogram, single-storied in the smaller, and doubled in the larger mausolea, is either plain above, or capped with floriated crenelles like spear-heads; many bear balustraded balconies of the most complicated patterns. The lower portion is invariably an arcade of pointed arches resting upon a raised quadrangular terrace of cut stone, which is ascended by four flights of steps. The prevailing colour is white, in some cases picked out with green. Each large tomb has its Mosque or *Musalla* (chapel), usually a wall or a hall-porch opening eastward, with a *Mihrab* (prayer-niche), to the west, and flanked by minarets on either side. These towers are also of one general type; the cap is a bulb and neck, somewhat like the mosque dome in miniature; the body is a shaft either circular or polygonal, with a floriated gallery, single or double; whilst the foot is a pillar of larger dimensions than that above. The minarets are either engaged or unattached, and the general effect is top-heaviness. Many also are toy articles, evidently never meant for use.

The interiors of the sepulchres are arbitrarily laid out with intersecting arches in infinite variety; and not a few of them deserve photographing. Flights of stairs, now rarely practicable, lead up to the unbalconied galleries above, and down to the graves contained in the arched and alcoved basements. In the midst lies the occupant under a tomb of black marble or greenstone, the fine produce of the Krishna river quarries. The shape is oblong, and stepped with six or eight slabs diminishing above. The top is either *bombé* or flat, in which case it is ornamented with a mimic *Mihrab* (prayer-niche), and the sides bear mortuary and devotional inscriptions in the Naskh and Nasta'alik characters. From the four corners of the slab resting upon the base, spring feet not unlike the claws of an old-fashioned sugar-pot; and one or more of the steps bears lines of the horns which distinguish the altars of classical Greece and Rome. Many of them have suffered from the iconoclast, and Mohammed Lal declares that the offenders are *Sahib Log*—Englishmen. This may be the case, for we are a race of relic-lovers. On the other hand the scribblings on the walls, another form of barbarism, are mainly Moslem. Let us not forget that Chateaubriand, when cutting his name on the great pyramid, called the process one of *les petits devoirs d'un pieux voyageur*.

The items most worthy of notice are (1) the Tomb of Sultan Abdallah, the easternmost of the repaired group, lying north of the highroad. It is the largest and the best, the lines are less broken, the corners of the parallelograms show noble monoliths, and the platform of cut stone is on the grandest scale. Whitewash has here been applied even to the granite; and shabby wooden doors lead to the three-stepped tombstone of fine porphyry. Ascending the range to the garden, where a holy beggar persistently offers us bad fruit, we turn to the right or northwards, and find, west of Sultan Abdallah's mausoleum, that of his mother Fatimah Sahib. No. 2 is apparently a copy of No. 1, but not so large nor so well finished: the door-jambs on the south are miserably painted with imitation Persian tiles. A few paces south-west lead to (No. 3) the noble pile of Mohammed Kuli Khan, supported by an arched basement containing the tombs of his relatives and friends. It is remarkable for its four porches, fronting, as usual, the cardinal points; for its deep bays supported by pilasters and thin monolithic pillars; and for ceilings of flat slabs reposing upon finely-cut stepped corbels. Too much stucco is the only fault of No. 4; and, curious to say, the resting-place of the founder of Hyderabad has not been repaired. Near it is a well-whitened Idgah (place of festival prayer) with a splendid tank of cut stone, vaulted over after the fashion of Syria. Further west rises (No. 4) the Chíní Gumbaz (china-dome) of Ibrahim Badshah, whose mosque and *Mahalleh* (station) we have just seen. The Persian tiles, fastened by large nails, still linger on all the faces, especially the southern, where there is an inscribed frieze. Our cicerone again charges the *Sahib Log* with sacrilege, but he stumbles in his facts, declaring the porcelain to be true Chinese. The tiles are evidently Sind work, possibly from Tattah; and our good friend, Mr. Gumpert of Bombay, now deceased, showed me a similar article taken from the excavations of Garapuri or Elephanta Island. This "china-dome" has buttress-claws, shaped exactly like those of the tombstones; one of the four is of brick-work evidently repaired. No. 5, the sepulchre of Kulsum Begum, is more curious than artistic; the tall double-storied basement gives it, like the Cathedral of Boulogne, the aspect of an immense pepper-caster.

At one tomb only, a small and mean specimen of its kind, the masons were at work. The modern hand was easily distinguished by its inferiority to the ancient, but no liberties were taken—evidently restoration is here not synonymous with destruction. A gang was also dawdling about a tank of noble size, partly cut in the rock, and built up with solid arches. After inspecting the ruins, which have been effected by time, by Aurungzeb, and by the fig-trees springing from the masonry; and which, strange to say, in a Moslem land, are not utterly neglected, we bade adieu with regret to the Tombs of the Kings. Their site is high and healthy, the wind is strong and cool; the place ought to become a sanitarium for sickly and etiolated children, and we only hope that the picknicers will have the grace to build, or to get built, a travellers' bungalow, and cease to desecrate poor Tháná Shah's tomb.

From grave to gay. The vulgar of Hyderabad, unlike most Moslem cities in India, is less fond of kite-flying and of pigeon-tumbling than of cock-fighting; while the latter is ignored by the higher classes. I could never understand, by-the-by, why we have abolished the classical sport as barbarous, whilst we conserve our ignoble pigeon-shooting; yet such is the case, and we have been imitated by Brazil and by Hyderabad. Here there are five or six cockpits, especially that of Káchí-Ghorá, where mains are fought every Sunday. The bird is large, often weighing 5 to 5½ seers (10 to 11 lbs.), equalling, in fact, a small turkey; it is one of the best in India; the price reaches 200 Rupees. You cannot depend upon your friend to send or to sell you an *Asíl*, or thoroughbred; and eggs, it is said, are generally boiled before given over to the outer world. The colours range from *púrí* (white), here a noble colour, to *chitú* (spotted) *kháki* (earthy) and black, deep as the Bhaunra's (bumble-bee's) wing. The *yákút* (red) and the *pílá* (yellow) have a vast variety of sub-shades, as *yálá-yákút*, black and red; *Dhunwár-pílá*, light yellow; *Abrash*, yellow hackles, back and tail on a chocolate ground; and Gherwá or Hyderabad *ká pílá*, yellow with white wing feathers. The birds are trained, physicked and sweated with more care than Spaniards or Mexicans can bestow upon them, and they are so heated with *Masálá* (spices), whose preparation is a secret, that they will fly at man or beast. Thoroughbred birds are practised with "hods," or leather spur sheaths;

but they are fought with the natural weapon trimmed to points, as their fine condition would suggest: the hackles and tail feathers are cropped before the combat, like ours, but the combs and wattles do not require removing;—all the best specimens are born without these unseemly appendages. Silver is rarely used; the favourite weapon for "dunghills" is a short scimitar, springing from a straight bar which is bound to the middle toe: thus the gladiator can spring and fly, but cannot walk. The experienced *Murghbáz* (cock-fighter) will have dozens of these articles, showing every variety of length, weight, and angle. He appears to ignore the fact that it is unfair to pit a thoroughbred against a dunghill when both have steel spurs: whilst the former is too enraged to settle down at once into thrashing "that confounded snob," the latter hastens to the attack, before his courage oozes out of his toe-ends, and often deals a fatal blow.

Partridges, quails, and the bulbul, a shrike here called a nightingale, are fought by Moslems at all seasons. Perdrix is a most pugnacious "party," as many of us can bear witness who have witnessed his duellos from the cover-side, where the ring is carefully kept cleared by the friends and relatives, chiefly male, of the combatants; they are trained and *musálá'd* like game-cocks; they travel in double cages with a single handle jealously covered over like a Moslemah belle, and the loud screams of the non-combatants testify the interest they take in the fray. Nothing prettier than this style of fight; the wing is strong, the short spur is sharp and well thrown out, and the bird is thoroughly game. The quail (*bater*) is trained like the partridge, and carried in long covered cages with room for four. When battle is to be given, the *teterrima causa belli* is placed in the ring, her little prison having open bars, and two males, let loose, at once begin to peck and jump and hustle for their lives. The little devils are perfect "gluttons" for fight, and they will stick to it for an hour or more. Rams (*bakre*) are fought chiefly by Hindús at the venerable festival called Makur Sankrantí, when the sun enters Capricorn, the winter solstice which with us means Christmas, and New Year's Days.

Their horns are covered for dignity with gilt paper, but they are a poor and mean lot after the noble animal of Gujrat (Guzerat) which seems to derive directly from *Ovis Musimon.*

Meanwhile the nobles of the land, despising these vulgar doings, disport themselves with shooting and hawking. The favourite birds are the Shah-baz (*Falco peregrinus*), for which even Iceland has been ransacked to supply the Indian market; the Shákín (royal white falcon); the Basha (Goshawk); the Bhairi, which is generally preferred as giving the best sport, and sundry small species, like our sparrow hawks, especially the Lagar and the Jagar. The riding ground about Hyderabad is not very dangerous, and I need hardly say that the "Bázdárs" (falconers) are perfectly versed in their craft.

CHAPTER IX.

THE NIZAM DIAMOND—THE DIAMOND IN INDIA.

IT would be unpardonable to quit Golconda without a word concerning the precious stone which, in the seventeenth century, made its name a household word throughout Europe; and, also, without noticing the great diamond whose unauspicious name Bala (little) Koh-i-noor, I would alter to "The Nizam." Not a little peculiar it is that professional books like Mr. Lewis Dieulafait's "Diamonds and Precious Stones" (London: Blackie, 1874), which record the life, the titles, the weight, the scale, the size, and the shape of all the historic stones, have utterly ignored one of the most remarkable. Mr. Harry Emanuel does not neglect even the Násik diamond, which fetched only £30,000: we must, by-the-by, convert for intelligibility his "Mahratta of Peshawur," into the "Peshwa of the Maharattas."

The history of the Nizam diamond is simple enough; like the Abaïté, and unlike the Koh-i-noor, its discovery cost at most a heartache, and did not lose a drop of man's blood. About half a century ago it was accidentally found by a Hindú Sonár (goldsmith) at Narkola, a village about twenty miles east of Shamsábád, the latter lying some fourteen miles south-west of the Lion City, on the road to Maktal. It had been buried in an earthen pipkin (*Koti* or *Abkhorah*), which suggests, possibly, that it had been stolen, and was being carried for sale to Mysore or Coorg. The wretched finder placed it upon a stone, and struck it with another upon the apex of the pyramid. This violence broke it into three pieces, of which the largest represents about half. With the glass model in hand it is easy to restore the original octohedron. The discovery came to the ears of the celebrated Diwan (minister) Rajah Chandú Lál, a friend of

General Fraser, who governed the country as Premier for the term of forty-two years. He took it very properly from the Sonár, before it underwent further ill-treatment, and deposited it amongst his master's crown jewels. Lately Messrs. Aratoon, of Madras, offered to cut it for three lakhs of rupees, a modest sum, considering the responsibility and the labour such operations involve; but the figure was considered exorbitant. A M. Jansen of Amsterdam, who died about a twelvemonth ago, volunteered to place it in the hands of Messrs. Costa, who certainly did not improve its big brother. This offer was also naturally enough declined. Let me hope, however, that it will not be cloven into a plate or flat slab *more Indico.*

The stone is said to be of the finest water. An outline of the model gives a maximum length of 1 inch 10·25 lines, and 1 inch 2 lines for the greatest breadth, with conformable thickness throughout. The face is slightly convex, and the cleavage plane, produced by the fracture, is nearly flat, with a curious slope or groove beginning at the apex. The general appearance is an imperfect oval, with only one projection which will require the saw. It is not unlike a Chinese woman's foot without the toes, and it will easily cut into a splendid brilliant, larger and more valuable than the present Koh-i-noor.

I can hardly wonder at this stone being ignored in England and in India, when little is known about it at Hyderabad. No one could tell me its weight in grains or carats. The highest authority in the land vaguely said "about two ounces or three hundred carats." * The blacksmith who made the mould was brought to us, and the rascal showed a bit of wood shaped much

* Our diamond weights are as follows:—

16 parts = 1 (diamond) grain = 4-5ths grain, troy.
4 diamond grains = 1 carat = 3-1-6 (3·174 grains, troy).

The Indian weights are—

1 Dhan = 15-32 grains troy, in round numbers half a grain.
4 Dhary = 1 Rati = $1\frac{7}{8}$ grains, troy.
8 Rati = 1 Masha = 18 ,, ,,
12 Mashas = 1 Tola = 180 ,, ,,

The "ounces" in the text probably represent "tolas," certainly not troy ounces of 24 grains.

like a clove of orange. Finally, I was driven to accept the statement of Mr. Briggs (i., 117): "Almost all the finest jewels in India have been gradually collected at Hyderabad, and have fallen into the Nizam's possession, and are considered State property. *One uncut diamond alone of three hundred and seventy-five carats is valued at thirty lakhs of rupees*, and has been mortgaged for half that money."

Let us now estimate the value of the Nizam's diamond. For uncut stones we square the weight (375 × 375 = 140,625) and multiply the product by £2, which gives a sum of £281,250. For cut stones the process is the same, only the multiplier is raised from £2 to £8. Thus, supposing a loss of 75 carats, which would reduce 375 to 300 (300 × 300 = 90,000 × £8), we obtain a total value of £720,000.

Allow me briefly to compare the Nizam diamond (uncut 375 carats, cut 370), with the historic stones of the world. The list usually begins with the Pitt or Regent, the first cut in Europe. When the extraneous matter was removed in unusual quantities, it was reduced to 136¾ carats, valued from £141,058 to £160,000. The famous or infamous Koh-i-noor originally gauged 900 carats; it was successively reduced to 279 or 280 (Tavernier) and to 186¼ (=£276,768) when exhibited in Hyde Park; its last treatment has left it at 162½ carats. Then we have the Grand Duke's or Austrian, of 139½ carats (=£153,682); the Orloff or Russian (rose-cut) of 195 (193?) carats; and the Abaïté, poetically called the "Estrella do Sul" (Star of the South), weighing 120 carats. The "Stone of the Great Mogul," mentioned by Tavernier, is probably that now called to Daryá-i-noor: it weighs 279 9-16 carats, and graces the treasury of the Shah. The nearest approach to "The Nizam" is the Mattan or Laudah diamond of 376 carats. Experts agree to ignore the Braganza, whose 1,680 carats are calculated to be worth £5,644,800: the stone is kept with a silly mystery which makes men suspect that it is a white topaz.

And now to notice the diamond-diggings of India, and especially of Golconda, their ancient history and their modern state. I will begin by stating my conclusions. Diamonds have been found in the Ganges Valley: they are still washed as far north as Sambalpúr, and in the Majnodi, an influent of the Mahanadi, on the Upper Narbada (Nerbudda), on the line of the Godaveri and on the whole course of the Krishna. The extreme points would range between Masulipatam and the Ganges Valley; the more limited area gives a depth from north to south of some 5° (= three hundred direct geographical miles), beginning north from the Central Provinces and south from the Western Gháts, a breadth averaging about the same extent, and a superficies of ninety thousand miles. A considerable part of this vast space is, I need hardly say, almost unexplored, and the sooner we prospect it the better. The curious reader will find the limits laid down in the "General Sketch," etc., of British India, by G. B. Greenough, F.R.S.

The history of the diamond in India begins with the Maharabháta (B.C. 2100). The Koh-i-noor is supposed to have belonged to King Vikramaditya (B.C. 56), and to a succession of Moslem princes (A.D. 1306), till it fell into the hands of the Christians. Henry Lord's "Discovery of the Banian Religion" quaintly relates how "Shuddery" (Sudra), the third son of Pourvus (Purusha), "findeth a mine of diamonds," and engenders a race of miners—this is going back with a witness, *teste* Menu. At what period India invented the cutting of the stone we are as yet unable to find out; the more civilized Greeks and Romans ignored, it is suspected, the steel wheel. The Indian diamond was first made famous in Europe by the French jeweller, Jean Baptiste Tavernier (born 1605, died 1689), who made six journeys to the Peninsula as a purchaser of what he calls the Iri (*hira*).

Tavernier's travels are especially interesting to diamond-diggers, because he visited the two extreme points, north and south. He began with "Raulconda," in the Carnatic, some five days south of Golconda (Hyderabad), and eight or nine marches from Vizapore (*hodie* Bijapur). In 1665 the diggings were some two hundred years old, and they still employed sixty thousand hands. The traveller's description of the sandy earth, full of rocks, and "covered with coppice-wood, nearly similar to the environs of Fontainebleau," is perfectly applicable to the Nizam's country about Hyderabad. The diamond veins ranged from half an inch to an inch in thickness, and the precious gangue was hooked out with iron rods. Some of the stones were valued at two thousand, and even at sixteen thousand crowns, and the steel wheel was used for cutting. He then passed on to the Ganee diggings, which the Persians call Coulour (*hod* Burkalún), also belonging to the King of Golconda. They lay upon the river separating the capital from Bijapur. This must be the Bhima influent of the Krishna, and the old jeweller notices the "coracles" which are still in use. The discovery began about A.D. 1565 with a peasant finding a stone gauging twenty-five carats. Here, we are told, appeared the Koh-i-noor (nine hundred carats), which "Mirzimolas" or "Mirgimola," the "Captain of the Mogols," presented to the Emperor Aurungzeb. The sixty thousand hands used to dig to the depth of ten, twelve, or fourteen feet, *but as soon as they meet with water there is no hope of success.* Tavernier then records the fact that the king closed perforce half-a-dozen diggings between "Coulour and Raulconda, because for thirty or forty years the yield of black and yellow had given rise to frauds." The Frenchman's last visit was to "Soumelpore" (Sambalpur), "a town of Bengala, on the river Gowel," a northern affluent of the Mahanadi. The season for washing the diamantiferous land began in early February, when the waters run clear; other authors make it extend from November to the rainy season; and the eight thousand hands extended their operations to fifty *kos* up stream. Gold and the finest diamonds in India—locally called "Brahmans"—were found in the river-bed and at the mouths of the various feeders.

So far Tavernier. In 1688 and 1728, the well-known Captain Hamilton (New Account, etc., etc.), in his twenty-ninth chapter, treating of "Maderass or China-Patam," describes the diamond mines, evidently those of Partiál in the Northern Circars, as being distant a week's journey from Fort St. George; and he records the fact that the Pitt diamond was there brought to light.

The precious stone was practically limited to Hindústan and Borneo before A.D. 1728, when diggings were opened in Brazil. At first the new produce was rejected by the public, till it found out that many Indian stones from the New World were sent to Goa, and thence were exported to Europe. Still the general view was not wholly wrong. The specific gravity of the diamond averages 3·6, and the difference of oxide in the crystallized or allotropic carbon does not exceed a third place of decimals. This, however, makes all the difference in lustre; and, even in England, we have lately found out that a small brilliant of perfect water, hung to the ear for instance, is far more effective than a stone much superior in size but inferior in quality. The Public, perhaps, do not remember that as far back as 1868 my husband's study of the formations which bear the Brazilian diamonds enabled him to forecast that the gem would be found in a variety of places where its existence had never been suspected. Thus, to mention no others, they were washed in the Cudgegong river, near Rylston, New South Wales; the Australian Diamond Company failed, however, probably by bad management, to pay its expenses. It has been otherwise with the South African diggings, which began with the Vaal river; the stones are inferior even to those of the Brazil, yet they have reduced the value of the latter by one-third. When another great revolution or other political trouble shall occur, the diamond will recover its old market price.

"The diamond miners of Golconda," says Mr. Briggs (ch. vi.), "derive their name from being in the kingdom of Golconda, and not from being near the Fort. They are at the village of Purteeali (Partiál) near Condapilly, about one hundred and fifty miles from Hyderabad on the road to Masulipatam.* The property of them was reserved by the late Nizam when he ceded the Northern Circars to the English Government. They are

* Mr. Maclean kindly drew my attention to the Treaty with the Nizam (Nov. 12th, 1766), which cedes to the E. I. Company "the five Circars or Provinces of Ellour (Ellore, north of Masulipatam), Rajahmondra Siccacole (or Chicacole on the Coast), and Moortizanuggur or Gunton. The four first named were added to the French dominions by De Bussy. "These Circars," we read, "include territory extending along the coast from the mouths of the Kistna (Krishna) northward

superficial excavations not extending ten or twelve feet deep in any part. For some years past the working of them has been discontinued, and there is no tradition of their having ever produced very valuable stones."

This *resumé* is so full of errors that we cannot but suspect that they conceal some design. The historian must have known that the Pitt diamond, one of the finest and most perfect of its kind, was produced at Gáni Partiál; and that the Koh-i-noor came from the so-called "Golconda mines." Again, Partiál, on the north bank of the Krishna, some fifty miles from the Bay of Bengal, is only one of many diggings in the vast area which I have before laid down, some being still worked, and the others prematurely, we must believe, abandoned.

The student will do well to consult that valuable volume, the "Geological Papers on Western India" (Bombay, 1857), edited by my husband's old friend, Dr. Henry J. Carter. Here he will find detailed modern notices of a multitude of mines. John Malcolmson, F.R.S. (p. 6), treats of the diggings at "Chinon on the Pennar," and the Cuddapah mines (p. 6). Of the latter Captain Newbold says (Geological Notes, p. 375): "The diamond is found in the gravel beds of the Cuddapah district below the *Regur*,"—the black, tenacious, and fertile soils of Central and Southern India. The same scientific officer, who died too early for his fame, describes (p. 67) the yield of Mullavelly (or Malavilly), north-west of Ellore, as "occurring in a bed of gravel, composed chiefly of rolled pebbles of quartz, sandstone, chert, ferruginous jasper, conglomerate, sandstone, and Kankar, lying in a stratum of dark mould about a foot thick." Both these geologists inferred the identity of the sandstone of Central with that of Southern India from the existence of the diamond at Weiragad, a town about eighty miles south-east of the capital. Malcolmson declared that the "celebrated diamond

to near Ganjour, and stretching some distance inland." Article No. 11 of the same treaty runs thus: "The Hon'ble E. I. Company, in consideration of their diamond mines with the villages appertaining thereto, having been always dependent in H.H. the Nizam Government, do hereby agree that the same shall remain in possession now also."

mines of Partel (Partiál), Bangnapilly and Panna, occurring in the great sandstone formations of Northern India, as well as the limestones and schists associated with them, exhibit from the latitude of Madras to the banks of the Ganges, the same characters, and are broken up or elevated by granite on trap rocks, in no respect differing in mineralogical characters or in geological relations."

The Rev. Messrs. S. Hislop and R. Hunter, who visited and described the Nagpur mines, object to this assertion, and endeavour to prove that the "diamond sandstone of the Southern Maharatta Country is a conglomerate, reposing upon the arenaceous beds, which have *never* yielded the precious stone, nor are there any data to prove that the conglomerate derived most of its materials from that source." Dr. Heyne contributed an excellent description of the mines of Southern India, especially those of Bangnapilly (p. 689); of Ovalumpilly, six miles from Cuddapah (p. 691); and of others on the Ellore district. This experienced geologist concludes, "All the diamond mines which I have seen can be considered as nothing else than alluvial soil." Major Franklin (Geological Translation, second series, vol. iii., part 1), who visited the mines of Pannah in Bandelkhand, before Victor Jacquemont's day, makes the diamond-sandstone, between the Narbada (Nerbudda) and the Ganges, belong to the "New Red," apparently an error. Others have described the diggings east of Nagpur (Central Provinces) as having been opened in a matrix of lateritic grit. Dr. Carter (Summary of the Geology of India, pp. 686-91) connects the "diamond-conglomerate" with the Oolitic series and its *débris*, and he offers (p. 688) a useful tabular view of the strata in the mines of Bangnapilly, described by Voysey, and Pannah or Punna by Franklin and Jacquemont. The most important conclusion is their invariable connection with sandstone.

Dr. Carter's volume quotes largely from the writings of Mr. Voysey (*Journal As. Soc.*, Bengal, second Report on the Government of Hyderabad), a geologist who maintained the growth of the diamond as others do of gold: he declared that he could prove in alluvial soil the re-crystallisation of amethysts, zeolites, and felspar. During his last journey from Nagpur to Calcutta he visited the diamond washings of "Sumbhulpore," in the Mahanadi valley, and he describes the gems as being "sought for in the sand and gravel of the river," the latter consisting of pebbles of clay slate, flinty slate, jasper and jaspery iron-stone of all sizes, from an inch to a foot in diameter.

We possess fortunately a modern description of the diggings, which, I have said, were visited successively by Major Franklin and by Victor Jacquemont. M. Louis Rousselet ("L'Inde des Rajahs:" Paris, Hachette, 1875), in his splendid volume (pp. 440, 443), gives an illustration and an account of the world-famous miner of Pannah, the Pannasca of Ptolemy (?), a little kingdom of eastern Bandelkhand erected in 1809. The Rajah sent a "Jemadar" (officer) to show him the diggings, which are about twenty minutes' walk from the town. The site is a small plateau covered with pebble-heaps; and, at the foot of a rise somewhat higher than usual, yawns the pit, about twelve or fifteen inches in diameter, by twenty deep (about one hundred and eighty feet). It is pierced in alluvial grounds, divided into horizontal strata, *débris* of gneiss and carbonates, averaging thirteen metres: at the bottom is the diamond-rock, a mixture of silex and quartz, in a gangue of red earth (clay?). The naked miners descend by an inclined plane, and work knee-deep in water, which the Noria or Persian wheel, turned by four bullocks, is insufficient to drain; they heap the muddy mixture into small baskets, which are drawn up by ropes, whilst a few are carried by coolies. The dirt is placed upon stone slabs, sheltered by a shed; the produce is carefully washed, and the silicious residuum is transferred to a marble table for examination. The workmen, each with his overseer, examine the stones one by one, throwing back the refuse into a basket; it is a work of skill on the part of both men, as it must be done with a certain rapidity, and the rough diamond is not easily distinguished from the silex, quartz, jasper, hornstone (corundum), etc.

Tradition reports that the first diamonds of fabulous size were thus found, and the system of pits was perpetuated; when one is exhausted it is filled up and another is opened hard by,—a deplorable system, as one hundred cubic metres must be displaced to examine one, and around each well a surface of twenty times the area is rendered useless. Moreover, much time is lost by the imperfect way of sinking the shaft, which sometimes does not strike the stone.

This diamond stratum extends more than twenty kilometres to the north-east of Pannah; the most important diggings are those of the capital, of Myra, Etawa, Kamariya, Brijpur, and Baraghari. The mean annual produce ranges between £40,000 and £60,000,—a trifling sum, as the stones are the most prized in the world, and sell for a high price in the country. They are pure and full of fire; the colour varies from the purest white to black, with the intermediate shades, milky, rose, yellow, green, and brown. Some have been found reaching twenty carats, and the Myra mine yielded one of eighty-three, which belonged to the Crown jewels of the Mogul. Of course the real produce must be taken at double the official estimate, despite all precautions; such is the case everywhere. The Rajah has established an approximate average amount, and when this descends too low, he seizes one of the supposed defaulters and beheads him or confiscates his goods. He sells his diamonds directly to Allahabad and Benares, and of late years he has established *ateliers* for cutting; these are the usual kind, horizontal wheels of steel worked by the foot.

Evidently here we have a primitive style, which has not varied since diamond working began. Good pumps are required to drain the wet pits. Instead of sinking a succession of shafts, tunnels should be run along the veins of diamond-bearing rocks. Magnifying glasses and European superintendence would improve the washing. I need hardly say the yield would double in the hands of Brazilians or South Africans.

The precious stone is still brought for sale from the nearer valley of the Krishna to Hyderabad: it occurs, I was assured, in a whitish conglomerate of lime locally called Gar-ká-pathar, which must be broken up and washed. As it is found in a region of crystalline rocks, common sense would suggest tracing up the material to the places where it may have been formed, but this is never done. During our week's visit my husband was consulted by two Parsee merchants concerning the rudimentary tests of scratching and specific gravity. In fact at Golconda, when the finest gems used to be worked, no one, strange to say, can now recognise a rough diamond.

The "Highlands of the Brazil" (ii., 113) has given a detailed list of the various stones associated with the gem; and specimens of the Cascalho or diamond gravel, the Tauá, the Canga, etc., have been sent to the Royal Society of Edinburgh by Mr. Swinton. It is advisable to remark that this Association has everywhere been recognised. In Borneo we are told that "the diamond is known by the presence of sundry small flints." The gem-yielding pebble-conglomerate of India, not usually a breccia, as was proved by Franklin, Newbold and Aytoun (*loc. cit.*, p. 386), contains quartz and various quartzose formations; garnet, corundum, epidote, and Lydian stone; chalcedony and carnelian; jasper of red, brown, bluish, and black hues; and hornstone, a kind of felspar, whilst "green quartz indicates the presence of the best stones." Fossil chert is yielded by the limestone; and the highly ferruginous and crystalline sandstone produces micaceous iron ores, small globular stones (pisoliths?), and almost invariably fragments of iron oxide. Finally there are generally traces of gold, and sometimes of platinum. At Hyderabad I was assured that such was the case on the Krishna river, but none of my informants had any personal knowledge of washing. Finally Dr. Carter's "Geological Papers" convinced me that the sandstones of the diamond area will be found to resemble the "Itacolumite,"—quartzose mica slate or laminated granular quartz, of Brazilian "Minas Geraes."

These considerations convince me and my husband that diamond digging in India generally, and especially in Golconda (the territory of Hyderabad), has been prematurely abandoned. In the seventeenth and eighteenth centuries the machinery for draining wet mines was not what it is now; and the imperfect appliances led to the general belief that all the deposits were purely superficial. Doubtless some were in the alluvial soil of the most recent rocks, but M. Rosselet's account shows that deep digging may still be practised to advantage. Voysey also saw the "sandstone breccia" (diamond conglomerate?) of Southern India "under fifty feet of sandstone, clay, slate, and slaty limestone." The Brazilian miners ("Highlands," ii., 121) have only lately learned to descend one hundred and eighty feet; and they find some of their best stones at the lowest horizon. The Vaal River, and other South African washings, opened in 1868, soon reached sixty feet.

Immediately about the Golconda Fort the rocks, almost wholly syenitic and granitic, supply only quartz, chalcedony, carnelian, and amethyst; but we had heard of chance diamonds being picked up by the accolents of the Krishna River, and Sir Salar Jung, with his usual liberality, proposed laying a *dák* for Captain Burton to Raichor; he was ready, in fact, to meet a wanderer's wishes in every possible way. I presently, however, learned from good authority that only crystalline rocks, like those which we had seen in the Golconda tombs, are produced by this central section of the Krishna, and that "Itacolumite" must be sought elsewhere. Evidently the precious stones have been rolled down from some unknown distance; and to follow the "spoor" demanded more time than I could command.

It would be wasting paper to insist upon the benefits of reviving the ancient industry. But India is slow, deadly slow. In her present impoverished state she wants an energetic cultivation of every branch of industry. She does nothing; worse still, she rages against those who advise her to be up and doing. There is a fatal lethargy in her air. England administered like Anglo-India would be bankrupt in a week. And, locally speaking, diamond-working is a necessity. Hyderabad is not a rich country, and her trade is well-nigh *nil*. But she has coal that wants only a market, and if to the "black diamond" she can add the white diamond, her future prospects are not to be despised. The first step is of course that of "prospecting," of systematically reconnoitring the ground, with the aid of a few experienced hands, imported from the Brazil and South Africa. If the search be successful, a Company or Companies would be soon found to do the rest. For me it will be glory enough to have restored the time-honoured "mines of Golconda."

14

We left at the week's end the country of "our Faithful Ally," greatly pleased with the courtesy and hospitality which seem to be its natural growth. And I have a conviction that, despite the inevitable retrograde party of all native states, the *codini* of the East, the warlike Zemindars, the "dissolute vagabonds," the "Pathan bravos," and the "cut-throats and assassins" of the Press, this realm has become, since 1859, the "greatest Mohammedan power in India."

The return journey to Bombay gave time for other reflections. At present our "enormous dependency, India, the most populous and important that ever belonged to a nation, and conferring a higher prestige on the ruling race than has ever been conferred by any other subject people"—as the judicial Trollope has it—is, has been, and, under present circumstances, ever will be, somewhat neglected by the general public of England. No home Britisher can interest himself even moderately in such a colony: it is too distant, and it can hardly be brought nearer by local parliaments and similar institutions. Although "taxation without representation is tyranny," we are not yet prepared to grant, what eventually must be granted, Representative Government. We are therefore driven to seek some other course.

Again, at Hyderabad, as in India generally, we are living upon a volcano which may or may not slumber for years. See how of late all soldiers have come round to the same opinion concerning the "scientific frontier." All, in fact, are tacitly agreed to treat our Empire in India like an army, with supports, reserves with outposts, vedettes, and similar martial appliances. The remedies hitherto proposed for the natural disaffection of the great native powers, kept as they are in a state of *quasi*-tutelage, appear to be mere quackeries, likely to do harm rather than good. For instance, to make the energetic Indian prince more powerful within his own jurisdiction, would be simply to arm him against ourselves.

But why not at once admit a certain number to seats in the House of Lords? Of those who claim salutes of twenty-one guns, there are, besides four foreigners, three Indian princes, the Nizam, the Gaikwár, and the ruler of Mysore, who all happen at present to be minors. Amongst those honoured by nineteen guns we find Scindhia, Holkar, and Udepúr, whilst Jaipúr, with twelve others, has seventeen guns. Of course it would be necessary to limit the number to six or seven, but the hope of eventually rising to the dignity should not be withheld from chiefs of lower grade.

Nothing would tend more directly to conciliate the princes of India, and to make them our firm friends, than to admit them to the highest dignity of the Empire, to a House where they would doubtless hasten to sit; where they would learn their true interests, and where they would find themselves raised to a real instead of a false equality with the ruling race.

Mr. Sowerby addressed a letter (April 25th, Broach) to the *Times* of India, entering into a discussion with my husband on the Diamonds of Golconda, to which the latter replied as follows:

THE UNDEVELOPED RESOURCES OF INDIA.

To the Editor of the "Times" of India.

SIR,—Amidst the hurry and worry of departure, I failed to find a spare moment for noticing the valuable communication dated Broach, April 25th, and bearing the name of your distinguished correspondent, Mr. Sowerby. The calm and quiet of my present home, the "*Minerva*," allow me leisure *à discretion*, and perhaps some of your readers may not be unwilling to see how much may be said on the other side.

The Madras Government would have done better to send a few experienced diamond-diggers to the Cuddapah country, instead of "driving the unfortunate diamond-seekers away from the fields;" but we have already heard something concerning the modicum of wisdom with which the world, even in Madras, is governed. Of course untrained prospecting and ignorant working end, as a rule, in "the most abject poverty, wretchedness, and starvation." Thus we explain the Spanish proverb, "A silver mine means misery, a gold mine ruin." The "Garimpeiro" or pick-and-pan adventurer in the Brazil could hardly keep himself alive on manioc and tobacco where the wealthy English companies, which took his place, filled their coffers. With the diamond the same is the case, and hence I have been able to draw up a "rose-tinted" account of the diggings in Minas Geraes. Capital and skilled labour succeed where the desultory attempts of untaught men breed nothing but failure. My "projects" are simply to place the true state of the case before the

English capitalist, and to enlist the sympathies of individuals and of the public: it would be a profligate waste of labour to attack the *vis inertiæ* of the Indian Government, and bepreach the caste whose Dharma it is to work the machine. It is hardly possible to believe that, whilst the diamond has been found in spots scattered over the enormous area, say, of five hundred direct geographical miles in depth, bounded north by the Mahanadi and south by the Krishna, the mineral resources of vast and almost unexplored tracts, like the highlands of Orissa, should continue to be neglected. And, although an attempt to revive the diamond mines of Sambalpore resulted, I am told, in failure, my advice would be to begin with the oldest diggings, which, as Tavernier shows, were systematically abandoned after reaching the depth of a few feet, because the owners ignored the art of pumping. Even if the deserted spots be so worked out as not to yield a single gem, they will make an excellent practical study of the formations in which the stone may be expected to occur elsewhere. My principal difficulty will be the utter unfamiliarity with the subject which belongs to the class whose interests are most concerned. The first attempt brings me the following answer: "I will give my opinion of the undertaking when I have studied the details, but Golconda is an ungodly place to invite the British capitalist to." As regards preliminaries, a friend, whose touching modesty induces me to withhold his name, writes to me: "The success in finding minerals and gems to the east of the Gháts is simply a question of prospecting; and the more prospectors the merrier. Why, there must be now ferreting in Australia, Tasmania, and New Zealand, little short of half a million of skilled hands. Geologists are valuable only so far that they indicate formations likely to prove fertile,—the real work must be done by prospectors."

I am far from thinking with Mr. Sowerby, that in a hopeful matter like this, of development of wealth, "native rulers will always take their cue from the paramount power," however rigidly our official seal is affixed to the mineral treasures lying dormant in the land. One of the commonplaces of the theoretical English writer is the exceeding conservatism of the East: practically I have found the reverse. True the Bombay "Kumbi" rejected the ridiculous windmills by which the late Dr. Buist proposed to abolish the cheap and all-sufficient water-wheel; and thus he incurred the vehement displeasure of that *perfervidum ingenium*, who had, they said, a monetary interest in the matter. But show the Hindú and Hindí (Moslem) that the novelty will pay or will save money; they will adopt it as readily as almost any nationality known to me. What nonsense has been written and read about the failure of Indian railways because nothing could persuade the Brahmin to ride side by side with the pariah! The truth is, Caste remains powerful as long as it pays; in the inverse condition it is a name, and nothing more.

But practically it is very little matter whether the Government of H.H. the Nizam take or take not the cue from the groovy and torpid rule which distinguishes British India in this section of the nineteenth century. That it will grant free and liberal concessions I am persuaded. Still, after all, the diamond-diggings in the Krishna Valley, though far-famed for their produce in days gone by, are a mere line of trenches compared with the depth of field which lies behind them.

Upon the subject of iron-making in India, Mr. Sowerby and I must agree to differ. Of course stone may be too rich for smelting purposes: my travels have shown me mountains of iron, in the United States and in South America, which are, perforce, neglected for poorer ores. But the common charcoal-smelted metal of the Brazil is preferred by the English mining companies, for instance at Sao Joao d' El Rei, to stampers of the best English steel; and I fail to see why the same should not be the case in India, when replanting of trees shall become the rule, and when the woods and forests shall be properly managed. In my former letter, however, I alluded especially to sword-blades and other costly articles, in which the least thing thought of is the value of the raw material. Mr. Sowerby asserts, "Not a single attempt has been made to manufacture arms in India on a European scale and on European principles, but it has ended in financial failure." Yet, further on, we are told that a "native smith of Salem makes the best of hog-spears and hunting-knives." European principles, I presume, mean the use of coal, whilst the native preferred charcoal. And why should the Brazil succeed so admirably with its thousands of little Catalan furnaces, and India fail? Evidently the quality of the fuel is, in both cases, the vital condition of success.

The specimens of Hyderabad coal shown to me at the Nizam's capital were of thicker formation and of superior quality to the "brown coal of Southern Austria," which is a mere lignite. And yet the latter pays, even for steamers, when mixed with a certain proportion of Cardiff. There *is* a demand for coal almost throughout the ancient kingdom of Golconda, where the land has been ruthlessly disforested; and there should, methinks, be little difficulty in inducing the people to abolish in its favour the use of "gobar" and other fuels to which their poverty drives them. Here the only want is evidently cheap and easy transport; and with this object I proposed Mr. Worsley's "wooden idea."

Your distinguished correspondent throws undue stress, it appears to me, upon the fact that these cheapest of tramways have been known in England for centuries, and have been supplanted by light iron rails. Because the latter are found cheapest in England, *argal*, as the grave-digger said, they should be adopted in India. But the mine-owners in the Brazil, where wood is hard and abundant as in India, still work with wooden rails; and in both countries the state of the thoroughfares, especially beyond the main lines of traffic, is that of England two hundred years ago.

Upon this subject the modest friend before quoted writes to me as follows: "I shall be much obliged if you will give me all the information you can about Worsley's wooden railways. I have five hundred acres of excellent timber at a point of the Tasmanian north-west coast, three hundred and fifty miles from Melbourne. I am within two miles of a shipping-place, and I shall have to make five miles of tramways with wooden rails, *as is always done in this neighbourhood*" (italics mine); "but the ordinary flanged wheels are used, and they drub the rails horribly. I understand your description of the rails, but I cannot gather from your letter to the *Times* of India what sort of wheels Mr. Cayley Worsley proposes to use. Could you send me a plan, or tell me where to get one?"

Mr. Worsley supplied me with a sketch-design of his invention or modification, but as it contains novelties perhaps unknown to Mr. Sowerby, whilst allowing me to put the public in possession of the outline of his scheme, he naturally enough insisted upon the details and the plan being kept secret. I have therefore referred my valued correspondent to the inventor himself, whose private residence is No. 62, Belgrave Road, London.

Finally, when Mr. Sowerby roundly asserts "it is rather too late in the day to teach us anything new in making cheap tramways," I presume that he has seen or has read about the "Pioneer," lately invented by my friend, Mr. John Haddan, C.E., and exhibited during last December at Mr. Lee Smith's offices, No. 6, Westminster Chambers; and "The Economical," belonging to Mr. Russell Shaw. If not, he would do well to master the subject, and then he will probably conclude with me that what has been done in tramways (as in other matters) is a very small part of what remains to be done.—Yours, etc.,

Aden, at Sea, May 18th, 1876. R. F. BURTON.

CHAPTER X.

HIS ROYAL HIGHNESS THE PRINCE OF WALES.

THE next event was the Prince of Wales's departure from Bombay; when that "Illustrious Visitor" left what romantic writers call the "palm-tasselled strand of glowing Ind." There was a feeling of gladness that the long and somewhat risky visit had passed off, not only without accident, but with no heavier *contretemps* than a night in the swamp, and the delaying of a mail train. The closing scene of a historic event has fallen to the lot of old Bombay, where the Prince leaves behind him the happiest memories. Many tales are circulated of his genial and hearty manners, sweet temper and good breeding; his frank, friendly, and thoroughly unofficial greetings to the Rajahs and Chiefs whom he visited, and who visited him, and these, they said, formed a refreshing contrast to the stiff dignity of *employé* manners, from the "big wig" down to the acting assistant sub-deputy collector. Hindí (Moslem) and Hindú (non-Moslem) have at length seen what they will not see again; but I will not describe, because the description would be too flattering, and flattery is no compliment.

H.R.H. entered, or rather re-entered, Bombay (which on both occasions greeted him with effusion) at a most anxious moment. Reuter's telegram, March 9th, had just announced that Her Majesty, by the sensible advice of Lord Beaconsfield, had taken the additional title of EMPRESS OF INDIA, a title thoroughly recognized throughout India since A.D. 1859. Curious to relate, one of the native Chiefs, who assisted in receiving the future Emperor at the Church Gate Station of the B. B. and C. I. Railway, bore on his breast a large gold plate, presented to him by H.M. in 1859, and bearing upon it "Empress of India." The ex-"People's William" on this occasion was greatly at fault. How could the superior rank of a Suzerain "affect the status of the independent Princes of India," except by making them the allies of an Empress instead of a Queen,—and moreover in India, where everything appertaining to rank is a question of how many guns are fired for one of our Indian allies? The man who has nineteen guns must think himself almost equal to the Queen, whose salute is only twenty-one; but when she is Empress with one hundred and one guns, then she is a Sovereign indeed in his eyes. India has not yet thoroughly learnt to master, and yet less to love, the British idea of a constitutional King, whilst that of an Emperor is as familiar to her as any other household word. The meanest subject of a petty Hindú Rajah always feels himself raised in the social scale when his liege lord becomes a Maharajah or Great Rajah.

It is amusing to hear the different disputes as to what the Hostani title ought to be,—Sarvabhauma Rájni (All Lands' Queen), or Máhárájni (Great Queen), Sháhansháh (King of Kings), Malikat el-Mulúk (Queen of Kings), Sultánàt el-Hind (Sultanah of India), but not Gamaná-gamanam (*i.e., coming and going between East and West*), Professor Monier Williams's hobby, which was awfully criticised in India. However, the great impression here is created by the Queen's hundred and one guns. *They* can range only as high as twenty-one guns, and think more of one extra gun than anything in the world, by way of importance, and they know that it is hardly right that a subject can be saluted by as many guns as his Sovereign.

The Hindús are delighted because the Prince has arrived at one of their great feasts,—a time-honoured festival, the chief of the four great solar epochs, solstices and the equinoxes. It is called Holi or Holika—when the sun has finished his annual southing, and returns to the north, bringing with him spring, warmth, growth, life, and love. The favourite ceremonies are the burning of the Catu, the dance round the fire, the swinging with hooks inserted under the shoulder-muscles, which gave one's girlhood shivers, and broadsides of chaff and abuse between the male and female votaries of the merry god, are memorials of Krishna in his solar aspect, and denote the sacrifice, the sportive games, and the chaffing of the Gopals and Gopís, the male and female cowherds of idyllic Mathura. The worshippers wear red-dyed faces and yellow-stained body-garments, trailing their jackets for a Hindú saturnalia; and during these days master and man, officer and private, may seize one another and rub on and in the *gulah*, or coloured flour. The Anglo-Indian is always testy about the Holi festivals. That is a stupid want of sympathy with a conquered race; for these same men would enjoy an Italian carnival, and be anything but displeased at the throwing of the *confetti*, which is our Western Holi. They do not mind wax lemons full of rosewater dropped on their hats and coats by fair Senhoras and Senhoritas of Lisbon, Rio, Seville, Rome. So the Prince finds Bombay in gala dress, with strips of coloured paper hung from house to house, and a host of faithful subjects disguised with *gulah*, merriment, worship of Krishna, and strong waters.

The other festivals are (1) the Dewalu, a Feast of the Lanterns; (2) Cocoa-nut Day, which is the feast of throwing offerings into the sea; (3) the festival of the eighth incarnation of Krishna.

At the Feast of Lanterns every home must be illuminated, from the grand house near the Mombadevi Chowki, to the fruitseller who (Maclean wittily describes), "with a small vegetable hole, and a dip stuck in a cocoa-nut or two in front, squats in a corner amongst his vegetables, crossing his thin black legs, and stares at his illumination with as much satisfaction as Nero looking at Rome in flames."

The Topasses have a passion-play at Bandora.

Flags of course hung out in abundance from every window and possible place, and Watson's Esplanade Hotel was gorgeous. Sets of double poles, blue painted, did duty for Venetian masts, and lined the way, each bearing its bunting. In front of the Municipality was a trophy or stand of arms,—ancient guns taken from native Princes, French, and Portuguese; Miss Frere's floral fount was hung with tropical blossoms, in which glowed a red "Farewell;" H.M.'s statue by Noble was garnished with scarlet trappings, and the dockyard sheds were beflagged.

The main entrance and exit, the largest dockyard shed, was some hundred feet broad, and perhaps two hundred yards long. It was red carpeted, and benches were erected in tiers on each side, covered with red cloth. It was decorated with flags of all nations, and Prince of Wales feathers, and arches of evergreens, and palms, and flowers; the front adorned with a large inscription, "God speed." Near the entrance was placed a large model of Elephanta—at which, however, the Prince had just then no time to look. On the benches and around were collected his devoted admirers—the ladies, the press, the municipality, and corporation, and all sorts of military display; band, escort, and officials waiting, the way lined with troops in white and in full dress, and "Souter's Canaries" (police, yellow turbaned). The Royal greeting was fired from the saluting battery. The bands struck up "God save the Queen," and the troops presented arms, the public rushed to the windows as the carriages and the travellers followed.

As the Prince neared to where the English, his loyal subjects, gathered round, and in the dockyard shed, then the native buzz was lost in the true British cheer. The Prince was looking strong and well, brown, handsome, and happy. He shook hands with the officers and officials, bowed to the ladies, and passed on to embark; and here the naval authorities took up the pageant as the Prince set foot in the boat, and were as important as gunpowder and bunting could make them.

The formal farewell was over, and the grand pageant faded for ever into the past. Despite smallpox * and fatigue, the Prince landed as a private person from the *Serapis* at seven p.m. on Saturday, and dined at Malabar Point with "His Excellency the Governor and high officials," and the "Palace" on the ridge was a blaze of light. With this exception the Prince did not quit

* The smallpox was raging, and so great was the fear that the Prince might catch it, he was made to avoid the native town, and go from station to ship, whilst the unpunctuality of the railway made him an hour late.

the ship. Smallpox cases were fifty a day, and he was entreated not to run the risk. On the 12th there was a dinner on board the flagship *Undaunted*, Admiral Macdonald, Commander-in-Chief, in honour of the Prince, and this day I write there is a luncheon party on board the *Serapis*. Towards three o'clock the shore was crowded, and house tops were gay, flags making Bombay a many-coloured city. Martial bands struck up, and salvoes of artillery, fleet, and city, announced that the *Serapis*, *Osborne*, and *Raleigh*, steamed out of Bombay harbour at 3.30, containing our Royal, Imperial Prince, and future Emperor, and with him the hearts of all his subjects, and the golden opinions of all true men and women.

We visited the Towers of Silence, or Parsee charnel-house (Dakhmeh), the burying place of the "Fire-worshippers." This is situated in a large garden on a hill-summit, which you ascend by a giant staircase, half a mile long, overhung by palms and tropical vegetation. Then you pass a clock, and a hand pointing to the following notice: "None but Parsees enter here." This eminence, a spur of Malabar Hill, appears to stand alone like a little knoll rising out of a plain, and it commands a lovely view, like the city of Rio de Janeiro, feathery palm-forest, glorious sky above, and sea all around.

This is one of the four splendid views of Bombay, with harbour, sea, and adjacent islands. Another is Kumballa Hill, one from Mazagon Hill over the harbour, a glimpse of the Konkan, the narrow plain which lies between the coast and the Western Ghâts, and the curious forms of the hills beyond it, which look like weird cathedrals, fortresses, and citadels; and the fourth is from Parell Hill, looking over the picturesque country of Suri, and over the tops of the palm and cocoa forests, with a glimpse of sea towards the west.

The palms, however, immediately around us, are thick with myriads of large black vultures, gorged with smallpox and cholera corpses. The air is heavy with their breath, and though people say it is impossible, I felt my head affected so long as we remained there. It stands to reason. These myriads of birds feed only on corpses. They must breathe and exhale what they feed upon. They fatten upon what bare contact with would kill us, and they cluster in thousands. This garden, or burial ground, is full of public and private family towers.

The great public tower is divided into three circles, with a well in the middle. It has an entrance and four outlets for water. First there is a place for clothes, and a tank, like a huge metal barrel, lying on its side, to bathe with. Here the priests, who are the operators, leave their garments. A large procession of Parsees having accompanied the body as far as this spot, turn and wait outside. The priests then place the body, if a man, on the first circle; if a woman, on the second; and if a child, on the third; in the centre of which is the dry well, covered with a grating. The priests are obliged to stop and watch. A body is picked clean in an hour by these vultures, who fly down the moment they see the procession coming, and have to be kept at bay till the right moment. It is considered very lucky if they pick out the right eye first, instead of the left, and the fact is reported to the relatives. When the bones are perfectly clean, the Parsee priest pushes them into the well. When the rain comes it carries off the ashes and bones, and the water runs through these four outlets with charcoal at the mouths, to purify it before entering and defiling the earth, which would become putrid and cause fever. They will not defile the earth by being buried in it, and it is an honour to have a *living sepulchre.* They have on an average, when there is no epidemic, three bodies a day. The priests then descend, wash, and resume their garments, when they are reclaimed from being impure, and the procession returns to the city.

Once descended from this melancholy height there was no smell, whilst Bombay itself smells of sandal wood and roast Hindú, as I will afterwards explain.

In the afternoon I had a charming sail with Miss Rose and her *Brother Jack*, in an affair of sixty tons, with a broad lateen sail. The breeze was stiff, and I enjoyed seeing the men crowding up the mast and rigging like monkeys, eight on one sail, and tacking it in with their toes in a moment. I went to supper at the house of a Persian friend of my husband's, whose wife

I like very much. They had a small relative to supper, aged five, who is very sharp. She is to be married eventually to the son of the house, aged seventeen, and they chaff each other; for instance, she says, "I don't want you," and he says, "Well, I am sure I still less want you."

Lieutenant Julian Baker, R.N., called next day; he is a nephew of Sir Samuel Baker: a pleasant youth, with a nice frank face and manners.

In the afternoon we went to the Town Hall, to swell the numbers of those who went to assist at the unveiling of the statue of Sir Cowasjee Jehanghir, father of Mr. Mannockjee Cursetjee. Mr. Dosabhoy Framjee read an address, Mr. Gibbes made a short and feeling speech. We arose and made a procession, and there was a hearty cheer as the covering was struck away, the Union Jack remaining above the head. It was the statue of a noble meditative Parsee, with hands strongly clasped, as if making a resolution. He is an upright, charitable man, who has used his immense wealth, with all his might, for good purposes, like Lady Burdett Coutts. He has long been bedridden, for he is a great age. Happy he whose only reward is *not* a statue, and may this little testimonial he so richly deserves, detract nothing from his eternal reward, for they say he has never done charity for show, but for charity's own sake.

We dined at Parel in the evening—a solemn Government House dinner. It was exactly like a gentleman's dinner at a good house in England, but naturally a little bit stiffer, as it was official.

Next morning we drove to Malabar Point, a delightful spot; a promontory or tongue of land running out into wild open sea, bound by rocks and boulders. The Point is covered with bungalows, having spacious verandahs all around, covered in with cool matting. The sea dashes up on both sides, for it is exposed to the full sway of wind and waves, and the trees are blown back, beginning about a foot from the roots, and have the appearance of being pegged down. This residence is the only thing I envy his Excellency the Governor of Bombay.

In the afternoon we drove to Lady Sassoon's beautiful palazzo and gardens, and found her surrounded by about fifty relations, pretty Jewesses, in costumes, and covered with jewellery. They were playing cards and smoking Narghilahs, and received us most cordially.

In the evening we went to a provincial theatre, the last representation, where we saw a not bad Pygmalion and Galatea; but the manager came out and made a funny speech, in which he abused all his own actresses so much, that I thought it was rather good-natured of them to perform afterwards.

Sir Charles Sargent and Mr. Melville gave us several very nice garden-parties. They had a villa and charming gardens overhanging the sea and rocks at Breach Candy, where we used to have games out of doors, ices, and refreshments; tea and cigarettes by moonlight, and private theatricals. The performance was masterly, and Mr. Melville, who is one of the most popular members of the society, for his amiability, cleverness, and hospitality, composed and spoke the following bright little epilogue, which deserves perpetuating.

EPILOGUE.

Ladies and Gentlemen, I must implore
Your kind indulgence for five minutes more.
I wish to preach a sermon, ere we part,
Upon a subject very near my heart!
You've been amused to-night; your looks confess
You think our play a moderate success;
And yet we feel, with a keen sense of shame,
There's not been much to praise, and much to blame.
I don't speak of the acting; *that* defies
E'en the most critical to criticise:
But how can the best actors play their part,
With no appliances of scenic art?
For stage a low verandah, which, albeit a
Cool airy place, makes but a wretched theatre;
Scant scenery; no properties; a curtain
Whose rise and fall is, like the funds, uncertain.
Ah! if we only had a proper stage,
Our entertainments would be quite the rage:
The Rivals, School, She Stoops to Conquer, Caste—
We'd act them all, each better than the last;
But as it is we can no higher aim
Than a poor farce like "Woodcock's Little Game."

This brings me to my sermon ; you've divined
No doubt the subject present to my mind.
My text is this : Oh grievous thing to say !
There's not a Theatre in all Bombay,
Except that unendurable abode
Of dirt and evil odours in Grant Road.
O my dear brethren, what a stain is this
On the fair fame of our metropolis !
We boast of our fine buildings, and we utter
Contemptuous remarks about Calcutta ;
Look at our splendid Sailors' Home ! "Yes, look :
It holds two sailors and a drunken cook."
Look at our University ! how grand !
There's not a building like it in the land !
"It cost ten lakhs," you say ? Humph, rather dear :
"Is it much used ?"—Well, only once a year.
Then our Museum ! what a gorgeous pile
Of architecture in Renaissance style !
"No doubt it's full of treasures ? Let us knock :
Ugh ! specimens of cotton, and trap-rock !"
Don't laugh. With all this money (oh ! 'tis sad),
Think what a Theatre we might have had !

Let us recall to mind the blessed day
When England's Heir first landed in Bombay.
We rose to the occasion : near and far
Millions of *bhuttees** blazed in the bazaar :
Triumphal arches spanned the roads : on one
"Please tell Mamma that we are happy" shone ;
And on another, writ in words of fire,
"Hail, Albert Edward, Prince of Wales, ESQUIRE !"
Much gratified, His Royal Highness passed
Through the thronged streets, and reached Parell at last ;
And having feasted like a prince (as all
Feast at Parell, who go there, great or small),
And having smoked, said in his cheery way,
"Now, Carington, let's go and see the play."
What words can paint the Prince's scornful pity,
When told we don't have plays in this dull City ?
His looks complete bewilderment expressed,
And he was heard to mutter, "Well, I'm blessed !"

Those precious words, from lips so honoured, still
Through every fibre of our bosoms thrill.
They've roused us from our torpor : come what may,
A Theatre we *will* have in Bombay.

* Candles ; lamps.

All that we want is money; if I read
Your looks aright, you'll soon supply that need:
Or, if our private means won't bear the brunt,
Pedder,* the People's William, to the front!
Now is the time for our Municipality
To show itself possessed of some vitality!
Go, all ye members of our Town Committee,
View every third-rate Continental city;
You'll not find one which does not yearly vote
The funds to keep a Theatre afloat.
These foreigners still hold in due respect
The maxim of old Rome, which we neglect,
That a wise ruler to the ruled dispenses
Not bread alone, but *panem et Circenses.*
If it must be, lay on another tax:
We'll not complain,—it will not break our backs:
But, if you're not incompetent *in toto*,
Give us a decent Theatre to go to!

Our Governor in Council, sure I feel,
Will lend his best support to my appeal.
O noble Wodehouse! shall the Muses own
In thy fair realm no house of wood or stone?
O Counsellor of the poetic name!†
Thyself a poet, is not ours thy shame?
O great high priest of the masonic guild!
Thou, and thy masons, up, arise, and build!

I see already with prophetic eyes
A pile of purest Bombay Gothic rise;
I stand within its walls: what perfect taste!
No vain display, but how extremely chaste!
Soft music floats upon the perfumed air:
Our beauty and our fashion all are there:
Our gilded youths (whatever that may mean)
Lounge in the stalls, and deck the festive scene:
And still more beautiful, and still more dear,
Our maidens crowd the boxes, tier on tier:
Their cheeks are flushed with happiness; the light
Of their sweet eyes is more than ever bright;
Their parted lips——but stay! I do declare
Your parted lips have quite a hungry air:
So, ere imagination gets the upper
Hand of us all, let's go and have some supper!

* Lord Mayor of Bombay, Mr. Pedder.

† Hon. Mr. Rogers.

One of my pleasures was the Chinese bazar, but that was greatly interfered with by the smallpox. Crawford market is also a sight to see, and the dockyards. Then came Lord Lytton's arrival, which was carried out in the same way as the Prince's departure, the same buildings and decorations being left to stand for the two occasions. I went, amongst others. Lord Lytton bowed courteously, was very well dressed,—which strikes one when in savage lands,—and had nice cordial manners. All the Bombay world was there, and Lady Lytton, I need not say, was conspicuously thoroughbred and graceful. I am always glad to see such important posts filled with blue, not golden blood. I spent part of the day in the Convent, with five simple English nuns sitting around me, and listening to my stories of travel and adventure. They do immense good by teaching.

Then came the departure of Lord Napier of Magdala. Everybody went to see him off. Besides the regular guard of honour, all his old Abyssinian Wallahs (21st), by force of habit, "off duty" and without arms, formed themselves into a guard to bid farewell to their cherished Commander. I saw several misty eyes, and got myself an unpleasant sensation in the throat as I saw the splendid old soldier move away from the crowd of "swells" after the first greetings, and go and speak touching words of parting to his men. It must be a strange moment in a man's life, resigning a command after a brilliant forty-eight years' career such as his was, and being turned out to grass ere the fire and energy of work has flickered out, if one may use such an expression regarding the Command at Gibraltar.

In the evening I had a pleasant little dinner and sensible talk with Mr. Martin Wood and his wife, to whose house I used to enjoy going.

We went several times to the old Girgaum burial grounds in the Sonápur Quarter, to find a lost grave, and at last, after an infinity of trouble, we did find it. He was a once celebrated man, and yet no one at present knew of his grave, except Richard Burton. Such is glory! After many hot hours and days and vain searching, in parties, amongst the twenty thousand tombs, we found a plain space containing a very old tombstone, with letters that required one to kneel down and trace with the finger. No "Sacred to," but only "Victor Jacquemont; born at Paris, 28th August, 1801; arrived at Calcutta in May 1829, and after travelling three years and a half in India, expired at Bombay on 7th December, 1832" (forty-six years ago). He was a man of letters, a botanist, and naturalist, who is supposed to have pioneered the French to India, and had the Legion of Honour ("Correspondance de Victor Jacquemont," 2 vols.: Paris, 1833, published a year after his death). He was a French Catholic, and a fellow Bohemian, so we paid a tribute to his memory. I recited a *De Profundis*, and my husband gave directions to have the letters picked out and painted afresh, to mark where he lies. Jacquemont died in the house of one Nicol, who wrote to his brother, M. Porphyre. He had three doctors,—MacLellan, Kemball, and Henderson,—60×60 leeches, salivated, blistered, etc. Got worse after a quarrel with his black servants, and died of abscess in the liver, which burst internally. He had "black vomit," *c'était un baquet de macération*, and was kept alive by animal soup and wine. He had a public funeral. These were all the details we were able to collect; but this is a great deal after forty-six years, considering that no one actually remembered where his grave was.

We then went to see the Brahm Somaj, a new Maharatta religious meeting place,—a building like a singing or lecture hall. The house is a small stone-carved house, like all Hindú temples. It is a compound between Hindú and Christian. A railed gallery runs all round. It is full of benches and chairs. There is a chairman's seat and a desk. On Sundays they meet, talk, and sing. The new sect believe in one God, no idol, no revelation. Miss Mary Carpenter goes to these meetings to draw them over.

There is an old-new church in Travancore, started by the Syrian Christians. It claims to have been founded personally by St. Thomas the Apostle, in the year of our Lord 57. It is like the church of Armenia; Christ Himself wrote to the Prince of Ur, and despatched Bartholomew and Judas to find it. However, the Syrian church in Travancore dates to the second century, showing the vitality of their faith, and the toleration of the Hindús, who granted them a separate village and full jurisdiction over their own tribe; these happy days lasted till the Portuguese came. Since the abolition of the Inquisition, the Church has grown again, and its members are returned, although Travancore is no bigger than Wales, at four lakhs. They have been indulging in revivals, and their present prophet is Justus Joseph, the son of a woman who was a singer in a Hindú temple, and of hysterical temperament. He has a flock of five thousand Syrian Christians, and eighteen priests, to the grief of the orthodox, and the scandal of British missionaries. The accounts of their doings are wonderful, and in the worst form of "revival meetings;" but this is only hearsay, I have not been there.

Malabar Hill, thirty years ago, had only two houses on it, now it is covered with the bungalows of the English. It is a charming drive from here to Breach Candy by the sea to Mahaluxmee.

Then we went to Walkeshwar, and I am sure most visitors and many residents do not know where that is. Just off the road to Malabar Point, and close to Frere Town, little as you would suspect it, lies a most interesting remnant of ancient India, pure and undefiled. You descend several flights of steps, and come in view of a splendid tank some hundred yards long and broad, which you reach by other flights of steps, and which extends the whole length and breadth of the tank. The water looks nasty and unwholesome, and was covered with insects, some stinging and venomous. The banks are surrounded by innumerable Hindú temples, great and small, dedicated to Mahadevi, and their other gods. As it was already evening, there was a lighting of lamps and a ringing of bells. The village around is inhabited entirely by Hindús. A holy Brahman pundit came out of a Hindú convent, or ascetic place, and good-humouredly escorted us to see everything.

We went one day to the Hindú Smáshán, or burning ground, in the Sonápur Quarter. The corpse was covered with flowers, the forehead reddened with sandal wood, and the mouth blackened.

The bier was carried by several men; one bore sacred fire in an earthenware pot. The burial-ground men, or sextons, made four holes in the ground with a crowbar, a little larger than the length and breadth of the body, into which they drove four stout stakes; then they piled up logs of wood, cross-barred, of the same length and breadth, six or eight layers high. It is teak wood (Saag), and cost about ten rupees. They lay the body upon it. Everyone walked up and put a little water in her mouth, first the husband, then the father, father-in-law, relatives, and friends, just as we throw dust on the coffin. They pile more layers of wood on the body, leaving it in the middle. Then the husband comes out and walks backwards to the fire, and takes, with his hands behind him, a burning brand, and applies it to the wood, and sets the first light to it; the whole party in similar order, as before named with the water, do the same, but facing the pile, not walking backwards, and they apply the fire to the four corners, one to each cardinal point. The rich burn with wood and ghee. The ashes and bones are thrown into the sea. The ordinary ceremony costs about sixteen rupees,—three hours consume a corpse. The burning of the Hindú reposes upon the idea of regeneration. He has three births: first, physical from his parents; his second, his religious ceremony, which makes him a Dwija, or thrice-born man; his third is the heavenly birth attained by passing through the purifying pyre.

There were two mourners, eleven employed over the fire, a guardian of the burial ground, a sepoy, a gatekeeper, eighteen or twenty spectators, accompanying the funeral—all were Hindú, except ourselves. They bring sugar, and on coming and going they throw some down to feed the ants. Shortly the clothes caught fire and then the feet, and then we saw no more except a great blaze, and smelt a smell of roasted flesh, which mingles with the sandal wood perfume of Bombay. The Smáshán, or burning ground, is a long, large enclosed yard, with a long shed or covered verandah, and seats for mourners. The yard is dotted with these burning places. A sacred cow is stalled at one end. Towards the entrance is a little garden, a Moslem cemetery, and a little burial ground for Hindú children, as these are not burnt.

All the burial grounds here extend almost to Chaupati (Chaw-putty), the inmost bend of the bight, but are now at Sowri (Suri), some ten miles from Bombay, and are very pretty. The groves of cocoa palm which belt the road of the Sonápur Quarter, make one forget the melancholy site, the heads tufted with luxuriant fronds, blown in every direction by the sea breeze, and their masses of dark verdure contrast well with the leek green of the plantain, the darker hues of the various figs, the glowing scarlet of the silk cotton tree, the gold yellow of the bignonia, the mauve bracts of the Bougainvillea, and the purpling red of the Poinsetta.

CHAPTER XI.

DEDICATED TO THE ANTI-VIVISECTIONISTS OF ENGLAND.

ANOTHER most interesting visit for me, who devote a great part of my life to "prevention of cruelty to animals," was the Pinjrapole, or hospital for animals sick, maimed, and incurable, in the heart of the Native Quarter called Bhuleshpsar, which establishment covers two thousand square yards. There were old bullocks that have been tortured and had their tails wrung off, which is the popular way here of making them go faster. There were orphan goats and calves, starved kittens and dogs, the blind, the lame, the wounded. It was founded forty years ago by Sir Jamsetji Jijibhoy, and is kept chiefly by the money and piety of the founder, and the well-known banker, Mr. Khamchund Motichand, and supported likewise by Hindú contributions, amounting to eight lakhs of rupees per annum. I was told that they were neglected and starved, but we took them quite unawares, and were well pleased.

I should think it far better to put a bullet through their heads; but I admire the religion that believes in animals having a kind of soul, and future, and that prompts their having a refuge where, at least, no one can hurt them, and where they get some kind of food, drink, and shelter. God is too just to create things, without any fault of their own, only for slow and constant torture, for death, and for utter annihilation. To me this is a missing link between Nature and Grace, and my hope is that God allows them, by their bitter expiation, to bear so large a share in the atonement due for Adam's fall, that they may win an immortal soul to save in some other state. Anyway, as God is just, there must be some way out of it, though we do not know it.

As I said, we took them unawares, and we saw but few faults; though some animals were too old, or had been too maltreated ever to grow fat on any amount of food. I am glad to know that since I wrote these lines the Bombay Society for the Prevention of Cruelty is in full work, and is reforming all kinds of dreadful abuses.

I remember, on one occasion, seeing a party of blacks working at the roads, and one of them nearly wrung off a bullock's tail to make it go. I flew out of my carriage, and the blacks all huddled up together like a covey of partridges in a fright. However, I pounced upon my man, as I thought, and had him transferred to the box of my carriage by the aid of a strong policeman, and we proceeded to the station, where the delinquent would probably have been fined five rupees, to him an awful big sum. But going along, I reflected that the blacks all huddled up together, and to me they are all as alike as a flock of sheep, so that without some distinguishing mark, I could not tell one from another. I should have to swear that I saw *this* man torturing the bullock,—supposing I had seized hold of the wrong man? On arriving at the door of the police-station, I took the policeman, who was an Englishman, into my confidence, and we agreed that he should interpret for me; so I told the black what he would be fined, and asked him, if I let him off, if he would promise to pull no more cows' tails, and try to get the others to leave it off; he promised most earnestly; we gave him a lecture and a fright, and let him go. A lady who used to walk that way every morning, and always had an early fight upon the same subject in that road, and who did not know of my adventure, related to me as a wonder that for several days she had not seen the men wrenching the tails off, which shows it had a good effect.

I would not recommend anyone to take pet dogs to India. I took out some bull and fox terriers to Syria, which produced eight pups, the youngest and best of which I brought away with me.

"Nip" accompanied me twice to England, all through France, Italy, Germany, and Austria, and finally to Arabia, India, and Egypt, being my constant companion for the five years of her life, and I loved her as dearly as a child. In India she caught a fever, which attacked her eyes; I attended her night and day for three months and a half, as did also my maid, who loved her as much as I did. We had six doctors one after another, and a most talented German oculist in Trieste kindly did all he could for her. Finally, it was no use. She lost both eyes, and used to knock herself up against the furniture. In going down stairs or out of doors we had to carry her, and lead her with a string, and put her food and drink into her mouth. When she got her fever attacks she suffered so much pain that it was pitiable to see her, and she would put up her poor little paw to my face, and beg of me to do something for her.

At last, seeing there was no hope for her, I determined to put her out of her misery—but how? Here, as in the East, nobody will kill anything. To give a sensitive, intelligent dog, who has been spoiled and petted all her life, to the authorities, who might try experiments, or to the professional slaughterer for the town, who would throw her aside in a yard for a day, and give her a knock on the head—or half a knock, when convenient, and she perfectly conscious of what was going on, was not to be dreamt of. How should we feel if, in our last day or two of agony, our dearest relations were to hand us over to a body of surgeons with leave to do as they pleased with us, alive or dead? How we should hate their return for our years of love and fidelity—and a dog the same. So there was nothing for it but to do it myself. I looked at my revolver, but I could not take courage. I inquired all the easiest ways of doing it, and after having heard all, chloroform sounded the pleasantest and easiest.

Having summed up desperate courage and resolution, I took her on my lap and petted her, and had two handkerchiefs soaked in chloroform hanging close to her, but she, being blind, could not see them; so she gradually went to sleep, knowing nothing, and the drowsier she became, the nearer I brought the handkerchiefs. When she seemed quite insensible, I laid her in a large box upon some hay, and in the corner, close to her nose, a dessert finger bowl, containing six ounces of pure chloroform. I shut the lid, and she passed away without a struggle. May I have so comfortable and easy a death!

I am still suffering from this sorrow, as every lady with a pet will know, and will not laugh at me that I have made her a little grave in a garden, in a lovely spot overlooking the Adriatic, the glorious Istrian coast, and Miramar, and erected a small tombstone and inscription.

I beg of ladies not to send their pets with a footman to the chemist to be poisoned. How can they tell what they go through? I never allowed the subject to be mentioned before my dog. She understood everything too well. It is dreadfully cruel of people to say, "I am going to shoot that dog, he's of no use," and similar other things. The dog understands every word, and so all animals do, only they can't answer you. I remember a lady once telling me that she was going to part with her dog, because she could not take him on a long journey she was about to make; how she loved it, and how grieved she felt, and I replied, "Oh! do take him with you. He is so fond of you; he will be heart-broken." The dog, a fine large handsome animal lying on the rug, had hitherto taken no notice of me, but now started up, jumped on my knees, and began to lick my hands and face. He knew quite well I was pleading his cause. The lady was so touched that I believe she did not part with him.

I should now like to tell you of some of the things which I have seen in my late expedition in Arabia, India, and Egypt. Perhaps I need not say much about Arabia, as I saw nothing except the pariah dogs treated with the same universal indifference or cruelty as in Damascus.

The dogs had a curious disease whilst I was in Suez lately. They appeared to be suddenly taken ill, and withered away. They became so nervous and weak as to shrink away from everyone, and stagger against everything, as if they did not see, and finally die. No one could say if it were distemper, or if they were poisoned by some unskilful hand. We shot several.

One case in particular struck me. A lady's little pet black-and-tan terrier suddenly started as if it saw a ghost; in fact, was quite scared, and continued yelping and trying to run up the wall or jump out of the window, and snapping at everything, with a glazed eye. This lasted about forty hours, and its mistress grew afraid of it and gave it away. We administered castor-oil after about six hours, which did a little good. It appeared more frightened of Arabs, and I thought perhaps some Arab had ill-used or frightened it. Some thought it was sunstroke. I thought it was rabies, and wanted to have it shot. Finally, a captain of a ship said it resulted from being over-fed, begged to have it, and took it away, and I never heard if it relapsed or died, or if it got well.

European dogs were more affected by the disease than pariahs, which get but little to eat. Captain Burton sent back two dogs from Midian. They were kept in a yard; they had every care and wholesome food. They were certainly not poisoned, nor allowed to associate with the street dogs. They both died in a few days after arrival of the same complaint, and had been perfectly well in Arabia. I used to keep all the scraps for the pariahs, and two or three were my regular pensioners. One afternoon I gave some meat to one of them, and whilst eating it he suddenly howled and ran into the sea, looking reproachfully at me, and would not come near me again. The Arabs standing by thought I had poisoned it, as they do themselves; but one of them who knew me said, "Oh no, she is not capable of doing it;" whereon I picked up the meat, and gave it to them to examine, and see how good it was—quite fresh from our table. When I left there were very few dogs alive, and the epidemic seemed to be over. From all accounts it must have lasted two or three months, say February and March, particularly cool months and pleasant climate. If anyone knows the symptoms I should be glad to learn something for future guidance. We only gave castor-oil, and shot those that suffered too much and had no chance of recovering.

In Bombay there is, I have said, a Society for Prevention of Cruelty to Animals; it does a great deal of good, and one or two residents are heart and soul in the cause; but the cruelty there is excessive, chiefly to "buggy" and "shigram" horses, which represent our cabs, and greater still to bullocks, which do all the heavy work. I have told you that they twist the bullocks' tails to make them run. I never saw a bullock with a whole jointed tail, and some were pulled right off. I saw one put hot coals under his bullock's tail, to make him draw too heavy a weight. It requires a large staff of European members to watch the natives. I was only a drop of water in the ocean, and my stay temporary. Moreover, if my husband did not keep me in order in this matter, I should always be in the "lock-up" for assault, for these sights make me forget that I am a lady.

In Aden, the usual way of driving is by poking the poor, weak, half-starved creatures with a sharp stick under the tail, and between their legs. But Cairo is the most disgusting of all. I saw, daily and hourly, mules flogged along drawing heavy loads, with broad stripes of flesh cut off their breasts, where the leather breast-plate goes by which they draw, for they have no collars; and many were also lame.

I saw pitiable bullocks; but worst of all is the treatment of their beautiful thoroughbred, sensitive donkeys. I saw three out of every four donkeys with two raw holes behind, that made one shudder, some *alive*, the strap or cord behind (which is *quite unnecessary* to keep the saddle in its place) eating into the flesh like a perpetual rasp or file. I saw them poked incessantly in these holes with a sharp-pointed stick, some with a metal prod; and also between their legs, and under their tails. I saw a boy driving a donkey with a knife, pricking holes in the most delicate part of the spine; and *all* look for a tender place, just under the back of the saddle. I saw them hit their donkeys between and under both legs, which made the poor beasts almost sit down with agony. Shortsighted human brutes, not to know that their animals lose half their time, and can only do half their work, with this treatment.

Directly a rider gets off a donkey, the boy ties the bridle to the back of the saddle so tightly as to gag the donkey's mouth open, into which blows all the hot wind and sand; and they will take them out fourteen or fifteen miles—a day's work—without a grain of food or a drop of water, unless the tourist takes the trouble to order it beforehand, which I am sorry to say they seldom think of, though their own luncheon is never forgotten.

The pariah dogs, on the whole, are not so deplorable as at

Damascus, but many have stripes of flesh torn out; and I learnt that it is a favourite pastime with the people, especially in *cafés* and cookshops, where the dogs hang round in hopes of a "bit," to pour the superfluous boiling water of the establishment upon them when the day's work is done. I saw one with a kettle tied to his tail, and one with a live rat set alight with spirits. I saw a boy carrying lighted braise for a *narghileh* with a pair of pincers, and he stopped and put it on a puppy's back that was lying in the street. It had only time to singe the hair before I knocked it off, and took advantage of being alone to box the boy's ears.

Much as I like Egypt, I had as soon live in a vivisecting hall. I tried two years ago to see H.H. the Khedive, to ask what many have asked before me, viz., a "Society for the Prevention of Cruelty to Animals," but I was, unfortunately, only there during the three weeks of the tragedies at Constantinople, and therefore I failed in my object;* the public mind was too agitated to think of so unimportant a matter, and H.H. has never known any other state of things. Many eminent people have before proposed it. General Stanton has done all he could, also Miss Whately, and others. All the Europeans, and most of the influential Moslems, would be glad to see it carried out, and to join it.

Miss Whately, at Cairo, is doing so much good; has an admirable school for about eight hundred children of all races, tongues, and creeds, whom she is inoculating with love and kindness towards the brute creation, so sadly needed in that country, of which more just now. I do heartily wish that every school under British dominion might take the *Animal World*, so that it could be translated into every tongue, and circulated throughout the world. A tax of three shillings would not hurt any schoolmaster or mistress, and the reward would be great.

I am told that the Khedive always says most agreeably that "it shall have all his support," and then the matter gets put away and forgotten, and this quivering mass of living agony has never been relieved by a word. What I say of Bombay

* This was in 1876, but in 1878 I began my work systematically, and mean to carry it out.

applies to all western and southern India, and what I say of Cairo means all over Egypt.

At Alexandria, the donkeys were nearly all in better condition, because the crowds of English daily landing, mostly turn with disgust from the donkey full of sores, and take the nice-looking, brisk, well-fed ones.

From my experience, and love of the lower animals, I have become convinced that all, even the wild beasts, would willingly live with man, and delight in serving him and doing his will; but man is such a brute to him, seldom approaching him but with a gun or stick, that fear and an instinct of self-preservation makes him shy or savage. No animal is bad until man has made him so. My panther in Syria was always free, and never attempted to leave me. Madame Omar Bey's hyena and lynx in the desert could have run away when they pleased, but they never did.

At Mar Saba, the most desolate spot of all Syria, near the Dead Sea, is a monk's penitentiary, amidst the rocks; at the sound of a gong at sunset, I have, with my own eyes, seen flocks of wild jackals clamber up from the depths of the fearful ravine to be fed. The monks and the jackals are the only living things there, and they fraternise instead of hurting each other. I had fifty pariah dogs under my windows in Syria, whom I used to protect and feed daily. They whined for me a year after I left, and would know me now if I went back, and any of them are alive.

I found on my return from India an innovation under my windows in Trieste, in the shape of a large stone-cutting yard, with a wild; savage mountain dog as guard. "Turco" was tied up with a short chain, in all the heat and cold, and though he had plenty to eat, the water was always dirty, and he never got a walk, so I went down and remonstrated with the master. He said the dog was too savage to do otherwise, and I noticed that whenever the men went near him it was with great caution, and that all but one or two gave his chain a very wide berth. So I fetched a bone and went up to him; the master expostulated, saying he would tear me to bits. However, with my conviction that dogs bite only cowards and cruel people, I went up and gave him my bone, and he ate it, and then I sat down by him and patted him, and put my closed fist into his mouth, and he wagged his tail, and then I let him loose and took him out for a walk, to his great surprise and joy.

However, whenever we met a soldier he set his teeth and made a spring at him, thereby telling me that some soldier had once used him savagely, so I had to collar him and walk him out with a chain, as this is a great military station. We soon became the best of friends. I took him out for a walk every day, and saw his water changed, and took him tit-bits to add to his dinner. I propitiated the men with a few pence for a glass of beer, and the whole yard, containing perhaps over a hundred hands, learned that "Turco" is the best fellow in the world. At night he is allowed a chain several yards long, so as to walk into the guardian's house if the weather is bad and storms come on, and the men and boys are now not afraid to play with him. As I passed along every one seemed to know his bad repute, and said, "What! can that be 'Turco' alone with a lady?" and they cleared out of our way most respectfully, but needlessly; for he has no grudge against anything but a soldier. He is now a family pet.

Everything living has instinct, and birds an immense amount, though unobservant people may not think so. In the stormy part of the year this last winter, a Peninsular and Oriental steamer encountered rough weather, and, as often happens at such times, many seagulls hovered near the ship and even came on board. One allowed itself to be caught, and it was found that it had a fish bone stuck in the eye in such a position as not absolutely to destroy the sight, but penetrating an inch into the flesh of the bird and projecting an inch and a-half (it might have had a fight with a fish or got transfixed seeking its prey). The doctor of the ship took the bird, extracted the bone, applied a soothing remedy to the wound, and let it go. It flew away, but returned the next day, again allowing itself to be caught. The doctor examined the wound, which was progressing favourably, applied more of the remedy, and let it go a second time. It flew several times around the ship, and then departed and returned no more.

I have read with great interest all that the paper says on the cruelty of keeping caged birds. I have a bullfinch, and I try to make his life as happy as I can; but when I read stories about caged birds, I put the cage by the windows, and left the door open five or six times, and he never went out; but he will go out in the room and fly about, and perch again, for two or three hours, and return of his own accord to the cage. If I put my lips to the cage, he will go and fetch a couple of seeds, and when he has cracked them and made them white and soft in his beak, he comes and puts them between my lips, thinking I am hungry, and want to be fed. I therefore do not think he can be unhappy, although a neglected cage bird must be most wretched; the only thing that could atone for confinement, would be the petting and companionship of its owner. I doubt whether my bullfinch would not be more unhappy turned adrift than kept, and I am sure he has wonderful intelligence.

Whilst in India I addressed the following note to the editor of the *Bombay Gazette*:—

Sir,—I have read with great interest, in your paper of to-day, the account of the meeting of the Society for the Prevention of Cruelty to Animals. As I am myself a member, and a very earnest one, I would ask you to say something in behalf of two very ill-used animals in Bombay. Firstly, the horses in the "buggies" and "shigrams," which seem mostly starved, few of which can show four sound legs, and all of which are beaten too much. Could not some member of the Society preside at the overhauling of these poor wretches, by competent persons, say once a week; always remembering that the night cabs, if there are such things in Bombay, are drawn by the most pitiable objects, that darkness may save their brutal masters from the police? I notice that even gentlemen's coachmen here drive without the slightest judgment. They do not know how much a horse can do, or how little. They drive up and down hill just the same as on a level road, and the crack of the whip is incessant; and what is stranger, nobody tells them of it. For the first week I was here, I used to threaten to have the whip inside my carriage, and my coachman does not use it now, and his horses go much better. The bullocks have, I see, protectors, judging by the number of cases of fines for torturing them.

The second animal is the snake. Conjurors come every day before Watson's Hotel, and show a great number of tricks, which are for the most part very amusing, *i.e.*, the mango and the basket trick, and others; but they ought to be prohibited from carrying about with them animals to torture. A favourite trick is to make a mangoose bite a snake till it bleeds and appears to be dead, then to pat it on the back and give it a little water to bring it to, in order to repeat the same scene at another house. It is a very ugly sight, and a very cruel one, and surely might be forbidden. I have been nearly two months in India, and I am bound to say, however, that I have seen less cruelty here than in many other places.

If you think that the Society would take these two cases into consideration, may I ask you to be so kind as to publish my letter?

I am, etc.,

Watson's Hotel, 31st March. ISABEL BURTON.

This was answered by a most amusing letter from a Shigram Horse, which tells the whole pitiful story :—

PITY THE SORROWS OF A POOR SHIGRAM HORSE.

To the Editor of the "Bombay Gazette."

SIR,—What a noble lady Mrs. Burton must be to take up her pen in the cause of us poor brutes of horses. May she be rewarded by living to see her distinguished husband become a Saint.

I am a shigram horse, and belong to a fat Sáhib of about my own weight, who lives at the very top of Malabar Hill. Every day in the week do I drag him in an old shigram that's as big as a labourer's cottage down to the Fort and back again. Oh! if his medical attendant would advise him to walk up the hill occasionally for the benefit of his health, how thankful I should be. We both take our "tiffins" (luncheon), down, only master has his put in a basket, nicely wrapped up in white cloths, and takes it inside with him; whilst mine is tied to the axletree of the hind wheels, and very often so carelessly made fast that some of the grass scrapes on the ground and raises a cloud of dust. Many a time I can't touch a morsel of it. Then the "gram" (grain) is served out to me in a bag, which, to my certain knowledge, has not been cleaned since it was made two years ago. The very smell of it, I declare, sometimes makes me nearly sick. You should see the harness they put on me. It's of country manufacture, was not made for me originally, and does not fit me a bit. No one ever oils it, so that it is as hard as if it was made of horn.

The bit is small and sharp, and has a high port; and, as I am driven from the lower bar, it makes my tongue and the roof of my mouth so sore that I can hardly chew my food. At each corner of my mouth there are sores that have been there for I don't know how long. Then —for no other reason in the world that I can see, except to torture me— they put on what is called a bearing-rein. It is made fast at one end to a thin piece of rusty iron, which goes in my mouth. My head is then pulled up, so that I can't see where I am going, and if I should happen to make a stumble I find it very difficult to recover myself; and the rein is then carried round a hook in the saddle. I believe sometimes in my struggles to ease my poor mouth, and get my head down into a more natural position, I should drag the saddle clean over my withers, only that vagabond of a driver takes care to prevent this by making the saddle fast to my tail. But oh! what I suffer from my tail!—I wish my master had one (as I am told his forefathers used to have), and that it was the fashion for Sáhibs to wear bearing-reins; he would very soon know how much better *we* should be without them.

But I was going to tell you about my tail. Well, it's a peculiar one, and I daresay you may have noticed it, for it is always made fast to the shaft of the shanderydan; that's to stop my wagging it, for fear I should get it over the reins. This once happened to me, and I was terribly frightened, but I did not kick or bolt; I wish to goodness I had, and smashed the trap all to pieces; for as soon as that fiend of a coachman had got the reins into his hands again, he set to and licked me most unmercifully, and the Christian gentleman, my master, sat there and looked on, and never said a word. But to return to my tail. What do you think makes me want to wriggle it about? "Why, to brush the flies off, of course," I know you'll say. No, you don't know everything. It's because my tail is covered with lice; so is my mane and forelock. And those ugly sores that you see on my hip-bones are caused by my rubbing the skin off at night while I am lying down on a bed scantily supplied with straw, and working my head and neck about to try and get some relief from the itching. Instead of my Christian master seeing that my tail and mane are dressed with carbolic acid ointment, so as to kill the animalculæ, and then kept clean, he has my tail tied to the shaft, and a little *mutty* (clay) dabbed on my sore hip-bones, so that they may not show. I should like to tell you what a happy home I have in the Christian gentleman's stable, and what a beautiful illustration it is of one of his pious sayings, that "Cleanliness is next to godliness," but I must reserve this for another time.—Yours, etc.,

Drudge.

I am trying to establish the same reformation in Egypt as

I did in Trieste with regard to cruelty to animals. As everyone knows, it is terribly wanted, and I have a gigantic work before me. As all the Europeans who visit there in winter, or are residents in Egypt, are interested in it, and wish it well, I hope I shall meet with their tangible support, and the moral support of the Press at home. The work is at the very commencement, and looks disheartening. The Press has always helped me like a "band of brothers;" I venture to hope that support will be continued by inserting my appeals and reports of work.

The expedition from Midian, commanded by Captain Burton, returned, and we were at Cairo for some time. This gave me the opportunity for sowing the first seed, which was an appeal for contributions, and I hope they will soon accumulate sufficiently to enable me to begin to offer prizes for Humanity, and to buy a little zeal from the Police. Any subscriptions will reach me at the British Consulate, Trieste, where I live, or the London Joint Stock Bank, 69, Pall Mall.

But I must make one thing known. English passengers landing from steamers homeward and outward bound at Alexandria and Suez, occasionally so ill-treat the donkeys, as even to disgust the donkey-boys, who complain bitterly of it, and make us ashamed of our compatriots. These persons—we cannot say gentlemen, although we suppose they would be highly indignant if they were not considered and treated as gentlemen—may be second or third-class passengers; may be Americans or Australians; but they have a tidy coat on, they speak some sort of English, are very tipsy and given to swearing, and to the poor Arab boy he is "one English gentlemens." They land for a few hours, hire and maim a donkey for life, and depart, leaving the poor donkey-boy with no knowledge beyond the name of the steamer the tyrant departed in, and no redress.

An English doctor was had up before the Consul at Suez, for repeatedly sticking his donkey in the back with his knife. He admitted the fact, saying the donkey would not go. The poor beast had, I believe, been ridden to death, and had scarcely had anything to eat for two days. When our troops were passing, in the time of the Mutiny, the residents told me that if a donkey did not please a soldier, he would draw his sword and lop off its tail, its ear, and in some instances cut its throat.

Whilst I was there lately (at Suez) a young man landed from the steamer *Nepaul* (in April 1877), and so thrashed a donkey, to make it gallop faster than it could, with a cruel instrument known as a "Penang Lawyer," that the donkey could not move for two days, and now drags its hind quarters after it. It is a matter of consideration how we are to prevent our own brutes from doing worse than the Arab, or with what face can we begin to reform the Arab? All that I *can* do I *mean* to do: to establish at Suez and Alexandria a book for entering the names, professions, and addresses of these persons, the ships they sail in, what they did to the animal they ill-treated as they passed, and the date, and publish it.

People in England would be ashamed and indignant to see many of our fellow-countrymen (passengers) land from ships for a day's amusement, looking extremely common and vulgar, and mostly drunk. One man I noticed, was being held on to his donkey, by his legs, by four small Arab boys; he was quite drunk, and beating the donkey and the boys unmercifully with a big stick. I am sorry to say this is an every-day sight. What must the poor Arabs think of enlightened and civilized England when this is the specimen they daily get of her sons? When will such people learn to think that they have really passed a pleasant day, even when they have not been drunk, and illused or maimed something? for that seems to be their realization of that popular chaff, "Oh! what a day we're having." If an English person offers an Eastern a glass of anything,—water or lemonade,—he naturally starts back in horror, and says, "No, thank you,—me no drink brandy," supposing it is our only sustenance.

Last March I saw a very bad case at Suez. It was a very small donkey; its spine was a mass of raw meat, its hind quarters the same; a white film covered one eye; it did not walk on its hoofs, but literally ran on its fetlocks, from weakness and fatigue, and was nothing but a bone. A heavy man was riding it, and the usual tormentor—small boy—with pointed stick, was driving it into the raw flesh, and going along a fair speed. I think had I let it alone it might have died in a few days, but I could not. The big man was soon off, the boy ran away; the donkey "shaykh," the master of all the donkeys, came and said I had no right to interfere—he would have £5. I took the donkey before the Governor, who said it was a shocking case, but there was no law, and that I had better do as I liked; so I cast away the saddle and bridle and the cruel hind leather strap, and with a little bit of rope led my donkey along, followed by a crowd of Arab boys saying, "O happy donkey, famous in history! Thy case was heard before the Governor!"

I put him in a yard containing a comfortable shed, belonging to the hotel; made him a nice bed of straw; watered, fed, and groomed him for a fortnight, treating the wounds with plain cold water; and I had him clipped to get rid of the dirt. At the end of the fortnight the white film had cleared off his eye, he stood well upon his feet, the trembling knees grew firm, the wounds healed, and I left him a fast-galloping, plucky little animal, full of fight and kicking if played with; but I had to keep him under lock and key during the cure, from the vengeance or tricks of the boys, his old tormentors.

When I found he could live and recover, I gave £2 to the shaykh, and made a present of the donkey to the children of Mr. Levick, the British Postmaster-General, and he is ridden and petted by their little son,* aged ten, or carries the baby's basket.

You can keep a donkey on the very best food for ninepence a-day—he cannot eat more. A large feed of split beans, and twenty bundles of a grass called "burseem," is enough; I have no doubt residents in the country can do it for less; and I should think the donkey-shaykh can do it for next to nothing. I cannot, therefore, think why they should be starved, except through heartlessness.

I have put up three notices at the Suez Hotel, two in English and one in Arabic, begging passengers to refuse to take a donkey with a sore, (look under the saddle,) and to set their faces against the leather strap behind, and against the mouth being gagged open when standing still. The hot wind

* I am sorry to say that they have sold him since, and I shall have to buy him back again. We called him El Muskeen—the poor wretched one.

and dust blows into their poor mouths all day, and they only drink when the day's work is done, and that is probably often forgotten. The gagging is done for style, on the principle of bearing-reins. I want to introduce the crupper-leather to the saddles, instead of the strap round the hind legs, which chafes and makes the first raw, which is afterwards enlarged and kept up by the pointed sticks; but until passengers refuse donkeys with these three faults, the donkey-boys may laugh and be happy with their pointed sticks.

On the 13th of last May the following letter appeared in the *Standard:* it was the cause of my receiving forty-seven guineas, in two separate sums, towards our undertaking, from a gentleman whose modesty is equal to his charity and generosity, for I am not allowed to mention his name. I feel it can only aid our cause if I perpetuate that letter in my book. The results of my labours in Trieste are, that scarcely ever a cruel thing is done, but if there is, I know it in two hours; and before twelve hours, by the concurrence of the authorities, the man is under arrest.

With regard to Egypt, I propose to solicit the patronage of His Highness the Khedive, and of their Highnesses the Princes and Princesses of Egypt. That we should ask Mr. Vivian, Her Majesty's Consul-General and Political Agent at Cairo, and Mr. Rivers Wilson, Minister of Finance, to be our Presidents; that our Patrons and Patronesses should consist of the *Entourage de la Cour*, Mrs. Vivian, and the Corps Diplomatique; that the Secretary and Manager should be Mr. Le Mesurier, at Cairo, who has been very active at Bombay in this cause; and that the first step we ask of the Khedive is to issue a proclamation to the Governors and Kaim Makams to lay half a piastre fine on all animals found with sores or marks of ill-usage. We must avoid the word sore-backed, as that would create evasion. This must apply to horse, mule, donkey, camel, cat, and dog, and include all animals. The fine must be increased to a whole piastre for hidden wounds under the saddle, and for the usage of the cruel strap behind that creates sores, and we must enforce the use of the crupper strap; the same fine must be levied for the mouth being gagged open whilst the animal stands still, as this permits the hot wind and sand to blow down its throat all day; and we all know that the best treated beast only gets water in the morning and at night, in that fearful heat, however hard they are worked.

A Plea for the Dumb.

To the Editor of the "Standard."

Sir,—The large number of English who come yearly to Cairo for health or pleasure, will, I am sure, take an interest in the subject of cruelty to animals in Egypt, which is, perhaps, more flagrant and less cared for or thought about than in any other country. The expedition from the land of Midian, commanded by Captain Burton, has now returned, and as we are stopping in Cairo, I have the opportunity of trying to lay a foundation for a similar reformation to that which has taken place at Trieste.

I have established at Shepheard's Hotel, in Cairo, and am preparing to establish at the Suez Hotel, and the "Europe" and "Abbats," in Alexandria, little books, which contain a printed account of the *fête* and the way we organized our method from the very beginning at Trieste. Also a subscription list, where people who care about this subject are requested to insert their names and the amounts of their donations, and to entrust them to the managers of the hotels, or to send them to me at the British Consulate, Trieste. When the donations are sufficient I will commence the same work in Egypt, and will address myself to influential people in Cairo to give us moral support, and procure a law for us from His Highness, if possible, making cruelty punishable. It must not be forgotten also that my second Trieste *fête* for prize-giving must come off on 1st of November next.* Having reformed such a large place as Trieste and its environs, with colleagues spreading it up all through Italy and Austria, I hope the animal-protecting public will not let me lose it for the want of £100, and I should lose it, and all the *prestige* of the affair, if I were to miss the second *fête*. Public interest would die out (I have it all on my side now), and the drivers would say, "It was only for once, and now we can drop back into our old ways."

I have prefaced the little books which are to lie on the hotel tables in Egypt as follows:—"I hope to succeed in an attempt to abolish the exceedingly cruel treatment of animals which is and always has been the custom in Egypt. If we all unite we can do it. It will cost a little money and two years' time. It was just as bad at Trieste a year ago, and everybody said that it had always been so, and there was no remedy.

* My appeal has been nobly responded to. The prize-winners have themselves asked to await my return to Trieste for their *fête*, that they may receive their money from my own hands.

I thought there was, and I collected in England a sum that yielded one thousand five hundred florins. I published an announcement on the walls that in eight months' time I would give a prize of twenty-five florins to every man who should distinguish himself for humanity during that time. I wrote several letters on humanity to the German and Italian press during the time of probation. I got the support of the authorities, called a commission of gentlemen and another commission of coachmen and ass drivers, who lived in the stables, and could report daily on the cruelties and neglects that were taking place; and, further, I paid the police to be a little zealous.

"I here subjoin an account of the *fête* I gave on the 1st November, 1877, at Trieste, at which the Governor-General and all the authorities supported me. From that day there has been an emulation amongst the men, a certainty that there is something to be gained. Cruelty is now rather the exception, and out of a cab-stand of thirty horses you will perhaps only find two bad ones. The omnibuses and truck carts are still bad, but improving. I am sure we could do the same thing here. We could begin to collect a little money. We could get the Viceroy to approve of and sanction our efforts, and to issue a circular to the Governors and the Kaim Makams to fine and imprison for cruelty. All the Europeans would join in it, and we should admit influential Egyptians to our undertaking, who would help to enforce the carrying out of our philanthropic object.

"We have even a better chance here; for whereas Triestines are turbulent and independent, a mixture of all nations and tongues, these people are docile and well disposed, and are only cruel from ignorance and thoughtlessness. They have yet to learn that an animal can suffer and feel like us, and they will give in much sooner than the Triestines. I have colleagues now doing the same thing all over Italy and Austria, and trying to work it up into France, and we report from time to time to our Head Centre, 105, Jermyn Street, London. I make no excuse for coming forward to appeal to the visitors or residents of Egypt, because I know they wish it as much as I do, and, having had experience of success, I should think it wrong to hang back and not to try.

"Please insert your names and the amounts you give in this book, and the manager of the hotel, Mr. Gross at Cairo, Mr. Adams at Suez, will receive the subscriptions for me. I do not know the managers of the two hotels at Alexandria, but will arrange on arriving there, or subscriptions will always reach me at the British Consulate, Trieste, where I live."

I am, Sir, your obedient servant,

CAIRO, *April 29th.* ISABEL BURTON.

I have said a great deal about what has been done at Trieste, but I have forgotten to explain our proceedings, which I will now do, hoping that it may be taken up in other places where it is required. In summer, 1876, I commenced writing a series of articles in the German and Italian papers,—on humanity, on training horses, and similar subjects, and made proclamations which were posted like handbills to the walls, of which the following is my first specimen.

In summer, 1876, I composed the following address in Italian from the horse to his driver, thus describing the actual condition of the cab horses and bullocks in Trieste:—

"To the Drivers of Carriages and Carts, and their Owners living at Trieste.

"Man! God made me for your benefit, but He also recommended me to your mercy. The only wish that I have is to love and serve you and obey your will. Do not, therefore, break my heart with ill-treatment. I have intelligence, memory, affection, and gratitude, only I do not know how to speak. I want to understand you, but I am often so terrified by you that I no longer know what it is that you want me to do. My head throbs from the blows you give me on my tender nose. I am full of pain from the kicks you have given me upon my stomach with your hob-nailed boots; my whole body writhes with your hide lash. My mouth and teeth ache with the hard bit which you incessantly tug at as if it were a bell-rope. My collar does not fit, and often it presses on me up-hill with a heavy weight and stops my breath, and instead of loosening it or giving me time, you cut me in two with your whip. Look at the sore near my spine which goes nearly to the bone. Look at that wound near my tail full of vermin. I am lame because you shod me so badly that I have a nail in the tenderest part of my foot, yet I must run up and down hill and over stony streets eight hours a day, in a burning heat or a cutting north-east wind, often overladen. And I would do it willingly if I were not so weak and ill. When you give me up to the ostler after the day's work he often forgets me, and goes out to amuse himself. I come home half dead of hunger, thirst, and fatigue, full of pain and misery, and he forgets to give me water. My food is poor and old and scant, my bed is the hard, cold, wet ground. I am weary and would sleep, but I am too full of aches and sorrows. Oh! if you do not love me as I wish, only think of this—all the good and rich people will choose the fine, well-treated horse, but will turn with disgust from a poor beast like me, so that the well-treated horse will make his master rich whilst I make you poor. But this is your fault—not mine. Then be my friend and not my tyrant. Treat me well, and you will see that I shall be able to do double my work. I shall last longer, and in making you gain more money I shall repay you for your goodness to me. We shall both be proud and happy because we shall have done our duty. And now I will tell you a secret, whispered in my ear by the best friend we poor horses have in Trieste. There is a good time coming for the well-treated horses and the humane coachmen. There will be prizes. Let us (you and I) win the first prize.

"(Signed) The most Broken-down Horse, in the name of all the ill-treated horses and bullocks of Trieste."

With the permission of the police, I caused this manifesto to be placarded on the walls like a large playbill at every cab-stand, bullock-stand, and public stables. It produced a very good effect, and was taken up at Nice and Florence, and many other towns in Italy and Austria, and to my surprise has been translated in English, and taken home to one or two towns there. I collected prizes for the drivers, some for the day cabs, some for the night cabs (which are by far the worst cases), some for the bullocks, and some for the asses, which are also shamefully treated, and a few (for policy's sake) to such of the police who have the courage and zeal to bring us bad cases for punishment.

We have a Society for the Prevention of Cruelty to Animals, of which I am a member; but it is a very weak affair, and we are only nominally supported by the police. The men don't like interfering for a very good reason. The populace are against them. They get stabbed or ill-used, and the culprit gets eight days in prison, which is as effectual as putting a child in the corner.

To succeed with these people, who are exceedingly independent, and have scarcely any laws over them, it is necessary to display the most courteous manners, and to encourage them with money, for the misery here behind the scenes is dreadful; but also be it said that a sum that would be despised in England by our poor, goes a long way here with *these* poor, although the place is very dear. I was eventually supported in my efforts by the Government, and the Police, and the Municipality, and our "Society,"* and in course of time announced by placards that, "After six months' probation, ending such a day, we shall give so many prizes, to such an amount, to such and such classes of drivers, to the most humane men, and for the best-treated animals;" that the prizes would be given with some pomp in a public hall, in the presence of the authorities, and the names of the winners published in all the newspapers. I forgot to say a commission was called to decide which were the most deserving cases.

The drivers were proud to be thus publicly brought forward before their own town as superior men, and it created an emulation. Most of them are needy enough to make the prize a great object to them. In the six months' probation, we were able to mark off the most brutal-natured men and procure their dismissal. The prizes are now becoming yearly, and I want to establish a fund that will bring us in £120 a-year. The first time we made forty-eight prizes at twenty-five florins, or fifty shillings each.

I have no one to look to but my own country-people, for no foreigner, however rich or charitable, and so many are, would give one shilling for an animal's comfort, and the lower orders do not yet know that an animal can feel; but nevertheless, if I have but the prizes, I am sure of the support of the authorities, not only because they are all my personal friends, but because they have always wished for this reform, and know that the present state of things is deplorable, and I believe that my northern energy, and a little English gold, will permanently turn the scale in favour of the poor beasts.

I wrote to the papers. Those who have already given, will be glad to know that there is already marked difference in the treatment of animals since I began: cruelty is now exceptional. Assisted by my own country-people, this reform will slowly but

* Moral support,—all the money is English.

surely be carried out. The oxen are labelled with a number, and a cruel driver is fined.

When the promised *fête* day arrived, it was conducted as follows:—

On the first of November, at twelve o'clock, all the highest Austrian authorities of Trieste, with the Municipality, my personal friends,—comprising sixty or seventy of the leading families of the town,—and all the English, by invitation, were assembled in the "Sala del Ridotto," a magnificent Hall of the city. The Sala was hung with flags of every nation, the Austrian and English crossed in the centre, and the Hungarian band of the Duke of Saxe-Meiningen's regiment was in attendance and played. The doors were thrown open to the public. We, the Committee of the Society for the Prevention of Cruelty to Animals, occupied a table and circle of chairs in front of the audience, and the forty men found worthy of prizes ranged on each side. As soon as the Governor-General and *suite* came in, the band struck up the Austrian Hymn, and we proceeded to our work.

The President, Baron Pascotini, made a short but effective speech, showing forth the object and use of the Society, enumerating its services up to the present date, and then invited me, as the Presidentess, to speak. I then stood up and addressed them in Italian, as follows:—

"I am going to ask your patience to let me say a few words. My difficulty is not to speak before the public,—a thing not quite unknown to us Englishwomen,—but to speak in Italian, which is not my language; so that if some faults escape me, I hope you will be kind and indulgent to me.

"It is not quite a year since I first conceived the idea of making these prizes. In December 1876 my first letter appeared in the English press, asking for subscriptions for this purpose, and has been most nobly responded to. You did not then believe, and I hardly dared hope, that my efforts would culminate in such a solemn and delightful *fête* as that we are now assisting at; but God has blessed all hands who have had to do with this affair, and I hope He will continue to do so.

"And now I am most proud and happy to be allowed to distribute this money, these diplomas and decorations to you. Your names will be in all the newspapers of Trieste, and will be read in Vienna, in London, in Florence, and everywhere. You stand to-day, before your own townspeople, the admired and envied of all, from your own good conduct, and for the marks of approbation you are receiving, in the presence of His Excellency the Governor-General and of all the high authorities and nobility of Trieste. You will be the most likely men to be chosen for good situations. I am only sorry there are not more of you.

"We have failed to find one humane omnibus-driver, one humane ass or mule-owner, or any inventor of humane means for catching stray dogs, or carrying fowls except by their legs. But I hope this, our institution, is only in its beginning; and, by-the-by, for this very reason, I will mention that I have received all kinds of private complaints, that some few who were worthy of prizes have not been called up to-day. To this I reply that the Commission decides, and not I, who are worthy and who are not; and that next year you must send in all your complaints and claims to the Commission a month before, and they shall be duly examined and justly dealt with. The Commission has been occupied with this for six months, and I know they have done their best. You know how difficult it is to obtain money; nevertheless, I shall do my best to renew this solemnity once a year, and if I can get sufficient funds, I will interest myself and others about the wives and children of the prize-winners.

"Don't think, however, that I am going to work for you for nothing. No such thing! I want my prize as well as you, and I will tell what it is to be. You shall help me in my mission by talking over your comrades, and by your example and influence you shall win them over to our way of thinking and feeling, which will considerably help our mission.

"I see such very respectable men amongst you, some very nice cabs, and good horses, but a great number also—and you know it as well and better than I do—are a perfect disgrace to such a city as Trieste, and there are horses that make one's heart ache. I am sure you would all like that your social standard should be raised as high as possible, and that the respectable half of you must be disgusted with many of your comrades. Truth and public opinion will always carry the day, and you can win over the others by your example, by your words, and by setting your faces against their manner of dealing with their animals.

"The Police can help you by not giving licences to those who, having lost all respect, and as a last means of gaining a livelihood, buy a dying horse for a few florins, and obtain a licence without a question; also, by punishing more severely special cases of wanton cruelty, by a vigorous surveillance, especially on hills where houses are building, and about the shipping and railroad; and a readiness on the part of the Police to sequestrate such animals as are unfit for work, without the presence of our Secretary, Mr. Chinchella, or mine being necessary.

"It is a terrible sight to see a coachman who never had a horse in his hands before. As a boy he never, perhaps, had a little cat or dog to play with; or if he had one, perhaps the only use he knew to make of it was to drown it. He never knew a beast could feel or suffer, but looks upon it as a machine; and therefore he lets it die of hunger and thirst, and beats it to death, to make it run as long as it can to get back his few florins; or else he makes it draw a weight fit for four strong horses. This is not respectable. Set your faces against it and stamp it out, and you will by so doing ennoble yourselves, and you will find every one whose heart is in the right place will applaud your conduct.

"They say we carry love for animals too far in England. I don't know that! We exact a fair amount of work from our beasts, in return for good food and excellent treatment; and when a horse begins to decline or suffer, if he has the good luck to be a rich man's pet, he is turned out to grass for the remainder of his life; otherwise, he is humanely killed. The law does not permit any man, however poor, to earn his livelihood upon the tortures of an animal. We have great brutes in England, too, but thank God they are heavily punished; and the law can go as far as three months' imprisonment and £5 fine.

"Our police see the law respected. They seize an ill-used animal in the street and consign it to the slaughter-house, where it is humanely killed; and our people, by common consent, side with the police. Thus we maintain order, and this union is the secret of our strength. The cabmen in England now take a great pride in their cabs and horses, and kindness to animals is popular in England, because we believe that by reason of their instinct and intelligence, they suffer the same as we do, only they can't speak.

"Our clergy diffuse the sentiment of humanity from the pulpit, which finds its way into the hearts of the people; and our schools teach tenderness to animals to our little ones, and punish and shame cruelty. You may therefore imagine that the report I shall send to London of to-day's Feast will give the sincerest pleasure to all, and especially to those generous persons who contributed the money I give you to-day.

"And now I have only to join our President in thanking His Excellency the Governor-General and the authorities and Municipality, singly and collectively, for the great kindness with which they have permitted me to carry out my mission, with their support and protection. As our 'Society' in England has already conferred its highest honours on our illustrious President, Baron Pascotini, and our zealous Secretary, Signor Chinchella, nothing remains for me but to thank them and the 'Society' of Trieste and the Commission, and that most warmly, not only on my own account, but from the Society of London, for the honour conferred on me, their country-woman and member, for the manner in which they have accorded me all the merit and glory of this day, and put me forward to share the direction with them, and even in trusting me to be a public speaker in so glorious a cause and on such a joyful and solemn occasion.

"Furthermore, I thank, on behalf of our English Society and on my own account, the German and Italian press of Trieste, especially the *Triester Zeitung*, the *Cittadino*, the *Adria*, the *Gazettino del Popolo*, *Independente*, *Osservatore*, *Tramway*, and *Sandro*, for their support, and for having, last winter, inserted gratis, and at a time when every line was precious, my long letters on humanity in behalf of my beloved mission—beloved because humanity is the bottom rung of the ladder of all future great things and the root of all good in after life in our transactions with our fellow-creatures. The man who tortures a cat in public does it also in private by reason of his depraved tastes. A baby would not be safe with him—a man, yes, because a cruel man is a coward and fears his fellows. The tender-hearted child will be a great and noble man.

"I now end my long speech, cabmen, by counting on your assistance, and thanking you for having allowed me, though only a woman and a stranger, to interfere in the cause I have at heart. It is greatly to the credit of Trieste, and I shall tell it to the whole world, that in most trying moments when I have rushed in between an angry man and his beast, and snatched his stick or whip from him, that, with very few exceptions, I have scarcely ever received an angry, rude, or unkind word. That tells me that the heart of this people contains a world of good, and that it will not be difficult for me to induce them to be merciful to their beasts, when they once quite understand it.

"Finally, let me thank all of you, my own dear and good friends, for having honoured me to-day by your presence in this Hall, and for the very touching kindness you always show me, and especially to-day. I shall always remain a good Triestine, I shall always be your faithful friend, and you shall see that, whether in public or private life, I shall always try to earn and deserve all the good things you have showered upon me."

My speech lasted about twenty minutes, and I am told that every word was heard distinctly in every part of the hall.

Then the trumpets sounded, and the names of those who had received diplomas in gold letters, twenty-four in number, amongst whom was Mr. John Colam, the Secretary of our London Society, and myself, were read out. Then were called out the men who were to receive prizes, forty in number; they were clean, well dressed, and well-mannered, and walked up and saluted, and received their honours in a manner that would have done credit to any gentleman. The trumpet sounded after each name was called out, and each man on coming up to the table saluted the President and myself, and I handed him his twenty-five florins, his diploma, and a tiny decoration, consisting of a small red silk English flag, with the Union Jack in the corner, and a silver safety-pin. These they pinned on to the left breast, and wore all day. When this was finished, one of the chief personages of our Society, Cavaliere Richetti, made a short but very touching speech. After this I was surrounded by the authorities, and decorated with a medal and ribbon, the third the town has given me in these last two years, and then all my friends surrounded me, and kissed me, and congratulated me, and we broke up.

Everybody, I have since learned, was delighted, and the press, without exception, have spoken most warmly of it, both Italian and German. It has produced the best possible effect in the town and environs. They now know it is a real thing, and one can see the most extraordinary difference in their manner of handling their animals, whilst the Police are taking up the thing with spirit.

I have regulated all the accounts, and fee'd all those who ought to be fee'd, and circulated reports of the *fête* to various towns. I had one thousand five hundred florins; one thousand two hundred were spent, and three hundred remained towards next year, and I have found generous souls to fill the purse again for 1878. It is such a very small sum, and has done untold good. I can assure my donors that not a penny has been wasted, but the sums carefully hoarded and put out to interest to accumulate, and every farthing so placed as to bring back a hundredfold in humanity. To fail one year would be to lose all we have gained with hard work, anxiety, and difficulties which no one will ever know but myself, but which may be supposed to arise in face of a woman and a stranger working single-handed in a foreign seaport of independent tendencies, and I heartily thank my donors, and Almighty God first, for the great success I have had.*

* It is a remarkable fact that God is holding out a great grace to England at this moment—the petition of millions of Her Majesty's subjects to have a total abolition of vivisection. We make a present of our share of medical cure to such doctors as practise this abomination. It is purchased at too great a price. There *have* been, I believe, clever, humane, and honest scientists who have thought to make great discoveries by such means, and using chloroform. Those great men are the very ones to come forward now to declare that vivisection has served its purpose. We know *all*, and any further experiments to illustrate what we know, come under the head of useless and sinful barbarity. I regret to find that in spite of the fact that atrocious abuses are now the order of the day, fifty-three licenses have lately been granted, with permission not to use anæsthetics (chloroform), and without obligation of killing the animal after the operation. I deplore that a large portion of English people, and even some ladies, are in favour of half-measures; but

this is only because they do not know what they are talking about. They hear the matter glossed over, in technical terms of which they know nothing, by some friendly doctor in whom they believe; and I am always met by the remark—"Oh! these things are *not* done in England—not in OUR hospitals." Right! for they are done, not *in* the hospitals, but in an outhouse attached to the hospital. Let us sweep down the quibble. This apathy can only arise from ignorance. I wish I dare write all I know, but the details are so *filthy*, that my book could not appear upon any table. People talk of "*insulting* scientists" by a doubt. When I know how that branch of science is prostituted, I have no fear of saying *anything* too insulting; and if *we* are afraid, God Almighty will not be afraid. How can parents approve of their warm-hearted youths having their finest feelings first outraged and then blunted? I mention no names, because those who can best tell, from experience, what goes on, would have their professional prospects destroyed by their preceptors and examiners; whilst the cleverest and best physicians, from some idea of *esprit de corps*,—a mistaken point of honour,—think it necessary to support their lower brethren; but let them beware, for God says, "The righteous man regardeth the life of his beast," "Blessed are the merciful, for they shall obtain mercy," "Open your mouth for the dumb." What, then, shall the man obtain who is the reverse of merciful? What shall we call the man who only sees a beast to torture it? What name shall we call a man, for instance, who sticks hot irons into his dog's brain, and beats it for howling for fear he should be found out; and after several experiments, finds a subject whose life he can prolong under that torture from 28th June till 14th August?* Did you, my reader, ever suffer from hot irons in the brain, and want medical advice for such a complaint, or ever hear of anyone who had?

The three really great discoveries (I am told) which that incarnate fiend, that inhuman animal which we may define as the *ignorant scientist*, attributes to vivisection are—

1. The discovery of the circulation of the blood.
2. The distinction between the nerves of sensation and the nerves of motion.
3. The use of chloroform as an anæsthetic.

These three discoveries are said to have been made without any experiments on living animals, except in the last instance, on the person of the discoverer, Sir James Simpson.

The British Association, at Belfast, in 1874, tried to prove that animals are a machine. If animals writhe, shriek, and howl under these awful, sickening processes; if these animals in health and happiness show more sensitiveness, and intelligence, and affection than many human beings do, and are still a machine, then the whole of *Nature* is *one enormous lie*.

Do not let these operators cant about "unwillingness and sorrow" in inflicting pain. They will have time enough to bewail their deeds in Eternity. God is sick of these bestialities. He is moving England to reject them as He previously did the Inquisition. Tremble, vivisectors! for your time is short. Repent and amend quickly. On your deathbed you will have to endure *every* torture you have *ever* inflicted; and if you have not even *that* mercy extended to you, you must endure it in the other world, *because God is just.*

---

* Monsieur Bouillaud, a *distinguished scientist*, and one of the most conspicuous physicians in the Medical School of Paris, *from his own reports.* We anti-vivisectionists are really not (as we have been termed) a set of sensational old women; we will give chapter and verse, name and hospital, for every heart-rending history we bring before the public.

CHAPTER XII.

BOMBAY.

THE society of Bombay, and indeed in any part of India I have travelled in, is not to be surpassed for hospitality. It is difficult to breakfast, lunch, or dine at home; and yet every book on Bombay manners and customs contains notes of regret, such as the "decline of comforts, urbanity, and hospitality," that "the high polish had debased the material, and the valuable ties of friendship and affection sacrificed to an ostentatious vanity." Again, "Etiquette, ostentation, and formality have supplanted urbanity, friendship, and conviviality, so delightful in former times." I daresay an old lady like Mrs. Hough, who had lived there for seventy-five years, would perceive the gradual change caused by wealth, population and civilization, which would tend much to break up a family party, or colony, however large.

Bombay shares, in common with all foreign stations, a little formality; which if one could but dispense with in hot places, society would become twice as charming and twice as attainable (I do not of course mean the formality of etiquette or good breeding). You are expected to call between twelve and two *en grande toilette,* at the risk of a sun-stroke, which makes a large acquaintance a labour, and detriment to health or pursuits. When you dine out you are naturally expected to make a toilette, it may be *grande toilette,* or *demie* (which takes just the same time), but to accomplish which you must forfeit your only possible breath of air, a drive or ride from six to eight. There is no dropping in after dinner from your drive in your bonnet, for an evening chat, and meeting from six to twenty of your acquaintance, which makes foreign society so easy, so pleasant, and so really conversable.

Then, just as you fancy you have made such a nice lot of acquaintance—nay, almost friends, and that everybody likes you so much and treats you as such an "acquisition," perhaps a Royal Prince, or a Viceroy, or some other big "swell" comes, and then they cluster round him, and drop you out of all their arrangements, in favour of Mrs. Ensign Jones, or Mrs. Brown of the steam packet agency, etc., because "you have no official rank in India," and are therefore periodically a worthless member of society. They do not seem to care that you would like to have basked a little in the sunshine too, and enjoyed a little of the fun; and when the "star" is gone, they like to pick you up again, and be as hospitable as before, but then you have learnt that "you are not one of *them*," and do not feel quite so enthusiastic.

When you dine out you must remember that India has three times, and you must not forget to ask whether eight o'clock dinner means Bombay time, Madras time, or Sekunderabád time.

The ladies soon become listless, their eyes are sad, their lives are dull. They always look tired, and I do not wonder. They get up about nine, breakfast, and pay or receive visits; then tiffin, siesta, a drive to the Apollo Bunder to hear the band, or to meet their husbands at the Fort, dine, and bed, is the programme of the day. Men live much the same, but the officers and men do better, for they have cricket and polo. Civilians have office work from ten a.m to four p.m. Merchants work harder. The amusements are balls, regattas, races, garden-parties, private theatricals, little dinners. Sport consists of snipe, when the paddy (rice) is buried after a monsoon (first week in November), the large grey quail when they dry up, and the black-breasted quail is found in the Deccan. At Tannah, and opposite Bombay, are snipe, duck, teal. At Penn, partridges and hares. We travel with ponies. You might get a good bag of duck, teal, snipe, partridges, and hares. Big game with a *shikári* farther off, for hog, deer, panthers, boars, bison, and tigers. The jungle is full of wild pig, cats, civet-cats, and porcupine.

I found nobody individually stiff, but society very much so, when they meet *en masse*, by reason of there being so much officialdom. There was none of that easy abandon, or *laisser aller*, which makes foreign society charming, because they forget themselves, and only think of pleasing others, or perhaps rather they make no effort at doing anything, so all that comes is natural, *i.e.* in *good* society, and this would make a hot foreign station so congenial. Your very finger-glass here seemed to be filled with red tape, and the "order of precedence" seemed to be uppermost in every mind. I daresay I should think it "awful fun" if my husband was an Indian Member of Council, or a Colonel, though I cannot fancy it; but as an outsider I gazed upon it as "ye manners and customs of ye Anglo-Indians," and thought how tedious it would be all the year round. My husband went to make a little excursion on his own account to Jhinjeera, which gave me time to take some notes on the personal appearance of Bombay: it is nearly the only subject I have not touched upon, concerning that city and its doings, during my stay.

They live very much here as they do at home, and dress the same, excepting the sholah topee, or pith helmet. Their cold weather lasts from November till February. The monsoon begins in May or June, and lasts till the end of September. I found it extremely hot in March. The average rainfall is eighty inches (I speak of Bombay). Poonah is the Head-Quarters of the Army, and is delightful during the rains. One should be at Bombay from November to February, in March at Mátherán or one of the sanitaria, in Poonah in May or June, and at Bombay again in November.

The money is the silver Rupee (a silver florin), which contains sixteen annas. An anna is 1½*d.*, a pie is a centime.

The first moment of landing was to me rather a disappointment. We do not see anything of "Oriental luxury" in the hotel or Fort St. George, but rather European discomfort. Those who reside in bungalows can of course accumulate what they please in them, but they all live entirely in English fashion. I had expected something picturesque, and I found myself in a regular European settlement, the Fort full of large, and seemingly empty, buildings, and I said to myself, "Every man here has his own public building."

"What is this?" and "What is that?" were my natural questions.

"That," said my friend and guide, "is the Sailor's Home, built by Khanderáo Gaekwar, at a cost of £25,000, and it contains two sailors and a drunken cook, though it is a magnificent pile, fit for a Residency. That is Convocation Hall, open once a year, with nothing to convoke. The University Senate Hall was erected partly by Sir Cowasjee Jehanghir Readymoney, and bears his name, and can seat one thousand persons comfortably, and is prominent in India for design and beauty. The University teaches Art, Law, Medicine, and Civil Engineering. There are five Colleges and thirty-five Public Schools. There are too many buildings to notice all, and I therefore only allude to a few of the best, as every rich man has erected a public building; and the names of Khanderáo Gaekwar, Sir Cowasjee Jehanghir, Wadia, Goculdas, and Sassoon, are connected with every improvement or charity. That is the University Library (but we have no books); and from the Clock Tower, two hundred and fifty feet high, you can have a view of the whole city. That is the Gothic High Court and Law Courts, costing £140,000, and that the National Bank; that the Bombay Club; and that the Public Works Office, costing £42,000; and that the Post Office and Telegraph Office, costing £60,000 and £25,000. That next to Watson's gigantic hotel is the Secretariat, which cost £130,000; and the Queen's statue, where the roads meet, was erected by Khanderáo Gaekwar for £18,000."

"I am quite startled at the number and size of the buildings; but where is the general Hospital?"

"We have none."

"And the Assembly Rooms?"

"We have none."

"And the Theatre?"

Again, "None."

"And the Lunatic Asylum?"

Also, "None."

Wonderful people!

The Catholic churches are the Fort Chapel, or Cathedral of N. S. de Esperanca, St. Xavier's, St. Mary's, and Nossa Senhora do Rosario. There are ten Protestant churches, five English missions, one Scotch, one Irish, one American, and seven Indian.

The greatest improvements and changes during the last fifteen years are said to be the reclamations, which are now overdone; the communications, which are perfect; and the (too many) public buildings.

They say twenty years ago, Apollo Bunder, the fashionable resort of to-day, was a foul and hideous sea-shore of pools and sewers. This has been regulated, and advanced into the sea below low-water mark, and five millions, spent upon the drainage, have been an enormous advantage; altogether since 1860 six and a half millions have been spent in improvements.

Then comes a spacious place for Rotten Row work, where you see about two riders once a week; and large grassy enclosures, a mile or two long, for regimental lines and tents, where polo and cricket and games have space, and this separates White Town and Black Town. Drive across that, and you come to Crawford Market, well worth seeing, called after Mr. Arthur Crawford, who erected it; he was Municipal Commissioner from 1865-71*; it is a most attractive bazar for food, and the spice stalls are curious. At last we drive down the Kalbadevi Road into the Bhendi Bazar, and for the first time I believe that I am really in India.† The most characteristic sight in

* He died lately.

† Where I pick up *bric-a-brac* there are three hundred and three jewellers and dealers in precious stones; and there are very fine diamonds, carved black-wood furniture (which I don't like), cocoa-nut fibre matting and reed matting, all sorts of brass and copper work, bronzes, ivory and tortoise-shell made into ornaments, Bombay box-work, carving in sandal-wood and ebony, turquoise ornaments, shawls, and all sorts of silver and gold work and old china. Mr. Grant Duff says that Bombay is to all Asia what Alexandria was during the earliest centuries of Christianity. The natives are strongly influenced by English education and ways of thought, without abandoning the Oriental dress or manner. Public meetings, and a wish to be brilliant speakers and writers, influence them. They read the papers, and form a tolerably respectable and wholesome public opinion.

Bombay is the famous Bhendi Bazar. It is unrivalled in India, and in the whole of the nearer East, and there one really sees what India is to-day. The roofed and shady Suks of Damascus, Cairo, and Jeddah are picturesque, especially Damascus, but this has a totally different *cachet.* We have the Hindú, Parsí, Portuguese, Chinese—every race, caste, and family between Cathay and Peru, Morocco and Pekin, Moscow and the Malay Peninsula.

How complicated the crowd you may judge from the fact that a friend, a hard student, whose average work was ten and sometimes fourteen hours out of the twenty-four, toiled through some five hard years before he could look out of the window and tell the caste, manners, and customs of the motley crowd passing below. The old Bombayites—veteran Japhetans dwelling in the tents of Shem—ignore the Bhendi Bazar; to their jaundiced eyes all between Frere Town and the Byculla Club (Dan and Beersheba) is desert; they would much prefer a workman's town, or a clump of semi-detached villas in the vicinity of English Babylon.*

Every block along the road and bazar has its own peculiar *cachet,*—some green, some blue, mostly cashmere-shawl pattern; most of them have a shady recessed ground-floor, with pillars; some, four stories, shed-shaped, with eaves and balconies, series of dwarf niches, yellow and white, pillars and vases heaped one upon another. The shop underlies and pays for the house; it is a den, or cave, shaded from sun and guarded from rain by projecting wooden eaves, supported by painted spotted pillars, elaborately carved, and coloured wooden buttresses. The names are written in English, Máhárátí, Guzeratí, and Hindústaní. The prevalent tinge is dark yellow or straw, especially the Pagodas or Dewals, as the Hindú calls them. The Marwári Temples are red with green columns and capitals, like the Sacred Tree of the Bhuddists, with all manner of decorations, paintings, bas-

* "Take the street scenes of Bombay," said Sir Richard Temple lately: "is there anything in Constantinople, in Cairo, or in Ispahan to equal the picturesqueness of the busy street scenes of Kalbadevi in Bombay?" Apparently not; for, though this picturesqueness and this kaleidoscopic variety so soon become part and parcel of the humdrum and routine surroundings of Bombay residents as to be overlooked or forgotten, every new visitor to our city is alike impressed.

reliefs, and alt-reliefs; some of them have five rows of statuettes of humans and bestials, all coloured; blue elephants upon a ground of cream, quaint flags and pennons, crescent and cross, towers for lamps, and the lumpy towers of three steps, which suggest dumpy Pyramids.

Every here and there are small oratories dedicated to different gods, for there are as many as races. These consist of a small square room, with a circular dome; a hideous black figure, with silver-white eyes, face painted red, and nude trunk, squats on a little square base for throne; it has a gaudy *sàri*, or mantle, and you are attracted to it by a black (almost naked) worshipper, dancing furiously before it to the jangling of bells.

Mombadevi Pagoda has a huge tank, goats, humped cattle, and blue-rock pigeons, is the godmother of Bombay, and is opposite the brass shops, which remind one of Damascus. The Mohammedan Mosque is white and green, an offset from the Jamma Masjid (mosque). The road is crossed with ropes, bearing triangles of coloured paper, left of the Mūhárram feast. This and the delicate lines of dome and minaret are adorned, but simply for effect (they are too thin to serve the Muezzin prayer-calls), and tell the tale of what has happened to El Islám in these soft lands.

Beyond the Nawwáb's Mosque turn to the right, into the quarter called the Umarkérí; the Imambárá; a handsome new church of the Moghuls, with Persian *façade* and gilt minarets; the huge Tank of Bab Ullah Shah, a famous devotee, backed by the battlements of the Jamsetji Hospital, and the grim old Debtor's Jail, with barred approaches and *chevaux de frise;* and then double back and resume the Bhendi Bazar.

Remark also the swell houses, especially those which have been adorned for a *shádí*, or marriage, with garlands, bouquets, couches, and quinquets. Some of the tenements are the quaintest things under heaven, from giant to dwarf; others a little ground floor, hardly eight feet high; these are square boxes, from one to six tiers high; those with white or spotted or stained glass windows, painted inside, outside, with every colour of the rainbow, and in violent contrasts,—red and green, black and yellow; fretted with wood-work, cut and carved like paper; posts or tiled eaves, every one with different pillars of various colours (all are covered with native tiles). The common house is a ground-floor shop, mats and shutters instead of windows, balconied upper storey, and dirty; and nose-ringed, bold-looking women, with bare faces, grin from the upper storey, dressed gaudily, and light up the windows in the evening that they may be seen. But many humble houses here contain the wealth of Ind.

It would be a capital question (in an arrogant voice) from an ignorant examiner to a timid boy going up for competitive examination: "Describe the architecture of the Bhendi Bazar in Bombay."

Timid boy: "I don't know, sir." (Plucked.)

Sharp boy's hand up: "Please, sir, *I* don't know, and *you* don't know, and *nobody* knows." (Passes, first class.)

A thing quite as ridiculous did happen (I do not believe in fairness at examinations, any more than I will believe "every care is taken" to avoid a railway accident, until we are allowed to tie a Director on to the cow-catcher in front of the engine). An arrogant and ignorant examiner asked a timid, humble boy, who was very anxious to pass for his mother's sake, to obtain some appointment, "How far is it from the city of São Paùlo in Brazil to the tropical line of Capricorn?"

The boy, radiant, answered, "Between four and five miles, sir."

"Go down, sir; you're plucked; it's twenty miles."

The boy grew red and white, and turned despairingly to go. Suddenly he remembered his mother, turned round, and said nervously, "Please, sir, of course you ought to know better than me; but—I lived there five years, sir, and I had to walk it twice a week to go home from school to mother's house from Saturday to Monday!"

Chorus of laughter at the examiner, and the poor boy passed.

I here insert a Frenchman's view of the Bhendi Bazar, Count Goblet d'Alviella, from an extract of a review in an Indian paper on his book:—

"Few travellers, however, have been so successful in conveying their freshest impressions to others as Count Goblet d'Alviella, whose views upon Anglo-Indian life we lately discussed. Native life he first witnessed in the native town of Bombay; and the first day spent there seemed to him like some dream under the spell of opium or haschich. In imagination he plunged 'into an orgie of lines and a debauch of colours;' he found himself amidst the very splendours of the Arabian Nights, which, after cradling his infancy in an 'orient of the phantasy,' had been rudely dispelled by the actual orient of the Levant. In Bombay he expected to see a parody of Liverpool or London. Instead of this he found bazars such as Arabia or Turkey could never imitate in the variety of lines, the richness of tints, the exuberance of outdoor life, which startled him at every corner. The irregular streets pleased him vastly, with their lofty houses, each differing from the other in style and colour; many with columns, balconies, belvideres, verandahs, balustraded galleries of carven wood; terraces after the Italian style, gables like the Dutch; designs borrowed from the pyramid or pagoda; façades covered with ornament and sculpture, and symbols, complicated and strange—all the colours of the palette, all the 'motives' of architecture jumbled extravagantly and fantastically together. But the people pleased him more; for the costumes that seemed to borrow every colour of the rainbow were after all only typical of the wearers, 'who ran down the complete gamut of human colouration, from the Aryans of the North, who are almost white, to the Dravidians of the South, who are almost black.' In death, as in life, there was the same variety: he met Hindús bearing their corpses to the burning pyre; Parsees carrying their dead to the vultures of the Towers of Silence, and Mohammedans starting for the sand-strewn burial ground by the shore. Nothing was wanting in local colour but the elephant; nothing jarred upon the fancy but the yellow staves of the blue-frocked policeman. Such was Bombay to a stranger, but to us it is still, unfortunately, Bombay, with a long-pending drainage question; Bombay, with as many stenches as Cologne; Bombay, with a present death-rate highest but one of all the great cities in the world.

"But with this strange scene before him, Count d'Alviella at once began an effort which he found almost insurmountable, to penetrate into the interior life of the Hindus. 'What do you know of that?' he first asked every English official he could meet; but the opinion and the information of each were all at variance. Then he went to natives themselves for information, and though he saw that caste exclusiveness is so much the more insurmountable as it is founded rather on social prejudice than on religious faith, he was introduced to some of the ceremonies of native domestic life. He was warmly received by Sir Munguldas Nathoobhoy, and was not only present at the marriage of his two sons, but taken 'behind the scenes' to see the female guests at their banquet. The repast lasted two hours, during which he could contemplate at his ease these twelve hundred women, 'draped in their beautiful robes of gauze,—white, blue, yellow, red, green,—fringed with gold or silver, squatting side by side in five long rows,' and eating soups, curries, and sweetmeats from leaves instead of plates. In the evening he came again to the nautch, and was as well sold as the Scotch padre in Aliph Cheem's verses. There were 'two nautch girls,' who, without being particularly pretty, are held in great reputation in Bombay. I was even told that one of them receives as much as four or five hundred rupees a night.' Unlike the 'Bayaderes' he had seen on the Paris stage, these nautch girls were very much more dressed in their public performances than in their ordinary costume. He had, however, a long conversation with his host, who is, as the Count writes, a good representative of the enlightened class of native society. Among other things, Sir Munguldas said that the loss of their English rulers, who alone are capable of assuring order and spreading education, would be far the greatest misfortune that could happen to his countrymen. But that he thought the English Government had two grave faults: first, that they would not admit the great poverty of the people, and so overstrained their tax-paying capability; second, that they were guided too much by abstract and exotic principles, and disregarded essential race differences. He was as frank about himself; for while he rallied the superstitions of his countrymen, and regretted the absurdity of their creed, he confessed that he was obliged to carry out every practice of his own sect,—supporting idols in temples, accepting the date fixed by astrologers for the marriage of his sons, and bearing on his temples the distinctive castes mark. In India, says the Count, perhaps more than elsewhere, religion is *une affaire de convenances*, and here it is no slight thing to lose caste, as Sir Munguldas said, when explaining away the restrictions he was compelled to observe in his relations with Europeans.

"The Hindú division into castes is sometimes said to have done good service in preventing the civilization of the Aryan from being lost in contact with the inferior races; but if even that be granted, its utility has disappeared, and as our writer puts it, the question to-day is between the decadence of that civilization and the regeneration of India by light coming from the West. The Count is perhaps too sanguine about the speedy approach of that emancipation, and seems to undervalue the immense force of conservatism in India,—all the stronger because latent. But it will come, he tells us, not from the efforts of missionaries, simply preaching the doctrines and dogmas of various Western Churches, but partly through the moral force of extending education and enlightenment, partly through the efforts of a free press, and, more than all, through the material means of railways and steamers and tramcars. What change in the national life has been wrought by all the efforts of all the Protestant missions ?. Not one-thousandth part of the population, he answers, have even *called* themselves converts. The native press, again, is too young to be fairly judged. At present, he says, 'it is capable of neither directing nor indicating public opinion.' But it is a grand experiment, for India is the only country in the world in which a press has ever been allowed to start free and untrammeled. It must, in the nature of things, be crude,—servile in one direction, ridiculously disloyal in another ; 'but, in despite of all its vagaries, it accustoms its readers to think for themselves, and while it educates the public it will also educate itself.' The progress that education has made is wonderful, even in the numbers who have passed through the schools,—if we consider the short period in which it has been scientifically pursued,—and wonderful in the results proved by the formation of theistic societies such as the Brahmo-Somaj. And for this the English alone are to be thanked. 'I know,' says Count d'Alviella, 'no civilized nation in which talent has so much opportunity of bringing itself to light in the organization of popular education ; and it may safely be affirmed, that among European States no Government could, without being accused of Socialism, interfere in so liberal a fashion for the development of the intellect of the poor.' But a still more potent change is being wrought by a thoroughly unexpected means—the railway. When railways were started here, returns were expected only from European travellers and goods traffic. Natives were left out of the question ; but by 1875 the natives had monopolized 97 per cent. of the whole passenger traffic, and the constant change and promiscuous society that this fact of necessity implies, have done much to weaken the distinctions of caste. Many, perhaps most of the advanced Hindús, are as anxious as Count d'Alviella himself to do away with the trammels of caste, but, like Sir Munguldas, they feel that at present it is too intimately bound up with all the ties and traditions of family life."

The crowd, seething and frying in the gorgeous glare of the tropical sun, is at least as remarkable as the houses which lodge it. The great mass consists of Konkani Moslems, with dark sub-Turanian features and scraggy beards, clad in chintz turbans, resembling the Parsí head-gear ; in long cotton coats,

A SIND MOONSHI.

whose waists, like our grandmothers' gowns, are just under the arm-pits; and in tights which, unlike those of our grandfathers, pucker all adown the lean, calfless leg; Konkani shawls on shoulder, shoes with turned-up toes, and short drawers, or *pajammahs.*

There are Persians (Shiahs), with lambskin extinguishers, shaved chins, and huge moustachios, *en virgule,*—grown in order to denote their horror of the Sunnis; the so-called orthodox Bohrahs, with white turban, all clothes white, and big *pajammahs.* Arabs from the Persian Gulf, sitting or lolling about the *kahwah* (coffee-houses) or the stables of Abd el Rahmán, or Ali bin Abdullah (they are known by the *burnous* and the *kuffiyyah,* the silk and gold fichu, which covers the head and falls on the shoulders), athletic Afghans, and Beloch Sindis, and Brahmins in wide *pajammahs* (drawers), and Mahmans who have now learned to affect the *Moghul* (Persian head-gear), Schismatic Shiahs, and Khiyahi and Wahhabis. The Kwajah (Shaykh) wears a gold cap, with thin rim, mid turban. The Mahman (Sunni), a gold cap, long skirt, and always the *sudréh,* or waistcoat. There are the conjurers and snake-charmers, the vendors of pipes and mangoes; Hindú women in colours that pale those of Egypt and Syria, with brass and silver bangles and nose-rings. There are two sorts of Parsees, one white turbaned, and the cayman, whose hat (one has no name for the seemingly useless and misshapen article, which looks like a chimney smoke-escape made of *papier maché*), purple black, spotted with red.

The women are the best dressed in India. They are often very pretty, and have *svelte* figures like the Copt women in Egypt, and look elegant in their *saris* (a sort of mantle, like a sheet), of every bright colour, tulip-tints, silk stockings cased in tiny slippers, down at heel, and unveiled, except at the back of the head. Where *they* are, all places seem like a garden. The Bhandari women wear yellow *sári* and parti-coloured *choli.*

There is nothing that startles one so much as the immense variety of *turban* in the men and the *choli* in the women. You see of the former every size and shape, and colour and manner of wearing. Some are the size of a moderate round tea-table, and others fit the head tight; some are worn straight, and some jauntily cocked sideways; some are red and horned. The *choli* is a bodice, which is put on the female child, who never knows stays; it always supports the bosom, and she is never without it, I believe, night or day, unless after marriage; and whilst she is growing they are always, of course, changed to her size. They are of all colours and shapes, according to the race. I bought some of every kind whilst I was there. No Englishwoman could wear one unless it was made on purpose for her, but I cannot explain why. The Maharattas wear *turban* and forked slippers, and the Konkanis peaky slippers.

To continue the crowd-staring. There is the Pattewálá, the local Janissary or Kawwás, meeting the equally black Portuguese; and the Sisters of Mary and Joseph, in black robes and white-frilled caps, glide meekly in and out the crowd, and make way for "Souter's Canaries" (policemen), and Sepoy riflemen in dark green. The Bheestic still creeps under his huge water-skin, looking like a live pig. Sulaymánis (Afghans) from the hills, and Rohillas, also hill-men, are not wanting. The mass of the crowd is evidently Hindú, as we have now learnt by the *tilak*, or forehead mark, applied after the daily bath; and here the subject is endless. The sign denotes his caste:—

● Tilak ● red and wafer-like, means nothing; it is put on, if possible, by Brahmins after bathing.
⌇ Váishnava, or Vishnuiti.
— Sháivya, worshipper of Shiva, the Third Person of the Triad.
||| Ramanaj, worshipping Ráma.
⊏⊐ Worn between brows (earth or white sandal).
≡ Kshatriya, military or regal caste.
U Vaisya, Banian, the traders.
● Shudra, the servile man, a large round spot, size of shilling.

The crowd is remarkable for violent contrast, and, clad in the raiment of the tulip, the pale-faced soldier in scarlet uniform strides past the almost naked Fakir. (Moslem), Jogi, or Sunyasi (Hindú), daubed *cap à pie* with ashes, and carrying the

NATIVES OF SIND.

instruments of his craft—the begging-bowl, the crutch, and the tiger-skin. The Rámosi, or red-turbaned policeman, comes in contact with Jack ashore, who has indulged in copious libations of cognac. The sleek warm Banyan, with red turban, horned in front, and *dhoti*, or waist cloth, hanging over his heels, glides among the pariah dogs and the coolies—whose toilet is a roll of rag—and the Borah, with his basket of shawls for sale. The Hindú waggon—a painted box on wheels, dating long before the birth of Jagannath—crosses the four-in-hand of a dragoon officer.

There is now a tramway, whose horses are provided with hats (sholah *topees*), and a continuation of protection down the spine, in consequence of so many of them falling down dead from the sun. It is a shame to drive horses in such a sun; steam ought to be used. It is also remarkable that the carriage of all these peoples is universally graceful,—especially the women, and more especially of those who have to carry water-pots or weights on the head. The prevalence of mendicancy, in all castes, is another remarkable item. The form here is not, however, as in London, a drunken father at home, and six little brothers, and ten with the small-pox, and mother can't work, etc., etc., but a whine that some happier brother has been able to buy a draught of water at a neighbouring stall, *i.e.*, a table upon which is a huge *ghará* (earthenware water-pot) and garnishings of flowers, mustard-and-cress, palm fronds, and plantain leaves.

The begging nuisance has been embodied by the English in the following classical lines, evidently between a "griff" and an old Indián:—

"What is the black man saying,
Brother, the whole day long?
Methinks I hear him praying
Ever the self-same song:
'*Sa'b merí bakshish do!*'

Brother, they are not praying,
They are not doing so;
The only thing they are saying
Is, '*Sa'b merí bakshish do!*'
(Gi'e me a 'alfpenny, do!)"

The word Sáhib is perverted to Sá'b by people who speak Hindústani much as a Frenchman would, who had learned English from his groom. Sáhib, an Arabic word, means in the classical tongue, Companion (of Mohammed understood).*

We were fortunate enough to arrive in time for two out of their four great galas or festivals,—the Tábút, the tenth of their month Mūhárram, corresponding this year with our February 7th, and Holi-day, 9th March. When the whole of Bombay is in the streets, then you can appreciate the crowd justly. You must end by going to Carnac Bunder at sunset, to see the remains of the Tábúts (biers) thrown into the sea. Persians content themselves on this day with the Tajyah, mourning for the survival of Johrab, killed by his father, Rustam. The Sunni crowd consider it a theatrical representation of the martyrdom, with the corpse being carried amidst a general wailing; and for this the two sects would willingly murder each other.

There was once a riot, when the Parsees were killed, and it used to be a season of terror to Christians in days when India

* Maclean says that "nowhere in the world are there so many varieties of race, nationality, and religion as in Bombay. Firstly the Hindú, with many diversities of type, such as the Banian of Guzerat and the Maharatta of the Deccan, whilst the Mohammedans include, beside Indian Mussulmans, Afghans, Persians, Arabs, Turks, Malays, and Abyssinians. There are besides colonies of Jews and Armenians, many thousand Indo-Portuguese (or Topazes), and it is the head-quarters of the thriving and prolific Parsees, and chiefly the Europeans. The Jains, Brahmins, Lakshmi, Lingaets, and Bhattias are of the Brahminical division of caste."

The Brahminical Hindús (orthodox) form three-fifths of the population of Bombay, and are subdivided into the worshippers of Vishnū and worshippers of Shiva, the Second and Third Persons of the Hindú Trinity.

Vishnū is known popularly through his incarnations—Rama, and Krishna, and Vishnū's wife, Lakshmi. These are the favourite deities in Bombay, also the elephant-headed god Gunpati. The worshippers of Shiva pay their homage chiefly to his consort, Kali or Bhowanee, patroness of the Thugs, to whom the Parbati Temple at Poonah is dedicated.

The Banians are also most important Hindús, and great traders, and include the Bhattias and the Jains, who love animals, and support them by money and care.

The Aaricks are seceders from Brahmin's doctrines.

The Marwarees are also another variety, and are chiefly bankers and usurers.

Buddhism, to which we owe such magnificent remains, was more popular two was a vast charnel-house; but now the mob is kept in order, and nothing is allowed save shillelaghs of sugar-cane.

The battle of Kerbela is represented by boys in tinsel gold and silver, painted yellow and black, in stripes like the tiger; eyes and muzzles dyed blood red, and represent the lion which guarded the tomb of Hosayn; and what looks like hoops are the bows and arrows of ancient Arabia. They rush to and fro like the whirlwind, brandishing their sugar-cane truncheons, headed by men in a light clothing of ashes. These are Indian howling Dervishes; and "rowdies" appear to be supported by their friends, staggering and singing as if they were drunk, which means intense emotion (they are only pretending). Flags and banners of every form and hue thicken the air; tinsel Tábúts, or biers, are supported on men's shoulders, each carrying figures, like our Catholic processions abroad; every sect or school has its own, and they dance before them frantically, the mob exciting itself to madness by noise and motion. The grand thing is for several to be carried off in what would be considered by us an epileptic fit.

Bridal processions cross the street; say bridegroom eight and bride six, mounted on a gold-covered horse, with a horned saddle, golden and jewelled, which the children grasp with their hands

hundred years before Christ, but now Brahmah has superseded Bhuddha. Maharatta is the universal language, but Guzeratee is the commercial tongue.

The Mohammedans form one-fifth of the population, and are subdivided into Sunni (orthodox Turks and Arabs), disciples of the Caliphs, after Mohammed, through Abubeker, Omar, and the Ommiade, Caliphs of Damascus and the Shiahs (Persians), who are all disciples of Ali, the fourth Caliph and of his sons, Hassan and Hossein, who were murdered by their Ommiade rivals.

In Bombay there are more Shiahs than Sunnis, and they include the well-known caste of Borahs, dealers in all goods,—who have Jewish features.

The Wahabees are like Moslem Jacobites, and fearfully dangerous; but they are fortunately, few. They do such deeds as the murder of Mr. Justice Norman.

The Parsees are the most intelligent, civilized, and prosperous: they follow the fortunes of the English. They are fire-worshippers from Persia. If you see anything nice in India, and you admire it and ask to whom it belongs, the answer is invariably "a rich Parsee."

The Topazes are nearly the only native Christians,—a cross between the early Portuguese and Indian; they make capital servants. The Jews are from Mesopotamia, whose chief family is that of Sassoon. Mr. David Sassoon's eldest son, Albert, was knighted in 1871 on account of his and his father's great charities.

The bridegroom wears a gold head-dress and cap, and carries a wooden sword; the bride is enveloped in flowers, so as to hide her face, like a little "Queen of May."

The Bombay servants are terrible; so dull and stupid. They never do a thing right if there *is* a wrong way. They break all they touch, and then burst into a "*Yah, yah, yah!*" like a monkey. Leave half a bottle of sherry, and they will fill it up with hock. "Are they not both white wine, Sá'b?" Your "Khitmadgar" does not know the name of the next street. Call for your tea: he brings up a saucer and stares at you. You wait awhile, and ask him why your tea isn't ready: he will run downstairs and fetch up a spoon, and so on through the whole business, till your tea has occupied one hour to put on the table. As he walks about barefoot, you never hear him approach. You think you are alone in the room: you are writing or reading; you look up, and if nervous, are made to jump by seeing a black face close to you, star-gazing.

I was there only a few months, and so had not time to get used to the infliction. If you have a visit, you will see the door slowly open and a black face protruded in at least six times in a quarter of an hour. They are so curious, and I never can think what can repay them for the trouble,—they are so stolid in everything else. As a child at school the Indian is quicker than a European, but he has no stay, he stops at a certain point; he can imitate but not originate. In a higher grade, if the Hindú scents rupees and rank, he is a sleuth hound till he has qualified himself for the public service and won the object of his ambition; but there he ends, instead of beginning, life. Hence the danger of trusting him with charges of high responsibility.

Anglo-Indian children are most frightfully spoilt. There is no nursery; they live with grown-up people. The natives indulge them to death, and even delight in being tyrannized over by them. They learn all sorts of bad things and language. Who dare send them to bed in the evening, or tell them to do anything they don't like? I pity the parents: they dread the climate; they are thinking of the long parting when the children (if they live) must be sent to England, and *they* must

NAUGHTY BOY!

remain there, and, perhaps, die there, and only see them now and again. Yet there is nothing to save health but England; no chance of reforming their manners and morals save in an English school. This struck me as being the saddest part of Indian life. The woman must go to the hills for to England or the six hot months of the year; the man must remain at his duty; the children must go away at six or seven to England, or earlier. There is no *home:* affections must be divided and broken up, or they must run the gauntlet of sickness or death; and all these compromises have to be effected on very small means.

CHAPTER XIII.

THE SANITARIA OF WESTERN INDIA.

ON the 16th April we started for Máhábáleshwar, the favourite of all the sanitaria, save the Neilgherries; the last, however, is a difficult business, being eight or ten days' journey by sea aud land; it is very expensive, and very rough travelling for delicate people from Bombay. Were it not for this, the Neilgherries, being the fashion, would leave the other poor stations quite deserted.

The sanitaria of the Western Gháts—the Sahyádri range, the stepped mountains nearest Bombay—have therefore to be used. They are Khandálá, Lanauli, Sinhgarh, Purundhur, Punalla near Colapur, and Kálsábái in the Deccan (the latter an eminence, five thousand five hundred feet high, of the romantic and quite neglected Sahyádri range); the three *main* items are, Tungá, in the Northern Konkan (1), the baby; (2) Mátherán, the hobble-de-hoy; and (3) Máhábáleshwar, with Panchganni, the middle-aged man.

Tungá is easily reached from Bombay. You take a ticket by the B. B. and C. T. Railway to Bassein, which is thirty-three and a half miles, telegraphing to the inn-keeper, Christopher da Souza, to have riding ponies, and men with bullocks for baggage, and drinking water. Don't hurry, for at a short distance to your right are the far-famed caves, Kánheri or Kánhá Hill (Kánhágiri the late Dr. Wilson called it, and Kennery Mr. and Mrs. John Bull call it now, in the same way they say Enery for Henry).

Salsette, old Sáshthi, is an island of sixty-six villages, and was loved by the old Cave-priests, as the tigers love it still. The tall walls of Mandip Eshwar rise on the left, just beyond Baroli, the thirteenth station. This word means,—Eshwar, "God" (and

God here means Shiva), and Mandip, "Threshold;" but the old Portuguese called it Mont Pezier. Here the Paulistas, as the Jesuits were called, built a church and college on the hill in which the caves are, and set up an altar in the latter; then it of course drove out Shiva, and became a Catholic crypt.

The first aspect of Tungá, which hides its towering head from Bombay, is dignified. You cross the broad, picturesque river of Bassein in the train. This is a sea arm, and it separates from the mainland of India, Salsette, which is the northernmost of nine little islands, now welded into one large one, composing the Mombadevi Peninsula. The crumbling walls and towers of Portuguese Bassein, the old Fort, and Port of the Fidalgoes, or Cavaliers, rise down stream.

In front, buttressing the right bank of the Indian mainland, towers the long Tungá ridge, two thousand three hundred feet above sea level, and is a formation something like Mátherán; and beyond it, up stream, the fort-crested cone of Káman (the sailors call it Bassein Peak), which from this aspect appears split by a nick. The scenery is picturesque. The leek-green watery lowlands are studded with brown ruins, and dotted with rich groves; the hills and mountains are of a warm red laterite, a natural brick, contrasting with the verdigris of the jambu tree, which gave its name to the Indian continent, and means Jackal-Land. The riverine sea arm reflects the pale blue sky, and bears on its broad bosom a fleet of tall-sparred native craft; and the piles that you see driven across the river support the Koli's fishing-nets.

Tungá is a holy hill, and has its legend, and was a place of pilgrimage. Parashu Ráma, or Ráma of the Battle-axe, who is supposed to have been an incarnation of Vishnú, and is believed to have flourished about 1170 B.C., did battle, in revenge for affronts offered to the Brahmans with certain Asuras, evil spirits headed by Vimala. The demons, driven by the sturdy god, beat a hasty retreat, until stopped by the western sea; and Vimala, carrying Tungá on his head, placed it amongst the waves, and established his fortified head-quarters. His defeat, however, caused him to repent and practise religious austerities, which pleased Shiva so much, that he was granted immunity from death, and other privileges, on condition of his desisting from being aggressive towards the Brahmans, in which case Vimala need fear nobody in the three worlds: the condition was acceded to, and the privileges were granted.

The fighting god, Ráma, having a tiff with the Hindú Neptune, Varuna, stood upon the Sahyádri range, our Western Gháts, and shot fourteen shafts seawards. The waters receded where the points fell, and the land thus reclaimed was divided into the seven districts composing the classical Konkan, and corresponding with its seven families of Brahmans, speaking seven dialects. We cannot despise the fanciful old legend, because it tells us the proto-historic changes, both geological and volcanic, still evidenced by the Deccan, and the battles of the pure Aryans with the an-Aryans, or "demons" as they were called.

Tungá is about nine miles and a half from the Bassein Station, and of these, five are utterly unfit for carriages, and even native carts. From the plain you cannot see the solitary bungalow built by the Hon. Mr. Hope, now member of Legislative Council, Calcutta. It encouraged M. da Souza to build an hotel, now three years old, which has, I believe, held three visitors. Naturally the tank is in a fearful state, and drinking water must be carried up on pain of fever, and other horrors. Tungá wants everything,—roads, houses, guide-book, and a superintendent. The man-eating tiger walks about without fear of man. Still, its height and position, open to the sea breeze, are in its favour; the ridge is easily reached from Bombay, and perhaps some Governor or Commander-in-Chief may develop it into a full-grown sanitarium; at present it is a *terra incognita* to the Bombayite, but it may become, like Mátherán, a hill station.*

Khandálá, Lanauli, and Mátherán I have already described.

* The road from Poonah to Máhábáleshwar goes, *via* the Katraj Ghát and tunnel, to Sherwal, thence to the Kamatki Ghát. Shortly after, the route leaves the Sáttárá road at Soorool, and branches off to Wahi on the Krishna river, and then ascends the Passernee Ghát to Panchganni, a small hill station, ten miles from Máhábáleshwar—the whole seventy-five miles. The new Ghát from Máhábáleshwar to Poladpoor is now opened for *palkees, tattoos,* and for *tongas* (little light pony carts, and ponies the size of rats).

Sinhgarh you see in the distance, going by rail from Poonah to Hyderabad; but both it and Kálsá-bai, like Tungá, are not formed. People go up for an excursion, but not to stay, because there is nothing there; yet these are spots which could be easily and advantageously converted into sanitaria.* It is no use waiting until you are sick to look for sanitaria. The first thing on arriving in a country like India, especially if you are healthy, is to seek them all out, and find out which suits you best. But no private family can form a sanitarium; some great official must go there with all his staff; then bungalows, and inns, and necessaries, and lastly comforts, begin to grow. Roads have to be cleared, water looked after, wild beasts to be hunted out, regular supplies for man and beast to be sent from the next greatest town, and presently things come round of themselves.

It only remains now for me to say a few words about Máhá-báleshwar, which owes its existence to the energetic Sir John Malcolm, Governor of Bombay, 1827-30 as also the Bhore Ghát road. This journey from Bombay is a far more serious matter, and hence, probably, the "superior fashion" which surrounds this great sanitarium like a halo, for it is certainly the favourite after the Neilgherries, the most difficult of all. First you must get to Poonah, and from this city the journey is seventy-five miles.

We left Bombay by the 1.15 train, *express*, reaching Poonah in seven hours, doing one hundred and nineteen miles,—and a

* Purundhur, in the Deccan, is about twenty miles south-east from Poonah, four thousand five hundred feet above sea level.

There are also plenty of desert spots little known, but salubrious.

Thirty miles north-east of Baroda is the once fortified hill of Pawangarh.

Far to the north, beyond Deesa, the famed Mount Aboo, the southernmost point of the Aravalli range.

In the Southern Konkan is Dapuli.

In the extreme south is the hill near the port of Carwar.

Along the coast from Balacherri, on the Gulf of Kutch, and Gogo, on the Gulf of Cambay, to Mangalore and Honore (at the mouth of the Gairsappa, leading to the celebrated falls) on the south, are several pleasant coast stations, with a south-westerly breeze.

There are Balsar Domus and Vaux's Tomb (near Surat, north and south of the Tapti's mouth), and Tithul, a good beach.

But notwithstanding the choice, the only sanitaria used are Mátherán by necessity, and Máhábáleshwar for pleasure, by those who cannot get to the Neilgherries.

very comfortable journey it was, saving the fact that the thermometer which I pinned to the cushion showed 105° F. The air, in spite of every luxury for coolth, was like blasts out of a heated furnace; and this was the 16th April. We dined at Poonah, and our Parsee landlord was most attentive, and sent us off in the evening laden with fruit and flowers.

Mr. Framjee Ardaseer, No. 14, Civil Lines, Poonah, sent us a magnificent prospectus of carriages from Poonah to Máhábáleshwar; the whole cost of the seventy-five miles, tolls and coolies included, to be thirty-five rupees. The prospectus also contained several inviting testimonials; so we ordered "a trap." However, the springs were broken, and projections were sticking through the hard, narrow cushions, in all directions, into our unhappy bodies; and the carriage was lop-sided, and bumped fearfully on my side; so it was not a paradise,—nevertheless we enjoyed the trip very much.

It was a charming night; the moon late, being in the last quarter. We saw a great Moslem *fête* coming out of Poonah at night. The hills were illuminated in patterns and letters. We slept when it was dark, and I remember we drank a great deal of water, for it was a most thirsty night. The scenery was first a cultivated plain. The Poonah road is picturesque, especially about the Katraj tunnel and the Kámátka Ghát, and the road is easy.

At six a.m. we passed a beautifully clean travelling bungalow at Soorool, when we brought down our basket, and ate and had tea, and milk from the cow belonging to the old soldier who kept it. At the foot of the third "stepped mountain," Pasarni, you pass through Wye (*Wahi*), the village capital of the Pándu Princes, which, according to the Hindú Pantheon, "enjoyed the privilege of killing beef for sale."

It is the name of the prettiest and most interesting place, with the prettiest women, in Western India; besides being a quasi-sacred settlement, enriched by the barefaced mendicancy of its Reverend men. This is a village of Temples and Holy Tanks; the former of various forms, covered with delicate tracery, which line the bed of the river, or peer out everywhere from their nestling-place among the cocoa trees. This heap of temples affords us an excellent study of the "Gumat," or Hindú dome, that covers the idols' *sanctum sanctorum.* The usual shape is a pyramid, with the faces broken by a multitude of steps and long tongue-shaped ovals, large and small. The general effect of the temples, which are strewed about *even* in the river-bed, is that of being dotted all over with *blanc mange* moulds. It is pretty, *bizarre*, and a most interesting scene.

The ascent was performed by sixteen coolies, from Wahi, up the steep Pasarni Ghát, which occupied about two hours, and was very hot and dusty, and dreadfully hard work; but they did it much better than horses could have done. At Panchganni we came to the travelling bungalow, sixty-two miles from Poonah, and stopped a few minutes to tie up some of our broken springs. After this we were very tired, and the last thirteen miles seemed almost insupportable. Everything appeared so far. When once we entered the verdure of Máhábáleshwar, at the summit, four thousand seven hundred and eighty feet above sea-level, the distances seemed intolerable, the plentiful vegetation and trees being cut so as to give no shade, though the luxuriant woods extend over seventeen miles long by five broad. The roads are so badly engineered, all up and down hill, and so heavy with loose, thick laterite dust and ferruginous clay as to tire horses very much. It is a large Mátherán, and, as I said before, its difficulty makes its worth, just as Palmyra is more valued than Baalbak.

We had been eighteen hours out, instead of the advertised twelve. We unpacked, bathed, dressed, breakfasted, and went off for a drive with Lady Agnes Danyell, who drove a pair of *tattoos*, each about the size of a big dog. These *tattoos* are immensely strong, and bear any work and hardship; but the hired ponies are over-driven and ill-treated.

The first settlement which one reaches, after a stiff pull up the last Ghát, should evidently be the head-quarters. It stands on a gravelly ridge, some four thousand feet high, at the very eastern edge of the block; the drainage is excellent, and the place is habitable all the year round. A European colony and schools have long been settled here—on paper. We went first to Prospect Point and Lodwick Point,—called after General Lodwick, an old officer of the Wellington type, in 1799, whose memory is perpetuated by an ugly pillar and medallion.

Lady Agnes left me near her own gates, and I drove her ponies back in the dark, without knowing the ground. There were no lamps, and other carriages constantly passed me. The *tattoos*, being still half-broke, did not answer their bits perfectly; and next morning I saw some places where the wheels had been unpleasantly close to. We dined and went to bed, thoroughly tired; we had been out twenty-five hours, and had had no sleep for forty-one hours. I did not even remember the end of dinner, or how we went to bed, from sleepiness.

We lodged with Dorabjee Sorabjee, a civil Parsee, Máhábáleshwar Hotel, where we each paid six rupees a day. We had decent food, capital mutton,—as good as Exmoor or Dartmoor, —and fair hock; the rooms were clean and comfortable.

Fountain House Hotel takes fifteen rupees a day (no diminution for servants) for the poorest fare.

18*th April.*—We got up at five, and drove in a *tonga*—a sort of tea-cart, with small *tattoo* ponies—to Elphinstone Point and the Máhábáleshwar temples. It was a most enjoyable excursion, but entirely spoilt by the driver cutting the poor little "tats" with a thick cowhide whip, for three hours and a half, over their eyes, ears, noses, mouths, legs,—using also the butt end, and this over ground that would kill any other kind of animal. The patient and willing nags were doing their best, and getting galled and being whipped when they went full speed the same as when they walked a little to ease themselves. These occasions are a *misery* to me. I get so nervous, bully the driver, take his whip away, promise him bakshish if he won't do it, and then drive myself. Then the foolish things stand still when *I* have the reins, and will not go without the whip. Then my husband swears at the driver for being cruel, and scolds me for spoiling an excursion by my ridiculous tender sensibilities. On this occasion my fox-terrier, "Nip," tried to bite the coachman for beating the ponies; and not being allowed, she laid her head on my shoulder and went into hysterics: the tears actually ran down her cheeks, for she was extremely sensitive and hysterical, and sometimes cried like a child.

I am told in the season these *tattoos* perform this journey three or four times a day. Only English visitors hire these tongas, and I am sure if they would not allow this treatment it would cease, and at least they might walk up the hills and promise the boy a rupee not to beat too much. Only think how you would like your own ponies to be treated so.

Elphinstone Point is one of the usual grand mountain scenes; it is most strikingly beautiful, with piles of Gháts on all sides, and the depression, or valley, is the broad bed of a river. The point runs out into the air with a fall of four thousand feet, into the Konkan, and the whole ravine looks as if a deluge had passed through it, bursting and tearing up all before it. In the distance on another eminence is Purtabghur, where Sivaji, the founder of the Maharatta Empire, murdered the Moslem general, Afzul Khan; whilst embracing him he stabbed him with a dagger, called *waghnak,* like a tiger-claw, worn on the hand like a knuckle-duster.

Sivaji, born in 1627, was one of the greatest leaders of light cavalry ever known. His character was fiery, and fascinated all bold adventurers. He formed a large body of wild horsemen, whom he led to great military enterprises, and at his death left a kingdom four hundred miles long by one hundred and twenty broad, though only a subject of the Rajah of Bijapur, with whom he broke faith.

The village of Máhábáleshwar is a Brahman settlement, where five rivers, and, at some seasons, seven, arise. The five are the Krishna, Yena, Koyana, Savatri, and Gavatri. This is the Krishna source. There are some ancient temples with carved bulls and tigers on them, and tanks of holy water conveyed through stone bulls; one temple has a very dirty bed with snakes behind and under it for the god Mahadeo, with a rude fresco of the god over it. Disease is cured and mortal sins washed out by sleeping on this bed. The villagers who believe this are Maharatta, a fine race. We returned at nine, going to Lingmálá, where lie utterly neglected the plantations of chinchona (quinine). You are shown the Dabdahá, or cataract of the Yena, which during the "season" is bone dry. If you are fond of walking you may walk to Kamalghar and to Purtabghar, a ruined hill fort, near which, as I have recounted, Sivaji's most famous murder was committed; but return before nightfall, for a horror of deep gloom settles upon the world.

We were glad to be housed, for even at nine a.m. the sun was very trying. I had a charmingly lazy day, much needed; sleeping and writing, and out at five in the cool afternoon. Lady Agnes drove us to call on the Petersons, and to Badminton Point. The Blue Valley is a misty depth, and the Point is another of those splendid scenes which do not differ enough to bear description. We dined with Lady Agnes, and met Mr. and Mrs. Moore, and Mrs. Pottinger. We went home in the dark, and talked about tigers, one of which is periodically seen at intervals. The tigers, bisons, and bears, have, however, been killed off, and nothing remains but snakes and panthers. So I think the tiger is a panther. Yet the late Dr. John Wilson, of Bombay, one of my husband's old friends, had a narrow escape from one.*

19*th April.*—My husband went to look at the iron mines, the best iron from which all the Damascus and Khorassan blades were made; it is soft and pliable, and when the blade is made they harden it. He brought away a lump of the iron, and Mr. Joyner, C.E., has since had it made into a very pretty inkstand, as a remembrance, which stands on my husband's writing-table.

There is a Protestant Church called Christ Church; it has a handy bier placed in the porch. Frere Hall contains the Station library, with very few books. The bungalows have funny names,—Apollo Bunder, Love Grove, Hog Island, Belle Vue, The Steam Tug, Paradise Lodge, and Hen and Chickens. The sun is very hot, as hot as Sind. The nights are cold. The thermometer gives for average temperature 66° 2′ F., the perfection of climate; but I find figures are no use in estimating the effect of the heat in tropical

* See his Life, by George Smith, LL.D.

lands. I have bullied myself for being half dead with heat at 75°, and thought myself as "hard as nails" for enjoying 115°. Can anyone tell me why?

Now one reason for liking Mátherán better than Máhábáleshwar, is that your eye is tantalized by yellow green Eugenia Jambo, the bright green mango, and the glaucous green of the wild olive, and yet you have no ease, because fashion has broadened the bridle paths to carriage roads, and abolished the shady dingly walks which still linger at Mátherán. Then Máḥábáleshwar is filled with life, Society is always on duty—it is not getting away from town life. Tall carriages instead of basket chairs, and sables capped with black chimney-pots look queer in the wild wood. Sets are the rule, and priggishness is rampant in the primeval forest.

There are plenty of "Points" to do,—Bombay and Scandal Point, Sydney or Lodwick, Elphinstone, Arthur's Seat, and Kates or Cates. The cliffs are higher, steeper, and more thickly wooded than at Mátherán, and the lowlands are lower, dustier, and more sunburnt.

The Dangar tribes still linger like the Todas of the Neilgherries. Mátherán has its Thakurs (Chiefs), and the Katkarís, or catechu-makers, haunt the lowlands. All are said to be pre-Aryan or an-Aryan, speaking a Dravidian tongue, and separated in manners and customs from their Máráthá neighbours. Presently I will give you a little *resumé* of what I have gathered concerning the various hill-tribes that I have seen.

Meanwhile, on this same 19th April, after a pleasant breakfast with Lady Agnes Danyell, we started at two for our return journey, and had a twelve hours' drive down, stopping again to admire Wahi, and for some tea at Soorool. The scanty moon showed us the dark and awful parts of the Ghâts, which suggested tigers and jackals, and in any other land, brigands. The wood was very winding, and the turns were very sharp for a dark night. We arrived at the station at two in the morning, ate from our basket, and entered the train at 4.45; got morning tea at Lanauli about seven, breakfast at nine in the train, arriving at 11.15 at Bombay.

CHAPTER XIV.

THE HILL RACES AND FOREST MEN OF WESTERN INDIA.

THE Hill races of our Bombay sanitaria in the Sahyádri, or Western Gháts, are chiefly the Kátkaris, who prepare the Kát (catechu); the Kolis, Walis, the Thakurs, and the Dhangurs. Some authors (and I think principally Mr. Sinclair of the Bombay Civil Service) divide the population between Poonah and Sholapur, into seven orders, Brahmans, Shankarjátya, or mixed races, soldiers, and cultivators; Parwaris (out-castes), wandering tribes, and, lastly, hill men and forest men; and it is in these last that I am most interested.

1. The Thakurs are found in the jungles near the Sahyádri range (Western Gháts), north of Bombay, between Násik southwards to Umbarkhind, and in the Kolaba Collectorate, and especially below the Khandálá sanitarium. About 1805 they were removed from the hilly parts of Salsette on account of their depredations. They are admirable *shikáris* (huntsmen), brave and skilful, and hold themselves superior to the Dhangurs, Kátkaris, Kolis, Walis, and all other hill tribes. During our excursion to Mátherán we saw a gipsy camp of these people. They were the long-legged hill-men, rather than of the long-backed mountaineer type, and had nothing in common with the black squat an-Aryan race of the plains, who are armed with spears and poisoned arrows. Their colour was a dark olive without any tint of red, and is said to become much deeper in the lower levels, covered with dense forest. The men wore the topknot of hair, and were quite different to the Máráthás (who neither marry nor eat with them), who were known by their Alpenstock and naked feet. The women, like those of the Kolarian "Hos," had their waistcloth tightly tucked up, like

the statues of the Kárlá Buddhist cave (B.C. 275-250). They wore the *choli* bodice, and ornaments of glass bangles and rings of brass and copper. Their lodging was of home-made blankets thrown over the trees to shelter the "cooking place" in the ground, and the babies were slung in hanging cradles to the branches.

2. The Dhangurs, also called Dángars, affect Máhábáleshwar chiefly, though some are found at Mátherán. Their boundaries are Maoli north, Sholapur east, Sátárá south, and the west open to the sea. There are two sets of Dhangur huts to the south-east. We saw some living at Sindóba, near the Sátárá road. They are well-grown men, resemble the Todas of the Neilgherries, but are much darker, have shaven beards, and dress like Máráthás. The women are tall and thin. The Chiefs are called Máliks (Kings). They occupied a spacious hut wattled with the Kárvi cane. They allowed us to drink out of a metal pot, and the women gave us milk in a *green hock glass.* They are great *shikáris,* using the gun as well as the bow and arrow, but not the boomerang of the Gujrat (Guzerat) Kolis. The bow is bamboo, the string wild hemp, the arrow-piles either flat or rounded, the feathers are of the wild pea fowl, and they are bound on, like the heads, with the silk of the Tusser (a cocoon).

3. The Kátkaris, or Kátodis, are governed by Naiks, elders or patriarchs, and are divided into two castes. I think it is Major Macintosh who divides them into four families,—Heloman, Jádu, Pawár, and Sindhi; others tell me into the Dhor, or Northern, and Máráthá, or Southern, which last do not eat beef. They intermarry more or less. The Dhor Kátodis eat cow, and the Tokrya Kátodis do not. They are not found above the coast ranges, but in that section of the Northern Konkan which lies under the hills between the Bhor and the Thál Gháts, and in the valleys east of the Sahyádri range to the Thánú, and the Kolaba Collectorates, and to the territories of the "Habshi." They consider themselves descendants of the demon Rávana of Lanká (Ceylon), which possibly alludes to a secondary migration from the south.

The Santals, numbering some two millions, look to the East as their origin. Their special occupation is to make catechu from the Khayar tree (*acacia catechu*), but not being allowed to eat this "Terra Japonica," they chew the gum, and the *khayar-sar*, or concretion of the tree, is considered good for asthma. The wood is cut to chips, infused and boiled to a paste in earthern pipkins, after which it is caked in wooden moulds; the white variety, much preferred by Kát-chewers, is made from the Areca-nut, and the Anblá, or Auli. Formerly there were several qualities, but now the Banyans have taken it in hand. Some say that the Kátkaris ignore the Hindú gods, and some that they worship idols of Bhawáru and Bhayrú, Kálká-ái, Chirobá, and other lower Hindú incarnations of Shiva, the third person of the Hindú Triad.

Since our Government forbid the felling of acacias, they sell grass and fuel, hire themselves for field work, snare, trap, and shoot game, and rob and plunder when they can. They live during the rains near the ordinary Hindú villages like outcasts, and in the fine season wander about where they get work, building frail huts of branches, or living in caves. They keep fowls, and they eat the black-faced monkey, jackals, squirrels, rats, snakes, and lizards, but they will not touch the food cooked by an outcaste. The men are shy when sober, and violent when drunk, preferring the Maúrá spirit, distilled from the flowers of the *Bassia latifolia*. The women are turbulent and intractable, even to their husbands, and it is said that if a stranger should chance to see them bathing, he is made perforce to join and to intermarry in the caste. Both sexes are feared as sorcerers and magicians. The men become tigers, bears, and Wandarú monkeys; the women, buffaloes, dogs, cats, and hens.

The Thakurs, Dhangurs, and Kátkaris, on and about Mátherán, live in the neighbourhood of the Máráthá villages; the Kátkaris close by, the Thakurs a little further removed, and the Dhangurs deeper in the jungle. They associate and will even eat together, but then the food must be cooked by one of the higher tribe. They do not intermarry, and they are monogamists, ignoring the polygamy of the Hindús, and the polyandry of the Todas. Their occupations are distinct. The first are agriculturalists; the second, like the Todas, are herdsmen, and own sometimes sixty herd of cattle; the third are fishers, hunters, and breeders of goats and fowl. The Thakurs are rarely well-to-do, and the Kátkaris are ever poor. The Dhangurs and Thakurs are said to be very healthy, to attain extreme old age, and to have large families, even numbering sixteen. There is more dissimilarity of feature and figure among members of the same tribe than might be expected, and the distinctions between the three are well marked.

The Dhangurs are the best looking, and although they lack tradition, they seem to have retained the purity of their race ever since they left their northern homes. The frontal and central cranial regions are better developed than in the other lower tribes, and the broad-pointed, flat-rooted, irregular nose, with wide-spread nostrils, becomes more or less aquiline and classical. All have large, but not over-high and prominent malar bones, subtumid lips, and deeply-sunk eyes, whose expression is genial and sparkling amongst the better sort; scowling and surly, unsteady and roving like the gipsy's, in the depressed races.

They do not show the rounded Santál face and cranium, somewhat suggesting the statues of Buddha, which contrasts so strongly with the tall, narrow-headed, olive-coloured Brahman. The limbs and extremities are shapely, the chest is of fair breadth, and the muscular system in the better fed is well developed. The straight, lank Tartar hair, like that of the Hindú and the Red Indian, sometimes (especially in the Thakurs) is replaced by a curly and frizzly mop; but this and other apparent traces of African blood are evidently accidental.

In 1851, when the first European house was built at Mátherán, there were twelve Dhangur *wárás* or settlements. They were built upon the level plateau, not far from the springs. Every hut was occupied by its own family, and afforded shelter for man and beast. The dimensions varied by the owner's means. The largest might be 80 × 30 to 40 feet, and a central partition-wall separated the family from the cattle.

The Thakur huts are much smaller, and the *wárás* contain a greater number; the materials are the same, the cattle head with the family, and a space is screened off for cooking. The household gods held a conspicuous place; their images are adorned with peacocks' feathers and the flowers of the Til (Sansk) and the Kunhil, while little *ágdán*, or fireplaces, for *dhúp* (incense) and *úd* (gum benzoin), stand before them.

The huts of the Kátkaris are wretched and filthy. They show fewer of the comforts of life than those of the other two hill tribes. Goats take the place of cattle. All these people eat mutton, game, fish, and fowls. The Thakurs will devour squirrels, but draw the line at rats, and musk rats, of which the Kátkaris are as fond as Chinamen. I am not certain about their eating monkeys, whose dead bodies the Máráthás will not even touch. The fish are chiefly the Malyá, a sort of carp; and when the rivers flood, the Sirjura, weighing eight to ten pounds, run up from the sea. All are immoderate drinkers, like the Santáls, whose debauched habits have lately engaged the attention of the Anglo-Indian Government.

Colonel Tickell has told us that the Santáls acknowledge a divine authority for the use of strong drinks, especially *hándiá*, or rice-beer. So it is with the Hos or the Larká Kols, the typical tribe of the true Kolarian Aborigines, whose Bacchus, "Sing Bonga," first brewed "Illi," or rice-beer. This drink is made like the *pombé* of Africa, simply by boiling the grain, and allowing the decoction to ferment. No spirit comes amiss to them, and the gratification is only limited, by their poverty, to a tippling match at intervals, and on all occasions of feasting and revelry, when it is allowed. Besides this Máurá spirit they draw the toddy of the Berhli-Mahr, or Fish-tail palm, a grove of which, mixed with other trees, clothes the northern slope of Panorama ridge.

When wandering about the hill sides or engaged in their daily work, the hill people have a way of hailing one another, which prevails, with modifications, in all mountainous countries. The voice rises with each successive word, and the message is delivered without drawing breath, the end being dwelt upon in a yell, which, like the "cooeing" of the Australians, fills the valleys with its echoes. The speaker will either continue standing, or dip behind the brow of a hill, to await the reply, which comes presently up, floating in the air from distances almost incredible. All strangers are struck by the cry of the Neilgherry Todas, the hill-men of the Himalayas, and the inhabitants of the West African Cameroons. The "hauk" in Sind *Sadha-pandhu*, or "shout," and the distance at which a man can be heard, is a common measure in the Konkan and elsewhere. The Dháwa, or length which a runner can cover without drawing breath, and the Wáo is a measure of depth, the space between the finger-tips with the arms extended.

The dress of these tribes, excepting the Thakur women, is scanty enough. The *kamli*, or blanket, thrown over the shoulders, and arranged on the head and body, with the *Langúti* (T-bandage), and the *dhotar*, waist-cloth, are the only articles of wear. They go bare-headed, and the *pagri*, or turban, is kept for ceremonies and great occasions. The Thakur women, besides the *choli* bodice, bind about the loins and thighs a long strip of dark-coloured cotton, but use no skirt. They often spend fifty rupees upon this article. The other women use the Máráthá "Sári," which is somewhat like our Damascus "Izar," a single piece of stuff, loose and flowing, acting as mantilla and petticoat. All men, women, and children wear all sorts of rings in the lobes and rims of ears; bangles, necklaces of metal, white porcelain beads, and nose rings, but they never load the ankles as the Santál and Ho women do. They do not care about their hair, whereas the hill people of other parts of India interlace it elaborately with shells and beads, and wreaths of leaves and creepers.

In point of religion, these people have a good deal in common with their Máráthá neighbours; and of late years it has become a general belief that the modern worship of Shiva has been modified by the Hindús from the cruel local god of the black races which preceded them. Their faith, like that of all savages, is one of fear, not of love. The Santáls asked a missionary, who was discoursing upon the omnipotence of the Creator, "What if that Strong One should eat us?" and the Kátkaris, when the philanthropist, Dr. John Wilson, was trying to teach them something about the love of God, remarked, "Even white men drive us from their homes; is it likely, therefore, that your God should allow us to approach Him in the future world?"

The chief hill god is Páshánáth, the "Lord of Cattle;" a Dhangur is his Pújárí or priest, like the *Ojha*, the Fetishman, who discovers what evil spirit entered the body and killed the man. The Birbhúm Highlanders preserve a trace of Monotheism; they say, "God is great, but He is too far off;" and I think many educated people, unluckily, feel like that too.

The Mátherán shrine is a gloomy sacred grove of Anjún. The chief figure (most likely the idol of Moab) resembles a limbless human body, smeared with vermilion; smaller forms surround it, supposed to be its Sepoys and servants. There are earthen vessels for oil and incense, rude figures of animals, and remains of offerings, amongst them a tile from the floor of the English church. The ground is stained from the blood of sacrificed goats, and strewn with fowls' feathers; a pillar stand for oil lamps, and a framework of three posts, like a small gallows, is covered with little bells, and stands opposite the idol. The Todas adore this bell god in memory of the bell borne by a succession of saintly cows. They place their offerings before the deity, pour rose-water and scatter flowers upon him; mark him with the Tilak, the sectarian wafer, burn camphor and frankincense. The worshipper then tells his wants through the priest, tingles one of the sacred bells, and goes aside to wait the answer. Two hollows in the breast of the image have been made to hold stones, placed by the priest, and the latter has some unexplained trick of moving them: according as one or the other first falls, the prayers are granted or refused. The goats and fowls are then eaten by the worshippers.

Smaller gods are in favour at the surrounding settlements, especially a sprite called "Zir," who is not honoured with paint, and is held in dread. The same with the Tiger-god, and the smallpox goddess "Mátá-Devi," an incarnation of Bhowanee, wife of Shiva, whose shrine is everywhere. We saw upon the Hill a *Hanuman*, or monkey god, cut in alt-relief upon a slab of basalt. Like all pagans, these people believe *everything*. They go to Hindú fairs; they worship at the shrine of a Moslem Santon or Fakir called Bháo Malang, and they go to the Roman Catholic church at Mátherán.

The hill people use calves' heads for charms, and tie branches of the *Pandri*, a small, crooked jungle bush, with white bark, and whose light, firm pointed leaves are placed about their huts to keep off evil spirits. They believe that they have no souls. The cry of the owl and the goat-sucker, and birds chirping, are auguries. The horrid hooting of the brown wood-owl is a bad sign; this devil-bird announces painful and certain death. The same is thought by the Krumen of West Africa. It is not unknown in England.

The ceremonies of birth, marriage, naming children, etc., so resemble those of the Santáls, and other hill tribes of Central India, that no description is needed; and the same of their singing, dancing, exercises, all of which are based upon religion. All tribes bury their dead, except in case of sudden death, or lingering disease caused by witchery. The Dhangurs are buried sitting, with face eastward, the others lying with feet to the north, the reverse of the Hindú position. The Kátkaris disinter the body a fortnight after burying; their lamentations are renewed over the half-decomposed remains, and, amidst a regular orgie, with the "devil dancing," as in our pantomimes, they are burnt. They do not exhume the victims of cholera or smallpox, because they died of a goddess. This race takes little notice of its deceased, and after death all is a blank. Ancestral worship occurs in the higher tribes, and for years after their death, influential men are honoured, and hence, probably, their "gods" and "devils."

The common names of the hill tribes are those of low caste men among their neighbours, but some are also distinctive. In the two higher races, Dhangurs and Thakurs, the men take surnames from their clans, and they are also assumed by their wives. For instance, one family of Dhangurs contained four brothers, Bájú, Dháku, Ráma, and Túká, all being surnamed Akadá. Thūs also with the Thakurs, where five sisters were Úmbi, Sirké, Gomé, Kani, and Shemré, and called themselves Úmbi Páradi, this last their family name, or the family name of the husband, just like us. But the Kátkaris only take the name of the tribe, as Rúpa Kátkari; their wives would be, for instance, Zánkí Kátkarin.

The intelligence, in some respects, of all the tribes is low. They do not know their ages, nor count above twenty. They know the week days, but not the months, only the changes of the moon. *En revanche,* ask them about their trees, the seasons of flowering and fruiting, the use of each plant in food or medicine, about the wild beasts, and numerous birds and insects of their jungles, and they will reply with astonishing minuteness and accuracy. Even women and boys show great readiness, and the best collector of plants on Mátherán Hill often brought his wife to assist in naming them correctly.

Living out of the world, and under the influence of "forest primeval," these tribes have generally a shy and quiet manner. They are gentle to one another, and crime is so uncommon they give the magistrates but little trouble. They settle their disputes amongst themselves, generally by privation of fire and water, a punishment popular throughout India; or they carry them before old Madhú Rad, their native Chief of Police, for whom their respect verges closely upon worship. Only the Kátkaris have a bad name: a fat sheep or a sleek goat is not safe from them, but their robberies at Mátherán go no further. They are the only tribe that wander beyond the immediate circle of the tribes, and it is probable that their morality has not been improved by enforced visits to the jails of Thánâ, Sri Sthánáká, and Ratnagiri. All are unarmed in the limits of civilization; even the Kátkaris have left aside their bows and arrows, except when hunting. A few are licensed to carry guns by way of keeping wild beasts in check, and an old Thakur, below Mal-dungar, has shot over fifty panthers, and some tigers.

In days not long past, when *Bandwálás,* or bands of brigands, were abroad, the hill tribes suffered; but if there was a foray in prospect, they were always as ready to join it as oppose it. The marauders who harried the lowlands, were mostly of the Koli caste, and their stubborn resistance often showed the same determination as that which characterised the Waghars of the present generation. There are some famous names among the hill men,—Paddú, Nármal, Kímia Gaulé, Bháo Keng, and Punia Gowaré, are the still far-famed Robin Hoods and Rob Roys. Their strongholds were Mátherán, Prabal (known as Purbal and Parbal), and Bháo Malang, which forms an isolated group in the middle Konkan. Prabal is a precipitous, scarped hog's-back, upon which Sivaji the Máráthá, so often named, built a fort.

Bháo Maláng is not the name of the Mohammedan saint, but refers to a particular class of Mūhárram Fakir. The Massif itself is the noble castellated basaltic spine which we spoke of as seeing from Panorama Point, and which is called the Cathedral. Each tribe has its own dialect, in which they use some Hindústani words. The natives declare that the Thakurs, Dhangurs, and Kátkaris speak a dialect only intelligible to themselves; can understand one another, understand the Bhils in the heart of India, and the Gonds; but to strangers they speak broken Maharatta with Hindústani words. Perhaps this arises from their mixing with Moslems. There are still semi-Hinduised Dhanwars at Máhábáleshwar, who formerly worked the famous iron used for Damascus blades; and amongst the Koli fishermen of Bombay there is a Moslem tribe, the Dáldi. But very little, if anything, is known of their dialects, and it would be a most interesting study for a resident there for some years.

CHAPTER XV.

WE LEAVE BOMBAY FOR GOA.

22nd April.—We sailed about six p.m. (my husband and I), in the British Indian Steamship Company's *Rajpootana*, Captain ———,—a middle-sized steamer, beautifully clean, with good table, excellent wines, airy cabins, great civility, ship very steady in wind and swell, fares extravagantly dear—one hundred rupees a head (£10) for thirty-six hours' passage; but there is no opposition, so they can charge what they like, and you can take it or let it alone, as you please.

23*rd, Low Sunday.*—The Protestants were upon their own ground, and had their service, but we, the rival creeds, Catholic and Mohammedans, were too much in the minority. I had my Bishop on board, the Right Rev. L. Meurin, S.J., Bishop of Ascalon, i. p. i. Vicar Apostolic of Bombay; and he suggested that as he and his secretary, a nun, and I were the only Catholics, we should read our service privately. It was calm weather overhead, but intensely hot and glaring, with a heavy swell, and many were ill. We read and studied a little, slept a good deal, and played with the monkeys. At about nine at night we reached Vingorla; the coast is very bad, and dangerous, and in the monsoon all but impossible; vessels are often wrecked,—so the steamers never go near, but boats are put off. The boats brought some charming fans, made of *cuss-cuss* grass, which, being whirled round, produce more air than any other fan, and smell deliciously, especially if wetted with cold water.

We disembarked a young man going to join his regiment, and Sister Marie, Fillé de la Croix, a young German nun, bound for some desolate spot where they are forming a convent for educating children, nursing the sick, and reclaiming the savages;

this young, interesting-looking girl of about twenty has to make her own way up the country. These are the true soldiers of Christ. Our hearts yearned towards her as she calmly and smilingly bid us good-bye and left the ship's side. The Bishop and his secretary went ashore with her, to see her safely lodged for the night, and her preparations for travelling next morning secure.

Whilst I was asleep the Bishop had returned, and we had steamed out; but the ship was so steady I thought, on awaking, that we were still at anchor, and waiting for his lordship.

24th April.—At daylight we did stop; it was about five a.m., but as the captain told me overnight not to hurry myself, as he should not steam on till seven, I got up leisurely: presently a black steward came down and said,—

"Please, ma'am, the agent's here with your boat, to convey you ashore; and the captain desired me to say he's going to steam on directly."

I was just at a juncture of toilette which rendered it impossible for me to open the door or come out.

I called out, "Please go with my compliments to the captain, and beg him to give me ten minutes or a quarter of an hour, and tell my husband what is the matter."

The answer was, "I'll go, ma'am, but I'm afraid the captain can't. It's his duty to go on."

"Go!" I replied. In two minutes down came the negro again.

"Captain says it's impossible; in fact, the ship's moving *now*."

Well, as we were tied to time and to many other things, and could not afford to miss our landing, which might have entailed a fortnight's delay, I threw on a shawl and petticoat, as one might in a shipwreck, with my hair down, crying to the steward,

"Bundle all my things into the boat as well as you can, and if anything is left, take it back to the hotel at Bombay." And so I hurried on deck, and, to my surprise, found the steamer was not moving on. My husband and the captain were quietly talking together, and when they saw me, asked the cause of my dress and agitation, and when I told them the captain said,—

"I never sent any message of the kind. I told you last night I should steam on at seven, it is now only five."

That is not a bad practical joke from a negro servant to a first-class passenger, paying £10 for thirty-six hours' passage; I thought it exceedingly independent and impertinent, but nobody was reprimanded, much less turned away, and I thought the captain much to blame in not enquiring into the matter. He must consider that if it were a delicate, nervous passenger, with a heart complaint, it might do a great deal of harm. I complained to the Bishop of it, and he told me he had been served exactly the same, the year before, on the same spot. These things arise from its being the only line, with no opposition: it makes them *do* independent, impertinent things. Although you receive, *personally*, the greatest civility, still they can always find little ways to make your hours bitter. This was quite uncalled-for and unprovoked, as I always treat everybody courteously; and certainly native servants should not have command of a ship after this fashion.

Mr. Major, the agent of these steamers at Goa, arrived with a large boat to take us and our little baggage ashore. We are cast adrift in the open sea, on account of an unbuoyed and doubtful shoal called La Clarinda, covered by twelve to twenty-four feet of low water, which at low tides is a mud bank some three cables long. We have eight miles to row before we can reach Goa (or Panjim). You may imagine what that is in a storm. Their agents ought to be right well paid, for they must do this unpleasant service with the mails, monsoon weather as well, all the year through, once a fortnight; besides living in a fetid hole where they can get none of the comforts of life, and never see a soul.

I do not know how it is, but the Portuguese, in the days of their glory, from A.D. 1500 to 1600, when they made all their conquests, not only built every town like Lisbon, and every church on the same pattern, but they actually made the features of the country all the same. Here is the same abrupt entrance from the sea, between mountainous cliffs, up a broad winding river, or sea-arm, with wooded rising banks, with the same white town perched on its banks as Santos, São Paulo, Brazil, about

24° south of the Equator. I thought I beheld not India but Brazil, and that we were about to enter the Rio dos Santos.

The bay is formed like a large crescent, the two points seawards. The one, near which we come in, is called the Castello da Agoada, as ships touch there to take in water. The opposite one is the Cabo do Convento, a monastery instead of a fort, which we shall afterwards visit. We had to ask leave to enter (everything is very official), and to land our luggage, whilst a sergeant bustled down, full of importance, protesting it was not right to inspect British luggage, and *he* would see it all right. We rowed about a mile and a half of open sea, five miles of bay, and one and a half of winding river, the Rio de Panjim (exactly like the Rio dos Santos), to a little stone pier, jutting a few yards into the water.

Panjim is situated upon a narrow ledge, between a hill to the south, and on the north the Rio de Goa, or arm of the sea, which stretches several miles from west to east.

There is a total absence of anything in Goa but the *barest* necessaries of life. If you have a friend to take you in, you are fortunate. The Bishop would have taken us, but he did not know *we* were unprovided. There is no inn, no travellers' bungalow, no tents; and you must either sleep in your filthy open boat and have fever, or you must take tents and everything with you. It is not healthy enough to sleep *al fresco.*

We wrote to Mr. Major to take us rooms, and did not know that there are none. So this kind-hearted man and his wife, Mrs. Major, conceded us a small room in their house, with their only spare single bed; and, I fear, put themselves to great inconvenience to do so; and a few yards' walk placed us under their hospitable roof. We had, luckily, one of those large straw Pondicherry reclining chairs, which I had just bought from the captain of our steamer, and a rug, so we took the bed in turns, night about, the other in the chair; for we had come to see Goa, and a little inconvenience does no harm if one is good-humoured over it, though I confess I like roughing it better out-of-doors than in-doors. The people who live at Goa rough it all the year round, but they have grown so used to it they do not know it. There is *nothing* to be had, and it has not the charm of tent life and moving on, which makes going without things a pleasure; but all that the residents have to give you they give with the warmest hospitality.

It is the worst climate I ever was in, and I have been in many bad ones. The thermometer showed only 87°; but, as I said before, I prefer 115° or 120° in any other place. The thirst was agonizing, and all the drinks were hot (no ice), and the more you drank the more you wanted. The depression was fearful, and never a breath of air, even at night; whilst a blazing sun poured into our little room all day, and baked it quite red hot for the night. I used to look upon the people who lived there as miracles, especially our kind good hostess. I do not know how she kept herself alive; her health was quite broken by it. If I had to live there I should say good-bye to all my friends, and use it as an expiation for past sins, a purgatorial preparation for death.

Portuguese India is, thank Heaven, only a strip of abont seventy miles long, which they would do much better to sell to the British Government; for of all the God-forgotten, deserted holes, one thousand years behind the rest of the creation, I have never seen anything to equal Goa. Do not let the residents who read this fancy that I am touching them in any way: I only remember them as charming, kindly, gentle, hospitable people whom I pitied for having to live there. I have lived in sandy deserts, and in primeval forests, and have suffered hunger and thirst, cold and heat, fatigue, privation, and danger, and thought it charming; but I hated the sort of life at Goa. It is *dead*, and nothing rewards one. However, we have come to see it, and I have a particular object in view, which is, to pay my respects to the shrine of the Apostle of India, St. Francis Xavier.

Our next step was to see if we could hire horses or a vehicle, and at last we found a little *gari*, a small open thing made of wood, in the year one, with room for two persons. The wheels were nearly off, at least wobbling, the step and the spring of one side were broken, the lamps were hanging, the hammer cloth, or box-seat, was a deal box, which I think once brought candles from Tucker's, in England. The harness was made of large old rusty chains and bits of string tied together. Our coachman and footman were two boys in little dirty shirts, and something round the loins, afterwards increased to a bit of scarlet cloth put on like the Order of the Garter, and waistbands ditto, kept together with bits of twine, and bare legs peeping out underneath like two sticks of chocolate.

But now about the horse, the only horse in the country, a poor old screw of a pony, broken down by mange, starvation, and sores. It broke my heart to look at him, much more to drive him. I hired him on condition of keeping him myself the whole time of my visit, and I think he did not know what had happened. He was put into a comfortable shed in Mr. Major's garden; he had as much as ever he could eat and drink, of the best and most nourishing sort, and he was groomed daily, and before I left began to look quite respectable. By this means, I ascertained that he only did my work, and no other person's. I used to drive him, and the boys used to run, as there was only room for us two.

We set out first for Cazalem, about half an hour away, along a good road; here there is a beach, and an open sea, and a few cottages, where the best people reside in summer, just as we used all to go down to the "Bar" at Santos, Brazil, to bathe and breathe. Here we made the acquaintance of the married daughter of our hostess and her children. The husband is Military Secretary to the Governor, a descendant of the ancient and historical family of Albuquerque; and Dr. and Mrs. Torres and children reside in the next door cottage; there we often passed a pleasant hour. They sup and play cards and games on the sand by lamps or torchlight.

The only bearable time of the day was from dawn to eight or nine; so next morning at daylight we drove to old Goa. The roads are good but hilly, and sandy here and there. Our poor horse at first had to be led by a rope by No. 1, the whip used behind, and the wheels rolled round by No. 2 boy, and a help; but I remedied all this in three days by having the animal in my own keeping. His sores healed, he began to assume a respectable appearance, he followed me about like a dog, and looked after me with almost human eyes. He seldom stopped needlessly afterwards, and if he did the *Gharawála* running in front of him for a moment was enough, without any stick. He treads his old forage under foot with contempt now, and uses it as litter. Poor beast! I am sorry that it will be such a short paradise for him.

The day after, we went at dawn to the Cabo (Cape) to visit the old Portuguese monastery, and lunched on return at Cazalem with Mr. Major, the Albuquerques, and De Torres, and visited the Da Gamas and Da Cunhas.

We had a great feast to-day (27th); Corpus Christi is kept at Goa. There are barbarous bands, flowers, lights, a procession headed by the Bishop—but the heat was dreadful. In the evening we drove all over and around Panjim. Mr. and Mrs. Major gave a little party in our honour, and the company were all native Portuguese and Canarins. We had some music, and I tried to get them to sing me some native music, which is so interesting, and of which I learned a great deal in Brazil; but they are ashamed of it, and will only sing in French and Italian, which does not suit their voices.

Now there are in Portuguese South America, three sorts of native music. The Lundù, with a very peculiar time and catch, is sung mostly by the lower classes; it is their comic song, their popular dance music. The Modinha is more used by the respectable classes, as our ballad, and is not striking; but the highly-educated affect only the recitative, as if they were too lazy to sing; they play a flowing accompaniment, and pitching their voices in a peculiar manner, recite you a tale of love or war. This is most strikingly characteristic and interesting.

There are several classes of people in Goa. It would be difficult to find an uglier or meaner-looking race, unless it were the Bengali. The black Christians, like the whites, are of two orders—converted Hindús, and mixed breed of European and Indian blood; Brahman Christians being descended from the Hindú pontifical caste, and common ones being a subdivision. The Mestiços Eurasians, or mixed breed, compose the mass, and include all the middle classes. The Government officials are mostly from home.

The white families settled here—I mean native Portuguese—were called Castissos, to distinguish them from Reinols, *i.e.*, "the Kingdom," the Portuguese who come from Europe, between whom and the settled whites there is very little difference to an outsider. Very few can consider themselves pure Portuguese, and those who can are very proud of it. Officials sent from Portugal are of course excepted; but the descendants of the first great families have intermixed with natives. There is a deep-rooted hatred between black and white. The blacks look upon an Englishman with dislike, mingled with fear, as he passes through to visit its monuments of antiquity. A corrupted Maharatta is spoken here.

The superior race are the Moslems, at Panjim, who number about one thousand. The Hindús are the most esteemed and advanced, however, and the most numerous, as are the Parsees in British India. The Europeans are divided into two distinct classes—the officials sent on service from Portugal, who are the great people, and the white families' descendants who settled here. The former must remain three years, and they count the moments to return. Few signs of dislike appear to the unpractised observer, because a hollow politeness is always observed when they meet.

Now I would explain that in all Portuguese India, which is, as I have said, a mere strip of seventy miles, the only things of interest to see, are the three Goas, but *they* are full of history and romance, especially to a *devotee* of St. Francis Xavier. All the rest of the country is simply a green, wooded, undulating tract of land, such as you may see anywhere in Maritime India.

No. 1 is the old Hindú Goa, a site now almost markless, —a salt plain and two hills, with a church upon each, as well as a third upon the plain. Nowadays it is called San Lourenço, and is about six miles from Panjim, upon the winding river; and two miles to the southward of Old Goa, about the centre of the island, more to the southern shore. The church we see on one hill is the Parochial Church of Sant' Andrè, and the one on the other hill is San Lourenço. It is pretty, seems healthy, and no one knows why it was deserted.

The Puranic name of Goa was Gomanta, and according to some inscriptions found lately at Belgaum, belonging to the Kaedambas, and published by Dr. Da Cunha in the *Indian Antiquary*, the name, not only of "Gopakapúra," but also "Goa," was applied to this City in ancient times. This is interesting, because it is a disputed point.

No. 2 is "Old Goa," Goa Velha of the Portuguese and of St. Francis Xavier. It is nine and a half kilometres from Panjim, by a good road along the winding river, and is a most picturesque locality, full of history and Catholic tradition. It was deserted, on account of malaria and fever, for "New Goa," called Panjim, situated on the river side nearest the sea, and where the few personages who are obliged to be there, vegetate, except with an occasional change to Cazalem, or Caramzalem, the six cottages on the open beach in the middle of the crescent of the bay, the fashionable sea-bathing retreat, corresponding to our *barra* at Santos.

The long, low coasts, the interior undulated and covered with vegetation, here chiefly the palm, the whole dotted with white and thatch villages, and white and green houses; little white fortresses, which a ten-pounder could demolish; long, barn-like churches, with big *façades*, all painted white, inside and out, peeping out of the vegetation, show how the Portuguese have formed the land upon the pattern of the mother country, and her colonies. We stand upon a Portugal—a strip of Brazil—in an Indian hemisphere.

The mesquin rhubarb-coloured race, are dressed either in a scanty, dirty-white bit of decency or the refuse of European rag-shops; they are deteriorated by a shabby, demi-semi civilization. The enervating climate, like a dirty Turkish bath with a thermometer only at 87°, makes people long to drink and sleep, sleep and drink. The poverty, the utter uninterestingness of everything, bears the curse of the Inquisition; but at any rate they bear one mark of St. Francis Xavier's teaching,—the manners of the lower orders are excellent. A beggar has the manners of a gentleman; the poor all doff their caps as you pass, and seem formed to exchange civilities with Europeans. St. Francis Xavier was a true gentleman, besides being a saint; he preached courteousness, and I have no doubt traditions of his manners were handed down from father to son. The higher orders (who are chiefly officials sent here by the Portuguese Government) are more sulky and slow in their demonstrations, unless they meet you *en intime*, when they are very pleasant; but there is much jealousy and cliquedom and bad feeling between the different races. If you take a letter of introduction to one, perhaps the two or three others will not call upon you because you did not also take one to them, not making allowances that you did not previously know of their existence.

There is but little wealth here, and not much want of it, to keep up the antiquated civilization and modern barbarism. A ball once in six months at the Government House; a few small dinner-parties, a *soirée*, a little quadrilling, ancient waltzing, mild flirting, and smoking, are the amusements. No serenades, no *guitarra*, no *cicisbeism*, but small scandal and ill-nature exists. As steamers have not done much for Goa yet, dress is mediæval and grotesque, when there is any *pretension;* when there is not, there is nothing to ridicule, and much to respect and admire, especially when the native costume is adhered to; but it is painful to see a black face peeping out of a would-be Parisian bonnet, which never was in Paris. Talking of dress, the poorest man, who considers himself a Portuguese twenty times removed, will wear a seedy, patched black coat, and a black "tile," in a cocoanut forest hut, to distinguish himself from the natives, and as a mark of respectability.

The education is confined mostly to prayers and embroidery, making sweetmeats, a little writing, reading, and music. Life is dull; domestic occupations, smoking, visiting, church, and sitting and lying *en déshabille*, riding in a *mancheel* (a sort of palanquin), and an occasional dance, sum up the round of life. They marry young, and are soon old. They rise early, have a light breakfast of rice *congee;* a heavy meal of bread, meat, soup, rice and curry, fish, sweetmeats, and fruit, all served together, which means dinner. The wine is Tinto and Branco, imported from Portugal. Then follows the siesta, five o'clock tea, and biscuits, a stroll at sunset, and supper,—fish, curry, and rice; and they smoke all day.

The animals are starved and ill-treated; the women scolding; and all the children, by their whining and crying, appear to be perpetually "teething." Captain Burton mentions this in his "Goa," when he was here thirty years ago, and devotes a whole page to the squabbling of the women, which he describes as being almost like pig-killing, and he had to change his lodgings to get away from their noise.

Panjim is a town of sixteen thousand inhabitants, and, as I said, is a God-forgotten place, without the necessaries or comforts of life; nor are things to be bought here; and to import and land everything from Bombay in so expensive a steamer as the *British India*, and then to convey it eight miles in a small boat from the high-running sea to Panjim, would cost a large fortune in a staff of men and boats, besides heavy duty.

There is no escaping the heat of Goa. There is no ice, no *punkahs*, or *tatties*. The houses are built for Lisbon, not for India; bare, without verandahs, or any sort of shade; the white-paint glare puts your eyes out; and the sun bakes the walls through, the first hour he comes out. There is no milk, no servants; there is no one to pull the only *punkah* in the town; and no one to milk the cow if you had one. Goa exports annually twenty-eight thousand excellent servants; but they won't stay at Goa, because they get no wages to speak of, and do better elsewhere; so you have, whether you are rich or poor, to live in the smallest of ways, and do everything yourself.

Panjim is a very clean and very cheap place, is larger than it looks, but its stiff, ordinary-looking houses are so scattered and straggling, and so badly laid out, that it makes no show. It has very few shops, and those very poor; I would not give a five-pound note for all that is in them. Its chief buildings are the Viceroy's Palace, the Archbishop's Palace, Custom-house, Barracks, and Government Offices,—all huge white buildings, with green jalousies. The poorer part of the town is the prettiest; the windows are framed with oyster-shells. It has huge but poor-looking official buildings. One statue of Albuquerque stands under a white-washed dome in the square opposite the east front of the Barracks. It has plenty of churches on heights; those are picturesque; but there is only one pretty villa with a garden. Everything is white-washed or painted white, and if it has any other colour it is a green jalousie.

If I had to live here (which God forbid!) I should bring a dozen tents, and pitch them under the trees; bring half-a-dozen horses, a tent servant, a first-rate cook who could market, a groom, and a general servant and messenger. I should make a contract with the British Indian steamers (through an agent at Bombay) to supply me with everything; keep a steam launch to go out and meet those steamers. The usual attempt at "home" and establishment is only a miserable failure, because the things are not to be had. But then, if I were rich enough to do all that, why should I go and live at Goa?

However, *we* were most lucky to have such kind friends as Mr. and Mrs. Major; and I am not speaking for ourselves, because they put everything they had at our disposition, but I am grumbling for those who have to live there, and must not grumble out loud. My husband came to re-visit an old scene, and I to make a pilgrimage to the tomb of St. Francis Xavier; and we did both. With our now respectable pony, and our broken-down vehicle, we used to drive most mornings at dawn to the object of my interest (Old Goa), and only return to Panjim in time to avoid sunstroke.

Of Old Goa (Goa Velha) nothing is left but churches, with monasteries attached to them, and these buildings are mostly situated on different hills; but the remains show that Goa must have been once a very extensive city. As we were about to enter Goa we were deluded by the distant view of white churches and towers, glittering steeples and domes, and I fancied we had come to a grand place, and was surprised to find myself wandering in a City of the Dead. A more suggestive scene cannot be conceived than the utter desolation which surrounded us. Everything that met the eye or ear seemed teeming with melancholy associations; the very rustling of the trees, and the murmur of the waves, sounded like a dirge for the departed grandeur of the city.

The Bom Jesus is the church dedicated to St. Francis Xavier —my favourite patron saint for his conversion of so many unbelievers. The church and house of the Bom Jesus belonged to the Society of Jesus, was dedicated to Xavier, and given to the Jesuits, in 1584. In 1761, when the Jesuits were expelled from Portugal, it was handed over to the Lazarists. When the new Viceroy or Governor arrives, he is invested with power, and is buried here if he dies. It is full of their tombs. They bury a Governor-General in great state. One, João Tavarez d'Almeida, died July 1877, on his return, of the fatigues of going to Delhi for the great event of the Queen becoming Empress. The pomp starts from Panjim, and the burial takes place now at the Cathedral of Old Goa, the Bom Jesus being full. Here is an account of the ceremonial:—

"It was ordered that the Governor's corpse should be embalmed, dressed, and put in a coffin, and be carried by the Council members from his quarters to the Palace Chapel, and there placed in a grand mausoleum erected for the purpose in the centre of the nave. On the 24th, by six p.m., the key of the coffin was delivered to the President of the Council. From the hour he died all the fortresses began to fire minute guns, which was continued until the body was carried to the vault in the cathedral. The ships in the harbour had their flags half-mast, and all the people went into mourning. The corpse, at four p.m. on the 25th, accompanied by the Confraternities of several churches, a large number of the clergy, including the Corporation of Canons, the members of the Municipal Corporation, the members of Tribunals, military and civil authorities, and all other corporations, and a large number of the public, was carried in funeral procession to the Cathedral, all the military forces lining the road on both sides. At the Cathedral the *officium defunctorum* was sung solemnly.

"On the 26th there was a High Requiem mass at the Cathedral, accompanied by regimental bands, at which all the above authorities and the public, etc., etc., assisted. After mass the coffin was taken down and placed in a separate apartment, to be conveniently removed to the convent of St. Caetano at Old Goa. During the above Mass all the military forces were present, in full uniform, posted in front of the Cathedral, and the artillery fired minute guns, concluding with a salute of twenty-one guns.

"For three days all the public offices were closed, and no public entertainments, etc., were allowed for the space of eight days."

The Bom Jesus is exactly the same pattern, inside and outside, as all other Portuguese churches,—a long, white-washed barn-shaped building,—but the much adorned altars are under arches of carved and gilded wood, which, although it looks tawdry, has lasted for centuries, and will last for many more. The object of my devotion (the tomb) is contained in a recess on a side altar,—dedicated to Xavier,—and consists of a magnificently-carved silver sarcophagus. This is on a magnificent base of black marble, from Italy; while on the silver sarcophagus are *alto relievi*, beautifully cast, representing different acts of his life: one, preaching a sermon to the multitude; two, his shipwreck; three, his baptizing the people; four, his death, alone in a shed upon the Indian sands. All this is surmounted by a gold and silver top. Inside is a gold box, containing the remains of the saint, shown to the people, with a great Feast, once in a century. It took place this 3rd December, 1878, on his Feast, and crowds flocked to Goa for the event, which was celebrated with great splendour and pomp in the presence of all the Roman Catholic Bishops in India and several from Europe, including a body of medical men, who took advantage of the Suez Canal, available for the first time, for the pilgrimage. The body was found to be in its normal state of freshness, and was enclosed, after the usual honours had been paid. An arm was sent to Rome!

If ever England takes Goa, I feel sure that tomb will be respected and conserved. If any other nation took it I should feel very unhappy about it. There is something conservative about an Englishman, and he generally respects other people's churches as well as his own; and as for Mohammedans, they would put a rail round it, as the tomb of a *nabi* (prophet), and only let people approach with their slippers on. But I should dread the sacrilegious Frenchman, the arrogant German (Prussian), or a *progressista* Italiano.

At the annual Novena a silver statue of the saint is placed upon the altar. This Novena is a nine-days prayer, which terminates on his feast, 3rd December. During this, High Mass is sung every day before the altar which contains the monument, and low Masses are said from daybreak till nine a.m. by priests, who flock from all quarters, with a concourse of people, to perform this devotion. On the festival the clergy come in procession, and sing the whole Church office, beginning on the eve with the first Vespers. The High Mass is pontifically celebrated at the High Altar by the Archbishop, in the presence of the Governor, the members of the Administration, the deputations from all the churches and convents of Goa, and crowds of people. The panegyric of the Saint is always preached on this occasion. During the rest of the year Mass is said every day, but especially on Fridays, in honour of Xavier, accompanied by hymns and organ.

The Sacristy is vaulted, and is the finest in Goa. There is a real old portrait of St. Francis Xavier, outside his chapel, before entering the cloisters. I here give you a reproduction of an old print, found in rags in a convent dust-hole, which is almost an exact copy of it. The original is a large oil painting done in 1552.

St. Francis Xavier was of middle height, he had well-bred hands, dark hair, eyebrows, moustachios, whiskers, and frill-beard; large brown eyes, with good dark eyelashes, and bronzed complexion, small mouth and straight nose. His picture looks about thirty-five; he wears a *soutane;* he holds a staff and a book; he looks thoroughly like a gentleman, as he was. On the High Altar, under the crucifix, is a wooden coloured image of Xavier. The Cloisters are of carved wood, and each partition is surmounted by a spread eagle, in centre of which is a pierced heart. There are four side altars.

We used always to leave our vehicle here, and have our horse taken out, and fed and watered by the boys, who rested whilst we scrambled the whole morning over the hills. We walked off to the church and convent of San Gaetano, or Cajetan. It is

TRUE PORTRAIT OF ST. FRANCIS XAVIER, FROM AN OIL PAINTING DONE IN 1552.

built in the form of a Cross, like St. Peter's on a small scale, and belongs to the Theatines; and the present Government palace is attached to it. All are the same whitewashed barns. The grand entrance to Goa was by a picturesque road along the river, which road runs under an archway, painted black and white, with armillary spheres, and deer picked out in yellow. A blue and white niche contains a figure of Vasco da Gama, and is exactly like our caricatures of "bluff Harry the Eighth," and of which "Murray" plaintively complains that Lieutenant Burton, in 1845, found it grotesque. I can assure Murray that in 1876 I found it exceedingly grotesque; and so will you, reader, when I tell you how Vasco da Gama dressed.

DOM JOÃO DA CASTRO.

I will begin at his head, which carries a large grey wideawake, turned up, say a "Gainsborough," under which are his jolly red cheeks and iron-grey long beard. His legs, which stand wide apart, wear brown knickerbockers; he has brown vest and dressing-gown, with chain armour peeping out here and there—especially about the loins; his right hand grasps a sword, and the left a *bâton*; he is surmounted by a figure of St. Catharine. João da Castro's hair is also funny; it might be an idea for our *Journal de Modes.* The pet joke of the Goanese used to be, "that any Governor taking charge of Goa Velha must pass under the feet of Vasco da Gama."

Near San Cajetan is a heap of ruins, once a splendid Vice-Regal Palace, of which only two small broken-off pillars stand. We then went to the Sê Primacial, or Cathedral of St. Catharine, whose *façade* is surmounted by the Goanese arms, St. Catharine stabbing a Moor,—rather a curious thing for a saint, and must be figurative. One tower has fallen, which makes the building look lop-sided. It is a much finer church than any other. One chapel holds a miraculous cross, and another is dedicated to O Santissimo, the Blessed Sacrament, and is very fine.

The Sê is situated on a large Square called Terra de Sabaio, and flanked by the Holy Office. Its deep bell booms out for dozens, where hundreds of thousands had once hearkened and obeyed its call; and it is now the only sound that tells us of man's presence. It is sad to see a Cathedral big enough for a Capital peopled by twenty or thirty native Christians, and monasteries, to fit these churches, inhabited by a single priest. The few human beings increase rather than diminish the dismal effect, as sepulchral as their city: their pallid faces and emaciated forms seem destined to live on and give evidence against what was. The Cathedral or Sê was dedicated by the Franciscans—who were the first priests here—to St. Catharine, on account of the Portuguese taking permanent possession of Goa on her feast; and this church and convent belonged to them, but they afterwards took Our Lady and St. Peter as additional patron and patroness. The Archbishop's palace is attached to it, and the site of the once misnamed Holy Office, or Inquisition, is on the right hand, a heap of ruins, covered with a luxuriant growth of poisonous plants and thorns—not one stone left upon another. Not a wholesome shrub springs between the fragments of masonry, which, broken and blackened with decay, are left to encumber the soil as unworthy of being removed, or of contaminating another building with their curse.

The Inquisition of Goa—the shapeless heap over which we toiled wearily in the heat—is in the main square, Terra de

Sabaio, and was in its day a massive stone pile, pierced with three magnificent entrances, of which the centre, larger than the two lateral, led to the Hall of Judgment, while the side doors communicated with the spacious apartments of the Inquisitors and the other offices of the Establishment.

St. Francis of Assisi's Church, to which the Convent is attached, has a good arch built after the time of Dom Manuel, and the sides are frescoed on panels, with the incidents of the saint's life.

The Aljuvar, or Ecclesiastical Prison (where Captain Burton formerly lodged), is razed to the ground. At Sta. Monaca, the only woman's convent, there is but one nun left. She is wonderfully old, and when she dies no more are to be admitted. What a curious fate, to outlive all her community, and to be a whole convent in herself! She has seen Goa lapse from grandeur to decay, its people vanish, and its buildings fall to ruin, but she cannot die nor move. When she dies, the convent becomes secular property; but by the law, although they can, and do, refuse to admit new ones, they cannot turn *her* out, so they say her life is miraculously prolonged to worry them.

The Church and monastery of St. Augustine is kept up, but all the others—Dominicans, Carmelites, Franciscans, etc., etc.—are in ruins.

Now I daresay you think we have been walking through comfortable paved streets to these different buildings. Not in the least; we have been scrambling through woods, over hill and dale, and the distances give us some idea of how large Goa must have been.

We had one very fatiguing scramble, up a roughly-paved way, an ascending stony Scala Santa, through briers and brambles, and we passed the place where victims used to be scourged; and after ascending a long and weary way, now and then stopping to breathe and wipe our brows, we came to the Cruz do Milagre, the Cross of the Miracles, formerly a church and convent of the Miraculous Cross, where now remains a round pedestal, which had once held a cross, and where now briers spring out.

A sharper and more tedious ascent brought us to the convent

and church of the Cross of the Miracles,—formerly belonging to Augustinians,—in ruins; the high altar and side altars being still discernible. It is on a beautiful site, commanding an exquisite view. I could see, on the opposite hill, at its base, the chapel where Xavier first started a school and chapel for converting and preaching, and where he nsed to educate children; and hard by, is the well where he took his morning bath. The only inhabitant of the Church and Convent of the Cross of the Miracles was a large cobra, which we left in undisputed possession of the stronghold.

After inspecting the whole country from this eyrie, we scrambled down almost on hands and knees, with the assistance of a bamboo pole, the sides of the height, through dried vegetation, over low stone walls and broad gaps, with a tree to replace the long since ruined bridge thrown over the mountain torrents which watered Goa below, until we got into the hollow and alighted at a Hindú village. Naked children, fowls, buffaloes, and black men and women stared surlily; but, at the sight of silver, boys went sulkily up the trees, picked off three cocoa nuts, and brought them down. With a hatchet they chopped off the little round piece at the top and handed them to us to drink. How beautifully white the inside of the nut, and how refreshing the milk! cold as ice, each nut containing enough to quench the greatest thirst; and besides one knew it was *clean*. It left a refreshing coolness in the mouth, throat, and interior.

Without any cant, does not Providence provide wonderfully for us? In a dry, parched, and thirsty land, without water, there is drink for you at the top of the trees that shade you, and harmless drink, iced by nature. These things make an impression upon you until you grow used to them, and you take these benefits as a matter of course,—just as if they were your due, as if you had earned them, and have a right to them; but, at any rate, the first time you have the true impression—you are grateful.

Thus refreshed we crawled half way up the neighbouring hill and visited the first school and chapel and well of Xavier, now a ruin, but distinct in all its details; and often on our return, kind Senhora da Cunha Rívara, wife of a high Portuguese official (the Civil Secretary), would send us down some delicious Portuguese wine and water and cakes to refresh us when we were too tired and dirty and hot to make a visit.

In this little chapel and school (his first) Xavier preached and converted. This was abandoned as unhealthy, and they built St. Roc on Mount Rosary, near the Augustinians. This became the novitiate; whilst the Provincial and the oldest members of this order were sent to inhabit the house attached to the Bom Jesus. To the left are some stone-cut steps in the bushes and shrubs leading down to his bathing well. At the top of this mountain or hill is the ruined convent and church of the Dominicans.

We then came upon a by-road with an arch, over which is a recess containing images of our Blessed Lady and some saints. Here, in the days of the Inquisition, they used to ring the bell for the executions to take place. It is one of the centre Gates, and leads out of the city nearest the river, and is close to the spot where the victims were executed and burnt. Nothing but the foundations of houses can be traced; the tall cocoa and lank grass wave over many a forgotten and unnamed building. In the few (some seven or eight) remnants I have mentioned, a window or two, dimly lighted up in the evening, shows that here and there dwells a solitary priest. It is like the Arab's "City with impenetrable gates, still, without a voice or cheery inhabitant; the owl hooting in its quarters, and night birds skimming in circles in its ruins, and the raven croaking in its great thoroughfare-streets, as if bewailing those that had been in it."

The moonlit scenery of the distant bay smiles in all eternal Nature's loveliness upon the dull-grey piles of ruined, desolate habitations, the short-lived labours of man; delicately beautiful are the dark hills, clothed with semi-transparent mist, the little streams glistening like lines of silver over the opposite plain, and the purple surface of the creek stretched at our feet. Musically the mimic waves splashed against the barrier of stone, and the soft whisperings of the night breeze alternately rose and fell with the voice of the waters.

We used then to return to the Bom Jesus, to pick up our vehicle and rested horse, and drive home. Our way wended through black figures, chickens, small naked brown children like gutta percha, and pigs, which peopled picturesque Goanese villages of thatched huts, mangrove, rice, paddy swamps, and cocoa-nut groves; then a vast mud announced our entrance to Panjim, the poverty of the people and the unhealthiness of the air being the two salient points to strike a stranger. We sometimes varied this programme by a drive to one of the two points of the crescent bay; the Cabo do Monastero, now kept as a palace for the Governor. It has spacious rooms, and a few old Portuguese pictures, chiefly saints' heads. It is built in a fine, open space, and has bold, craggy heights on all sides. It boasts of the purest air in Portuguese India. The pleasantest part is in the cloisters on the upper floor, whilst the ground floor is a garden containing a curious old fountain with figures of women, and beds of flowers enclosed in little walls a foot or two high. There is a small whitewashed chapel, containing a handsomely carved wood pulpit, and side altars, a very old choir of carved work, and a still older picture (but probably worthless) of the Holy Family over the archway.

A very interesting feature is the tanks, built some three or four hundred years ago by the monks (on this height), who were afraid to leave themselves in the power of the rest of the world without water, when, perhaps, the wells might be poisoned. They cover a large surface of ground in the convent enclosure, and are full of pure, cold, fresh water, and have several apertures from whence the people come now with pitchers to draw. Certainly the Catholic clergy, especially the Jesuits, were the first to pioneer civilization into all lands, and to choose the healthy sites, and to teach the people. And how are they rewarded now?

We made a slight detour on the way home from Goa Velha to Panjim, near Ribandar, a large village directly *en route* and half way between Panjim and Panelly, the beginning or suburb of Goa. Ribandar is two miles to the east of Panjim, and connected with it by a long stone bridge, built by the Viceroy Miguel de Noronha. This village throve upon the ruins of its neighbour Panelly, another old village laid waste by the devastation of the first Old Goa (Gomanta) from intermittent fever. Our object was to visit the convent of the Misericordia. It is a picturesque spot, containing a Convent and Church with a *façade,* the whole building embosomed in palm trees.

Here are kept under surveillance, both religious and civil, sixty or seventy girls, orphans, of all colours, classes, and ages. They are educated by the nuns, and when grown up remain in the house till they receive an offer of marriage. It was six o'clock at dusk when we reached it, and what with the severity of the regulations, which do not permit opening after five o'clock to strangers, and the anxiety of the poor girls to open and let us in, and see and hear something of the outer world, there was some discussion between the now peopled windows and *terra firma.* They looked like birds in a cage, and I pitied them sincerely. One spoke English and was shut up for an *affaire de cœur* not approved of. I thought there must be many an aching heart in that picturesque, desolate spot; for, with the world full of nice, pretty girls, and love affairs that come spontaneously, who would think of going to the world's end to overhaul this cage of forgotten captives, kept there for the purpose of respectable *mariages de convenance,* and who would look upon any suitor as a deliverance from the house of bondage? However, in these cases it is a blessing to remember that they are not brought up with an English education, which would make such circumstances unendurable.

"Come to-morrow, before five," they cried down to us. "We want so to see you."

"Alas!" we shouted up to the windows, "we cannot, for we sail to-morrow for Bombay."

These were the parting sounds on the evening air.

We made two boat expeditions; one to see Mr. Major's coffee plantation, which he calls Louisiana, in which is a petrified forest; and Captain Burton made one also to Seroda; the distance of the latter is fifteen miles: each expedition occupied two or three days.

We embarked for the first in a filthy boat full of unmentionable vermin, and started down the river in the evening, with storms of thunder and lightning and wind preluding the monsoon. After an hour along the south-east coast, we entered a narrow channel formed by sea and innumerable little descending streams, and wound through a dense mass of bright green underwood. On arrival we toiled up two miles of steep rocky path, through cocoa groves. It is on Mr. Major's estate.

At the bottom of the hill you find a little rivulet, and pieces of petrified wood are sticking out of the bank; ascending the hill to the east of the bungalow, you find them scattered over the ground. They appear to be the same as those near Cairo, of which several are existing; they are composed chiefly of palms and a small number of pines,—the peculiarity of this one is, that some of the sections appear to show marks of mankind, as if cut with a sharp instrument. They are of any antiquity, have always been known, and therefore excite but little curiosity.

Captain Burton went up to Seroda alone, and described it as lying in a long, narrow hollow, surrounded by hills,—a Hindú town of houses, pagodas, tombs, tanks, lofty parapets, and a huge flight of steps; people, trees, and bazars all massed together. It is fearfully dirty, hot, and shut in on all sides. It used to be a nursery for nautch girls, Hindús of the Konkani caste; dancing girls connected with the Hindú temples, not allowed to marry, and it has some legends attached to it.

The petrified forest was most interesting; albeit there only remains a few stones lying on the ground in the shape of trees. We returned with our skins in a state of eruption from the bites of the l—— and the stings of mosquitoes, and thought Panjim charming, for at least half a day.

CHAPTER XVI.

THE CIVIL AND RELIGIOUS HISTORY OF GOA.

THE bald account I have given of Goa shows its present state. The site is well worth visiting, and its history well worth learning; for it is one of those kingdoms that *has* been, that grew, reigned in magnificence, declined, and is now a pauper. I will not apologise for giving a short account of it, having studied its history on the spot in Portuguese, for there are actually no English books whatever upon it, or the few that are, are not worth reading, containing the scantiest accounts.

Governed by a succession of Viceroys of the bravest, wisest, and highest of the Portuguese nation, then in her zenith, Goa shot up like a mushroom, to a height of power, wealth, and magnificence almost incredible. It is described as the finest, largest, and most magnificent city in India. Its villas were like palaces showing the wealth and magnificence of the owners. In the merchants' houses all was gold and silver. They coined and made pieces of workmanship; the very soldiers were enriched After nine years' service in Goa, on account of the deadly climate, all were entitled to some command, by land or sea; but they despised Government employ, being more profitably employed. The Viceroyalty was one of the most splendid appointments in the world. There were five other Governments—Mozambique, Malacca, Hormus, Muscat, and Ceylon; the worst was worth £2,000 a year, a great sum in those days.

Vasco da Gama, in 1504, who landed at Calicut 1498, with the first Portuguese fleet in India, was the great Discoverer, and the first Goanese hero.

Dom Francisco de Almeida was the first Viceroy of Portuguese India in 1505, and resided at Cochin.

Goa, upon the Island of Tissuary, was built by the Mohammedans, and belonged to Hindú Kings, or Rajahs of Beejanuger, and is first mentioned under Mujahid Bahmani, the third of the Bahmani dynasty, who began his reign in 1374.

Affonso de Albuquerque, called *O Conquistador*, and the greatest hero of Portuguese Asia, succeeded Almeida as Viceroy 1509, and he captured Goa on the 7th February, 1510. The Portuguese were surprised by Idul Khan, who retook it, and had to retire; but they returned and retook Goa finally, on the 25th November the same year, the feast of St. Catharine; they therefore chose St. Catharine as patroness; and the first little chapel erected there by the Franciscans, the first religious who accompanied the expedition, was dedicated to her, as was afterwards also the great Cathedral.

Protestants must not confound the Franciscans with St. Francis Xavier, the greatest theological hero of Goa. The Franciscans means a very ancient order of religious, founded by St. Francis of Assisi, and is divided into first, second, and third orders; whereas Xavier did not arrive at Goa till 1542.

Linschoten, a Dutchman, who was in Goa 1582-83, says that the walls of the old town were still standing in his time, and that it was *twice larger;* he seems to speak of it as three-quarters of a mile long, and a quarter broad, and in later MSS. it is spoken of as one mile and a half long, and the same broad, and six miles in circumference, not counting suburbs; and indeed from the distances we had to walk from one holy site to another, I should say that would be the most correct.

In such a little sketch as mine, I must only give a general outline of Goanese history, without entering into long details, and so I will only notice the most remarkable Viceroys, Governors, and Captain-Generals, as the various representatives of the King of Portugal were called, although I have a complete list of them all, from the first, 1505, to the last, 1878, a period of three hundred and seventy-three years, with most of their notable events, which I have made into an Appendix.

Vasco da Gama (the discoverer) was the sixth representative in India (1524), but he unfortunately died at Cochin, four months after he became Viceroy. His successor was one Enrique de Menezes (1525), who had the good taste to permit of no rejoicings until he had paid the last duties to his illustrious predecessor, saying "it was much more becoming to bewail the loss of that great man, than to rejoice at *his* assuming the administration.

In 1529 Nunho da Cunha succeeded as Governor. During a siege a soldier near him having his head struck off with a cannon ball, Da Cunha exclaimed coolly to the bystanders, who were filled with terror, "Humiliate capita vestra Deo" ("Humble your heads before God"); using some words from the Roman Liturgy taken from the Scriptures.

In 1539, Estevão da Gama, the hero's son, came as acting Governor. He undertook a celebrated expedition to the Red Sea, and went as far as Mount Sinai in Arabia to make a pilgrimage to the shrine of St. Catharine, patroness of Goa,—a great feat in those days,—for which he raised himself to the honour of Knighthood, and bestowed it also on his comrades in the expedition,* amongst whom were Alvarez da Castro, son of the afterwards celebrated Viceroy of that name, and Louis de Almeida, who afterwards distinguished himself gloriously in Germany, under Emperor Charles V., who would then have knighted him, but that he had already won his spurs. And the Emperor declared that Almeida was more proud of having been knighted by the son of Da Gama on Mount Sinai, than for the victory he had just gained; whilst the father of Alvarez da Castro set such a value on the distinction bestowed upon his son, that to perpetuate the memory of it, he put the wheel of St. Catharine in his family arms.

In 1542 Martim Affonso da Souza arrived as Governor, bringing with him St. Francis Xavier, of whom more anon.

João da Castro arrived in 1545, the fourth and last great hero of Portuguese India, who, having just been made Viceroy, died in 1547-48 in the arms of Xavier.

* This was a custom, and allowed in those days, when such a feat was remarkable.

The four great heroes still honoured at Goa are :—

1. Vasco da Gama, 1504 and 1524.
2. Affonso de Albuquerque, 1509.
3. Dom João da Castro, 1545.
4. Dom Francis d'Almeida, 1505.

I do not put them in order of *date*, but in order of veneration and hero worship.

João da Castro, their last hero, defeated the King of Bijapoor, and secured to the Crown of Portugal, Salsette and Bardez. He sent his son Ferdinand to assist the Governor of Diu, who was besieged by the King of Guzerat. Ferdinand was killed, upon which he immediately sent his second son, Alvarez, who had been knighted on Mount Sinai. Being in want of money to continue the war, he sent one of his whiskers as a pledge to Goa, which was received with great honour; and the women of Goa and Chawl sent him all their jewels, which Castro courteously refused, praising them, however, for their patriotism. He returned in triumph to Goa, pulling down part of the wall, according to ancient custom, to erect a triumphal arch.

Some time after, he fell ill, and, disgusted of all earthly things, turned his thoughts towards Eternity. Xavier returned from the Moluccas and became his director. Castro repenting his proud entry into Goa, and wishing to humble himself before God, caused a second entry to be made, giving all the glory of his victories to the Almighty; and having a great devotion to the Apostle Thomas and St. Martin, he set up their images in place of his own. Presently despatches arrived from Portugal making him Viceroy, and continuing him in office for three years. The people made public rejoicings on getting the news; but Castro, hearing the shouts and seeing the illuminations from his bedroom window, turned to Xavier and said, "How deceitful is this world, which promises three years' honours to a man who has but a few moments to live." He expired some days after in the arms of Xavier, who assisted him to his last breath. Happy Da Castro! The last Hero of Goa died, attended by the most illustrious Apostle of that part of the world. Castro died so poor that the city had to pay for his funeral.

In 1551 Affonso da Noronha was Viceroy. In his time Xavier died in the island of Sancian (San Chan), near Canton, China, on the 2nd December, 1552; his body was brought to Goa, 16th March, 1554, and exposed publicly for many years at St. Paul's, and for the last time in 1783. It was then locked up in its present sarcophagus at the Bom Jesus, which has three keys—one with the Archbishop, one with the Senate, and one in Lisbon.

In 1558 Constantine de Braganza, a Viceroy of Royal blood, reigned there. He protected Camoens, author of the "Lusiads." He was dear to the Portuguese of Goa, and is not forgotten; but in spite of his good qualities, is hated by foreign historians, because the tribunal of the Inquisition was established in Goa in his time (1560); although lenient authors say that he had no hand in it. Of course it is difficult to form an opinion. He is also much ridiculed on account of having refused to cede to the King of Pegu, a monkey's tooth, revered as that of Buddha, in a temple of Ceylon, although the king offered three hundred thousand cruzados for it. He was placed in rather a difficult position. If he ceded the tooth, the Inquisition would have found him guilty of participating in idolatry for the sake of gain, and so would posterity. On the other hand, if he kept the tooth, he would have descended to us as a bigoted fool, which is just what has happened. He threw it into the sea. I have always been told by Anti-Catholics, that the Inquisition's whole object was to grasp property and money; but here is one instance to refute it. They would not allow Braganza to accept three hundred thousand cruzados, and perpetuate an idolatry, and it is the only good thing I ever heard of them.

In 1759, Viceroy Albuquerque (a descendant of the great man) transferred the Regal Palace from Goa to Panjim, the Goa of to-day.

In 1812 the Inquisition was abolished by the interference or request of the British Government, and the palace of the Inquisition at Goa was shut up in the reign of Bernardo José Lourena, Count of Sarzedas, who was Viceroy and Captain-General from 1807 to 1816. It is only fair, however, to say that the Inquisition had long before this time become only a name.

Most of these Viceroys, and Governors, and Captain-Generals stayed but two, three, or five years, probably on account of the climate, which is fearful. During these three hundred and seventy-three years, from the time of the first to the present day, many have died at their posts, and are buried at the Bom Jesus.

The religious history of Goa is more striking than its Civil Government. When one knows all about it, it appears to have been a huge collection of churches and convents in a desert place. I must explain that in England we say monastery for a monkery, and a convent for a nunnery; but abroad we do not say *monastero.* We only use the word *convento* for both; and if it be for women, they generally say the nunnery, or the Sisters. I shall therefore use the word convent, and as in Goa there was only *one* for nuns, I can well afford time to specify it.

Goa was made a Bishopric in 1534,—the first bishop was an Albuquerque,—and an Archbishopric and Primary of the East Indies in 1557, by Pope Paul IV. The Province was in its meridian, both civil and religious, three hundred and seven years ago, in 1571. It contained about one hundred and fifty thousand practical Catholics; it owned half a million of subjects in Portuguese India; it contained eight parishes, and the extra Parochial Church of the Arsenal, not including suburbs. The much-abused Archbishop was Fray Aleixão de Menezes, who became Archbishop in 1595, and Acting Governor in 1607. In 1613 he was transferred to Braga, when he became Viceroy of Portugal for Philip III., King of Spain, and died 1617. In his time there were about two hundred thousand inhabitants in the city, fifty thousand Mohammedans and Hindús, and one hundred and fifty thousand Catholics. He was much beloved at Goa, and is handed down to posterity as having done an immense deal of good; but is abused by all English writers, who fancy he forced the Catholic religion upon the Pagan with fire and sword. Tradition and the MSS. say he only committed the imprudence of burning idols, pagodas, and temples, which caused a massacre and retaliation.

The decline of Goa began under Philip de Mascarenhas, Viceroy from 1645 to 1651. This Viceroy was an expert poisoner, and always dined alone, even excluding his own family. He was the richest Portuguese that ever left the East, and had parcels of diamonds, all between thirty and forty carats' weight. The Goanese hated him, hung him in effigy before he departed, and when he died on the voyage, reported that he had been poisoned in the ship—a judgment from Heaven.

Its decay actually began in 1603-1643, and so quickly did the city wither, that Tavernier, who was here in 1642 and 1648, says that people who owned two thousand crowns per annum in '42, were in '48 secretly begging for alms. Goa flourished *absolutely* during a space of one hundred and thirty-five years.

Francisco da Souza, writing in 1697, and printed 1710, says, that from being once a large and oppulent metropolis, it seems to be the chief town of a most miserable country, or province; and he was doubtless right.

Even in 1830 the convent of St. Monaca had thirty nuns. Goa, the city, had one thousand five hundred communicants at Easter, and a total of three thousand two hundred persons of all kinds, most of them residing in the suburbs; chiefly at the village of Ribandar, half-way between Panjim and Old Goa. The twenty-four parishes, and the whole island of Goa, contained then not more than fourteen thousand persons of all kinds.

When Captain Burton was here in 1845, there was still something more to be seen than now, for, as I have described in my few pages, only a solitary church or ruin peers out of a wilderness of cocoa-nut trees. *The* convent owns one ancient nun, and the whole place at the outside contains a dozen of priests, inhabiting different buildings, whilst the whole population may arrive at one hundred persons. All that *is* of dead-life exists at Panjim, New Goa.

How it must have been cursed by the victims of the tortures of the Inquisition, till God heard their cry and avenged their blood, so that not one stone remains upon another, whilst the only thing that lives is the shrine of the one saint and gentleman, Xavier, and the tomb of the Christian hero, João da Castro; as if God had preserved them, to shine out as everlasting treasures from the ruins of Crime.

I would sum up for my readers a list of the buildings, and a general state of things existing in the palmy days of Goa.

The only *profane* buildings we hear of were—

The Viceregal Palace, transferred to Panjim 1812.
The Arsenal.
The Senate House (first the old, and then the new).
The Landing Stairs.
The Slaughter-house.
The Bazar.
A Bridge.
The old Custom-house, and private houses.

The religious buildings were—

The Archiepiscopal Palace.
The Archbishop's Prison (Aljuvar).
The Santa Casa (Inquisition).

And a list showing eight parishes (one extra, not counting suburbs), which included twenty-four churches, nine colleges, two seminaries, ten convents, three hospitals, three Houses of Misericordia, one convent of nuns, and seven religious orders, *i.e.*—

Franciscans.
Jesuits.
Dominicans.
Augustinians.
Carmelites.
Theatins.
St. John of God (Brothers of Charity).
Oratorians.
Confraternity of Laymen attending the Houses of Misericordia.
Italian Lazarists (Vincent of Paulites).
And the Convent of St. Monaca (Nuns of the Order of St. Augustine).

In my short recital I have already mentioned—

The Cathedral, or Sê, dedicated to St. Catharine, Our Lady, and St. Peter.
The Church and Convent of St. Francis (Assisi).
The Church and House of the Bom Jesus.
The Church and Convent of St. Augustine.
The Convent of Nuns of St. Monaca.
The Church and Convent of the Miraculous Cross (Cruz do Milagre).
The Church of St. Paul, Santa Fé, with its Seminary and College,

made over to Xavier on his arrival, from which the Jesuits were called Paulistas, and of which only the little chapel which I have mentioned, stands, near his well.

The Church and Convent of St. Cajetan, or Gaetano.

These are the only remnants left of all these churches and convents, which are said to have been magnificent, and were—

A little Chapel of St. Catharine, the first built on landing, by the Franciscans.

The Parochial Chapel of the Five Wounds, at the Arsenal (the extra parish).

Three Churches, with three Houses of Misericordia,—one for old men, one for widows, and one for girls. These were served by the Brothers of Charity of the Convent and Church of St. John of God, who waited on the hospitals and the Misericordia; in fact, an order of lay brothers for serving the sick.

The Chapel of St. Antony of Padua.

The Parochial Church of the Rosary (Dominicans).

The Parochial Church of A Luz (Our Lady of Light).

The Parochial Church of the Trinity.

The Parochial Church of St. Thomas Apostle.

Church and House of Nossa Senhora do Monte (Augustinians).

Parochial Church of Sta. Lucia.

Church and Convent of St. Dominic.

The Church and Convent of the Carmelites.

The Parochial Church of St. Alexis.

The Parochial Church of St. Peter (Pannely).

There were besides all these—

The College of St. Bonaventura the First (Franciscans).

The College of Augustinians.

The Seminary of St. Antony of Padua.

The College of St. Roc (Jesuits).

The College of the Rosary.

The College of Luz.

The College of St. Paul (Xavier's).

The College of Carmelites.

The College of St. Thomas Aquinas (Dominicans).

The old Senate House (became a hospital).

The old City Hospital.

The Hospital of St. Lazarus, where Xavier used to spend his nights tending the sick; which tells me it must have been for the poorest and most abandoned, for it is said he "much affectioned it, and there he loved to pass all his leisure hours.

Of the above-mentioned Houses of Misericordia, one was set apart for young girls, who, after (it is said) "a suitable instruction, were at liberty to marry, and received a settlement from the funds of the house." It is the same mentioned in Captain Burton's "Goa," visited in 1845, and published in 1851, which tells us that the dower was £10; and it is the same we visited on our last evening there.

In 1739 the Bare-footed Carmelites (Discalced) were expelled on account of a dissension with the Archbishop concerning the spiritual jurisdiction of Bombay, in which the Carmelites were supported by the Propaganda. In 1780, Dom Fray Emanuel, of Santa Catarina, who was one of their Order, was made Archbishop of Goa. The Carmelites thought they were going to have it all their own way, and waited upon him at his arrival; but he answered them in one sentence: "Reverend Fathers, before I became a Carmelite I was a Portuguese;" and the dissension broke out worse than ever.

The Franciscans, as we have learned, were the senior religious order in Goa, having accompanied the first expedition to India as chaplains.

When St. Francis of Assisi died, after founding his Order, he left this will, by which you will see that it is quite different to that of Xavier; but after his death it was divided into three sections—the Conventuals, the Observants, and the Third Order. The Observants observe the rule to the letter, and in a greater spirit of poverty; and the Third is for people who are obliged to live in the world, but who wish to belong to a religious order. There are four religious orders, provided each with a third order for seculars living in the world,—that of St. Francis, the Carmelites of St. Teresa, the Dominicans, and one more whose name I forget. In France the Observants are called Cordeliers, because they wear the knotted cord of St. Francis, as do the Third Order also,—but under their worldly garments.*

* THE WILL OF OUR HOLY FATHER ST. FRANCIS.—Our Lord has given me the grace (to me, Brother Francis) to begin a life of penance. When I was in a state of sin, it seemed to me a terrible thing to have the care of lepers; but our Lord having led me Himself amongst them, I did works of mercy towards them, and in leaving them I felt that what had at first seemed so bitter and repugnant to me,

The Jesuits, disciples of Loyola, were the Second Order, by rank of antiquity, at Goa; the richest, most highly educated, influential, and powerful,—of which Xavier was the second in command.

The Augustinians were the fourth Order. St. Augustine was born at Tagasta, in Africa, and he founded his Order there before he became a bishop, and afterwards at Hippo.

was changed into wonderful sweetness both of mind and body. After this I lived very little in the world. I was, as it were, set apart; and our Lord gave me such faith in the Church, where He is ever present, that I could do nothing but simply adore Him, saying, "We adore Thee, O Saviour Jesus Christ, both here and in all Thy Churches throughout the world, and we bless Thee that Thou hast redeemed the world by Thy Holy Cross." Our Lord gave me also such faith in His priests, that even were they to persecute me, I, having regard to their office, should always seek them and look up to them; and if I had all the wisdom of Solomon, and I came to a place with only poor secular priests, I would not preach in their churches contrary to their will, for I should wish to fear, love, and honour them as my masters. I will not think of their faults, because I recognize in them the Son of God, and thus am subject to them. I do this the more readily, because they alone can consecrate, and receive, and dispense to others the precious Body and Blood of the Son of the Most High. I wish those sacred mysteries to be everywhere revered and honoured above all other things, and that they should be deposited in some safe and honourable place. I wish also to respect all theologians, and those who dispense to us the Holy Word of God, as the ministers to us of life and grace.

After our Lord had given me a community, no one taught me what I should do, but the Most Highest Himself revealed to me that I must try and live as far as possible according to the rules of evangelical perfection. I drew up the Rule in a few and simple words, and our Holy Father, the Pope confirmed it. Those who came to embrace this state of life gave all they could to the poor. They contented themselves with a single habit, often mended within and without, with a cord for a girdle, and drawers. We wished for nothing else. We who are priests said Office like other priests; the lay brothers said the Pater Noster. We were content with poor and neglected churches; we were simple poor people, obedient and submissive to everyone. I worked with my hands, and I wish to work. I wish also that all the other Brothers should occupy themselves with some manual work, and that those who do not know how to work should learn, and that not from the hope of recompense, but to give a good example to others, and to eschew idleness. If we obtain no wages for our toil, let us throw ourselves on Providence, and beg our bread from door to door. It has been revealed to me that the Brothers and Sisters should salute one another with the words, "Pax Vobis" (*God give you His peace*). Let the Brothers be very careful not to accept churches, houses, or anything which may be built for them, if inconsistent with the holy poverty we have vowed by the Rule, and let them always remain as strangers and pilgrims on the earth. I strictly forbid any of the Brothers, by their vow of obedience, to ask for any letter from the Court of Rome, either for their churches or for any other thing, under pretext of preaching, or even for the security of their persons in case of persecution; but when

Martin Luther was a member of this Order, and on account of his apostacy they obtained leave from the Pope to change their habit from black to white, which is like the Dominicans; they are distinguished from the latter by a black leather girdle, and never use a cloak or mantle, but on all great occasions they are obliged to resume their black habit. Their monastery, on Mount Rosary, was the most beautiful and stately of Goa, and, it is said, would have been remarkable even in Europe.

The discalced Carmelites is the oldest Order in Christendom. *We* consider in England, St. Simeon Stock, of Kent, to have been the founder on Mount Carmel; but *they* believe the prophets, Elias and Eliseus, or Elijah and Elisha, who established themselves on Mount Carmel, to have been their first founders,

they are persecuted in one place, let them flee unto another, and there let them do penance with the grace of God.

I promise absolute obedience to the Father General of this Brotherhood, and to the guardian he may please to appoint over me; and I wish to feel myself so bound in his hands that I should be unable to do anything or go anywhere without his permission, because he is my master. If I should be weak and infirm, I yet will always have a clerk to say Office to me, as is appointed by the Rule. Let all the other Brothers be equally obedient to their Superiors, and say Office regularly according to the Rule. And should any be found who either neglect or wish to make changes in it, or who are not good Catholics, let such be delivered over to the Father Rector, and kept close prisoners until given up by him to the Cardinal of Ostia, who is the Master, Protector, and Corrector of the Brotherhood.

Let not the Brothers or Sisters imagine this is another Rule; for it is but a memorial, a warning, an exhortation, in fact, my *will*, which I, Brother Francis, your very humble servant, address to you, my Brothers, so that with the blessing of God we may observe the rule with greater fidelity, as we have promised our Lord to do.

The Father General and other Superiors of the Order are commanded under obedience to add nothing to these words, and to retrench nothing. Let this my will be added to the Rule, and when Chapters are held and the Rule is read, let them equally read these my words.

I forbid positively, in virtue of obedience, any of the Brothers, whether priests or laymen, to gloss over the Rule or my will, and say, "These words are to be understood in such or such a sense;" but as our Lord has given me the grace to write the Rule and these words clearly and simply, so let our Brothers understand them with equal straightforwardness and simplicity, and put them in practice unto the end.

Whoever shall observe these things shall be filled with the heavenly benediction of the Father Most High, of His dearly-beloved Son, and of the Holy Ghost the Comforter, together with the virtues of the Saints. And I, Brother Francis, your poor and humble little servant, confirm, as far as I can, this holy benediction within you and without you. Amen.

before Christ; that they had successors till the coming of Christ; and that certain members of their body were at Jerusalem on the day of Pentecost, when the Holy Ghost descended on the Apostles. They were present at St. Peter's first sermon; they put themselves under the protection of the Blessed Virgin, then living; and went back to their convent on Carmel; that upon their report of what they had seen, all the Order declared themselves disciples of Jesus Christ. It is certain they existed in the time of the Crusades. In 1607 they established a convent at Goa. On account of the dissensions before mentioned, with the Archbishop, their church and convent was handed over to the Oratorians, and later the Archbishop of their own Order gave them the convent of Chimbel, between Ribandar and Panjim; but it was of an inferior grade altogether, and they never recovered themselves in Goa.

The Oratorians were instituted by St. Philip Neri at the same time St. Ignatius instituted the order of the Jesuits. They are secular priests, with simple vows, live in common, and their duties are preaching and instructing youth. The Church of the Miraculous Cross on the mountain, which belonged to the Augustinians, was given to them.

CHAPTER XVII.

THE CAREER OF ST. FRANCIS XAVIER.

ST. FRANCIS XAVIER was certainly one of the most wonderful men, in every sense of the word, that the world ever saw, either in ancient or modern times,—religious or otherwise,—wonderful for his virtues, labours, and achievements. He shed a lustre over the East during his ten years' Apostleship, and dead, his memory alone draws any interest to his headquarters, Goa, which city would otherwise be dishonoured, if remembered at all in the world's history; but is hallowed by his remains—an incorruptible body.

Xavier was a saint and an apostle in gifts and works. His was a double mission: on one hand to reform the manners of the Europeans in the Indies, whose lives were a disgrace to the Christian profession; and on the other, to carry the Gospel to the pagan population of the East. He stands before us as the father and founder of missions for the conversion of the natives of the East, whilst his marvellous successes testified to the reality of his apostolic gifts.

About three hundred and fifty or four hundred years ago there stood at the foot of the Pyrenean Mountains, between twenty and thirty miles distant from the town of Pampeluna, the fine old Castle of Xavier. The family to which it belonged was one of the noblest in Spain, being descended from the Royal House of Navarre. At the time of which I write, this Castle was in possession of Don Juan de Jasso, a nobleman of great merit, holding one of the chief places at the Court of John III., King of Navarre. He married a lady remarkable for beauty, talent, and virtue, whose name was Maria Azpilcueta Xavier. She was heiress to two of the most illustrious families in the kingdom.

The Castle, from which her name was derived, had been granted some centuries before to one of her ancestors as a reward for his past services to the Crown. Her surname of Xavier was an aristocratic and historical family name, and was perpetuated in the family by being conferred upon her children, who would have been called, as the Spanish custom is, De Jasso y Xavier, from father and mother. Francis, the youngest, was destined to render the name immortal.

This young Spanish hidalgo (noble) was born on April 7th, 1506. Francisco was an active, lively boy, full of health, strength, and courage; with the gentle, winning manners which mostly accompany birth, united to great strength, so that he was loved by all. He loved to join his brothers in all manly sports; to climb the rugged sides of their native mountains to the chase, and where there was difficulty or danger Francisco was always to the fore. They would sit together in a wild spot, and relate the brave deeds of their ancestors, and talk of what they would do when old enough to bear arms and fight for their king and country, and emulate deeds of knighthood and valour. He had great energy, and he courted obstacles for the pleasure of conquering them; but his intelligence was of a higher order than that of his brothers: he loved literature and study, and all the hours that he could not pass with his brothers, were spent in poring over the old manuscripts in the library of his father's castle. When he was seventeen his parents sent him to the University of Paris, which was then the fashion for the youth of Spain, Italy, and Germany; and there he worked hard at philosophy. He was so ardent in his studies that in due time he took his degree as Master of Arts, and was appointed Professor of Philosophy; he gave public lectures, which drew down such applause that the youth was rapidly rising to fame, with a splendid career before him.

Francis, from his first entry, had for companion in his room at the college of St. Barbara, a fellow-student named Peter Faber, the son of a poor peasant in Savoy, who employed him to keep swine on the mountains; but this boy pined so for learning, that, through some interest, he was sent to school, where he soon learned Latin and Greek, and showed surprising ability. These two lads, so far separated by social position, became warmly attached to each other.

Whilst Francis was giving his lectures on philosophy, another man came to lodge at the College. He was of middle age, poorly clad, and lived in the poorest way. He had been a distinguished soldier, but feeling himself called to the Church, gave up all, and came to acquire the necessary studies for his new career. This was Ignatius Loyola, the Founder of the Order of the Society of Jesus. The heart of this honest man warmed to these two talented youths, and he took every opportunity of conversing with them. Faber listened to him gladly, but Xavier proudly resented what he considered the uncalled-for interference of an unlearned stranger. He laughed at his conversation, made game of his dress and poverty, and joined with the other professors in showing him dislike and contempt. One day, as Faber was sitting at his books, Xavier entered the room, exclaiming,—

"What an odd man that Ignatius is! I have never said a civil word to him since he came to Paris; on the contrary, I have shown him marked disrespect, and yet he goes on as if he were my dearest friend. Just now at lecture he brought two new students to hear me, and has been speaking in the most flattering terms of me. Really, if there were not such a calm dignity about him, I should think he wanted something of me. But if so, he has got hold of the wrong man."

"Xavier," said Faber, looking up and speaking with considerable warmth, "you do not know what you are saying! If you knew that man you would not speak of him or treat him as you do; and I can only say, if you mean pecuniary help, so far from seeking it from you, he is conferring it on me. I could not remain here but for him. He often shares with me and other poor fellows, money sent from Flanders and from England for his own necessities."

"You do not mean it, Faber! That he should do *you* a service would be quite a sufficient reason for me to like him. I own I don't understand him; but his conduct yesterday, when the Rector publicly asked his pardon for an insult he had offered him, struck me forcibly. I thought I had never seen so noble a face. Who and what is he, Faber?"

"I only know that he comes from one of the first families in Guipuscoa, and that he was greatly distinguishing himself in arms, when he suddenly gave up all for Christ's sake, and came here to study for the Church."

From this short conversation Xavier's manner entirely changed towards Loyola, and so far from avoiding him, he began to feel a growing pleasure in his society, and they used always to walk together in the University garden. One day Francis had given a lecture in which he had surpassed himself: his thoughts were full of the applause he had gained. Ignatius was also full of interest about it, and the three friends walked up and down, as usual, discussing the matter, and talking of learning, talent, and glory, when Ignatius pensively, and half to himself, muttered, "What shall it profit a man if he gain the whole world and lose his own soul?"

Francis had heard the words a thousand times, but to-day, whispered by Ignatius, they sank so deeply into his soul as to take root there; he speedily left him, and sought his room. He *never forgot those words;* he tried to banish them, and to turn to his books; but his mind was so perturbed, he could not. All his projects of honour and renown seemed like a child's castle of cards, beside the solid glories of the eternal Kingdom of Christ which He has promised to those who devote themselves to His service.

One by one the long-cherished hopes of youth passed in array before his mind's eye, and Francis sorrowfully, but willingly, let them go, embraced the poor, hard, mortified life of a soldier of the Cross, and became, as Peter Faber already was, a disciple of Loyola. He never could do anything by halves, and with all the natural ardour of his character, now governed by Grace, he set to work to subdue a proud, vainglorious temper, and to acquire the meek and humble spirit of the Gospel.

He led a life of constant self-denial and mortification. He fasted for two, three, and four days together, and occupied himself with prayer and divine contemplation.

When their studies were completed, Loyola, Xavier, and Faber, and others who had joined them, entered on a life of constant journeyings, amidst many privations and sufferings. They divided themselves into twos and threes, passing from place to place, devoting themselves to the works of mercy, corporal and spiritual. The future Saint served in one of the hospitals at Venice. During this time took place a great event. I mean the formation of the wonderful Society of Jesus, begun by this small *réunion* of pious friends headed by Loyola, and of which Xavier and Faber were the first members. Then followed his preparation for the priesthood, and his first Mass. All these men were filled with a longing to go to the Holy Land, and Francis made a vow to do so if it were possible. Thus seven years passed away, and we find him labouring in Rome, by the Pope's command, with nine companions, who, like himself, had joined Loyola.

There was at this time, in Rome, a Portuguese named Iago Govea, who had known Xavier, Ignatius, and Faber, at Paris, in the College of St. Barbara. Seeing the wonders they were working, and knowing how anxious John III. of Portugal was to find zealous missionaries to send to the Indies to convert the heathen, he wrote to him about Loyola and his disciples, describing them as wise, humble, charitable men, inflamed with zeal, unwearied in labour, lovers of the Cross, who aimed at nothing but the honour of God. John III. wrote to his Ambassador at Rome, Pedro de Mascarenhas, to obtain of the Pope (Paul IV.) an order that some of these apostolic men should be sent on this enterprise. The Pope sent for Loyola, who gladly acceded to the plan; but as they were only ten in number, he could spare but two, and fixed upon Simon Rodriguez and Nicolas Bobadilla, for the Indian mission. But Bobadilla was taken so ill as to be unable to go.

Loyola was then inspired that his most loved disciple, Xavier, was the one whom God would have preach His Word in the Indies. He was so impressed with this, as a revelation from above, that, much as the sacrifice cost him, he sent for Xavier. He was so absorbed in contemplation that he did not perceive

Francis till he knelt and asked his blessing. Then looking upon him with deep affection, and speaking slowly and with emotion, his eye kindling and his manner animated, he said:

"Xavier! I had, as you know, named Bobadilla for the Indies, but the Almighty has this day chosen you, my son; and now I bid you, in the name of the Vicar of Jesus Christ, receive the Mission entrusted to you by His Holiness, and delivered by my mouth, as if our Lord Himself conferred it on you. Rejoice that it is granted to you to satisfy the fervent desire wherewith we are all filled, of carrying the Faith to distant lands. You have not here a narrow Palestine, or a single Asiatic province, but a vast extent of country, and innumerable kingdoms. Nay! a whole world is given to you wherein to work; and nothing less is worthy of your energy and zeal. Go then, my child, my brother, where the voice of God calls you, whither the Holy See sends you; and set the unknown natives on fire with the flame that burns in your own breast."

The tears filled Xavier's eyes, and a deep blush spread over his whole face. He deeply respected and loved his Chief, and he could find no answer. When he could speak, he humbly expressed his surprise that one so weak and unworthy should be chosen for so great a mission; but he cried,—

"I am only too ready to obey. I offer myself, with all the powers of my soul, to do and suffer all things for the salvation of the Indians. I dared not say it, but I have longed for years, to be sent on this mission. I have dreamt of vast oceans full of storms and tempests, of savage rocks and desert islands and pathless wilds; of hunger and thirst and nakedness; of toilsome, solitary wanderings, cruel persecutions, and constant danger of death; and my soul dilated at the encounter, and I called out, 'Yet more, my God! yet more.' What an honour if amongst these idolatrous nations the glory of dying for Christ should be my fate."

He was to begin his journey next day. He sat down and patched his well-worn habit. He bid farewell to his companions, took a tender leave of Loyola, his Master, and threw himself at the feet of the Pope to obtain his blessing. The Holy Father

22

received him with the greatest kindness. He told him that however he might think so high a mission above his strength, He whose work it was, would never fail or forsake him; that he must be prepared for toils and sufferings, whereby alone a Christian can conquer, and that he who would be an Apostle must tread in the footsteps of Apostles, whose lives were a continual Cross and a daily death; that he was called upon to revive the Faith in that land where the great Apostle St. Thomas had first planted it; and that, if necessary, he must be ready to shed his blood for the honour of Christ.

The words of the Holy Father sank deep into Xavier's heart, and his reply was full of humility and trust in God, but so plainly told of the high courage and firm purpose in his soul that the Pope had from that moment a strong presentiment of the great things he would do in India. He embraced him several times, and dismissed him with his benediction.

It was in March 1540 that Xavier, now thirty-four years of age, without scrip or purse or shoes, taking only his breviary, his rosary, and crucifix, and clad in his old patched cassock, set out with the Ambassador and his party for a three months' journey to Lisbon. The whole journey was a series of acts which endeared Xavier to every member of the party,—his great and unaffected humility, his winning qualities of Nature and Grace, his manly daring and hardy mountaineer strength, which came to notice when any feat was to be performed from which the city-born gentlemen shrunk in horror. Twice one of the party fell over a precipice, and whilst all held their breath in terror, Xavier, accustomed from his youth to the mountains of the Pyrenees, accompanying his father and brothers in war or chase, was scaling the rugged sides like a chamois to rescue those in danger.

He would sometimes be with the Ambassador or his gentlemen, joining in all the interesting topics of the day; now, with sweet humility, cheering the attendants, keeping them in good humour, drawing them to talk of their own concerns; then lending a hand to groom and feed the horses; letting them ride his when tired; often giving up his bed and sleeping on the straw by the horses; yet so thoroughly a gentleman in his humility that nobody ever forgot his dignity.

The most touching event of the journey, and one that is too perfect for my understanding, is as follows. The Ambassador and party are now descending the Spanish side of the Pyrenees. The old and dearly-loved scenes of his boyhood come before the eyes of Xavier. There is the spot from which he used to fly his hawk; there a rugged pathway where he used to climb with his brothers. The very trees and favourite haunts greet him as old friends. How short the distance, how well known the way to his ancestral home and his idolized mother, who little thinks that her Benjamin is so near, or on what distant and perilous mission he is bent.

He is not insensible; he does not forget. Crowds of familiar associations and tender memories rush into his heart, but he rides on calmly by the Ambassador's side, courteous, self-possessed, attentive to the wants and wishes of others, so that none guess that this region has any particular interest for him. None saw the conflict going on in his young heart, or the agony of this first moral crucifixion. A lovely scene lay beneath them: a rich fertile valley, large flocks and herds grazing; the cheerful song of the mountain shepherds, and the murmur of streamlets gliding down from the mountain sides to feed the broad river in the plain, reached their ears. The land was richly wooded, groves of orange and citron trees were luxuriant, and the rays of the setting sun fell upon the landscape and upon the turrets of a noble's castle situated amidst the embowering foliage.

"What a lovely spot!" cried Mascarenhas, reining in his horse, that all the party might enjoy it; and after some moments—"Why, surely, Father Francis, we must be close in the neighbourhood of your home? Is not that Castle Xavier? You have said nothing, and it well-nigh slipped my memory. We will halt here, and give you time to visit your mother and family."

Francis tried to steady his voice, and to check the natural tears.

"Noble sir," Xavier answered, "with your permission we will go on. I have no home now."

"But consider! You are about to sail for India; you may never return; and anyhow, seeing your mother's age, you are not likely to see her again."

"I thank you, noble sir, for your great kindness, but I have put my hand to the plough; to go down there would unman me. I wish to make this sacrifice. Pray let us go on."

One sob arose to his throat, and he rode forward. He had sacrificed all that he held dear on earth to his God. It was one straight career, without let or hindrance, evermore, from this moment to his death, twelve years later. The men now knew they were travelling in company with a Saint.

They reached Lisbon at the end of June 1540, but did not embark for the Indies till April 1541. In Lisbon Xavier found his old companion, Father Rodriguez, who had left with Bobadilla, the priest who had remained behind with fever; and so much good did these two effect in these nine months, that the King of Portugal requested the Pope and Loyola to be allowed to retain one of them in Portugal. Rodriguez was chosen to remain, and Xavier to go on, accompanied by Father Paul da Camerino, a priest, and Francis Mansilla, not yet in orders; they set sail with Martim Affonso da Souza, who was going out to replace D. Estevão da Gama, son of the hero, as Governor of Goa. Their vessel was called the *St. James*, or Sant' Iago, and sailed April 7th, 1541. Xavier was thirty-five years of age.

On board, as everywhere else, Xavier gained all hearts. A terrible disease broke out; Xavier was the priest, the nurse, the friend of everybody, to the smallest cabin-boy. Dom Martim always kept an especial place at his table for him, but Xavier excused himself, and only accepted a grand cabin, and delicacies from the Viceroy's table, to nurse the poor and the sick thereby, sleeping on the hard deck, and eating bits that the sailors gave him; and this though he suffered wofully from sea-sickness, and the results of attending on his many patients.

They did not reach Mozambique till August, from contrary winds; and then, the monsoon being too violent, they landed and wintered on an island a mile distant from the mainland, and conveyed the sick to a quickly-constructed hospital, Francis and his two companions following and serving them, administering the medicines with his own hand, assisting the dying, and giving them the Last Sacraments. All wanted to have him near them, and declared that only the sight of him bore them up, body and soul. Nature gave way under such continued labour, and Xavier was seized with a violent fever and delirium; but he only thought of his sick and poor, and used to creep along, holding on by the beds for support, with a mantle thrown around him. One day the physician caught him in this act, and he said, "I assure you, Father Francis, there is not a patient in the hospital in half so great danger as yourself, and you make your recovery impossible."

"I promise," said Xavier, "to obey you, only let me do one thing,—the salvation of a soul depends upon it,—and then I will do as you like."

He crawled to where a poor ship-boy was lying on a little straw. He knew the boy had led a bad life, and to his despair saw him insensible, and knew also that he would not be allowed to wait till he recovered consciousness. He called out to his two comrades to carry the boy back to his own bed, and then placing him in it he sat down beside him. The boy recovering his senses, Xavier long and earnestly spoke to him of his past sinful life, and the Saviour's love, and all he had done for sinners. The dying lad at length turned to him, and with tears besought the Holy Father to do what he could for him; he confessed his sins with deep contrition and breathed his last. After that Xavier kept his word to the physician.

They stayed six months at Mozambique, and set sail on 15th March, 1542, touched at Melinda, on the African coast, and the Island of Socotra, and arrived at Goa, the chief city of the Portuguese in India, on the 6th May, thirteen months after they had left the port of Lisbon, and two years from the time that Francis had left Rome. He was now thirty-six years old.

Xavier had at length reached the long-wished-for scene of his labours, and it only remains to give a little sketch of his remaining ten years.

In the time of Thomas the Apostle, there had stood without

the walls of the great city of Meliapore a stone pillar, on which was engraved his prophesy—"That when the sea, then forty miles distant, should wash that pillar's base, white men should land upon the shores who would restore the true religion in India."

The Pagans had long laughed at this; but little by little the sea had gained upon the land, and after one thousand four hundred years the Portuguese cast anchor off the shores at an hour when the tide was in and the waves were dashing against and breaking themselves round the pillar's foot.

Still the missionaries made but little way. About forty years before Xavier arrived, a martyr, Pedro de Couillan, expiring, prophesied that God would raise up in his Church a new Order, which should bear the name of Jesus, and that one of its first fathers, conducted by the Spirit of God, should be the Apostle of this land. When Francis arrived, things were in the saddest state. Everybody was living in the grossest profligacy, and worst of all were the Europeans, who professed to convert and give example to the Pagans. Idolatry, bigotry, and persecution; polygamy, slavery, and extortion; murder, usury, injustice, and tyranny of every sort were rampant.

The Viceroy on landing, before entering his carriage, turned to Xavier and said, "Father Francis, I need not say that my Palace is your home."

Xavier answered, "I thank your Excellency for this, and all favours, but my home must be the Hospital."

The Viceroy replied, "If I thought I could induce you, I would go on entreating, but I know you too well; so pray for me, and whenever you require my services remember me."

So they parted, and Xavier was conducted to the Hospital, where he passed the night in prayer, amongst the sick and poor.

Next morning he repaired, after saying Mass, to the Palace of the Bishop, Dom João d'Albuquerque, a holy Prelate and a Franciscan, who deeply grieved over the state of his diocese. Francis respectfully explained to him why he was sent, and showed him the briefs from the King and Pope; but he concluded, "Of these, my Lord, I shall make no use without your sanction."

The Bishop was struck with Xavier's humility and modesty, and the impress of holiness on his countenance, and raising him tenderly as he knelt for his blessing, said, "An Apostolic Legate sent by the Vicar of Jesus Christ has no need of any other orders. Use freely the powers the Holy See has given you, and if ever my Episcopal authority be wanting to enforce them, I shall never fail you."

A friendship sprang up between these holy men, and their union tended greatly to facilitate matters. Francis began his day by saying Mass, and then went from hospital to hospital on his mission of love, begging alms for the poor, and especially was he merciful to the lepers. Thus he continued observing the position of affairs and learning the native language, considering what he had best do.

One day, in the cool of the evening, Francis passed along the streets ringing a little bell, and they recognised the stranger priest, the good Father, who was devoted to the people : the little children used to cluster around him, catch hold of his hands or his robe, and he used to talk to them, and his little stories and prayers instructed them, and he wrought such a difference in the children, that the parents flocked to hear him preach. He never shrank from those who were leading wicked and scandalous lives, but became their friend, and drew them to God. The people came in crowds to the Confessional, and Xavier was so busy in administering sacraments, preaching and catechising, that he said he wished he were ten people, instead of one, to be in many places at once.

By the Bishop's order, the children were now catechised in the Church ; the gentlemen and merchants endeavoured to promote virtue in their families, and gave large sums to the Father for the poor and hospitals. The Viceroy himself attended to the sick one day in the week, waiting upon them with his own hands ; and when the Viceroy did it, it became the fashion with all ; in fact, there was a universal change of sentiment, life, and manners at Goa.

There was no Inquisition in Xavier's time. He established a reign of love and courtesy, and taught it to the Pagans ; and when he worked miracles, of which I shall speak perhaps as I go on, instead of turning things into ridicule, as our present shallow-pated youths do, without inquiring, they simply called him the *God of Nature*, which name he retained during his whole ten years. One day he was told that the Vicar-General of the Indies, Dom Miguel Vaz, a man of great piety, wished to have an interview with him. He told Xavier that along the east coast of India, extending from Cape Comorin to the island of Manaar, lived a people called Paravas, the pearl fishers, that they wanted pastors, but the land was so barren and the heat so insupportable that no one would go.

Francis set out at once, and the only thing he would accept was an old pair of shoes from the Viceroy, to protect his feet from the burning sands. There he had to learn the Malabar language. He used to apply himself first to translate the Paternoster, Ave Maria, and the Creed, the Ten Commandments, and the principal points of the Christian doctrine, and learn them by heart. Scoffers always say, "How could he speak?" Firstly, Spanish and Portuguese are very quick, as most Southern foreigners are, at acquiring languages. When a man knows Latin, and has acquired a few languages, he reduces it to a method. Captain Burton, who is certainly not aided by miracles like Xavier, can, in a fortnight, acquire quite enough of any language for ordinary purposes. English are, as a rule, a dull nation at acquiring languages, but they can do it if they try. I do not believe the French *can*, at least all I have met speak everything abominably, except French.

When Xavier had learnt his lesson, he used to take his bell and proceed through the towns and villages as before, and we have learnt that it was impossible not to love him and be attracted to him, first for himself, and then for God's sake. His noble air, his adorable dignity, and sweet humility and charity, his voice and manner, and face beaming with the love of God and the love of his neighbour, all drew the people, accustomed to be treated like slaves, or dogs, blacks without souls or rights, to listen to the words of one who appeared to them like a god, by comparison with the other Portuguese, and who not only was superior to their tyrants and oppressors, body and soul, but who, far from despising them, lived *with* and *for* them, and only asked them in return for their *own* sakes to adore *his* God. He loved to send some of his dear convert children to work miracles for him, to *show* that it was not by *his* power that he wrought wonders, but by the power of the great God he preached, who, if *He* willed, could use a little black child to perform mighty works.

The Brahmins believe in a Trinity—Brahma, Vishnu, and Shiva. The first is the creative and ruling power, the second is the preserver, and the third the destroyer. Vishnu is their Christ. To their own doctrines they added scraps borrowed from St. Thomas. Xavier had to suffer many persecutions from the Brahmin priests. He returned after a year's mission, miraculous in its success, to Goa, to bring out other priests, as there was far too much work for one. Francis then went to Travancore, where he pursued the same plan, and soon forty-five churches were erected. He wrote home, begging for more of the Society to come out to him. A prince of the island of Manaar, called King of Jafanapatan, sent him a deputation, in answer to which he despatched one of his missionaries.

A terrible persecution of the new Christians ensued. Francis set out to Cochin, thence to Cambaya, to meet Miguel Vaz, the Vicar-General of the Indies, whom he induced to return to Portugal at once and lay the state of the case before the King, and wrote also himself, praying for a reformation of all these abuses. He afterwards set sail for Nagapatam, thence to Meliapore and Malacca, to the Moluccas, to Ternate, and the Isle of Moro; also to Macassar, in the Celebes, and a second time to Malacca, and thence to Cochin. His old friend, Peter Faber, died at Rome, August 1st, 1546, and Francis in his writings, praying in a storm, said "he prayed through the Dead, and addressed himself particularly through Peter Faber to appease the wrath of God." He now revisited Parava and Ceylon.

In each of the places I have mentioned he established religion, and then returned to his College at Goa, to mature plans for converting Japan. When everyone tried to dissuade him from going, and represented to him the dangers, he replied, "I am only ashamed that I have not led the way to this enterprise, and cannot endure to think that a merchant has shown more courage for gain, than a missioner for God's honour. God, who saved me from the lances of the Badages, the prisons of the Isle of Moro, and from shipwrecks, will not abandon me. India was not my boundary: I was ordered to carry the Faith to the uttermost ends of the earth." So he wrote to Ignatius and Rodriguez. He settled all the affairs of the Society at Goa, gave written instructions for all the Jesuits in various parts of India, and set sail for Japan in April 1549.

On the way he went to Cangoxima and Firando. In the first of these places he endured great persecution from the *Bonzes*, the native priests of Buddha; thence they went to Amangughi and Meaco. What touched these pagans most, was, that when presented at the Court of any place he arrived at, instead of asking for place or wealth, as all the other new-comers did, he only asked leave to preach the word of God. This generosity and disinterestedness was so unusual, that all exclaimed, "How unlike this European *Bonze* is to our covetous priests, who only care for money and interest!"

In Bungo, Xavier, with his old patched cassock, all travel-stained; bare, swollen, bruised feet; crucifix, breviary, and *berretta* on his head, excited great contempt.

Then, to their astonishment, some Portuguese ships arrived, and all the gentlemen and merchants and officers formed a cavalcade to meet him, and found him toiling along the road, carrying his own baggage, and the Japanese lords riding along at either side of him. The Portuguese, who were held in high respect by the Japanese, dismounted and knelt before Xavier, begging his blessing, and wished him to mount; but on his declining, they walked, and insisted on carrying his burden. The ship was decorated for his reception with flags and banners; the bands were playing, the streamers flying, the men in glittering armour drawn up to receive him, and as he approached, salutes were fired from all the cannon.

King Bungo resided with his Court at the city of Fucheo, near the port of Figen, and took fright, thinking it was an attack, and sent in alarm a gentleman of the Court to enquire the cause of the noise. Da Gama, smiling, led the messenger forward and showed him Xavier, and told him that this was a small testimony of the respect due to one so dear to Heaven, and so highly esteemed at the Court of Portugal. The Japanese, who saw before him only a mean, insignificant, poor, ordinary priest, in a torn cassock, foot-sore, covered with dust,—to him only worthy of contempt,—showed his amazement.

Da Gama said, "You see a man meanly dressed, but he is born of kingly blood, and is heir to great wealth; but the great and generous spirit in him, makes him give up all, and appear as he is, for the love of God." And he then added a short account of his wonderful life.

The messenger was almost afraid to return to the King, as they had all treated this treasure of the Portuguese with contempt; but he did return, full of admiration, and told the King that the Europeans appeared more happy in the possession of this poor holy man, than if their vessels were laden with ingots of gold. Then Bungo wrote to Xavier a beautiful letter, begging him to come to his Court; it was carried by a Prince of the Royal blood, attended by thirty young Lords of the Court; and they said to one another, "What a great God theirs must be, when he can make these wealthy merchants obedient to so poor a man." The Ambassador told the King that the European *Bonze* must be very differently treated to their own *Bonzes*. The Portuguese were resolved to read the Japanese a lesson, as to how they wished Xavier to be treated; and much as it shocked his humility, he acceded to the plan, for the furtherance of religion in Japan.

With the same pomp as above mentioned, they made him leave the ship in grand array,—in a cassock of black camlet, over which was a surplice and a stole of green velvet, brocaded with gold. Thirty Portuguese gentlemen, richly attired, with gold chains around their necks, accompanied him. The sloop was lined with the costliest Chinese tapestry: other similarly equipped boats followed; silken banners waved, there were accompaniments of music, and booming of cannon. Da Gama, bare-headed, led the way, with a wand of office: five Portuguese followed, carrying the Father's catechism in a white satin bag: another, a Bengalese cane, tipped with gold; a third, a pair of slippers of black velvet; a fourth, a picture of Our Blessed Lady, enveloped in a scarf of violet damask; and the remainder bore a magnificent parasol, or canopy, such as in Japan is used for Royalty. Then came Francis himself, looking noble and dignified, but modest and simple, followed by the rest of the Portuguese nobles, with their gallant bearing and robes of state. The streets, windows, and balconies of the houses in the line of march were filled with spectators, and gaily decorated; six hundred of the King's Guard, armed with lances, were drawn up before the Palace.

Then Da Gama turned round and saluted the Saint respectfully. One presented him the cane tipped with gold, another the velvet slippers; those who bore the parasol spread it over the Father's head, and those who carried the book and picture ranged themselves on either side. The Japanese were enchanted, and said that this was a very different *Bonze* to what had been represented. The reception was magnificent; all the nobles of the Court were assembled in dresses of damask, embroidered with gold, and richly variegated. The extraordinary condescension and familiarity of the King, and his new mode of reception of Xavier, so excited the jealousy of the *Bonzes* that there were insurrections in the city; notwithstanding which, religion made rapid strides, and Francis laboured there two years and four months.

Whenever there was persecution or fighting, Xavier never shirked or ran away, but stayed with his flock like a gentleman and a soldier, and stood between them and danger, so long as it lasted; and not only in dangers of war, but pestilence as well. On the 20th November, 1551, he sailed from Japan, leaving four hundred thousand Christians there.

He went back to Malacca and to Cochin, and Goa in February 1552, and was overjoyed to find the good and altered state of religion there; for his greatest sorrow had been the infamous lives of the Portuguese from Europe; the harm that they did, and the scandal that they gave, made converting the pagan an irony. Another source of joy was that the Paravas (the pearl fishers) mustered five hundred thousand Christians.

Francis, having laboured in Bassein, Cananor, Cochin, Cape Comorin, Manapar, Malacca, Careapatam, Japan, Moluccas, and other countries, now occupied himself with organising an expedition to China. He set sail on Maunday Thursday, April 14th, 1552, with a little band of Apostles. A shipwreck drove them to Malacca, which was visited by the plague, where Francis found work to do; the Governor ill-rewarded his labour of love by opposing his mission to China, and detaining his vessel. In fact Xavier, in his writings, said that nowhere had he suffered such persecutions as at Malacca. Sending on his brethren for their own safety to Japan, he kept a Chinese named Antonio, a young Indian (both converts), and a lay brother. The Governor sent Xavier's vessel, the *Santa Cruz*, forcibly to trade at the island of (San Chan) Sancian, off the coast of China, with orders to erect no buildings save huts of mats and branches. Francis resolved even so to embark, with his three companions, hoping to be able to get somehow to China.

Sancian was reached after storms and calms, difficulties and hardships. It was a desolate and sandy region, infested only by tigers.

At last all turned against Xavier; the merchants and men, who owed their lives to him, put every obstacle in his way, to break his spirit, and to deter him from his project, even to denying him sufficient food, imagining his project to be detrimental to trade; so he suffered desertion of friends, desolation, and abandonment He was struck down with a violent fever, and had an intimation of his end; he therefore begged to be put ashore.

On a morning of late November 1552, the waves broke with a dreary sound on the shores of the barren little island of Sancian; the cold north wind and the scorching sun made themselves each felt in bitterest intensity. The *Santa Cruz* lay at anchor, and presently a boat was lowered from the ship's side, and made towards the island. The lay brother, the Chinese convert Antonio, the Indian, and the Portuguese merchant Alvarez landed, and ascended a sandy hillock which commanded a slope beyond. Then they hurried along to the prostrate figure of a man which they had just descried.

There, on a bed of sand, lay the great Apostle of the Indies; his head, grey with toil and suffering, exposed to the wind and sun. His noble face was flushed with fever, his breath came convulsively, his thin hands clasped his crucifix, and beside him was a little knapsack containing the necessaries for Mass.

THE DEATH OF ST. FRANCIS XAVIER.

They bore him to a shed of mat and leaves which belonged to Alvarez. They bled him, but for want of knowledge, pricked a vein which only produced convulsions, and the operation was twice repeated. He was delirious, and muttered only, "My Lord and my God," "Jesus, Son of David, have mercy on me," "O most Holy Trinity," "Queen of Heaven, show thyself a Mother." He came to his senses, smiling sweetly, and thanking those around him, never alluding to their previous unkind treatment, and told them his end was near.

At two o'clock on Friday, 2nd December, 1552, he kissed his crucifix, and saying, " In Thee, O Lord, I have hoped; let me not be confounded for ever," whilst a gleam of joy lighted up his heavenly countenance, he yielded his pure soul to God.

When those who were on board the *Santa Cruz* heard of his death, they hastened ashore, and one and all—even those who were the servile creatures of the Governor of Malacca, Dom Alvarez d'Atayde, and had ill-treated him—knelt down and kissed Xavier's hands, begging his pardon, and asking his prayers in heaven.

He was forty-six years of age, and these events happened three hundred and twenty-six years ago.

George Alvarez, the merchant, put the body in a large Chinese chest, filled up with unslaked lime, to consume the flesh; and they buried it, and set up a cross, and two heaps of stones at the head and feet.

In the old Castle of Xavier was a life-size crucifix, before which, as a boy, Xavier had been in the habit of praying. During the last years of his life, when the Saint was in the midst of his greatest labours and sufferings, this crucifix sweated blood every Friday; but on this Friday, upon which Xavier died at Sancian, the sweating ceased.

On the 17th February, 1553, by the Captain's orders, the coffin was uncovered, but when the lime was taken off the face, it was found ruddy and fresh-coloured, as though in sweet repose; and on making a puncture, the blood flowed as if in life, the priestly vestments were unhurt, the body entire, exhaling a delicious perfume.

They bore the Saint's remains to sea, and landed at Malacca, 22nd June, 1553. All the clergy, nobles, and chief inhabitants came out to receive the body, each with a wax taper in his hand, and bore it to the church of Our Lady of the Mount, followed by Christians and Mohammedans, in so great a crowd that it is thought not a soul able to walk or ride was missing, save the wicked Governor, d'Atayde, who mocked at it, and resumed his cards, at which he was engaged. Shortly after, he was deprived of his government, for extortion, cruelty, and other crimes; his goods were confiscated, and he was thrown into prison, where he died of a loathsome disease, the result of his evil courses.

Preparations were made for transferring the body from Malacca to Goa. Twenty leagues from Goa the vessel was becalmed; but the Viceroy ordered a light galley to be manned without delay, in which Father Melchior Nuguez, Vice-Provincial of the Jesuits in the Indies, and three others of the Society, proceeded to fetch the body of the Saint. When it was half a league from the town, eighteen barques, having on board the flower of the Portuguese nobility, and eight hundred of the principal inhabitants, each with a lighted taper, and every barque dressed with flags, and having a band of singers and musicians on board, went out to meet the galley. The body of the Saint, covered with cloth of gold, lay under a noble canopy, with lighted flambeaux and streamers waving on each side. The whole town gathered on the shore, and when the galley neared, cries of joy and tears of devotion testified to the life of the Saint, and the estimation in which he was held. Some flung themselves into the sea and swam back with the galley.

On the shore stood the Viceroy, the guards, the Members of the Royal Council, the Magistrates, and remaining nobility, all in mourning; and, with salvoes of artillery, the body was received, 15th March, 1554. Then the procession, chaunting "Blessed be the Lord God of Israel," moved on. The children in white, crowned with flowers, bore olive branches; the Brotherhood of Mercy carried a splendid banner; the coffin was borne by the Fathers of the Society, followed by the Viceroy, his Court, and the people. The streets were hung with tapestry, and the people from the balconies, windows, and house-tops, flung flowers upon the coffin. The miracles that occurred are chronicled, but this is no place for them. The procession proceeded to the chapel of St. Paul's College, where the body, fresh as in life, was exposed to the veneration of the people.

He was canonized by *the people,* and after the usual judicial formula and a strict inquiry as to his life, virtues, and miracles,

Pope Paul V. beatified him on the 25th of October, 1619; and his canonization was completed by Gregory XV., 12th March, 1622, and promulgated by Urban VIII. This bull contains a compendium of his miracles, which were astounding, during life and after death; and it said that the new Apostle of the Indies received, in a *spiritual* sense, the blessings vouchsafed to the patriarch Abraham in a *temporal* sense, that he was the father of many nations, that his children (meaning his converts) were multiplied more than the stars of heaven, and the sands of the sea; that his apostolate was garnished with the gift of tongues, the gift of prophecy, the gift of miracles, with all evangelical virtues in perfection.

His feast is kept by the Church on the 3rd of December, and this year the body was exposed; there was a great religious festival, and crowds went to it. If any take an interest in the subject I would advise them to procure the Life and Writings of Xavier in full, by Father Coleridge, S.J. The usual way that the Church honours him is by a nine days' prayer or Novena, finishing by Communion on the feast. This devotion was invented by Father Mastrilli, to whom the Saint appeared; and telling him that his influence with our Saviour was very great in heaven, *promised to intercede with God* for all those who implored his aid by this Novena, whether in spiritual or in temporal wants. I can only say that I frequently have had recourse to it, and the Saint has never failed me, so I can honestly recommend any one who has some case of distress, some great want, to ask St. Francis Xavier *to pray to God for it*, and see whether they will not get it.

The Novena may be performed privately at any time. The Church keeps it publicly, beginning on the fourth and ending on the twelfth of March. It was the same Father Mastrilli who erected the splendid mausoleum over the body of the Saint at Goa. There is a second devotion called the Ten Fridays of St. Francis Xavier, which appears never to fail in obtaining requests. That is going to the Sacraments of Confession and Communion every Friday for ten weeks, and reciting some prayers which, as well as the Novena, are found in a little book called "Preces

Xavieranæ." We make it on a Friday because Xavier died on Friday.

He composed a prayer in *Latin* which we often say, called *O Deus Ego amo te.* It is a splendid prayer, showing what noble sentiments filled his soul,—no servile fear of hell, no idea of reward; only honest, loyal love. Here is its literal translation as used by us, with its old spelling:—

"O God! I love Thee, not to get
Thy favour to be saved; nor yet
To shun that sad eternal lot
Designed for those that love Thee not.
Thou, Thou, my Jesus, to Thy losse,
Would'st needs embrace me on the Crosse,
Thou would'st endure both nayls and lance,
Disgrace and dolours; with a trance
Of bloody sweat, and boundless seas
Of anguishes and bitterness;
Nay, even death's last agony,—
And this for *me*, a foe to Thee.
Most loving Jesus, shall this move
No like return of love for love?
Above all things I love Thee best,
Yet not for hope of interest;
Nor to gain Heaven's promis'd land,
Nor to stop Thy threatening hand;
But as *Thou* lovedst *me*, so do *I*
Love *thee*,—and ever shall,—meerly
Because Thou art my King, my God,
Of love the source and period. Amen."

There is a little book which I am sure would strongly interest my readers. It is the "Life of Catharine Burton," an English Carmelite, whose religious name was Mother Mary Xaveria of the Angels. She became a nun in the English Teresian Convent at Antwerp. The book is a collection of her writings by Father Hunter, and is published by Burns and Oates, Portman Street.

The MSS. was in possession of the Carmelite nuns of the Order of St. Teresa at Lanherne, Cornwall, the same community as that to which Catharine Burton belonged. The first Prioress was an English lady, of the Worsley family, and she was trained by the famous Anne of St. Bartholomew, friend and companion of St. Teresa, in whose arms she expired. The nuns left Antwerp in 1794 for Lanherne, Cornwall, and I may be pardoned for mentioning a curious coincidence that Catharine Burton was an ancestor of my husband, and that Lanherne belonged to my family (the Arundells of Wardour), who gave it to the nuns, and so it is believed that Mass has been said, and the Blessed Sacrament preserved without interruption through all the centuries of Catholic persecution in England. I allude to this book chiefly to illustrate the power of Xavier, whose memory, so far from dying out, has constantly received fresh honours. In 1748 he was proclaimed "Defender of the East."

Father Hunter, the compiler, was a man of powerful mind and extensive information, as well as a reader versed in spiritual literature. He had learning, experience, and judgment. He was born in 1666, made his early studies in the English Jesuit College at St. Omer, entered the Society in 1684, was professed in the early eighteenth century, and for many years was Chaplain and Missioner to the Sherbornes of Stonyhurst, and died in 1725, soon after compiling this MSS.

Catharine Burton was born at Bayton, near Bury St. Edmunds, Suffolk, 4th November, 1668. After passing a virtuous childhood and youth, she was seized with a violent and extraordinary illness, which lasted seven years, from beginning to end; and God restored her, first her health, and then the use of her limbs, in a miraculous manner,—each time after making the ten Fridays of St. Francis Xavier. It happened in the sight of her own family, and was witnessed by the whole town where she lived.

And if we may trust this account, Xavier promised her that he would procure blessings for all those who should read what she wrote by his order and dictation; therefore as I wrote on the subject, and whilst residing at Goa, I could not, to avoid the criticism sure to be showered upon such remarks in this enlightened nineteenth century, omit the mention of the only interesting object left at Goa, Xavier's tomb; and I hope to incite some of my readers to profit of these blessings if possible, and to read his Life and Writings, and also those of Catharine Burton.

I may mention that Father Hunter forwarded her MSS. to her native town, where it was signed and witnessed by all the important residents there, in attestation of its truth. Catharine Burton's father was Mr. Thomas Burton, of the Yorkshire Burtons. Her mother was Mary, only daughter of Mr. Christopher Suttler, in Norfolk; she left nine children behind her, four sons and five daughters, and died of her tenth child at thirty-five years of age. The father, after having brought up his children most admirably, when they stood in no further need of him, went to join the Society of Jesus; five of the brothers and sisters became priests and nuns in different monasteries and convents. Henry Burton, the grandfather of Catharine, was cast into prison on account of his religion.

The English Carmelites at Antwerp were founded by Lady (Mary) Lovel, daughter of Lord Roper, Baron of Teynham. She was the widow of Sir Robert Lovel, and her sister was Elizabeth Vaux, the friend of Father Gerard.

Catharine Burton died one hundred and sixty-four years ago, 9th February, 1714, at the age of forty-six—like Xavier,—having been twice re-elected as Superior of the Convent. The compilation of her career was finished in 1725.

In short, the life of Catharine Burton is one of those rays of glory, that occasionally play around the memory of my favourite Saint, who is no fictitious Hero of romance, but a more wonderful man than most great historical characters. Xavier was a hero who is not like one dead and gone, but exercises his influence on posterity; and cares for, and communicates still with this visible scene from his realms of light and glory.

His ten years were passed in prayer, attendance on the sick, going from hospital to hospital, relieving and comforting the sufferers, and the lepers, begging alms from door to door to supply their needs, and showing untiring charity to all; preaching, catechizing, and instructing, confessing, and administering sacraments, studying languages and dialects to perform his labours, curing diseases, working miracles, and prophesying, suffering persecutions, insults, dangers, privations of hunger, thirst, cold, heat, fatigues, and often foot-sore, sea-sick, ill and feverish, reduced by want of food and sleep and the barest necessaries. He was never surprised out of his sweet charity and gentle dignity of man and gentleman by these sufferings, he never deserted his people in pestilential diseases, in foul infections, in persecutions by arms and violence; on these occasions Xavier was ever to the front, as became one of the race of the Kings of Navarre. He converted many hundred thousand pagans, including their Kings, Queens, and Princes. He broke forty thousand idols, and threw down heathen temples by their votaries' own consent. He erected innumerable churches, and baptized with his own hand alone one million two hundred thousand persons.

Baldæus, a Protestant, in his history of the Indies, says: "Had Xavier been of the same religion as ourselves, we should have esteemed and honoured him as another St. Paul. And notwithstanding the difference of religion, his zeal, vigilance, and the sanctity of his life ought to stir up all good men not to do the work of God negligently; for the gifts he had received for the fulfilment of the office of a Minister and an Ambassador of Jesus Christ were of so high an order as it surpasses my ability to express. If I consider the patience and the sweetness with which he proffered to both great and small the holy and living waters of the Gospel; if I regard the courage with which he endured injuries and insults, I am constrained to cry out with the Apostle, 'Who, like him, is sufficient for these things?'" and he concludes by apostrophizing Xavier thus,—"Oh that it had pleased God, *that being what you were, you had been, or might have been, one of us.*"

Hackluyt the traveller, an Anglican minister, writes: "Sancian is an island on the confines of China, and nigh to the Port of Canton; it is famous for the death of Xavier, the worthy preacher of the Gospel and divine teacher of the Indians in the matter of religion, who, after great labours, many injuries, and innumerable crosses, suffered with much patience and joy, died in a cabin, on a desert mountain, on 2nd December, 1552, destitute of all earthly conveniences, but replenished with all spiritual benedictions, having made known Jesus Christ to many millions of Eastern peoples. Modern histories of India are filled with the eminent virtues and miraculous works of this holy man."

Tavernier (a Huguenot), endowed with every good quality, says: "Xavier here ended his mission with his life, having established the Christian faith with astonishing success in all places through which he passed, not only by his zeal but also by his example and the sanctity of his life. He never reached China, but probably the religion he planted in Japan spread into the neighbouring countries, and multiplied itself through the labours of this holy man, who may be justly called the St. Paul and true Apostle of the Indies."

These are only a few of the Protestant and other testimonies adduced by Bonhouse at the end of his biography.

Reading and studying all these works on the spot, and finding myself at the bourne of a long-formed wish, a pilgrimage to this Tomb, and having great faith in the prayers of St. Francis Xavier, I made an earnest petition to receive a great boon *through his intercession with* our Saviour. When I receive it, as I am confident I shall, I will not fail to make it known for the honour of God, and as a testimony for St. Francis Xavier, and to fulfil the promises I have made in event of obtaining it.

CHAPTER XVIII.

ON THE INQUISITION OF GOA.

I DO not know why we find many Catholics, even at the present day, who dislike writing or talking about the Inquisition. I always conclude that it results from a want of reading or from ignorance. I cannot say that I feel any difficulty about it. I think that there is but one opinion for an educated, well-read, honest-minded Catholic to hold upon the subject.

There is no doubt that in poring over old books and MSS. in Portuguese, one feels that much may have been exaggerated by hatred and terror, but that in any case, horrors were committed by unscrupulous people in the name of Christ, which can never be glossed over and excused, and *that* especially in so far-off a land as Goa, where Civilization would never hear of the crimes committed by those in full power. Torture was in those barbarous days the custom, and what was practised in the Civil Tribunals—witness the Torture Chambers in Venice—the Council of Ten—who handed the criminal with his sentence over to the fatal Three, who enforced it; whence he was transferred to the *Pozzi* (wells) or *Piombi* (leads under the roof), to fry or freeze until torture and death put an end to his misery.

We may likewise look at our own thumb-screws and rack in the Tower. So torture was practised by the Church in the short but terrible reign of the Inquisition, chiefly in Spain and Portugal, where it was in vogue long before it reached Goa,—its acme. What makes the crime so salient amidst the horrors of civil tribunals was to torture in the name of Heaven.

What would be felt now-a-days were a midshipman lashed to the mast-head in a gale, as our grandfathers and even our fathers were? What a howl of execration would run through

England were a soldier flogged to death for a slight fault. How long is it since these things have ceased to be?

Goa used to complain bitterly in 1812 that Great Britain was very intolerant to her Inquisition, but that she ought to look to her own windows before flinging stones. How did you treat Joan of Arc? they ask. She was captured at Compiègne, she was betrayed to the English, and they handed her over to the Inquisition, who burnt her to death. "Bishop of Beauvais," said the victim, "I die by your hand and I summon you before God." Her *sanbenito*, or paper mitre, bore the following inscription at the procession to the stake, "Heretic, relapsarian, apostate, idolatress;" and her *samaria* (mantle) bore amongst the flames, "Joan who calls herself The Maid is a liar, a pernicious deceiver of the people, a superstitious blasphemer of God, boastful, cruel, dissolute, an invoker of the devil," and several other titles. They burnt her alive and threw her ashes in the Seine.

As Captain Burton went to Dahome as Her Majesty's Commissioner in 1863, to try and induce the King to abolish his "customs," *i.e.*, the slaughter of some thousands of victims yearly, and as Captain Burton tried to induce him to use the blood of animals instead of human blood for this religious ceremony, so Inquisition has given place to Vivisection, and animals are now tortured under the plea of Science, as a century ago human beings were tortured under the plea of Religion. The lust of cruelty, like the volcano, must have its outlet, its safety valve, till Civilization and Education slake and absorb it. If we could catch an Inquisitor now-a-days the Pope would excommunicate, and the Civil Law would hang him. In the next century refinement and Civilization will cause people to look upon the Vivisectors of *our* century, as we now look upon the Inquisitors of the *last* century. They will pass away like the Inquisitors to their Eternal *Un*rest, and pave the place which is falsely said to be paved with good intentions.*

* To my Fellow-Workers against Vivisection.—I have perhaps said enough about Vivisection in my note to Chaper X., but I was told a story to-day, from some of the official reports, I think, to be found in the Blue Book, viz., that eight medical students had operated at the same time on eight different parts of the body of the same horse, and that after the unhappy beast had served their purpose for one, two, or more days,

I have read every word of Dellon, all the accounts in Portuguese, in fact all the local notices down to the present day, and made all my extracts from them. Dellon was a French physician attached to the Inquisition, a volunteer; it was only by enrolling oneself as a "Familiar," that any person could hope for safety, for which reason many good souls enlisted without doing any harm. But it was not until it was abolished that anyone dared write about it, if within reach of the long arm of the so-called Holy Tribunal; the latter had power over all except the Viceroy and the Archbishop, and even *these* dared not openly interpose in behalf of any prisoner under pain of being reported to the head Inquisitor in Portugal, and possibly recalled: even Papal threats were disregarded by this dread Tribunal.

The Palace of the Inquisition faced the New Senate House, and was on the south side of the Cathedral Square. Its front was adorned with three lofty vaulted gates, which were reached by large stone steps,—by all accounts a very handsome building,—

was left to die as best he might. Now, I should have given those eight embryo doctors each a month on the tread-mill without the option of a fine.

However, I am told, by the most humane, kind-hearted, and sensible men of this country, that we anti-vivisectionists are going on quite a wrong tack; that what we want, however right, is unattainable at the present period; that we have too much influence counteracting our cause; that we are expending money, time, energy, and good feeling in vain, and exhausting ourselves needlessly. If this is so, do not let us, as it were, go on taking useless headers against a dead wall, doing no good; but, much as I hate half measures, let us shift our sails, and go on another tack, that is sure to fetch the port at last. Do not let us, because we cannot close ALL the doors, leave the biggest ones open.

Let this be our petition to Parliament. No reasonable Government could refuse us. We should have it endorsed by the *whole* Public Voice.

1. Let *unauthorized* Vivisection be forbidden under pain of punishment, which shall be *imprisonment with hard labour*, and no *option of a fine*.

2. The only exceptions should be, such well-known eminent men of science, who can, from their position, humanity, and probity, be trusted to carry out their work with as much humanity as possible, specifying the *use of anæsthetics* and the *obligation* to *destroy* the animal *as soon as possible after the operation*.

3. The term "men of science" is too general. The class must be limited to the highest members of the scientific medical profession, who are known to be making experiments for the benefit of suffering humanity.

4. In all cases they must take out a licence, and if in the course of their work any *abuse* of their privileges should occur, and come to knowledge, they should be

raised one storey above the ground-floor. In India it used to be rare to have anything higher than the ground-floor. The breadth, which was seventy feet, and the length, was enclosed in walls covering two acres of ground (*duas geiras*).

The burning place was near the river, and not far from the Palace, as the Viceroy and Court had to attend, for it was part of the policy of the Inquisitors to make the punishments appear to be the work of the State.

It was in 1812 that the British Government had a garrison in Goa, and orders came from the Court then at Rio de Janeiro, by the recommendation of the Court of St. James's, London, for the total abolition of the Inquisition. The Inquisitors, four in number, had choice either to go to Portugal, or to remain in Goa and enjoy their salaries, as pension, for their remaining years, in private life.

Goa was the place where the Inquisition was at its worst, yet in 1812 it is said that there was not a single prisoner in its walls; and that no one at Goa recollected to have seen any *auto da fé*. But middle-aged men of 1812 had heard their fathers relate that they had witnessed some; so that for at least eighty

subject not only to condemnation by the public voice, but to the severest penalty the law could exact.

5. The *public* have a right to *require* that the names of those who receive such a licence should be made known monthly in print by the Press.

6. *Under all circumstances, medical students should be prosecuted, and most severely punished unless their operations are performed in a public operating theatre, beneath the eye of those high professors who obtain this licence.*

7. As there are *grave doubts*, that any *great* benefit to science can arise from such powers being permitted to mere students, it is hoped that men of science will refuse their permission and approval, unless under some most exceptional case, which should be made public, and then in form of a written certificate.

8. Any persons being aware of these laws being transgressed, and will give information of the same at the Society for Prevention of Cruelty to Animals, 105, Jermyn Street, or to the office of the *Home Chronicler*, 11, Ave Maria Lane, E.C., will be rewarded, and their confidence not betrayed.

I do not believe that we shall succeed in getting *all* we wish, but meantime I think we might succeed in closing up the Great Gates of Cruelty by this sensible and moderate petition to Parliament, and that the rest would follow. "Half a loaf is better than no bread," and I beg of my fellow-workers to think over these few suggestions. They do not satisfy me, but if we cannot run let us walk, and we shall arrive at the winning post quicker than by jumping and springing on one spot of ground, which is evidently what we are doing now.

years (that would be 1732) no such thing had taken place, nor had anyone been executed by order of the tribunal. I suspect that this was owing to Pombal's reforms, which were not thoroughly carried out, and that a modified form went on secretly, just similar to the half-measures about Vivisection to-day. Now the question is, to look round and see what state our civil tribunals were in, as to torture, at the date of 1732, and that in most civilized and non-Catholic countries, and then we shall arrive at a temperate and just conclusion with regard to what was done by the clergy of the Inquisition, whose abominable acts were *legal.*

Tavernier visited the Inquisition at Goa, and narrowly escaped. Twenty-five years later Dellon was entangled by it, and suffered. About the beginning of the last century Captain Hamilton, a sturdy old merchant militant, infested the Eastern Seas, just when it must have been at its worst. He says there "were eighty churches, convents, and monasteries within view of the town, and these were peopled by thirty thousand church vermin," as he calls them; and the whole of his book is written in that rough-and-ready style.

In more modern times, the Rev. Denis L. Cottineau de Kloguen went there; he died in 1830, and his short and useful sketch of Goa was published in 1831. Captain Burton went there in 1845, and we went there together in 1876. Dellon's MSS. was published in Holland two hundred and eleven years ago.

The Inquisition found but little favour in France, Italy, and Germany. In 1221 it was introduced by Pope Innocent IV., and in 1255 by Pope Alexander III., in concordance with St. Louis of France. In the thirteenth century it crept into Spain, but it was in Portugal where it took root and flourished, and in 1478 was regularly organized by Cardinal Don Pedro Gonsalvez de Mendonça; and in the reign of Ferdinand and Isabella of Spain, Torquemada, the great Chief Inquisitor, worked it up to its maximum of full energy and bloodthirsty ferocity, and brought in eighteen years 105,294 people to the Tribunal, actually burnt 8,800, and 6,500 in effigy.

The first of these Inquisitors sent to Goa were Don Fray

Aleixão Dias Falcão, and Francisco Marques de Botelho, secular canons. This was in 1560, after the death of Xavier and the good Bishop Albuquerque. This vile institution is said to have existed two hundred and fifty years. The Marquis of Pombal tried to reform it, and gave an order to that effect in the name of the Court, 1774. The last person burnt was a Jesuit, named Malagrida. Donna Maria allowed a revival of it in a minor degree in 1779. It was finally extinguished in Goa by an order from Lisbon, October 8th, 1812, and the revolution of 1820 washed out its execrated memory in blood.

Every writer says that Goa was the worst city of all those that had admitted the Inquisition. They used chiefly to burn the poor Jews, whom they called the new Christians. Whenever the Holy Office was afraid of sedition on account of their cruelties, they used to employ assassins or poison, to rid themselves of their enemies. It was really by this means that the Portuguese lost India. They subjected foreign ships to examination by spies, and ships preferred to trade elsewhere. People grew afraid to settle there, and all who could, fled from the horror of these so-called religious severities. One cannot conceive anything more ill-judged than such dealings with ignorant men, Pagans whom they wished to convert, men of all tongues, races, and creeds.

Barret Mirando said the cruelties which were practised in the name of a religion of love and peace were carried to far greater excess in India, where the Inquisitors were surrounded by a luxury that exceeded that of royal potentates, and whose pride was to make all things submit to them, even indirectly the Viceroy and Archbishop. The *Gazette de France*, August 12th, 1680, contained an article on the spirit of the times, which showed that it was bad everywhere, but nowhere so evil as at Goa. The two celebrated cases of Padre Ephraim de Nevers, and that of Boulaye de Goux, did much to open the world's eyes to their proceedings.

The rule was that every person enrolled, and especially those who served the Inquisition House, should be Portuguese of virtuous life, old Christians, of pure Portuguese blood, and without black or Jewish descent or intermingling. They must never have been prisoners, or descendants of any race possessing the above-named obstacles or objections. They must also be personally of good conduct, and worthy of important and secret missions; but, however, in Goa all these rules were broken and set aside.

Linschoten, a Hollander who came to Goa in 1583, and was thirteen years in India, says that the Pagans were much better doctors than the Portuguese, for that they understood the diseases of the country, and the herbs, which the latter did not, and therefore usually had resort to bleeding, which is almost certain death in those climates, where the heat exhausts the frame.

Dellon was seized on August 24th, 1673. He gives a pitiable account of the humidity and fetid filth of the prison. The victims were subject to an illness called Mordixim, which began with a violent fever, then tremors, vomiting, terror, delirium, and death. They used to do for this what they do for everything in Syria,—burn with a red-hot iron; there it was applied in the hardest part of the sole of the foot, and in Syria in the head; until the patients scream and show consciousness. This may also have been quoted as one of the cruelties of the Inquisition, but it is not; it is a remedy much in vogue amongst certain peoples. This disease, according to all European dictionaries, was a bilious colic, a frightful indigestion, and finally sporadic cholera morbus.

In Goa they never use the term Inquisidor-Mor, or Chief, but First Inquisitor, or Inquisitor of the First Class; and the Chief Inquisitor, who resided in Lisbon, was called Inquisitor-General; the post should have been occupied by a Dominican and a secular priest. Prison was a general name; *Carcere* was the term for the Inquisition cells, *Aljube* for the ecclesiastical prison. The *Cadêa*, anciently called *Tronco*, was the civil prison, and *Calhabouço* was the military prison. The *Aljube*, or *Aljuvar*, is now levelled to the ground, and a small private house occupies a little portion of its site. There used to be a life-size crucifix in the Inquisition Hall, which had some celebrity, and which is now in the Sacristy of the Chapel of the Palace of the Governor.

They never say in Portuguese—as we do—Santa Casa; that word is only applied to the Misericordia; but they say either

Holy Office of the Inquisition, or simply Holy Office. The Inquisition at Goa was held in the Palace do Sabaio, and the Palace of the Viceroys adjoined it till the time of Mascarenhas, 1554, who was too old to get upstairs; it was raised a storey above the ground, unusual in tropical climates until English settled there; and the old Viceroy sought an easier residence.

The personal Staff of the House consisted of three Inquisitors, three Deputies *with* pay, and *without* as many as they pleased, one Promoter, four Notaries, two Procurators of prisoners, as many Reviewers as were needful, one Bailiff, one Judge, four Guards of the secret cells, one Porter, three Solicitors, one Dispenser, three Bailiff's-men, two Doctors, one Surgeon, one Barber, one Chaplain, one Guard of the penitential prison—a Staff of about forty-four regularly employed and paid. Every maritime port had a Visitor, a Writer, a Guard, and an Interpreter. Each City, town, and notable place had a Commissioner, a Secretary, and "Helps," or, as they are called in Inquisition jargon, "Familiars."

They had amongst their list of crimes, for which people were burnt alive, one of which I myself am guilty—Catholics who married with heretics and non-Catholics. A century ago I should have perished at the stake for the same act for which Cardinal Wiseman obtained for me the permission and blessing of Pope Pius IX. He moreover undertook to perform the marriage ceremony himself, but being exceedingly ill in bed on the morning of the wedding, requested his Vicar-General to perform the ceremony in his name, and desired me to consider myself as married by him, which I had greatly set my heart upon. How quickly Civilization, Progress, and Education are marching.

Finally, the first who dared write to the King of Portugal against the Inquisition was the Viceroy of Goa, João da Gama, a descendant of the hero Da Gama. In 1729 he informed His Majesty that the decline of the Portuguese in India was caused by the failure of commerce, as no ships would subject themselves to the chances of such horrors, nor would anyone willingly live under such a rule who could escape to free lands. He proceeded to detail the cruelties committed by the Inquisitors, and he advised the King to make a law that none should be punished except those who made *public* scandals by their crimes, but to interdict all secret prying into private houses and underhand information.

After his time, Captain-General Francisco da Cunha e Menezes wrote about the arrogant pride of the Inquisitors, how they tried to intimidate the Government, how they frightened commerce away, and how they alienated the souls of the Pagans instead of attracting them to religion.

In all Portugal and its dominions there were four centres of Inquisitors: Lisbon the chief, Evora, and Coimbra in Portugal, and the fourth and worst, Goa in the Indies. The only persons *personally* safe were the Archbishop and his Vicar-General (who was a bishop), and the Supreme Authority, who was either a Governor, a Captain-General, or a Viceroy, and, as I have before said, even *they* could be misrepresented to the Court of Lisbon and recalled if they interfered too much.

The Supreme Tribunal met every fifteen days, unless some extra case was in hand. The common tribunal met from eight to eleven and from two to four daily, and in extraordinary cases late in the evening up to ten o'clock. Dellon was first summoned before them 11th January, 1676, and again on 23rd of the same month. They made him swear, kneeling, with his hands on the Gospel, to keep inviolable secrecy for ever on all that passed, and on all that he should see whilst in their hands, which was a period of four years.

One of their principal crimes was to say anything against the Holy Inquisition. It is a pity that they could not peep into the future.

The Rev. Dr. Claude Buchanan, Vice-Provost of the College of Fort William, Calcutta, seems in 1808 to have worried the Inquisitors considerably. He went there for that purpose, and he could afford to do it. He tried to worm out their secrets, insisted on seeing everything, and going into the prisons; the last, however, he did not succeed in. He told them to take the consequences of refusing him anything, and then showed them Dellon's book and other works against themselves which till then they had never heard of.

At first, not knowing who he was, or why he had come, they evidently, by his own account, tried to weave a spider's web around him. They lodged him in a comfortable house with a charming, polite, frank, mild old reverend gentleman, who delighted in religious discourses with his Protestant visitor in the long evenings, and who turned out to be the Chief Inquisitor. But Buchanan's regiment, the 78th, was at Panjim, only eight miles off, which would have blown the Inquisitors into the air if anything had happened, so they were obliged to chafe and restrain themselves. Even a cup of coffee would not have been safe.

Buchanan said that there was Goa Velha, Old Goa, and Goa Nova or Panjim, eight miles distant from each other; that the Viceroy was residing at Panjim, at the river's mouth, amongst the forts, but that the old City, where are the churches and the Inquisition, was deserted by all except the ecclesiastics—the unhealthiness of the climate and the dominion of the priests being the cause. All that was as it is to-day, except that to-day Old Goa is bare of Inquisition, and priests, and even almost of churches, by comparison with what was. In fact it was a Sacerdotal Republic, whose power lasted some three centuries, and whose business it was to persecute heretics and especially preachers of heresy, and from whose sentences and authority there was no appeal; in short, they appear, like Moses and Mohammed, to have carried religion by fire and sword.

Buchanan speaks of "*two hundred* churches, chapels, seminaries, colleges, hospitals, and misericordias, and *two thousand* priests. He said that even the Viceroy had no power over them, and that if the British Governor preferred any complaint to him he could get no redress." In 1808 in all Goa there existed eighty-seven churches known as parochial, thirty-six in the *island* of Goa, twenty-seven in Salsette, and twenty-four at Bardez. Seven extra ones newly began are not included.

Buchanan appears to have been much impressed by the booming of the Cathedral bell, which had tolled so many to their *auto da fé;* and so were we. He was also much affected by the writings of Dellon; he is very eloquent on the riches of the churches and the beauty of the edifices. The Dominicans had ten convents, two actually in Goa and seven outside. The Inquisitor told him that it was believed that the city of Goa has only been preserved by the prayers of St. Francis Xavier, and Buchanan replied that "Xavier was accounted a first-rate man, even amongst the English."

Dom Fray Aleixão de Menezes was the Archbishop who founded the Church and Convent where Buchanan resided. He also remarked that the Augustinians have a white habit for common use and a black one for ceremonies. In Buchanan's time the Inquisition, which had been abolished in 1770, was re-allowed, but under great restrictions, in 1779, and he was there during this period, four years before its final and total abolition. Protestants, however, at that time (see Kirk Sessions) considered it a sin for a Scotchman to live in a Catholic country, and they were advised to abstain from trading with Catholics. An innkeeper might not give shelter to a Catholic, he was anathematized by Scotch clergy, and excommunicated from all salvation.

The old *régime* of the Inquisition was even more palatable to the unhappy sufferers than the modified *régime*, between 1779 and 1808, for at least parents, husbands, wives, and relatives saw their unhappy ones once a year, at the *auto da fé*, and if condemned they assisted at the death; but under the new rule of secret punishment and execution they never knew if the sufferer were alive or dead.

One of the peculiarities of the Holy Office was that after long incarceration, no one ever dared, on coming out, to tell what they had seen, nor to show the terror they felt, nor even any sign of having lived in it; this was called the "Mark of the Holy Office" (Dellon wrote nothing until years after, when he was in free lands and under safe protection); they were so afraid of being indirectly betrayed or decoyed back within their reach, when destruction would be inevitable.

The so-called reforms were made by the famous Pombal, whose memory is equally praised and execrated, according to men, politics, and religion. He was a man who lived before his time, and doubtless had an understanding with the English. His orders date 10th February, 1774, but people do say that they only had the effect *at Goa* of torturing and killing secretly, instead of openly, which I suspect to be the reason that in 1812 no living man could remember to have seen an *auto da fé*. It is like the present abolishing the slave trade. During the process the slaves are only packed closer, and worse treated, and longer and harder driven to reach a safe creek, in order to embark and fly before our slavers at night, and consequently more die; whereas before they had space, and light, air, food, and drink, and reached their destination in comfort; still of course the *end* will be Freedom. *They* should have hanged the Inquisitors. *We* should hang the Slave dealers and Vivisectors.

Buchanan told them that he did not see that it mattered, their boasted humanity of attending to their prisoners' health and comfort, if they only kept them to burn them, as we fatten a beast to kill it, but he wisely added, "If you want to convince me, show me the prisons, because I am writing on them." However, they would not. From the time he showed them Dellon's and others' works, the Inquisitor, in whose house he had been lodging without knowing it, never recovered his calm or frankness. Colonel Adams, of the 78th, when Buchanan went up to old Goa, said, half in joke, half earnest, "If we don't hear from you in three days I shall march the 78th up, and take the Inquisition by assault." Buchanan did forget to write, and at the end of three days the Colonel sent him a note, begging him come down to Panjim every night to sleep in the fortress, a ride of eight miles, "on account of the unhealthiness of Goa."

In 1812 the correspondence between the Courts of Lisbon and Goa, orders liberty of conscience and the total annihilation of the Inquisition, being, as the King said, "so terrifying to all nations, *and so contrary to the true spirit of the Institution, so opposed to the original pious intention of his august and royal Ancestors.*" And this I devoutly believe, that it was instituted for some laudable religious purposes, by holy people, which we shall never know, and was converted by a rapacious, blood-thirsty, intriguing, grasping race, arrogant and bloated with power and riches, never sated, into a means of grasping wealth and assuming the reins of Government, and that it degenerated to lust of blood and cruelty, and to be a huge machine for all petty jealousies and spite, enmities and calumnies, lying and cowardice, and secret prying into families, until God, who had so blessed and raised up Portugal until she forgot herself in her pride of success, used England as His instrument to crush the head of this cruel serpent; for God does love England, and shows it every day. Shall we continue to try to deserve it, or will vice creep into our land too, with our new fashions, and shall we lose our proud and respected pedestal? That is a question we ought sometimes to think of.

The letters go on to relate, that the then reigning prince, being of the same mind as his august grandfather, Don José, who had decided upon its abolition long ago, and *as the motives for its existence* had ceased, he condemns it to utter annihilation, and commands liberty of conscience, without fear of violence, to all races, creeds, and tongues, the same as that which exists amongst the most civilised nations on earth.

Conde de Sarzedas, 20th December, 1812, answered, expressing the great benefit Goa would derive from this clemency, and advised that the enormous quantity of processes and documents might be burnt, as too great scandals would result therefrom, and be handed down to posterity; which was carried out.

Conceive what a pity! What histories they would have furnished to posterity! We have lost about forty thousand *procés* and inexhaustible matter for historians, novelists, and melodramatic writers, showing the manners and customs of those centuries in Portuguese India.

The first Inquisitors of Goa were (1560) the priest Aleixão Dias Falcão and Francisco Marques de Botelho, before-named, and the last at the date of abolition (1812) were Fray Luiz de San José de Ribamar, Fray José das Dores, Gabriel Archanjo de Carvalho, who died at the time of the abolition, and Antonio Gomez Pereira da Silva, who was changed to some other higher office, whilst the two first were pensioned off for life.

There is no question that in every country where the Inquisition was established, it was a cruel scourge on the human race, a sanguinary and ferocious tribunal that could be used in secret by any innocent man's enemy against him, or for envy of talent or riches ; it was a perennial font of incalculable evil, and especially in a conquered land of so many races, tongues, and creeds, who had to be conciliated for religion; and likewise it was ruinous to trade.

It only shows what the Catholic religion is, and that "Hell's gates cannot prevail against Christ's Church," when the Faith could stand unmoved, and flourish, under three centuries of this tribunal of fire and woe, composed of serpents in its own bosom, traitors in the camp; worse than internal civil war, covering its own members with infamy, and which fixed its brutal claw upon this far-off fertile country. It was a monster before which *all* fled,—Godliness, Manliness, and Nature.

Moreover Arabs, Persians, Armenians, Jews, and Indians found the Christian God even more cruel than Bramah or Allah ; they deserted the country and commerce, and fled from low envy, vile cowardice, and calumny, which dealt brutally and safely—like vivisection—not with crime alone, but with the most trivial actions of their home life. Sufficed a little success in an enterprise, a few more thousands, a gallant action winning praise, a rise in the social scale, public esteem for a good work done,—anything that raised a man above his fellows was quite enough.

It is, perhaps, the same now, as far as evil tongues can wag, and will always be, and people wince with moral pain; but it breaks no bones, scorches no skin, and the object of envy may still breathe fresh air and light, and enjoy life and liberty, though a few *soi-disant* friends may fall away. Nay, the fact of being of a different race, tongue, and creed, a variance of opinion, family rivalries, an unhappy love, a little spite or jealousy,—all was turned to account, all was of use to denounce one's enemy on a religious ground. It was enough for a "Familiar" to open his mouth to make people lose their judgment and reason.

A story is quoted of a mother of five children whose youngest was eight years old. The mother was the victim of a joke amongst the gay "Familiars," who told her she would be burnt at the stake. She believed it, lost her head, and threw herself out of the window. It is said that abortion, from fear, always took place, if a woman, when *enceinte*, was arrested. There are worse things handed down, but I cannot write about them.

All the few writers upon this subject have depicted the torments and iniquities of Goa. Lord Talbot, of Malahide, believes them to have been beaten by Nuremberg—at least, he says he never saw anywhere such a variety of tortures, or so horrible, as those shown in the Museum there. I have had a sight of all the documents existing, exclusively Goanese, by the present descendants of the Inquisitors, and the authorities of that time.

In Captain Marryat's "Phantom Ship, The Flying Dutchman," he gives three chapters on Goa, than which a better description cannot be read. It correctly describes the great Viceroyalty in the middle of the seventeenth century, when its glory began to fade. His account of the Inquisition taken entirely from Dellon, is quite correct. I insert a short but beautiful, as well as truthful bit of Marryat's :—

It was a bright morning when the Portuguese vessel on which Amine was on board entered into the bay and roadstead of Goa. Goa was then at its zenith,—a proud, luxurious, superb, wealthy city—the capital of the East—a city of palaces whose viceroy reigned supreme. As they approached the river, the two mouths of which form the island upon which Goa is built, the passengers were all on deck; and the Portuguese captain, who had often been there, pointed out to Amine the most remarkable buildings. When they had passed the forts, they entered the river, the whole line of whose banks was covered with the country seats of the nobility and hidalgos—splendid buildings embosomed in groves of orange-trees, whose perfume scented the air.

"There, signora, is the country palace of the viceroy," said the captain, pointing to a building which covered nearly three acres of ground.

The ship sailed on until they arrived nearly abreast of the town, when Amine's eyes were directed to the lofty spires of the churches, and other public edifices; for Amine had seen but little of cities during her life, as may be perceived when her history is recollected.

"That is the Jesuits' church, with their establishment," said the captain, pointing to a magnificent pile. "In the church now opening upon us lie the canonised bones of the celebrated Saint Francisco, who sacrificed his life in his zeal for the propagation of the Gospel in these countries."

"I have heard of him from Father Mathias," replied Amine; "but what building is that?"

"The Augustine convent; and the other, to the right, is the Dominican."

"Splendid, indeed!" observed Amine.

"The building you see now, on the waterside, is the viceroy's palace; that to the right, again, is the convent of the barefooted Carmelites; yon lofty spire is the cathedral of St. Catharine; and that beautiful and light piece of architecture is the church of our Lady of Pity. You observe there a building with a dome, rising behind the viceroy's palace?"

"I do," replied Amine.

"That is the Holy Inquisition."

Although Amine had heard Philip speak of the Inquisition, she knew little about its properties; but a sudden tremor passed through her frame as the name was mentioned, which she could not herself account for.

"Now we open upon the viceroy's palace, and you perceive what a beautiful building it is," continued the captain. * *

* * * * * Amine went on shore with Father Mathias; she refused the palanquin which had been prepared for her, and walked up to the convent. They landed between the Custom-house and the viceroy's palace, passed through the large square behind it, and then went up the Strada Diretta, or straight street, which led up to the Church of Pity, near to which the convent is situated. This street is the finest in Goa, and is called Strada Diretta from the singular fact that almost all the streets in Goa are quadrants or segments of circles. Amine was astonished. The houses were of stone, lofty and massive; at each story was thrown out a balcony of marble, elaborately carved, and over each door were the arms of the nobility, or hidalgos, to whom the houses belonged. The square behind the palace and the wide streets were filled with living beings; elephants with gorgeous trappings; led or mounted horses in superb housings; palanquins, carried by natives in splendid liveries; running footmen; cyces (native grooms); every variety of nation, from the proud Portuguese to the half-covered native; Mussulmans, Arabs, Hindús, Armenians; officers and soldiers in their uniforms, all crowded and thronged together,—all was bustle and motion. Such was the wealth, the splendour, and luxury of the proud city of Goa,—the Empress of the East at the time we are now describing.

I now extract the pith of Dellon's narrative:—

The cells and dungeons, numbering about two hundred, lay in the rear, each with double doors opening upon one of the two long galleries, where the watchful keepers could overhear every word. They were about ten feet square, and the most comfortable admitted the goodly air and light, forbidden fare to the others. The inmates were kept separate; this rule was broken only when prolonged solitude appeared likely to endanger reason or life. Perpetual silence was enjoined, and strictly kept; those who lamented, or wept, or even prayed aloud, were forced by blows to hold their peace. The dreadful maddening stillness was broken only by the cries and shrieks of the tortured, which rang through the whole length of the galleries, terrifying those who in solitude and darkness lay expecting the same fate. As regards food they were well treated, and care was taken to prevent them suffering from the indigestion produced by want of exercise. Surgical attendance was also allowed; but no priests were admitted, except for confession, unless on particular and especial occasions. Thus the consolations of religion, and the sacraments of Eucharist and Extreme Unction, were denied. Those who died in confinement, whether proved guilty or not, were buried without ceremony, and tried subsequently; in case of sentence being passed, its execution took place upon their disinterred bones. This was another horror to a superstitious age, and seems intended to make the wretches regard death with redoubled fear.

The Grand Inquisitor and his Lieutenant were invariably Dominicans,—those Zouaves of the Catholic Church: in their examinations and judgments they were assisted by the Deputies of the Holy Office, a large body chosen from the other religious orders, but attending only on summons. There were also officials called Familiars of the Inquisition, a Procureur, a Public Accuser, and others whose duty it was to export, *à l'index*, all books not approved of. The lawyers had a bad name; they were charged with pleading the prisoners' causes, but their chief business and interest was to worm out secrets and to betray their victims. The highest nobles held it an honour as well as a security to be enrolled among these Famuli; and thus there was in society a *haute police* which brought every careless word or jest to the ears of the Holy Office. A summons was never opposed; in such cases the whole population would have risen to enforce it.

The first question put to the newly-arrested was concerning his property. He was ordered to declare on oath everything he was worth, being informed that mental reservation would incur the wrath of the Inquisition; and that, even if proved innocent of the special charges, he would be liable to arrest and punishment for perjury. The reason for this procedure was evident. If the accused confessed his crime he was usually allowed, after a long purgation, to go free, but he left all his property behind him.

In the procedure of the Court we find that *summum jus* which is proverbially *summa injuria*. While two witnesses justified an arrest, seven were required for convicting a prisoner; but the witnesses being subject to torture, often swore away other lives to save their own; besides which, they were never confronted with the accused. The crimes chiefly noticed were—in Europe, sorcery, heresy, blasphemy, and what was called Judaism; in India, accusations of magic were most common, arising from the customs and ceremonies of the Hindús. These people, like the hosts of African slaves, were often induced to profess Christianity, but they lost by the change. If baptized, they were subject to the punishment of fire on relapse; but those who refused were chastised only by flogging, imprisonment, or the galleys.

The crime of Judaism, so frequent in Spain and Portugal, arose with the expulsion of the Jews by the bigoted and short-sighted Ferdinand and Isabella of Castile. Those who embraced Christianity, or who appeared to do so, were called New Christians, as opposed to Old Christians; and the people, with the truth of instinct, despised them and suspected them. After a time the two were intermingled by marriage; but this was always a disgrace to old and noble families, and the descendants were taunted as having a taint of *new* blood. They lost caste, and were at the mercy of the Holy Office whenever denounced for Judaism, that is, for returning to the ceremonies of Moses and the old practices, such as keeping the Passover, and crucifying a cock at Easter. Thus the Catholic Church opposed what appears to be the especial tendency of the Protestant or so-called Reformed sects, which are remarkable for their reversion to Hebraism.

An accusation of Judaism worked as follows:—A New Christian was arrested by the Inquisition, and was ordered to make declaration of his property; this, if strong in innocence, and expecting a speedy release, he readily did. But hardly had the cell-door closed upon him, than all his goods were sold by public auction, it being well understood that they would never be restored. After imprisonment for months he was summoned to the Hall of Judgment, and asked if he knew the reason of his confinement; and he was earnestly advised to confess, and to conceal nothing, this being the only way to liberty. He declared his innocence, and being sent for several times, persisted in it. But the *auto da fé*—the public execution of the condemned which took place every three or four years—was approaching. The Public Accuser then came forward, and stated that a number of witnesses had charged the prisoner with Judaism. If he acknowledged his guilt, he was condemned to the fire; if he maintained his innocence, he was sentenced by *convicto in votivo*,—found guilty without confessing guilt. After this he was followed to his cell; exhorted, and promised pardon if he would make a clean breast of it; and these appeals continued till the eve of execution. Often the wretch, terrified by the horrors which awaited him, confessed the crime which he had not committed, little thinking that thereby he had entangled himself without hope of escape. It was important to the Inquisition that such confession be made; the act, with the signature affixed, being publicly read, proved to the world that the Holy Office was impartial and just, and even merciful, as it pardoned those who had been proved guilty. But whether the accused owned his sin, or died asserting his innocence, in either case his property was confiscated.

Upon a confession of Judaism, the victim would be told, "You have acknowledged observing the Laws of Moses. These ceremonies are never performed alone; you cannot have eaten the Paschal lamb alone; tell us the names of those present, or you go to the stake!" Thus the wretch has accused himself in vain, and if he would save his life he must as falsely accuse others,—of course, his friends and acquaintances, and often his family and his relations. He was now ready for destruction, and he was returned to his dungeon without the least idea of what his fate was to be,—a terrible uncertainty, which lasted till the morning of his execution.

When the Act of Faith was to take place, the jailers, shortly after midnight, led their charges from the several dungeons into a large, dimly-lighted hall, where all the victims were gathered together in an agony of suspense, worse than the agony of death. Here the crowd, dressed in the same black and white, received their wax candles, about five feet long, and were ordered to put on over their dresses the *sanbenitos*, a paper mitre, and the *samarias* (a sort of long scapular) with the reversed flames, showing they were not to suffer. In another, and a similar hall, the women were exposed to the same doubt, fear, and terror. But there was a third chamber, smaller than these two, reserved for the *relaxed*,—such was the mild term, denoting death at the stake. Each was attended by his confessor; and presently the head jailer appeared with the *samarias* whose flames were turned upwards. The dresses were loose *blouses* of grey stuff; and at the lower part, before and behind, was the likeness of the wearer, the face only resting on a burning faggot surrounded by flames and demons, and inscribed below with the crime for which he was to suffer. Sugar-loaf caps, also powdered with flames, were put on their heads, like stiff paper mitres.

The procession has been described in "Gil Blas," and many other books. In Goa it took about two hours, promenading every important street, and the feet of the accused suffered severely from the hard roads. At last they reached the Cathedral, which was hung with black cloth, and lighted by thousands of tapers. On one side was a throne for the Grand Inquisitor, on the other a raised *estrade* for the Viceroy and his staff. The nave had benches for the prisoners and their godfathers, the other members of the procession falling off right and left to the aisles, and there mingling with the other spectators. As the prisoners entered the Cathedral they were led to their seats, the least guilty sitting nearest the altar. A Dominican monk then preached the sermon, which illustrated the tender mercies, the paternal love of the Holy Office. It was compared with the Ark of Noah, but with this difference (highly in favour of the Inquisition), that whereas all the animals walked out of the former after the Deluge no better than they walked in, those who had entered the Santa Casa with the hearts of great wolves came out mild and patient as lambs. The Public Accuser then mounted the pulpit, and read out the crimes of the condemned, with the punishments attached to them. Each prisoner, as his sentence was passed, was brought forward by the officers, and placed to hear it, standing with the lighted candle in his hand. Those who were spared were sprinkled with holy water, the Grand Inquisitor and other religious putting on their priestly robes to handle the asperges; thus was removed the ban of excommunication under which they had fallen.

When this part of the ceremony ended, the relaxed in the flesh, and the effigies of those who had escaped by death, were brought up one by one to hear their sentences, which all concluded with the same formula: "The Holy Office found it impossible to pardon them, on account of the hardness of their hearts and the enormity of their crimes. With great sorrow it handed them over to the temporal arm to undergo the last penalty of the law, exhorting the authorities at the same time to show clemency and mercy to the unhappy wretches, and if they must suffer death, *that at all events it might be without the spilling of blood.*"

Then followed the last tragical scene. The accused, who had been spared, were led back by their godfathers (*padrinhos*) to the Casa Santa, and those who had been condemned, supported by the Familiars, were taken down to the large open space on the river-bank, to the left of the Custom-house. Here, as in the Cathedral, were raised seats for the Grand Inquisitor and for the Viceroy, who in state headed the procession, followed by an immense concourse of people. The executioners were ready at the stakes, to which the wretches were chained, and surrounded by faggots and piles of wood. The head executioner then asked the confessors whether the culprits died in the true faith. If answered in the affirmative, a rope was passed round their necks and twisted to the stake, so that they were garroted before the fire was lit. The others were burnt quick, and the only mercy was throwing on the pile a heap of wet straw, which emitted a dense smoke before it burst into flames.

Our last day came, and Dr. Da Gama gave us a breakfast. We were ten at table, native and European. He owned the coolest, largest, airiest house and rooms in Goa, and it looked upon a garden full of flowers, the only one. We had every variety of native food and fruit in abundance, good cool air and water, the latter produced by hanging the *chattis** in the window, clothed with wet hay or grass. We had much speechifying after dinner, as is the Portuguese custom, and a little music. After breakfast I paid a farewell visit to my Bishop (Meurin) of Bombay, and to the Archbishop of Goa (Monsignor Omello), an excellent man, who denies himself even necessaries, to give all to the poor.

In the evening Mr. Major took us an excursion in his boat to Cazalem. We coasted along for an hour and sang glees under a fine moon accompanied by a heavy swell. We were carried ashore through the surf on natives' shoulders, and were hailed first by the watch dogs and then by the inmates, who did not expect us; they were assembled in a verandah, playing cards by the light of torches. We passed a merry evening, after which one of the party, Dr. Torres, insisted on our going back in his private carriage. Up to this time, we had not been aware that there was any other vehicle or horse than ours, and when we saw his (the only other one) we found it was an exact pendant to our own. The seat gave way, and we sat on the edges. The horse walked all the way, and was led by the coachman, and even so fell down twice, which by this time mine would not have done.

It only remains for me now to relate how one leaves Goa. We had waited four days idly and anxiously for a steamer which would repass to Bombay. They are due once a fortnight, but this one was long past her time. On the morning of our departure

* Earthen water-bottles.

we had a telegram to say, "The steamer will pass Goa at midnight." Telegrams are the only sign of civilisation here. We started in a large open boat with Mr. Major and his secretary, four men to row and one to steer. We rowed down the river and then the bay for three hours against wind and tide, bow on to heavy rollers, and at last reached the mouth of the bay, where is the fort. We remained bobbing about in the open sea in the trough of the great waves for a considerable time. A violent storm of rain, thunder, and lightning came on, and Mr. Major proposed we should put back to the fort at the entrance of the bay and take shelter under some arches, which we did. Then we went to sleep, leaving the secretary and the boat-wálá to watch for the steamer.

At 1.30 I was awoke by the sound of a gun booming across the water. I sprang up and aroused the others, but we could see no lights in the storm, and returned to sleep. An officer passed out of the fort, and I fancied he said to another man that he was the Government officer, and that the ship was in, but he looked curiously at us and passed on. Presently I felt more fidgety, and leaving the others went to the water's edge, and making a trumpet of my hands called to the secretary, who answered back, "That the ship had been laying to three-quarters of an hour, and that we should have come off when the gun fired."

People become so lazy and indifferent in this climate that he had not let us know that before, until he saw me anxious, although he was left there for that purpose, albeit he was an excellent and even sharp youth for Goa. If we had not happened to have the mails and the agent with us, the ship would have gone on without us. We should have lost our passage to Europe, and in the next ship must have encountered in the Indian ocean the monsoon; and, worst of all, had to return for another fortnight to Goa, which we were heartily tired of and knew by heart, only to renew the same scene a fortnight hence.

After a few moments' delay we were under weigh again and out to sea, and by-and-by saw the lights of the steamer, which looked about three miles off. Knowing the independence of these captains, and the monopoly, and the futility of complaints, I trembled lest she should put out further to sea as soon as the Government officer left her; and determined that no effort of mine should be spared to prevent it.

My husband slept, or pretended to sleep. Mr. Major really slept, but I managed adroitly to be awkward with a boat-hook, and occasionally to prick his shins. The secretary good-naturedly stood up and waved a lamp on a pole, which they might see through the storm, and I urged the boat-wálás with perpetual promises of "Bakshish." Everybody except myself was behaving with Oriental calm and leaving it to Kismet.

At last I began to quarrel with our kind host, who had been during the whole evening blowing up the boat-wálás because the boat was dirty, making them bale out the horrid-smelling bilge water, pouring in clean water and baling out till all was right, and now we wanted his lungs he was asleep and as good as gold. "Can't you shout 'Mails?'" I cried to him as we got nearer. "They might hear you. You can shout loud enough when nobody wants you."

At last, after an hour of anxiety, we reached the ship, and heavy seas kept washing us away from the ladder; no one had the energy to hold on to the rope or take the boat-hook to keep us to her, so at last I did it myself, my husband laughing all the while at their supineness, and at my making myself so disagreeably officious and energetic, but it was absolutely necessary. An English sailor who, I suppose, sees this bad weather once a fortnight threw me the rope. "Thanks," I said, as I took advantage of an enormous wave to spring on to the ladder, "I'm the only man in the boat to-night." All came on board with us, and we had a parting stirrup-cup and said farewell; and often now my good host and his wife laugh over it together, and write to me, "the only man in the boat."

CHAPTER XIX.

A PEEP INTO THE FUTURE OF NOTRH-WESTERN INDIA.

I DO not say anything about Sind, because Captain Burton has already published two volumes on this expedition—"Sind Revisited;" but I would fain enter a vehement protest against the spirit and the manner in which the relative positions of Great Britain and Russia are treated by Englishmen, and I hope to show the immense detriment to which this treatment has subjected, and still subjects, our prestige and our good name.

We were lately asked by an educated native of Bombay if the Russians are not ready to throw fifty lakhs of men—five hundred thousand bayonets!—upon British India; and not a few of the lower classes, Mussulmans all, had told me that the "Moskoff" is about to attack the Panjáb.

Men now, just middle age, whose youth saw the virulent attack of Russophobia which in 1838-39 led to the Afghan War, the severest shake, next to the Sepoy Mutiny, which our Indian Empire has ever endured, find it difficult, with the proverbial difficulty of mastering new ideas after the tenth lustre, to appreciate the complete change in the positions of the two great rival Powers. As early as 1791 Russia prepared to invade India from Orenburg, *viâ* Ashur, Ata, and Asterabad, "the line of least resistance," Meshhed, Herat, and Kandahar.

Let us suppose that in 1835 she had taken heart of grace and resolved to follow in the footsteps of Nadir Shah. The road to Delhi lay completely open to her. She had only to point to India, the "traditional plunder-ground of Central Asia," and all the rugged robber-hordes, from the Sutlej to the mouths of the Euphrates, would have rushed to the "loot" like wolves and

ALLIGATORS NEAR KÁRÁCHÍ' (SIND).

vultures to the quarry, and Persia was only waiting to see the offensive action taken. Afghanistan was ever ready to renew the pleasant scenes of Paniput. The whole line of the Indus, Mooltan, Bahawulpore, and Sind, under the Talpur Amirs, would have hurried to the flank attack. The direct line lay through the dominions of our good friend and bitterest enemy, Runjeet Singh, whose gallant heart was broken by the easy successes of the British in Afghanistan, where he flattered himself they had fallen into his trap. With the Punjab would have sided Cashmere, Nepaul, and even Bhootan; in fact, the whole region south, and possibly north, of the Himalayan range.

But Russia did not take the opportunity, which means she had other things to do; and that cautious, far-seeing Power saw no advantage in a raid like the "Chapáo," of Nadir Shah, now the conditions of our frontier are completely changed. From the modest line of the Sutlej and the great North-Western Desert we have occupied a thousand miles of the Indus frontier, extending from Peshawur to the sea; the Punjab is ours; Cashmere, Nepaul, and Bhootan exist on sufferance; they may be ours at any moment we please.

Persia might still join Russia, but we have operated more than once with fatal effect upon her vulnerable heel, the Gulf; her strength has been wasted by famine; her exchequer is empty; and the chivalry of the Desert, her Iliyát or Bedawin, have been crushed by the contact of a so-called Regular Army. The Afghans would still flock to enrol under the banners of the North, but they would be met by their hereditary foe, the Sikh. How secure we are upon this point may be judged by the way in which the military authorities have dismantled the whole Indian fortress. Our native army has been converted into an irregular machine, which could not meet even the Abyssinians without sending for reinforcements of officers to Madras and Calcutta.

The hare-hearted Sepoy—undoubtedly the worst soldier in Asia—has been reduced to eight European officers per regiment, with all the combatants mounted, so as to secure their being swept away by the first fire.

We have no army in England beyond what is required for police purposes; nor shall we have one until the Britons, still happily separated from the total world, determine, by a general onscription, to march with the rest of Europe, and to exchange a small standing army for a national force. And whilst we literally hold India with eighty thousand white faces, we freely allow the Native Powers to levy and to drill troops in numbers exceeding our own. Evidently our authorities are very sure of their affair. Possibly, they rely upon the fact that the game is no longer worth the candle; that India, that golden land, has been squeezed till no more is to be got out of her. "Poor India, every hair of her head is numbered!" said a mercantile traveller when I explained to him the figures on the date trees; and, certainly, between the Abkari (excise) and the salt-tax, we have thoroughly emptied the pockets of the breechless population.

But, happily, things are gradually getting to the worst, and we may fairly hope that they will surely mend. Presently we shall take a lesson from Russia, who manages her trans-Caucasian Provinces by a mixture of foreign and native *employés*. Nothing more offends the patriotic Russian than to doubt that he is wholly European; and yet to the dash of Asiatic blood he owes many of his highest national gifts,—his facility in acquiring languages; his devotion to his Emperors, the "Shadows of Bog upon Earth;" his subtle and persistent policy; his love of conquest and military glory; and his fatalistic calmness under fire.

We shall remedy the chronic discontent of a pauper population by opening up new sources of wealth in reproductive works, in manufactures and mines. At present India is administered for the benefit of England, or rather, of the English trading classes, who must supply the public offices with paper and sealing-wax; and the soldiers and sepoys with broadcloth and ducks. The national religion of England will become the State Church in India, and we shall cease to foster and encourage, by a fatuous and absurd toleration, the fanaticism of Pagan idolatry. We shall borrow from Russia another lesson of economy, by substituting military law and rule for the pseudo-constitutionalism with which we, like Portugal, have afflicted India: we shall relieve our great colony, or rather conquest, of such an incubus as Presidency Governors and Commanders-in-Chief; members of Council and Chief Justices. We shall reserve High Courts and similar preserves for lawyers' game; but we shall confine them to the various capitals, where wealthy natives may play at law, and ruin themselves *à discretion.*

With this money, now profligately wasted upon civil establishments, we shall maintain an efficient native army, which will deliver us from the feeble politic of "purpose and no power." At home a general conscription, or a revival of the Militia Act, will give us a force, between actives and reserves, of two million of men. The first serious "shake" in the East or the West will show us that our national existence depends upon this measure, or rather, that the alternative will be subsiding into the position of Belgium and Holland. And finally, when Russia begins her railway from Tabriz to Teheran and Baghdad, we shall check her by the Euphrates Valley Line, at present our principal Colonial want. And thus the "Ikbal," or good fortune, which apparently departed with the defunct East India Company, will be inherited by the Home Rule.

The Government of the Company, it must be remembered, was aristocratic,—an aristocracy of bales and barrels if you please, but still, to a certain extent, a rule of honour. Its successor acts upon the latest and most modern rules of political economy; it buys its labour in the cheapest market, and it demands only a fair day and a half's work for a fair day's wage. It notably borrowed from China its system of competitive examinations, which examine all least worth examining,—that is the memory and the receptivity, not the moral and physical value of its Mandarins. Some day, perhaps, we shall see a return of the well-abused system of patronage, whose evils can so easily be checked by the administration of proper tests, and by provisional appointments to be confirmed only after a sufficient period of practical trial.

To an Englishman, who has at heart the honour and interests of his native land, nothing is more offensive than the low standing taken by our writers in treating of the Central Asian Question, and the tone of despondency which contrasts so disparagingly with the high grounds assumed by the Russians. England accepted as a kind of boon the creation of a neutral zone,—a string of independent semi-barbarian States, separating the frontiers of the two great Asiatic Powers. Russia, with the moderation engendered by her intense vigour and vitality, throws this sop to Cerberus, perfectly certain that the measure is merely temporary, whilst the powerful war party which looks upon the Cesarewitch as its head, openly expresses its scorn and disgust. We are told by our Pundits that "all we want is rest—rest from foreign wars, rest from political disturbance." We want nothing of the kind: our only want is, *de l'audace, de l'audace, et toujours de l'audace.*

We are assured that we are conservative, not aggressive; whereas our rivals are aggressive, not conservative; in other words, that they are young and active and strong, while we are old and stiff and weak. We are advised to push forward, because any check upon our frontier would raise a host of enemies in our troubled rear,—which means that our position in India is more or less precarious. We are informed in the same breath that Russia has certainly not contemplated anything like an invasion of India; and yet we are advised to take the strongest steps in order to secure ourselves from invasion.

A curious comment, by the way, upon the first dictum is the tone of the young Grand Duke Nicholas, letters published by Miss Fanny Lear, in which he considers an appointment to the Caucasus as the first step of a Russian march upon India. Again, we read the alarming sentence, "If there was danger to British India from the attitude and possible designs of Russia twenty-eight years ago, that danger must be increased a hundredfold at the present day." Furthermore, we are threatened with the "moral leverage" which Russia, by menacing India, can bring to bear upon us in Europe; and with the chronic conflagration which would result from the mere contiguity of a rival European Power; in other words, we are told that Russia can make India too hot to hold us,—as if we could not make, by means of China, Turkestan too hot to hold Russia. Her troops are ever moving on resistless as fate, whilst we are thoroughly alarmed by their advance: that is, Russia swoops like the hawk, whilst we cower like the pigeon.

Hence the perpetual reports of new invasion rontes from the North which fill our Press, the old Buroghil Pass being the latest "fad." And hence the trembling anxiety with which the Anglo-Indian eye was fixed upon the late Amirel-Muminin, Ya'akub Khan of Kashgar, as if a struggling little Moslem Prince, who would assuredly be crushed between the rival Colossi, Russia and China, held the destinies of British India in his weakling hand. Hence the exaggerated importance attached to what is called the "Indian situation," to the "Russian glacis" on the north-east of Persia, and to the strategic approach from the south-eastern corner of Persia, "which is so stealthily but steadily progressing." And hence finally, the forcible feeble stand which we are making about the independence of villainous Bokhara, and the inviolability of pauper Merv,—a village which once numbered a million of souls.

This tone of excited despondency, this symptom of weakness and violence, have travelled far, and have already done great damage to our name. It has thoroughly complicated our relations with Afghanistan. As may be proved by any old map, that turbulent land of robber chiefs has gained enormously, both in territory and in population, by our intervention. Yet Shere Ali Khan sulks and pouts because Lord Lawrence acknowledged his elder brother, the friendly Afzul Khan; because Lord Mayo did not anticipate his every wish, and because Lord Northbrook did not pay his subsidy—"tribute" I would rather call it—with all the regularity he desired. Hence he refused to receive the Kashgar Mission, under pretext of being unable to protect the members,—"Their blood be upon their own heads if they come to Cabul!" Hence he will admit no English resident Agent; and the native *Aakil i-Sarkar-i-Wngriz* is hardly permitted to address him in Durbar. The fact is, this miserable Highland Chief believes, and has been taught by us to believe, that he holds "the road to the English." He is convinced that he has only to offer aid to the Russians in order to drive us out of India. That he hates us we know: during the Sepoy Mutiny he urged in vain his wise old father, Dost Mohammed, to invade the Panjáb, a measure deprecated by Afzul Khan. That he despises us we cannot fail to see; and not less can we fail to feel that our policy has given him a right to despise us.*

What, then, should we do in this matter? The "repose of Strength" is liable to be interpreted by the Oriental as supineness; moderation means fear; and "compromise," the basis of public and private life in England, has no synonym in the East. *De l'audace*, etc., is the only rule of conduct in the Afghan hills. At the first opportunity—and any day may bring one—we should break openly with Shere Ali;—tread boldly upon the coat-tail which he is trailing for a fight; withdraw that phantom of a Native Agent, and offer the subsidy, a lakh *per mensem*, to the successor who promises us his friendship and his confidence. The latter measure has been characterized as a premium on rebellion. Sit, so be it!

We have nothing to fear from the Afghan chief, most of whose snbjects would right willingly exchange his barbarous sway for our civilized rnle. We have nothing to hope from him; he would take, Afghan-like, our money with one hand, and stab us with the other. Here, if anywhere, is the time and place to assume the tone and position of a "dominant race." We have talked too long and too loudly about "our fellow-subjects in India" and our "Afghan allies;" let us now change the terms for "conquered races" here, and for "paid partizans" there.

Curious to say, the latest form of Russophobia was developed by our grand national blunder, the great artillery-duel in the corner of the Black Sea, which history will call the "Crimean War." After nearly incurring national bankruptcy by our rabid hostility to Napoleon I., we were cozened by Napoleon III. into an alliance, whose sole object was to give his house a status amongst the old and aristocratic dynasties of Europe. But to do the latter justice, he proposed to take upon himself the chief onus of the campaign.

It was Lord Palmerston—the statesman who saddled us with the Fenian embroglio; the man who, believing about as much as

* All this was written two years ago, before the present Afghan war began.

Epicurus, never missed a Sunday morning service; the Irishman who knew the English public better than it knew itself—that rejected the Frenchman's offer to send the army, whilst England supplied the fleet. Thus, upon the obsolete principle that one Englishman can beat three *Mossoos or Johnny Crapauds*, we were allowed to contribute a mere contingent. Thus we were condemned to play, as is commonly said, second fiddle, without the least hope of rising in the world; whilst the want of ability amongst our superior officers, the normal English deficiency of organization, and a few miserable blunders, glorious like the Balaclava charge, and inglorious like the run from the Mamelon, duly printed abroad throughout the civilized world, combined to form an ample "vengeance for Waterloo."

The world has not yet learned that we entered half-hearted into that war; that we were thoroughly ashamed of our Turkish allies and their cause; that many of our leading statesmen determined upon not abasing Russia; that Cronstadt was allowed to exclude us from St. Petersburgh, when the late Captain Cole's turret-ship would have set the fortress at defiance; that Kars was given over to starvation because the Russians refused to make peace without a set-off for the southern half of Sebastopol, evacuated after a resistance of eighteen months; that Napoleon insisted upon coming to terms with Russia, because his Crimean army was mutinous, and he had won his point; and lastly, that our allies, ignoble jealousy confined us to a game at long bowls in the Crimea, when, with the assistance of the Turks, the Kurds, and the Persians, we might easily have driven Russia once more behind and beyond the Caucasus.

All this, and more, we have been told by the late Lord Strangford, in the two volumes of his pleasant works published some years ago by the Viscountess, whose late gigantic charitable undertakings in Bulgaria must be the envy and admiration of every woman. But, in determining that Russia had gained by the war as much as Great Britain lost, my clever friend was not so happy as in the rest of his judgments; in fact, he neglected one great item in the account which determined the balance in our favour. The Crimean War prevented the march of the Russian empire southwards,—the general rule of northern conquest. It compelled her to go and grow eastward.

This necessity of growth in the Northern Giant is treated by our writers with a luxury of explanation. It is attributed to a steadfast political purpose; to the preponderating impulse of irresponsible military ambition thirsting for distinction; to a traditional creed of the Empire, which aims at augmented power in Europe through extension in Asia; to obeying the natural law of increase, and to all these causes combined.

For the anthropologist, one amply suffices. The body politic, like the individual, must grow to attain full development; and "earth-hunger," as it is called, characterizes all young peoples in the lusty prime of life. At present the only great conquering races are the Slav, especially Russia, and the English, especially the Anglo-Americans. The former conquer by invasion, the latter by occupation and colonization.

Why Great Britain, at the present moment of her history, has turned her sword into a ploughshare, is apparently little understood by the mass of foreign writers. The truth is, we are still in a period of reaction. During the first quarter of the present century we meddled with—and often, it must be confessed, we muddled—European affairs which least concerned an insular people.

About 1850 the counter-action set in with peculiar violence. Lord Palmerston was rebuked by the Crown for his officious interference in Continental matters. Mr. Cobden was at the summit of his fame. The Great Exhibition of 1851 was to inaugurate the reign of peace and goodwill amongst men, and international commerce was to cement the union of the Pan-European family. The Frenchman would never invade us: if he attempted so obsolete a step, our touching and charitable reception of him would melt the heart of the bearded Zouave, and the *Sapeur* to whom nothing is sacred. The army should be turned into a body of navvies; the navy was to be converted into police ships and emigrant ships. Posterity will marvel at this peace mania, and perhaps will sneer at the part which the peacemakers took in precipitating the Russian war of 1853. It reads like a tale of Bedlam, but it is not the less true; the secondary symptoms of the dread malady still ferment in the national constitution, and possibly we may not escape without tertiaries. But the perfect cure must come at last.

About 1863, when Russia had recovered from the fatigues of the Crimean campaign, her "manifest destiny" began to show itself in what we vaguely term "Central Asia." It is not my purpose to trace her steps: England, and especially India, looked on uneasily, although a "large portion of the thinking public, including the optimist class of Anglo-Indian politicians to a man, declared in favour of the Russian advance." And no wonder. The actual civilization of the Russian Empire may not yet be of the highest order, yet it is long centuries in advance of the reckless barbarism which characterizes the Great Horde and the Usbeg Khanats. Whilst annexing the barren steppes, the eastern shores of the Caspian, the lands about the Aral and the noble valleys of the Oxus and the Jaxartes, Russia's mission was *terram aperire gentibus*. She opened military roads, and proposed railways; she built forts and meditated canals. She rendered the country passable to the traveller and the trader: the European had no longer to fear being plundered, or reduced to slavery, or being foully murdered. She enlisted sundry marauding tribes; she made them disciplined soldiers and peaceful subjects; whilst many "bad neighbours" were converted by example into "good neighbours."

Again, the dash of Eastern blood in the veins of Russia enabled her to curb the fanatic spirit of her new lieges. Her enemies had predicted that she had disturbed a hornet's nest; that her lines were now cast in unpleasant places, amongst the most violent and bigoted of Mohammedan races. Even our latest writers dwell upon the prospects of an anti-Russian Jehad, or Holy War.

But Russia is the only European Power which can successfully abate the evil; and we must seek the reason of her success in her despotic rule,—the only regimen which the Oriental understands. She knows how to handle her Sáyyids and her Súfis; she "grasps her nettle," and this is the only treatment to which the ecclesiastical throat—priest or parson, Mullah or Brahmin—unconditionally submits.

We, on the contrary, with our excess of toleration and *penchant* for liberty, too often degenerating into licence, make the natives subjected to our rule far more bigoted than they were when we first conquered them. Formerly the Hindú would allow the "Mlenchha" to drink out of his metal pot, which only required scouring to become pure once more; now he pours the water into a doubled leaf, or into the European's hand. Twenty-five years ago, when entering the mosques or mausolea, we removed our hats and wore our boots; now the Moslems insist upon our conforming to a practice which, in our case, means degradation. At Jeddah, the guardians of Eve's Tomb only laugh when a terrier runs in and out of the doors; after a few years of British rule they would object to admitting, not only the terrier, but the terrier's master. In her early relations with Persia, the Russian was as fanatical as the Persian, till the murder of an envoy taught him the more prudent way of dealing with Moslems. We have notably failed in this matter, and I should be sorry to see the experiment tried elsewhere.

Some six years after Russia's first decided move eastwards (1869) she abandoned the direct Persian line, and adopted the new plan of turning her friend's flank by annexing the Bulkan or Krasnovdsk Bay, and exploring the northern valley of the Atrek river, the road popularly known as the "Atok," or hill-skirt. Thereupon the alarmist openly denounced the annexation of the eastern coast of the Caspian, and the subjugation of the Turkomans, as a "violation of treaty." The good sense of the public refused to be scared. What sympathy, indeed, could England have with wretched Khiva, whose main industry was kidnapping Russians and enslaving Persians? What with hateful Bokhara, the very focus and head-quarters of Islamitic fanaticism; the city of barbarians, whose murderous chief, Nasr Allah, had foully put to death Stoddart and Conolly? Could we forget that, unable to reach this double-dyed assassin, despite the proverbial length of her arm, England was compelled to leave the slaughter of her envoys unavenged,—to sit down and cry, like an impotent crone?

Again, the thinking public saw no objection to the two great

Powers, Russia and England, dividing between them the Empire of the East. Not a few of us were put to shame by the importance attached to establishing a craven "neutral zone" of independent Native States. The "friendly partition of Asia, leaving no intermediate zone," was the favourite idea of the Russian press and of the public, especially the powerful and influential War Party, or Party of Progress. Here again we took theoretically lower grounds than Russia: we were afraid to meet her; she did not fear to meet us. After all, the prize, such as it is, will fall to the better man: *detur digniori* will be the verdict of the world. If we can win the day, let us do so; if we cannot, let us cease to accumulate futile obstacles in the path of those who deserve to win.

And we shall gain little or nothing by the strong flanking position secured by the re-occupation of the open country of Shaul, of Candahar, and even of Herat. Men are ever hankering after Herat and its "stupendous earthworks." A still better line of outlying frontier—namely, Khelat, Quetta, and Jelalabad—would avail us as little. Wanting an army, English or native, we shall be driven to moral influence, to sympathy and moral support, to moral disapprobation, a pretentiously feeble tactic without the *gros bataillons* to give it *vis*. So the late Macgregor Laird defined moral influence in West Africa as a sixty-eight pounder worked by British seamen.

Our present policy must be a lively trust in the chapter of accidents, and looking forward to the day when we can place two millions of bayonets in the field. Russia has internal dangers of her own. She works cheaply; her invasion of Khiva cost her, we are told, £70,000, whilst we paid £15,000,000 for our occupation of Afghanistan. Still capitalists are beginning to inquire curiously about her budget, and she refuses to satisfy their curiosity. "Russians" fell two per cent. in one day during last autumn, and a chilling report pronounced them to be "shaky." The fact is, a portion of the English press has so long been preaching the doctrine of repudiation, that the world of debtors begins to lend its ear to the charmer: there are so many nations which can afford to keep house, but which cannot afford to *payer les Anglais.*

South America may be pronounced to be "going," Turkey to be "gone;" and the influence of such failures on a gigantic scale, especially when they extend to Europe and to England,—where at the present moment nothing is safe beyond ground-rents, railways, and three per cents.,—must sooner or later weigh upon Russia. Even she cannot go to war without the sinews of war; even her ingenuity will be puzzled to make *la guerre nourrir la guerre* amongst the impecunious peoples of Central Asia.

But our highest prospect of happy deliverance from this terrible northern rival is still to be noticed; and that so little attention has been paid to it by our writers, is not a little astonishing to the student. In Russia it must have caused a vast amount of anxious thought; and it readily explains the cautious system of her approaches, parallels, and encroachments in the East; her provisional system of indirect until ready for direct rule over her new conquests; her strategic lines of observation and demonstration; and her carefully-disposed apparatus of supports, reserves, and bases of operations. *Nolens volens*, will-we nill-we, Russia must eventually absorb Kashgar; she must meet China face to face, and then her serious troubles begin.

The dash of Tartar blood in Russian veins cstablishes a remote consinhood with China. There is something of physical, and more of moral, likeness between the two peoples. Both are equally sturdy, hardy, frugal, energetic, persistent, aggressive, and brave in facing death. Both have a national speech, a peculiar alphabet, and, to go no further, a religion which distinguishes them from the rest of the world. Both are animated by the sturdy vigour of a newly-awakened civilization. During the war of 1842 we facetiously said that it was rank murder to attack the Chinese troops with any missiles but oranges. Presently the ever-victorious army led by Gordon, one of England's noblest and best neglected sons, showed the might that was slumbering in a nation of three hundred millions.

And now China is preparing herself, with that slow but terrible stedfastness of purpose which distinguishes her, to exercise her influence upon the civilized world,—upon the other three-fourths which compose the sum of humanity. After a hundred checks

AMIRS OF SIND.

and defeats she has utterly annihilated the intrusive Mohammedan schism which attempted to establish its independence in Yunnan. She will do the same in Kashgar, although the dilatoriness of her proceedings, unintelligible to the Western mind, tends to create a false feeling of security. She is building a fleet and rolling her own plates. Her army is being drilled by Europeans; the men are armed with Remingtons, and she has six manufactories for breech-loading rifles. Securely cautious of her coming strength, she declines all little wars with England and France, till another dozen years or so shall enable her to meet her enemies on terms which, forecasted in 1842, would have appeared the very madness of prophecy.

Such is the nation which is fated to contend with Russia for the glorious empire of Central Asia. This is the power which our Press and its teachers have agreed to ignore. In the coming struggle we shall see the direct result of the Crimean War, and then, perhaps, we may reap the reward of sacrifices and losses which hitherto have added little to our honour or to our power.

CHAPTER XX.

WE LEAVE INDIA.

THE day of departure came round. I was both glad and sorry,—glad to leave the now almost intolerable heat, and to escape the coming monsoon, this being the last ship that could expect to run free of it, nor was that even certain,—glad at the prospect of seeing Trieste; sorry to leave the now ever-increasing interest and daily accumulating friends. I longed for home letters, and was content with my six months' trip and all that I had seen and learnt. With these mixed and contending emotions we embarked, attended by a handful of friends, on board Austrian Lloyd's *Minerva.*

I have a few words to say about Austrian Lloyd's, yet, if I find a fault, it is sure to be unpopular, like maternal counsels to the self-willed, obstinate child; but I mean them in the spirit of true friendship, for I am a good Austrian and Triestine citizen. I take a pride in their institutions, and if I can worry them into making a second-class line a first-class line, I will turn knife and cautery on to their little faults, although, as I am always at home on their ships, and always spoiled, it will seem at first sight, ungrateful.

Lloyd's has a fleet of sixty-nine keel (sixteen paddle-wheelers), covering twenty-two different lines. She is reasonable in her charges. Her *cuisine,* which is Italian, is excellent, and plentiful for reasonable people. Everything is served up with the perfection of cleanliness, and in a certain style and refinement. Her agents, captains, officers, and stewards are more than civil and kind, nay, devoted to the care and comfort of their passengers. She is safe; she has never lost a keel. Her captains and officers are prudent, and her capital Dalmatian crews from the Bocche di

Cattaro are a brave, seafaring race, quiet, docile and sober, stalwart, honest and civil, who mind their ship in a storm. They sing beautifully on fine nights. I have heard worse opera choruses than the native glees (which make a quiet moonlight night charming) issuing from those untutored throats. I know of nothing pleasanter than a voyage in Lloyd's in fine weather, when there are few passengers. It is perfect repose.

In spite of all these good qualities, we were very uncomfortable during this voyage, and I never hear an Englishman bound from India without a volley of grumbling. The boats are well fitted for the Mediterranean, but not so for passengers from India, and I will explain how: they steam very slow, eight knots an hour (the captains have a premium on coal). I do not find it any fault not to carry a stewardess or a doctor,—the steward waits upon you and cleans your cabin much better than the stewardess. Ship-doctors are never first-rate, they generally bleed you when you want a tonic, and you are far less likely to die when you have none.

There are, however, three things which it is absolutely necessary to provide for Indian voyages, in the hot weather: one is ice and soda water; secondly, to have a skylight let into the saloon to put a wind-sail down; and number three is to provide three awnings instead of one, like three roofs raised one above another, with a little space between, and turn the hose on sometimes in the heat. Punkahs and tatties are a great luxury, but even that one can rough it without. We had to sit on deck clad in our pith helmets, with umbrella and spectacles, and that means *frying alive* in the Indian Ocean and Red Sea. It is nonsense to say "we don't care about you passengers, we only want cargo." You do care about making money, and yet you turn a blind eye to the source from which it flows, or you would be making fourteen or fifteen per cent. instead of six or seven.

I want to urge the Directors to make a few hundred pounds' worth of changes in their Indian boats only.

There is commerce enough for three lines down the south-western Indian coast, which is monopolized by one. This one does not suffice to the needs, and makes fifteen per cent.; the same applies to the north-western coast. Why should not Lloyd's run another two lines and enrich herself? But she is too slow. She has people who stop her prosperity by childish mistakes, and being penny wise and pound foolish. Young blood in this direction may change all that.

If she kept her reasonable prices, and gave three months' return-tickets to Indian civilians, she would have more business than she can do with the same number of ships, and become one of the five or six "crack lines" of the world. On our return from India we wrote three despatches to convince the Directors of all this, and we had been to the trouble of collecting every item of information, and detail of ways and means, as a simple, honest return for the kind and civil treatment we had met with from the whole service, whether from the agents ashore, or from the captain down to the smallest *mousse* at sea. I concluded that some foolish old gentleman in the Board of Directors fancied that we expected to get something out of it, as we only got for answer to our long despatches, "That the Directors could not make any distinctions." This speech was so unintelligible to us that we shrugged our shoulders, laughed, and forgot it. Our sole motive was our *esprit de corps* which made us wish to see an Austrian Lloyd line doing well wherever there is money to be made. After England is served, there is a surplus for others, and I should like to see Austrian Lloyd pocketing it.

Our little ship *Minerva* is one thousand eight hundred and sixty-one registered tons, engine four hundred horse-power, length two hundred and seventy-four English feet, crew forty-eight men, schooner yacht rig—a capital boat, but ill-provided for the Indian seas. She is small, lumbered up with cargo, and smells like an unclean chicken pen, from negro deck passengers and onions, which are stacked up for the Commissioners outside my window. We have no wind-sails because there is no skylight, nor punkahs nor tatties; no ice or soda water, so our drink is lukewarm, and there is only one awning. These boats are all well built, all on the same pattern, and you are happy if you can secure one of the six cabins on the upper deck.

We were seventeen first-class passengers, nine ladies, three second-class, two third-class, thirty-one deck passengers,—Negro, Hindí, Somal, Moslem, and Jew. We have our Captain, first and second officers, four engineers (the Chief is always an Englishman), and a crew of forty-eight; in all, one hundred and eight souls. Another fault I have to find with Lloyd's is, that there is a certain amount of jealousy shown to the English engineers. After all, they have taught everything to the Austrian Lloyd's engineers, and now they know their business they wish to rid themselves of the English, who consist of seventy-five families at Trieste who have served them faithfully and have worked well for them these forty years.

I do not, however, by any means side with my travelling compatriots in their grumblings on board these steamers. They are as troublesome at sea as a mustard-plaster. Nothing is right. They want their huge lumps of beef and mutton four times a day. They eat up the provisions like locusts, and drink the cellar dry almost before we get to Aden. Accustomed to Indian luxuries ashore, and the old P. and O. by sea, notwithstanding reasonable prices, extreme cleanliness, nice food, and the united attention of Captain, officers, and two stewards, they are irate with everything and everybody. In the "White Star" and "Royal Mail," and about four other lines, you are in a floating palace; but you pay palace fares, and yet you do not grumble; you cannot have your cake and eat it; you cannot travel cheaply and exact the same living as on one of those lines. You must be fair.

What would last Italians and Greeks six weeks, does not last an Englishman one. They want less, and give far less trouble than we do. We want to eat and drink enormously, be well served, and give an infinity of trouble for comfort, but then we should not mind paying for it. So either economize and be content with excellent fare, and do not grumble, or go by the crack lines and pay.

The Italians and Greeks have quite another form of being troublesome; they will send every half-hour for the Captain to ask if there is any danger, if the sea and wind are going to be worse or better, to tell him they feel very bad, and to ask him what they shall take. He, with the greatest good nature, instead of giving them a hearty "blessing," as I expect ours would, recommends a little *eau sucrée*, and says we shall be in smooth water in another hour, though he knows quite well that the glass is down, and that we are going straight into a gale of wind which may last several days.

My husband and I are exceedingly comfortable, and as we are used to going about, and have opportunities of judging of all sorts of ships, we cannot help laughing to hear "our boys," as we call our fellow passengers, swearing at the Triestine stewards in Hindústani. The English generally do not know Italian, German, or Slav, and the stewards are innocent of English or Hindústani; and when they do not understand, the English speak louder, in a rage, to make them comprehend. We have two most excellent stewards, Fernando and Frantz, who deserve to get good bakshish and promotion for toiling from dawn to midnight to minister to our slightest wants, notwithstanding the killing heat. They wring their hands in despair, only too anxious to serve us. We hear all day shouts of "Where is Mrs. Burton?" (this is to interpret; Captain Burton is busy, and not to be disturbed.) I am, on this occasion, the connecting link between Lloyd's and the discontented Britishers.

Feeling my responsibility, I collected all the ladies on starting, and said, "I daresay we shall be very hot and uncomfortable, and I will tell you how we will manage to have a very pleasant voyage. We must all be as kind to one another as possible, and everyone must do exactly as they please, without any remarks being passed on it, or any offence taken." They all agreed, and kept to this rule. Every night we slept on deck, in rows, whilst in the Indian Ocean and Red Sea; for the cabins were like heated ovens, and we darted down only to dress as quickly as we could.

At six a.m. we went, in our dressing-gowns, to the saloon, and took coffee; and then we read, talked and slept on deck in the day; my husband and I a little apart when seriously employed with literature. In the evening we sang glees and duets. We abolished *toilette*, and dressed in loose white or coloured cotton, or linen, dressing-gowns. I am sure that we were all sorry when the voyage was over; I heard that some of them cried when we had to break up.

John Bull's "grumbles" usually come on at feeding time. Let that only be to his taste, and "a child might play with him." And then the Captain and officers and stewards upon this, and every other of Lloyd's ships, are so obliging and civil, so anxious, and inventive to lessen woes which they cannot help, and do not suffer from themselves, such as sea-sickness in a small, full ship in burning seas; and despite steady head-winds, and long swells, and that all, except four of us, were more or less ill crossing the Indian Ocean, we had a merry passage.

And well they might be ill, fresh from India, where the liver always suffers; for, Captain Vogelhaus remarked, as Captain Bogojevich did in March (going out) of the north-east monsoon, "If this is not the south-west monsoon it is his brother." We have a jolly, fat old captain, and we call him Captain Vogelhaus, because he always brings home thousands of birds, and passes his whole leisure hours in making bird-cages. I tell him, that when he goes to heaven he will have a gigantic bird-cage shop. He sits holding his chair by the two arms, as if it hurt him to sit down, the perspiration streaming off his face, and puffing "Corpo di Bacco." The dear old thing would like to have all the windows shut for fear of rheumatics, and we want every hole open to catch a breath of air. "Sehr komische Leüte sind diese Engländer," said the steward to me; "they *will* have everything open." "Yes, Fernando," I said, "we're all like that. We like lots of fresh air, and plenty of cold water—*per uso externo* only; you take it inside and we outside, that's the only difference."

On a fine May morning Captain Pietro Mersa (Chief Officer), one of Lloyd's best officers, and in every way a most praiseworthy man, passed under my cabin, and said, "Safe under the lee of Socotra, Signora!"—six words full of meaning at the end of May to homeward-bound passengers from India. As I said before, any day the monsoon may burst with fury upon your cockle-shell, or you may be gathered into a cyclone, which not only engulphs ships in its centre, but some are also twenty-two days getting from Bombay to Aden, whereas in ordinary times a P. and O. passage is six days, and Lloyd's nine days as we do not stack on the coal. As it is, we dance like a cricket-ball in the water, and this is child's play to what it would be in the monsoon.

In case children read my book, I ask permission to say a few elementary words about the monsoon.

Monsoon (Arabic *mausim*) means "a season." There are north-east and south-east trade winds, and there is a north-east and a south-west monsoon, and it is the latter that we have to do with now. The wind blows steadily in India during eight months from the north-east, and for four months from the south-west.

The south-east trade wind gradually develops, gathering fury as it goes, and becomes, by deflection, a south-west monsoon. It reaches Galle (Ceylon) in May, and by the end of May bursts with fury, and fills the Indian seas with rain, thunder, lightning and furious winds, that raise the sea mountains high. You see the equinoctial gales twice a year in England. This is much more furious, and lasts four months. It is caused by the intense overheating of the land. The cold air rushes in from the south-west, and passes over the Atlantic overcharged with moisture, the sun acting like a great pump upon the sea. The Himalaya mountains are one of the great causes, on account of the accumulation of snow thereon. These storms are sometimes augmented by cyclones, or circular storms, which arise chiefly at Mauritius, and when they penetrate into the Indian seas play the mischief, the difficulty being to get out of them. The centre is perfectly calm, but it is a whirlpool or vortex, which engulphs many a ship, for once in the focus there is little, if any, hope of escape. Ships now steer somewhat more northerly than in old days, from Bombay to Socotra, not to get into these storms.

"Safe under the lee of Socotra," under all these circumstances, meant a good deal to us, especially to the nine of my sex out of the twenty-two passengers; and still more to the thirty-one deck passengers, who lie out under the open heavens. We should all have been battened down under the hatches, and the heat being intense, and the very air like blasts from a furnace, it would have killed us. The next ship must catch it, and we have only shaved

H.H. THE KHEDIVE'S PALACE OF SHUBRAH.

it, with the monsoon wind in our teeth, and a heavy sea until now.

At Aden on the 19th of May we drove over to the camp. My drive was a martyrdom to me, as the negro coachman drove his poor, lean, starved beasts by poking them with a stick under the tail; who, when I interfered, said, in his defence, that he only did it to the weakest of the two *miseries*, because the other did not require it so much.

First we drove to the Convent of the Good Shepherd, visited the Tanks and the Camp, the town and bazars; then we went to the mess-room, where our military friends of the regiment gave us a capital luncheon, and met nearly all the male portion of our seventeen first-class passengers, who each had friends to invite them. We drove back and rejoined our ship. We left here, to our regret, a nice married couple,—the lady preferring Aden to India, on account of not having the monsoon between her and Alsace, when she wished to return home. I should not like to live at Aden at all; it is so hot and desolate, in spite of being a military station; and one would be expected to live in a sort of civilization. We met a P. and O. at Aden, and it was so hot in late May, that a young lady on board, despite all the precautions and preventives of those steamers, had brain fever from the excessive heat.

20*th*.—We pass the Straits of Bab-el-Mandeb, with its single white factory-looking house on the French side, and the flag-staff on Perim island, where an officer and his wife and a small detachment are quartered, to her great discomfort. We are now in the Red Sea, and passed the great and little Harnish and several steamers, and on the coast we see Mocha and Jebel Sakkar. One cannot speak sufficiently about the Red Sea's dangers; it is full of reefs and shoals, barely covered with water, and no beacons or lighthouses on them, so that ships are wrecked every year. The Red Sea has three lighthouses, and wants at least fourteen more. England expects the Khedive to do it, and he cannot.

The Khedive is a most ill-used ruler. I believe the refuse of Europe go to Egypt, fatten upon him, suck his very blood, and retire rich, and then go away and abuse him. If he were what they say he is, he would have remained rich, and they would have remained poor; and Egypt would not have been plundered by everybody who had taken out a patent for the smallest invention. Small blame to His Highness if he is beginning to get cautious and suspicious of Europeans, and not risk too much till he knows if it is a real thing. We cannot cry out for lighthouses from the plundered treasury. Our good chief officer, Capitano Mersa, never slept those eight days, was always at his charts, and if obliged to take a nap, had some one stationed close by, to call him at a moment's notice.

Foreign ships do not respect *our* law of hospitality to birds at sea, who come for rest on a long flight, and perhaps to pick up a few crumbs. They have no "Ancient Mariner." They wanted always to shoot or catch them, and one unhappy dove left all its back feathers in a sailor's rough hand. I always work upon their superstition in these matters.

It was now fearfully hot. There were only two hours in the night which might be considered cool, and we used anxiously to wait for them. We all suffered from prickly heat.

On the 23rd we passed Jeddah. The sea is here about one hundred and twenty-five miles broad. I may say that on this day we sensibly changed climate, leaving the Indian heat behind us, for it became very rough, with a cool head-wind. The poor sailors were glad, and the weak felt uncomfortable.

24*th*.—We passed the Dædalus lighthouse (one of the three). They dipped flag to us, as the Captain paid us the compliment of flying the red Union Jack for the Queen's birthday. Lloyd's made us an extra good dinner for this occasion, and I brewed a claret-cup, and we drank Her Majesty's health "three times three," with a fervent "God bless her!" at the end.

Then followed the healths of Emperor Franz Joseph and the Empress, the Captain and the officers. The old Captain was quite affected by this unusual scene, for we made the old Italian ship ring with British cheers, and he ordered champagne and drank to our Queen and to us, in a very pretty speech; we afterwards sang "God Save the Queen" on deck, and then the

AN ENGLISHMAN WITH THE "SPLEEN" AT VENICE.

Austrian national hymn. It was quite cold, and blew hard all night.

25*th.*—Ascension Thursday we sighted Shadwán at ten o'clock, and passed Jobal at twelve. We were steaming between the two mainlands of Africa and Arabia, and the north-westers rush down the narrow passage like a funnel.

26*th.*—After a very rough night we anchored before Suez, at 7.30 a.m. Here eight of us left the ship, to have a run through Egypt, and the agent kindly took us and our baggage in his steam-launch. Ships anchor out so far that we were not landed till nine, and those in sailing boats arrived much later. We were soon surrounded by a little band of my husband's old friends of Meccah days, especially Mr. and Mrs. Levick, British Postmaster-General. Captain Roberts, P. and O. Superintendent, kindly lent us his steam-launch, and Mr. Alfred Levick and two of our fellow-passengers—Mr. Bonny, of San Francisco, and Mr. Mitchell—accompanied Captain Burton and myself, and put off to the Arabian shore.

It was a most lovely scene, familiar to all who know Suez, with its blue sea, yellow sands, azure sky, and pink and purple mountains. Our visit was to Moses' Wells, about three miles in the Arabian desert. The sun was hot, but the pure desert air blew in our faces as we went across the sand to the picturesque spot. The wells, or springs, are surrounded by tropical verdure, intermingled with Fellah huts, divided into distinct patches: they extend over a good tract of country, which if cultivated might prove most valuable. The most romantic spot was a single tiny spring, under an isolated palm-tree, standing all alone on a little hillock of sand in the desert, far from all else, as if that tree and that spring had been created for each other to live alone.

We took our *Kayf* there for some hours with the Arabs; we had some delicious Arab coffee and Narghíleh with them; and on returning we procured for our American friend the novel emotion of riding a camel. The sea homewards was rough, and we shipped so much water that we had to cover our fires.

We remained till the 12th June in Egypt, seeing as much as

possible. It was during the troublous time of Abdul Aziz's death. I wrote three chapters on Egypt, and have since passed three months there; but I have promised not to write anything about it at present, and as I fancy I shall see a great deal more of that country if my life is spared, I shall be better able to produce a book like that which I have produced upon Syria, because my knowledge will be more sound and more intimate than if I jotted down the ideas of one or two cursory visits, which I should perhaps afterwards have to unwrite.

We embarked on June 12th for Trieste in another Lloyd's, the *Apollo*, and suffered much from the cold after India. The journey from Alexandria to Trieste in these steamers is very interesting for thoughtful people.

We begin by going straight in a north-westerly direction to the Isle of Candia, which we leave on our right, passing also on our right the island of Gavdo, Cape Spaltra, and the two islands Cerigotto and Cerigo; then we glide by Cape Matapan, on the Greek coast, which continues for a long way. We pass Cabrera and Sapienza, two islands which are called *Le* Sapienze, because Cabrera is uninhabited, and of no account.

We leave the lighthouse on Strophades to the left, and pass Zante, a lovely island, with a large, picturesque town, and run between Cephalonia and Ithaca (of Ulysses), the first to the left, and the last to the right. Then we change the Greek coast for Arcarnania, and pass Santa Maura, or Leucadia, with Sappho's Leap, which does not look very high, and we are told, by not very educated Italians, that she took that leap because she was jealous of *Dante*.

We change to the purely Albanian coast, gloriously green to the water's edge, with cliff and cave, with the Cimariote Hills and its wild people and their lawless legends behind them; and then pass two islets, Anti Paxo and Paxo, to Corfu. We continue to coast along Albania, passing Capo Linguetta and Isole Sasseno. We afterwards change to the Dalmatian coast, passing Bocca di Cattaro and Ragusa, and the islands of Lagosta and Cazza; then Lissa, where the two great battles were fought, one 13th March, 1811, and one 20th July, 1866; then the islands of

Spalmadore, Lesina, Incoronati, and Grossa; then Punta Biancha, and the island of Sansego. Here we change to Istria and are upon our own ground, beginning with Punta di Promontore and Pola, our great Austrian Naval Station, with its Coliseum and most interesting ruins; then Rovigno and Parenzo, harbour towns on the coast. At Punto Salvore we enter into our own Golfo di Trieste, passing Pirano, which we see from our windows, and finally Trieste.*

The beautiful little city, nestled in its corner in the mountains at the very end of the Adriatic, seemed to me the greenest and most beautiful spot I had ever beheld, after hot India and barren Egypt and Arabia. The hills, plumaged to the sea, dotted with white villages and villas, Miramar standing well out to sea in the warm haze, the splendid Carniola mountains on the opposite side still slightly tipped with snow, was most refreshing to our eyes, and we settled down in our little home with a feeling of rest.

After our ever-warm reception from Trieste friends on our return from long voyages, we resumed our old life of literature, and all sorts of pleasant studies and occupations. I resumed my avocations amongst my poor people, and the protection of the poor animals of our district; for the greatest happiness anyone can know is to feel that one is of some use in ever such a small corner. I think if a person has not time for long prayers, that two ejaculations I was taught to say, on getting up in the morn-

* The voyage is divided thus:—

	Sea Miles.	
Going.		
Trieste to Port Said	1304	
Canal	80	
Suez to Aden	1296	
Aden to Bombay	1660	
		4310
Returning.		
Bombay to Aden	1660	
Aden to Suez	1296	
(Through Egypt) Suez to Cairo and Alexandria	280	
Alexandria to Corfu and Trieste	1460	
		4696
Total		9006

ing, at my convent (the Holy Sepulchre), go a long way: "Mon Dieu! mon Dieu! donnez votre grâce à l'âme qui va vous offenser!" "Oh, mon Dieu! que je sois utile à quelqu'un aujourd'hui!"

One's heart glows, and it attaches one to life, to see many glad at one's coming; and it is so easy a thing to accomplish that I am afraid that we grow to take a selfish pleasure in it, instead of meriting by it. I have set *one* law for myself wherever I am stationed, which simple rule contains, for me, the whole First Commandment, and the broad base of Religion, and it makes life happy and independent, come what may; and that is, never to hear a cry of distress from man or beast without responding to it *as well as I am able;* and for this simple service I get too much rewarded at Trieste in affection and kindness from all classes, high and low; no wonder, then, that I am happy and at home there.

My husband has been twice to Egypt and Arabia since we returned from India. In his old Arab days, wandering about with his Korán (twenty-five years ago), he came upon a gold land in that part of Arabia belonging to Egypt. As I have told in my preface of his last book, he was a romantic youth, with a chivalrous contempt for "filthy lucre," and only thought of "winning his spurs;" so setting a mark upon the place, he turned away, and passed on. After twenty-five years, seeing Egypt in distress for gold, he asked for "leave," went to Cairo, and imparted his secret to the Khedive. His Highness equipped an expedition in a few days, and sent him there to re-discover the land. He has given an account of that trip in "The Gold Mines of Midian."

The Khedive was desirous of sending him out last winter, with a view to learning exactly every item concerning this rich old country; and Captain Burton's leave having been granted, he set out October 1877 in command of a new expedition, on a much larger scale, and was out seven months in the desert of Arabia doing hard work. He discovered a region of gold and silver, turquoise, agate, lead, and six or seven commoner metals, extending some hundreds of miles either way, and pearls on the coast, a Roman temple, and thirty-two old mining cities. The expedition mapped, and planned, and sketched the whole country, and came back, bringing twenty-five tons of the various minerals for assay or analysis. The ancients had only worked forty feet, whereas, with our appliances, we may go down twelve hundred. Captain Burton is about to produce a most interesting work on this expedition, which is now in the hands of Mr. Kegan Paul.

To my great annoyance I was left behind, October 1877, to bring the first book through the Press, with leave to join the expedition as soon as my work was done. I accomplished it in January 1878, started and got as far as Suez, where I met with a check I was not prepared for. My readers will understand that the land of Midian is not in Egypt, but in the opposite land, Arabia, with the Red Sea running between, and I found it utterly impossible to get any farther. It is a desert place, where none go; there is no communication. The expedition was then working five or six days up country. To cross the Red Sea in an open *Sambúk*, with head winds blowing, and afterwards to fight my way across the desert alone upon a camel, would have been both dangerous for me, and *infra dig.* for my husband's position; nor was it exactly the moment to ask the Khedive to organize a second expedition to send me out with no definite object, except my own pleasure.

Once an Egyptian man-of-war was sent by the Khedive, but only to bring them back (there was to be a choice between two). I went down and inspected them both. The Captain received me with all honour, all hands were piped on deck, and a guard and everything provided for me. They would have liked to take me, would have done all to make me comfortable, and were most courteous, but I saw that the accommodation was of too public a nature; in short, it would be impossible for any woman to embark without her husband on an Egyptian man-of-war,—it would lower her in *their* eyes. Besides turning them out of their only quarters, when my husband came to re-embark the men of his Staff, I should be excessively in the way; so thanking them exceedingly for their courteousness, I returned to the town (much to the relief of the excellent energetic Governor, Said

Bey, who was on thorns for fear I should go), took some small rooms, and commenced literary work.

Mr. and Mrs. Adams, of the Suez Hotel, were exceedingly kind and attentive to my wants and comforts. A stone's throw from my rooms was a little Franciscan convent of Italian monks, a mere hut, with a room decorated as a chapel, where I used to pass an hour or so every day, and visit the monks. Mr. Consul West and Mrs. West were most hospitable, and wanted me to live with them, and they lent me a gigantic white donkey, more difficult to ride than any horse I ever mounted, for he ate his head off in the stable and never was ridden, so I had some little desert rides.

I commenced my work for the poor animals in Egypt, and had the pleasure of being present at the Khedive's magnificent *fête* in Cairo, where I returned for four days, a *fête* which is one of three engraven on my memory. There were theatricals (amateur), ball, and supper at the Abdin palace, lately burnt to the ground.

In April, the expedition returned, and I was the first to greet them. We could see the ship two hours away in the horizon; it was for that I remained at Suez instead of Cairo. The Khedive sent a special train for us, and we went to Cairo, and at his wish made an exhibition of the minerals, which he opened in person. After three weeks of that work and French report writing, we returned to Trieste, where my husband had to remain at his post on account of the expected war, but was released in a few weeks, and allowed to come to London to arrange matters for the further working of Midian. On our arrival, we went over to Ireland, to tell the British Association something about Midian, and were most warmly and hospitably entertained by Lord Talbot and his family at Malahide Castle, where I finished my MSS.

And now in conclusion, having made all my political jottings in 1876, I find myself obliged, on publishing in 1878, to make a *resumé*, correcting them as one adds a codicil to a will, but more especially as regards the "partition of Turkey."

> "Now whether he kill Cassio,
> Or Cassio him, or each do kill the other,
> Every way makes my gain."

When we were at Jeddah my husband addressed to the *Daily Telegraph* a letter upon the "Partition of Turkey." This paper had not pronounced itself in January 1876 as decidedly as in Jannary 1877, so the missive was published on March 7th, with the heading only changed to "The Future of Turkey." Captain Burton did not then know that the Duke of Wellington had put forth exactly the same views upon the critical point, the main question, What is to become of Constantinople? nor could he forecast that Mr. Grant Duff, who probably glances, like other men, at the *Daily Telegraph*, would see in a dream what my husband saw when wide awake,—the Kingdom of Byzantium revived.

During the last two years and a half of war and massacre, which must have cost the lives of a million human beings, the situation has shifted, but the truth remains untouched. Still the Sick Man's constitution is breaking up fast; and the political doctors and patent drugs have done him no good. What peace he now enjoys is accompanied neither by honour nor by honours. Instead of removing proud flesh and amputating gangrened limbs, the rough surgeons have cut into the very vitals of the patient. They should have pruned the tree; they preferred to bark it. Under such circumstances vitality is impossible. With acephalous governments and dynastic demoralization, diminished States and autonomous Provinces, to say nothing of utter impecuniosity and of a paper money that threatens to be cheaper than *assignats*, ruin is a mere matter of time.

Resolved to maintain the "integrity of Turkey," the doctors have disintegrated it. Turkey has become, not "a scattered Empire like England," but a mere "geographical expression," as was the Italy of the past. And now the Sick, or rather the Dying man, has only to look forward to financial ruin, to Russification, to the reign of dementia, to spoliation, to partition :—

> "The dull grey close and apathetic end."

During the last quarter of a century the preservation of the putrid Power has cost us forty thousand lives and four hundred millions sterling. We are not likely to spend much more.

The first letter was written, it will be remembered, under the reign of Abd el Aziz, the suicided and "forbicated" Vitellius, when the troubles began at Podgorizza. In those days (1875-76) the general reader knew nothing of Dalmatia, Servia, and the Herzegovina, beyond what he had learnt from our late friends Gardner Wilkinson, Alexander Paton, Miss Muir Mackenzie (the late Lady Sebright), and from the present Viscountess Strangford. Mr. Arthur Evans had not published either his brilliant book, or his still more brilliant letters in the *Manchester Examiner*. The older writers did indeed bring out the fact, afterwards ignored by a host of "Our Correspondents," that the Turk of the Slav Provinces has not one drop of Turkish blood in his veins, that he cannot speak a word of Turkish, and that he detests the Turk, especially the Effendi from Constantinople, with the bitterest hate; witness the murdering of two Pashas, Mehemet Ali and Saad el ed din, by the Albanians in September 1878. Even the dress of the Slav "Turk," his big turban, his tight jacket, and his bag breeches, are those of old Slavonia, and contrast strongly with the flowing robes of the Osmanli, whom you insult by calling a "Toork," *i.e.*, a wild wanderer, a nomad. He is by blood a cousin of the Russian Slavo-Finn, an element which peoples nearly half of the great Empire, which forms thirty-four out of seventy-one millions. In creed he is simply a renegade Christian, an Islamised Paulicean or Bogomil, with all the malignant animosity of a renegade, with a horror and abomination of the creed which he abandoned. Hence the tenacity and fury which he displayed at Plevna and the Balkan Passes, where Russian met Russian, where heretical Jugo-Slav struggled with orthodox Slavo-Finn. This is the true history of the "gentle and gallant Turk," as far as the Bosniac element is concerned. And that element supplied Turkey with one hundred thousand of her best regulars.

Like most outsiders, I cannot see the difficulty of settling the Eastern Question (*malè pereat!*), but I thoroughly see the danger of leaving it, as at present, half settled. Of course the distribution of the spoil and the Turkish debt favour the conservation of Turkey. But although the *haute politique* makes all kinds of delays, ambiguities, considerations and mysteries, the eye of common sense can detect none. As regards matters of finance, if the Powers that profit by annexation will only guarantee, as in fairness they should, the liabilities of Turkey, one prop of the rotten old pile is at once knocked away. And even total loss is better than this chronic state of irritation now afflicting the European system ; this disturbance of trade and industry ; this fool's paradise of the gaming table; this armed peace, which has many of the evils and little of the good that war brings.

Our great diplomatic triumph in the second half of the nineteenth century has removed from us the fatal necessity of propping up "Turkism" in Europe. The late occupation of Bosnia by the Austrians shows what are the Bosniacs and their Beys. Savage and brutal as Krevosjes or Cimariots, they have all the Moslem vices, none of the simple and noble virtues which distinguish their peasant co-religionists in Caramania, Anatolia, and other parts of Asia Minor, where the Faithful number three to one. Their bullying tyranny was exasperated for many a generation by the conviction that despite numerical inferiority of one to three (3,380,000 to 9,500,000), theirs was the ruling class ; and that the Mudir, the Wali, the Ministry, and the Sultan himself would invariably support their iniquities, unless compelled by the Great Powers of Europe to do simple justice under threat of war. His temper was not improved by the aggravating presence of the Kafir; and his habit of carrying weapons enabled him to gratify every whim by a stab of the ready *yataghan*. He had never heard of the classical policy embodied in Sultan Selim's will—*Farriku baynhumá wa Sallitu alayhumá* ("breed dissensions between them both, Moslems and Christians, and rule them both.") Selim El-Fátih (the conqueror) left a will, you see, like Peter Velika, and their merits were, being the expressions of hereditary racial thoughts, like Lord Palmerston and M. Thiers. Yet he recognised the working of this obsolete Machiavelism as it still prevails throughout the Turkish Empire. Whenever a dispute arises between the rival religions about a field, a woman, or a boy whose face has been slapped, the Nazarene applies officially to the Pasha. The Pasha lends an attentive ear to the complaint, quotes all the Hatts

Sherif, Humayoon, and so forth, and exhorts the petitioner to remember that under a Constitutional Government (Heaven save the mark!) men of all faiths are equal. When the Mussulman proffers his counter complaint, the same Pasha swears by his beard that no earthly power can make the Infidel take rank with True Believers. This was the tactic that caused the Syrian massacre of 1860. My theory stands proved by the fact that, in the out-lying villages and hamlets, where no Turks were, the Mohammedan peasants fought against the emissaries from Damascus, in defence of their Christian neighbours.

Austria has at length adopted the course prescribed to her many years ago. Prince Eugene was the first name of note that advised the Holy Roman Empire to abandon her worse than useless Italian conquests, and to bring her weight to bear upon the Ottoman. Bosnia and the Herzegovina are in these days political necessaries to her; and the visit of the Emperor to Dalmatia was the beginning of the present policy. It would have been carried out two years ago, only circumstances then tied the hands of Count Andrassy, who throughout the affair has shown himself a statesman. Without these inner regions the stout Dalmatian kingdom cannot hold in the world the rank which it deserves to hold. The country of Diocletian, the mother of Emperors, was the narrowest realm of Europe, a mere masque, a face without a head. She had the finest ports in the Mediterranean and the noblest maritime population, while she had nothing to import, nothing to export, nothing to transport. Meanwhile the barbarous and exclusive policy of the Porte cut off the interior from the outer world. The precious metals, the "Dalmatic gold," famed by the Romans, silver, copper, iron and coal, remained undug; and the timber, the cattle, and the wool never saw the sea. Building was confined to forts; entrenchments took the place of roads, and whenever a traveller passed through the country he carried his life in his hand.

But things are now changed. After an occupation which has been a campaign costing some four thousand lives, Austria, by the mandate of Europe, has pacified Bosnia and the Herzegovina. She has taken the first step towards becoming a great Slav power. These modern Sarmatians and Saythians are divided by ethnologists into a multitude of races, Slovaks, Slovenes, and so forth. I know only two halves. The majority would be the Northern (Russo-Orthodox), the minority the Southern (Jugo-Slavs) and Catholic. Here religion, not race, draws a hard and fast line. Dual empire has now become virtually a *Triregno,* as she would have been but for Count Beust, so much more distinguished as an Ambassador than as a Minister. The conquest of Bosnia, for such it is, puts an end to Dualism; the Slav will now have his rights. Austria may lose her "better half," Hungary, which threatens to renew the scandals of 1849. The land of the Magyar, once the *Antemurale Christianitatis,* the outlying bulwark of Christendom, has now become a country of white Turks, of "Ogres" as Mr. Freeman calls them, of Ugro-Altaics, more Turkish than the Turks. There is nothing to prevent her becoming a great Jugo-Slav power, ever extending herself to the south-eastward till she meets the Greek. Thus she will halve with Russia the Slav world. By cultivating the Christian populations on the Lower Danube, and by a league with Old Bulgaria (Servia, Roumania, Roumelia, etc.), added to Bosnia, she would invest the Muscovite rival to the south and the south-west, while Germany hems it in to the west and north-west. Indeed, Russia declares that such a union, forming a state of siege impossible to endure, would be a calamity second only to the restoration of the Polish Kingdom.

Here, then, has begun the distribution of the Dying Man's estate. The characteristic of the situation is its purely provisional nature. No one is satisfied as matters now stand. All are, without exception, claimants, and urgent claimants, for something more than "administrative autonomy," either municipal or provincial. The "rebellious principalities," Montenegro and Servia, have enlarged their boundaries at the expense of Bulgaria; but both want more, and will have more. The new "tributary principality" of Bulgaria Proper, as I suppose we must call her, will not be satisfied with quasi-independence. As soon as she is strong enough she will fight again, and unless amalgamated with the "Servian accession" she will insist upon becoming

Russian. Meanwhile the Russians have not withdrawn their armies, and they are justified in not doing so as long as Austria holds Bosnia and England holds Cyprus. Eastern Roumelia, which is Southern Bulgaria, will obtain her freedom only by uniting with Bulgaria Proper and Russia.

By the way, I must notice the notable injustice of the European Press that expects the wretched Bulgarians, who have been treated like wild beasts for the last five hundred years, to show all the virtues of freemen. There is an old prejudice against them since Pushkin sang :—

> "Be a Pole, or be a Russian,
> Frenchman, Austrian, or Hungarian,
> Englishman, or Dane, or Prussian,
> Anything but base Bulgarian."

Nothing can palliate their "atrocities ;" but what horrors have they not to revenge? We all remember Lord Macaulay's answer when the Jews were taunted with their preferring low and immoral callings. But fair play in English politics threatens to be a thing of the past. At least the Bulgarians have as yet enjoyed very little of our boasted national quality. And Bulgaria literally has been what Turkey will be, broken up, distributed into Roumania, Servia, and Roumelia. She is, the world without knowing it, a Southern Poland.

Another sturdy claimant is Greece, not including her neighbour and old congener Albania. The writings of Messrs. Gladstone and Freeman have told the public of Turco-Græcia's wrongs. Since 1827, when her independence was recognised, she has been shut up in the barren Morea and the rocky deserts, north of the Gulf of Corinth. Her name is strong in the nostrils of the financial world as a turf-defaulter ; and the massacre of Marathon is better known to our generation than the battle of Marathon. But she now begins to see the error of her ways. She makes roads, she proposes to pay her debt, and she puts down brigandage. She behaved with exemplary patience during the Russo-Turkish war ; and we must excuse the irritability which presses for the proposed concession—a miserable slice. But her turn will come. Her manifest destiny is to divide with Austria the broad lands between Albania and the Despoto Dagh, the Rhodope range. Meanwhile, Albania—classic land of ruffians—hemmed in by Montenegro, Servia, and Greece, clamours for self-rule. Let her take it, and supply bath-men to Byzantium.

So much for Turkey in Europe. In Asia Turkey has lost her most valuable possessions: Kars, the great base of military operations; and Batoum, the port which commands the Bosphorus. The Russians intend to run their fine harbour against Trebizond, and to divert as much as they can of the caravan-trade that enriches the latter. Hence their obstinacy in the matter of that "interesting tribe," the Lazes. The Muscovite wants nothing more at present in Western Asia, and it was a second masterly stroke policy, our pledging ourselves to defend that which needs no defence. The Russian has nothing to do with the bleak and barren mountains of Armenia, which must also count amongst the rebellious provinces; and they are sturdy fellows, the men of Adana, of old Cilicia. Nor is she tempted by the rocky wastes of Kurdistan, where every brigand "subject" would want waiting upon by a soldier. She may assist and laugh till she cries at the pleasant spectacle of Mrs. Britannia performing the part of "Reform by Moral Force," and proposing an honest gendarmerie, just tribunals, and tax-gathering publicans turned to saints. If England were "doctrinary" she would either let the task severely alone, or she would appoint to every Wiláyat (province) a "Resident" after the fashion of British India. But compromise is her specific, her panacea for home use. She will do neither this nor that; she will use *mezzi termini* (half-measures), rely on the rule of thumb, and in fact meddle and muddle. Her position between the two stools, Do-nothing and Do-everything, will be the normal one. Liberal measures of reform have been freely promised, but that stale trick now deceives nobody. It is very well to command; but what is the use where none obey? Europe has had so much dust of this kind thrown into her eyes, that she now endures the process without writhing. And the Turk virtually says: "Pay us, and we will give ear to you; no loan, no reform." Which means, if you do not pay him he won't reform; and if you do pay him he will do ditto. The truth is he can't reform, and if he could he wouldn't. When Turkey assented to the proceedings of the Berlin Congress, the credulous dreamed that she intended to keep her treaty engagements. Not she! When Turkey promises, suspect a lie; when she swears, be sure of a lie. What to her are treaties, save things to be broken? Talk of a treaty between a dog and its fleas!

My beloved Syria and Palestine must also be withdrawn from the vampire claws of Turkey,—this daughter of chaos. The Holy Land for many past centuries has not enjoyed a gleam of prosperity, except when connected with, or, rather, when placed under, Egypt. It was a miserable and mistaken policy of Lord Palmerston in 1840, which, arresting the progress of Mohammed Ali Pasha, made England the cat's-paw of Russia. The old Bash-Buzuk of Cavala, as Sultan of Turkey, would have given fresh life to the obsolete and effete, the battered and broken empire of the barbarian; and his ambition was, naturally enough, dreaded by the northern pretenders to Constantinople. Let one sentence suffice to show the difference of development between the two Pashaliks. Syria has not one made port, Egypt has three; Egypt has a dozen railways, Syria boasts only of one carriageable road,—the Beyrout-Damascus,—and that one French. Of late years many efforts have been made to restore the Israelites to their own; and there is, I believe, a project of the kind—financial, not sentimental—actually in hand. The idea is to obtain the consent and the subscriptions of the Jews in every part of the world, and to purchase the tract between Dan and Beersheba by means of a loan to the Porte. Jerusalem cannot, in the present state of Europe, become the exclusive possession of any one European power. But already the land has been almost all bought up by the Jews, and the city, like its holy sisters, Hebron, Tiberias, and Safet, now virtually belongs to them.

Moreover, Syria is fated to become in a few years most important to England. The Euphrates Valley Line, under the surveillance of the Duke of Sutherland, has at last fallen into shape. Instead of a Levantine port, Alexandretta, Tripoli, or Tyre, and the great river for termini, it will set out from Constantinople and pass, *viâ* Baghdad, to Persia and India. This great highway—the only means of consolidating Turkey in Asia Minor—has hitherto been delayed only by the activity of Muscovite agents, and by the systematic self-effacement of our own. Before many years are past a branch of the main trunk-line will connect it with the Syrian coast opposite Cyprus. Baalbek and Palmyra are not yet "played out." These main stations, on the first and best of the many "overlands," will presently hear the whistle of the railway, and in the evening of their days they will again be made happy. The Euphrates Valley system will be to the Suez Canal what the "Egyptian Bosphorus" has been to the Cape of Good Hope.

And then we shall recognise the full value of Cyprus. After the melancholy policy of the pedagogue-demagogue in 1862, that restored and ruined Corfu, where some few years ago there was a popular tumult in favour of bringing back the old masters, England must secure ports and stations for her ironclads. The marvellous excitement caused by our last scrap of annexation shows the way the popular wind blows. Such a cackling over such a very small egg: we do not wish to make the Mediterranean an English lake, but we object to her being a French lake or a Russian lake, like the Black and Caspian Seas. Candia and Mytilene would certainly not oppose the hoisting of the Union Jack. Of course, those possessions will at first be unpopular; they will cost money; soldiers will die of fever, and officers will grumble. The Turks, after making the noble islands howling wildernesses, will propose to raise loans upon their "surplus revenues." But British gold will drain these homes of fever; ports will be laid out, and population will be introduced. We are not justified in failing where the Crusaders and the Knights succeeded so grandly.

The destiny of Turkey in Africa is equally manifest. France, who has by no means abandoned her claims to "hegemony," would add, if she pleased, to her Algerine provinces the fair lands of Tunis as far east as the plains of Jafara, where the southern bend of the coast ends in the Gulf of Sidra. The limits are roughly east long. (G.) 8° to 12°, a linear length of two hundred and forty direct geographical miles. Already there is a report that the offer has been made to her, despite the active opposition of Italy. This latter might be contented with Tripoli, as far as the eastern shore of the Gulf of Sidra. But, since her emancipation, she has shown a turbulent spirit, which threatens the peace of Europe. I lately met a young Italian diplomist, who would hardly speak to an Englishman because we hold Malta as our *Haupt-Piquet*. The occupation of Cyprus was a severe blow; the three standards in St. Mark's Square, Venice, represent Cyprus, Candia, and the Morea. "Unredeemed Italy" means an Italy "free from Etna to Trieste." It represents, I have shown, amongst the moderates, the annexation of the Trentino, the Duchy of Gorizzia, and the Peninsula of Istria. The immoderates add the whole of Dalmatia and part of Albania, in fact wherever the Roman "*regiones*" reached.

I say "Tripoli as far as East Sidra," the knob projecting into the Mediterranean eastward of Sidra, and including Barca and the Cyrenaic, should be added to Egypt, which would thus be prolonged from east long. (G.) 24° to 20°, also about two hundred and forty direct geographical miles. Grennah, of Old Cyrene, has a noble port, lying at a short distance south-east of Malta, and this will be the terminus of a future railway, connecting the glorious lands lying along the Mediterranean, with the Nile Valley. By this line passenger-traffic shall escape the sea-voyage between Malta and Egypt, whilst the Cairo-Sioot, prolonged to Cosseir, will save the mortification of the Suez Gulf.

As regards Egypt, we are only beginning to take into consideration the grand results brought about by the great Mohammed Ali Pasha and his family. We want from her nothing but the free right of transit and transport; we are resolved that the highway of the nations shall not be barricaded. We may eventually be compelled to annex her, but that measure is still distant, although lately advocated in England and feared in France. Meanwhile, we might be a little kinder to her. Whilst the Turks are allowed freely to repudiate their debts, poor Egypt must pay her usurious Christian creditors the uttermost farthing. The powers of Europe unwisely and wickedly compelled her to take part in the last Russo-Turkish campaign. We have hitherto refused to set her free from the immense "benevolences" and other *douceurs*, heavier than any tribute, which perpetually find their way into the Seraglio and into the ministerial pockets at Stamboul; and now that all the family income is mortgaged, the head of the house will still be obliged to hold his position by bribery. Surely the absolute independence of Egypt has now become a necessity.

Remains the real "bone of contention"—Constantinople. Europe has generally assumed that, with this Queen of the Golden Horn added to her dominions, the great Muscovite power would become irresistible; men and statesmen have made it an article of faith. I am far from believing in such results; at the same time, it would be unwise to allow Russia the chance. The problem to be worked out is this: How, when the Eastern half of Europe is almost wholly Slav, to exclude the Slav from Stamboul? To create another island like Roumania, breaking the Slavonic flood? Practically it was solved many years ago. Volney narrowly escaped the Bastile for advocating a Franco-Russian coalition against Turkey. When the Emperor Joseph I. of Austria had shaken the equilibrium of Europe by his alliance with Catharine II., the great traveller saw the political necessity of his project, namely, a Christian State having command of the Bosphorus. The Duke of Wellington, as has been told, recommended it in the same words, and the Russians have never refused to accept the measure. What says the Turk himself? "For Turkey, Roumelia is the Past, Anatolia is the Future." Pleasant prospect, by-the-bye, for poor Anatolia! And what say his serfs? "Avoid the Turk if you can; for either he eats you out of very love, or in his rage he tears you to pieces."

I would abolish the very name of Constantinople, whose hateful sound reminds us of religious cruelty and hypocrisy. Let us substitute a Kingdom or Principality of Byzantium,—a Hanse town mediatized by Europe. Her territory would extend northwards, through Eastern Roumelia, to the Balkans, and westwards to Rhodope, a fair and fertile country, somewhat larger than increased Servia. Protected by the Great Powers, she would be governed by a prince chosen from amongst the ruling families of Europe. She would be neither Greek, nor Bulgarian, nor Jewish, nor Armenian, nor Roumelian, nor Frank, but something of all. The Hellene would make her illustrious by his political aptitude and literary gifts; the Israelite and the Armenian would enrich her by banking and commerce; the Bulgarian and the Roumelian would be her hewers of wood and drawers of water; and, finally, the Frank would connect her with the civilization of the west. I know nothing in Europe which shows a finer combination of intellect and labour than this would be. No stronger dyke could be opposed to the Muscovite flood.

Turkey would thus be confined to Asia Minor proper, with Broussa or Koniah, the old Iconium, for a capital. Her new frontier, bordering on Russia and Persia, would remain untouched, and southwards she would be barred by a line drawn from Alexandretta, *viâ* Aleppo, to the Euphrates. She would thus cease to be an incubus on Europe, especially on south-eastern Europe, whose "neutral armaments" must last till relieved of her hideous presence. Thus the evil effects of her extended influence, which exists by acting upon the hates and fears of her neighbours, would presently be abated, leaving behind them the battle and the wrack. Thus her hopeless misgovernment and her inveterate maladministration would at once be confined within comparatively narrow limits. The old and venerable kingdoms, the Syria of the Seleucidæ, for instance, which her iron heel has trodden and trampled into wastes and deserts; where ruins are the sole remnants of a glorious and memorious past; where even hope, man's last delusion, can hardly cheer the prospect of the future, would soon recover a prosperity now all but forgotten. Christendom would once more be free from the deadening presence of that Mohammedan Mongol, whose hateful boast it ever was that—

> "Where once the Sultan's horse have trod,'
> Grass neither grows, nor shrub, nor tree."

Ay, truly quoth Mazeppa,—

> "The year before
> A Turkish army had marched o'er;
> And where the Spahi's hoof hath trod,
> The verdure flies the bloody sod."

"This is a mere spoliation of Turkey!" I hear someone cry. Well, yes; the Osmanli rose to empire by spoiling others, and it is now his turn to be spoiled. What he won by the sword he must keep by the sword, or the sword will snatch it from him. His presence in Europe is in these days an anachronism; it might be tolerated for good, certainly not for evil. He is fit only for Asia Minor, where, untrammeled by rival Plenipotentiaries and unscrupulous Ambassadors, he can throw off the tights that embarrass his limbs, and become once more the "man on horseback." There, at least, he can clean abolish his Irádes, his Tanzimát, and other bastard forms of constitutionalism, which, combined with so-called reforms, have destroyed the old forms without substituting anything new; which have weakened his material powers, spoiled his temper, and debased his character. There he can revert to those mediæval institutions that made the race what it was; to the eternal "*non possumus*," to the "Paçha of many Tales," to the slave and the concubine, to the eunuch and the mute, to the bowstring, the bastinado, and the bag for the light o'love. There *la gent qui porte le turban* may cultivate its mixture of childishness and senile cunning; its levity of mind, cloaked by solemn garb and mien; its mental indolence, with spasmodic efforts by way of change; and its conscious weakness warring with overweening arrogance. But Europe will no longer bear in her bosom this survival of the Unfittest. *Apage Sathanas!* Return, Tartar, to that Tartary whence thou camest. These are the words of St. Louis, and they shall be heard.

Our work in London is to analyze our minerals, subject them to every possible assay, report officially to the Khedive, and form and carry out some immediate plan of action, in regard to the land of Midian, in concurrence with the Khedive and the permission of our superiors, and to go back in February.

This, with seeing our friends and relatives, as much as we are able, buying our supplies and necessaries, bringing out each our new book, with some law-business, a variety of literary work, the inevitable daily correspondence and reading, leaves no idle time on our hands, and makes our "leave" all too short.

Dear reader! be as kind to me as you were three years and a half ago, even if we differ in religion, and disagree in politics, as might occur. Wish us all success and God-speed, and do not utter that unlucky word, "Good-bye." Let me sail from my dear Native Land with a "God bless you," and "au revoir' thrilling in my heart.

14, Montagu Place,
Montagu Square, London, W.
January 1879.

APPENDIX A.

NOTE TO CHAPTER XVIII.

Before I left, Dr. T. Gerson da Cunha, the most educated and cultivated native of Goa I have ever met, son-in-law of Dr. Da Gama, presented me with the following interesting account of the English and their monuments at Goa, which I am sure will be so interesting to Englishmen that I venture to introduce it here.

TO
THE DISTINGUISHED TRAVELLER,
CAPTAIN RICHARD F. BURTON,
BRITISH CONSUL AT TRIESTE,
I DEDICATE,
AS A TOKEN OF FRIENDSHIP,
THESE PAGES,
RELATING TO AN INTERESTING, THOUGH LITTLE KNOWN,
HISTORICAL EPISODE OF HIS GREAT NATION IN INDIA.

PREFACE.

A SUDDEN interest having been evinced by the British public in the existing and past relations of the English and Portuguese Governments of India on account of the new treaty to be signed between them, the author has deemed it advisable to reprint, in an accessible form, from the *Journal of the Bombay Branch of the Royal Asiatic Society*, the following "paper," read before that learned body in the month of March 1877.

While some organs of the Anglo-Indian press have insisted on the fact of the British having once been complete masters of the situation, when holding Goa for seventeen years with their garrison, and then generous enough to return it to the Portuguese on the general peace in 1815, the Portuguese journals have refused to place such a liberal construction on their evacuation of that Settlement. The evidence embodied in this *brochure* will, however, clear up all doubt on the matter.

Bombay, 29th May, 1877.

THE ENGLISH AND THEIR MONUMENTS AT GOA.

During that remarkable period from 1798 to 1815, when almost the whole continent of Europe was the theatre of wars by the army of Napoleon, Goa was occupied by English troops. So uncommon an incident, notwithstanding the just remark of Goldsmith that all history increases in value the nearer it approaches our own time, has been so lightly touched upon by historians as to be almost lost sight of in the stream of great events that have with unusual rapidity followed each other from the beginning of this century.

Soon after the French Revolution, all the Indian settlements belonging to that nation having been captured by the English, and the possessions of other European powers, except the little Portuguese settlements of Goa, Diu, and Damaun, having by degrees fallen into their hands, India appeared to be blessed with profound repose. Under such an appearance, however, a most formidable conspiracy was going on in the interior of Hindustan; and the French, under the control of the mighty Bonaparte, were again trying to establish an empire in Asia, of which the rival arms of Great Britain had deprived them.

The opportune possession of Bourbon and the Isle of France, in the Indian Ocean, their treaties of alliance with Tipû Sultân, and the influential position of their officers in the service of different Marâthâ chieftains and at the court of the Nizâm, organizing native armies on European principles, appeared to the French to be a favourable occasion to regain their former prestige and power. But, to carry out such a project with success, they were much in need of a central point on the Malabar Coast from whence to direct their operations; and that much-coveted point was Goa.

The desire of the French to possess Goa is evidenced by the following extract from a MS. entitled "Mémoire sur l'importance actuelle de l'Inde, et les moyens les plus efficaces d'y retablir la nation Françoise dans son ancienne splendeur," which was obtained for the British at Pondicherry, written by a French officer named Stanislas Lefebre, who accompanied General Decaen to India. "Bombay et Goa," says Lieut. Lefebre, "sont sans contredit les deux pointes les plus essentielles de la côte occidentale de la Presqu'île de l'Inde, mais dans l'alternatif et l'impossibilité d'attaquer les deux à la fois, Goa semble présenter aux François beaucoup plus d'avantages réels : d'abord en raison du territoire considérable qu'en dépend, et pouvoit entretenir l'armée par ses revenus; ensuite par la beauté de son port, et sa position avantageuse en regard aux états Marattes, avec qui l'on ne sauroit trop le répéter il est désormais indispensable d'entretenir étroites liaisons. L'importance de cette conquête en temps de paix ne seroit pas moindre en raison de la facilité qu'elle offre de communiquer avec la Mer Rouge, et il est aisé d'entrevoir que par la suite cette communication peut rendre à nouveau cette ville, autrefois si florissante, l'entrepôt de toutes les richesses de l'Asie, en bouleversant totalement le système commercial actuel, et faisant réprendre aux productions de l'Indostan la route que les Arabes et les Venétiens leur faisoient avant le découverte de Cap de Bonne Espérance par Vasco de Gama."*

Amidst such conflicting interests, there arrived at Calcutta, on the 17th May, 1798, Lord Mornington (afterwards Marquis Wellesley) and his brother Colonel Wellesley (afterwards the renowned Duke of Wellington). On succeeding Sir John Shore, Lord Mornington found the state of affairs in India extremely critical. Tipû Sultân, the ruler of Mysore, had sent an embassy to the French Governor of the Isle of France to propose an alliance with the object of driving the English away from India. The French flag had in the meanwhile been carried in triumph from Alexandria to Suez, and Napoleon was awaiting his opportunity for invading India. Under such circumstances one of the skilful measures of Lord Mornington, of whom it is said that "wherever he saw a Frenchman, there he was prepared to discern a foe," was to counteract by all means within his reach the designs of the French against Goa, by immediately despatching an Envoy thither, to be soon followed by troops to garrison its principal forts.

The first document relating to this affair is a letter by Lord Mornington, dated Fort William, 14th July, 1798, addressed to Lieut.-General Stuart, which runs thus :—"It appears certain by the last accounts from Europe that the French will soon either conquer Portugal, or compel that power to sign a disgraceful treaty of peace, in which case the French will endeavour to obtain possession of Goa."† After some lengthy reflections, he adds that he would make every effort to secure Goa from such a fate, and with this view offer to the Portuguese Governor the terms proposed to the several Dutch Governments in

* *Wellesley Despatches*, vol. iv., pp. 657, 658.

† *Ibid.*, vol. i., p. 128.

India,* and if the terms should be rejected he would directly attempt the reduction of Goa. He asks Lieut.-General Stuart whether the Governor of Goa would admit a British garrison into that settlement, and requests him to state what other measures would be likely to frustrate the supposed designs of the French against Goa, and what force would be necessary for its reduction. Lieut.-General Stuart replied, and although both were so early impressed with the importance of providing in the most effectual manner for the safety of Goa, the extensive preparations that became necessary in consequence of the conquest of Egypt by Bonaparte on the 1st July, 1798, combined with the hostile proceedings of Tipû Sultân, precluded the possibility of their furnishing a force for the protection of Goa. The fall of Seringapatam, however, followed on the 4th May, 1799, and Lord Mornington from that moment lost no time in adopting means for the accomplishment of that object, rendered more urgent by the discovery, at the conquest of Mysore, of papers consisting of a letter from Tipû Sultân to the French Directory, and a note of demand by Tipû's ambassadors, their aim being the alliance of the two Governments in opposition to the English, the Portuguese colonies playing a conspicuous part in the division of conquests between the two allied nations.† He selected Joseph Uhthoff, one of the Commissioners of Malabar, for the post of British Envoy at Goa, and his conduct in the course of these important and delicate transactions is said to have obtained for him the approbation of the Honourable Court of Directors.

The British troops employed in the defence of Goa were chiefly drawn from Bombay, and the question respecting their payment was agreed to be referred to the respective Home Governments of the two nations, and in the meanwhile the accounts of their expenses were kept in a separate form. The troops consisted of a detachment of about eleven hundred rank and file, furnished by H.M.'s 75th, 77th, and 84th Regiments, under the command of Colonel Sir William Clarke, Bart., of whom I shall speak more at length hereafter.

From a despatch by Lord Mornington to the Secret Committee of the Honourable Court of Directors, dated Fort William, 25th October, 1799, we learn that the British troops were admitted into Goa on the 6th September of that year, "with every demonstration of the most perfect cordiality and distinguished attention" on the part of the Governor of

* The Dutch held then the settlements of Chinsura on the Hooghly and Negapatam on the coast of Tanjore, which were made over to the English in 1824, and they received in return the English possessions on the coasts of Sumatra.

† *Wellesley Despatches*, vol. i., pp. 710-712

Goa, Francisco Antonio da Veiga Cabral. Lord Mornington adds that the importance of providing for the safety of Goa by garrisoning it with British troops was strongly impressed on his mind as early as the month of June 1798, but that subsequent to this, Egypt was occupied by the French, and he could realize his idea only after the fall of Seringapatam, in consequence of a negotiation which he had opened with the Governor of Goa.

But from some correspondence between Lord Mornington and Henry Dundas it appears that the former was not quite satisfied with the mere admission of British troops into Goa; he wanted more than this, for he writes:—"You ought to endeavour to negotiate with Portugal the cession of Goa, for which you might give Malacca in exchange, as the French look to Goa, and will labour to obtain it, either by force or intrigue."* Again, in a letter dated 24th October, 1799, and addressed to the same gentleman, he says, "You are already informed of my opinions with regard to the importance of the possession of Goa to our security and interest in every point of view, and I should hope that the present might prove a favourable opportunity for accomplishing the great advantage of obtaining the cession of Goa, either to the Crown or to the Company, in exchange either for Malacca or the Spice Islands, or for some equivalent pecuniary compensation. It appears to me that the attempt to obtain this cession ought not to be delayed, and, as I know you concur with me in my estimate of its value, I rely on you that the negotiation with the court of Lisbon will be immediately opened." †

Lord Mornington was, however, prevented from indulging further his scheme to add Goa to the British possessions, by the Governor of Goa, instead of allowing the English Governor-General to take Goa away from his hands, putting forward his own claims to a part of the territory of Canara, then recently conquered by British arms, and secured to them by the treaty of Mysore.

In reference to this subject, Lord Mornington, under the date of 24th October, 1799, writes to the Right Honourable Henry Dundas thus:— "The claims of Portugal to any part of the Canarese dominions of the late Tipû Sultân are so obviously weak, that I do not think it necessary to trouble you further on that subject than to request you to advert to the length of time during which the places claimed by the Portuguese have belonged to the State of Mysore, and to the nature of the conquest which brought them under our power. The Governor and Captain-General's pretensions to be considered as an ally in the late war appear

* *Wellesley Despatches*, vol. ii., p. 42.

† *Ibid.*, vol. ii., p. 129.

to be founded principally on the share which His Excellency bore in issuing an order for a royal salute to be fired from Fort Algnada (Aguada) on the occasion of the fall of Seringapatam, and of the death of Tipû Sultân. Although this claim is certainly more powerful than any which can be alleged for His Highness the Peishwa, I do not expect that, in the most liberal construction, this meritorious effort of forward and active zeal of His Excellency the Governor and Captain-General will be deemed to entitle Her Most Faithful Majesty (D. Maria I.) to any portion of our conquests. Even if the principle could be applied to cases of alliance in war, I doubt whether any degree of promptitude and alacrity manifested in rejoicing over the destruction of our late enemy could justify a claim on the part of the Governor and Captain-General to the right of an accessory after the fact." * This is true, though sarcastic enough, for the claims advanced by Cabral were unutterably unreasonable; but Lord Mornington forbore speaking so plainly to the Governor of Goa himself, and wrote him instead—in reply to his letter of the demand, which probably arose from the courteous reception he had accorded to the British Envoy and garrison at Goa—that his claims should be submitted to the decision of their respective governments in Europe. This answer may perhaps have been conformable with his politics.

The position of the British Envoy and troops at Goa had another advantage for the English Government, besides that of protecting the settlement against the French invasion. Lord Mornington writes to Jonathan Duncan, Governor of Bombay, thus:—"It has occurred to me that this communication between the E. I. Company and Purushram Bhow (a Maratha chieftain of Chittledoorg and Bednore, and once the arch-enemy of Tipû Sultân) can best be opened and maintained from the coast of Malabar (perhaps from Goa), from which place to the residence of Purushram Bhow the route would probably be found sufficiently easy and secure. It is my wish that Lieut.-Colonel Little and Mr. Uhthoff should be employed on this mission, and that for this purpose they should proceed with as little delay as possible to Goa." †

The above letter is dated the 30th April, 1799, and it was soon after that Mr. Uhthoff was sent to Goa, and about a couple of months after the monsoon (rainy season) the British troops entered the port of Goa.

I have so far confined myself to the despatches of the Governor-General. Now let us turn our attention to those of Colonel (about this time General) Wellesley. While the former treats of Goa as far as it affects his political situation, the latter indents on its resources for the

* *Wellesley Despatches*, vol. i., pp. 128, 129.
† *Ibid.*, p. 563.

comfort of his troops in the vicinity of Goa. In a letter dated the 21st September, 1799, and addressed to J. Uhthoff, British Envoy at Goa, he informs him that Sunda is taken possession of, and the European troops being far away from the source of supply of articles of most need to them, he is induced to look towards Goa for some of them, such as arrack for soldiers, and wine for officers, and promises liberal payment if those articles are sent to Sûpâ, only thirty miles from Goa.*

On the next day he writes to Colonel Stevenson thus:—"I have written to Mr. Uhthoff at Goa to request that he will endeavour to prevail upon the traders there to bring supplies for the European officers and soldiers from thence to the army at Sûpâ. I beg that you will desire the officer proceeding there to communicate with Mr. Uhthoff as soon as possible after he will arrive there, and to assist with small guards any traders that may wish to come to the army." The principal articles required were, as above remarked, Portuguese wine and Goa arrack. Respecting the latter article General Wellesley writes on the 13th October, 1800, to Uhthoff thus:—"I don't imagine that the Goa arrack is of so good quality as that made at Batavia or Colombo, and as it is more liable to adulteration * * * * no more may be purchased for the use of the army." † The editor of these despatches adds here a note stating that the Batavian arrack is made from rice, and that of Colombo from the juice of the cocoanut flower, and the Goa arrack is a less pure spirit because it is made chiefly from the date palm. It must be observed here, however, that the date palm is a very rare plant at Goa, and that the Goa arrack is obtained from the same source as that of Colombo.

During the year 1800 the British garrison of Goa consisted of one European regiment and two battalions of sepoys. During the monsoon of that year, when it was very improbable that an attempt would be made by the French against Goa, one of these battalions was sent up to Sunda.

About the middle of the next year (1801) a sudden change of an ominous nature was observed in the political horizon of Europe; and General Wellesley, who had hitherto maintained a confident tone respecting the security of the British interests at Goa, now became exceedingly apprehensive about its fate. On the 15th June, 1801, he writes from Seringapatam to Sir William Clarke thus:—"The consequence of affairs in Portugal will probably be a peace between that kingdom and France, the first condition of which peace it is likely will be either that

* *Wellington Supplementary Despatches*, vol. iv., p. 329.
† *Ibid.*, pp. 334, 335.

Goa shall be surrendered to the French, or that the detachment of British troops now at that place shall be sent away. In either case it is not probable our Government will give up the footing which has been gained at Goa; and our efforts must be directed to retain it,—at least till the orders of Government are received to abandon it." * Elsewhere he writes:—"You must be the best judge whether, with your present force, you will be able to retain your position at Goa as long as the British Government should think it proper. In my opinion, it is desirable that you should keep secret from the Governor of Goa the intelligence received from Lisbon, and that you should not add to your strength at Goa immediately, even if you should think that you will eventually require troops, unless you should be of opinion that the force will be wanted at the moment that the intelligence of the state of affairs in Portugal will arrive at Goa. If the consequence of the state of affairs in Portugal, as represented in Mr. Frere's letter, should be that you are to maintain your position at Goa against the inclination of the Portuguese Governor, * * * you must look forward to the mode of supplying your detachment with provisions, at least until navigation of the western coast shall again be open. I don't exactly know in what manner you live at Goa. * * * You may depend upon it that if you are to remain at Goa contrary to the inclinations of the Government, the first step on their part will be to endeavour to distress you for provisions." †

Sir William Clarke replied stating that should the Governor of Goa desire him to withdraw at a short notice, he would retort that he could not do so without orders from the Governor-General; should the demand, however, be insisted on, then he would immediately take a more central position in the island of Goa,—at the Arsenal, for instance—and with the remainder of his force secure his magazines at Gaspar Dias and Cabo, and occupy the port of St. Iago, this being the principal pass into the island from the eastward (and a pass that has, moreover, an historical import, being the place of encampment of the redoubtable Adil Khân, when he tried for the second time to reconquer Goa from the hands of Albuquerque, about the beginning of the sixteenth century). Sir William adds that should orders be given him to seize the place, he would immediately make the Grenadier battalion from Sûpâ penetrate by the Tinem Ghât as far as Pondâ, instead of prosecuting the route from Sadâsivagadh, and having to encounter in the neighbourhood of Margao one of the European Portuguese regiments. Pondâ, he says, is about ten miles from St. Iago, and on the approach of native troops there he

* *Wellington Supplementary Despatches*, vol. iv., p. 447.

† *Ibid.*, vol. iv., p. 449.

would push three hundred men of the 84th, with two field-pieces, across the river from St. Iago, to cover the advance of these troops into the island, and then join in an attack upon the post of Margao. The most difficult operation would, however, remain to be performed, and that is "carrying the fort of Aguada." But the accession of the native troops would allow of his detaching six hundred men of the 84th against the fortress, and he had little doubt of succeeding against it by escalade or assault. Having done this, "the Portuguese territory in this quarter," Sir William exultingly adds, "would be our own." * And so it would, but that no such violent measures did ever become necessary.

In consequence of the above reply, General Wellesley, writing to Captain Lewis on the 2nd July, 1801, says: "You may tell Colonel Stevenson that I have heard from Sir William Clarke, who thinks himself very secure with the assistance which I have proposed to afford him against any effort which the Portuguese can make to remove him. You can depend upon it that I am fully aware of the advantages of our situation at Goa, and very unwilling to give it up." †

About the end of October 1801, the position of Sir William Clarke at Goa was, however, not so secure as his former communications had led General Wellesley to believe. A communication from the General to Lieut.-General Stuart states that he had received letters from Sir William regarding his situation at Goa, from the perusal of which he infers that Sir William does not think himself strong enough to take possession of the place while the Governor of Goa has a strong disinclination.

In course of time, however, the difficulties were smoothed, and the Governor of Goa not only consented to receive a company of native infantry in place of about fifty recovered sepoys belonging to different corps who had been left at Goa, but the negotiations were carried on by Sir William with such tact as to succeed in procuring orders from the Governor for the introduction of British troops into Damaun and Diu, in disobedience to the orders which the Governor had received from Portugal.‡

In reference to the result of these negotiations, General Wellesley writes to Jonathan Duncan on the 5th November, 1801, thus:—"Are you not astonished at Sir William Clarke's success in his negotiation with the Government of Goa regarding Damaun and Diu? We must, notwithstanding, secure Goa, and upon this subject I have lately urged General Stuart." §

Within one month, however, circumstances were altered. The Governor

* *Wellington Supplementary Despatches*, vol. iv., p. 491 *et seq.*
† *Ibid.*, p. 490. ‡ *Ibid.*, vol. ii., pp. 610-616. § *Ibid.*, vol. ii., p. 613.

of Goa had changed his mind, and desired Sir William to withdraw the British troops from Goa; but General Wellesley interfered in the affair, stating that, the occupation of the country being merely military, he would have no scruple in advising Sir William not only not to withdraw from his position, but to draw in to Goa forthwith as large a body of troops as would secure his stay there, taking the precaution, however, by the adoption of so violent a measure, not to create more extensive political complications, which it was necessary to avoid.*

About the beginning of the year 1802 all the obstacles had been more or less overcome, and that happy turn affairs had taken was, it seems, materially aided by a letter from Lord Mornington to the Governor and Captain-General of Goa. As this letter gives an insight into the intricacies of the political situation of the time, I shall offer no apology for inserting it here *in extenso*:—

No. CLXVII.

"THE MARQUESS WELLESLEY TO HIS EXCELLENCY THE VICEROY OF GOA.

"*Cawnpore, January 17th*, 1802.

"SIR,

"1. By authentic advices which I have just received from Europe, I am apprised of the conclusion of a treaty of alliance between the Governments of France and Portugal, by which Her Most Faithful Majesty has been compelled to abandon the relations hitherto subsisting with His Britannic Majesty, and to unite with the Government of France in hostile proceedings against the British Empire.

"2. Under the knowledge of this event, it becomes my indispensable duty to adopt the necessary measures for precluding the Government of France from the means of applying the resources of the Portuguese possessions in India, under the provisions of the late treaty of alliance, to purposes injurious to the interests of Great Britain.

"3. The security of this object manifestly requires that the Portuguese Settlements in India should be immediately placed under the authority of the British power, and should continue subject to that authority until these possessions shall be restored to Her Most Faithful Majesty by any arrangement which may take place at the conclusion of a general peace in Europe, or which may be hereafter established between His Britannic Majesty and the Court of Lisbon.

"4. Anxious that the measures which my duty compels me to pursue with respect to the Settlement of Goa should be carried into effect without injury to the persons and property of its inhabitants, and desirous to combine with the execution of those measures the utmost consideration for your Excellency's high rank and exalted station, and also wishing to make every

* *Wellington Supplementary Despatches*, vol. ii., pp. 636, 637.

practicable provision for your Excellency's convenience and accommodation, I have directed Sir William Clarke, previous to the employment of the force placed under his command, to propose to your Excellency terms for the peaceable surrender of the civil and military Government of Goa and its immediate dependencies.

"5. Your Excellency's wisdom and discernment will suggest to you the inutility of opposing any resistance to the accomplishment of this measure, and your Excellency's justice and humanity will not permit you to expose the lives and property of the inhabitants of Goa to the danger of an unavailing contest with the superior power of the British army.

"6. In expectation of this, I have directed Sir W. Clarke to receive and to communicate to me any representations which your Excellency may desire to convey to me relating to the concerns and interests of the Portuguese Settlements, also relating to any points connected with the execution of the orders and instructions with which he has been furnished. It will afford me satisfaction to conform to your Excellency's wishes, on all occasions, to the utmost extent compatible with the obligations of my public duty.

"7. It is proper that I should inform your Excellency that I have transmitted orders for the introduction of the British authority into the Settlements of Damaun and Diu, similar to those which I have deemed it necessary to issue for the occupation of the Settlement of Goa.

"8. I refer your Excellency, for a more ample communication upon all these points, to Sir W. Clarke.

"I have the honour to be,
"With great consideration and respect, Sir,
"Your Excellency's most obedient, faithful servant,
"WELLESLEY." *

A similar letter was addressed to His Excellency the Governor of Macao.

It has been said that one of the most rigorous measures ever displayed by Lord Mornington in his Indian policy was the establishment of subsidiary alliances with the native princes, with the intention to make the Company a paramount power, and to secure the tranquillity of the country. It was perhaps from his possessing such a genius for consolidating an empire that he has, not inaptly, been termed "the Akbar of the Company's dynasty." But he did more than this. Besides establishing subsidiary alliances, and garrisoning with British troops the Portuguese and Dutch settlements, he had treaties made with the native princes stipulating the total exclusion of Europeans hostile to the English from their armies. Here is, for instance, a clause relating to the subject in the treaty of Bassein, signed about the end of the year 1802:—"Whereas it has been usual for His Highness Rao Pundit Pur-

* *Wellington Supplementary Despatches*, vol. ii., p. 617, *et seq.*

dhaun Behander to enlist and retain in his service Europeans of different countries, his said Highness hereby agrees and stipulates that, in the event of war breaking out between the English and any European nation, and of discovery being made that any European or Europeans in his service belonging to such nation at war with the English shall have meditated injury towards the English, or have entered into intrigues hostile to their interests, such European or Europeans so offending shall be discharged by his said Highness, and not suffered to reside in his dominions."*

Within a short time, however, all these precautionary measures were deemed unnecessary, since the treaty of Amiens, signed on the 22nd March, 1802, reinstated the French in their former possessions, and the British troops received orders to evacuate Goa. But the Government of France resuming, under the provisions of that treaty, its Indian possessions, made such demonstrations as to clearly reveal their intention to establish, on the foundation of those possessions, a political and military power, and to strengthen and augment it by every practicable connection with the native states. The reluctance, therefore, with which the British troops quitted Goa may be easily imagined.

Joseph Uhthoff had in the meanwhile resigned his post of British Envoy at Goa, and Lieut. Dillon was then the Acting Resident. General Wellesley, in a letter addressed to the latter dated the 17th November, 1802, says, "By a letter transmitted to me by Major Budden, I observe that the Governor-General has ordered that the troops may be withdrawn from Goa. I hope, however, that you are to remain; and at all events, I beg that you will remain there till you receive the further orders of Government. In the present situation of affairs in this part of India, it is essentially necessary that a person should reside at Goa, on the part of the British Government, who possesses the confidence of, and has an influence over, the persons at the head of the Government of that settlement."†

Again, in a letter addressed the next day to Lieut-General Stuart, General Wellesley writes thus :—"The Governor-General has informed the Governor of Goa that he has given orders that the troops may be withdrawn from thence. . . . It is necessary that the Acting Resident, Lieut. Dillon, should remain at Goa, this place being a most important source of supply for an army in the Mahratta territory, and there is no chance of using that place in that manner unless they have a person residing there in whom the Portuguese have confidence, and who has

* *Wellington Supplementary Despatches*, vol. ii., p. 402.

† *Wellington Despatches*, vol. i., p. 120.

some influence over the persons at the head of their Government, Lieut. Dillon being of this description."*

In January 1803, General Wellesley writes to Sir W. Clarke:—"It gives me great satisfaction to observe that everything has been brought up from Goa with so much speed."† Respecting the contracts for the supply of arrack and other articles from Goa for British troops, he writes elsewhere, "I suspect that the merchants of Goa are not the only people concerned in these contracts for the supply of our troops, but that the members of the Government have some share in them. If that be true, we shall be sure of having the use of that convenient station as a link in our communication with Bombay, as long as they have a beneficial contract in view."‡

The peace resulting from the treaty of Amiens was of so short a duration that a rupture between France and England took place on the 22nd May, 1803, and on the 7th June General Wellesley writes to Lieut-General Stuart thus:—"It appears to be the Governor-General's intention that, if the Viceroy of Goa will receive a British garrison, British troops should be sent to Goa without loss of time. . . . There are already at Goa two companies of the garrison of Hâlihâl . . . but the Governor-General anticipates the refusal of the Viceroy of Goa to receive the British troops at present, which I acknowledge I think more than probable; and in that case he wishes that troops should be so stationed as to prevent the French from carrying into execution their plans, or to drive them from Goa in case they should get into that place."§ In a short time, however, the difficulties, it appears, were arranged, and a force was ordered to proceed to Goa; for the General, writing to Lieut.-Colonel Montresor on the 9th July, says, "I observe that you have been directed to make arrangements to send a force to protect Goa from the French grasp."||

The Governor-General, Marquis Wellesley, in a letter addressed to Lord Hobart on the 15th November, 1803, writes:—I have the satisfaction to inform your Lordship that a British garrison has occupied the important fortress of Goa, with the entire concurrence of the Portuguese Government of that settlement."¶ Their detachment entered, with the consent of the Portuguese Government, into Goa on the 3rd September, 1803. Besides this detachment, the squadron under Vice-Admiral

* *Wellington Despatches*, vol. iii., p. 407.
† *Ibid.*, p. 511.
‡ *Ibid.*, vol. iii., p. 522.
§ *Ibid.*, vol. iii., pp. 162, 163.
|| *Ibid.*, vol. iv., p. 134.
¶ *Ibid.*, vol. iii., p. 455.

Rainer, stationed off the coast of Malabar, had its attention particularly directed to the defence of Goa.*

At that time, however, the troops were so thinly scattered over all India that only a small force could be spared for Goa. General Wellesley, writing on this subject to Sir William Clarke, says, "Your situation at Goa is precisely the same as that of every other commanding officer in India. You have not the number of troops you would wish to have to defend your post."†

Complications with the Portuguese Government soon arose. General Wellesley, in a letter of the 2nd November, 1804, to Sir W. Clarke, says, among other things, that the Governor of Goa is not disposed to allow them to retain their footing there; and, to avoid further misunderstanding, he recommends Sir William to have a conference with the Governor. He adds that on no account shall the settlement of Goa be given up to the French; that the Portuguese troops should coöperate with the British, their pay being made equal to the pay received by the British troops, the extra expense being paid by the British Government, and that at the conclusion of the war with France they will deliver over the settlement intact to the Crown of Portugal. These instructions appear to have been carried out with success. To these were added others by the Marquis Wellesley, who, on the 11th December, 1804, writes, through his Private Secretary, N. B. Edmondstone, to Sir W. Clarke thus:—"In case of the demise of the Viceroy, the Envoy should follow the general principles on which were founded the instructions of H. E. the Governor-General of the 11th December, 1801, and 6th and 17th January, 1802, and 17th June, 1802, to negotiate with the existing Government to place it on the same state of British power as before, and proving his exertions ineffectual, to proceed to assume, in the name of His Majesty, the civil and military government of Goa.‡

But there never was the least need of the British assuming the civil government, while their military occupation continued almost uninterrupted, until the general peace in 1815.§ Thus Goa was for seventeen long years, with the exception of a short interval in 1802, in the hands of a British detachment, who had, however, in compliance with the terms of the agreement, to give it up, although till the end complete masters of

* An event of some historical importance, worth notice here, is that some men belonging to the squadron of Vice-Admiral Rainer lost their lives in the great fire in Bombay on the 19th February, 1803.—*Huma viagem de duas mil legoas*, etc., part ii., p. 16, and the *Annual Register* for 1803.

† *Wellington Despatches*, vol. iv., p. 192.

‡ *Ibid.*, vol. iv., pp. 55, 56.

§ *Ensaios sobre a Estatistica*, etc., por J. M. Bordale, Lisboa, 1862, p. 37.

the situation, when they saw it incurred no longer the danger of a French invasion.

The period from 1804 to 1815 is devoid of any political interest as far as the British occupation of Goa is concerned, although not absolutely destitute of some curious incidents worth recording in the annals of the country.

It is but natural that within such a period there should have occurred frequent changes in the appointments of the Commanding Officer and Political Resident, as well as those of the officers and men belonging to the subsidiary force at Goa.

Sir William Clarke, Bart., who while at Goa kept himself on the best terms with the Portuguese Government, the proof of which lies in the rank of Major-General which he, not unlike several British officers in the Peninsular War, held in the Portuguese army with the sanction of H.M. the King of Great Britain and Ireland, was compelled by ill health to sail on furlough to England in 1804.

On his return to India in 1807, Sir William was posted to the command of troops at Seringapatam, where he died in 1808. Sir William Clarke was one of the most distinguished officers in the British army at the time, and was replaced in his command of the military force at Goa by Colonel Adams. When Goa was visited by Dr. Claudius Buchanan, in January 1808, the British detachment consisted of two European and two native regiments, and were under the command of Colonel Adams, of H.M.'s 78th Regiment. Dr. Buchanan informs us, in his *Christian Researches in Asia*, that when he was going to visit the palace of the Inquisition in the old city of Goa, accompanied by Lieut. Kempthorne, of H.M.'s brig *Diana*, and Capt. Stirling, of H.M.'s 84th Regiment, which regiment was then at Goa, Colonel Adams facetiously told him that if any accident should befall him within the walls of the Inquisition, he would at once march with the 84th Regiment to Old Goa and take the palace of the Inquisition by assault. Fortunately, however, nothing untoward happened to the reverend tourist, although he had not a little difficulty in attaining the object of his visit—information on the Goa Inquisition from the priest at the head of that dreadful tribunal.

The post of British Envoy at Goa also underwent several changes, the last incumbent being Captain Courtland Schuyler.

The Governors of Goa were changed only twice during this long interval of seventeen years, a circumstance rather unusual in the annals of the Goa Government, though fortunate enough for the British commander, who would, under other circumstances, have had to change his tactics in conformity with the caprice of each new Governor. The two Governors above alluded to were the before-mentioned Francisco Antonio da Veiga Cabral, 89th Governor and Captain-General, who governed from May 1794 to May 1807, and B. J. de Lorena, Conde de Sarzedas, 90th Viceroy and Captain-General, who governed from May 1807 to November 1816.* Of these two the former appears to have been friendly towards the English, although anecdotical tales are not wanting among the people of Goa of how he once offended the whole British detachment by pulling down their flag in their own encampment and hoisting his own. But altogether he seems to have maintained himself on the most cautious of terms with the English officers; while the second appears to have been affected with Anglophobia, and the letters he has left behind cannot but be extremely displeasing to the English, as they are to an impartial historian.

During the administration of Lord Minto, Portugal was occupied by the invading army of France, and orders were received from the English ministry to take possession of the Portuguese settlements in the East,—a measure quite unnecessary with regard to Goa, Diu, and Damaun, where from 1799 an arrangement had been made reserving the civil government to the Portuguese, and assigning the military authority to Great Britain. It was not so, however, in reference to Macao, where in 1801 a reinforcement of British troops to garrison its fort was sent when it was known that the French Government intended to make a descent on it, and which was prevented at one time; but it appears to have subsequently evacuated the settlement altogether.† An expedition was therefore sent, which sailed from Calcutta and Madras in the month of July 1809, and arrived off Macao on the 11th September, to the utter astonishment of the Governor of that settlement, who was without instructions from Lisbon, and refused to receive the sanction of the Viceroy of Goa for giving up the colony to the British on an arrangement similar to the one existing in the Indian settlements. Force was, however, employed, and the English troops were soon in possession of it, although this occupation very nearly provoked a war with China,—for the Celestial Empire thought that it had some right to be consulted on so delicate a matter before undertaking it,—which led to the complete stoppage for some time of the British trade with that country.

Of the several letters from the Viceroy, Conde de Sarzedas, to the Minister at Lisbon, only two bear on the question of the British occu-

* *Bosquejo Historico de Goa*, por M. V. d'Abreu, Nova Goa, 1858, pp. 56, 57.

† *Wellesley Despatches*, vol. i., pp. 612, 613. Also see a letter dated 20th November, 1801, addressed by the Governor-General to James Drummond, President of the Committee of Supercargoes, Canton: *ibid.*, pp. 612, 613.

pation of Goa.* One is dated the 8th October, 1808, addressed to the Visconde de Anadia, and refers to the damage caused by the English troops to the fortresses and houses occupied by them at Goa and Damaun.

He also gives a circumstantial narrative of how the English troops landed at the "Cabo," at first without the consent of his predecessor, the Governor and Captain-General Veiga Cabral, under the deceitful machinations of a Hanoverian engineer, by name Blister, in the Portuguese service, who then advised the Governor to declare, in order to avoid public scandal, that the reinforcement had entered the Goa territory with his consent. He adds that on his arrival at Goa he met the British Envoy there, by name Courtland Schuyler, and the British detachment was under the command of Lieut.-Col. A. Adams; while Major-General Sir William Clarke, who had left for Europe in 1804, was then in the command of troops at Seringapatam. We have already learnt that it was at Seringapatam that he died soon after, in 1808. The Hanoverian engineer Blister was then dead.

The other letter is dated the 18th December, 1812, and is addressed to the Conde das Galveas. It gives a long list of the expenses incurred by the Portuguese Government in the repair of edifices, such as the Convent da Graça at Damaun, occupied by British troops, and the fortress of Mormugão at Goa; the latter fortress, he adds, was occupied by them in the month of May 1808, and evacuated in that of November 1812. The fortress of Aguada was, according to the Conde de Sarzedas, occupied for the first time on the 2nd January, 1802, and evacuated on the 1st April of the same year. The English, he adds, would then have willingly taken possession of Goa, but for the treaty of Amiens being signed just about that time, which compelled them to quit the place. On the first occurrence of a rupture between France and England they again entered that fortress, in the month of November 1804, the troops crossing the mouth of the river in a large number of boats from their encampment on the opposite hill of the "Cabo," under the command of Colonel Spray. They did not enter, as before, by the gate, but by escalade, and the first announcement of their having taken possession of the fortress was conveyed to the Governor of Goa by their firing twenty-one guns, and by their warm hurrahs and cheers, which were distinctly heard at the Governor's palace at New Goa. Their occupation of this fortress was so precipitate that no time was allowed for the making of a regular inventory of articles contained in the magazines belonging to that fortress; and therefore, while the damage caused by the British troops to the fort-

* *Bosquejo das Possessoēs Portuguezas no Oriente*, etc., por Joaquim Pedro Celestino Soares, Lisboa, 1853, vol. iii., pp. 177, *et seq.*, and 188 *et seq.*

ress of Mormugão is clearly made out, that to the fortress of Aguada is left out of calculation.

This letter is altogether a deliberate indictment against the British troops of carelessness, making insinuations even against their probity in having quitted Goa without paying their debts. The Viceroy can nevertheless not deny, in spite of his anti-English policy, that considerable profit accrued to local trade from the presence of the British troops there. He confesses that their grasp of the country was so firm that the Portuguese might have lost their settlement altogether, had it not been for the timely interference of St. Francis Xavier, the palladium of Goa, who somehow prevented the English from taking possession of his sacred trust. The tradition still current in the country goes beyond the spiritual protection accorded by the Apostle of the Indies against foreign invasion, by ascribing to him the assumption of the bodily form to drive away the English by his miraculous might and power.* Be this as it may, the belief is still rooted among the people of Goa that as long as the saint's body remains there, no earthly monarch will be able to wrest that settlement from the hands of His Most Faithful Majesty the King of Portugal.

The Viceroy at last vents his indignation on some half-caste Portuguese officers who were unpatriotic enough to exchange the Portuguese for the English uniform, in order to flatter the English and get better pay from them.

Now let us pass on to describe the English monuments at Goa. These consist of three tombstones on the hill of "Sinquerim," only a few yards distant from, and to the eastward of, the lighthouse, and a pretty large cemetery on the southern slope of the hill called "Cabo," almost opposite to "Sinquerim." The three tombs at Sinquerim consist of an obelisk and two mounds, one of which had an inscriptional slab, which has been removed, and the other is now reduced to stone and mortar.

The English cemetery at Goa consists of an oblong area, about 180 yards long by 145 broad, walled all round; and the gate, with some architectural pretensions, has massive teakwood doors. The key of this door is in the hands of the chaplain in the neighbouring old convent, now reduced to the Governor's summer residence, with a chapel attached to it. There is a gatekeeper, who takes care of the cemetery, and is paid by the English Government six rupees a month. To the right of the gate, let into the wall, is a two-feet square slab, all the letters being worn out except HIS M's. .... The whole area is studded with tombs, forty-one in number, eight of which have a four-sided wall

* See my *Memoir on the History of the Tooth-Relic of Ceylon*, p. 57.

around. Interspersed among the tombs are thirteen trees,—six mango, six cashew-nut, and one jack-fruit tree.

Besides these relics of the English at Goa, there were until lately the ruins of the barracks and hospital of the English troops at the "Cabo," which were demolished in 1848 by the order of the then Governor, José Ferreira Pestana, but at present no vestige of them remains.*

In the English cemetery there are six epitaphs, but none in the state of being easily perused. I had no little difficulty in deciphering them, and I beg to present them to the Society just as I copied them in the month of October last.

It will be observed from the dates on the tombstones that some persons were buried there subsequent to the time of the British occupation, and even now the English and American residents at Pangim continue to bury their dead in this same cemetery.

Among travellers who have visited the English monuments at Goa, I find only one who has deigned to leave us a record of his impression of them. It is Mr. W. Walker,† who writes :—"I visited the burial-ground at Cabo, built and used by the British force of 10,000 ‡ men when they held possession of the seaboard points of Goa, to prevent the French entering India by this route in 1805.§ The massive laterite stone wall which surrounds it is as perfect as the day it was built, the laterite in this neighbourhood being the best I have anywhere seen; but the lofty arched entrance gates have long ago been despoiled of every particle of wood.‖ The burial-ground is used for rice cultivation, and the very tombstones are worn down from the sharpening of native tools on them; where not cultivated, it is overgrown with high, rank grass, said to be alive with the deadly *cobra de capello*. If it be true, as I have heard, that the Collector of Belgaum allows an annual sum to keep it in order, I can assure him that not a pice-worth of care is bestowed on it . . . and I do not think it is desirable to do so, for if people who build memorials over the remains of friends do not like to build deep and solid foundations for tombs, and let inscriptions into deep side panels, with an outside protection of plate-glass half an inch thick, they must expect them to fall to decay with more or less rapidity; and it is absurd to

* I am indebted for this information, and for a great deal more, to my friend Sr. Luiz Xavier Correa da Graça, ex-Judge of one of the Courts at Goa, who had, besides, the advantage of being an eye-witness of the events above recorded.

† *Jottings of an Invalid in Search of Health*, published under the *nom de plume* "Tom Cringle." Bombay, 1865, pp. 265, 266.

‡ This number is very much exaggerated.

§ The British occupation began in 1799.

‖ There is now a wooden door, of which care is taken.

think that posterity is to keep gravestones in repair for ever; and if not for ever, why a day? Mourners, don't build *shams* as brick and mortar expressions of your grief!"

Here follow the inscriptions:—

SACRED
TO
THE MEMORY OF
CAPTAIN JAMES GRAHAM,
OF THE 7TH REGIMENT BOMBAY N.I.,
WHO DIED ON BOARD OF THE
"LADY EAST,"
OFF VINGORLA,
ON HIS PASSAGE TO ENGLAND,
ON THE 11TH APRIL A. 1829,
AGED 44 YEARS.

J. G.

SACRED
TO THE MEMORY OF
THEODOSIA DORCAS,
THE BELOVED WIFE OF CAPTAIN E. MESSNER, 39 M.N.I.,
WHO DEPARTED THIS LIFE THE TWENTY-SECOND SEPTEMBER, 1838,
DEEPLY REGRETTED BY ALL WHO KNEW HER, FOR HER
MANY INESTIMABLE VIRTUES.

SACRED
TO THE MEMORY OF
MARGARET REEL,
WIFE OF
JOHN WILLIAM REEL,
CONDUCTOR IN THE
HON'BLE COMPANY'S SERVICE,
WHO DEPARTED THIS LIFE
THE 19TH OF DECEMBER,
1808.

SHE WAS A VIRTUOUS WIFE,
AN AFFECTIONATE MOTHER,
AND A FAITHFUL AND SINCERE
FRIEND.

SACRED
TO THE MEMORY OF
SUSANNA JANE PULTON,
WIFE OF CAPTAIN PULTON,
OF THE 3RD REGT. M.N.I.,
WHO DEPARTED ON THE 5TH
SEPTEMBER, 1826,
AGED 23 YEARS.

ERECTED
TO THE MEMORY OF
CAPT. ISW * * * SMITH,
* * No. 2 BAT * * 10 N.I. * * *
BO * * * * * * * * *
AMAR * * * * * * * *
* * * * *
EST * * * * *

SACRED
TO THE MEMORY OF
OLIVER * * * BLE,
* * * WHO DEPARTED
THIS LIFE * * * 10
* * OF OCTOBER *
* * * * 15

APPENDIX B.

CHRONOLOGICAL TABLES FOR HISTORICAL REFERENCE OF THE VICEROYS, THE ARCHBISHOPS, AND THE RELIGIOUS ESTABLISHMENTS OF GOA.

SECTION I.

CHRONOLOGICAL TABLE OF THE VICEROYS AND GOVERNORS OF GOA AND PORTUGUESE INDIA, from the Conquest to the present time, with the most memorable events in each Administration.*

DON FRANCISCO D'ALMEIDA, first Viceroy of India, in 1505, resided commonly on the Island of Angediva, or at Cochin. This officer, the seventh son of D. Lopo d'Almeida, first Conde de Ahrantes (De Barros), left Lisbon on March 25th, 1505, with an armada of 22 sail and 1,500 fighting men; reached Angediva September 12th, and, on October 24th, Cananor, where he assumed his title. Thence he passed to Cochin, where he delayed for some time, and built a fortress, with others at Cananor, Anjediva, and Sofala. He took and destroyed Kilwa (Quiloa), Mombasah, Panani (Punani), and Dabul in Sind; and he gained great victories over the Turks and the Soldan of Egypt. In 1506 his son, D. Antonio d'Almeida, discovered the islands of Ceylon and Sumatra. After governing for four years, he was returning homewards when, on March 1st, 1510, at the age of sixty, he landed at the Agoada de Saldanha, near the Cape of Good Hope, and was miserably killed by the Kafirs (Caffres) with a wooden assegai, which pierced his throat. The untimely death, sad as that of Lord Mayo, is eloquently deplored by Camões.

1509.—ALFONSO D'ALBUQUERQUE (No. 2), second son of Goncalo d'Albuquerque, Lord of Villa-Verde, the greatest hero of Portuguese Asia, succeeded Almeida this year in the month of November,—others say at the end of October,—with the simple title of Governor, after running imminent danger at the court of the "Zamorin" (*Samorim*), or Samire, Rajah of Calicut, whence he extricated himself by his invincible courage and the love of his soldiers. He had already (February 17th, 1510) taken Goa from the

* This Chronological Table has been corrected and extended by Sr. Miguel Vicente d'Abreu, the Portuguese translator of De Kloguen. The latter borrowed his materials from the *Biographias dos Vice-Reis*, and *A Galleria* of the same author, by Sr. Delorme Collaco; the *Colecções dos Facsimiles dos Governadores e Arlebispos*, by Sr. F. N. Xavier; the *Almanak de Goa*, by Sr. C. J. Peres; the *Dialogos de Varia Historia*, by Sr. Mariz, and other trustworthy documents.

Mohammedans, on which occasion he found in the city 40 large guns, 55 falconets, and smaller pieces, with hand-grenades, and all kinds of weapons and ammunition: upon the stocks were 40 vessels large and small, amongst them 17 "foysts" (*fustas*) ready for sea; the royal stables contained 160 Persian horses, and the Custom-house revenue was 82,000 xerafins per annum. The future capital had been recaptured, three months after the conqueror's departure, by Adil Shah (Idal Khão); but he returned to attack it a second time on November 25th, the same year, with a fleet of 800 Portuguese and 200 Malabar auxiliaries. The "Historia dos Descobrimentos," etc. (vol. ii., pp. 111-12), speaking of the second conquest of Goa, which cost only 80 lives, declares that the spoils there for three days were exposed to the soldiery, amounted to an enormous sum, besides the precious stones and specie carried off by the enemy, and the plunder hidden by the conquerors. The Royal fifth of the booty amounted to 200,000 crusados (= 500,000 xerafins). The heroic Governor captured Malacca the year following, and built a fort at Calicut, and another at Goa: he discovered the islands of Banda and the Moluccas; drove the Arabs* from Aden, thus opening the navigation of the Red Sea, and received a number of embassies from the kings and princes of the East. In 1514 he built the church of N. Sra. da Serra, in consequence of a vow for the salvage of the ship *Santa Maria de Serra*, which had grounded on a shoal near Camaram Island, at the entrance of the Red Sea. In 1515 he sailed for Ormuz (Persian Gulf), but hearing that he had incurred the displeasure of his Sovereign, and had been superseded in the government of India, he returned to Goa and died, aged sixty-three, after ten years' service in India. The death took place on December 16th, 1515, as he entered the harbour. His remains were buried in his own chapel of N. Sra. de Serra. Albuquerque was truly a great man in every respect. When tardy justice was at last done to this victim of an ungrateful king, his remains were transported from Goa, and, with great pomp, were placed (April 6th, 1566) in the church of N. Sra. de Graca, of the Order of St. Augustine in Portugal. This transfer was not without much opposition and regret on the part of the Goanese. For the subsequent vicissitudes of the hero's ashes, see the Viagem de Lisboa á China (vol. ii., pp. 45-47), by Sr. C. J. Caldeira.

1515.—Lopo Soares d'Albargaria, the next (3rd) Governor, left Lisbon April 7th, 1515, with 13 keel and 1,500 men-at-arms, besides sailors; reached Goa September 8th, and took possession whilst his predecessor was at Hormuz. He attacked the port of Jeddah (*Judá*) and made its chief a vassal of the Crown; built the fort of Ceylon, rendering the Island-King a tributary, and on December 20th, 1518, after three years' rule, handed over the power to his successor at Cochin. Thence he passed to Cananor, and returned to Portugal on January 20th, 1519, richer in worldly goods than in renown.†

1518.—Diogo Lopes de Sequiera (No. 4), left Lisbon with a fleet of 9 ships and 1,500 men, on March 18th, 1518; reached Goa September 8th; and took charge at Cochin, on December 20th of the same year. He built the fort of Chaul, and governed till January 22nd, 1522, on which day he embarked for Portugal. He died at home on October 14th, 1530, *æt.* sixty-

* Or rather the Arabs of Aden drove him away.

† Various details concerning the rule of this and other governors, distributed in the chronological order of the Portuguese kings, will be found in the "Compendio da Historia Portugueza," by Tiburcio Antonio Craveiro (p. 111, *et seq.* Rio de Jan. edit. of 1833). The curious will also consult the "Bibliographia Historioa Portugueza," by Jorge Cezar Figaniere, an officer in the Secretariat of State for Foreign Affairs (Part II., tit. 3rd, Lisbon edit. of 1850, 1 vol. 4to.) There are many other monographs whose names are omitted for brevity

four, and was buried in the Ermida (chapel) under the invocation of N. Sra. da Consolação, near the villa or town of Alandral.

1522.—D.* DUARTE DE MENEZES (No. 5), Lord of the House of Tarouca, left Lisbon April 5th, 1521. In the following September he reached Cochin, where he awaited the return of his predecessor from Hormuz, and took possession on January 22nd, 1522. During his rule he built the fortress of Ternate in the Moluccas; and the body of Saint Thomas the Apostle was discovered at Meliapur, seven leagues from the port of Paliacati.† His salary, exceeding that of all former Governors, was raised to 30,000 crusados, not including the disbursements for justice and general government. Unfortunate in all his undertakings, he was superseded, and gave up charge on December 4th, 1524.

1524.—D. VASCO DA GAMA (No. 6), Admiral, Count of Vidigueira. Discoverer of the way to India by the Cape of Good Hope, and created the first Admiral in the Indian Seas, left Lisbon April 9th, 1524, with 16 ships, and 3,000 soldiers; arrived at Goa about the end of September, when D. Duarte was at Hormuz; took provisional charge, and returning to Cochin was formally installed on December 4th. His name sufficed to make the name of Portugal respected in the Eastern Seas; he re-established order and instituted the *tres Vias de Successão.* After a reign of three months and twenty days, this second Viceroy (the first being d'Almeida) died, at Cochin, on December 24th, 1524, and was buried in the High Chapel of the Franciscan convent of that city. His remains were brought home by his son in 1538, and his tomb in the High Chapel of the Convento do Carmo, at Vidigueira, bore the epitaph: "Aqui jaz o grande Argonauta D. Vasco da Gama, 1° Conde da Vidigueira, Almirante dos Indias Orientoes, e seo famozo descubridor." ‡

1525.—D. HENRIQUE DE MENEZES (No. 7), called *O Roxo* (the Red), son of D. Fernando de Menezes, of the House of the Counts of Castanheda, and succeeding by the *Primeira via* or first nomination, followed Da Gama as Governor; he would not enter into office nor allow any rejoicings on that occasion, until he had performed the last duties to his illustrious predecessor, saying that it was much more becoming to bewail the loss of that great man than to rejoice at his assuming the administration. He supported the Fortress of Calicut against the whole army of the Rajah; governed from January 17th, 1525, till February 20th, 1526; died at Cananor, *æt.* twenty-eight (Mariz says thirty), and was buried in the Chapel of S. Thiago, in that city.

1526.—LOPO VAS DE SAMPAYO (No. 8), succeeded in the *Terceira Via* (third nomination), and governed for three years, till November 18th, 1529. He sent to Lisbon in chains the nominee of the *Seconda Via,* Pero Mascarenhas, who was received by the King with great honours. During his administration, Tidor in the Moluccas, Mangalore on the Malabar Coast, and the Island of Mahim or Bombay (*Bombaim*), were taken possession of by the Portuguese. He routed 10,000 Malabarians at Cananor, and 64 galliots of Paliana, commanded by Ali Shah, War-Captain of Cambay. Finally, by

* M. de Kloguen neglects the "Dom:" in those days it was an important item in the style and title of the Portuguese Fidalgo, who could not assume it without just claim.

† Near Madras: St. Thomé has a literature and library of his own.

‡ The Abbé A. D. de Castro e Souza patriotically proposed to Government that the hero's ashes should be removed to Belem, near Lisbon; and Sr. J. S. Ribeiro, Civil Governor of Beja, 1845, supported the petition by reporting the scandalous neglect of the tomb. What it was in 1853 may be learned in the pages (ii., 47-49) of Sr. Caldeira before mentioned.

order of the Court, he was made prisoner and sent to Portugal, where, after two years in irons, he was condemned to banishment in Africa and to indemnify Pero Mascarenhas for the salary which had been drawn by him in India, besides a fine of 10,000 crusados. All these pains and penalties were remitted by the Royal Alvará; and his energetic address to D. João III. has been printed at full length in the Decades of Do Couto. He died April 18th, 1538.

1529.—NUNO DA CUNHA (No. 9), was the son of Tristão Vas da Cunha, in whose company he aided the Viceroy d'Almeida in winning his famous victories against the "Moors." He left Lisbon on April 18th, 1529, with 11 ships and 2,000 men-at-arms, including his two brothers Simão and Pero. Arriving at Goa on October 22nd, he took charge at sea off Cananor on November 18th. He captured the cities of Bassein (*Baçaim*) and Daman from Bahádur Shah, King of Guzerat, and afterwards the stronghold and island of Diu, on the coast of the same peninsula, now called Kathiáwár, after the long and memorable first siege. It was during this affair that a soldier having had his head struck off by a cannon ball, Nunho, who was standing near, exclaimed coolly to the bystanders, who were filled with terror and bewailing their danger, "Humiliate capita vestra Deo," the words of a well-known part of the Roman Liturgy. He so encouraged his men that Antonio da Silveira, with 600 Portuguese, put to flight the 76 galleys of Sulayman Pasha. By the terror which his name inspired, his successor, after the capitulation, concluded an advantageous and glorious peace with Bahádur Shah, whom the Portuguese authors call, after his chief seaport, "King of Cambay." This Prince made a formal cession of Bombay, Chaul, Bassein, Daman and Diu, where the Portuguese built a fortress. Nuno da Cunha, one of the heroes of his race, had been profoundly hurt by the order to imprison his predecessor, thus taking away the privilege of nobility (*tomar a menagem*), and he seemed to foresee a similar fate for himself.* And so it happened; after governing nine years, till September 14th, 1538, he was ordered back to Portugal. He embarked in January 1539, and in the following month he died off the Cape of Good Hope, quoting Slipio's words, "*Ingrata patria, ossa mea non possidebis.*" In his will he ordered that the price of the iron thrown with his corpse into the sea, should be paid to the King, as the only debt with which his conscience charged him.

1538.—D. GRACIA DE NORONHA (No. 10), third Viceroy of India, and a nephew of Albuquerque, had already served with high distinction in 1511, commanding a squadron of six ships in the Eastern seas. He left Lisbon in mid-March, 1538, with 12 ships and 3000 men-at-arms; amongst whom were many Fidalgos. He reached Goa on September 14th, and at once taking possession, governed for nineteen months, till April 3rd, 1540. He attacked the Turks (*Rumes*) at Diu, and put them to flight. Died at Goa, and was buried in the Cathedral choir.

1539.—D. ESTEVÃO (STEPHEN) DA GAMA (No. 11), son of the hero of that name, succeeded as acting Governor, *em via*; in fact, in *seconda Via*, because the nominee of the first, Martim Affonso de Souza, the hero of Brazil, had a little before his arrival returned to Portugal. On the day of the "opening" (of the road), April 4th, 1540, when he took charge he ordered an inventory of his property, which was large and well gained; he did homage before the Captain of the city, and took the oath before the Ouvidor Geral (or Chief Judge of the Supreme Court). He undertook the celebrated expedition into the Red Sea, and went as far as Mount Sinai, to visit the

* "Annaes d' El Rei D. João III.," by Fr. Luis de Souza, p. 278, 3rd Edit., by the late Sr. A. Herculano, one of Portugal's noblest *littérateurs*.

shrine of St. Catherine, patroness of Goa; here he assumed the arms of knighthood, and granted the same honour to all his companions, among whom were D. Alvaro de Castro, son of the great and celebrated D. João de Castro, afterwards Viceroy; and D. Luis d' Almeida, who presently distinguished himself so gloriously in Germany, under Charles V., that he would there have obtained knighthood from that Emperor, had he not already possessed it. On this occasion the Emperor said that he esteemed more the honour done to D' Almeida, that is of being knighted by the son of Da Gama, on Mount Sinai, than the victory he had just gained from the Duke of Saxony. Similarly the Viceroy D. João de Castro, father of D. Alvaro, set such a value on the distinction bestowed upon his son, that to perpetuate the memory of it he inserted the wheel of St. Catherine in his family arms. During his reign the Collegio da Santa Fé was built in the street of Goa known as the Carreira de Cavallos (race-course); it was an imitation of the seminary founded by Antonio Galvão in the Moluccas for the propagation of Christianity. His reign lasted till May 6th, 1542; on the following day he gave up charge to his successor, and presently retired to Pangim. A second inventory of his property showed that it had diminished by 50,000 xerafins. After wintering (*i.e.*, passing the rainy season) there, he returned to Portugal during the following north-east monsoon.

1542.—MARTIM AFFONSO DE SOUZA (No. 12), nominated in January 1541; left Lisbon on the 7th of the following April, wintered at Mozambique till March 15th, 1542; and, reaching Goa on May 6th, disembarked after sunset, and found quarters in the church of St. Pedro. At midnight he had announced his arrival to D. Estevão; on the next day he took charge in the place where he lodged, and shortly afterwards he made his solemn entry into the city. His Governor brought with him the celebrated FRANCIS XAVIER. Japan was discovered, and the first spiritual labours and achievements of that holy apostle signalized his administration. He subjected the kingdom of Moluccas, and united to the State the Custom-house of Hormuz, and the peninsulas of Salsette and Bardez.* Besides the Cathedral, Goa city was increased by three more parishes, and its population, not including the suburbs, was rated at 300,000, of whom a quarter were Gentiles. After three years, ending on September 10th, 1545, De Souza returned to Portugal.

1545.—D. JOÃO DE CASTRO (No. 13), called by some authors "*O ultimo heroe Portuguez no Oriente*" (the last Portuguese hero in the East), equalled the most illustrious of his predecessors in virtue and in glory, both as a warrior and a statesman. He succeeded De Souza as a mere Governor and Captain-General (*Capitão-Mór*) in January 1545. He left Lisbon March 17th, reached Goa on September 10th, and two days afterwards took charge with the usual ceremonious entrance. He defeated Ibrahim, King of Bijápúr; and he secured for the crown of Portugal, and incorporated with, as *Ilhas de Goa*, the two peninsulas Salsette and Bardez, which encompass the main island. He afterwards sent his son, D. Fernando, to succour Governor D. João de Mascarenhas who was besieged in the citadel of Diu by Mohammed, King of Gujerat, successor of Bahadur, assisted by a Turkish fleet, and by the troops of the King of Bijápúr, under Allahdád Khan, his Prime Minister. This was the second siege of Diu.† Fernando having been killed, Castro did not hesitate

* See in the "Annaes" before alluded to (p. 413) a remarkable letter of this Governor on the continental lands of Salsette and Bardez and the 300,000 xerafins given to him by a "Moorman."

† The reader may consult "The Life of D. João de Castro," by the classical writer Jacintho Freire d' Andrada (Lib. 2, § 7), for the celebrated speech put into the mouth of Coge Cofar (Khwájeh Safar). The Moslem recapitulates all the Portuguese conquests

to send there his second son, D. Alvaro, the same who had been knightep at Mount Sinai. He afterwards went himself * with an Armada; penetrated into the citadel, from which he sallied to attack his enemies and gained a complete and glorious victory. Afterwards, wanting money to continue the war, which was not ended, or rather to rebuild the city, he sent to Goa to borrow the 20,000 xerafins required, with one of his whiskers—some say a few hairs of his beard—as security. The unusual pledge was received with due honour, and more than the sum required was procured. The ladies of Goa and Chaul even sent him all their jewels, which Castro courteously refused, highly praising their patriotism. After having put all his enemies to flight, and having concluded peace, the great Governor returned to Goa, where he was visited at sea by the Bishop, the Captain-General, and the Regent. The latter begged him to delay at Pangim, whilst the capital prepared to greet him with a triumph; and gave such good reasons for according the honour that D. João could not refuse. The ceremony was magnificent; the Governor was received at the Cathedral by the bishop and clergy with a *Te Deum;* and, after offering his thanks to the "Author of victories," he returned to the Palace. The ceremonies, though shortened, could not be completed in one day.†

Shortly after this event, at the age of forty-eight, he fell into a lingering disease, a languor which, disgusting him with things mundane, presently made him turn his thoughts to the solid goods of eternity. S. FRANCIS XAVIER having about this time returned from the Moluccas, he chose him as the director of his conscience.‡ In October 1547, being confined to his bed, he received despatches from Portugal, conferring upon him the title of Viceroy, and re-appointing him to his office for three years. The people made public rejoicings, and a great display of fireworks; but De Castro hearing their shouts, and seeing the lights from his windows, said to SAINT XAVIER, who was seated at his bedside, "How deceitful is this world, which promises three years' honours to a man who has but a few moments to live." He expired fourteen days after, June 6th, 1848, with the same Christian sentiments, in the arms of the holy apostle, who assisted him to his last breath. It is a remarkable circumstance that the greatest Christian hero of the East should have died attended by the most illustrious apostle of that part of the world in modern times. Castro died so poor § that the city was obliged to defray the expenses of his funeral. The Life of De Castro (Lib. 1, p. 329) gives us

in the East, with one notable anachronism: he speaks of the city of Macáo, founded by the Portuguese some years afterwards.

* There are three *Roteiros* (log-books) of this celebrated captain,—1, of his first journey to India, printed at Oporto (1843) by Sr. Diogo Klopke; 2, from Goa to Diu in 1538-39, the original being in the hands of Sr. Klopke, and a copy in the *Bibliotheca Eborense* (see catalogue by Sr. Cunha Rivara, vol. i., p. 4); 3, from Goa to Suez in 1541, the so-called *Roteiro do Mar Roxo*, published in Paris (1833) by Dr. Antonio Nunes de Carvalho. Notices of the three are given by Sr. Rivara in his panorama, and by M. Ferdinard Denis in his "Portugal" (p. 230, Paris edit. of 1846).

† See the Life, by J. Freire, before quoted (Lib. 3, § 39). M. de Kloguen gives the event altogether a wrong turn. According to him, D. João celebrated, on re-entering Goa, a triumph, after the vainglorious manner of the ancients, pulling down a part of the walls to raise the triumphal arch.

‡ Equally erroneous are De Kloguen's accounts of the second triumph. According to him (p. 31) the Governor, having gone back to Goa, in order to correct the impression of his former triumph, so opposed to Christian humility, celebrated a second, attributing the whole glory to the Almighty, and to the intercession of the Apostle St. Thomas and of St. Martin, and he ordered their images to be set up in the place of his own.

§ The Life says that after his death his desk was found to contain "*tres tangas larins*" (three small Persian coins of silver) "*e humas disciplinas com signaes da uzar muito dellos*" (well-worn scourges).

some touching details concerning the end of this hero, who was wasted less by years than by the fatigues of his continual campaigns. When repeated fainting fits announced that his end was near, he summoned the principal authorities of the city, civil and military, ecclesiastical and laical; and made over to them the charge of the State to which his many victories had assured peace with all its neighbours. He addressed to them a pathetic speech, reminding them that he came to the East to serve, not to trade, and that he had pledged for the safety of his fellow-citizens the bones of his son and the hairs of his own beard. In regard to his wants, for he had not money enough to buy a fowl, or to enjoy the comforts of a private soldier in hospital, he prayed them to allow a small sum from the Treasury, as long as his illness lasted. He then, calling for a missal, swore upon it that he did not owe a *crusado* to the Crown, nor had he received aught from Christian or Moor, Jew or Gentile. The speech was inserted in the city archives, as a lasting memorial to posterity. His remains were temporarily interred in the convent of St. Francisco. After some years they were transferred to Portugal, and were carried on the shoulders of four grandsons to the convent of St. Domingo, in Lisbon. After magnificent obsequies, he was finally buried in a decent tomb in a chapel of St. Domingo de Beinfica, by his grandson, Bishop and Inquisitor-General, D. Francisco de Castro. The family is still one of the noblest in Portugal.

1548.—GARCIA DE SÁ (No. 14) succeeded in the "third *Via*," because D. João Mascarenhas, of the first, and D. Jorge Tello of the second, had returned to Portugal; under him the King of Tanôr came to Goa, and embraced Christianity. After one year of rule he died (June 13th, (1549), and was buried in the Priory Church of N. Sra da Rosario.

1549.—JORGE CABRAL (No. 15). He succeeded in *quarta Via*, opened to him by the death of his predecessor. As he was Captain of Bassein, the government of the Capital was provisionally held by the Bishop, the City Captain, and the Supreme Judge, till his arrival at Goa on August 15th, when he took possession at Pangim. He built the (new) Chapel of Saint Catherine* near the Porta da Ribeira (water gate), which had admitted the Portuguese captors of the city; and he afterwards committed it to the charge of the Municipal Chamber (*Senado da Camara*). He was preparing to attack certain Malabar chiefs, when, after four years' rule, his successor arrived, about mid-November 1550.

1551.—D. AFFONSO DE NORONHA (No. 16). This Viceroy, a brother of the Marquez da Villa Real, named in January 1550, left Lisbon on May 1st; reached Cochin in November; took charge at once from his predecessor, and embarked on May 1st for Goa, where he made his solemn entrance. During his reign the Fort of Califa was taken from the Turks, and a great defeat was inflicted upon the Java kings who had blockaded Malacca. On December 2nd, 1552, S. FRANCIS XAVIER died in the Island of Sancian (*Sanchão*), near Canton, and his body was transported, first to Malacca and then to Goa. Another important event took place, the arrival of Luis de Camões, "Prince of Portuguese Poets." D. Affonso governed for four years, till September 23rd, 1554, when he gave up the reins to his successor, and retired to Pangim. He then went to Cochin, and thence he embarked for Portugal, January 15th, 1555.†

1554.—D. PEDRO MASCARENHAS (No. 17). This Viceroy, Lord of Palma

* See Appendix I., "*B.*—The Religious Establishments," for the error of De Kloguen.

† De Kloguen is wrong when he says (p. 33) "Noronha died (*i.e.* at Goa) after four years of his administration."

and Alcaide-Mór (Chief Magistrate) of Trancozo, named January 1554, left Lisbon in latter March, reached Goa September 23rd, and governed till June 16th, 1555, when he died, *æt.* seventy. He was buried in the High Chapel of the Cathedral, and some years afterwards his bones were removed to the Church of S. Francisco do Alcacer do Sul, Portugal.

1555.—FRANCISCO BARRETO (No. 18) succeeded by *primeira Via* opened on the death of his predecessor. He took the Fortresses of Assorim and Manorá, and in the last year of his reign the King of Cambaya, upon the rebellion of Cide (*Sidi*) Bofeta the Abyssinian,* ceded Daman to the Portuguese. He governed till September 8th, 1558, when he embarked for Portugal *viâ* Cochin. He was afterwards sent to reduce the Empire of Monomotapa; he died at the Rios de Sena, and his mortal remains were carried to Portugal.

1558.—D. CONSTANTINO DA BRAGANÇA (No. 19). This Viceroy, of the the blood Royal, was fourth son of D. Jaime, fourth Duke of Bragança, sailed from Lisbon at the age of thirty-one years on April 7th, 1558; reached Goa on September 3rd, and made his entrance on the 8th of the same month. His many good qualities have endeared his name to the Portuguese of India. He was the constant friend and protector of the celebrated Luis de Camões, author of the Lusiads. Firm, wise, mild, polite, and benevolent, he has nevertheless incurred the hatred of foreign historians, because the too famous tribunal of the Inquisition was established in Goa during his administration; yet he had no hand in the matter, which took place before in Portugal. D. Constantino is also blamed and ridiculed for having refused to give to the King of Pegu, who offered 300,000 crusados, a tooth, which some affirm to have been that of a monkey, but which had been revered as a relic of Buddha in a temple of Jafnapatam (Ceylon).† Although in this business D. Constantino acted as a conscientious and religious man,‡ he consulted the archbishop and clergy, as he was afraid on the one hand of participating in an act of idolatry and superstition, and on the other of defrauding the king, his master, of a considerable treasure. When it became clear to him that conscience and natural reason forbade his taking part in the affair, and least for money, which would only incur the imputation of avarice, he consented that the "infamous relic" be thrown into the sea. Had he preferred the money he would have been represented by prejudiced authors as a greedy and dishonest man; but as he acted otherwise, they call him a fool. It is very difficult, or rather it is impossible, to please those who are bent on blaming their fellow creatures. D. Constantino governed till September 7th, 1561, and January 1562; and after three years this nobleman returned in the ship *Constantino* § to Portugal.

1561.—D. FRANCISCO COUTINHO, Count of Redondo (No. 20). This Viceroy sailed from home on March 15th, 1561, reached Goa September 7th, and governed till February 19th, 1564. After two years he died, and was buried in the Convento de S. Francisco da Cidade, Goa.

1564.—JOÃO DE MENDONÇA (No. 21), acting Governor (*em Via*), succeeded by *seconda Via* on the death of his predecessor (D. Antão de Noronha, the first claimant, being absent), on February 4th, 1564. He governed till September 3rd, and returned to Portugal.

* His title "Sidi" suggests that he was a Msawáhili, or Zanzibar Negroid.

† The celebrated bit of ivory, rudely representing a canine tooth, which passes for a relic of Buddha in Ceylon, has been lately the subject of a "Memoir" by Dr. J. Gerson da Cunha. London: Thacker and Co., 1875.

‡ See "Do Couto," Decade vii., Lib. 9 cap. 17.

§ This ship weathered the Cape seventeen times, and carried four Viceroys during her life of twenty-five years. See "Oriente Conquistado," c. i., d. ii., p. 193.

1564.—ANTÃO DE NORONHA (No. 22). This Viceroy, who was beloved almost as much as D. Constantino, named in January 1564, left Lisbon on March 18th, and on September 3rd reached Goa, where he erected that long wall along the creek subtending the eastern shore of the Goa Island that defends it from the Continent. He sent succour to Malacca, and built the Fortress of Mangalore; governed till September 10th, 1568; passed to Cochin, and died in the same year on his passage home.

1568.—D. LUIS D' ATHAIDE (No. 23), Viceroy, Lord of the noble house of Athouguia, was sent out in January 1568, left Lisbon in March, reached Goa on September 10th, and at once took possession. Under his reign Goa was afflicted with a pestilence, believed to have been caused by the carcase of an elephant, stuck fast in the *alagôa* (pond) adjoining the Igreja da Trindade (Trinity Church). During the early part of his administration Goa was besieged by Ali Adil Shah, or Idalkão, King of Bijapur. The enemy, however, was decisively routed, and the Viceroy ruled with much prosperity till September 6th, 1571, when he returned home and was received with magnificent ceremonies.

1571.—D. ANTONIO DE NORONHA (No. 24)*, a relation of the former Noronha, was named Viceroy in January 1571; left Lisbon during the south-west monsoon; reached Goa on September 7th, and governed till December 9th, 1573. A Royal Letter of the preceding March recalled him home, as his term of office was ended, at the same time naming his successor. After two years he returned to Portugal, and died of disappointment.

1573.—ANTONIO MONIZ BARRETO (No. 25) was named on March 12th; took charge on December 9th, and governed till September 1576; after three years he was recalled.

1576.—D. DIOGO DE MENEZES (No. 26) succeeded in *primeira Via*, the nominee Rui Lourenço de Tavora having died in September 1576, a little before reaching Mozambique. He governed till August 31st, 1578, and after two years returned home during the south-west monsoon.

1578.—D. LUIS D' ATHAIDE (No. 27) was named Viceroy for the second time; left Lisbon in November 1577; reached Goa August 31st, 1578, and governed till March 10th, 1581, when he died of grief after the hapless battle of Alcaçar-quivir. After his death the title of Marquez de Santarem was conferred upon him. He was buried in the tomb of his brother D. João d' Athaide, and his bones were afterwards removed from the Reis-Magos of Goa to the Church Bom Jesus de Peniche, Portugal.

1580.—FERNÃO TELLES DE MENEZES (No. 28) succeeded by the *primeira Via*; took possession on March 13th, 1581, and governed for seven months, till September 17th of the same year.

1581.—D. FRANCISCO MASCARENHAS (No. 29) was appointed Viceroy by Philip II. of Spain, who in this year took possession of the throne of Portugal. This Count de Villa d'Horta left Lisbon April 11th, 1581, reached his government on September 16th, and ruled till early November 1584. When his successor was appointed he fell ill at Cochin, committed the power to the Archbishop, and embarked for Portugal on November 22nd.

1584.—D. Duarte de Menezes (No. 30), descended from the Governor of that name, and Count of Tarouca, left Lisbon April 10th, 1584, and arrived at Cochin October 25th. This Viceroy of India governed till May 4th, 1588, when, after more than three years, he died in Goa, *æt.* fifty-one. His remains were buried in the High Chapel of the Reis-Magos, and were afterwards transferred to the Convento da Trindade, Santarem.

* De Kloguen (pp. 40-41), calls Antonio *Antão*, (quite different names) de Noronha the First, and Antonio the Second; moreover, he makes the latter a son of the former.

1588.—MANOEL DE SOUZA CONTINHO (No. 31) was named in the second place, and took possession when the first nominee, Mathias d' Albuquerque, returned to Portugal. He built the *Couraca* or battery of the Fortress Reis-Magos. After governing three years he embarked for Portugal May 15th, 1591, and was wrecked on the Baixos (shoals) de Garajáu.

1591.—MATHIAS D' ALBUQUERQUE (No. 32), named Viceroy, left Lisbon May 8th, 1590, and reached Goa on May 15th of the following year. He built in 1594 the Church and Convent of N. Sra. do Cabo upon an older Ermida (chapel) of Na Sra. da Conceiçao. On May 25th, 1597, he returned home, having governed more than six years.

1597.—D. FRANCISCO DA GAMA (No. 33), Count of Vidigueira, Admiral of India, great-grandson of Vasco da Gama, was named (*æt.* thirty-one) in July 1595; left Lisbon April 10th, 1596, reached Goa May 22nd, 1597, and disembarking at the College of the Reis-Magos, took possession on the 25th of the same month. He solemnized his entrance (Couto Dec., xii., cap. 15) on June 1st, the centennial of the discovery of India by his ancestor. On December 25th, 1597, the Aldermen (*Vereadores da Camara*) placed the portrait of D. Vasco in their Session Hall, and shortly afterwards a statue of the discoverer was placed over the archway forming the gate of the Rio da Cidade. He built in 1598 the Fort of Gaspar Diaz in the palm ground of a proprietor of that name; and, governing till December 25th, 1600, after three years' administration returned to Portugal.

1600.—AIRES DE SALDANHA (No. 34), appointed Viceroy; reached Goa on December 25th, 1600. During his administration the Hollanders blockaded the city for the first time. He governed for four years, till the middle of January 1605, and returned to Portugal.

1604.—MARTIM AFFONSO DE CASTRO (No. 35), son of the hero of the same name; reached Goa with the title of Viceroy in mid-January 1605, and during the south-west monsoon of 1606, by orders of the Crown, he set out for Malacca, which was besieged by the fleet of the King of Java. He delivered the place, but he died of sorrow June 3rd, 1607, after being beaten in battle by the Dutch, and was buried in the Church of N. Sra. do Monte, Malacca.

1607.—D. FRE ALEXIO DE MENEZES (No. 36), Archbishop of Goa,* administered as Acting Governor in the absence of his predecessor; and when the nominee, D. João Pereira Forjaz, Count of Feira, died on his journey, continued to rule till May 27th, 1609, when his successor arrived. In his day the Dutch besieged Mozambique twice and Malacca once.

1609.—ANDRÉ FURTADO DE MENDONÇA (No. 37) conquered the kingdom of Jafnapatam; took Cunhalle, and with 160 Portuguese supported a great blockade in Malacca against the Dutch, whose 11 ships and 7 smaller craft (*patachos*), were aided by 327 keel belonging to the seven Kings of Java. On this and other occasions before and after he did many acts of prowess; and, after ruling three months and eight days, he left Goa for home on September 5th, 1609.

1609.—RUI LOURENÇO DE TAVORA (No. 38), took charge on the day when his predecessor left and governed till December 15th, 1612.

1612.—D. JERONIMO DE AZEVEDO (No. 39) was the first Viceroy, nominated during his stay in India. He took possession on December 15th, 1612; governed till November 18th, 1617, and after four years returned home.

1617.—D. JOÃO COUTINHO (No. 40), Count of Redondo, son of the Viceroy of that name, took charge on November 18th, 1617; governed till November

* Of this prelate further details will be found under the Archbishops.

10th, 1619; died after about two years, on November 10th, 1619, at the Palacio da Fortaleza, and was buried in the Reis-Magos, Goa.

1619.—FERNÃO DE ALBUQUERQUE (No. 41), who was before Governor of Colombo, in Ceylon, and had been fifty-one years in India, succeeded on November 11th, 1619, as Acting Governor of all India. He remained in office till December 19th, 1622, more than three years.

1622.—D. FRANCISCO DA GAMA (No. 42), Count of Vidigueira, and Admiral of India, Viceroy for the second time, named January 22nd, 1622, reached Goa and took charge in the Reis-Magos on November 19th, regoverned during five years, till the end of January 1629, when he returned home with permission of the Crown.

1627.—D. FR. LUIS DE BRITO (No. 43), of the order of St. Augustine, Bishop of Meliapor and Bishop-elect of Cochin, who had been twice Governor of the Coromandel Coast, succeeded, in January 1627, as acting Governor of India, and died July 29th, 1628, in Goa.*

1629.—D. MIGUEL DE NORONHA (No. 44), Count of Linhares, was named Viceroy on February 7th, 1629; reached Goa October 21st, and took charge on the next day. During his rule the Empire (!) of Monomotapa was annexed to the Crown of Portugal, and many rich mines were there discovered. He made himself respected by all the Princes of India, and recovered Mombaseh; he united to the State the Island and Fortress of Carambolim; built, with heavy expenditure of his own property, the Hospital da Piedade, which he left, with a foundation, to the Senate of Goa. This establishment, by a *concordat* of 1680, was administered by the Brotherhood (*Irmandade*) da *Misericordia;* and in 1706 it was united to that of Todos os Santos, built in 1547. During the six years of his rule he caused several useful works to be executed, amongst others the great bridge of Pangim, in which he was assisted by the influence of the Jesuits. He built the Casa da Polvora and (1633) the Church of S. Lourenço de Linhares, in the Aguada Fortress: he fortified the lands of Bardez and the Island of Goa by redoubts and other works attached to the long wall. All this was done with the surplus of the Treasury, which Philip II. had directed him to remit to Portugal: yet he was hung in effigy by the discontented, who are never wanting.† He governed till December 8th, 1635, when he returned to Portugal.

1635.—PERO DA SILVA (No. 45) came to Goa as Viceroy on December 8th, 1635; died June 24th, 1639, in Goa, and was buried in the Church of St. Domingo. Under his rule the plague appeared in the city.

1639.—ANTONIO TELLES DE MENEZES (No. 46), who commanded the fort of Diu, was appointed acting Governor in *segunda Via*, the Archbishop and Primate, D. Fr. Francisco dos Martines, acting for him till the next October, when he took charge in the Government House, Pangim. During his reign, which ended September 21st, 1640, the Hollanders gave great trouble.

1640.—JOÃO DA SILVA TELLO DE MENEZES (No. 47), Count of Aveiras, was named Viceroy on February 25th, 1610; left Lisbon March 26th, and on September 21st took charge in the Church of Reis-Magos. Under him Goa was often attacked by the Dutch. In this year the Duke of Bragança was acclaimed king, under the name of D. João IV., and Portugal again became an independent State. On December 30th, 1646, after five years, this Viceroy left Goa, and returned to Europe.

* After this Governor the *segunda Via* was opened, the nominees being Nuno Alvares Botelho, Counsellor of State; D. Lourenço da Cunha, Captain of the City; and the Chancellor Gonçalo Pinto da Fonceca. They took charge on August 1st, 1627, and when the first-named went to succour Malacca, the second and third governed till October 20th of the same year.

† See fol. 59 of 2nd edit. of the "Instruments of the Marquez d'Alorna." (Goa, 1856.)

1646.—D. FELLIPPE MASCARENHAS (No. 48), named on April 10th, 1644; reached Ceylon December 10th, and began to govern; at the end of the next year (December 30th, 1646) he reached Goa, and was installed in the Reis-Magos. It was under this Viceroy that the decline of Goa became so sensible, as Tavernier, who then visited it, informs us. He governed till May 31st, 1651, and died, on his way home (1652), in the Jesuit College of Loanda.

1651.—D. FRE FRANCISCO DOS MARTYRES, Archbishop of Goa, ANTONIO DE SOUZA CONTINHO, and FRANCISCO DE MELLO DE CASTRO (No. 49), governed by interim, having learned the death of the Viceroy, D. João da Silva Tello de Menezes, Count of Aveiras, who, appointed for a second time Viceroy, died on his passage to India, and was buried at Mozambique. When the way of succession was open, the first and the third at once took charge, and the second, who was commanding at Daman, pledged his oath before the Captain of Bassein; and ratified it on December 8th of the same year, in presence of his associates. His government lasted till September 6th, 1652.

1652.—D. VASCO MASCARENHAS, Count and Alcaide-Mór of Obidos (No. 50), appointed Viceroy on January 19th, 1652; left Lisbon on March 25th, reached Goa September 3rd, and on the 6th took charge in the Reis-Magos. He sent aid to Ceylon and the fortress of Canará, both besieged by the Hollanders, and showed many excellent qualities; yet he was deposed, on October 22nd, 1653, by a sedition, and compelled to embark for Europe. On that day D. Bras de Castro, the ringleader, took forcible possession of the post, and kept it till August 24th, 1655.*

1655.—D. RODRIGO LOBO DA SILVEIRA (No. 51), Count of Sarzedas, nominated in January 1655; left Lisbon on March 23rd, with four vessels, disembarked at Mormugão on August 21st, and two days afterwards, acting under direction of the Supreme Court (*Relação*) of the State, assumed charge in the Reis-Magos, as though the Government were vacant. He at once seized and kept in solitary confinement D. Bras the usurper and his followers. He showed prudence, wisdom, rectitude and singular disinterestedness, and he governed till January 3rd, 1656, when he died, not without suspicion of poison. He was buried in the Dominican convent.

As there were no ways of succession, the three Estates met and chose MANOEL MASCARENHAS HOMEM, who ruled provisionally from January 14th to May 22nd, 1656. On the latter day a caravel brought the nomination of the same Homem, of Francisco de Mello e Castro, and of Antonio de Souza Continho. The latter two, returning from their governments at Colombo and Ceylon, swore in presence of the third on May 22nd, 1657, and governed till September 7th of the same year. Learning that the Viceroy elect, Conde de Villa-Pouca d'Aguiar, had died on his voyage to Goa, they found the first way of succession open, and continued to govern. On September 25th, 1657, Manoèl Mascarenhas Homem died, and the other two kept charge till June 14th, 1661. A new *Via* was thus opened, and the nominees were D. Manoel Mascarenhas, who refused in order to keep command at Mozambique, and the two officials whose names follow.

1661.—LUIS DE MENDONÇA FURTADO and D. PEDRO DE LANCASTRE (No. 52), governed jointly till December 14th, 1662.†

1662.—ANTONIO DE MELLO E CASTRO (No. 53), named Governor on March 11th, 1662, and one year afterwards allowed to style himself Viceroy;

* A justification of his conduct, forwarded to the Court on January 2nd, 1654, and that of his successor, D. Rodrigo, will be found in the "Pregoeiro da Liberdade" (No. 8, of 1838), printed at Bombay.

† De Kloguen separates the two, making Mendonça govern for one year (1661), and D. Pedro for a short time in 1662.

he arrived at Bombay September 29th, and, much to his disgust, gave over that island to the English, in consequence of the Matrimonial Treaty of 1661. During his rule the Dutch became masters of Cochin and other establishments upon the coast of Malabar.

1666.—João Nunes da Cunha (No. 54), Count of S. Vicente, and Gentleman of the Chamber to the Prince D. Theodosio, named Viceroy on March 11th, 1666, reached Goa on October 11th; took charge in the Reis-Magos on the 17th and governed for two years till November 6th of 1668, when he died, and was buried in the Church of Bom-Jesus, belonging to the professed house of the Jesuits.

1668.—D. Antonio de Mello de Castro (No. 55), a relation of the last Viceroy but one, together with Luis de Miranda Henriques, Captain of the fortress of Diu, and Manoel Corte-Real de Sampaio, Counsellor of State, governed conjointly between November 7th, 1668, to May 22nd of 1671. D. Antonio was brother of the first Count of Galveas, Diniz de Mello de Castro, and father of Julio de Mello de Castro, who wrote a life of his uncle the Viceroy.

1671.—Luis de Mendonça Furtado d'Albuquerque (No. 56), Count of Lavradio, appointed Viceroy on March 9th of 1670; took charge on May 22nd, 1671. After governing nearly seven years, till October 30th, 1677, he embarked for Portugal. The ship struck upon the shoals of Pinda, and saved herself by running into Mozambique; this notwithstanding, the Viceroy died at sea.

1677.—D. Pedro d'Almeida (No. 57), first Count of Assumar; named Viceroy on April 8th, 1677, took charge in the Reis-Magos on October 30th. By order of the Crown he embarked for Mozambique on January 27th, 1678, and, after finishing the work entrusted to him, he died there in March of the same year.

1678.—D. Fre Antonio Brandão (No 58), Archbishop Primate of Goa; Antonio Paes de Sande, and the Chancellor, Dr. Francisco Cabral d'Almada, administered jointly during the late Viceroy's absence. On the death of the Chancellor the two others continued in power, and the Prelate dying in July of the same year, the survivor became sole acting Governor, by direction of a Junta of the three Estates, for more than four years, till September 12th, 1681.

1681.—Francisco de Taura, Count of Alvor (No. 59), became Viceroy on September 12th, 1681. He carried on a successful war with Sambaji, the Maráthá; fortified the Island of Angediva, administered till December 3rd, 1686, during four years, with zeal and activity, and returned on December 16th to Portugal.

1686.—D. Rodrigo da Costa (No. 60), acting Governor, held power between March 26th, 1686, to June 23rd, 1690. He was Captain-General of the fleet of Indian galleons, and with that rank he served in India and Africa. His recovery, from Sambaji, of the Serra de S. Cruz, of Asserim, and of the city of Pate, won for him the promotion to Viceroy and the title Conde d'Assumar. He died after ruling three years, and was buried in the Church of Bom-Jesus.

1690.—D. Miguel d'Almeida (No. 61), acting Governor, succeeded in *segunda Via* the Conde d'Alvor, and governed alone after the death of the other two nominees till January 9th, 1691, when he also died, and was buried under the high altar of N. Sra. dos Remedios, in the college of St. Thomas Aquinas (*S. Thomaz*), which is now razed to the foundations.

1691.—D. Fernando Martim Mascarenhas de Lancastre (No. 62), and Luis Gonsalves Cotto succeeded in *segunda Via* D. Rodrigo da

COSTA, and administered jointly; but the latter dying on June 4th of 1691, D. FR. AGOSTINHO DA ANNUNCIAÇÃO, the new Archbishop, who had lately arrived in Goa, was associated, in the following September, to the Government, and the two kept in power till May 28th, 1693.

1693.—D. PEDRO ANTONIO DE NORONHA (No. 63), Count of Villaverde, was named Viceroy on February 5th, 1692 (*æt.* thirty); he left Lisbon on March 25th, wintered in Mozambique, and on May 28th of 1693 took charge in the Reis-Magos. This Viceroy visited the northern forts, where he sent aid to Mombaseh twice. He beat the Arabs, and governed till September 20th, 1698, and three months afterwards returned to Europe on the arrival of his successor.

1698.—ANTONIO LUIS GONSALVES DA CAMARA (No. 64), sent out on December 11th, 1697, took charge in the Reis-Magos on September 20th, 1698; sent an army to Hormuz, and aid to Mombaseh, which was lost to the Portuguese. On September 17th, 1701, with leave from the Crown, after administering during three years, he left Goa and died at Bahia, in Brazil, on his way home.

1701.—D. FRE AGOSTINHO DA ANNUNCIAÇÃO (No. 65), Archbishop of Goa, and D. VASCO LUIS COUTINHO, Field-Marshal of the Horse belonging to the local force, administered jointly as acting Governors from September 17th, 1701, to October 2nd, 1702.

1702.—CAETANO DE MELLO DE CASTRO (No. 66), installed as Viceroy at the Reis-Magos on October 2nd, 1702, sent a fleet of seven frigates, which fought the Arabs at Surat (February 2nd, 1704); levelled the fort of Ambona, belonging to the Bounsuló or Bhonslá (July 4th, 1705), and marching in person on the lands of Bicholim, captured and razed the Hindu fort (December 6th). In May 1706, he took the Islands of Carjuem and Ponelém from Quemá Saunto (Sáwant); fortified them; and finally, concluding peace, he gave up his government (October 29th, 1707), after ruling Portuguese India for five years with courage and activity.

1707.—D. RODRIGO DA COSTA (No. 67), named Viceroy on February 25th, 1707; took charge at the Reis-Magos on October 28th, and governed also for four years till September 21st, 1712.

1712.—VASCO FERNANDES CEZAR DE MENEZES (No. 68), sent out as Viceroy on March 8th, 1712; left Lisbon April 14th; took charge at Goa on September 21st; sent an army to the Poço, or Well of Surat, where it defeated the Arabs of Muskat, and other enemies at the mouth of the Danda Rajpuri river; built a new fort on the frontiers of Bardez, and returned home (January 13th, 1717) after governing for the same period as his two predecessors.

1717.—D. SEBASTIÃO D'ANDRADE PASSANHA (No. 69), Archbishop Primate of Goa, acted as Governor from January 13th till October 16th of the same year.

1717.—D. LUIS DE MENEZES (No. 70), Count of Ericeira, Viceroy and Brigadier of the Serpa Regiment; took charge on October 16th, when under thirty-eight years. He promoted the happiness of the State by prompt justice, and by encouraging agriculture and trade. He made himself respected by his enemies; sent a fleet to burn the ships and magazines in Por Patan; chastised the pirate Angria; defeated the Arabs in three several actions, and began to build the upper fortress of Chaporá. He received embassies from the Grand Mogul and the Shah of Persia; to the latter he sent an embassy in return, and afterwards a fleet to succour that prince against the Arabs. After three years of glorious rule he gave up charge on September 14th, 1720, and returned to Portugal, suffering much on the way from tempests and pirates.*

*In the same year, and shortly after his departure, a fire completely consumed the great *Bambual* (bamboo plantation) defending the Province of Salsette, upon which he had expended 20,000 xerafins, a sum imposed upon the neighbouring villages.

1720.—FRANCISCO JOSÉ DE SAMPAYO E CASTRO (No. 71), named Viceroy on March 31st, 1720; left Lisbon April 13th, and took charge (September 14th) in the Bom-Jesus. He warred with Angria and ended by concluding an advantageous peace. After governing for three years he died at Goa (July 13th, 1723), and was buried in the Bom-Jesus.

1723.—D. CHRISTOVÃO DE MELLO (No. 72), acting Governor from July 13th to September 3rd.

1723.—D. IGNACIO DE SANTA THEREZA (No. 73), Archbishop Primate of Goa; D. CHRISTOVÃO DE MELLO, Counsellor of State, and CHRISTOVÃO LUIS D'ANDRADE, the Chancellor, administered jointly, by virtue of letters received to that effect from the Court of Portugal, until October 28th, 1725.

1725.—JOÃO DE SALDANHA DA GAMA (No. 74), named Viceroy on January 20th, 1725, and took charge in the Reis-Magos. During his term of six years Goa and all the northern provinces were in perpetual fear and consternation, occasioned by the neighbouring states and the progress of the Maráthá armies. He conquered Bicholim from Phond Sáwant (Fondú Saunto), and entrusted it to that Rajah's son Nagobá; and he recovered Mombaseh, Pattá (Patte), and Zanzibar, which soon afterwards were finally lost. After governing till January 23rd, 1732, he at last obtained leave to return to Portugal.

1732.—D. IGNACIO DE SANTA THEREZA (No. 75), Archbishop Primate of Goa; D. CHRISTOVÃO DE MELLO, and the Secretary of State, THOMÉ GOMES MOREIRA, took charge, the two former *in Via*, and the third in virtue of a Letter Patent (*Alvará*), on the death of the third nominee, JERONIMO CORREA FREIRE. During the joint government, which lasted till November 7th the same year, they made peace with the Maráthá.

1732.—D. PEDRO DE MASCARENHAS (No. 76), Count of Sandomil, appointed Viceroy on March 23rd, 1732; left Lisbon on April 26th, and took charge in the Reis-Magos on October 7th. In his time, Tanna and the whole Island of Salsette (Bombay), the important city of Bassein (*Baçaim*),* with its dependencies, Trapôr and the Island of Caranja; in fine, all that composed the Province called del Norte, except Daman and Diu, were taken by the Maráthás; these plunderers had also invaded the Goanese territory; they attacked the peninsula of Salsette, and the Bhonslá that of Bardez, while both threatened the capital itself.† To complete the calamities of the Portuguese, their fleet was destroyed (1740) by the Angria pirate. The unfortunate Viceroy governed nearly nine years, till May 18th, 1741, and returned to Portugal in 1742, after the arrival of his successor with powerful forces.

1741.—D. LUIS DE MENEZES (No. 77), fifth Count of Ericeira and first Marquis of Louriçal, was re-appointed Viceroy, with the title of Marquis, April 21st, 1740; left Lisbon May 7th, and took charge on May 18th, 1741. He brought with him 12,000 men from Brazil; routed the Maráthá on the plains of Bardez, thereby recovering five forts, the Island of Carjuem, and other great advantages; he granted peace to Quemá Saunto, making him a tributary of the State, and charging him for all the damages; he took the fortresses of Sanguem and Serpem, and finally he ordered the famous fort of Pondá, on the mainland, to be besieged. The very day (June 12th, 1742) it was taken by the Portuguese, the Viceroy died in the Palace da Casa de Polvora, in the suburb of S. Pedro, or Panelim, and his body was transported with great pomp to the professed house of the Jesuits, where it was interred at the foot of the altar of St. Francis Xavier.

* It capitulated on May 19th, 1739. A long and interesting account of the siege is given by Dr. da Cunha, in the volume before alluded to.

† They were bought off only by the cession of the Praça (*place forte*) de Chaul.

1742.—D. FRANCISCO DE VASCONCELLOS (No. 78), Bishop of Cochin, D LOURENÇO DE NORONHA, Counsellor of State, and D. LUIS CAETANO D'ALMEIDA, were found, at the death of the late Viceroy, jointly named in three Letters Patent of Declaration. The first, however, being in his diocese, and the second at his government in Mozambique, the third alone assumed the administration, which he filled till December 20th, 1742; on that date the Bishop of Cochin arrived in Goa, but died (March 30th, 1743) in the Polvora Palace, and was buried in the church of Bom-Jesus. Almeida, consequently, again governed alone till May 18th of the same year, when his colleague arrived from Mozambique. After this they governed jointly for more than a year, till September 24th, 1744.

1743.—D. PEDRO MIGUEL D'ALMEIDA E PORTUGAL (No. 79), third Count of Assumar and first Marquis of Castello-Novo, was appointed Viceroy on March 24th, 1744, with the title of Marquis; left Lisbon on the 29th, and took charge on September 24th. During the second year of his rule he waged a just, severe, and bloody war with the Bhonslá Rajah; who, encouraged by successful forays in the days of the Conde de Sandomil, made himself very troublesome. On May 5th, 1746, the Viceroy took in person the fort of Alorna,* and in consequence his title was changed by Royal Letter (November 9th, 1748) to "Marquez d'Alorna." Crossing the Arandem river in front of the enemy, he captured the Fort of Tíracol and the Praça de Rarim, the latter considered the strongest on this coast, together with the fleet, warlike instruments, and ammunition of his opponent; and, finally, on December 3rd of the same year, he made himself master of Neutim, the last maritime work belonging to the Bhonslá. He carried on a successful war with the Maráthás, from whom he took the fortresses of Bicholin and Sanguelim, on the mainland, to the east of Bardez, with the surrounding territories, which still belong to Portugal. After the arrival of his successor he resigned his place (September 27th, 1750), and returned to Europe.

1750.—FRANCISCO D' ASSIZ DE TAVORA (No. 80), third Marquis of Tavora, and sixth Count of S. João, was named Viceroy on February 18th, 1750, and assumed charge at Goa on September 27th of the same year. He carried in person aid to Neutim, and raised the siege, which the Bhonslá was pushing by land, and the Maráthá by sea. In 1751 he chastised the Canajá Rajah, who infested the seas of Diu, razing the Fort of Neubandel (*Nau-bandar*), and burning all the ships in port. On October 31st, 1752, he took from the Rajah of Sunda the fortress of Piro, and on the following day that of Ximpem; he also captured Conem, and laid waste the lands of Pondá and Zambandim. In fact, he carried on a successful war, by sea and land, against the Maráthás, and after four years (till September 18th, 1754) he returned home. During his rule the Governments of Goa and of the Mozambique, including the Rios de Sena, were separated.

1754.—D. LUIZ MASCARENHAS (No. 81), Count of Alva, was appointed Viceroy, on March 22nd, 1754, and took charge at Goa on September 20th. He continued the war with the Maráthás, and made peace with the Bhonslá, by ceding the Praças of Rarim and Neutim. At last, having in person besieged Pondá, which had been retaken by the Maráthás, he was killed in the attack, on June 28th, 1756. His body was transported to Goa, and interred in the Bom-Jesus.

1756.—D. ANTONIO TAVEIRA DA NEIVA BRUM DA SILVEIRA (No. 82), Archbishop of Goa; JOÃO DE MESQUITTA MATTOS TEXEIRA, the Chancellor of State; and FILIPPE DE VALLADARES SOUTO-MAIOR administered during the

* A description of the campaign, together with the instructions given by D. Pedro to his successor, was re-printed by Sr. F. N. Xavier, at Goa, in 1856.

vacancy. The two first, and JOSE CORRÊA DE SÁ, succeeded in *primeira Via*, opened by the last Viceroy's death; and, when Corrêa returned home, the first Letter Patent of Succession was found to name D. Antonio José da Costa, also deceased. The second *Alvará* appointed Filippe de Valladares, who, with his companions, assumed charge on July 1st, 1756. During this rule the Bhonslá broke the peace and invaded the provinces of Pernem, Sanguelim and Manarim. The triumvirate lasted till September 23rd, 1758.

1758.—MANOEL DE SALDANHA D'ALBUQUERQUE (No. 83), Count of Ega, appointed Viceroy on March 10th, 1756, took charge on September 23rd.. He continued the war, and concluded an advantageous peace with the Maráthá, for which a solemn *Te Deum* was sung in Goa, on the 25th July, 1759. On December 1st, the same year, he transferred his residence from the Polvora Palace in Panelim to that of Pangim, where his successors continue to reside. This change caused an enormous expenditure of the municipal revenue. The Royal Hospital, near the Arsenal, having been pulled down, the old Polvora Palace was converted into quarters for infirm soldiers and sailors, and it still continues to be the Royal Hospital. The Palace of Goa was reserved by the Viceroy for certain solemn occasions. During the same year (1759) the Jesuit Fathers were apprehended in Goa, were sent to Portugal, and their goods were confiscated. In 1761, by order of the Crown, he made over the forts of Piro and Ximpem to the Rajah of Sunda, and shortly afterwards that of Bicholim and Alorna to the Bhonslá. On May 31st, 1763, the fort of Pondá, called "Mardan Goddo," yielded itself, and he ordered its demolition. He made himself master of the provinces of Pondá and Zambaulim, and the forts of Pernem and Cabo di Rama, the latter, with its jurisdiction, including the province of Canacona. Pondá and all the new provinces of the mainland were to be given up to the Maráthás; but in consequence of the new wars, in which these plunderers were involved by the contentions between the English and French, and the Nabob of the Carnatic, the Portuguese remained in possession, though they had forcibly to maintain their hold against the contending powers. The Count of Ega made himself unpopular by his arrogance, despotism, and other bad qualities; and he disliked his position so much that, hearing the appointment of a successor, D. João de Lancastre, the Count de Louzaa, and ignoring the death of that nominee, he opened the *Vias*, resigned charge on October 19th, and making over charge to the Archbishop and colleagues, on December 25th, 1765, set out for Portugal. Arrived he was imprisoned in the Torre de Outão, with his secretary, Belchin José Vas de Carvalho; the latter was set free after a year, but the Viceroy, after eighteen months' confinement, died of grief. The principal charge preferred against him, by the Procurador (Solicitor-General) of the Crown at Lisbon, in the act of accusation, was his wilful waste of public money on the occasion of the confiscation of the Jesuits' property.

1765.—D. ANTONIO TAVEIRA DA NEIVA DA SILVEIRA BRUM (No. 84), Archbishop of Goa; JOÃO BAPTISTA VAS PEREIRA, Chancellor of State; and JOÃO JOSÉ DE MELLO, Controller-General of the Treasury, took charge, by virtue of the way of succession on the death of the Count de Louzaa, and administered the affairs jointly during three years, between October 19th, 1765, and March 12th, 1768.

1768.—D. JOÃO JOSÉ DE MELLO (No. 85), one of the three mentioned above, was named titular Governor by the Crown, on April 14th, 1767, and took sole charge of the administration from his two former colleagues. This was a rule of retrenchment under orders from home, suggested by the ex-Controller-General. The salary of the Viceroys* was reduced to 20,000 xerafins (order

* The salaries are given in the Institutes of the M. D'Alorna (p. 76, 2nd edit. of 1556)

of the Royal Treasury, April 25th, 1771), and the *personnel* of the Palace was greatly diminished. The exchequer (*Casa dos Contos*) of Goa, the collectorship (*Recebedorias*) of Salsette and Bardez, and the troop of cavalry, called the Viceroy's Guard, were suppressed. A law (*Carta da Lei*) of April 10th, 1769, created the Junta da Fazenda (Treasury Committee) of Goa, with a new way of book-keeping and many other reforms. D. João died on January 10th, 1774, six years after, and was buried in the convent of Na. Sra. do Pilar, of the order of the Recollet Franciscans, outside the city.

1774.—FILIPPE DE VALLADARES SOUTO-MAIOR (No. 86), acting Governor from January 13th to September 24th, 1774.

1774.—D. JOSÉ PEDRO DA CAMARA (No. 87), Governor and Captain-General of India for five years. The new title of Captain-General had been substituted for that of Viceroy by the celebrated Marquis of Pombal, Prime Minister of D. José, King of Portugal. Named on February 4th, 1774; he took charge on September 24th. Various orders of reform were sent out by the Marquis,* and the Crown ordered some streets of the old city to be rebuilt, under the inspection of the Brigadier Henrique Carlos Henriques, and a tax of half per cent. was raised. The first Captain-General governed till May 24th, 1779, and returned to Europe.

1779.—D. FREDERICO GUILHERME DE SOUZA (No. 88), named March 18th, 1778, Governor and Captain-General, and took charge May 26th, 1779. He once more united to the Crown of Portugal the provinces of Bicholim and Sanquelim, on the mainland, in 1782. He reduced the *Fortal d' Alorna*, and the *Casa forte d'Arabó*, and he strengthened the defences of S. Thiago, S. Braze, and Naroá. By order of the Crown, the three infantry regiments of seven companies each were changed to two of ten; and the second legion of the volunteers of Bardez were enrolled. The Supreme Court (*Relação*), extinct by law of January 15th, 1774, was restored, the fleet was increased, and the northern possessions about Surat and Bombay were visited. D. Frederico administered for seven years, till November 3rd, 1786, and returned to Portugal.

1786.—FRANCISCO DA CUNHA DE MENEZES (No. 89), named on December 19th, 1785, Governor and Captain-General, and took charge on November 3rd, 1786; when Bahadur Saunto Bounsolo, threatened by the King of Kolapur, claimed his aid, according to the Treaty of January 29th, 1788 (*Livro dos Pazes* by which the Rajah had ceded his Province of Pernem.† Consequently 12,000 men were sent under the Marechal Veiga Cabral. This Governor was urgent in economising the Treasury issues, and he built at Daman, with money raised from the agricultural communities, a great *langebote* (long boat), and four flats (*chatas*), intended to clean out the Goa river. The attempt was never made, as he applied for recall; and after governing eight years, till May 22nd, 1794, he went back to Europe.

1794.—FRANCISCO ANTONIO DA VEIGA CABRAL (No. 90), was appointed August 24th, 1793, Governor of Goa, where he was serving as Lieut.-General and Commander-in-Chief, and took charge on May 22nd, 1794. During his rule the embarrassment of affairs in Europe caused Goa and the settlements in India to be much neglected by Portugal. The first Napoleon made vigorous efforts with Tipu (Tippoo) Sahib, to secure the city, as a nucleus for his ardently desired French Empire in the East. After the fall of Seringapatam the Marquis of Wellesley sent Joseph Uhthoff as British envoy to Goa, and

* Printed in 1841 at Goa, with copious notes, by the Secretary of the Governor-General C. Lagrange M. de Barbuda.

† Both in this and in the succeeding reign De Kloguen (p. 48) confuses Pernem with Piro, and makes the former province belong to Tipu Sahib instead of the Bhonslà.

on September 6th, 1799, an English auxiliary force, of about 1,100 rank and file, commanded by Colonel Sir William Clarke, took possession of the forts of Aguada in Bardez and of Cabo. They were received with every demonstration of the most perfect cordiality and distinguished attention by the Governor. The Treaty of Amiens (March 1802) caused reluctant evacuation; but a fresh rupture with France, in November of that year, led to a second occupation, which lasted till 1815, and the force at one time consisted of 10,000 men.* On November 15th, 1806, Governor Cabral was created, by Letter Patent, Governor and Captain-General. He ruled with rigour, and with much political ability, for thirteen years, till May 30th, 1807, when he left Goa for Rio de Janeiro. Here the King received him well, and granted him the title of Viscount de Mirandella.

1807.—Bernardo Jozé de Lourena (No. 91), Count of Sarzedas, and nephew of the unfortunate Viceroy, Marquis of Tavora, was named, October 17th, 1806, with the double title of Viceroy and Captain-General of Portuguese India. He took charge on May 30th, 1807, and remitted to the agrarian communities the sixth of their taxes, in order to liquidate the debts of his predecessor, who, in order to carry on the campaign, had raised from these establishments one-third of their revenue. In 1812, at the persuasion of the British Government, the Court of Portugal, then residing in the Brazil, abolished the branch Inquisition in Goa, and demolished the Palace. Under his rule, in 1815, when the general European peace was established, the English finally evacuated Goa. After administering for nine years, till November 29th, 1816, he retired to Rio de Janeiro, and died there in 1818.

1816.—D. Diogo de Souza (No. 92), Count of Rio Pardo, named Viceroy and Captain-General, on January 4th, 1816, and reached Goa November 25th. He captured and razed the *Casa forte de Uspá*, and wasted the *Campos de Rarim.* He ruled with prudence, military success, and economy. During his reign the Supreme Court and the Treasury were removed to Pangim.

1821.—In consequence of the political changes in Portugal, a revolution took place at Goa in 1821. The Viceroy was deposed by the Provisional Junta on September 16th, arrested, and confined in the fort *alias* the convent of Cabo. A Junta or Council of five members, elected by the inhabitants, was appointed to govern the Colony, on the principle of the Cortes then sitting at Lisbon. This first Provisional Junta was composed of two Field-Marshals—Manoel Godinho da Mira and Joaquim Manoel Corrêa da Silva e Gama—and of three Desembargadores (Judges of the Supreme Court)—Manoel Jozé Gomes Loureiro, Gonçalo de Magalhaes Teixeira Pinto, and Manoel Duarto Leitão. They were deposed by a new revolution of December 3rd, 1821.† The Viceroy embarked from Cabo for Bombay on October 22nd; returned to Goa on February 7th, 1822; sailed (March 4th) in the sloop-of-war, *Laconia*, for Rio de Janeiro, where the Court was; and died July 12th, 1829.

1822.—D. Manoel de Camara (No. 93), appointed Governor and Captain-General July 19th, 1820; arrived in December of the same year, and after much difficulty was allowed to land and take lodgings in a private house. He became President of the second Provisional Junta, named by the revolution of December 3rd, 1821, composed of the Archbishop of Croganor, D. Fr. Paulo de S. Thomas d' Aquino; Brigadier Antonio José de Mello Souto-Maior Telles; Desembargador João Carlos Leal, and Dr. Antonio José de

* See "The English and their Monuments at Goa," reprinted from the journal of the Bombay Br. R. As. Soc., by Dr. da Cunha.

† For a list of the ephemeral publications which on this occasion flooded the Colony, see Note A, pp. 165-66 of the "Bosquejo Historico."

Lima Leitão; and the latter, elected Deputy to the Cortes, was replaced by the "Captain of Sea and War," Joaquim Mourão Garcez Palha. In 1822 Captain Luis Prates d'Almeida e Albuquerque, editor of the *Goa Gazette*,* was barbarously murdered by a conspiracy; and the Archbishop of Craganor retired to Sunquerim, in Carwar, under the protection of the British Government. In 1824 King João VI., having recovered his power and dissolved the Cortes, sent orders to Don Manoel de Camara, by Royal Letter of August 22nd, received on February 23rd, 1825, to govern India after the ancient forms, and to assume the title of Viceroy and Captain-General. This step was taken on March 10th; tranquillity was restored, and the Archbishop returned to Goa. The Viceroy set free the political prisoners confined in the Aguada Fort; and, suspecting the fidelity of the disorderly Ranes and Sar-Desháis chiefs of Querim and Gululem, he interned them in that building, destroying at the same time all their strong places in the Satary Province. He built the Pangim Cemetery, and organised as private establishments the lotteries of the Misericordia and the Military Monte Pio. He ruled till November 16th, 1825, when he died of a cruel disease at the Convento do Cabo, and was buried in S. Francisco of the old city.

1825.—Upon the death of the Viceroy, D. Fré Manoel de S. Galdino (No. 94), Archbishop of Goa, and two others, namely, the Superintendent of Marine, Candido José Mourão Garcez Palha, and the Desembargador, Antonio Ribeiro de Carvalho, assumed the administration of public affairs, according to the ancient custom, and governed till October 9th, 1827.

1827.—D. Manoel de Castro e Portugal (No. 95), of a natural branch of the Royal Family, arrived in October with the title of Governor and Captain-General, and was solemnly invested with the administration by the Archbishop in the church of Bom-Jesus.†

1827.—D. Manoel de Castro e Portugal (No. 95) was raised by Royal Letter Decree of April 7th, 1830, to the rank of Viceroy and Captain-General. To him are owing the embellishments of Pangim. He levelled the ground, and filled up the three great rice-fields and fetid marshes which deformed the centre of the town, one facing the Palace and the Casa dos Camotins, where the fine quay now stands. He built six bridges, of which two are over the riverine sea-arm to the west of the Capital. The space between them, once a sand-waste, is now the "*Campal*," a kind of Champ de Mars, surrounded by trees, and serving for military parades and public promenade. He opened spacious squares and straight streets, some 40 palms (=26 feet 8 inches) in width, for private houses and public offices. Among the latter were the great Quartel Militar (barrack), which, according to the *Refutação Analytica*, published at Bombay, cost the Public Treasury 312,165: 0: 30 (=£12,486 12*s.*); the new Alfandega (custom-house) and its mole, which took the place of a shed standing in a swamp; the Cadêa (prison) of two stories; a *pakka*-house, which served as a Casa de Moeda (mint); and the Fountain, called Cabeca da Vacca (the Cow's head), from the form of its spout, at the foot of the hillock near the Hindu Pagoda.

He also added to the Revenue Office the Monte Pio Militar (military *Mont de Piété*), which before was a private establishment. He established, at the expense of the State, four schools for primary instruction. He reorganised

* A superior officer in the secretariat of the Governor-General—a man of liberal ideas, who had taken part in the rising at Pernambuco, and much loved in the colony. He was assassinated openly at mid-day on July 15th.

† Here ends the Chronological Table, etc., the work of M. de Kloguen (pp. 25-50). The following "Addition or Continuation of the Series of Viceroys and Governors until 1857," is the work of his translator, Miguel Vicente d' Abreu.

and improved the army, according to the Tarifa or Regulations of 1816; and compelled candidates for commissions to study in the mathematical schools of the Military Academy. He formed a flying corps of six *Partidos* or companies of Sepoys, including the *Mouros* (native irregulars), whom he had detached from the Line, and who on State occasions mustered in the Palace Hall. He also organised a picket of cavalry, which lasted, with his government, till January 1833.

During his reign (May 5th, 1858) the landowner, Pedro Joaquim de Miranda, established the *Sociedade Patriotica dos Baldios* (waste or uncultivated lands) *das Novas Conquistas*, and a section of it took the name of *Campos de Portugal e Castro.* This company of shareholders (limited), with a capital of £12,000, and paying only a nominal quit-rent to Government, afterwards became important by the energy of its members. D. Manoel was censured for inordinate expenditure upon the works of the capital. Besides the large sum lavished on the barracks, he disbursed 368,806 xerafins (£14,752 4*s.* 6*d.*), out of the sixths of the Rural Communities' Revenues, and 197,603 from the coffers of the *Senado da Camara das Ilhas* (municipality of the Islands), or a total of 878,574. He governed till the arrival of his successor on January 14th, 1835, and shortly afterwards he returned to Portugal. Here he was made, in 1847, *Vedor da Casa-Real* (Controller or Administrator of the Royal Treasury) and Minister of Marine and the Colonies. When the "Conselho Ultramarinho" was re-established in 1852, he was offered, but declined, the post of President, and he died on July 12th, 1854.

1835.—Bernardo Peres da Silva (No. 96), of His Majesty's Council, named Prefect of the State of India by Royal Letter (May 7th, 1834), reached Goa on January 10th, 1835, in the *Charrua* (ship-of-war), *Princeza Real*, and on the 14th took charge in the *Paços do Senado da Goa* (Senatorial Palace, Old Town). He was born at the Neurá village (also called Aldêa Grande) in the Islands of Goa, and he had thrice been named Deputy to the Cortes of Portugal. After protesting in the cause of constitutional liberty against the usurpation of D. Miguel, he emigrated to London and other cities; and when D. Maria II. was restored to the throne, he was appointed by the Regent, Duke of Bragança, to the highest position of his native country, under the title of *Prefeito* (Prefect), as in legislative use at that time. He brought out with him the decrees for reorganising the Law Courts and the Treasury, and the Legal Letter for reducing the *Sizas* (or tithes) from 10 to 5 per cent., losing no time in carrying out this measure. He was also empowered to make the necessary reforms and economies, as well as to dismiss *employés* appointed by the Crown. During his short reign of seventeen days he enforced, amongst other changes, the remission of a sixth part of the Revenues of the Rural Communities, carried to the Treasury account.

On February 1st, 1835, he was deposed by a faction, and sent on board the corvette *Infanta Regente*, which carried him on the 3rd to Bombay. After giving up the idea of returning with an expedition to Goa, he went to Daman, and governed that fort, with its neighbour Diu, till November 1837, when relieved by his successor, Barão de Sabrozo. On the day of his deposition the ex-Viceroy, D. Manoel de Portugal, reassuming the reins of government under the title of *Governador-General*, issued a proclamation; on the 3rd, however, he resigned, and called an Assembly at Government House, which named to the head of affairs the first Counsellor of the Prefecture, Field-Marshal Joaquim Manoel Corrêa da Silva e Gama. On February 10th a reactionary movement recalled the Prefect, but the measure was prevented by a new military revolt on March 3rd; which, on the following days, caused some bloodshed. Field-Marshal Corrêa consequently resigned; and the mutineers, forming an irregular assembly, chose a Provisional Government in the name of the Queen, composed of (President) Colonel João Casimiro da Rocha Vasconcellos, and two members, Surgeon-General Manoel José Ribeiro, and the *Pai dos Christãos* (Father of the Christians), Fr. Constantino di Santa Rita. D. Manoel, who retired to Vingorla, and the "Dezembrista," Manoel Venancio Moreira de Carvalho, refused to take part in this Government. On December 7th, 1836, the third member died; and another Assembly, determining to have a Council of Five, added to the two survivors Colonel João Cabral de Estifique, Lieutenant-Colonel Antonio Maria de Mello, and the Desembargador Joaquim Antonio de Moraes Carneiro. Shortly afterwards, when the latter resigned, and Dr. Ribeiro died (April 10th, 1837), a third Assembly, on the 18th of the same month, replaced them by the Major of Goa Engineers, José Antonio de Lemos, and Major (in the Home Army) Antonio Mariano d' Azevedo; the latter as Secretary of the Governor, Barão de Sabrozo, had arrived at Goa before his chief. The two Majors were compelled to resign by chronic dissensions with their colleagues; and the three others, after provoking a movement of the troops, administered the affairs of the colony till November 22nd, 1837.

During these years the principal Legitimist families of Goa suffered much in person and purse. The slaughter at Gaspar Dias, Tiracol, and Gululem, the destruction and plunder of the Arsenal, and the imprisonments and fines will not readily be forgotten. The events of this unhappy time have been amply and minutely described, of course with passionate partisanship, in the *Manifesto do Governo Provisional*, in the *Refutaçao Analytica* of the same Manifest; in the Goanese Journals, as the *Chronica Constitucional* and the *Echo da Luzitania*; in the Bombay and Daman papers, *Investigador Portuguez*, the *Sentinella da Liberdade*, and *O Portuguez*; and finally, not to mention any more, in the *Resumo Historico da Revolução*, published at Bombay. It is to be noted that the Military Governor, Fortunato de Mello, who had taken the side of the mutineers, was made prisoner, and sent to Portugal by the partisans whom he had commanded. Prefect Peres, again elected Deputy, returned home; and the Goanese successively reappointed him to represent their interests till the day of his death, on November 14th, 1844.

1837.—Brigadier Simão Infante de Lacerda, Moço Fidalgo Com Exercicio,* Barão de Sabrozo (No. 97), named Governor-General by Royal Letter of May 2nd, 1836, brought out new decrees for the administrative and judiciary establishments of the Provincias Ultramarinas, issued in December 1836 and January 1837. Early in the latter year he left Lisbon in the frigate *D. Pedro*; he reached Goa on November 19th, and on the 23rd he assumed charge of his post, after ancient custom, at the Bom-Jesus Church and Convent. He began by a Royal Amnesty conceded to those implicated in the troubles following January 1835, but confined to the Legitimists that had taken part with his predecessor, the Prefect. This Governor was involved in troubles with Commander (R.N.) Joaquim Pedro Celestino Soares, commanding the frigate in which he had sailed; and with the Acting President of the Relação (Supreme Court); the two latter resigned their posts and left Goa. In consequence of a fall from his carriage (June 13th, 1838), on September 28th he delivered over charge to the Council in virtue of the "Organic Decree," and he died on October 14th, 1838. His remains

* The Fidalgo (*Edler*) or third class of Portuguese patricians, not title-holders, are divided into six branches,—1, Fildagos do Conselho e Fidalgos Cavalleiros; 2, Fidalgos Escudeiros; 3, Moços Fidalgos; 4, Moços Fidalgos Com Exercicio (*i.e.*, doing actual service in the Royal Household); 5, Escudeiros Fidalgos; and 6, Fidalgos da Geração.

were temporarily placed in the house of the Brotherhood of the Church of Pangim for transmission to Portugal, as had been his desire expressed in writing; but the Governor, Conde d' Antas (in 1842), after pompous and solemn obsequies at the Cathedral, deposited them in the Catacombs of the Convent of S. Caetano, where they still rest.

The same Decree established during his Viceroyalty an Official Journal, *Boletim do Governo do Estada da India.* The first number was issued on December 7th, 1837, under the three editors, A. M. d' Azevedo (Secretary to Government), Canon C. J. Peres, and C. F. Pereira Garcez. No. 88, of 1856, gives a curious account of the phases of the paper, and of the other political and literary journals published at Goa, Bombay, and Daman.

1838.—(No. 98). On September 28th, when the Governor-General resigned his post, the Administration lapsed, according to law, into the hands of the Government Council, composed of (President) the Archbishop elect, D. Antonio Feliciano de Santa Rita Carvalho, and the three members, Colonel (Home Cavalry) José Antonio Vieira da Fonseca, commanding the troops; José Cancio Freire de Lima, Acting President of the Supreme Court; and Domingos José Mariano Luis, Deputy of the *Junta da Fazenda Publica* (Treasury Committee). On November 21st was committed the treacherous murder of A. M. d'Azevedo, Secretary to Government; and on the morning of February 1st, 1839, the Archbishop died. The other three continued to govern till a decree (December 27th, 1838) appointed one of them, provisionally, to the post.

1839.—COLONEL J. A. VIEIRA DA FONSECA (No. 99), who had accompanied the Barão de Sabrozo, as military commandant, took provisional charge in the Bom-Jesus on March 5th, and governed till November 14th of the same year.

1839.—FIELD MARSHAL and COUNSELLOR MANOEL JOSE MENDES (No. 100), first Barão do Candal, was the first to travel *viâ* the Mediterranean, as all his successors have done. Named on August 5th, 1839, he left Lisbon on November 12th; on the 15th he took charge in the Bom-Jesus, and he died on April 18th. Assisted by his learned secretary, Lagrange, he appointed several committees of reform during his five months' rule; and he died generally lamented. His remains had the same honours as those of the Barão de Sabrozo.

1840.—(No. 101). The Government Council, composed of (President) Colonel José Antonio Vieira da Fonseca, and members José Cancio Freire de Lima,—both before mentioned; of Antonio João d'Athaide, Capitular Vicar, and of D. J. M. Luis (also before mentioned), with the two counsellors elect; Captain (Goa Engineers) José da Costa Campos, and Colonel (Mozambique Militia), Caetano de Souza Vasconcellos, took charge on April 19th, 1840; and on September 24th vacated in favour of the nominee of the Decree of July 7th, 1839.

1840.—CAPITAO TENENTE (First Lieutenant R.N.), afterwards Capitão de Fragata (Commander R. N.), JOSÉ JOAQUIM LOPES DE LIMA (No. 102),*

* This is the celebrated author of the well-known "Ensaios" (Essays), etc. Lisbon: Na Imprensa Nacional, 1846; two volumes only being published during his lifetime. The third, treating of Goa and the Indian colonies ("Ensaios sobre a Estatistica das Possessoes Portuguezas na ultramar. Estado da India: Lisbon, 1862") was printed, after his death, by José Maria Bordalo, with additions of his own. Other works on the same subject are, 1, "Memorias des Estabelecimentos Portnguezes a l'Este do Cabo da Boa Esperança:" pelo Conselheiro Manoel José Gomes Loureiro. Lisbon, 1835; and 2, "the "Bosquejo das Possessoes Portuguezas no Oriente," por Joaquim Pedro Celestino Soares. Lisbon, 1853. I need hardly refer to the "Annaes Maritimes e Coloniaes," five volumes, of monthly publication, full of valuable notices on the history and geography of Goa.

was Superintendent of the Goa Marine when a decree appointed him Acting Governor. On September 24th, 1840, he took charge at the Bom-Jesus; and on April 27th, 1842, he was compelled to resign by a meeting of the Provisional Battalion from Portugal. He sailed for Bombay; and, after vainly attempting to resume his post, returned home upon the appointment of the Conde das Antas.

This Governor made many useful reforms. He changed the system of farming the Custom-House, organized the Council of Public Health and schools of primary and secondary instruction in the country, together with classes of history, geography, chronology, and statistics; of English, French, and mutual instruction at the capital. He regulated the Arsenal and the Accountantship-General; and, after changing the Military Academy into the *Escola Mathematicae Militar*, he prescribed its several grades, together with the course of military drawing for the three arms. He discontinued the twelve-months' course of navigation, taught in the Academy, and established a lecture-room for pilotage. He reorganized the army,—which gratefully offered him a medal,—and transferred the military hospital from Panelim to Pangim, in the houses of Diogo da Costa d'Athaide e Teive,—vulgarly *Mequinez*,—for which the Public Treasury disbursed 15,000 xerafins. He issued receipts, or public *apoliçes* (bonds), for paying the servants of the State. He ordered the streets of the capital to be lighted,—an improvement which lasted but a short time;—he renewed the old *Pharol da Agoada* (Aguada lighthouse) with sixteen beaks, which complete the circle in ten minutes, and which show from three sea-miles; besides which he placed, in the neighbouring tower, a large bell and repeating clock. He opened in Pangim the street named *Quatro d'Abril*, through the middle of the quarter known as *Fontainhas*. He laid down pipes for draining the wintry rains, and built the useful wharf, with its crane, at the quay of the chief Custom-House. Amongst many other reforms he abolished the taxes known as Bagibabos and Xendim; * and for the tobacco monopoly he substituted stamped paper and spirit licences. He gave life to the "Patriotic Society of Agriculture" in the *Novas Conquistas*, and hence a part of the reclaimed lands took the name of *Campos de Lopez de Lima*.

On his return home he was made Civil Governor of Coimbra, and resigned in consequence of a mutiny among the students. Being then appointed to the Government of Timor, he was made prisoner by royal order. He died in 1853, on board the corvette which was carrying him home; and he was buried in the city of Batavia.

1842.—(No. 103). The Government was carried on peaceably, till September 19th of the same year, by the Council,—composed of (President) Antonio Ramalho de Sà, President of the Supreme Court; members, Brigadier Antonio José de Mello Souto-Maior Telles, and the Rev. Antonio João d'Athaide, Capitular Vicar; with the counsellors elect, José da Costa Campos and Caetano de Souza Vasconcellos.

1843.—LIEUTENANT-GENERAL (Home Army) FRANCISCO XAVIER DA SILVA PEREIRA (No. 104), first Baron, first Viscount, and first Count das Antas: named July 18th, 1842; reached Goa September 16th; took charge on September 19th, and kept it till April 25th, 1843. On this date he received the news of his successor's appointment, by Decree of January 31st, 1843. He read his "Carta da Prego" † at Government House, before the

* These now obsolete terms denoted certain taxes in the *Novas Conquistas*.

† The "Carta da Prego," literally, "letter with a nail," was the royal rescript which each Viceroy or Governor brought with him to India, and whose seal was not broken till his death or removal. It is, in fact the old *tres vias de successão*.

Municipal Chamber of the Islands, and next day he returned to Portugal, *viâ* Suez. He made some economical reforms in the military branch; reduced two army corps, and increased the infantry by two companies; and he abolished the Provisional Battalion, which cost the Goa Treasury 150,000 xerafins per annum. Instead of the primary schools founded by his predecessor, he instituted a promiscuous course and two primary establishments at Daman, with four in the chief towns of the *Novas Conquistas*, besides which, the provincial interpreters were ordered to teach Maráthá. He regulated the seminaries, the Government Secretariat, the Marine Arsenal, the Telegraphs, and the English and French schools. He established the military archives and abolished the house of Catachumens and the Mint. In his time Pangim was raised to the rank of a city; for which reason he erected the monument in the *Praça das Sete Janellas* (seven-window square), for accommodating the statue of "O Conquistador," Affonso d'Albuquerque, that stood fronting the *Recolhimento* (orphanage) *da Serra da Cidade Velha*. Finally he visited the forts of Daman, Diu, and Angediva, and made improvements in the two former.

On returning home this Governor-General was made Vogal Effectivo (ordinary Member)* of the Supreme Council of Military Justice; and in 1846, during the Revolution of Minho, President of the Junta, or Committee of Oporto. He died on May 20th, 1852.

1843.—Joaquim Mourão Garcez Palha (No. 105); Pensioned Chief of Division in the Goa Marine; appointed Governor-General by the "Carta da Prego" (before mentioned); took charge on April 23rd, and governed till May 20th, 1844. He reduced the number of private soldiers and the two infantry companies, which his predecessor had preserved as the remains of the Provisional Battalion. He re-established the Marine School, and created one of Maráthá; and he stopped all the public works which were not absolutely necessary. Finally he allowed the physicians, surgeons, *Sages-femmes* and apothecaries to practise; whereas the Conde des Antas, by a "Regulation of Public Health," had forbidden them so to do without licence. Finally, after receiving the thanks of His Majesty by an Order in Council, he died on July 26th, 1850.

1844.—José Ferreira Pestana (No. 106); Royal Counsellor, Honorary Minister, and Secretary of State; and Mathematical Lecturer at the University of Coimbra; named Governor-General on January 20th, 1844; left Lisbon March 28th; reached Goa May 17th, and took possession in the Bom-Jesus May 20th. His term was prolonged for three years, and several parishes offered solemn acts of gratitude. At the end of his second triennium he made over charge to his successor, on January 15th, 1851; and on March 25th returned home.

This literary Governor-General established at the capital a school for girls, and others of philosophy (national and moral), the principles of natural rights, the art of oratory, poetry, and classical literature, and a French school at Margão. At the military hospital he established a medico-chirurgical school, with a course of four years, and two of pharmacy. With great zeal he finished building the corvette *Goa* and the Session House of the Treasury Committee. He also collected private subscriptions and completed the Albuquerque monument, the fine Bazar Quay, and the Chapel of St. Thomas, near the barracks of the Municipal Guard. He regulated the religious brotherhoods of the capital, the powder manufactory, and the public printing press. He abolished the barbarous *Zatrá dos Enganchados*.† He assisted the province

* Thus distinguished from the Vogal Substituto, or Extraordinary Member.

† Literally "the festival (*yátra*) of the hooked;" the swinging-fête so well known

of Macáo, although independent of Goa, with a detachment of troops, paid by the Goa Treasury. He ably repressed an attempt at military mutiny. During his rule, the tributary Regulo (rajah, or chief) Bounsoló de Saunt-Vary (the Bhonslá of Sáwant-Wari), holding the lands to the north of Goa, took up arms against the English, and was compelled to fly, with many of his followers, into Portuguese territory.* The Governor-General, with much tact and success, by cutting off the supplies sent from Goa, assisted the Bombay Government in repressing the movement without having to winter in the field; and, at the same time, supported the rights of asylum and hospitality, and the inviolability of his territory against all the pretensions of his powerful neighbours. Ably assisted by his Secretary to Government, the amiable Custodio Manoel Gomes,† he established the "Commercial Company of Goa," which offered him a medal on his retirement. During his six or seven years of rule he showed, when necessary, the severity which justice demands; and he treated the rich and the poor alike. Upon his return home he became one of the Ministry, and after some time Vice-President of the Conseltho Ultramarino.

1851.—José Joaquim Januario Lapa (No. 107); Baron, and afterwards Viscount of Villa Nova d'Ourem; Peer of the Realm (whilst governing India), Honorary Minister and Secretary of State, and Brigadier of the Royal Army. Named Governor-General October 30th, 1850; left Lisbon in December; reached Goa January 12th, 1851, and took charge on the 15th. Reappointed for three years, he was compelled by ill health to make over—with the permission of the Crown—the Government to his Council, and he returned home on May 6th, 1855.

This official made the useful distribution of the *Novas Conquistas* into four fiscal administrations; he changed to money payments the paper bonds assigned for public salaries; and he organized a corps of veterans, and another of Municipal Guard, attached to the old company of "Mouros." He began a new road in Cuessim (*Novas Conquistas*), but this work was stopped by the rising of the Ranes de Satary (feudatories of Satary),‡ led by Dipu, or Dipaji Ranes; a movement which began on January 27th, 1852, and which lasted throughout his Government. The robberies and destruction caused by the revolted, compelled him to declare a state of siege in the provinces of Bicholim, Sanquelim (or Satary), Pondá, and Embarbacem; and to levy a forced loan for the expenses of the campaign. At last he marched in person, accompanied by the greater part of the army, upon Satary; and a full account of his proceedings is in the "Boletim" (No. 41, of 1852). He abolished the Accas (Hakk, or vested rights); the Inamas (In'áms, or gifts), and the Mocassós§ (or grants of land), made to the Dessais (Desháis, or petty chiefs) of this province. He re-established the agricultural commu-

in England, when devotees were seen hanging by a hook passed under the shoulder-muscles. These victims of their vows were once common at Goa, as at Poonah and elsewhere.

* My husband has described his meeting with Phond Sáwant and his merry men in "Goa and the Blue Mountains," p. 34. Sáwant-Wári is a small State under British protection, and bordering the Goanese territory on the north.

† Still living, I am told, at Lisbon.

‡ The "Ranes" are what we English call "Desháis," or large feudal landholders, subject to the Portuguese Crown. They belong to the same caste as the people of Sáwant-Wári; and they occupy all the Satary, or north-eastern province of the Goanese, and almost the whole of the *Novas Conquistas*. Their chief, "Dipu Ranes," was a famous ruffian in his day.

§ Mocassó is, properly speaking, a village in the *Novas Conquistas* granted free of quit-rent, by Government, in return for favours received.

nities, and he equalized the predial tithes of the communities of the Velhas, Conquistas, and the Deshâis of Bicholim, with those of private proprietors. He regulated the arsenal, converted the military hospital into a regimental establishment; changed the Pagadoria (or soldiers' pay-office) into a *Repartição Fiscal da Contabilidade de Exercito;* improved the stamp office, and protected the forests of Goa, Daman, and Diu. He established an English school at Mapuçá, a normal school of primary instruction at New Goa, two of Latin at Salsette and Bardez; two for girls in the chief towns of the latter divisions, and one of promiscuous instruction at Diu. He organised the National Lyceum of the capital, with its six classes of secondary instruction,—in Latin, philosophy, history, English, French, and Márathá. He instituted free fairs at Goa and Daman, and he imposed annual taxes upon shopkeepers and retail dealers, payable to the Municipal Chamber of the Islands. He ordered the lower classes to appear decently clad in public. He opened, on the sea-board of the Fontainhas Bairro (or quarter), a handsome street with parapet, called the "Rua Nova d'Ourem." He built the Phenix fountain,—in the same division,—with a fine façade and a porch, opposite the barracks of the Municipal Guard, now serving as a Bazar. The two latter works were at the expense of the Municipality of the Islands. He also began a medico-chirurgical school, attached to the Hospital, and he laid the foundations of the great bridge over the Rio de Siridão. He visited Angediva and the Northern Forts, and he received a medal from the army and another from the inhabitants of Satary.

1855.—(No. 108). On the day of the Governor-General's retirement his place was taken by the Council of State, composed of (President) D. Fr. Joaquim de Santa Rita Botelho, Bishop-Elect of Cochim, Capitular Vicar and Temporal Governor of the Archbishopric of Goa; and of (members) Brigadier (Army of Goa) Luis da Costa Campos, and Francisco Xavier Peres, Acting Writer to the Junta; with the Counsellors-Elect, Bernardo Hector da Silveira e Lorena (General Treasurer of the State); and Captain (Engineers) Victor Anastacio Mourão Garcez Palha. During their rule, on September 8th, the dogma of the Immaculate Conception was solemnized at the Primatial Cathedral; a French school was opened at Mapuçá, and the lectures of medicine, chemistry, and natural history established by His Majesty, began their course. The Council governed till November 2nd, 1855.

1855.—FIELD-MARSHAL (Home Army) and COUNSELLOR ANTONIO CEZAR DE VASCONCELLOS CORREA (No. 109); Viscount (afterwards Count) of Torres Novas, and an officer holding a plurality of dignities, was named Governor-General by Royal Letter of May 24th, 1855; left Lisbon September 23rd, and arrived at Goa on November 1st. The voyage is described in a volume printed at Goa in 1856, by the Secretary to Government, Sr. J. H. da Cunha Rivára, a well-known *litterateur*, who was still holding his appointment in 1877.* The new Governor-General took charge at the Bom-Jesus on November 3rd, 1855; and, on the 3rd of the following December, King D. Pedro V. was solemnly acclaimed in the Primatial Cathedral.

This officer regulated the tax called *Liberdade de Tabaco*, extinguished the Corps of Veterans,—by dismissing the privates, who were pensioned,—abolished the fairs (called *Feiras Francas*) of Goa and of Daman; reformed the National Lyceum, the Normal School, and the Arsenal; established a Post-Captain at Sinquerim d'Aguada; abolished the penalty of transportation (*pena di degredo*) in the case of the *Gentios* (heathen); beautified the

* In June 1877, we had the unexpected pleasure of a visit from this gentleman at Trieste.

Bairro de Fontainhas with many new streets; began various sanitary works in the capital; opened the King's highway from Verem to Sunquervale, besides other thoroughfares and bridges; and restored the Accás (Hakks) and Mocassós (grants of villages), after pardoning Dipú Ranes, to the Desháis and the Ranes of Satary.*

His period of government having expired in 1858, it was twice prorogued, for three years each time. During his unusually long reign, the revenue was considerably increased, and was well spent in public works. Besides the highway above named, he began the tracings of the following thoroughfares: 1. From Usgão to Tinem, near the foot of the Gháts, crossing the provinces of Bicholim and Embarbacem, and reaching the British district of Dhárwár. 2. From Sanquelim to Massordem, across the province of Satary. 3. From the old city of Goa to Cumbarjua; and 4, from Pangim, across Santa Cruz, to S. Lourenço, intending to carry the latter through Salsette and Canacona to the English frontier of Sadasewgarh. His was one of the most popular of governments; the only fault that alienated the sympathies of the people, towards the latter part of his reign, being his interference (through interested counsellors) with the election of a *deputado* to the *Cortes*, in the electoral circle of Nagoa, on the 11th August, 1861, when the popular candidate was set aside, and the Government nominee was proclaimed, through the brute force of two hundred bayonets. And the outcome of all these violent manœuvres was that the Government *deputado*, a half-caste (*mestiço*), by name Mendonça, was sent up to the *Cortes*, and when the Conde de Torres-Novas was arraigned before the Chambers for his illegal act, Mr. *Deputado Mendonça* did not say a word in defence of his protector. The upshot of this unpleasant episode was too bitter for the old Count, and the ingratitude of Mendonça was ever present to his mind,—in fact, he carried it to the grave. This *faux pas* and subsequent events rendered him extremely unpopular, and undermined his health; notwithstanding which, he married, at the advanced age of above sixty, the fourteen-year-old daughter of the Count of Sarzedas, of Goa. At last he left India, on January 9th, 1865, for Lisbon, where, soon after his arrival, he died from aortic aneurism.

An event of some importance during his reign was the exposition of the body of St. Francis Xavier, from December 3rd, 1859, to January 8th, 1860; during which time many Catholic pilgrims and others visited the old and decayed capital of Portuguese India, with spiritual benefits proportioned to the occasion.

1865.—José Ferreira Pestana (No. 110), Honorary Minister and *Olim* Professor of Mathematics at the University of Coimbra, was re-appointed, and returned to Goa in May 1865. His second reign was a period of quiet and routine affairs; but as the end drew near happened the military mutiny of Marcella, which was put a stop to by an inglorious compromise with the mutineers. He left Goa in May 1870.

1870.—Antonio da Correia e Almeida (No. 111), Visconde de São Januario, reached Goa on May 7th, 1870 He was a man of unusual activity; he introduced postage-stamps; imported copper money coined at the Mint

* In writing this Appendix I have taken de Kloguen for my skeleton or plan. He Chronicles, after a meagre fashion, the Viceroys up to 1827, and the Ecclesiastical Government up to 1812. I then added the list made by his Portuguese translator. I have enriched and embellished the original sketch from Portuguese MSS., old hooks, and conversation with aged natives; and added the still remaining unchronicled period from 1812 to 1878 (68 years) from notes collected by me from the above mentioned sources at Goa itself. I have submitted them to our friend, Dr. da Cunha, who has been so kind as to correct and amplify them.

of Bombay; and attempted, but in vain, to raise from Messrs. Nicol and Co. a loan for public works at 3 per cent., guaranteed by a tax upon custom-dues. He was about to introduce new measures, when his rule was cut short by the mutiny of Volvoy. He was transferred to the Government of Macáo; and thence, after about three years, he returned to Lisbon. His Secretary to Government was Thomas Ribeiro, the poet, who did not add to the morality or the decency of the two years' reign.* On the 20th December, 1871, a literary institution, by name "Instituto Vasco da Gama," was inaugurated under the auspices of both the Governor and his Secretary.

1872.—Joaquim José de Macedo e Couto (No. 112) was sent out to introduce military order. This old General was accompanied to Goa by the Prince of Portugal, D. Augusto, the first of the royal family that ever travelled to India. A reign of economy in every department,—of retrenchments and of salary-reductions in all the official grades,—produced much opposition, enmity, and quarrels on the part of one section (the half-castes) of the press. The local battalions were suppressed under General Macedo, and the colony was garrisoned by troops from home: the *Academia de Goa* was changed to the *Instituto Professional*, and the military organization of the former was merged into the civil constitution of the latter. The arsenal at the old city was finally closed, and some valuable guns, cast at Goa in the sixteenth century, were sold by auction.

During this Government a band of banditti, organized in the *Novas Conquistas* by dismissed soldiery and others, whose interest it was to show that security to life and property was endangered through the abovementioned retrenchments, gave him some trouble, but the ruffians were at last safely lodged in the jail of New Goa.

Despite his unpopular measures, the old General escaped unscathed, and left Goa for Portugal in May 1875.

1875.—General João Tavares d'Almeida (No. 113) also undertook the work of retrenchment and reform; but his measures were just, and the public did not complain. The Treasury was not without funds, although trade was stagnant, and the value of cocoanuts (here the staple article of commerce) fell in the Bombay market. The Home Government directed the Treasury, by special decree of the Crown, to pay certain salaries of officers serving in Portugal; the local papers protested against the injustice, but the Governor-General was not blamed for obeying orders. He left Goa on December 19th, 1876, for Delhi, where he was present at the Imperial Assemblage, and returned after about six weeks of absence, during which the Chief Secretary, the Counsellor J. H. Da Cunha Rivara, carried on the government of the colony.

* Dr. da Cunha remarks of this sentence that it is perfectly true, but "nem todas as verdades se dizem." I have ever laboured, and I ever shall labour, to imitate that "admirable pagan," Ammianus Marcellinus, the historian, who "never willingly corrupted Truth, either by falsification *or by silence*."

Section II.

THE RELIGIOUS ESTABLISHMENTS.

Proceedings and Documents concerning the Erection of the Episcopal, and afterwards Archiepiscopal, See of Goa.—The Chronology of its Bishops and Archbishops.—Its Provincial Councils.—The Erection of its Religious Buildings and Religious Institutions.*

1510.—Goa, having been captured in the beginning (February 17th) of this year by the great Albuquerque from Adil Sháh (Idal Kão), King of Visapúr or Bijapúr, had no religious establishments before that Prince retook the place shortly afterwards, and drove the Portuguese on board their ships. Albuquerque having wrested a second time the town and island from the Moslems on November 25th, 1510, the day consecrated to the memory of St. Catherine, the Martyr of Alexandria, solemnly chose that virgin as the patroness of Goa, and the protectoress of the Portuguese in the East, and built the first Christian church or chapel† to God in her name.

The Franciscans of the "Observance," who accompanied Albuquerque from Portugal, were the first spiritual pastors of the Portuguese in Goa. They soon laid the foundation of the oldest religious building, a convent, which has since been enlarged.‡ Adjoining it was a conventual church, still much admired for its architecture and its decorations. These religious also erected at the public expense a parochial church near their convent.§

The Dominicans came to Goa shortly after the conquest, but they did not

* This Table, like the former, has been enriched with the labours of the Portuguese translator of De Kloguen, Miguel Vicente d'Abreu, with other documents and native information.

† This oldest religious building was the nucleus of the Igreja da Sé, or Cathedral. De Kloguen here and elsewhere (p. 12) confounds it with the (new) chapel of St. Catherine lying behind or west of the Franciscan Convent; it stood at the ancient water-gate *(Porta da Ribeira)* by which the conquering forces of the Portuguese entered the city. It was founded shortly after A.D. 1549 by Governor Jorge Cabral, at the expense of the Royal Treasury, and on his return home he made it over to the Senate of Goa. This is proved by an inscription on the outer wall of the (new) chapel at the corner of the Franciscan Convent. We must not trust De Kloguen when he says (p. 52): "It subsists still as a chapel, though it must have been repaired and probably rebuilt several times. Every year on the festival of the saint, after the morning service in the cathedral is over, the Franciscans perform a second one with the greatest solemnity in the chapel, in the presence of the Viceroy (who wears a red cloak, as a member of the brotherhood or confraternity of the saint), the clergy of the cathedral, a deputation from all the churches and convents, the Senate, and all the authorities, civil and military." The ceremony is celebrated by the clergy in the old chapel; but the "function" at which the Governor and all the officials "assist," takes place in the cathedral, whose patron is the same Virgin Martyr.

‡ See the Portuguese translation (Note C, p. 174). This convent, in which the first mass was said, had been a mosque, and was given to the Franciscans by Albuquerque. They resided there till 1521, when their new church, built by order of Dom Manoel, was completed; it was consecrated in 1603 by the Archbishop D. Fr. Aleixo. In 1661, when the building was renewed, the old portal was preserved as a specimen of early architecture.

§ De Kloguen (p. 53) makes the same error when he says that this convent "became the cathedral, and was afterwards considerably enlarged, as e shall see."

form themselves into a community for about half a century. They built the church of N. Sra. do Rosario on a hill commanding the western part of the city. It was afterwards converted into a parochial and collegiate church, and it is still standing (1831). Near this church is the chapel of St. Anthony of Padua, called "of Lisbon" by the Portuguese, who acknowledge him as the patron of their nation. This fane, also erected soon after the conquest, and those already mentioned, together with the church of our Lady of Light (*Da Luz*) on a hill towards the south, the chapel of our Lady of the Mount in the eastern part, and the hospital of St. Lazarus, were the principal religious edifices in Old Goa.

1514.—The Bull *Pro Excellenti* of LEO X. submitted in spiritual matters all the conquests of the Portuguese in Africa and Asia to the Vicar of Thomar, Grand Master (*Prior Mór*) of the Order of Christ, and invested him with the episcopal character and consecration.

1515.—Erection, by the same Pope, of the Bishopric of Funchal (Madeira), the diocese to comprehend all the Portuguese possessions beyond seas. The first Bishop of this see was DOM DIOGO PINHEIRO, Vicar of Thomar, and Grand Master of the Order of Christ. A Royal Letter (March 15th, 1518) established the *Dizimos*, or tithes upon goods possessed by the Portuguese. In this matter great changes took place till the final settlement in 1745.

1533.—The city of Funchal, capital of Madeira, was erected into an archiepiscopal or metropolitan see by CLEMENT VII.

1534, November 1st.—PAUL III., successor of Clement VII., by the Bull *Æquum Reputamus*, established the following bishoprics: Angra, in the Island of Terceira (Azores or Western Islands); Santiago (St. James) in the Cape de Verd Archipelago; the Island of St. Thomas (Bight of Biafra, or south coast of Guinea), and Goa, whose diocese comprehended all the Portuguese settlements from the Cape of Good Hope to the extremities of the East. All the sees formed the province, whose bishops were the suffragans of the Metropolitan of Madeira; but the latter see soon became again a simple bishopric; and, together with its four suffragan bishoprics, made a part of the ecclesiastical province of Lisbon.

1537.—D. FR. JOÃO D'ALBUQUERQUE, a Spaniard and Franciscan monk, not related to the hero of that name, was the first bishop that reached Goa.* The cathedral chapter was founded in the year of his arrival.

1541.—The foundation of the seminary of the Holy Faith (*Santa Fé*) was laid by the exertions of two secular priests, R. P. Miguel (Michael) Vas and Diogo (James) de Borba, and by the liberality of the Governor, D. Estevão da Gama, for the instruction of the newly-converted Indians. Padre Diogo de Borba became the first Superior of this establishment.

1542.—The illustrious S. FRANCISCO XAVIER arrived in India with the new Governor, Martim Affonso de Souza. After a few months he entirely changed the wicked and debauched morals of the Portuguese in Goa, and re-established the practice of religion and the use of the sacraments. The year ended, this apostle proceeded to Connah of the Parvás,† or the fishermen on the coast extending towards Cape Comorin; but during the remaining decade of his life in the East, Goa was his chief place of residence, and here he established the "capital house" of his order in India.

* The first nominated was D. Francisco de Mello, who died before embarking. João, appointed his successor, arrived in 1538 with the Viceroy, D. Garcia de Noronha, and died on February 28th, 1553. He was followed by the Dominican D. Fr. Jorge de Santa Luzia, transferred from the Bishopric of Malacca to Goa in 1559. The collection of facsimiles of the archbishops made by Sr. F. N. Xavier bears the names of more than fourteen elected to Goa, and extracted from the archives of the Franciscan Order.

† Not to be confounded with the outcast Parwáris (Pariahs).

1543.—PADRE BORBA publicly ceded the church and seminary of Santa Fé to Xavier and his companions, of the Order of the Jesuits; thus they became the second Order settled in a regular community at Goa. The seminary of Santa Fé was changed to S. Paulo, from a picture of the conversion of that apostle, which was placed over the church altar. From this accident, and the celebrity which their College soon acquired, the Jesuits were known throughout India as the "Paulistas," or Fathers of St. Paul, and sometimes as "the Apostles," they being the chief apostolical preachers in the East.

1545.—This year, which was the last of the administration of Governor Martim Affonso de Souza, and the first of that of D. João de Castro, Goa city, hitherto a single parish, was divided into four, viz., 1, the Cathedral; 2 and 3, the churches of the Rosary and Luz (already mentioned), which became Collegiates; and 4, that of St. Luzia, in the eastern suburb of the city, near the river.

1548.—The foundation of the great convent and church of the Dominicans was laid in the western part of the city. Their order was the third regularly established there. During this year, Christianity made great progress in the capital and island of Goa, in the neighbouring smaller islands, and even on mainland. Also, in this year, the three first Christian Japanese, Angirao and his two servants, after having been thoroughly instructed, were solemnly baptized *in albis* on Whit Sunday by Bishop Albuquerque, in the church of St. Paul, whence Angirao took the name of *Paulo de Santa Fé*, in honour of the double name of the house. His first servant was called *Antonio*, in honour of the patron of the Portuguese nation, and the second *João*, in memory of the bishop who baptized him. Shortly after, Xavier, together with the three "new Christians," and a priest and a lay brother of his order, set out for Japan.

1552.—On the 2nd of December FRANCIS XAVIER died in the island of Sanchão (Sancian), on the coast of China, whither he was going to preach the Gospel.

1553.—BISHOP DOM JOÃO D'ALBUQUERQUE died, and the see remained vacant for seven years.

1554.—On March 16th the body of ST. FRANCISCO XAVIER, which had been transferred from Sancian to Malacca, was carried to Goa in triumph, attended by all the clergy and confraternities, by the Viceroy Noronha, the Senate, and all the authorities. It was deposited in the church of the College of St. Paul, and remained for many years exposed to the sight of the people, in a perfect state of preservation.

1557.—POPE PAUL IV.* erected Goa into a metropolitan or archiepiscopal see, and assigned it to two suffragans. The first was the bishopric of Cochin, whose diocese began at Cranganor, comprehended the whole south of the peninsula, and the whole coast of Coromandel as far as the mouths of the Ganges, including the whole Portuguese settlements; and to the east the new diocese of Goa, which then embraced the settlements north of Cranganor, and continued westward and southward to the Cape of Good Hope.† The

* As has been said, the bishopric was established by Pope Paul III.; the archbishopric was the work of this Pope, at the instances of Dom Sebastião, by the Bull *Et si docta et immaculata.*

† The suffragan bishoprics of Goa, afterwards created were: 1, Macáo, for China and Japan, created in 1575; 2, Funay, capital of Bougo, for all Japan, created in 1588, and now extinct; 3, St. Thomé de Meliapor, created in 1606; and 4, Nankin-cum-Pekin in China, created in 1690. All these sees, except No. 2, as well as those of Cochin and Malacca, are still in existence, although they are generally vacant, or their titular prelates reside in Portugal; but their spiritual concerns are administered by priests named by the archbishop of Goa, and delegated for that purpose by the King of Portugal.

second suffragan, created on the same date, is the bishopric of Malacca, containing the peninsula from Pegu to China, with the adjacent islands of Sumatra, Java, and the rest of the archipelago as far as the Moluccas.

1558.—Although the Chapter (*Cabildo*) of Goa governed the diocese, according to the ancient statutes of the Catholic Church, the episcopal functions were performed by D. JOÃO NUNES BARRETO, Patriarch of Ethiopia, and first bishop of the Jesuit Order. Unable to penetrate into Abyssinia, he came to Goa, and, fixing his residence in the small neighbouring island of Chorão, he was chiefly instrumental in converting its inhabitants to Christianity. Here, also, he founded a house of his Order, which became afterwards its Noviciate; it is now one of the two archiepiscopal seminaries. Shortly afterwards, the adjoining island of Divar also embraced Christianity, and was divided into two, and then into three, parishes.

1560.—D. GASPAR DE LEÃO PEREIRA, Canon of Evora, named and consecrated first archbishop of Goa, arrived at the capital and performed the first episcopal ordination in India in the church of St. Paul. The new archbishop assisted by the Patriarch of Ethiopia and by the Bishop of Malacca, consecrated the Jesuit Father Melchior Carneiro under the title of Bishop of Nicea, and Second Coadjutor of the Patriarch. On the evening of the same day, and in the same church, in the presence of the four prelates, 409 persons chiefly from the peninsula of Salsette, received baptism. As the Patriarch was never able to enter Abyssinia,* he was named first bishop of China and Japan, and he died at Macáo after resigning his see. At that time Salsette had only one Church and Mission house in the fort of Rachol; this establishment, after having been given to the Jesuits, afterwards became the principal archiepiscopal seminary, its situation being more healthy than that of Chorão. During the ensuing half century, all the inhabitants of Salsette embraced Christianity,† and the parishes numbered twenty-eight.

In the same year (1560) was founded the too celebrated tribunal of the Inquisition, against which so much has been said and written. "Though we‡ are very far from justifying its proceedings, we are at the same time obliged to declare that many falsehoods and exaggerations have been advanced respecting it. It must be owned, it is true, first that this tribunal, both in Spain and Portugal, greatly degenerated from its original institution; secondly, that many of its forms were extremely vicious and cruel, though it might be observed at the same time, particularly as to the tortures it inflicted, that it had them in common with all the civil tribunals existing in the time it was

as Grand Master of the Order of Christ, according to Convention between the Courts of Rome and Lisbon. It is the same with the archbishopric of Cranganor, created at first in Angamale, for the union of the Christian Malabars of St. Thomé. It became a simple bishopric in 1600; and nine years after, being restored to archiepiscopal dignity, it was transferred to Cranganor; and it is without suffragans, but its prelates are enjoined to assist at the provincial councils of Goa, as constituting a part of that ecclesiastical province. Macáo is the only see which is regularly filled, and which has a chapter that administers during vacancies. It is likewise the only one now subject to the King of Portugal, but he is still considered as patron of all the other sees; he names the prelates when he thinks proper, and he pays their *congruos*.

* P. André d'Oviedo, who had been named the first coadjutor of the Patriarch, and who had been consecrated with him in Lisbon, was the only bishop who went to Abyssinia, and resided there several years.

† Here we see the origin of the "black Portuguese."

‡ These are the words of the Abbé de Kloguen. I beg to record my dissent from every word of excuse offered for an establishment which is a lasting disgrace to Christianity. Between 1600 and 1773 were seventy-one "Acts of Faith," many of whose victims are not registered. Among the few noticed are 101 men and 16 women *relaxed in the flesh* (burnt), and 64 *relaxed* in effigy. ("Historia dos principaes actos, etc., da Inquisição en Portugal." Lisbon, 1845.)

erected; and thirdly, that the Governors, powerful men, and the corrupted part of the clergy took too often advantage of the vicious way in which justice was administered in that tribunal to satisfy their private vengeance and hatred, as is evident in the case of Dellon, and of several other persons whom he mentions."

"But, on the other hand, it must be confessed that the cruelties of that tribunal have been greatly exaggerated; whereas we see in the first place that the Inquisitions, during the greatest part of the time, sincerely desired to save the lives of their prisoners, and that at every Auto da Fé,* of the great number of the accused and supposed convicts, very few suffered death, and almost all of these were strangled before they were burnt; secondly, that the greatest care was taken of the lives, health, and cleanliness of the prisoners, at a time when all the public prisons in all Christian countries were kept in a most wretched and inhuman state; thirdly, that the rigours of the Inquisition were never exercised but against Christians,† and not even against individuals out of the Catholic communion, unless they relapsed, and that they never forced any one either to embrace Christianity or to become a Catholic. Thus much we have said to show our entire impartiality, but by no means to approve the institution itself, nor to excuse it from all that has been advanced against it; it is merely to correct false and unwarranted statements, which can have no other effect than that of leading the readers into erroneous opinions and of propagating falsehood—a thing always very blameable, whatever may be the intentions of the authors of it."‡

1567.—The first Provincial Council of Goa was presided over by the Archbishop, D. Gaspar de Leão Pereira. There were also present D. Fr. Jorge Themudo (of the order of St. Dominic), the Bishop of Cochin, the Deputy (*Procurador*) of the Bishop of Malacca, the Vicar-General of Mozambique, and the Prelates of the Convents§ of Goa. Thirty-eight decrees regarding church discipline were pronounced in this assembly.

1568.—D. Fr. Gaspar de Leão resigned his See, and was succeeded by D. Fr. Jorge Themudo, who was transferred from Cochin. The latter died (April 29th, 1571) in the College of S. Paul, and was buried in the Cathedral.

1572.—The foundation of the Augustinian Convent was laid on the Monte do Rosario. This order was then the fourth established in Goa. During the same year Pope Gregory XIII.‖ granted to the Bishops of Cochin the right of administering the Archbishopric of Goa during vacancies.

1573.—On the death of D. Fr. Jorge de Themudo, second Archbishop of Goa, Dd. Gaspar de Leão Pereira, under new Bulls, assumed the archiepiscopal functions. He arrived at Goa in November 1560, and governed the Diocese till September 1567, when his resignation was accepted, and he retired to the Convent da Madre de Deos, which he had founded. He returned a second time, in 1574, to administer the Diocese. Died on August 15th, 1576, and was buried in the High Chapel of his own Convent.

1575.—The second Provincial Council of Goa was composed of (President)

* In p. 106 the Rev. de Kloguen, who visited Goa in 1828, declares that "no one living there recollects to have seen an *Acto de Fe*" (Auto da Fé).

† Not the case; see Dellon, chap. xvi., p. 89.

‡ "All this is clearly proved by Dellon's own account of the Inquisition of Goa, though that very account is so often cited as a monument of shame to that tribunal."—*De Kloguen.*

§ The Rev. de Kloguen says "Monasteries," which is quite another matter.

‖ By his Bull of December 13th *Pastoralis Officii*, Pope Leo X., on December 12th, 1826, ordered that in default of the Bishop of Cochin, the administration should be assumed by the Archbishop of Craganor, and in default of him by the Bishop of Meliapúr.

the Archbishop, D. Gaspar de Leão; and Members, D. Henrique de Tavora, Bishop of Cochin; of the Deputy of the Bishop of Malacca; of the Grand Inquisitor, and of sixteen secular and regular Priests, deputed by the Chapters of Goa and Cochin, the Prelates of the Convents, and the Vicars-General. Of the three sessions, the first pronounced three decrees; the second, twelve; and the third and last, eighteen.

1578.—D. Fr. Henrique de Tavora, of the Order of St. Dominic, Bishop of Cochin, succeeded, in the Archiepiscopal dignity, D. Gaspar de Leão Pereira (deceased), and governed the diocese during three years.

1580.—The Convent of St. Augustin, rebuilt in its present state, became the finest in Goa.

1580.—D. Fr. Vicente da Fonseca, of the Order of St. Dominic, became Archbishop of Goa. He arrived at the Capital in 1580, administered for three years, and died during the voyage home.

1584.—The foundation of the professed House of the Jesuits, whose church is so often mentioned in local annals, was and is still called *Bom-Jesus.* Here was transferred the body of St. Francis Xavier, and here it remains to this day.

1585.—The third Provincial Council of Goa was composed of (President) Archbishop D. Vicente da Fonseca; and members, D. Fr. Matheus de Medina, Bishop of Cochin; the famous Mar Abraham, Syrian Bishop of Angamale; the Deputy of the Bishop of Malacca; the deputations from the three Chapters of Goa, Cochin, and Malacca, and several other secular and regular priests. Its five sessions issued eighty decrees; ten relating to the Archbishopric of Angamale, and to the Christians of St. Thomé or of Malabar. Mar Abraham abjured the Nestorian heresy, to which he again returned several times. On his death-bed, however, he protested that he died a Catholic; and this was of his own free will, for he was not then under the power of the Portuguese.*

1588.—D. Fr. Matheus de Medina, of the Order of Christ, fourth Bishop of Cochin, was named Archbishop of Goa.

1592.—The fourth Provincial Council of Goa was presided over, as usual, by the Archbishop, and sixteen decrees were issued. In the same year the Archbishop resigned, and the Diocese was administered till 1595 by the fifth Bishop of Cochin, D. Fr. André de Sta. Maria.

1595.—D. Fr. Aleixo de Menezes, an Augustine, became Archbishop of Goa. He had three episcopal coadjutors, all of his order.

1599.—The famous Synod of Dampier, on the coast of Malabar, for the union of the Christians of St. Thomé with the See of Rome, was held by Archbishop Menezes. Concerning this Synod much has been written, but the subject is foreign to our purpose.

1600.—Before this year the second Convent of the Franciscans was founded, in the outer eastern suburb near the river, under the invocation *Madre de Deos.* In the following century it was separated from the congregation of the Observantine Franciscans, and was incorporated with that of the Recollets or reformed. Thus it became the local head of a new religious order, having several other filial convents in India; and it was the residence of a Provincial. The monks of this Order are improperly called in Goa *Capuchos,* though they are quite different from the Capuchins.

* This Prelate was the competitor and successor of Mar Joseph, both of whom went several times to Europe, either forcibly or of their own accord, in order to obtain confirmation in their sees. Mar Joseph is the man whom Yeates and other English authors pretend to have been arrested by order of Archbishop Menezes, who at that time was only five years old.

1602.—Foundation of the College *Populo*, for the Augustine novices, close to their great Convent, with which it communicates by a flying arch thrown over the street. The Dominican College of St. Thomas Aquinas,* in the western suburb of St. Pedro or Panelim, close to the river-bank, was begun shortly after this date, as well as that of St. Boaventura for the Franciscan Observants, also on the shore, within the limits of the city, and at a short distance to the west of their old Convent. The Jesuit College of St. Roque, close to the Church of N. Sra. do Monte do Rosario, had existed since several years.

1606.—The fifth Provincial Council of Goa, presided by Archbishop D. Fr. A. de Menezes, who, as his successors have done, entitled himself *Primaz d' Oriente* (Primate of the East). One hundred and forty-nine decrees were passed in four sessions. This was the last Catholic Council held in India.

1607.—Foundation of the Convent of the Descalços (discalceated or barefooted) Carmelites, near that of St. Dominic.

1610.—Assembly of Bishops, presided over by the Archbishop, for assigning the respective limits of the four dioceses, viz., Goa, Cranganor, Cochin, and Meliapúr. During the same year† D. Fr. Aleixo de Menezes was transferred to the Archbishopric of Braga in Portugal. "This Prelate issued from one of the noblest houses of Portugal, being the son of D. Aleixo de Menezes, Governor (*Aio*) of Dom Sebastião. Notwithstanding the calumnies advanced against him by the English writers, he was most virtuous and exemplary, and very humane in all his conduct. It is false that he used violence at the Synod of Adampiere (Dampier), to force the Malabar Christians to unite with the Catholic Church. All the authentic records of that assembly prove that he only made use of gentle and persuasive means for that purpose. Some acts of violence by the Portuguese agents may have been committed, both before and after him, but they are not to be imputed to him. It is equally false that, followed by the officers of the Inquisition, he went armed with fire and sword, to compel the inhabitants of Salsette (Salcete) to embrace the Christian religion. The Jesuits converted a great part of them by the usual and most laudable means; but in order, as they thought, the better to detach the remainder of the inhabitants from the worship of idols, they destroyed all the temples and pagodas. This, however, had a contrary effect; and the Pagans, exasperated at this circumstance, rose up in arms, murdered five Jesuits and several Portuguese. The Governor then felt himself obliged to use arms likewise, to reduce the rebels; and of course did not afterwards permit the temples to be rebuilt. But in all this the Archbishop had nothing to do; and what is certainly better proved, are the good works and the pious establishments of Goa, of which he is the founder. It was he who induced the confraternity of *Misericordia* to build three houses, one for aged and infirm men, one for widows, and one for young girls, who, after a suitable instruction afforded to them, were at liberty to marry, and received a settlement from the funds of the house. These institutions still subsist, notwithstanding the reduced state of Goa. He also founded the Monastery of the nuns of St. Monica,‡ of the Order of St. Augustine, on Mount Rosary (*Monte de Rosario*), near the great Augustinian Convent. And lastly, erected another parochial church in the centre of the city, not far from the Cathedral, which he dedicated to St. Alexius, whose name he bore. Since the division of Goa

* De Kloguen calls him (p. 67), evidently by misprint, "St. Thomas of *Acquinas*."

† De Kloguen (p. 68) postpones the date to 1613. I quote his description, or rather defence, of D. Aleixo, from pp. 68-71.

‡ A history of this foundation was written by Fr. Agostinho de S. Maria, and printed at Lisbon in 1699.

into four parishes, under the Governor (Martim Affonso de) Souza and the first Bishop Albuquerque, three other parishes (parochial churches) and an extra parochial chapel have been erected. They were the parochial church of St. Thomas (S. Thomé) the Apostle, in the south-eastern part of the town; that of the Blessed Trinity, in the south; that of St. Peter, in the western suburb, called Pannely (Panelim), near the Dominican College of St. Thomas Aquinas (*S. Thomás d' Aquino*); and the extra parochial chapel of the Five Wounds of our Saviour, in the King's arsenal. So that from this time the city and suburbs contained eight parishes and one extra parochial church, which still subsist, though with hardly any parishioners, except the two churches of the Blessed Trinity and St. Alexius, which are abandoned and in ruins, since more than fifty years. Archbishop Menezes, soon after his removal to Braga, became Viceroy of Portugal for Philip III., King of Spain, and died as he had lived, in 1617."

To this account the Portuguese translator adds that after being consecrated, D. Aleixo sailed for Goa on April 12th, 1595, and took charge of his diocese in the same year. In 1599 he visited in person the churches of the Serra or Highlands of Malabar; and on June 20th held the Synod above alluded to. He then went to Angamale, the residence of the Archbishop of the Christians of St. Thomas, burnt the ancient archives, and caused the new synodical decrees to be proclaimed in all the churches. Returning to Goa on November 16th, he despatched missionaries to Socotra, Bussorah, Melinde, Persia, and Ceylon. During his administration 113 parish churches were built. Returning home in 1610, he left as Governor of the Archbishopric his coadjutor, D. Fr. Domingos da Trindade, Bishop of Salé, who discharged the episcopal functions till December 30th, 1612.

1616.—D. FR. CHRISTOVÃO DE SÁ E LISBOA, of the order of St. Jerome, and third Bishop of Malacca, was transferred to the archiepiscopal see of Goa. This archbishop began to rebuild the cathedral of Goa; and, when the body of the church was finished he transferred to it with splendid ceremony the Holy Sacrament, on Sunday, the Festival of the Guardian Angel. A Royal Letter (September 30th, 1622) disapproved of his wishing to enter Bassein on horseback under the *Pallium*, with a *Fidalgo* (roble) leading his animal. He administered till his death, on March 31st, 1622.

1629.—D. FR. SEBASTIÃO OF ST. PEDRO, of the order of St. Augustine, first Bishop of Meliapúr, and subsequently sixth Bishop of Cochin, after governing the archbishopric for three years till 1623, became Archbishop of Goa. As Bishop of Meliapúr he three times defended that town with great valour, and all at his own expense, against the obstinate attacks of the Hollanders, taking from them the fort of Palicat, and another from the King of Bisnagar. He completed the building of the Cathedral in its present state and consecrated it anew. Being named to the Government of India by the *Via de successão*, he excused himself, pleading his age and his occupations, and he died on November 7th, 1629, two hours after midnight. Upon this event the Cabildo or Chapter took charge of the administration, and the instances of the Viceroy caused the Dean, Gonçalo Velloso, to be named as Governor of the Archbishopric. In the latter charge he was succeeded by D. Fr. João da Rocha, Bishop of Hierapolis, whom the Chapter nominated between 1632-33. In 1634 there were troubles about Church rule between the Cabildo and the Bishop; the former removed the latter and commissioned a Canon to report the case in person to Her Majesty; and the Bishop put the Canon in irons, and confined him in the public jail. A Royal Letter (March 27th, 1635) ordered the Bishop home, and reproved the Chapter, directing the Viceroy, in case of further disorder on the part of the Cabildo, to commit the administration to the Inquisitor, according to the Apostolic Brief of March 10th, 1635.

1633.—D. Fr. Manoel Telles de Brito, a Dominican named to the Primacy, died on his passage out (July 4th, 1633), and his body was buried in the Cathedral of Goa. The Diocese was then governed by the eighth Bishop of Cochin, D. Fr. Manoel Rangel, who probably began to administer when the Chapter removed the Bishop of Hierapolis. He continued in power from March 16th, 1634, for a year and seven months; and he also got into trouble by defending the nuns of St. Monica.

1636.—D. Fr. Francisco dos Martins, a Franciscan, appointed to the Primacy, took charge on October 21st, 1636, and administered till November 25th, 1652, when he died, *æt* sixty-nine years, one month, and four days. The Diocese remained vacant for more than twenty-three years, a period of ecclesiastical dissension and scandal, rivalling the political disorders of D. Braz de Castro. The Chapter at times reserved the power for itself, and then deputed it to Governors, which it arbitrarily named and removed. In 1660 the Chapter having appointed to the post Fr. João de S. Jacintho, the latter was induced, on June 17th, 1661, to give up charge, in consequence of the troubles caused by the Cabildo.

1659.—The church called Cruz dos Milagres (the Miraculous Cross), which had been built ever since 1608, and which belonged to the Augustinians, was rebuilt in its present state, on a hill to the south, near the parochial church of A Luz: it commands a beautiful view, not only of all the city, but of all the island and harbour of Goa.

1672.—D. Fr. Christovão da Silveira, of the order of St. Augustine, named and consecrated archbishop, left Lisbon in 1672, reached Bahia, and died on the way to Goa.* "It was a little before the arrival of this archbishop that the French physician Dillon was committed to the Inquisition of which he afterwards gave an account, though it contained some expressions unwarrantable for a Catholic, and which favour of his private resentment, is nevertheless far from being too exaggerated, and even on many points rather justifies than accuses that tribunal. He had been arrested ostensibly for some bold and even erroneous assertions, though excusable in a layman, who is not so much obliged to know the mysteries of divinity; but the chief cause, however, of his misfortune, was the jealousy of a Governor of Daman, who misrepresented his case."

1675.—D. Fr. Antonio Brandão, of the Cistercian Order, reached Goa on September 24th, 1675; took charge on October 7th; and died (*æt.* fifty-seven years, seven months, and sixteen days) on July 6th, 1678. He was buried in the cathedral.

1681.—D. Manoel de Sousa e Menezes, a secular priest; became Archbishop of Goa; and held charge from September 20th, 1681, to January 31st, 1684, when he died.

1687.—D. Alberto da Silva, Canon Regular of St. Augustine; created archbishop; reached Goa September 24th, 1687, and governed till April 8th, 1688, when he died. The diocese being vacant, was taken in charge (1689) by D. Fr. Pedro da Silva, coming from Portugal as Bishop of Cochin. He held it from 1689 to March 15th, 1691, when he died, and was buried in the convent N. Sra. da Graça.

1691.—D. Fr. Augustinho de Annunciação, of the Order of Christ, was consecrated archbishop during the preceding year. He established at Goa

* The Abbé de Kloguen says that "he arrived and took possession of the see, which had been vacant for twenty years." The following lines are quoted from him (pp. 72-3.)

the fund called "Cofre da Fabrica da Sé," in 1693, contributing to it the third of his salary; and he died July 6th, 1712.

Before the end of this century was founded the convent of the Theatins, or of St. Cajetanus (St. Caetano), by the Italians of that order. Their church, which had been built on the plan of the Roman St. Peter,* is, though small, the most perfect edifice in Goa. Originally the viceregal chapel, it lay, like the convent, near the palace. Some time afterwards, about the beginning of the eighteenth century, was founded the convent of the Irmãos de Caridade (Brothers of Charity), or S. João de Deos (St. John of God), to whose care the hospitals were committed.

1716.—D. SEBASTIÃO DE ANDRADE PESSANAH, secular priest, reached Goa September 17th, and administered till January 25th, 1721, when he resigned his see and returned home.

1721.—D. IGNACIO DE S. THEREZA, Canon Regular of St. Augustine, reached Goa on September 20th, 1721, and administered till 1739. On May 20th, 1722, this fighting ecclesiastic being on a visit to Ansolna, armed 300 men, and demolished three pagodas in the territory of the Rajah of Sunda. And this was not his only feat of the kind. He caused other and tremendous disturbances,—imprisoning the seculars, placing the Supreme Court (*Relacão*) under an interdict, and indulging in other excesses which misbecame his position. The tradition survives that when summoned before the High Tribunal he appeared in his pontifical robes, thus ignoring the laical jurisdiction. He was afterwards transferred to the bishopric of Algarves, in Portugal.

1741.—D. FR. EUGENIO TRIGUEIROS, of the order of St. Jerome, fourth Bishop of Macáo, was transferred to Goa, but died on the journey. His body was coffined and received burial at sea, north of Calicut Port. D. Francisco de Vasconcellos then governed the diocese from December 20th, 1742 (when he arrived at Goa), until his decease on March 30th, 1743. He was buried in the church of Bom-Jesus.

1742.—D. FR. LOURENÇO DE S. MARIA, named archbishop, reached Goa September 19th, 1744; administered till September 1750, and next year returned to Portugal, where he was transferred to the bishopric of Algarve.† In 1745 an Apostolic Brief imposed the *Dizimos* or tithes upon all the inhabitants of the "Old Conquests," including the religious orders; but with the difference that the village communities paid only half-tithes (Order of Treasury Council, September 30th, 1745, and confirmed by Conselho Ultramar, March 27th, 1750). This arrangement lasted till 1852.

1750.—D. ANTHONY TAVEIRA DE NEIVA, of the military order of Sant-Iago, Archbishop of Goa.

1761.—The Jesuits were expelled from the Portuguese dominions, and at Goa their professed house, Bom-Jesus, was given to the Italian missionaries of St. Vincent of Paul, better known by the name of Lazarists, with the view of establishing there the episcopal seminary. The noviciate house at Chorão, on the island of that name, was transferred to the Fathers of the Congregation of St. Philip of Neri, chiefly natives and descendants of Brahmans. These priests also took possession of the Jesuit house at Rachol, in Salsette, which is now the chief episcopal seminary.‡ The colleges and churches of

* De Kloguen erroneously asserts that it was *rebuilt* by the Theatins in this, which was its original form.

† M. de Kloguen errs when he states that this dignitary "never comes to Goa."

‡ In 1786 the seminaries were established in the three houses above referred to; and they were placed under the Vicentine Fathers (Italians), who afterwards made way for the Portuguese priests of the same order from the Rilhafolles Convent. That

SS. Paul and Roc (Roque) were abandoned and suffered to fall in ruins, as they may now be seen. The principal house of the priests of S. Filippe Neri had been founded some time before, close to the church Da Cruz dos Milagres (Miraculous Cross), which formerly belonged, as we have said, to the Augustinians. The religious built near it a large convent, which is now one of the finest, richest, and healthiest in Goa (1828). They also obtained possession of the ancient convent of the Barefooted Carmelites. The latter, about 1739, were expelled the city on account of the dissension between them (with the support of the Propaganda) and the archbishop concerning the spiritual jurisdiction of Bombay Island, a question which is not yet entirely settled (1828).* Their convent became the private college of the Philippians or "Congregationalists" as they are called. These monks, now all of the Brahman caste, are very rich, and to their care are entrusted, not only the two episcopal seminaries, as we have said, but likewise the missions of Ceylon in the diocese of Cochin.

1774.—D. Francisco da Assumpção e Brito, of the order of St. Augustine, Archbishop of Goa, arrived on September 21st, 1774; took charge in March, 1775; and administered till February 5th, 1780. "This prelate, who was the true creature of the famous Marquis of Pombal, gave great offence by his innovations. Though a monk, he rejected the title of Frei, according to the custom of the Portuguese prelates. He despoiled the library of Goa of its most precious manuscripts and other works, which he sent to Lisbon. He was disliked generally by all his clergy and the people at large. After the disgrace of the Marquis of Pombal he was suspended by Pope Pius VI., along with three others of the Portuguese dominions, and died in 1780."†

1780.—D. Fr. Manoel de St. Catharina (Barefooted Carmelite); named fourteenth Bishop of Cochin, and by especial Bull, preceding the royal nomination, constituted October 13th, 1779, Apostolic Governor of the Archbishopric; took charge in February 1780; confirmed on July 19th, 1783, and assumed the Pallium in the Primatial Cathedral November 21st, 1784. On the same day he consecrated D. Fr. José da Soledade, Bishop of Cochin; and on October 23rd, 1785, D. Fr. Amaro José de St. Thomas, Bishop of Pentacomer and Prelate of Mozambique. He published, with slight alterations, the "Constituçoes Goanas" (Goanese Ecclesiastical Regulations), ordained by his predecessor and approved by the Primatial Chapter, the Archbishop of Craganor, and the Bishop of Cochin. He gave statutes to the Carmelites; he represented to His Majesty the inconveniences of contracting espousals by public registering, and he obtained an *Alvará* (January 12th, 1798), allowing them to be made before the parish priest and three witnesses. He died (*æt.* eighty-six) at Quepem, February 10th, 1812, and was buried in the Cathedral.

branch which occupied the Bom-Jesus professed house, the greater part of which was burnt down, gradually died out; the other two were entrusted to the "Nerys" of the congregation, "Do Oratorio da Santa Cruz dos Milagres." When the religious orders were extinguished at Goa, the seminaries were committed to secular priests, chosen by the prelacy.

* An order from Portugal commanded the foreign priests settled in Goa to swear fidelity to the sovereign: the Theatins obeyed, but the Carmelites refused, and in 1707 their convent was made over to the Oratorians, or "Padres Nerys," by a Royal Letter of April 2nd, 1707.

† These are the words of the Abbé de Kloguen. The student of history will accept with great reserve the statements of a Catholic priest in the Inquisition days, relating to the great Pombal and his friends, who were enemies to the so-called Holy Office. In short, anyone praising Pombal would have been sure of the stake.

It is related of this archbishop that, shortly after his arrival in India, some Carmelites of the Bombay mission presented themselves before him and expressed a hope that His Excellency being of their order, matters would soon and satisfactorily be settled. The prelate shrewdly replied, "Reverend Fathers, before I became a Carmelite I was already a Portuguese." In truth, the dissension, far from subsiding, was renewed with more warmth than ever, under Governor Duncan, in Bombay. About 1798, by the exertion of Miguel de Lima, an influential native, who, highly esteemed by the English, declared himself for the Archbishop's jurisdiction, the dispute ended by dividing the four parish churches then existing on the Island between the Bishop (Vicar Apostolic of the Grand Mogul). at the head of the Carmelite mission and the Archbishop. The latter protested against this act, and at last submitted to it only because approved of by the Pope. Fr. Manoel was a simple and holy prelate; notwithstanding what has been said of him, he was much attached to his order. Unable to furnish the Carmelite convent with Portuguese monks, he established a community of Secular Fathers, a Society of the Third Carmelite Order, who pronounced only simple vows, like the priests of St. Philip of Neri, but who wear the Carmelite habit. He built for these religious a church and a convent in Chimbel, near the Temple of St. Barbara, between the villages of Ribandar and Pangim. As the convents of the Theatins, or St. Caetano, and that of the priests of St. Philip Neri received exclusively Brahmans,* that of Chimbel was consecrated entirely for the second native caste, called at Goa *Charodós*.

1783.—In this year the remains of St. Francis Xavier, which had been before constantly exposed to view in the church of Bom-Jesus, and which were afterwards shown on certain occasions only, were publicly exhibited for the last time. "Since then it has been locked up in its beautiful brazen shrine, under three keys, one of which is kept by the Archbishop, and the other by the Senate, whilst the third is at Lisbon."†

1790.—The Italian Lazarists, who, since the expulsion of the Jesuits, held the house and church of Bom-Jesus and the Archiepiscopal Seminary, were expelled Goa, for resisting some regulations, contrary to their statutes, which the Governor and the Archbishop determined to impose upon them. The house and church were then entrusted to the care of a secular priest, sufficiently salaried, under the title of Administrator. This place is commonly held by one of the canons of the cathedral.

1812.‡—D. Fr. Manoel des. Galdino, a reformed Franciscan, or Recollet of the Arrabida Province (Portugal), was named Bishop of Macáo in 1803, and was thence transferred to Goa, as coadjutor, in 1805. He arrived during the following year, and succeeded to the Archbishopric on the death of his predecessor, February 10th, 1812.§

* By Royal Avizo of 1750, natives were admitted to the Convent of St. Caetano, of which, indeed, the first professed inmates were Padre Agostinho Barreto de Rachol (November 21st, 1751), and Fathers Francisco Furtado de Margão and Jacintho Manoel de Rega de Verná (June 1st, 1752). There is a tradition that amongst the Brahman monks only one of the Charodó, or Charoddo (Khshatriya ?) caste was admitted.

† In the days of the Abbé de Kloguen (1828), whose words are quoted, the coffin was supposed to be of brass (p. 78), copper (p. 114), bronze (Port. trans.). The dirt of ages was presently cleaned, and it was found to be of pure silver.

‡ In 1812,—as has been said in the historical portion,—the Inquisition was suppressed at the instance of the British Government. The two Inquisitors, F. Luis de Rihamar and Fr. José dos Dores, retained their salaries (= 1000 xerafins) till death; and Fr. Thomas, the Promoter or Public Prosecutor, had 600. The Public Treasury on this occasion was the gainer in money by 32,428 : 1:30 besides 1,318 xerafins worth of plate belonging to the Secretariat ("Inst. of the Marq. d'Alorna," p. 11; edit. of 1856).

§ Here ends the "Chronological Table of Religious Establishments," etc., the work of

D. MANOEL was elected Bishop of Tunkim (Tonquim) on October 19th, 1801; was afterwards transferred to Macáo, and was consecrated on March 27th, 1803; he reached his bishopric on September 7th of the same year, and Goa on March 14th, 1806. He governed the Church there from February 18th, 1812, to July 15th, 1831,—the day on which he died of cholera. He was buried in the High Chapel of the Cathedral. He built and endowed three churches,—two in Salsette, S. Jozé do Areal, and da Ilha de S. Jacinto, and that of Marcella in the Novas-Conquistas. He consecrated, in the College of S. Thomas, the Archbishop of Craganor, D. Fr. Paulo de S. Thomas d'Aquino, and the Bishop of Cochin, D. Fr. Thomas de Noronha. Finally he carried out many wise measures for the benefit of his diocesan clergy and ecclesiastical discipline.

(21) 1831.—JOSÉ PAULO DA COSTA PEREIRA E D'ALMEIDA; Dean of the Cathedral; named Capitular Vicar by the Chapters of the vacant see; governed till January 11th, 1835, when he died. He founded the church and establishment of Quepem.

(22) 1835.—PAULO ANTONIO DIAS DE CONCEIÇÃO; born in Cavelossim (Salcete); High Treasurer of the Cathedral; elected Capitular Vicar on January 18th, 1835, and ruled till November 19th, 1837, when he was succeeded by—

(23) 1837.—D. ANTONIO FELICIANO DE S. RITA CARVALHO, D.D.; Theological Professor at Coimbra; named Archbishop-Elect and Temporal Governor of the Archbishopric of Goa by His Majesty; brought to the Chapter a royal letter, dated September 20th, 1836, conferring upon him unreserved jurisdiction, and consequently appointed by that body Capitular Vicar, under an order of November 19th, 1837. He took charge on December 2nd of the same year. He published, in pamphlet form, a learned dissertation upon the rights of Portuguese patronage (*padrado*), in reply to Dr. O'Connor, Apostolic Vicar of Madras; and he died, generally regretted, on February 1st, 1839.

Thereupon the Chapter of the Cathedral assumed the direction of the diocese, and on the eighth day was proceeding to elect a new capitular vicar, when the High Treasurer, Paulo Antonio Dias da Conceição, published a circular, claiming that title, independently of the Chapter, and declaring that he had resigned the dignity under reserve, and only in favour of the Archbishop Elect. The result was a reference to His Majesty, pending whose decision the Chapter provisionally governed the diocese. The claims of the Treasurer were set aside by a decree of September 20th, and on October 3rd, 1839, was elected.

(24) 1839.—ANTONIO JOZÉ D'ATHAIDE, a native of Sirulá in Bardez; Chaunter of the Cathedral. He governed till March 7th, 1844, and after twelve years of vacancy the See was conferred upon—

25 (1844)—D. JOZÉ MARIA DA SILVA TORRES, D.D., and Archbishop Primate; named by the Decree of January 27th, 1843; confirmed by Papal Bull of June 20th (same year); reached Goa on March 2nd, 1844, and took possession on March 7th. He was the first to voyage overland *viâ* the Mediterranean, and he was received with great ceremony. He regulated the two archiepiscopal seminaries and reformed the studies; he bravely defended the Patronage-right in the *Jornal da Santa Igreja Luzitana do Oriente*, which was appended to the official gazette. On March 26th, 1849, he returned to Europe, in virtue of a royal Avizo, appointing him coadjutor and future successor of the Archbishop of Braga; and he was there made a peer of the

M. de Kloguen (pp. 51-79). The following list, which brings the date down to 1859, is by his Portuguese translator.

Real, etc., etc., etc., with the title of Archbishop of Palmyra. On retiring he appointed to the government of the diocese, with the title of *Governador do Arcebispado*, D. Joaquim de S. Rita Botelho, Bishop-Elect of Cochin. When he was confirmed in the coadjutorship of Braga, by His Holiness, in the Consistory of February 17th, 1851, a royal letter, dated March, 1851, enjoined the Chapter of Goa to elect its Capitular Vicar, and on May 7th the choice fell upon—

(26) 1851—D. JOAQUIM DE S. RITA BOTELHO, a native of Goa, formerly in the extinguished order of Reformed Franciscans, Bishop-Elect of Cochin, who became Capitular Vicar and Temporal Governor of the Archbishopric on May 9th. In 1852 the Governor (Viscount d'Ourem) determined that the village communities, which since 1745 had paid only half-tithes (5 per cent.), should pay full *dizimos* (10 per cent.), thus equalising their taxation with that of individuals; at the same time he abolished other imposts. Early in March 1853, by order of the Home Government, came D. Jeronimo José de Matta, Bishop of Macáo, who, having ordained many priests to supply Missions of the Royal Patronage, returned to his diocese on October 28th. This visit gave rise to the celebrated brief *probe nostis*, against which the Ministry of H. F. Majesty protested, as a violation of patronage rights. Several publications were the result, especially the *Reflexões sobre o Padroado Portuguez no Oriente, applicadas a Proclamação Pastoral do Rev. Fr. Angelico, Pro-Vigario Apostolico de Bombaim, Por. um Portuguez* (*i.e.*, the Secretary, J. H. da Cunha Rivara), published in Nova Goa, 1858. He died at his post on February 8th, 1859.*

(27) 1859.—D. ANTONIO DA TRINDADE VASCONCELLOS PEREIRA DE MELLO, Canon of the See of Lisbon, was appointed Archbishop-Primate of the East, on May 26th, 1859; but was transferred October 22nd, 1860, to the Bishopric of Beja. He appointed, as his substitute to govern the diocese of Goa, the Canon of the See of Goa, Rev. Caetano João Peres, a learned native of the place, who died on January 24th, 1860. Canon Antonio José Pereira was thereupon nominated to fill up the vacancy.

(28) 1860.—D. JOÃO CHRYSOSTOMO DE AMORIM PESSOA was transferred from the Bishopric of Cabo Verde to the Primacy of Goa, on October 22nd, 1860. As he was unable to take up his diocese, through some objection of the *Curia*, the Chapter of Goa elected, *sede vacante*, to the Capitular Vicarship the Canon of the See of Evora, Antonio Ribeiro de Azevedo Bastos, on January 12th, 1861. Some time after, however, the Archbishop came to Goa, and after staying there for about five or six years, returned to Lisbon.

(29) 1875.—Dr. D. AYRES D'ORNELLAS made his solemn entry into the old city of Goa on December 29th, 1875. He is a popular prelate, young and zealous in the discharge of his duties; he has visited most of the missions southward, as far as Ceylon; and he has the reputation of, and the respect of the people for, being both pious and charitable. I frequently visited him, and was charmed by his simplicity and humility. He sells all he has to give to the poor, and keeps for himself the bare necessaries of life. Higher praise one can record of no man. May this Archbishop long live to fit his high station so nobly.

ISABEL BURTON.

* The two following notes were given to me by my friend Dr. da Cunha.

FINIS.